IMPORTANT

HERE IS YOUR REGISTRATION CODE TO ACCESS MCGRAW-HILL PREMIUM CONTENT AND MCGRAW-HILL ONLINE RESOURCES

For key premium online resources you need THIS CODE to gain access. Once the code is entered, you will be able to use the web resources for the length of your course.

Access is provided only if you have purchased a new book.

If the registration code is missing from this book, the registration screen on our website, and within your WebCT or Blackboard course will tell you how to obtain your new code. Your registration code can be used only once to establish access. It is not transferable

To gain access to these online resources

1. **USE** your web browser to go to: **www.mhhe.com/jonesintro**

2. **CLICK** on "First Time User"

3. **ENTER** the Registration Code printed on the tear-off bookmark on the right

4. After you have entered your registration code, click on "Register"

5. **FOLLOW** the instructions to setup your personal UserID and Password

6. **WRITE** your UserID and Password down for future reference. Keep it in a safe place.

If your course is using WebCT or Blackboard, you'll be able to use this code to access the McGraw-Hill content within your instructor's online course.

To gain access to the McGraw-Hill content in your instructor's WebCT or Blackboard course simply log into the course with the user ID and Password provided by your instructor. Enter the registration code exactly as it appears to the right when prompted by the system. You will only need to use this code the first time you click on McGraw-Hill content.

These instructions are specifically for student access. Instructors are not required to register via the above instructions.

The McGraw-Hill Companies

McGraw-Hill Irwin

Thank you, and welcome to your McGraw-Hill/Irwin Online Resources.

Jones
Introduction to Business, 1/e
0-07-322317-4
978-0-07-322317-9

D1402969

BWKP-4GWN-3MQC-T3VY-DGER

REGISTRATION CODE
REGISTRATION CODE

The McGraw-Hill Companies

McGraw-Hill Irwin

Introduction to
Business

How Companies Create Value for People

Introduction to
Business

How Companies Create Value for People

Gareth R. Jones

Texas A&M University

Boston   Burr Ridge, IL   Dubuque, IA   Madison, WI   New York   San Francisco   St. Louis
Bangkok   Bogotá   Caracas   Kuala Lumpur   Lisbon   London   Madrid   Mexico City
Milan   Montreal   New Delhi   Santiago   Seoul   Singapore   Sydney   Taipei   Toronto

The McGraw-Hill Companies

**McGraw-Hill
Irwin**

INTRODUCTION TO BUSINESS: HOW COMPANIES CREATE VALUE FOR PEOPLE
Published by McGraw-Hill/Irwin, a business unit of The McGraw-Hill Companies, Inc., 1221 Avenue of the
Americas, New York, NY 10020. Copyright © 2007 by The McGraw-Hill Companies, Inc. All rights
reserved. No part of this publication may be reproduced or distributed in any form or by any means, or
stored in a database or retrieval system, without the prior written consent of The McGraw-Hill Companies,
Inc., including, but not limited to, in any network or other electronic storage or transmission, or broadcast
for distance learning.

Some ancillaries, including electronic and print components, may not be available to customers outside the
United States.

This book is printed on acid-free paper.

3 4 5 6 7 8 9 0 VNH/VNH 0 9 8

ISBN-13 978-0-07-352456-6
ISBN-10 0-07-352456-5

Editorial director: *John E. Biernat*
Senior sponsoring editor: *Kelly H. Lowery*
Senior developmental editor: *Christine Scheid*
Editorial Coordinator: *Allison Clelland*
Executive marketing manager: *Ellen Cleary*
Producer, Media technology: *Damian Moshak*
Lead project manager: *Mary Conzachi*
Senior production supervisor: *Sesha Bolisetty*
Coordinator freelance design: *Artemio Ortiz Jr.*
Photo research coordinator: *Lori Kramer*
Photo researcher: *David A. Tietz*
Senior media project manager: *Susan Lombardi*
Senior supplement producer: *Carol Loreth*
Cover design: *Dave Seidler*
Cover illustrator: *Chip Wass*
Interior design: *Jenny El-Shamy*
Typeface: *10.25/12 Baskerville*
Compositor: *Precision Graphics*
Printer: *Von Hoffmann Corporation*

Library of Congress Cataloging-in-Publication Data
Jones, Gareth R.
    Introduction to business : how companies create value for people / Gareth R.
Jones.
        p. cm.
    Includes index.
    ISBN-13: 978-0-07-352456-6 (alk. paper)
    ISBN-10: 0-07-352456-5 (alk. paper)
    1. Industrial management. 2. Business. 3. Industries--Social aspects. I. Title.
HD31.J5977 2007
658--dc22
                                                            2005056249

www.mhhe.com

Brief Contents

Detailed Contents

Part 1 The Environment of Business

Chapter Three   Entrepreneurs, Managers, and Employees   64

Chapter Four   Multinationals and the Global Environment of Business   102

Chapter Five   Business Ethics and the Legal Environment of Business   138

Chapter Six   Leadership, Influence, and Communication in Business   174

Chapter Seven   Motivating and Managing People and Groups in Business Organizations   208

Chapter Eight The Structure and Culture of a Business Organization   238

Part 3   A Functional Approach to Business

Chapter Nine   Information Technology and E-Commerce:
Managing Information, Knowledge, and Business Relationships   272

Part 3 A Functional Approach to Business

Chapter Ten — Marketing and Product Development:

Creating and Positioning Goods and Services 304

Chapter Eleven — Sales, Distribution, and Customer Relationship

Management: Reaching and Satisfying Customers 340

Chapter Twelve   Operations and Materials Management:

Managing the Production and Flow of Goods and Services   370

Chapter Thirteen   Human Resource Management:

Acquiring and Building Employees' Skills and Capabilities   398

Chapter Fourteen   Accounting: Measuring How Efficiently and Effectively

Resources Are Creating Value and Profit   434

Part 3 A Functional Approach to Business

For Nicholas and Julia

In framing and writing *Introduction to Business* my goal has been to inform and familiarize students with what business is, how it operates, and how it affects them. The intention is to help students understand the many fundamental ways in which business affects people and society—by shaping the kinds of occupations they will pursue and the careers they can expect, for example. This is an important goal because people often fail to understand how business impacts them personally.

We are all used to going to school, going to work, going into restaurants, stores, banks, and buying the goods and services that we need to satisfy our many needs. However, the actual business activities and processes that are required to make these goods and services available to us commonly go unappreciated. Similarly, we know that businesses exist to make a "profit." But what is profit, how is it created, who does this profit go to, and what is profit used for in the future? Moreover, what are the actual activities involved in creating goods, services, and profit? And why is it that some companies seem to be more effective or make more money—that is, are more "profitable" than others?

This book has been structured and written to address these issues. Its goal is to explain in a thorough but succinct way why business is so important to people and the societies in which they live. Over time, many introduction-to-business textbooks have forgotten this fundamental goal. They have become huge compendiums of descriptions about different kinds of business and management practices. In chapter after chapter they overwhelm students with detailed information about the minutia of business and fail to provide the overall "big picture" of what business is and how it affects people. With such an approach to business, students fail to see "the forest for the trees."

In general, this book has been written

To be comprehensive and inclusive but concise, engaging, and to the point.

Introduction to Business provides students with an integrated, or "big picture," approach to business that covers all the most important functional areas of business. However, it does this in 15 chapters that engage students while clearly and concisely covering the main concepts and theories they need to know to understand business today. The coverage in the book is wide-ranging and thorough, providing them with the essential knowledge of the main building blocks of business without drowning them in details. In short, it explains the concepts and theories of business in an engaging, accessible way, unlike other introduction-to-business books. In addition, the book pays considerable attention to creating and developing both in-chapter and end-of-chapter features and exercises that offer the most learning value to students while economizing on their valuable learning time.

To be contemporary and up-to-date, yet grounded, relevant, and student-focused.

Introduction to Business contains state-of-the-art content and descriptions of current business practices yet explains the nature of business with an emphasis on its applications for people and companies. Moreover, the coverage in several chapters of the book is unique and not found in any other introduction-to-business books, such as coverage on the evolution of business systems as well as information technology applications. In particular, the text provides a detailed examination of the essential, value-chain business functions necessary to create goods and services that people will want to buy. Using the value-chain approach, each of the principal functions involved in business commerce is examined in turn. And, as the table of contents suggests, the book discusses functional activities in an applied way, so accounting, for example, is not about "number crunching" but about "measuring how efficiently and effectively resources are being used." This functional approach offers a contemporary, integrated account of business that always focuses on the big picture and not on minutiae that can both confuse students and waste their time.

with four main goals in mind:

To include rich, relevant examples plus a hands-on, interactive learning approach.

Introduction to Business uses an applied, hands-on approach to help students understand the many ways in which business affects them today—by shaping the kinds of occupations they will pursue and the careers they can expect in the global world today, for example. With the use of carefully selected and written stories and illustrations about small and large companies, *Introduction to Business* makes the complex concepts and terminology found in other books, which often intimidate students, easy to grasp. This learning is then facilitated by the use of a rich set of hands-on, experiential, end-of-chapter exercises designed to allow instructors and students to interact, discuss, and explore the meaning and implications of the chapter content. The goal is to involve and interest students in the business concepts explained in the chapter and give them the opportunity to actively think about how to make business decisions.

To be accompanied by state-of-the-art learning support materials, videos, and pedagogy.

The learning approach developed in the book is supported by the widest and most comprehensive set of support materials and videos available in the introduction-to-business market. A chapter-related video feature in each chapter offers students useful insight into real-world issues. In addition, an end-of-chapter section consisting of relevant and engaging stories taken from the pages of *BusinessWeek* magazine offers additional insight into many of the human and functional issues covered in the chapters. In addition, the instructor's manual, test bank, and many other supplements have been thoroughly developed and tested to provide instructors with a solid support foundation.

In short, *Introduction to Business* provides students with a comprehensive, integrated account of business that provides them with the most *essential* knowledge of the main building blocks of business but which does not drown them in detail. In a first course in business, students should gain a solid understanding of the nature and functions of business so they can make better career and life choices. This is better accomplished in a focused, integrated account of business that gives students all the knowledge they need but in a book far shorter than the typical 1,000 page text that few people, even instructors, want to read.

ORGANIZATION OF THE BOOK

The book provides a broad overview of the nature, form, and functions of business and helps to unravel the many hidden and intertwined meanings that business has. It facilitates students' understanding of how business operates and how it affects their lives and society in general. Part 1, "The Environment of Business," provides the big picture of what business is about. Chapter 1 develops a three-pronged approach to understanding business based on business as commerce, business as an occupation, and business as an organization. It also brings out the essential meaning of terms such as specialization and profit and tells students why companies exist to provide goods and services to customers. Finally, it describes the plan of this book and introduces the concept of the value chain, which will be used to structure the discussion of the principal business functions in Part 3. Chapter 2 looks at how business has evolved over the centuries, the factors of production, and their role in the business process. We trace business back to the Stone Age and then explain, for example, how wars were once waged to obtain land and labor. We then move on to the Industrial Revolution and the development of unionism and socialism on through to the age of information technology. Chapter 3 examines the essential functions of the entrepreneur and manager. It also looks at the role employees play and provides students with an in-depth account of the stages of the career process. Chapter 4 then provides an overview of the main issues facing multinational companies operating in today's changing global environment.

All these chapters, but especially Chapter 5, "Business Ethics and the Legal Environment of Business," make it clear that business is about the pursuit and creation of profit and wealth and that individual people engage in the same quest for wealth to satisfy their needs. The result is competition and self-interested behavior. While much of this competition is healthy and promotes the well-being of both people and society, competition can lead to fraud and deceit. Hence, management and entrepreneurship are always linked to ethical and legal issues. Chapter 5 therefore puts business in the wider framework of ethics, law, and society.

Part 2, "The Human Side of Business," discusses the nature of the individual and group processes that must be managed when people work together in a business organization. Chapter 6 examines the role of leadership, influence, persuasion, communication, and politics in making a business organization function efficiently and effectively. Chapter 7 looks at the role of individual motivation and group processes, including teamwork in the value creation process. It also examines how self-interest and competition lead to bargaining and negotiation. Both these chapters discuss basic processes that lie at the heart of business commerce—processes that frequently revolve around occupational issues, such as contests between people in the same function and between functions. Chapter 8 then discusses how organizational structure and culture motivate and coordinate people and reduce the bargaining and negotiation costs related to getting peoples' cooperation—the essential role of business organization, in other words.

Part 3, "A Functional Approach to Business," then provides a detailed examination of the essential business functions and occupations necessary to create valuable goods and services that people will want to buy. Using the value-chain approach, each of the principal functions involved in business commerce is then examined. As you can see by perusing the table of contents, the book uses a hands-on approach to discussing these functions and their activities. So, for example, finance becomes not about interest rates and numbers but about how firms, just like people, have to figure out how to fund their activities and manage their cash and other assets. Using this functional approach, the book offers a contemporary and integrated account of business that always focuses on the big picture.

In-Chapter Learning Features

Nothing makes the practice of business come alive more than vivid stories and examples about people and companies that demonstrate clearly the meaning of the chapter material, as well as hands-on exercises that offer students the opportunity to actively think about and engage in business issues and decision making. This book pays considerable attention to creating and developing both in-chapter and end-of-chapter features and exercises to offer the most learning value to students while economizing on their valuable learning time. The companies highlighted in each chapter, for example, were specifically selected to appeal to and engage students.

A Question of Business

Each chapter opens with a hands-on question about one or more companies that illustrates the issues that are dealt with in the chapter. These lengthy stories bring to light the substance of the business issues involved, and this theme is then carried on through the chapter.

A Question of Business
Kroger, Wal-Mart, and Supermarket Competition
How and Why Do Companies Provide Goods and Services for Customers?

Suppose you walk into one of your local supermarkets such as Kroger, the largest supermarket chain in the United States in 2005 (www.kroger.com). You are walking into a business enterprise or company that is there to sell you an assortment of food, drinks, and consumer products selected to appeal to you and to satisfy your needs. What makes you want to shop or trade with Kroger rather than with, say, Albertson's or Wal-Mart? And why has Kroger spent billions of dollars to build and stock its store to attract you to shop there? Moreover, what factors determine the kinds of goods and services Kroger's chooses to offer you and the prices that it charges for its products?

Kroger is *in business* to make money for its stockholders, the people who have used their savings or capital to buy shares of its company stock. Kroger's stockholders' goal is to increase the value or "get a return" on their investment in the company's business. This will happen if (1) Kroger's managers select the right mix of products and attract more customers, then (2) can sell these products at a price high enough to generate sales revenues (the money it receives from selling the products) that (3) more than exceed the costs of operating the business (including payroll costs, the cost of purchasing the many products it sells, and the cost of leasing store space).

When Kroger's sales revenues exceed its operating costs, it is said to make a *profit*, the difference between its total revenues and total costs. If Kroger can show its profit is likely to increase over time, more people will want to buy its stock. Then Kroger's stock price goes up, and so does the value of its stockholders' investment. The increase in stock price is its stockholders' reward for the *risk* they have taken in investing their money in its business: If a company ultimately performs poorly and its profits start to fall, the value of its stock falls; if it goes out of business entirely, stockholders lose all of their money.

Because the grocery business is competitive, finding ways to increase profit is not easy. Many of Kroger's rivals are trying to lure its customers away by offering them lower-priced or higher-quality products. Wal-Mart has become Kroger's major rival. Wal-Mart is rapidly expanding its

WHY IS THIS IMPORTANT ?
What if you went to your supermarket and found only one brand of toothpaste? Suppose there was only one pizza shop in your town and it charged $25 for a small pie. Economic principles such as the laws of supply and demand create the selection and prices we find when we buy, whether it's gasoline or hamburger.

This chapter will help you understand how business principles work and why companies try to add value to products and services that will appeal to customers and create a competitive advantage. The products we select compete with others for our attention and dollars. That means creating a business model that, for example, effectively brings customers to Home Depot instead of Lowe's. When we spend our dollars, we decide which companies will be profitable enough to survive.

Why Is This Important?

Students today are more and more interested in why and how business topics relate to them in their everyday lives. The "Why Is This Important?" feature, written by Judith Bulin of Monroe Community College, speaks to them directly in terms of what each chapter means to them and how it affects them personally.

Throughout each chapter, short "Did You Know" boxes highlight interesting factoids, statistics, quotes, and even trivia relating to business. This feature, written by Monty Lynn of Abilene Christian University, is designed to spark the interest of students and make them realize how truly interesting the world of business is.

Each chapter contains several "Business in Action" insight boxes, which have been carefully selected and written to increase the interest of students, but which also integrate seamlessly into the text so as not to disrupt its flow. Many books have examples that disrupt students' thought processes or distract them with enormous amounts of unnecessary detail. *Introduction to Business* avoids these pitfalls.

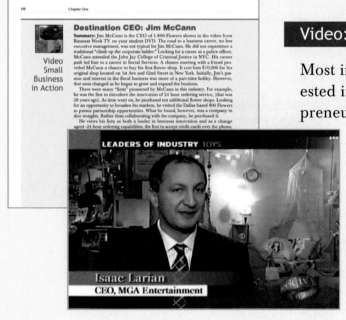

Most introduction-to-business students are interested in small-business examples and how entrepreneurs actually achieve success. The "Small Business in Action" boxes, written by Anthony Chelte of Midwestern State University, discuss videos prepared for each chapter. All of these videos can be found on the Student DVD for *Introduction to Business.*

Developing Business Skills

The end-of-chapter learning features, entitled "Developing Business Skills," is composed of a series of exercises that offer additional insight into the chapter material to improve the real-world learning experience of students. Designed to create lively discussion for the whole class, small groups, or at the individual level, six of these exercises represent a variety of ways for an instructor to engage students. In practice, an instructor will have to decide which of these exercises to select and use in any particular class period, or which to use as homework assignments. Frequently, instructors find that varying the particular exercises they use over the semester is the best way to engage students.

Questions for Discussion and Action

"Questions for Discussion and Action" are a set of chapter-related questions and points for reflection, some of which ask students to research actual management issues and learn first-hand from practicing managers.

Developing Business Skills

QUESTIONS FOR DISCUSSION AND ACTION

1. What are property rights and how do they affect the use of productive resources?

2. In what ways can the use of money lead (1) to a more productive use of resources, and (2) to a more profitable use of resources?

3. What is the difference between feudalism and mercantilism? How are the two connected?

4. What is the relationship between capital and enterprise? How did capitalism affect the use of productive resources?

5. What caused the Industrial Revolution, and why did it take so long?

6. How did the emergence of business organization forms based on (1) the hierarchy of authority (2) the joint-stock arrangement and (3) limited liability help to further business commerce and occupations?

Ethics in Action

"Ethics in Action" is an exercise that can be used at the class, group, or individual level. This feature challenges students to apply ethical principles as they try to figure out the right response to a business issue or problem. Generally, the best discussion arises in a group or class context as students express opposing views of the issues involved.

ETHICS IN ACTION

Ethics and History

Each of the three main kinds of business systems–feudalism, mercantilism, and capitalism–is associated with a particular kind of ethical or moral position: for example, different views about the rights workers should have relative to the owners of land or capital.

- Identify differences in the ethical or moral positions that explain how labor is treated in each of these three business systems.

- Do you see any themes going through them? Would you say the treatment of workers improved over time from an ethical point of view or did it get worse? Why?

- What basic kinds of rights do you think workers should have in business organizations today? For example, do you think rights, such as the rights to unionize, or to receive fair and equitable treatment are appropriate? What about workers' rights to privacy? Do employers have a right to monitor workers' e-mail and telephone conversations, for example?

- What ethical principles do you think multinational companies should abide by when deciding where to locate their operations or how to treat their workforces in the countries in which they operate?

SMALL GROUP EXERCISE

Adventures in Barbecuing

Read the following and then break up into groups of three or four people and discuss the issues involved. Be prepared to share your discussion with the rest of your class. (This exercise can also be done individually).

You and your friends have decided to work together to create an outdoor barbecue catering service in the summer months to raise money for next year's college fees. Your business model is to offer customers a worry-free party service with high-quality food and all the accoutrements. The activities you need to perform include food buying, food preparation, setting up the party at the customer's home, serving the food, and clearing up afterwards.

1. How can you create most value for customers? List the various elements of your business model.
2. How will you divide up the work among yourselves to create the most value for customers?
3. What will be the main factors that determine the profitability of your business?

Small Group Exercise

This exercise is designed to allow instructors to utilize interactive experiential exercises in groups of 3–4 students. Each exercise contains a chapter-related issue guaranteed to lead to debate among students. The instructor calls on students to break up into small groups, simply by turning to people around them, and all students participate in the exercise in-class. A mechanism is provided for the different groups to share what they have learned with each other.

Developing Good Business Sense

This exercise presents a realistic scenario in which some kind of business challenge, problem, or opportunity is presented and students offer advice and a recommended course of action based on the chapter content. Because managers and organizations frequently need this kind of help, these exercises provide students a real, hands-on way to take an action-oriented approach to solving "real" problems by applying what they've just learned.

DEVELOPING GOOD BUSINESS SENSE

Which Job in Which Company?

You are in the process of searching for a part-time job to help pay your way through college. You want to find a job that you will be able to keep for at least two years—a job in a company where you feel you will be able to develop skills that will help you later in your business career. You are currently considering several job options.

1. What factors should you consider when deciding upon the best job to look for (assuming you have a choice)?
2. What factors should you consider when deciding upon the best company to work for?
3. How would you go about finding out about the pros and cons of a particular job or a particular organization?

BusinessWeek   **CASE FOR DISCUSSION**

The New Nike: No Longer the Brat of Sports Marketing, It Has a Higher Level of Discipline and Performance

In many ways, the sleek, four-story building that houses Nike Inc.'s Innovation Kitchen is a throwback to the company's earliest days. Located on the ground floor of the Mia Hamm building on Nike's 175-acre headquarters campus in Beaverton, Oregon, the Kitchen is where Nike cooked up the shoes that made it the star of the $3.5 billion athletic footwear industry. In this think tank for sneakers, designers find inspiration in everything from Irish architecture to the curving lines of a Stradivarius violin. One wall displays models of every Air Jordan ever made, while low-rise cubicles are littered with sketches of new shoes. The Kitchen is off limits to most visitors and even to most Nike employees. The sign on the door says, only half in jest: "Nobody gets in to see the cooks. Not nobody. Not no how."

This is where, nearly 20 years ago, Nike star designer Tinker Hatfield came up with the Air Jordan—the best-selling sports shoe of all time. Right now, Hatfield and his team are tallying the results of the Athens 2004 Olympic Games. Hatfield and his design geeks produced an array of superfast sneakers for the Games, including the sleek track spike called Monsterfly for sprinters and the Air Zoom Miler for distance runners. As befits a global company, Nike's sponsored athletes hailed from all over the world. They took home a lot of hardware from Athens, including 50 gold medals and dozens more silver and bronze. And Nike apparel had its day in the sun, too. The top four finishers in the men's 100-meter race all wore the sign of the Swoosh.

GOING ESTABLISHMENT. The most telling events for Nike didn't take place on the track, however. The brash guerrilla marketer, famous for thumbing its nose at big-time sporting events, was showing a new restraint. Eight years ago in Atlanta, Nike ambushed basketball sponsor Champion (a brand of Sara Lee Corporation) by sneaking giant Swoosh signs into the arena. When the cameras panned the stands, TV audiences saw the Nike logo loud and clear, while Champion had nothing. Nike has even signed up to become an official U.S. Olympic sponsor in four years in Beijing, and it has toned down its anti-Establishment attitude. For good reason: These days, Nike is the Establishment when it comes to global sports marketing. With revenues exceeding $12 billion in fiscal 2004, the company that Philip H. Knight started three decades ago by selling sneakers out of the back of a car at track meets has finally grown up.

The kind of creativity that led Bill Bowerman, the University of Oregon track coach who co-founded the company with Knight, to dream up a new kind of sneaker tread after studying the pattern on his wife's waffle iron, is still revered at Nike. When it comes to the rest of the business, however, it's a whole new ball game. Gone are the days when Nike execs, working on little more than hunches, would do just about anything and spend just about any amount in the quest for publicity and market share.

But in the past few years, the company has devoted as much energy to the mundane details of running a business—such as developing top-flight information systems, logistics, and (yawn) supply-chain management—as it has to marketing coups and cutting-edge sneaker design. More and more,

BusinessWeek Case for Discussion

Each chapter ends with one or more cases from *BusinessWeek* magazine that can be used for further analysis of the chapter's issues. Each case has been carefully chosen to reflect contemporary issues and problems in business and to offer further information on the topics in the chapter or career-related issues. The accompanying discussion questions encourage students to read about and to analyze how managers approach real problems in the business world.

BUILDING YOUR MANAGEMENT SKILLS
Know Thyself

You, as do most people, probably hope to have a career working at something you enjoy, feeling that you do it reasonably well, and making a decent income. We might think that intelligence, drive, and opportunity will make that happen, You can improve your chances of achieving your career goals. Knowing which careers best suit your thinking and problem solving style, satisfy your primary motivational needs, and make you feel passionate about what you do will help you to succeed. You can start to develop the self-knowledge you need to make good career decisions by doing the self-assessment exercise on your Student DVD titled "Career Planning Based on Brain Dominance and Thinking Styles Inventory".

The "Building Your Management Skills" exercises are flash-based self-assessments and learning exercises that can be found on both the Student DVD and Online Learning Center to accompany this book. Students are able to complete these exercises on their own and receive instant, comprehensive feedback to their responses. There are nearly 50 exercises to choose from in all, and relevant ones for each chapter are highlighted within the end-of-chapter material for students to complete.

Chapter Video

CHAPTER VIDEO
Todd McFarlane

The video features a discussion with Todd McFarlane, CEO of McFarlane Companies in Tempe, Arizona. This global company spans comics, sports, monsters, and toys. In fact, it is the world's largest and most successful toy company. McFarlane is a very successful entrepreneur who started as a college baseball player looking to break into the major leagues. Unfortunately, this venture was not successful. Instead, he fell back on his self-taught ability to draw comics. After 300 rejections from various companies, Marvel Comics hired him. In 1990, Todd was the highest paid comic cartoonist in the industry.

He still wasn't satisfied, however. He left the company at the peak of his career and took 6 of the leading artists with him and formed his own company. Success came fairly quickly with the publication of the comic book *Spawn* which sold 1.7 million copies. This success was despite the predictions by industry insiders that Todd McFarlane wouldn't last a year on his own.

McFarlane knows that the two most important elements to successfully generate wealth are entrepreneurship and knowledge. Both of which he possesses in large measure. In a dynamic business environment, there are several areas that need to be addressed in order to be successful. (1) Economic environment–in McFarlane's case it is focused in the area of intellectual property laws; (2) technological environment–McFarlane sees technology as a tool to push the creative environment; (3) competitive environment–he sees the opportunity to earn less per unit profit by taking advantage of the opportunities to produce a higher quality product; (4) social environment–he keys in on his target demographic; (5) global environment–which affects all the other areas.

1. From Todd McFarlane's perspective, what is the key element of his business model?
2. What are the four main productive factors in business organizations?
3. What influences people to buy or not buy a product such as the comic book *Spawn* created by McFarlane?

Along with the "Small Business in Action" videos for each chapter found on the Student DVD, each chapter has a corresponding video accompanied by relevant discussion questions. These chapter videos can be found on both the VHS video collection and the Instructor Video DVD.

Introduction to Business offers a variety of resources to help you organize and bring to life the classroom experience for your students.

Instructor's Manual

(ISBN: 10-digit: 007-320980-5, 13-digit: 978-007-320980-7)

Prepared by Judith G. Bulin of Monroe Community College, the Instructor's Manual contains material above and beyond what you need to prepare an effective classroom experience. Bulin has had many years of experience preparing instructor's manuals, student study guides, Web-based study guides, and test banks. The

Instructor's Manual for *Introduction to Business* includes a "road map" for each chapter, teaching tips, and other useful information that can be used to capture the interest of students. In detail, the manual includes the following:

- Lecture outlines with embedded figures, tables, and PowerPoint slides notations.

- Teaching Tips
    - "Think about It" questions to stimulate classroom discussion.
    - Discussion points.

- Discussion questions based on each chapter's learning objectives.

- PowerPoint notations.

- Figures-library references.

- Instructions on how to use the Active Classroom Resource Manual (more later in the Preface on this new manual).

- Instructions on how to use the "Build Your Management Skills" exercises (more later in the Preface about these self-assessment exercises).

- Answers to end-of-chapter material and discussion questions.

VHS and DVD Video Collections

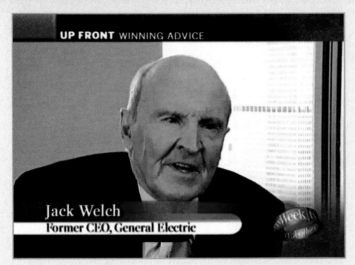

(VHS ISBN: 10-digit: 007-320984-8, 13-digit: 978-007-320984-5
DVD ISBN: 10-digit: 007-320983-X, 13-digit: 978-007-320983-8)
The VHS Video Collection that accompanies the text contains one video for every chapter from sources such as BusinessWeek TV, NBC News, PBS, and even originally produced material. Topics range from marketing and product development at 3M, to motivation at The Container Store, to leadership and influence with Sylvia Rhone, formerly of Elektra Records. The Student DVD contains the "Small Business in Action" videos highlighted in the boxes in the text, and the entire collection of videos that are found on the Instructor VHS and Student DVD, respectively, can be found on the Instructor Video DVD.

Printed Testbank and Computerized Testbank

(Print ISBN: 10-digit: 007-320981-3, 13-digit: 978-007-320981-4)
Prepared by Jim Steele of Chattanooga State Technical Community College, the Testbank contains a variety of true/false, multiple-choice, and essay questions, as well as "scenario-based" questions. These questions are application-based and use a situation described in a narrative. Three-to-five, multiple-choice test questions based on the situation described in the narrative are then included. The Computerized Testbank can be found on the Instructor's CD-ROM.

PowerPoint Slides

Prepared by Ray Polchow, Zane State College, the PowerPoint collection contains everything from an easy-to-follow outline, to additional slides with embedded video clips and Web links, to figure downloads from the text. This versatility allows you to create a custom presentation suitable for your own tastes and needs.
The Instructor's Manual, Computerized Testbank, and PowerPoint slide collection can all be found on the Instructor's CD-ROM. (ISBN: 10-digit: 007-320985-6, 13-digit: 978-007-320985-2)

Active Classroom Resource Guide

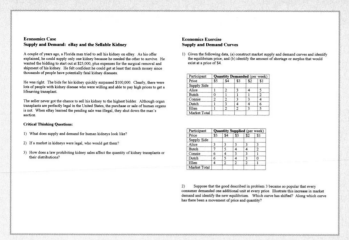

(ISBN: 10-digit: 007-319276-7, 13-digit: 978-007-319276-5) For those of you who are looking for additional material for in-class or out, McGraw-Hill/Irwin has developed the Active Classroom Resource Manual, containing cases, exercises, and project ideas (and accompanying Instructor Notes) for nearly every introductory course topic, including economics (supply and demand), ethics and social responsibility (whistle blowing), and entrepreneurship (SWOT Analysis). Many of the exercises were the result of reviewer feedback indicating that they wanted to delve into more difficult introduction-to-business topics.

Online Learning Center (OLC) with Premium Content

www.mhhe.com/jonesintro

Access everything you need to teach your course through our convenient Online Learning Center (OLC). A secure Instructor Resource Center stores your essential course materials to save you prep time before class. The Instructor's Manual, PowerPoint, and additional material for your students are now just a couple of clicks away. You will also find useful packaging information and notes on the Online Learning Center.

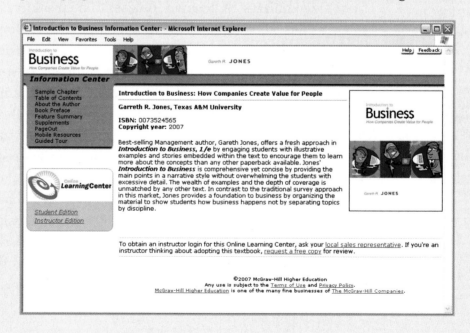

CPS (Wireless Classroom Performance System) by eInstruction

Have you ever asked yourself: "How can I measure class participation?" or "How do I encourage class participation?" If so, then CPS might be the product for you. CPS enables you to poll students and record their responses to questions posed on a PowerPoint slide as well as monitor their attendance. CPS also offers a variety of reporting features, including grade books that are easy to export to WebCT or Blackboard. For your students, CPS is as simple as using buttons on a remote control. Questions can be designed by you, or you can choose from a set of 20 per chapter available for the book. Ask your local McGraw-Hill/Irwin Sales Representative how to get CPS for your classroom.

Homework Manager

McGraw-Hill's Homework Manager (MHHM) uses selected problems from video quizzes and chapter quizzes to help students develop problem-solving skills. The students log in to complete the homework assignments and submit them for immediate, automatic grading. Each class has its own unique homepage that contains assignment material specific to the course and instructor. The assignments can be used to determine part of the overall grade your students receive. You control the rules and policies surrounding the assignments, which can range from low-stakes, self-study sessions to homework sessions and high-stakes, proctored exams. When an assignment is published, you determine when it is available to students and establish the due date and grade parameters recorded in the system's grade book. The system provides students with a graded assignment report that can include feedback about incorrect answers and other helpful study information. Ask your local McGraw-Hill/Irwin Sales Representative how to get the optimal package of Homework Manager and related textual material for you and your students.

Instructor Supplements

Printed Study Guide

(ISBN: 10-digit: 007-320986-4, 13-digit: 978-007-320986-9)
The Student Study Guide contains:

- Chapter summaries.

- Key-terms mastery exercises, including matching and fill-in-the-blank questions.

- Multiple-choice quizzes.

- Scenario-based quizzes.

Student DVD

(Packaged with text, ISBN: 10-digit: 007-322436-7, 13-digit: 978-007-322436-7)
Corresponding to the "Small Business in Action" boxes in the text, the Student DVD contains the videos that are highlighted in these boxes. Among the entrepreneurs featured in the videos are Jim McCann, the CEO of 1-800-FLOWERS, and Isaac Larian, the creator of the Bratz dolls. Other small-business topics featured in the videos include starting a business, franchising, and what it's really like to "be your own boss." The DVD also contains quizzes on these videos as well as the other chapter videos, chapter quizzes for self-study, and the related "Build Your Management Skills" exercises. (The videos on the Student DVD can also be found on the Instructor Video DVD.)

Online Learning Center (OLC) at

www.mhhe.com/jonesintro
More and more students are studying online. That's why we offer an Online Learning Center (OLC) that follows *Introduction to Business* chapter by chapter. It doesn't require any building or maintenance on your part, and it is ready to go the moment you and your students type in the URL. As your students study, they can refer to the OLC Web site for such benefits as:

- Internet-based activities.

- Self-grading quizzes.

- Learning tools.

- Additional video and related video exercises.

Developing Business Skills

Finding a way to integrate and present an overview of the rapidly changing world of business and business activities as well as make it interesting and meaningful for students is not an easy task. As I wrote and revised the several drafts of ***Introduction to Business,*** I was fortunate to have had the assistance of several people who contributed greatly to the book's final form. First, I am grateful to Andy Winston, our original sponsoring editor, for his constant support and commitment to the project that led to its realization. Second, I am grateful to Kelly Lowery for taking on the task of ensuring that the book would meet the needs of its users, satisfy students, and for finding ways to provide the resources needed to continually improve and refine a new product. Third, I am grateful to Christine "Chipper" Scheid, our internal developmental editor, for so ably coordinating the book's progress and Ellen Cleary, our marketing manager, for providing us with concise and timely feedback and information from professors and reviewers that have allowed us to shape the book to the needs of its intended market. My external developmental editor, Amy Ray, also has my gratitude for refining and sharpening the text of the book so that students are better able to grasp its key ideas. All these people have been instrumental in creating a product we hope will meet its goal of helping students better understand business and the many ways in which it affects them.

I also wish to thank Artemio Ortiz for producing a student-friendly engaging design, Mary Conzachi for coordinating the production process, and Patsy Hartmangruber of Texas A&M University for providing excellent word-processing and graphic support. Finally, I am indebted to the many colleagues and reviewers who provided me with useful and detailed feedback in several rounds of reviews and testing, and for their perceptive comments and valuable suggestions for improving the manuscript. They include:

Sally Andrews
Linn-Benton Community College

Vicki Befort
Arapahoe Community College

Maida Bessler
Los Angeles Trade Tech

Dennis Brode
Sinclair Community College

Deborah Brown
North Carolina State University

Judith G. Bulin
Monroe Community College

Lana Carnes
Eastern Kentucky University

Dana Dye
Gulf Coast Community College

Leatrice Freer
Pitt Community College

Steven Gilbertz
Richland Community College

Kris Gossett
Ivy Tech State College

Claudia Green
Pace University

Dennis Heiner
College Of Southern Idaho

James P. Hess
Ivy Tech State College

Kristen Hislop
University of Colorado at Boulder

Monty Lynn
Abilene Christian University

Richard Magjuka
IUPUI, Indianapolis

Roanne Angiello
Bergen Community College

Katherine Conway
Borough of Manhattan Community College

Mark Doubeck
Collin County Community College

Karen Eboch
Bowling Green State University

Dale Feinauer
University Of Wisconsin-Oshkosh

Richard Hilliard
Nichols College

Martha Laham
Diablo Valley Community College

David Leventhal
Queens College CUNY

Robert Matthews
Oakton Community College

Marla Mutis
Roosevelt University Chicago City College

Darrell Neron
Pierce College

Andy Nowel
North Carolina State University

Mary Padula
Borough of Manhattan Community College

Vinny Quan
Fashion Institute of Technology

Anthony Racka
Oakland Community College

Greg Westby
Portland Community College

Kathy Williams
St. Johns River Community College

John Wrigley
Portland Community College

Maxine McGarvey
Kingsborough Community College

John Mozingo
University Of Wisconsin, Oshkosh

Therese A. Maskulka
Youngstown State University

Roy R. Pipitone
Erie Community College, South

Janet Seggern
Lehigh Carbon Community College

Jim Steele
Chattanooga State Technical Community College

Tom Voight
Aurora University

Richard Westfall
Cabrillo College

Jennifer J. Wright
Drexel University

Gareth Jones

Texas A&M University

Introduction to
Business

How Companies Create Value for People

Part 1

The Environment of Business

Part One, *the Environment of Business,* provides the big picture of what business is about. Chapter 1 develops a three-pronged approach to understanding business based on business as commerce, business as an occupation, and business as an organization. It also brings out the essential meaning of terms such as specialization and profit and tells students why companies exist to provide goods and services to customers. Finally, it also describes the plan of this book and introduces the concept of the value chain, which will be used to structure the discussion of the principal business functions in Part 3. Chapter 2 looks at how business has evolved over the centuries to identify the factors of production and their role in the business process. We trace business back to the Stone Age, through war waged to secure land and labor, the industrial revolution, the development of unionism and socialism, through industrialism to the age of information technology. Chapter 3 examines the essential functions of the entrepreneur and manager; it also looks at the role of the employee and provides an in-depth account of the stages of the career process. Chapter 4 then provides an overview of the main issues facing multinational companies operating in today's changing global environment.

All these chapters, but especially Chapter 5 on business ethics and the legal environment of business make it clear that business is about the pursuit and creation of profit and wealth. Also, that because almost everyone is engaged in the same quest for wealth to satisfy their needs the result is competition and self-interested behavior. While much of this competition is healthy and promotes the well-being of both people and society, competition can lead to fraud and deceit. Hence, management and entrepreneurship are always linked to ethical and legal issues. Chapter 5 therefore puts business in the wider framework of ethics, law, and society.

1 What Is Business?

Learning Objectives

After studying this chapter you should be able to:

1. Differentiate between the three meanings of business as commerce, business as an occupation, and business as an organization, and identify the four main kinds of productive resources.

2. Understand how the forces of supply and demand determine fair, or market, prices.

3. Appreciate how a company's business model is the source of its competitive advantage and can mean the difference between merely making a profit and profitability.

4. Recognize the way specialization and the division of labor lead to increasing profits and wealth via the market's "invisible hand."

5. List the reasons why business organizations are created and how they facilitate commerce and lower transaction costs.

WHY IS THIS IMPORTANT ?

What if you went to your supermarket and found only one brand of toothpaste? Suppose there was only one pizza shop in your town and it charged $25 for a small pie. Economic principles such as the laws of supply and demand create the selection and prices we find when we buy, whether it's gasoline or hamburger.

This chapter will help you understand how business principles work and why companies try to add value to products and services that will appeal to customers and create a competitive advantage. The products we select compete with others for our attention and dollars. That means creating a business model that, for example, effectively brings customers to Home Depot instead of Lowe's. When we spend our dollars, we decide which companies will be profitable enough to survive.

A Question of Business
Kroger, Wal-Mart, and Supermarket Competition

How and Why Do Companies Provide Goods and Services for Customers?

Suppose you walk into one of your local supermarkets such as Kroger, the largest supermarket chain in the United States in 2005 (www.kroger.com). You are walking into a business enterprise or company that is there to sell you an assortment of food, drinks, and consumer products selected to appeal to you and to satisfy your needs. What makes you want to shop or trade with Kroger rather than with, say, Albertson's or Wal-Mart? And why has Kroger spent billions of dollars to build and stock its store to attract you to shop there? Moreover, what factors determine the kinds of goods and services Kroger's chooses to offer you and the prices that it charges for its products?

Kroger is in *business* to make money for its stockholders, the people who have used their savings or capital to buy shares of its company stock. Kroger's stockholders' goal is to increase the value or "get a return" on their investment in the company's business. This will happen if (1) Kroger's managers select the right mix of products and attract more customers, then (2) can sell these products at a price high enough to generate sales revenues (the money it receives from selling the products) that (3) more than exceed the costs of operating the business (including payroll costs, the cost of purchasing the many products it sells, and the cost of leasing store space).

When Kroger's sales revenues exceed its operating costs, it is said to make a *profit*, the difference between its total revenues and total

costs. If Kroger can show its profit is likely to increase over time, more people will want to buy its stock. Then Kroger's stock price goes up, and so does the value of its stockholders' investment. The increase in stock price is its stockholders' reward for the *risk* they have taken in investing their money in its business: If a company ultimately performs poorly and its profits start to fall, the value of its stock falls; if it goes out of business entirely, stockholders lose all of their money.

Because the grocery business is competitive, finding ways to increase profit is not easy. Many of Kroger's rivals are trying to lure its customers away by offering them lower-priced or higher-quality products. Wal-Mart has become Kroger's major rival. Wal-Mart is rapidly expanding its chain of superstores and grocery stores throughout the United States and offering customers lower prices than Kroger's. To fight back, Kroger has had to reduce the prices of it products. Whereas in the past, Kroger might have made a five-cent profit by selling a can of soup it now makes only three cents. Although this difference might seem trivial, it is not. The supermarket business has low profit margins, meaning the difference between the price at which Kroger buys products from manufacturers and sells them to customers is very small. Thus, a small drop in profit on every product it sells, such as a two-cent drop in profit on each can of soup, adds up to a major problem.

Kroger's managers have responded to Wal-Mart's competitive challenge in two ways. First, they have found ways to reduce Kroger's operating costs by using new information technology such as scanners and automated, self-service checkout lanes. So, even though Kroger must sell its products at lower prices, because it's managed to lower its other costs, it has been able to maintain its profit margins. Second,

Kroger has tried to attract customers by offering them a much wider selection of superior quality meats and vegetables than Wal-Mart. Third, it has built attractive new stores to make Kroger a more enjoyable place to shop. The catch is that these latter tactics have *raised* Kroger's operating costs because buying higher-quality products and building new stores is expensive. But this strategy will not be a problem if Kroger manages to attract *more* customers willing to pay *higher prices* to obtain better-quality food and enjoy surroundings that are more attractive. If customers are willing to pay prices that are higher, Kroger will be able to increase its profit margins, and its profit will increase over time.

Recently, the battle with Wal-Mart has reduced Kroger's profit margins, although it is still making a substantial profit. But finding new ways to keep customers happy is its managers' major priority: If Kroger's customers continue to leave to shop at competitors like Wal-Mart, its sales revenues and profit margins will fall further. Stockholders will begin to sell their shares, and Kroger's future will be in jeopardy.[1]

Overview

So far Kroger has met the challenge posed by Wal-Mart because its managers were aware of the changes taking place in the supermarket business; in June 2005 Kroger reported a much bigger than expected increase in profit. Many of its managers have risen through the ranks; many more have business degrees, and they all have wide experience of the supermarket business. This made them alert to the threat posed by Wal-Mart's fast growth and low prices. They also knew it was necessary to build attractive new supermarkets, offer a better shopping experience and superior produce. Many people, however, have not had much contact with the world of business and are not familiar with the way it operates.

Take the "business" of babysitting, for example. What do potential babysitters think about when they are deciding how much to charge a new family for their services? Do they think about the number of children involved or their ages when setting the price? Do they consider the kinds of activities they will be expected to perform such as preparing food or doing laundry? What about the time and gas it takes to drive to and from the family's house? Does a babysitter include these costs in deciding upon the price to charge? Suppose the parents guarantee they will be home by 10:30 p.m., and then don't get back at 11:00 p.m. Should they pay a higher "overtime" charge? Plumbers or electricians would factor all these kinds of things into the price they charge for their services, but do babysitters?

One reason that people may not understand what being "in business" means is that they often don't appreciate the way business operates around them. At a supermarket, for example, we take for granted that there will be a wide selection of fresh meat and produce and plenty of checkers and baggers to get us through the checkout process quickly. Often, it is only when supermarkets don't work as we expect—when there are too few checkers so we have to wait in line, or when we find that the food we bought is old or stale, that we wonder why the business is not working properly.

In this chapter, we start the process of building an appreciation of what business is and how it affects us in so many ways. First, we identify the three main meanings of the term: business as commerce, business as an occupation, and business as an organization. We describe the nature of business commerce and trade, along with how the forces of supply and demand determine the price of a product. We then discuss the way business occupations develop because of the process of specialization and the division of labor. Then, the way business organizations emerge to provide a stable platform on which people can engage in business commerce is described.

Finally, the relationship between the chapters in this book and the way they work together to provide an overview of how business creates value for people or the "value-creation process" is outlined. By the end of this chapter, you will understand what business is about and why business has always been a crucial factor in determining the occupations, wealth, morality, and culture of people and society.

What Is Business?

"Monkey business" is one of many sayings, or adages, connected with the word *business*.

"The great game of business," "the world of business," "monkey business," "I'm going into business for myself," "big business," "the business of America is business," even "mind your own business," are some of the many sayings, or adages, connected to the word *business*. Business is a complicated word to define and understand because it has several different, but related, meanings. Let's pull apart these meanings to understand what business is about.

Business is goal-directed behavior aimed at getting and using productive resources to buy, make, trade, and sell goods and services that can be sold at a profit. **Productive resources**—*land, labor, capital,* and *enterprise*—are the four crucial ingredients that make this possible. Typically, a business (1) operates from a specific location and facility (*land*); (2) employs one or more people (*labor*); (3) needs money (*capital*) to buy raw materials, inputs, machinery and computers, land, and labor; and (4) requires the foresight, drive, knowledge, ability, and ingenuity (*enterprise*) of one or more people—its owners or managers. Together, the cost of acquiring and using these four resources to make and sell goods and services determines a company's **operating costs.** This is illustrated in Figure 1.1.

Figure 1.1
Productive Resources and Operating Costs

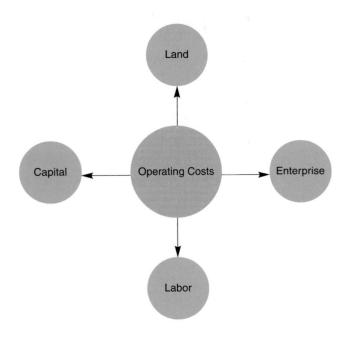

The role of the business owner and manager is to be *enterprising,* to sense an opportunity to acquire and use all the other productive resources to create a product. A product is any kind of *good* or *service* that other people value and want to buy. Value refers to how much utility a product gives customers, that is, how well it satisfies their desires or needs. In business, the most common way of measuring the value of a product is by how much customers are willing to pay for it, that is, by its price.

A company's business model outlines its plan for using its resources to create valuable products that will give it a competitive advantage—*the business model specifies how a company is going to create value for customers.* A company has a competitive advantage when it can offer customers a product that has more value to them than similar products offered by other companies. If the business model is competitive, and customers are attracted to the company's product, the company generates money, or income, from the sale of the product. This is called sales revenue. The profit a company earns is the total amount of money left over after operating costs have been deducted from its sales revenues. If sales revenues are less than operating costs, a company has made a *loss.*

Profit that is kept in a company and invested in its business increases its capital, the total monetary value of its financial assets such as cash, property, land, stock, patents, and brand name. The total capital invested in business activity is a major part of a society's wealth the sum total of the resources, assets, riches, and material possessions owned by people and groups in that society. The definitions of all these key terms are listed in Table 1.1. They are a basic part of the language of business.

The founding of the Blockbuster video rental chain, described in Business in Action, illustrates how a business model can give a company a competitive advantage.

Table 1.1
Key Business Terms

Business	Goal-directed behavior aimed at getting and using productive resources to buy, make, trade, and sell goods and services that can be sold at a profit.
Productive resources	The four crucial ingredients—land, labor, capital, and enterprise—that are needed to profit from business.
Operating costs	The costs of acquiring and using the four productive resources to make and sell goods and services.
Product	Any kind of good or service that other people value and want to buy.
Value	How much utility a product gives customers; that is, how well it satisfies their desires or needs.
Price	A way of measuring the value of a product by how much customers are willing to pay for it.
Business model	A company's plan of action to use resources to create a product that will give it a competitive advantage.
Competitive advantage	A company's ability to offer customers a product that has more value to them than similar products offered by other companies.
Sales revenue	The amount of money or income that a company generates from the sale of the product.
Profit	The total amount of money left over after operating costs have been deducted from sales revenues.
Capital	Profit that is kept in a company and invested in its business.
Wealth	The sum total of the resources, assets, riches, and material possessions owned by people and groups in society.

Business in Action

A Blockbuster Adventure

In the early 1980s, the number of VCRs in peoples' homes was expanding rapidly, and thousands of small video stores were opening up to rent the videotapes that people wanted. Many of these "mom and pop" stores were small, offered only a limited selection of titles, and were often located in hard-to-find locations in remote shopping centers. Many of the stores also rented X-rated movies. Of course, parents and their children—the biggest segment of the video market—were reluctant to visit these stores.

David Cook, who was searching for a new business opportunity at this time, realized that there was a market for a new kind of video store: one that would appeal to families and satisfy their needs in a way that no other store could. In 1985, Cook opened his first Blockbuster Video Store.

What were the elements of Cook's business model? To encourage families to come in and browse, Blockbuster stores were free standing, brightly decorated and lit, and in good locations with lots of parking. Cook made sure the stores were full of titles that appealed to children, and no X-rated movies were offered. He also pioneered the practice of renting out tapes for three-day periods and adopted a marketing campaign aimed at attracting the family viewing audience. Finally, he took advantage of new technology such as bar codes and scanners to speed up the checkout process and improve the shopping experience. As a result, Blockbuster became a smash hit. Every store Cook opened was immediately successful, grossing $70,000-$80,000 a month in revenues. Because each store's operating costs were only $20,000-$30,000 a month, profit margins were enormous. Cook soon

David Cook, the founder of Blockbuster, set out to change the focus of the adult-oriented, video rental business to one that focused on the needs of families.

franchising
A business practice whereby investors are allowed to purchase the right to own and operate a business using a company's name and business model.

franchised his video superstore concept—that is, he sold investors the right to own and operate their own Blockbuster stores using his business name and model. He later took the company "public," meaning shares of stock were issued and sold to investors. The chain's high profits caused the price of Blockbuster's shares to skyrocket, and it became one of the 100 fastest growing companies in the Fortune 500. Today, Blockbuster is the largest video rental chain in the world with over 5,000 stores. Cook had clearly found an opportunity to create a company that offered customers more value than they had previously been getting.[2]

nonprofit organization
An organization that is not in business to make profit but to provide value to the people and groups it serves.

Before we go on, we should recognize that while *for-profit* companies need competitive business models so do *nonprofit* organizations, such as government and state agencies and charities. By definition, nonprofit organizations are those that are not in business to make profit for stockholders but to provide value to the people and groups they serve. Nevertheless, nonprofits still need a business model that allows them to control their operating costs and to find ways to use their resources to create the most value they can. Charities, for example, compete to obtain donations. Suppose you have to decide which charity to give your money to. Would you give it to the charity that is able to send 85% of your money to needy people after it pays its operating expenses or just 45%? If a particular charity is known for paying its managers high salaries and having high operating costs, people will give less to this charity. Just like for-profit companies then, nonprofits must have a business model to guide their decision making.

**Video
Small
Business
in Action**

Destination CEO: Jim McCann

Summary: Jim McCann is the CEO of 1-800-Flowers shown in the video from Business Week TV on your student DVD. The road to a business career, no less executive management, was not typical for Jim McCann. He did not experience a traditional "climb up the corporate ladder." Looking for a career as a police officer, McCann attended the John Jay College of Criminal Justice in NYC. His career path led him to a career in Social Services. A chance meeting with a friend provided McCann a chance to buy his first flower shop. It cost him $10,000 for his original shop located on 1st Ave and 62nd Street in New York. Initially, Jim's passion and interest in the floral business was more of a part-time hobby. However, that soon changed as he began to grow and expand the business.

There were many "firsts" pioneered by McCann in this industry. For example, he was the first to introduce the innovation of 24 hour ordering service, (that was 28 years ago). As time went on, he purchased ten additional flower shops. Looking for an opportunity to broaden his markets, he visited the Dallas-based 800 Flowers to pursue partnership opportunities. What he found, however, was a company in dire straights. Rather than collaborating with the company, he purchased it.

He views his firm as both a leader in business innovation and as a change agent–24 hour ordering capabilities, the first to accept credit cards over the phone, the first to have an Internet presence on AOL. Now, 70% of his sales are from the Internet. Total sales this year reached $650 million, up 8% from the previous year. McCann credits his success as a business leader to his family roots that emphasized hard work and diligence. Prior to becoming CEO of this multimillion dollar enterprise, Jim McCann was a social service worker. He credits much of his innovative and creative abilities to working with his clients in that sector.

Discussion Questions

1. Identify four central business terms that would directly apply to the Jim McCann story.
2. What type of business model did McCann develop as he moved from his hobby to a multi-million dollar business?
3. Based on the facts presented in the video, how would you determine whether the company has used its productive resources to create valuable goods and services?

The Three Meanings of Business

business system
The combination of commerce, occupations, and organizations that result in the production and distribution of goods and services people value.

Three different but related meanings of the word "business" can be identified: business as commerce, business as an occupation, and business as an organization. We need to consider each of these three meanings to understand what business is and how it operates. This chapter discusses these three meanings, which together form the basic building blocks of the business system. The business system, illustrated in Figure 1.2, is the combination of commerce, occupations, and organizations that result in the production and distribution of goods and services people want. In Chapter 2, we look at the evolution of business and changes in business systems over time.

Business as Commerce

Business commerce is the process through which people produce and then trade, barter, or exchange valuable goods and services to better fulfill their wants and needs. The difference between trade and barter is that trade involves the exchange of products using money whereas barter does not. When people barter, they exchange one product directly for another. The goal of business commerce and the

Figure 1.2
The Business System: Commerce, Occupation, Organization

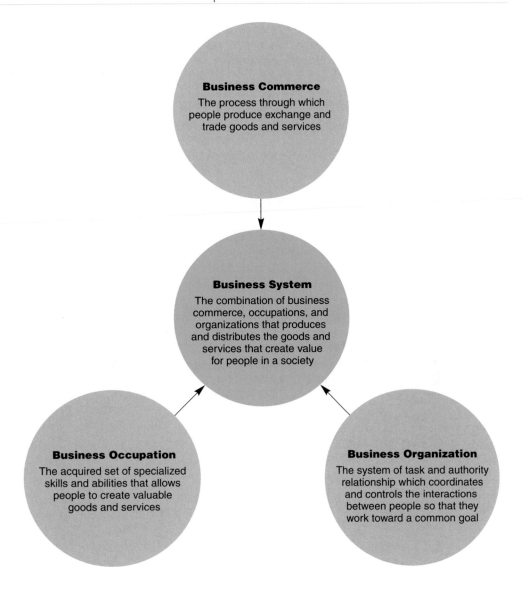

Business Commerce
The process through which people produce exchange and trade goods and services

Business System
The combination of business commerce, occupations, and organizations that produces and distributes the goods and services that create value for people in a society

Business Occupation
The acquired set of specialized skills and abilities that allows people to create valuable goods and services

Business Organization
The system of task and authority relationship which coordinates and controls the interactions between people so that they work toward a common goal

business commerce
The process by which people produce and exchange valuable goods and services that fulfill their wants and needs.

trade The exchange of products through the use of money.

barter The exchange of one product for another product.

trading or bartering of goods and services is to allow people to increase their *utility or satisfaction*–to make themselves better off by fulfilling their needs for security, food and clothing, entertainment, and so on. This occurs through exchange whereby people obtain products that are more valuable to them than the money or products they have to offer for them. For example, suppose I have plenty of potatoes but little wheat. By contrast, you have plenty of wheat but few potatoes. So, we decide to barter potatoes for wheat. We can both increase our utility and gain from the exchange as long as the wheat I get from you is more valuable to me than the potatoes I have to give you in return. People *profit* from trade or barter when the exchange increases their utility.

Whether a person has profited or increased his or her utility by obtaining a product is purely a personal *judgment.* Of course, people differ widely in their judgments. A product that one person perceives as satisfying may be perceived by another as being unsatisfying. I might believe that paying to go to a gym and work out is a painful waste of my money, time and effort. But you might believe it as an uplifting experience that makes you alert and feel better about yourself and that your money has been well spent.

People also use price as a measure of how much they profit from exchange. The price of different products is a measure of their relative value to different people. In general, the more that a particular product is valued, or *demanded,* by people, or the harder it is to find, the higher will be its price. To better understand the way business commerce works it is necessary to understand the relationship between demand, supply, and the market price.

Demand, Supply, and the Market Price

At what point do we cease to benefit or gain from the exchange of products, such as wheat and potatoes, as we continue to trade or barter? The answer from economics is that it is the *scarcity* of a product, in conjunction with our *need* for it, which determines its value and thus the price we are willing to pay for it. In barter, this price is expressed in terms of how many "units" of a product, for example, bushels of wheat, a person is willing to give up to obtain a bag of potatoes, and vice versa.

Suppose we start to barter wheat and potatoes. I have no wheat but a great desire to eat bread, so I am willing to give you quite a few bags of potatoes to obtain my first bushel of wheat. However, as we barter more and I now have two, three, or four bushels of wheat, its value goes down for me. I have more of it, so it is simply not so scarce to me. So, when I am deciding whether to buy a fifth or sixth bushel from you, I am judging how much that extra bushel is really worth to me. The reverse is true for you. You are willing to give me much more wheat to get the first bag of my potatoes than the fifth, simply because the first four bags have gone a long way to satisfy your need for potatoes.

diminishing marginal utility The principle that the value people receive from an additional unit of a product declines as they obtain more of the product.

The fact that the value or utility we receive from additional units of the *identical* product declines as we possess or consume more of it is known as the principle of diminishing marginal utility. Its result is to make the demand curve for a particular product slope downward from left to right, as shown in Figure 1.3a.

**Figure 1.3
Supply, Demand, and Market Price**

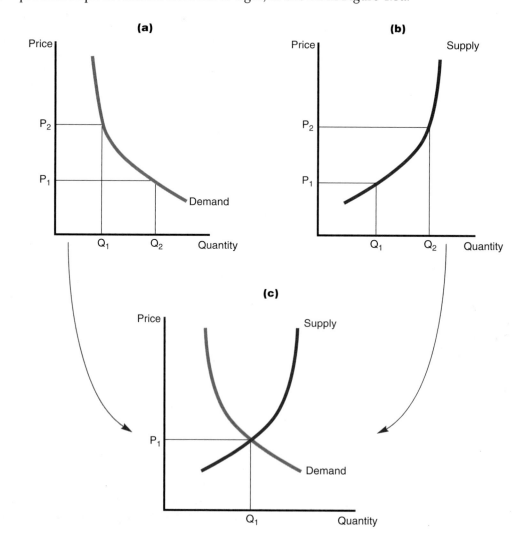

Note that this is a *marginal* curve because it shows how much *extra* utility a person will obtain from consuming each *additional* unit of a product as the total amount of the product consumed increases. The curve slopes downward, because, as just noted, the extra or marginal utility obtained falls as more and more units are consumed. The practical result of the law of diminishing marginal returns is that the quantity of a product demanded depends on its price: Specifically, consumers buy more of a product when the price of it falls and less of it when its price rises. This is called the law of demand.

law of demand The principle that states as the price of a product rises, consumers will buy less of it, and as the price of it falls, consumers will buy more of it.

On the other hand, from a supply point of view, it follows that the scarcer a product, the more valuable it is (it confers *extra* utility). This will cause the supply curve to slope upward from left to right as in Figure 1.3b. If only a small amount of a product is available people will compete to get it, and its price will be bid up. Once again, this is a *marginal* supply curve; it measures how much a supplier, the maker of a product, is willing to pay for the additional resources necessary to provide the marginal or last unit of a product. Obviously the higher the price that a product commands, the more a supplier will be willing to accept higher costs to produce the product. Thus, in general, the higher the price of a product, the more of it will be supplied. Conversely, the lower the price of a product is, the less of it will be supplied. This is called the law of supply.

law of supply The principle that states that as the price of a product rises, producers will supply more of it, and that as the price of it falls, producers will supply less of it.

market Buyers and sellers for a particular product.

DETERMINING THE MARKET PRICE In economics, the laws of supply and demand operate together to determine the price at which products will be sold in a market. A market consists of all the buyers and sellers for a particular product. Figure 1.3c shows that competition among buyers to buy a particular product, and competition among sellers to provide the product, leads the demand and supply curves to cross or intersect at the point where Quantity Q_1 is being bought and sold at a price of P_1. At this point, bargaining between buyers and sellers in a particular market has established the "going," or *market* price. As much of the good is being supplied as people want to buy, so the price is neither increasing nor decreasing.

It is important to realize that the price of all products are determined at the *margin*—the point at which the supply of the product just meets demand for it. At the margin, people have to assess carefully what value or worth a particular good or service has for them. The margin is like the center rod on a teeter-totter or a knife-edge, where people go one way or the other—buy or not buy, or sell or not sell. The price of a company's stock is determined like any other product. This is why the value of a company's stock, like Kroger's, rises and falls, often quickly. Investors buy, hold, or sell a company's stock based upon their subjective perceptions of how competitive they think its goods and services are. If they believe customers will be attracted to a company's products and the company's profits will increase, investors will bid up the price of the stock. If, for example, investors think Wendy's hamburgers are going to become increasingly popular, the demand for and price of Wendy's stock will increase. If investors think customers are switching to a competitor's products such as Subway's sandwiches and McDonald's chicken salads and that Wendy's profits will suffer as a result, they will sell Wendy's stock, and its price will decline.

Did You Know?

General Motors Corporation—assisted by Firestone, Standard Oil, and Phillips Petroleum—purchased and then dismantled more than 100 electric streetcar systems in Philadelphia, St. Louis, Los Angeles and other cities. They replaced them with GM busses. Competition, customer service, or collusion?[3]

The Business Model and Profitability

Companies are in business to make a profit. As the opening case notes, companies like Kroger or Wal-Mart are in business to maximize profits and returns to their stockholders. To achieve this goal, all companies must have a business model to guide their choices—choices about which products to make and how to use their resources most productively to maximize their profits.

As noted earlier, a successful business model allows a company to outperform its competitors. Thus, to determine how well

industry A group of companies that make similar products and compete for the same customers.

a company is performing in a particular industry, it is necessary to look at its performance *relative* to its competitors. An **industry** is a group of companies that make products that are similar or close substitutes for each other. Essentially, industry companies are competing for the *same* set of customers. The most common way of comparing how well one company is performing relative to its competitors is by measuring its profitability relative to its competitors.

THE DIFFERENCE BETWEEN PROFIT AND PROFITABILITY   You might think that *making a profit* and *profitability* are one and the same. But, in fact, the two concepts are different: Profit is simply the total or absolute monetary difference between sales revenues and operating costs; if a company's sales are $10 million, and its costs are $8 million, it has made a profit of $2 million (ignoring other complicating factors). Profitability measures how well a company is making use of its capital by investing in resources that create goods and services that generate profits.

profitability
A measurement of how well a company is making use of its resources relative to its competitors.

The important difference is that the size of the profit that a company makes in one year says little about how well its managers are making use of resources and its ability to generate future profits. In the car industry, for example, in good economic times, companies like Ford, GM, and Toyota may make billions of dollars of profit each year, but this tells us little about their relative profitability—which company is performing the best now—and which company has the best future prospects. Profitability, by contrast, gives managers and investors much more information to assess how well one company is performing against others in its industry—now and in the future. To see why this is so, consider the following example.

Imagine that there are three large companies in an industry and each pursues a different business model. Company A decides to make and sell a no-frills low-priced product; Company B offers customers a state-of-the-art, high-priced product; Company C decides to offer a mid-priced product targeted at the average customer. The company that has invested its capital in such a way that (1) it is making the most productive use of its resources (which leads to low operating costs) *and* (2) has created a product that customers are clamoring to buy even at a high price (which leads to high sales revenues) will have the highest profitability.

Suppose, for example, that Company A makes a profit of $50 million, B makes $25 million, and Company C makes $10 million. Does this mean Company A has outperformed Company B and C and is generating the most returns for its stockholders? To answer this question, we need to calculate the relative profitability of the three companies. This is a two-step process. First, it is necessary to compute a company's profit, which is the difference between total sales revenues and total operating costs. Second, it is necessary to divide that profit by the total amount of capital the company has invested in productive resources—property, plant, equipment, inventories, and other assets needed to make and sell the product. Now we know how much capital each company has invested to generate that profit.

Suppose we find out that Company A has made $50 million profit on $500 million of invested capital, Company B has made $25 million on $100 million of invested capital, and Company C has made $10 million on $300 million. Company A's profitability is 10%, Company B's is 25%, and Company C's is 3%. In other words, *Company B is generating profit at two and a half times the rate of A, whereas C is only marginally profitable.* Company B has done the most to build its stockholders' wealth because its higher level of profitability will have increased the demand for and price of its stock. The importance of considering the relative profitability of companies, rather than differences in their total profits, is clear.

A company's profitability is usually considered over time because it is seen as an indicator of its ability to generate future profits and capital. Figure 1.4 depicts how the profitability of these three companies has changed over time. Company

Did You Know?

California's total annual economic output exceeds that of Russia, Mexico, Spain, and South Korea.[4]

**Figure 1.4
Differences
in Profitability**

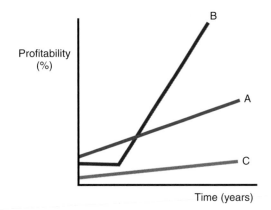

Profitability
(%)

B

A

C

Time (years)

B's profitability has been increasing rapidly over time, Company A's at a much lower rate, and Company C's has hardly increased at all. As an investor, which company's stock would you buy? Because the stock of a company normally rises as its profitability rises and vice versa, Company B would have been the most profitable company to invest in by far. Its managers created and pursued the most profitable business model. Company A is also making a respectable return for its investors; it is profitable and holding its own in the industry. However, like Kroger, it needs to find new ways to compete with Company B, perhaps by copying or imitating aspects of Company B's business model.

Company C is making a profit, but it is only marginally profitable. Its owners have to decide if the benefits of staying in its business outweigh the costs—the falling value of its shares and possible future losses. With such low profitability, a company's managers are forced to search for a new business model that can make better use of its resources and increase its profitability. At such a competitive disadvantage, however, it might become clear to managers and investors that Company C's capital would be better used in some other business. In fact, Company C might go out of business as its stockholders sell their shares and buy those of other, more profitable, companies.

INCREASING PROFITABILITY   In any industry, companies are in competition (1) to develop new and improved products to attract customers, and (2) to use their resources more productively in order to reduce their operating costs. Competition from Wal-Mart, for example, forced Kroger to find better ways to use its capital to maintain and increase its profitability. Kroger invested its capital to build attractive new stores and installed new kinds of information technology to lower its operating costs. This investment enhanced the shopping experience of Kroger's customers, which won their loyalty and allowed the company to charge higher prices than Wal-Mart. Those companies that succeed in attracting many customers (especially customers willing to pay a higher, or premium, price) *and* lowering their costs will have the highest profitability. (A **premium price** is the higher price a company is able to charge versus what its competitors can charge.) One company presently working hard to increase its profitability is Home Depot, profiled in Business in Action.

premium price The higher price a seller is able to charge versus what its competitors can charge.

**Business
in Action**

Home Depot Needs a Do-It-Yourself Fix, Too

Home Depot shot to corporate fame when it developed a business model based on offering customers a wide range of low-priced, home improvement products and excellent customer service. For example, Home Depot's well-informed salespeople offered customers good advice and even conducted classes showing "do-it-yourselfers" how to install bathrooms or tile floors. The company's business model made it the home-improvement market leader, and, until 2000 its high profitability had led to a high stock price.

All this changed in 2002 when Home Depot's stock dropped 53% after investors realized that the company's profitability had fallen sharply. This occurred both because Home Depot's business model was no longer working well and because it was experiencing intense pressure from competitors like Lowe's.

The problem began in 2000 when Home Depot's new CEO Robert Nardelli searched for a quick solution to restore the company's profitability. Nardelli's strategy was to try to reduce operating costs that had increased sharply as the chain had expanded throughout the United States. He centralized purchasing decisions hoping to realize savings in purchasing costs. He streamlined the range of products carried to reduce inventory costs. He instructed store managers to employ more part-timers to save on pensions and health-benefit costs.

But reducing operating costs will not lead to increased profitability if a company's customers lose interest in its products as a result. This is what happened to the Home Depot. Centralized purchasing decisions meant that local store managers were unable to stock products that best met the needs of their customers. When it streamlined its product range, Home Depot stopped stocking the newest, most up-to-date products customers wanted. Its new part-time employees only had limited home improvement knowledge, and they were increasingly unable to answer customers' questions. The competitive advantage Home Depot had built by providing customers with the broadest range of innovative products and excellent service was in shambles.

Meanwhile, Lowe's was rapidly expanding its chain of stores. Although Lowe's stores were also the warehouse type, they were brightly lit, had wide aisles, and provided a more attractive shopping experience than many of Home Depot's older stores. Lowe's had also imitated Home Depot's strategy of providing excellent customer service by employing highly trained associates. Finally, Lowe's had altered its product mix to appeal more to female customers, who made many of the big-spending decisions. These competitive moves created a business model luring away Home Depot's customers, and Lowe's revenues and profitability increased as Home Depot's fell.

Home Depot was a highly sought-after company until 2002 when investors realized its profitability had fallen sharply. Its stock dropped 53%. How did this happen to a company that was once at the top of its game? Could the drop have been avoided?

In 2003 Nardelli decided that once again he needed to change Home Depot's business model to respond to Lowe's competitive threat. Nardelli invested $500 million to buy new inventory like fashionable bathroom hardware and kitchen fixtures and rugs. New employee training programs were introduced to try to rebuild Home Depot's reputation for great customer service. The company also began to introduce self-service checkout counters to speed customers out of the store.

Although these moves increased operating costs, by 2004 they also had significantly increased the number of Home Depot's customers, especially those who bought expensive, big-ticket items. Home Depot's profitability also increased sharply, as did its stock price. By 2005, with rising sales and profit, it was clear that Nardelli has fashioned a successful new business model for his company.[5]

The challenge to improve profitability faces companies large and small as well as individual people doing business. Consider babysitting: Suppose a student agrees to baby-sit for a price of $8 per hour. So, for three hours work, he or she expects to earn $24. It takes thirty minutes each way and three gallons of gas to get to the babysitting location. Now consider the fact that the parents for whom the student is baby-sitting come home thirty minutes late but don't pay for the extra time. If the student subtracts all these operating costs from the $24 earnings, perhaps a small profit was made. But if the student then considers how much he or she had to "invest" to make this profit–the time and money to travel to and from the job as well as what he or she could have made working elsewhere–then the trade looks much less *profitable*. In fact, the student would probably not want to work for that family again. Experienced babysitters learn to work only for families willing to make it "worth the time." Alternatively, they can and do try to find jobs that make more profitable use of their time and effort.

Business, Self-Interest, and the Potential for Deceit

All people involved in a business exchange wish to increase their utility and profit from it. To watch out for and protect one's own welfare in an exchange, people behave in a se*lf-interested way.* Some people view the idea of people behaving self-interestedly in a negative way because it implies the intent to harm others or profit at their expense.

Business activity is inherently competitive, so the need to behave in a self-interested way forces people to make their decisions at the margin. Given that everyone is trying to profit from an exchange, each person is now required to think carefully about whether or not they will in fact increase their utility from a particular exchange. If all parties to an exchange do this–both buyers and sellers–then together they determine the fair market price for a product and *everyone* gains from the exchange. As noted earlier, our choices at the margin determine the supply and demand for a product and its fair market price. The greater the demand for, or the lower the supply or availability of, a particular product or resource, the higher will be its price, and vice versa.

Self-interested behavior thus leads to positive outcomes for all parties involved. It leads to the best use of resources because resources go to *their most highly valued use*–the use that creates the most utility for the people involved in the exchange. (See Figure 1.5.)

Figure 1.5
Positive and Negative Effects of Self-Interested Behavior

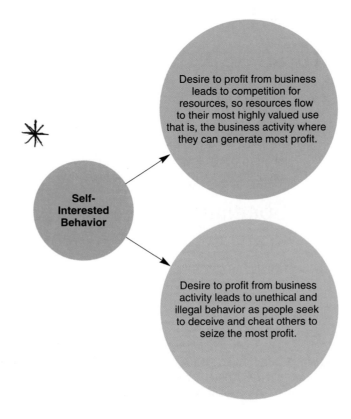

Nevertheless, no rule or law says that *all* people will or must benefit equally from an exchange. Some may benefit much more so than others. They may, for example, be better able to spot an opportunity and recognize a product that is a bargain. They may simply be better at bargaining and negotiation, an important skill discussed in Chapter 7.

Moreover, because business is based on the intent to profit from the exchange, there is always the possibility that ruthless or unscrupulous people might try to lie to and cheat other people to seize most or all of the profit from the exchange. In trade, for example, sellers might exaggerate the value of what they have to sell. Words and phrases like "racket," "crooked," "monkey business," and "buyer beware" came into being to describe exchanges where one person or company deliberately tries to defraud other people to maximize personal gain or profit. The prospect of being cheated always exists and must be guarded against.

Even if there is no intent to defraud the other people, because business is an inherently self-interested, competitive activity, people usually try to strike the best deal they can for themselves. Competition is always part of business even though we may not always be aware of it. Our decision to shop at Kroger's or Wal-Mart, for example, is ultimately determined by the way these companies have chosen to compete for customers. Kroger and Wal-Mart strive to attract us by offering that selection of products and prices that will generate the most profit for us and them. Similarly, as individuals we need to realize that we are always in competition with other people for scarce resources. For example, people are in competition with each other for the best grades in school, for highly-paid satisfying jobs, for promotion, or for entry into colleges and schools that provide a good education. These are all scarce and valuable products most people want.

Considerable negotiation and bargaining might be needed to determine the fair or market price for a product, hence the need for informed and savvy buyers and sellers. Sometimes the government intervenes when one party to a transaction has more information than the other. For example, some states have what are known as "lemon" laws to protect unsuspecting car buyers from purchasing vehicles that are flawed. Other products carry warning labels, such as prescription drugs and clothing. Determining what is fair and acceptable, or unacceptable and "sharp," business behavior is an ethical issue discussed at length in Chapter 5.

Business as an Occupation

If people wish to trade or barter goods and services to increase their utility and profit they have to have *something* to trade with. Most commonly, people trade their value-creating skills, or labor. For example, I might agree to fix your computer, if that were something I were good at, in exchange for something you are good at, say, hanging wallpaper I'd like put up in my apartment. As noted earlier, we both profit from the exchange as long as we each obtain something from the other that is more valuable to us than what we have to give up in exchange.

specialization The process by which people become more skilled and productive when they perform a narrowly defined range of tasks specific to an occupation or job.

Specialization, the Division of Labor, and People's Well-Being

People have learned that specializing can make them more prosperous. Specialization is the process by which people become expert in a narrowly defined range of tasks, such as those involved in an occupation or job. This helps them become *more skilled* and *productive* at what they do. (There's truth to the phrase "practice makes perfect".) When people specialize, together they are able to produce a greater quantity of *total* goods and services. This greater productivity gives them *more* products to exchange with one another, and makes them better off. For example, it might

Did You Know?

20% of the population in developed nations consume 86% of the world's goods.[6]

take you a very long time to fix your own computer. I, on the other hand, might be able to do it faster and fix lots of computers in a day. That would give you more time to hang wallpaper for me and other people in exchange for additional things you might want.

In essence, to do well in business and improve your standard of living, you need to have an occupation you are good at. A business occupation is the acquired set of specialized skills and abilities that enable a person to create valuable goods and service that can be traded at a profit. A person's job description, profession, trade, or "calling" are terms used to describe the kinds of occupations a person can pursue. To succeed in business is to try to excel in an occupation and perform at a high level to profit from exchange and increase one's personal capital and wealth. This is the origin of sayings like "minding or taking care of your own business" or "none of *your* business," which both imply the importance of protecting and building occupational skills to profit from them.

So, for example, mechanics must take good care of their toolsets if they are to make the most productive use of their time; lawyers must take steps to learn about changes in the law to preserve their expertise; and computer programmers must learn how to use new software as it is developed if they are to maintain their value in the job market. There is a market for occupations and jobs just as there is a market for wheat and potatoes.

Over time, the pursuit of business leads to increasing specialization and division of labor. A wider and wider set or range of occupational skills emerges in a group or society. This happens because people specialized in a particular occupation such as farmer, computer programmer, lawyer, or restaurant owner become more productive and start to earn more money. With their increased income, they can now afford to purchase the products of other specialized people who are more skilled at making those products than they are.

In essence, increasing specialization and division of labor lead to greater productivity and rising profitability across occupations and business commerce in general. In turn, this leads to an increase in the standard of living and well-being of a people or society. This process is illustrated in Figure 1.6.

business occupation
The acquired set of specialized skills that enable a person to create valuable goods and service that can be traded at a profit.

Physical therapy is one example of a set of acquired skills necessary to pursue a business occupation. Physical therapists must graduate from an accredited training program and pass a licensing exam before they can start working.

✳ Specialization and Profitability over Time

To see how profitability increases over time, take the situation in the food business. Supermarkets, and the companies like Kroger and Wal-Mart that own them, are a relatively modern invention. Early humans were hunters and gatherers and collected their own food; their problem was obtaining enough food to survive. Later, people learned how to grow their own crops and raise their own livestock. With more food available they became more secure. This gave them extra time to plan ahead and improve their farming and livestock-raising skills thereby increasing their overall productivity. As a result, country markets developed where farmers could meet to barter and trade their surplus food products. Soon, specialist food suppliers such as butchers, bakers, and brewers emerged to handle the growing food trade. Dry goods stores opened up when foods started to be canned and bottled.

All this specialization gave people access to better quality more varied food—something that has always had high utility for most people. It also greatly increased

Figure 1.6
How Specialization and the Division of Labor Increase Capital and Wealth

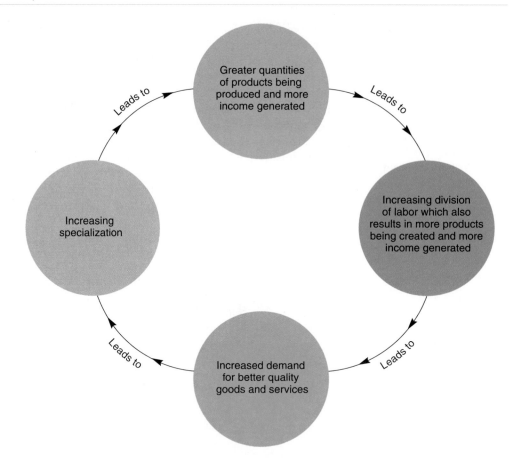

profitability because food was being made and sold much more cost-effectively. Eventually, improved technology, particularly refrigeration and better transportation, made it profitable to bring together the selling of a wide variety of foods and other consumer products under one roof. Thus, the modern supermarket came into being. When many different kinds of products can be sold together retailers can use their resources more productively. Buyers operate more efficiently, too. Imagine if you had to drive around all day looking for a baker, a vegetable grower, and a rancher with whom to trade!

Today, superstores sell everything from soap to appliances, from food to electronics, clothing, furniture, and even eyeglasses This has led to an even greater quantity of high-quality goods and services produced more efficiently and traded more profitably. In turn, people and society have become wealthier.

✳ The Invisible Hand of the Market

There is a key point to understand here. People choose an occupation to pursue in a self-interested way based on their desire to profit personally from their improved skills. People opened dry goods stores and supermarkets, for example, when changing technology provided an opportunity for them to make more profit.

All these decisions about what kind of skill to develop, or what kinds of store to open, are being made *independently* by self-interested people seeking personal gain. In the process, however, the decision made by each person indirectly helps everybody else because, *collectively,* it furthers the gains that can be derived from specialization. This increases the total amount of goods and services available for trade.

The development of occupational specialization is an example of Adam Smith's famous **invisible hand** of the market in action. (Smith was an 18th century philosopher, who, today, is considered the "father" of the economics discipline.) Smith believed that the self-interested economic behavior of individual people ultimately

invisible hand The principle that the pursuit of self-interest in the marketplace naturally leads to the improved well-being of society in general.

monopoly A situation in which one company controls the supply of a product and can charge an artificially high price for it.

makes society better off as a whole. Of course, Adam Smith also was clear that abuses that prevent the market from operating efficiently, that is, from establishing a fair, competitive market price, must be outlawed. For example, deliberate fraud, deceit, or the creation of a **monopoly**, a situation in which *one* person or company controls the supply of a particular product—and thus can charge an artificially high price for it—has to be prevented (or at least regulated by the government).

The invisible hand of the market *only* works to create a public good and higher utility for most people if a system of rules and laws exists to allow free and fair competition for resources and products. The wealth of a society as a whole will not increase if some people can unfairly gain power over products and resources and thereby distort the way the forces of supply and demand determine prices.

In summary, through the invisible hand of the market, the interaction of business commerce and occupations determines the standard of living, wealth, and prosperity of people, groups, and society. It also determines how profit will be *shared* between people and groups in a society. Remember, no rules exist that specify how the profit created from business commerce or occupations will be distributed or even who will receive it. Your chance of pursuing a profitable occupation that allows you to accumulate capital depends on your ability to take part in the "great game of business."

human capital
A person's stock of knowledge, skills, experience, judgment, personality, and abilities.

This is not just capital in the form of money but also your personal or human capital. **Human capital** is your stock of knowledge, skills, experience, judgment, personality, and ability. People invest in an occupation to develop human capital so they can generate future profit and build financial wealth. In a business context, your human capital is what you personally "bring to the table"; it is what you have to offer others and can trade with. The human capital you develop now, and in the future, will determine what kind of life you lead, which kind of people you are attracted to, and even which person you might marry and have children with. It is important to appreciate the major impact business, and particularly the pursuit of a business occupation, has on each person's "life chances," as well as on the well-being of a society as a whole. For example, imagine if people such as Michael Dell, Bill Gates, and Steve Jobs had decided to pursue some other line of work than advancing computer technology. The world might be a very different and less interesting place today.

Business as an Organization

We noted earlier that people in business have to spend a considerable amount of time bargaining and negotiating with each other to trade goods and services and establish their fair market price. The division of labor in a society increases the number and complexity of business activities and makes the bargaining process much more difficult and time consuming. There is a much wider range of goods and services to trade, for example, and much greater variation in their quality, so it is more difficult to determine their fair market price.

Transaction Costs Related to Business

transaction costs
The costs of bargaining, negotiating, monitoring, and regulating exchanges between people in business.

The costs of bargaining, negotiating, monitoring, and regulating the exchanges between people in business are called **transaction costs**. These costs are the necessary costs of "doing business." They have to be borne to allow business commerce to occur. There are several sources of these costs (Figure 1.7).

First, transaction costs are high when people are in business for themselves because each person has to individually bargain and negotiate with others over the price of resources and products. This is an extremely time consuming process and time *is* money. Like every

Did You Know?

Only three companies have risen to the #1 spot on the Fortune 500 list since 1954: General Motors, ExxonMobil, and Wal-Mart.[7]

Figure 1.7
Sources of
Transaction Costs

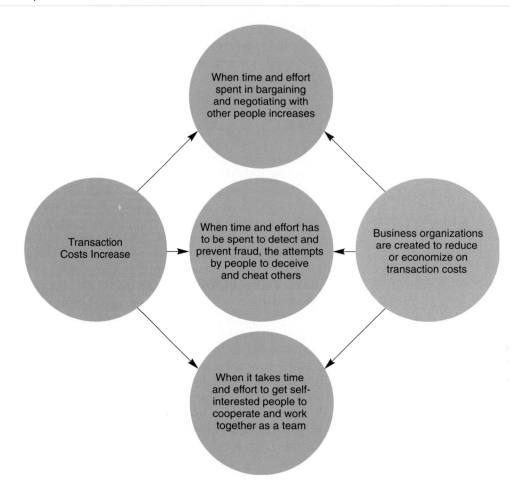

other valuable thing, time is a scarce resource. Time spent in bargaining over prices, for example, is time *not* being spent in learning new skills or becoming better at making goods and services.

Second, transaction costs are also high when people have to be on the look out for others who might act unethically and try to cheat or deceive them. Business people have to spend time and effort to guard against fraud or deception. They have to collect information about other people and the products they wish to trade. And, they may have to monitor the way the other party abides by their agreement; for example, will the painter I hire really put two coats of paint on my house or try to get away with just one? All this time spent bargaining with and monitoring other people leads to high transaction costs.

A third, very important, source of transaction costs is as follows: Often, people cannot perform many kinds of complex activities *unless* they can work together and cooperate. For example, one person cannot possibly raise a new barn, or perform all the activities necessary to get a new cargo ship into the water, or run a hospital single-handedly. To perform complex activities **teamwork,** a process in which people agree to combine and pool their skills to create a more valuable product, is needed. This results in a new problem of business commerce that also leads to high transaction costs. *How do you get people to cooperate and work as a team when each of them, as noted above, has the incentive to pursue his or her own self-interest?* How do you convince specialized people they will get their fair share in return if they work together?

Considerable bargaining and negotiation will be necessary to convince people that they will be better off if they agree to pool their skills and resources. Each person will want to ensure they will receive a higher price for contributing their skills; they also will want assurances that the other team members will do their best and will not shirk or "free-ride" on the hard work of their co-workers.

teamwork
A phenomenon that occurs when people pool their skills to create more valuable products than they could create alone.

People have a strong incentive to find ways to *reduce* or *economize* on transaction costs. Historically, the way people and groups have accomplished this is by using some form of business organization to manage and control exchanges between people. We discuss this next.

How Business Organizations Lower Transaction Costs

business organization A tool that empowers people to shape and control the behavior of other people to produce goods and services.

A **business organization** is a tool or instrument created to give people (its owners and managers) the *power* they need to shape and control the work behavior of other people (the organization's workers or employees). Those who found these organizations risk their valuable money and capital to buy productive resources, such as labor. In return for their labor, the employees of a company accept the right of its owner or manager to assign them to work in a particular task or role in exchange (trade) for a monetary reward, such as a salary and health benefits.

organizational structure The framework of task and authority relationships that coordinates people so they work towards a common goal.

The business's **organizational structure** is the framework of task and authority relationships that coordinates people so they work towards a common goal. A well-designed organizational structure reduces transaction costs and results in the production of larger quantities of valuable products—both of which increase a company's profitability. There are many reasons for this. First, many bargaining and negotiating costs are eliminated when people are assigned to a task or job and no longer have to bargain among themselves over every aspect of what they do. Second, managers can pool and combine employees' skills as they see fit to achieve the gains from specialization and the division of labor. Third, organizations overcome the problem related to getting self-interested people to cooperate with another because managers have the authority to ensure everyone performs well. Managers can also take corrective action as needed.

Finally, as the terms business *enterprise* or *venture* suggest, by combining the talents and resources of many different people, a business organization can pursue new opportunities and take more risks to create profitable goods and services. For example, business organizations enable two or more people—say, plumbers, carpenters, accountants, or lawyers—to pool their resources, attract more clients, and reduce their risks, as well as lower the transaction costs of running the business. By contrast, when a single person takes such risks, they are behaving as an entrepreneur. The way one entrepreneur confronted the challenge of designing an organizational structure to compete in the roofing business is profiled in Business in Action.

Business in Action

How to Restructure a Growing Business

In January 2005, Jeff Millard, the founder of a small roofing business in Houston, Texas, was facing a major problem. How should Millard organize his growing roofing business to maintain the high-quality standards and fair prices that had led his company to grow so rapidly?

Millard got into the roofing business in 1998 when he was 27 years old after having worked for a roofing contractor for six years. In 2001 he decided to branch out on his own, and he hired a couple of other experienced roofers for his crew. Millard also began advertising in a few local papers, and soon he had enough roofing jobs to keep his crew working fulltime. As word of mouth spread about his quality work, he soon had more business than he could handle.

Not wishing to turn down business, in 2002 Millard searched for a way that would allow him to take on and profit from his growing business yet not burden his company with too much debt. His answer was to approach other small roofing companies that did not have enough work but were eager and willing to work on Millard's jobs for a set price. Millard then pocketed the difference between the amount he charged his customers and what he paid the other roofing companies or contractors. Soon he has making as much from utilizing the other contractors as he was from his own company.

For a while all went well. But then in 2003 following a major storm, Millard began receiving complaints from customers about leaks around chimneys and where rooflines met at odd angles—places where a quality-roofing job was vital to avoid water damage. Although he always inspected the work done by the other companies and requested they fix any problems he discovered, Millard was surprised by the sheer number of complaints he was getting. When he informed his contractors about these problems, he found out they were very reluctant to follow up with his customers and fix the problems. He also found out that several of the problems were the result of one particular contractor's work and that the flashing used to stop water from penetrating into the home was not the expensive 25-year flashing he had ordered. It was an inferior type of flashing. Clearly, this contractor was substituting much cheaper flashing for Millard's. Of course, the contractor denied knowing about the problems and refused to fix them.

Soon, Millard found that he was spending a lot of his time talking and negotiating with his contractors to fix old problems. He also set out to find new contractors he hoped would be more trustworthy and reliable, but this also took a lot of time. Meanwhile, the amount of time and energy he had to spend on his own roofing jobs decreased, and he had to rely more and more on the goodwill of his crews to solve ongoing problems and get the job done right. By this time, he had six crews who worked separate jobs, and once again, the time needed to adequately supervise their activities and solve unusual problems was increasing.

In fact, the time he spent to manage all these activities was hurting Millard in another way. When his business was smaller, he had much more time available to find customers, meet with them, and get new business as well as explore new roofing products and techniques they might be interested in. Now, he often had to make customers wait for a week before he could even bid for their work. Tired of waiting, many potential customers simply found other contractors even though they knew Millard did quality work and did fix problems promptly.

Millard was searching for a way to handle these issues. He knew it was no longer possible to rely on other contractors to do the work because he could not control the quality of their work. Even the time it took to find other contractors and negotiate with them was no longer cost effective. On the other hand, with six crews he knew he was stretched to the limit to supervise his own employees. He could not possibly expand the number of his crews until he found a better way to control their work. Last, but not least, he knew he needed to give his employees more training in the finer points of roofing, particularly cutting the shingles to fit around chimneys and other weak spots and installing flashing properly. He also knew that he would have to find a way to motivate his employees to do good-quality work even though he could not be there to look over their shoulders.

Jeff Millard has proven that it's important to "try, try again" in order to succeed in the world of business. Millard could have given up his growth plans and settled upon a smaller customer base. But instead, he continued to find ways to reorganize and expand his business while still maintaining quality. In the end, his perseverance paid off.

Figure 1.8
Millard Roofing's Business Organization

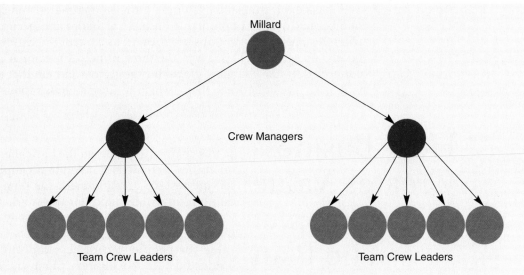

Essentially, Millard needed a structure of task and authority relationships that would allow him to solve *all* these problems. Believing that in the future he could easily find work for ten three-man crews, he decided to structure his business as shown in Figure 1.8.

First, Millard split the ten crews into two groups of five crews, and then he appointed his two most experienced roofers to be the managers of each group. The job of these managers would be to supervise each group of five crews and order the roofing materials needed to complete all the jobs they were assigned. In each three-person crew, one roofer became the crew leader responsible for controlling the job and for making sure the crew worked quickly and carefully to finish the job and minimize the amount of waste material such as cut shingles, which could increase the cost of a job by as much as 10%.

To motivate his employees to perform at a high level Millard decided to offer them reasonably priced health insurance—a benefit unheard of in the low-paying roofing business. He also developed a bonus system based on the number of jobs completed per month and what they cost as a way to reward all ten teams for any increases in productivity they achieved.

Millard's new system led to some radical new attitudes on the part of the team members. For example, they started stopping off at roofing yards on their way to work to pick up supplies they knew they might run out of and cause a slowdown. They also became more willing to improve their roofing skills, so the number of leak complaints fell dramatically. As the work quality increased, the obvious enthusiasm of the crews impressed customers. Once again the reputation of Millard Roofing spread.

As for Millard personally, once his new organizational structure was up and running, he was able to focus on his main task: attracting customers and keeping business flowing in. He even trained two of the crew leaders as estimators to help him quickly get bids to customers.

As a result, Millard soon saw the profitability and volume of his business skyrocket. With ten crews it was already one of the biggest roofing companies in Houston. In 2006, his once "small" business earned over $5 million in revenue.

Given the pace of Houston home building, Millard decided to give serious thought to growing to 15 crews within one year, and 20 within the second. He was also wondering if he could take his business model and use it to open new branches of Millard Roofing in Austin, College Station, and San Antonio, Texas. Of course, that would require a change to his business model and a new organizational structure. Was he up to the challenge, he wondered?

A business organization *facilitates* business commerce and specialization. A greater number and variety of profitable business activities and occupations become possible when business organizations are formed to control the production and exchange of goods and services. This is why the three principal meanings of business are so interconnected. In the changing global business environment that exists today, the issue is to manage the fit between them, which we discuss in Chapter 4.

How Business Creates Value for People: The Plan of This Book

In this chapter we outlined the basic meanings and terminology of business activity and noted that people are in business out of self-interest—to create wealth for themselves. Via the Adam Smith's "invisible hand" of the market, this, in turn, creates wealth for the people with whom they trade. The chapters in the rest of this book examine in detail how companies create value for people and discuss the multitude of factors both inside and outside a business organization that affect the way in which it does so.

In the first part of this book, titled "The Environment of Business," we provide an in-depth account of the context, or setting, in which business activity takes place. Chapter 2 examines the origins of business and the factors affecting the way business has evolved over time. This chapter directly follows from Chapter 1 because it also shows how the nature of business as commerce, as an occupation, and an organization has changed over time. In doing so, it fills out and elaborates on the concepts introduced in Chapter 1.

In Chapter 3, we look at the three main kinds of people involved in creating, managing, and operating a business company—entrepreneurs, managers, and employees—and suggest ways in which students can prepare for entry into the workforce. Chapters 4 and 5 examine two major forces profoundly affecting the way business is conducted today: Chapter 4 discusses the effects of the increasing globalization of business, as companies extend their activities around the world; Chapter 5 examines why increasing attention is being given to ethics and laws in an effort to curb the ruthless pursuit of self-interest that destroys the fabric of business and society.

Part 2 of this book, "The Human Side of Business," takes an in-depth look at the complex individual and social processes that take place inside business organizations as people and groups pursue their own interests while, at the same time, they contribute to the value of the goods and services organizations create. Chapter 6 examines the nature of leadership and social influence. It also discusses the importance of business communication as a means of harmonizing the efforts of managers and employees to produce high-quality goods and services. Then, in Chapter 7 we discuss what motivates employees at work as well as the kinds of group and team behaviors that affect how much value people create when they cooperate at work. Chapter 8 discusses how to design the structure and culture of a business organization to motivate and coordinate people as individuals and in groups to accomplish the principle organizational goal—creating value for customers.

Parts 1 and 2 provide a detailed account of the most important factors inside and outside the organization that affect how much value a company can create. Part 3, "A Functional Approach to Business," examines the main kinds of functional activities of a business. Functional activities are the task-specific processes that need to be done to convert resources into finished goods and services sold to customers. Figure 1.9 illustrates these different kinds of functional activities or *functions*, which together comprise a company's value chain. A

functional activities
The task-specific operations needed to convert resources into finished goods and services sold to customers.

Did You Know?

Nearly 1,500 separate industries are identified in the North American Industry Classification System (NAICS).[8]

Figure 1.9
Primary and Secondary Value—Chain Functions

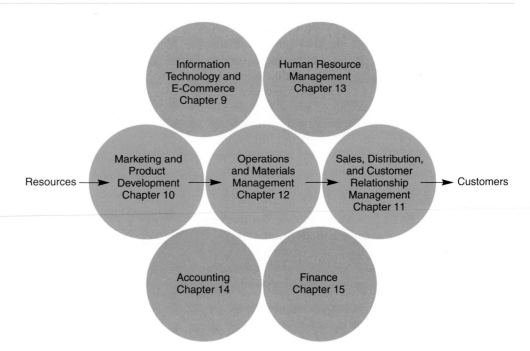

value chain The coordinated series or sequence of functional activities necessary to transform resources into the products customers want to buy.

primary functions Functions directly responsible for utilizing scarce resources most efficiently and effectively to create goods and services.

secondary functions Functions not directly responsible for getting products to customers but whose activities contribute to the efficiency and effectiveness of other functions.

company's value chain is the coordinated series or sequence of activities necessary to transform resources into the products customers want to buy.

The functions in the middle circles of the value chain, marketing and product development (Chapter 10), operations and materials management (Chapter 12) and sales, distribution, and customer relationship management (Chapter 11) are called primary functions because they are the ones *directly responsible* for utilizing scarce resources most efficiently and effectively to create goods and services. The functions in the upper and lower circles are called secondary functions because they are not directly responsible for getting products to customers. But, each function's activities *increase the efficiency and effectiveness with which all the other functions perform their activities.* The four main secondary functions discussed in Part 3 are information technology (Chapter 9), human resource management (Chapter 13), accounting (Chapter 14), and finance (Chapter 15).

In a similar way, the very sequence of the chapters in the book were designed to help you understand and appreciate business as efficiently and effectively as possible—how it affects you, the companies we work for, and the societies in which we live. In other words, I wanted to help you spend your time and effort reading this book in the most productive way.

Many people do not understand the way business affects them as they move from school to school, to part-time job to job, and then to college and into the world of full-time work. People are often so fully involved in learning and working that they do not appreciate the many ways their decisions and actions are being influenced by the business system around them. This certainly was my experience. In writing this book, I was motivated by my desire to help other people quickly gain the knowledge that took me a much longer time to acquire.

Did You Know?

"The value of history is not scientific, but moral: Liberalizing the mind, deepening the sympathies, fortifying the will, it enables us to control, not society, but ourselves, and to live more humanely in the present and the future." –Carl L. Becker[9]

Summary of the Chapter

In this chapter we have described the nature of business and discussed the ways in which business creates profit and wealth in a society. As we have discussed, the three meanings of business are interrelated. Each is a necessary ingredient for the production of the valuable goods and services on which both personal wealth and the wealth and prosperity of a society or country depend. To understand why some countries are wealthier, or more peaceful, or more enterprising than others, look at the nature of their business commerce, occupations, and organizations. Look also, at the legal and ethical rules that govern how business is to be conducted in a society. The chapter has made the following main points:

1. Business has three main components, business as commerce, as an occupation, and an organization. Together these three components make up the business system.

2. The four main productive factors are land, labor, capital and enterprise. A company utilizes these resources to produce goods and services.

3. Business commerce involves the trade or barter of products (goods and services) to create profit. The forces of supply and demand determine a product's market price. In turn, supply and demand are the result of peoples' personal judgments about the utility, or satisfaction, they will get from supplying or buying a product.

4. A company's business model describes the way it intends to use its productive resources to create profitable goods and services.

5. A company's profitability is a measure of how well it has used its productive resources to create valuable goods and services as compared to other companies.

6. It is important to recognize that while all business activity is self-interested and competitive, this competition benefits society because it directs resources to their most highly valued use. Nevertheless, there is no business rule that says that all people need to profit from business commerce equally.

7. Some people or companies will always ruthlessly pursue their self-interest and try to cheat or defraud others. Governments can sometimes prevent this from happening by passing laws and regulating certain business activities.

8. Through the process of specialization and the division of labor, business occupations develop that increase the amount of goods and services people can produce and trade. Increasing specialization, through the invisible hand of the market, leads to increasing profitability and the generation of more capital and wealth.

9. Business organizations are created to reduce transaction costs, the costs that arise from business commerce and from the process of specialization and the division of labor.

10. Business organizations develop an organizational structure, a set of task and authority relationships, to reduce transaction costs and increase their profitability.

Developing Business Skills

QUESTIONS FOR DISCUSSION AND ACTION

1. What is the relationship between business commerce, business occupations, and the business organization? In what ways do they work together to affect how the business system operates?

2. What is the principle of diminishing marginal utility? Why is it important to understand business decision making at the margin?

3. What is a company's business model? What is profitability? Why is a company's business model a major determinant of its profitability?

4. *Action.* Find an owner or manager of a small business in your city and try to determine the nature of that company's business model. What are the main components of its business model? What is its competitive advantage? Who are its main competitors?

5. Why is business activity self-interested and competitive? In what ways can self-interested behavior benefit or harm the way the business system operates?

6. How does Adam Smith's invisible hand of the market work? What is its result?

7. What are the main sources of transaction costs in business? How does the use of a business organization reduce these costs?

ETHICS IN ACTION

Ethics and Self-Interest

Ethics, discussed in detail in Chapter 5, involves a person deciding on the right, moral, or appropriate way to act towards another person. To begin our study of business ethics, either *individually or in a group,* decide how you would behave in the following situations:

- You are trying to decide whether or not to work with another person on a school project. What kinds of factors do you use to decide how that person would be to work with—someone you can rely on to do a fair share of the work—or someone who is likely to do very little?

- You want to buy a car, but you know it is priced $3,000 below its fair market value. Would you tell the seller of the car they are asking too little for it? If no, why not? If yes, why would you?

SMALL GROUP EXERCISE

Adventures in Barbecuing

Read the following and then break up into groups of three or four people and discuss the issues involved. Be prepared to share your discussion with the rest of your class. (This exercise can also be done individually).

You and your friends have decided to work together to create an outdoor barbecue catering service in the summer months to raise money for next year's college fees. Your business model is to offer customers a worry-free party service with high-quality food and all the accoutrements. The activities you need to perform include food buying, food preparation, setting up the party at the customer's home, serving the food, and clearing up afterwards.

1. How can you create most value for customers? List the various elements of your business model.

2. How will you divide up the work among yourselves to create the most value for customers?

3. What will be the main factors that determine the profitability of your business?

DEVELOPING GOOD BUSINESS SENSE

Which Job in Which Company?

You are in the process of searching for a part-time job to help pay your way through college. You want to find a job that you will be able to keep for at least two years—a job in a company where you feel you will be able to develop skills that will help you later in your business career. You are currently considering several job options.

1. What factors should you consider when deciding upon the best job to look for (assuming you have a choice)?

2. What factors should you consider when deciding upon the best company to work for?

3. How would you go about finding out about the pros and cons of a particular job or a particular organization?

EXPLORING THE WEB

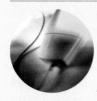

In Business to Make Cars

Research Ford Motor Company's website (www.ford.com) and locate and read the material on Ford's history, evolution, and business perspectives over time. What is Ford's business model or business mission? How has the nature of its business activities changed over time? How is Ford currently trying to increase its profitability, which is quite low? **For More Web activities, log on to www.mhhe.com/jonesintro**

BusinessWeek   **CASE FOR DISCUSSION**

The Ritz of Doggie Day Care

This past winter, just days before Ray Goshorn and his wife were leaving for a trip to Cancún, Mexico, their beloved bichon frise, Frosty, had surgery that required serious post-operative care. That put the Aurora, Colorado, couple in a bind: Who would watch their 9-year-old pooch and give him the proper love and medical attention while they were on vacation?

Goshorn turned to Camp Bow Wow, a Denver doggie day-care company. With a veterinary technician on site, the outfit tended to Frosty's needs – changing bandages, giving medicine, taking him in for checkups. "When we picked him up, he was running around with all the puppies," Goshorn says. "It was an incredibly comforting feeling to know that Frosty was OK while we were away, especially in that kind of emergency situation."

Camp Bow Wow, the nation's only franchised doggie day-care center, is much like a children's nursery where working parents drop off their tots. Pet owners leave their canines during the day or check them in for overnight stays. In climate-controlled facilities, they romp with toys, run on exercise machines, and swim in "paw pools." Overnight campers are given their own beds to curl up on, rather than kennel-style cages. "I wanted to have a comprehensive, safe, fun, place for dogs," says Heidi Flammang, Camp Bow Wow's founder and CEO.

DOGGED DREAMER. For most owners, dogs have long been considered part of the family. But families today are spending more and more money keeping Fido happy, as an increasing number of goods and services become available for those on four legs: Pet therapists, designer doggie shampoo, and aromatherapy products, to name a few. Indeed, this penchant for pampering now feeds a $34 billion industry, up from just $17 billion in 1994, according to the American Pet Products Manufacturers Association.

"There are two groups that are feeding this," says Bob Vetere, the APPM's chief operating officer and co-managing director. "The baby boomers and young professionals who are delaying marriage or having families. And they're turning to their pets as companions. They have more disposable income that they're putting into the marketplace, which has ramped up the total spending."

About 10 years ago, Flammang and her husband Bion channeled their love of dogs into a business plan for Camp Bow Wow. But when Bion was killed in a plane crash in 1994, Flammang, then a pharmaceutical sales rep, put her dreams on hold. She briefly switched careers, and in 1996 she became a certified financial planner. But her original dream kept nagging at her. "I'm an entrepreneur, and it was really my passion," she says.

CHECK UP ON YOUR PUP. In 2000 she decided to move forward and plowed her savings of $100,000 into Camp Bow Wow. She took care of the marketing and enlisted her brother, Patrick Haight, to handle operations. In order to entice her target upscale clients, she went to dog parks with buckets of milk bones and talked to people walking their pooches. She also tapped into her experience in pharmaceutical sales by networking with area veterinarians for referrals.

The first site was located in an old Denver war veterans' hall. Immediately, clients began dropping off their dogs to be cared for. The venture proved so successful that within six months, Flammang expanded the operation to include overnight boarding. A year later she opened a second location near Boulder. The idea caught on.

With the success came copycats, but Flammang distinguished her business from the start by providing an expanded menu of services. Unlike many facilities, Camp Bow Wow will care for older, sickly pets as well as puppies. Other features include on-site vaccinations and grooming care. And the strategically placed Webcams that ensure owners can check in on their "babies" anytime, from anywhere in the world, have become a hit. Prices run between $20 and $25 per day session and between $30 and $35 for overnight boarding.

OVERSEAS INTEREST. Flammang's original plan was to establish just three or four centers in the Denver area. Then, in November, 2002, a regular client who happened to be a sales representative for Mrs. Fields Cookies suggested franchising, and the idea clicked. "For me, franchising took the best parts of my personality," Flammang says. "I got people excited about building a concept, and I could get more of these places up and running while growing a system."

Flammang sold her first franchise in August, 2003. Today Camp Bow Wow has 11 locations. By the end of 2005, Flammang plans to have 75 sites, from Florida to Indiana. In two years, she predicts, the count will be 150 centers across the country. "We're on target," she says.

The concept has drawn lots of interest, with inquiries coming from as far as Germany. Franchisees pay an initial fee of $30,000 for a license and an additional $125,000 to $300,000 in capital costs, such as real estate and renovations. In addition, franchisees pay a typical 6% royalty fee on gross sales and 1% toward advertising.

Flammang says her goal is for each franchise to make between $750,000 and $2 million in revenue annually, depending on size and location. In turn, they get the kind of support and training that will allow each unit to succeed using the company's proven system as well as its brand name.

LOOKING FORWARD. Wendy Caldwell opened one of Camp Bow Wow's first franchises in Broomfield, Colo., in October, 2003. Laid off from her account-supervisor job with Weyerhaeuser, she decided it was time to make a change. And as a dog lover, she figured Camp Bow Wow was a natural fit. "In five months we were bursting at the seams," she says. "We were getting 40 to 45 dogs a day." So the following November she opened a second location in nearby North Glen. Caldwell says each shop is on target to make $500,000 in sales this year.

In fact, business is going so well that in March, Caldwell decided to sell her franchise and move to her native Calgary, where she'll head Camp Bow Wow's Canadian operations. She expects to open at least 15 franchises in the next two years. "I think there's really a need for a place for dogs to have fun instead of being left alone," she says. "Owners are more concerned with their dogs' mental and social welfare. And this is a much better alternative than leaving them in a cage."

Now, Flammang is readying the business for phase two. In May she'll open the first of a planned series of retail kiosks in malls, beginning in Durham, N.C., that will sell branded logo T-shirts and dog accessories. At the same time she'll open Camp Bow Wow Barkeries at the kiosk sites, offering doggie treats. A dog's life indeed.

Source: Stacy Perman, "The Ritz of Doggy Day Care," *BusinessWeek Online,* April 12, 2005.

QUESTIONS

1. How would you describe Heidi Flammang's approach to doing business?

2. In what ways is Camp Bow Wow's business model creating more value for dog owners than its competitors? How has Flammang altered her business model over time?

3. In what ways will Flammang's business model and her use of franchising affect the profitability of her company?

BusinessWeek CASE FOR DISCUSSION

Southwest: Dressed to Kill . . . Competitors

Gary C. Kelly is a steady, mild-mannered former accountant. But don't let that fool you. The new 49-year-old chief executive of Southwest Airlines Co. is also spearheading some of the most aggressive moves that the low-fare king has made in years.

The youthful and energetic Kelly is a good fit for the Southwest image. "Gary brings a lot more of a 'change agent' element here" than his predecessor, says one insider. That was abundantly clear at last year's Halloween party, when Kelly shocked co-workers by showing up as Gene Simmons, front man for the rock group Kiss.

Perhaps Kelly, who joined Southwest as its controller in 1986, has simply figured out that no one was buying the airline's old "Aw, shucks, we're just an underdog" act anymore. Says America West Airlines Inc. CEO W. Douglas Parker: "They really were at one point the scrawny kid who was lifting weights in his basement. Now they come out and they're bigger than anybody else and stronger than anybody else." In fact, Southwest now carries more domestic passengers than any other U.S. airline. For his part, Kelly insists there's nothing different about Southwest's behavior: "We've always been a growth airline, and have always been a maverick, and have always been very competitive."

The difference now is that Southwest, with the lowest costs and the strongest balance sheet, appears to be permanently shifting the balance of power to low-cost carriers. So it should come as no surprise that Southwest is on the offensive again. It plans to increase capacity at least 10% this year, adding 29 planes to its fleet of 417. Like other airlines, it hunkered down after September 11 and the crippling recession that brought four years of industry losses. Southwest grew by just 4% in 2003. But with travel improving, it's seizing opportunities as big competitors struggle to return to profitability in the face of costly fuel and shrinking fares.

GROWTH OPPORTUNITIES. Yet Southwest's game plan is defensive, as well. Its 2004 earnings of $313 million were just half what it earned in 2000. Without financial hedges that helped it manage fuel costs, Southwest would have lost money in three of the last eight quarters. The best way to improve future returns, says analyst Gary Chase of Lehman Brothers Inc. in a research report, is for Southwest "to take advantage of the growth opportunities created by industry duress." That's now important because formidable low-cost rivals, especially Air-Tran Airways and JetBlue Airways are eager to grow in the same lucrative markets Southwest is targeting. And they can promote arguably better products, including assigned seats, business class, and seat-back televisions.

Thus Southwest is rushing to stake its claim in places like Philadelphia and Pittsburgh, now dominated by bankrupt US Airways Group Inc. US Airways and other hub-and-spoke giants are working furiously to survive by slashing labor and other costs. They're still a long way from matching Southwest, but some are likely to emerge much nimbler. Southwest needs healthy expansion to help keep its own unit costs under control. It boasts the richest wages for pilots of narrow-body jets—38% above those at United Airlines Inc., after that carrier's deep pay cuts. By growing, Southwest averages in new, lower-paid employees and spreads its costs over more seats. At the same time, it is pushing for higher productivity from its already highly efficient workers. Southwest's pilots say they're being asked to fly 70 hours a month, up from about 65. Pilots at the traditional carriers average less than 60.

SHAKING THINGS UP. How much of the recent aggressiveness—or "assertiveness," as they prefer at friendly Southwest—reflects new opportunities or a new boss is the subject of much debate. After all, company co-founder and Chairman Herbert D. Kelleher, 73, is still firmly in charge of strategy and route plans, as he was when Parker, a reserved lawyer, was CEO. "We just didn't have these kinds of opportunities in 2002 and 2003," says Kelly.

But Kelly has been shaking things up inside the company, too. One of his first moves was to realign his management group to improve accountability and cooperation between departments. And while Southwest has long been known for its warm labor relations, those relationships were frayed during Parker's bitter contract negotiations with flight attendants. Feeling demonized by union leaders, Parker turned the job over to Kelleher, who reached a richer-than-expected settlement. Parker retired soon afterward, citing "personal reasons," but many believe the contract dispute was a key factor. Kelly created a new department focused on labor relations and now meets quarterly with union leaders to discuss finances and strategy. He's also insisting that all employees get regular scorecards on productivity and profitability measures.

For all of the changes, Kelly hasn't yet introduced such complications as international flights or the use of smaller regional jets, a move planned by JetBlue. He's even cautious about assigning seats, a service that new technology would easily allow but that many passengers, believe it or not, have said they would detest. But if Kelly's early months in office are any indication, Southwest is sure to keep rocking the industry.

Source: Wendy Zellner, "Southwest: Dressed to Kill . . . Competitors," *BusinessWeek Online,* February 21, 2005.

QUESTIONS

1. Why is Southwest the most profitable U.S. airline company?

2. How is Gary Kelly changing Southwest's business model to keep the company profitable?

3. In what ways has Kelly changed Southwest's organizational structure to help improve relationships with the company's employees?

BUILDING YOUR MANAGEMENT SKILLS
Know Thyself

You, as do most people, probably hope to have a career working at something you enjoy, feeling that you do it reasonably well, and making a decent income. We might think that intelligence, drive, and opportunity will make that happen, You can improve your chances of achieving your career goals. Knowing which careers best suit your thinking and problem solving style, satisfy your primary motivational needs, and make you feel passionate about what you do will help you to succeed. You can start to develop the self-knowledge you need to make good career decisions by doing the self-assessment exercise on your Student DVD titled "Career Planning Based on Brain Dominance and Thinking Styles Inventory".

CHAPTER VIDEO
Todd McFarlane

The video features a discussion with Todd McFarlane, CEO of McFarlane Companies in Tempe, Arizona. This global company spans comics, sports, monsters, and toys. In fact, it is the world's largest and most successful toy company. McFarlane is a very successful entrepreneur who started as a college baseball player looking to break into the major leagues. Unfortunately, this venture was not successful. Instead, he fell back on his self-taught ability to draw comics. After 300 rejections from various companies, Marvel Comics hired him. In 1990, Todd was the highest paid comic cartoonist in the industry.

He still wasn't satisfied, however. He left the company at the peak of his career and took 6 of the leading artists with him and formed his own company. Success came fairly quickly with the publication of the comic book *Spawn* which sold 1.7 million copies. This success was despite the predictions by industry insiders that Todd McFarlane wouldn't last a year on his own.

McFarlane knows that the two most important elements to successfully generate wealth are entrepreneurship and knowledge. Both of which he possesses in large measure. In a dynamic business environment, there are several areas that need to be addressed in order to be successful. (1) Economic environment–in McFarlane's case it is focused in the area of intellectual property laws; (2) technological environment–McFarlane sees technology as a tool to push the creative environment; (3) competitive environment–he sees the opportunity to earn less per unit profit by taking advantage of the opportunities to produce a higher quality product; (4) social environment–he keys in on his target demographic; (5) global environment–which affects all the other areas.

1. From Todd McFarlane's perspective, what is the key element of his business model?

2. What are the four main productive factors in business organizations?

3. What influences people to buy or not buy a product such as the comic book *Spawn* created by McFarlane?

2

The Evolution of Business

Learning Objectives

After studying this chapter you should be able to:

1. Understand how property rights affect the way productive resources are used in society.

2. Define the system of feudalism and how combining land and labor speeds the accumulation of capital.

3. Appreciate the functions of money in business and how the development of money promoted the rapid development of capital and enterprise.

4. Describe the system of mercantilism and appreciate how merchants and bankers hastened the development in global trade.

5. Explain the causes of the Industrial Revolution and the development of capitalism, unionization, and the class system as we know it today.

6. Explain how and why the form of business organization used to manage business commerce has changed over time.

WHY IS THIS IMPORTANT ❓

From the beginning of time, individuals have wanted the things that would give them security, comfort, and beauty. A family needs a variety of goods to survive, so those with special talents, abilities or resources trade with others. How should society's resources be allocated? Who will get what and how much of it? Political and economic systems have evolved to answer these questions. What is it about those systems that make it possible for an individual like Andrew Carnegie to accumulate great wealth, but results in poverty for others?

This chapter will help you understand why capitalism and corporations were crucial to the Industrial Revolution and mass production in factories and how entrepreneurs are able to raise the capital needed to grow companies like FedEx or Microsoft.

A Question of Business
Andrew Carnegie and the U.S. Steel Industry

How did Carnegie change the nature of business commerce?

Andrew Carnegie was born in Scotland in 1835. Carnegie was the son of a master hand-loom weaver who, at that time, employed four apprentices to weave fine linen tablecloths. His family was well to do, yet ten years later they were living in poverty. Why? Advances in weaving technology had led to the invention of steam-powered weaving looms that could produce large quantities of cotton cloth at a much lower price than was possible through hand-loom weaving. Handloom weavers could not compete at these low prices and Carnegie's father was put out of business.

In 1848 Carnegie's family, like hundreds of thousands of other families in Europe at the time, decided to emigrate to the United States to find work and survive. The Carnegies settled near Pittsburgh, where they had relatives, and Carnegie's father continued to weave table-cloths and sell them door-to-door for around $6 a week. His mother, who had come from a family of cobblers, repaired shoes and made around $4 a week. Carnegie found a job as a "bobbin boy," replacing spools of thread on power looms in a textile factory. He took home $1.20 for working a 60-hour week.

Once his employer found out he could read and write, a rare skill at this time, Carnegie became a bookkeeper for the factory. In his spare time he became a telegraph messenger and learned telegraphy. He began to deliver telegrams to Tom Scott, a top manager at the

Pennsylvania Railroad, who came to appreciate Carnegie's drive and talents. Scott made him his personal telegrapher for an astonishing sum of $35 a week. Carnegie was now 17; only seven years later when he was 24 he was promoted to Scott's job, as superintendent of the railroad's western division. At 30, he was offered the top job of superintendent of the *whole* railroad! Carnegie had made his name by continually finding ways to use resources more productively to reduce costs and increase profitability. Under his oversight, his company's stock price had shot up—which explains why he was offered the railroad's top job. He also invested cleverly in railroad stock and was now a wealthy man with an income of $48,000 a year, of which only $2,800 came from his railroad salary.

Carnegie had ambitions other than remaining in his top railroad job, however. He had noticed U.S. railroads' growing demand for steel rails as they expanded rapidly across the country. At that time, steel was made by the method of small-batch production, a labor-intensive process in which small groups of employees worked together to produce quite small quantities of steel. This method was expensive and the steel produced cost $135 a ton.

As he searched for ways to reduce the cost of steelmaking, Carnegie was struck by the fact that many different companies performed each of the different operations necessary to convert iron ore into finished steel products. One company smelted iron ore into "pig iron." Another company then transported the pig iron to other companies that rolled the pig iron into bars or slabs. Many other companies then bought these bars and slabs and made them into finished products such as steel rails, nails, wire, and so on. Intermediaries who bought the products of one company and then sold them to another connected the activities of these different companies.

The many exchanges or "handoffs" involved in converting iron ore into finished products greatly increased operating costs. At each stage of the production process, steel had to be shipped to the next company and reheated until it became soft enough to work on. Moreover, these intermediaries were earning large profits for providing this service, something that also raised the cost of the finished products.

The second thing that Carnegie noticed was that the steel produced by British steel mills was of a higher quality than that made in U.S. mills. The British had made major advances in steelmaking technology, and U.S. railroads preferred to buy their steel rails. On one of his frequent trips to Britain to sell U.S. railroad stock, Carnegie saw a demonstration of Sir Henry Bessemer's new "hot blasting" method for making steel. Bessemer's famous process made it possible to produce great quantities of higher-quality steel *continuously,* as a process, not in small batches. Carnegie instantly realized the enormous cost-saving potential of the new technology. He rushed to become the first steelmaker in the United States to adopt it.

Carnegie subsequently sold all his railroad stock and used the proceeds to create the Carnegie Steel Company, the first low-cost Bessemer steelmaking plant in the United States. Determined to retain the profit intermediaries were making in his business, he also decided his company would perform *all* the steelmaking operations necessary to convert iron ore into finished products. For example, he constructed rolling mills to make steel rails *next* to his blast furnace so that iron ore could be converted into finished steel products in one continuous process.

Carnegie's innovations led to a dramatic fall in steelmaking costs and revolutionized the U.S. steel industry. His new production methods reduced the price of U.S. steel from $135 a ton to $12! Despite the cheaper price, his company was still enormously profitable. Most of his competitors could not compete with his low prices and were driven out of business. He ploughed back all his profits into building his steel business and constructed many new low-cost steel plants. By 1900, his company became the leading U.S. steelmaker, and he was one of the richest men in the world.

Although this might seem like "business as usual" there was a dark side to Carnegie's business activities, and he is regarded as one of the early U.S. industry's "Robber Barons." Critics say he increased profitability "on the backs" of his workers. Despite the enormous increase in productivity he had achieved by using the new steelmaking technology, he was driven by the need to find every way possible to reduce operating costs.

To increase productivity Carnegie gradually increased the normal workday from 10 to 12 hours, six days a week. He also paid his workers the lowest wage rate possible even though their increasing skills were contributing to the increase in productivity. He also paid no attention to improving the safety of his mills where workers toiled in dangerous conditions. Thousands of workers were injured each year because of spills of molten steel. Any attempts by workers to improve their work conditions were uniformly rejected, and Carnegie routinely crushed any of the workers' attempts to unionize.

When Carnegie decided to get out of the steel business he sold his company "lock, stock, and barrel" to a consortium of New York investors for $485 million. The company was renamed U.S. Steel, and it is still one of the largest U.S. steelmakers today. The investors paid a high price for Carnegie's company because they knew they could use its low-cost, competitive advantage to create a monopoly in the steel industry—which is exactly what they did. U.S. Steel kept the price of steel high and made huge profits for decades. Of course, Carnegie sold his company knowing this would likely happen. This further tarnished his reputation.[1] •

Overview

Does your city have a Carnegie Library? If so, it is probably a well-built brick building containing the original mission-style furniture of the late 1800s, the time at which Carnegie constructed his libraries. Almost every small town in Texas has one. Carnegie created these libraries because in his youth, a rich Pittsburgh merchant decided to open his personal 400-volume library to the public, allowing anyone to take out one volume a week to read. Carnegie read most of them, and all his life attributed his business success to the knowledge he had gained from books. Carnegie decided that an important way he could help other people succeed in business was to provide them with access to valuable knowledge. So he built his new libraries in places such as small Texas towns where books were a rare sight.

However, as one of Carnegie's workers commented: "A library is small use for a man who works hard twelve hours a day."

Biographers claim it was the guilt Carnegie felt later in life that led to his great philanthropy—guilt because of the way he had treated his workers and the fact that his former company monopolized the steel industry for decades. He ended up giving away most of his huge fortune, establishing the Carnegie Foundation, which remains today one of the richest nonprofit organizations in the United States.

We can tell a lot about why business is the way it is today by looking at how it has evolved over time. The history of business is the story of people's constant struggle to obtain scarce resources to increase their well-being—resources such as the food, shelter, land, money, and savings people need to survive, protect their futures, and improve the future prospects of those they care about. The story of Carnegie's rise from poverty to wealth and power illustrates just this struggle.

In this chapter, we look at the evolution of business and how and why the nature of business has changed over time. We go back in history and trace the way the control of land and labor have been used to build capital and wealth. First, we chart the development of Feudalism, a business system based on the control of property rights to land and labor. Second, we look at the operation of money in a business system, the way it facilitates trade, and promotes the accumulation of capital. Third, we examine mercantilism, the business system in which products are traded across markets and countries until they are put to their most highly valued use.

We then describe the Industrial Revolution and the emergence of capitalism. Capitalism is the economic or business system in which private property rights become the basis for the production, trade, and distribution of goods and services. Finally, we take a look at the different forms of business organizations that have emerged over time to make more productive use of resources, enabling people to build capital and wealth. By the end of this chapter you will appreciate how business has always centered on the quest to obtain capital, wealth, and the power and influence that goes with them.

Feudalism: Land, Labor, and Property Rights

The earliest writings about business date back to Mesopotamia in 3000 BC and were discovered by archaeologists in what is now the Middle East. Business goes back to the Stone Age, however. Economists regard the clan, or tribe, as the earliest form of organized "business" activity. The division of labor between a clan's members into skilled hunters, food gatherers, craftspeople, priests, shaman, and sages is a good example of how these people organized their activities. (See Figure 2.1.) In fact, their very survival depended on it. Only by working together could people gather sufficient amounts food and perform the other activities necessary to protect themselves and survive in harsh conditions—such as through wars, severe winters, and so on. Only a cooperative group of hunters could bring down the biggest game or make the canoes and nets possible to fish on a large scale, for example.

The Emergence of the Hierarchy

To facilitate goal-directed activity, some form of power and control is needed to decide who will perform which task and how much each person should receive for his or her work. The need to reduce the transaction costs involved in exchanges led to the development of a hierarchy of authority in a tribe, clan, or any other "organized" setting. The hierarchy of authority is a ranking of people according to their relative rights and responsibilities to control and utilize resources. People at one level in the hierarchy have the right to make certain kinds of resource decisions, and they have the right to expect obedience from those below them in the hierarchy. At the same time, the people who make these decisions also bear the responsibility for whether or not their decisions work out. A person's ranking in a hierarchy will

hierarchy of authority
The ranking of people according to their relative rights and responsibilities to control and utilize resources.

Figure 2.1
Division of Labor in a Tribe

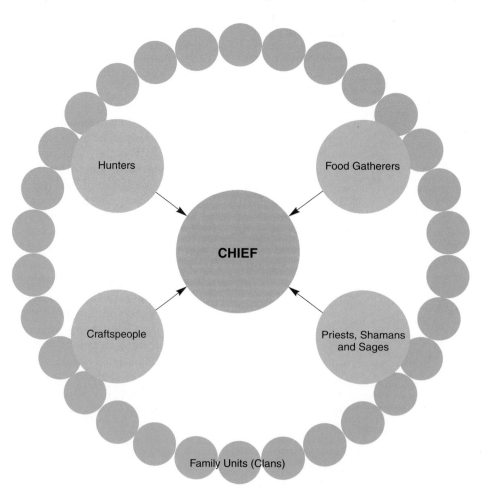

Hunters

Food Gatherers

CHIEF

Craftspeople

Priests, Shamans and Sages

Family Units (Clans)

change if they can show their ability (or inability) to use resources profitably to the advantage of the organization and its members. If the person succeeds, he or she will be promoted; if the person fails, he or she will be fired or deposed.

At the top of the hierarchy emerged the ruler of the tribe who, as tribes became allied with one another, took on the title of chief, prince, king, or emperor. Commonly, the ruler used power and status to create a dynasty, or ruling family, that then claimed the perpetual right to govern. The present Emperor of Japan, for example, can trace his family's royal bloodline back over five thousand years, while the present Queen of England traces her right to the monarchy back for almost 2000 years.

Hierarchy and Property Rights

property rights The right of people to own, use, or sell valuable resources.

At the heart of any claim of a right to rule or govern and to direct the activities of others is the possession of property rights. Property rights are the claims by people to own, use, and sell the rights to valuable resources. In earliest times, the claim to property rights was a matter of brute force. Today laws provide people with a legitimate claim to own and use a resource. Since earliest times land has always been considered the most secure resource, hence the term "property" right, implying control over land (property) and the things on it. Today, property rights pertain not only to land but also to any valuable resource such as the use of one's own labor; the tangible results of enterprise such as patents and copyrights; and ownership of financial capital in the form of bank accounts and stock. This is illustrated in Figure 2.2.

In the past, the ruler of a tribe or people claimed the legitimate power to assign the property rights to control land to whomever they chose. Commonly, monarchs, who were always the largest landowner in a country, granted their most powerful supporters the rights to control (not own) large landed estates. In this way they attempted to retain the loyalty of their most powerful followers and prevent them from trying to seize the crown for themselves! Thus came into being the **aristocracy**, the landed nobility that had the right to control all the resources, including the people on their estates. Consequently, they were given the power to direct all business and social activity within their particular domains.

aristocracy People given the right by a ruler to control a country's resources, including its land and labor.

Once aristocrats were in control of their estates, they had the incentive to be *enterprising*–to find ways to use the estates' land and labor more profitably and increase their personal wealth and power. Indeed, improving the land to make it more productive

Figure 2.2
Property Rights and Resources

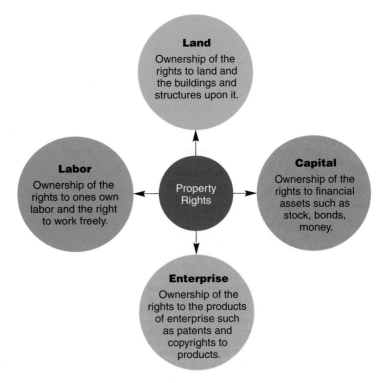

Figure 2.3
The Hierarchy of
English Aristocrats

King and Queen

Prince and Princess

Duke and Duchess

Marquess and Marchioness

Earl and Countess

Viscount and Viscountess

Baron and Baroness

Baronet and Lady

Knight and Lady

Commoners

was the principal way of building capital and wealth at this time. In most societies, a hierarchy of aristocrats came into being. An aristocrat's position in the hierarchy was largely determined by the income their estates generated. Such a hierarchy, the one that developed in England, is depicted in Figure 2.3.

Aristocrats were required to be loyal to the monarch in return for being granted the rights to control estates. They were also obligated to perform various important services for the monarch. For example, in times of war, which was often the most usual situation, aristocrats had to furnish soldiers and arms to the monarch in proportion to the size and wealth of their estates.

In most societies, ordinary "land-less" people had no property rights; they were simply a resource owned by the estate as laborers and slaves in bondage. In Russia, for example, the slaves who worked the aristocrats' estates were called serfs. Large Russian estates might have hundreds of thousands of serfs whose rights were determined at the whim of their owners. It was not until 1861, that Tsar Alexander II freed the serfs and allowed them to buy land from their former owners.

Feudalism

feudalism The business or economic system in which one class of people, aristocrats, control the property rights to all valuable resources, including people.

The business or economic system in which one class of people (aristocrats) control the property rights to all valuable resources, including people, is known as **feudalism**. (See Figure 2.4.)

Throughout the Middle Ages (A.D. 500–1500) this business system endured. Gradually, however, laborers began to receive more rights and rewards. In large part this was because people with few or no rights had little motivation to perform at a high level because they did not share in the profits. So, to increase the motivation of workers, and increase the productivity of land, the system of tenant farming evolved.

To make their estates more profitable landowners assigned the most able workers to take control of specific farms on their estates. Landowners then charged these workers, or tenant farmers, rent to work the farm per year, payable either in the form

Figure 2.4
Feudalism,
Mercantilism,
and Capitalism

Feudalism
Business or economic system in which one class of people, aristocrats, possess property rights to all valuable resources, including people.

Mercantilism
Business or economic system in which merchants and bankers organize the trade of products across markets and countries until they are put to their most valued use.

Capitalism
Business or economic system in which capitalists or industrialists privately own the physical capital of industrial production and use it to produce, trade and distribute products.

of produce or money. Tenant farmers could either give the landowner a share of their produce each harvest time, or they could sell the produce in the local markets and keep any profit or surplus over and above that necessary to pay the rent.

The amount of the rent a tenant paid depended on the value of the goods and services a particular farm produced and sold. Landlords had the incentive to charge as high a rent as they could get. But, to keep their tenants motivated to work well and improve the land, they had to let the tenants profit from their efforts. Thus, bargaining and negotiation between landowner and tenant to determine the fair market rent was common. From these negotiations arose the familiar terms we use today of landlord, lease, and tenant.

The conflict between aristocratic landowners and tenants over how to share the profits from farming is just one example of the kinds of problems that arose under feudalism, however. Conflicts arose between the aristocrats themselves. Throughout history wars have been fought between opposing aristocratic families, both inside a country and between countries, to possess the others' land, labor, and capital. "Enterprising" aristocrats tried to conquer their "enemies" and seize their property by force. At the time this was legitimate because different tribes and countries did not recognize each other's property rights. "Might makes right" and "to the strongest goes the spoils," were the principles of doing business.

The Hundred Years War, for example, was fought in England between the Lancaster and York families to secure the rights to the English throne—and thus gain control of England's property rights and resources. The fighting lasted for more than a century, from 1337-1453, during which time the need for more soldiers and armaments drained England's labor and capital. At the same time, England's land and estates were ruined by the constant warfare that also resulted in the deaths on the battlefield of most of the aristocrats themselves. When Henry Tudor claimed the English throne based on a distant royal bloodline (those most directly in the bloodline were dead), more vicious fighting ensued. After he finally secured the throne and founded the Tudor dynasty, Henry protected his family's future claims by executing most of the remaining "old" aristocratic families and then granting their estates to his loyal supporters. Another, but very different, example of the way in which the drive to possess private property rights has affected business and society is discussed in Business in Action.

Business
in Action

The Southern Kwakiutl Indians

The Southern Kwakiutl (Kwa'kee'oot'l) Indians lived among the inland waterways between Vancouver Island and the adjacent mainland of British Columbia, Canada. When Europeans first encountered the Kwakiutls around 1800, they were amazed at their custom of "potlatching." Every year at the Kwakiutl potlatch ceremony, the 28 different Kwakiutl clans, or extended families that formed the tribe, gave valuable gifts, or potlatch, to other families in the tribe. Moreover, the richest clans competed to give away the most valuable potlatch gifts, and thus a significant part of their wealth, to other clans in the tribe.

Europeans, used to living in a society where gift giving outside a family was unheard of were shocked by this custom. Anthropologists became interested in discovering why, when most people behave in a self-interested way, potlatching existed among the Kwakiutls. After much study they found some interesting answers.

The Kwakiutls' prosperity and wealth was based upon their ability to catch and preserve the salmon that swam up the many rivers to spawn each year during their annual summer migration. Salmon fishing was the Kwakiutls' business. Each of the 28 clans had the right to fish a different river, and some of these rivers contained many more salmon than others. As a result, some clans caught significantly more fish because their rivers were richer with salmon.

Apparently, in the past, the different clans had fought many wars against each other to obtain the rights to the best rivers. This had resulted in much bloodshed and rivers changed hands often. This fighting also resulted in high transaction costs–the enormous amount of time and effort each Kwakiutl clan had to spend protecting its stream from being taken away by other clans. This time and effort could have been used more productively in catching and drying salmon, making fishing nets, and all the other kinds of products necessary to improve their well-being.

The Kwakiutl's solution to this business problem–fighting over salmon streams and high transaction costs–was to permanently assign the property rights to a particular river to one of the clans. This had two main advantages. First, this gave each clan the incentive to learn about its river and find better ways to fish it because the clan members knew it would be theirs in the future. Second, private property rights also protected each stream from overfishing. Each clan knew that if it caught too many salmon in any one year, this would reduce its salmon catch in future years.

The Kwakiutl, a North American tribe, "potlatched" in the 1800s. The richest clans of the tribe gave some of their wealth to the poorer clans in return for fishing rights to the best rivers. This helped to preserve harmony among the clans and quell strife in the tribe.

To remove the incentive of the poorer tribes to wage war to obtain the best streams, potlatching emerged as a way of redistributing wealth between clans. To create a fairer distribution of wealth within the whole tribe, the richer clans gave away a significant portion of their wealth (potlatch in the form of dried salmon, blankets, canoes, and so on) to the poorer tribes, although all the clans exchanged gifts. Potlatching did not result in all clans having *equal* wealth. Some clans might be more skilled than others in fishing or in crafts, or more enterprising, and these differences in profitability between clans were recognized in the gift giving process. Higher-performing clans were wealthier than lower-performing clans.

There was another important reason why the richest clans competed among themselves to give away the most valuable gifts to the other clans, however. Those that gave the greatest gifts obtained the most respect, status, and prestige in the tribe. They were the ones who gained the most power to influence the tribal government. In a sense, they were the tribe's "aristocrats."[2]

Money, Capital, and Commerce

The fight for the right to own and profit from land and labor underlies the history of business. Just as the Kwakiutl's rivers varied in their productivity, so land also differs widely in its fertility. Thus, it was rare that any farm, or even estate, was self-sufficient, meaning it could supply all its own needs. For example, one estate's land might be particularly suitable for growing wheat or raising cattle or growing grapes. Rarely, however, can all three activities be pursued successfully on the same piece of land. Given differences in the characteristics of land and labor across estates, regions, and countries, people have to engage in barter and trade to obtain products they cannot make themselves.

From Barter to Money

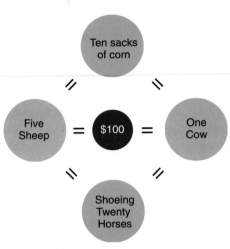

Figure 2.5
Money as a Standard of Value

When people meet to barter one kind of good or service for another, a problem economists call the *double coincidence of wants* arises. The problem is that each person has to want the product that the other person has to offer for the exchange to be successful. For example, if I specialize in raising pigs, and you specialize in raising cows, you have to want my bacon, if I am to be able to obtain your beef. Moreover, a cow is worth far more than a pig. For exchange to take place I would have to be able to offer you, say, six pigs in return for your cow—but you might have no use for six pigs. You might want three pigs, a horse, and five sacks of flour.

At some point in history, people started to use money to overcome this exchange problem. When people will accept some commodity, like coins made from gold or silver, in exchange for their valuable goods or services it becomes much easier to trade goods and services. This is because money acts as an exchange standard or measure against which the value of different goods and services can be compared and their relative prices determined. (See Figure 2.5.)

As we discussed in the last chapter, the forces of supply and demand determine the price of a product. The price of a cow, pig, or share of Kroger stock, is determined by its buyers and sellers. Its price will go up when there are more buyers than sellers of the product (and therefore the product is in short supply). Its price will go down when there are more sellers than buyers (and therefore there is an excess amount of the product being supplied). In our example of trading cows and pigs in the local market, the price of cows and pigs is determined by how much buyers are willing to pay for a cow or pig, and how willing suppliers are to sell a cow or pig at that price. The market tells us how much a product is worth in terms of money. This makes it easier to compare the relative value of different products in order to trade them.

One important economic consequence that arises when people agree to use money to buy and sell products is that it increases the profitability of trade because it is possible to structure exchanges more efficiently. To see how, let's continue with our example of cows and pigs. Under a barter system, only whole animals can be exchanged. But when money is used, animals can be butchered and their meat sold on a piece-by-piece basis according to the specific needs of a particular buyer. In effect, money makes the product "divisible." The effect of this change in trade is that there will be more buyers for the meat, which increases its value and price. We therefore will receive *more money* for our products. Furthermore, we can then use the money from the sale of our products to buy *exactly* what quantity and combination of goods or service we need—a round of beef, a leg of pork, two sacks of corn, and the services of a blacksmith. This makes these products more valuable to us. By using money to trade, both buyers and sellers can better fulfill their needs and profit from exchanges.

There is another important way in which money increases the profitability of trade. Beyond making the exchange process easier, the use of money *creates many new kinds of profitable business opportunities*. For example, rather

Did You Know?

Two of the oldest businesses with offices in the United States are the Takenaka Corporation, an architecture firm established in Tokyo in 1610, and Zildjian, a musical cymbal and drumstick manufacturer, founded in Constantinople in 1623. America's oldest family firm is the Shirley Plantation, in operation since 1638.[3]

than take on the task of trading for a cow and butchering the animal ourselves, we could sell our cow to a butcher–a person *specialized* in preparing meat. The butcher would then assume the responsibility for selling our meat, and we could take the money we get from the butcher and buy exactly what we need. In addition, and very importantly, we now have more time available and we can develop better skills to improve our land or raise better quality animals. *Thus, we can use our time in ways that allow us to create more future profit and capital.* In short, the use of money as a medium of exchange facilitates occupational specialization and this increases the wealth that can be generated from labor and land.

As noted in the last chapter, we have to be careful that while engaging in business activity we are not cheated by an unscrupulous butcher who tries to convince us our animals are poor quality and offers us a price far less than they are worth. On the other hand, the butcher must be careful not to buy poor quality or sick animals from unethical farmers who might disguise the poor condition of their livestock. Such unethical behavior does occur and must be guarded against. The problems of ensuring that an exchange is fair, and the need to avoid being cheated, led to the coining of the famous phrase "caveat emptor" or "buyer beware" by the Romans.

From Money to Capital

Why would people accept commodities like gold or silver in exchange for their products? First, gold and silver coins are scarce and in short supply, so their scarcity gives them value. Second, coins are a country's legal currency, and in the past, their

The owners of capital recognize the opportunity to "grow" their capital and increase their wealth by lending it out.

purchasing power or value was personally *guaranteed* by the ruler (hence the king's head on the coin). Thus, at a time when wars were commonplace and survival itself in doubt, the ability to carry, store, and hide gold and silver to protect against future unknown threats was, and still is today, perceived as offering substantial security. As such, money is considered *a store of value.*

When money serves as a store of value, the money *itself,* not just ownership of land and labor, becomes an important form of capital that can be used to purchase any good or service its owner desires in the *future.* Money can also be loaned out to increase the owner's future wealth. People are always looking for new opportunities to profit from enterprise, but capital is frequently required to buy the resources needed to engage in commerce. To obtain capital, these people offer its owners incentives to *lend* it to them.

When capital is available in the form of money and is not tied to land or labor, it is much easier to loan it to prospective borrowers. The owners of capital recognize the opportunity to "grow" their capital by lending it out. Bargaining then takes place between lenders (capital suppliers) and borrowers (capital buyers) over the price, or interest rate, at which capital will be loaned. A capital market then emerges, like a market for any other product.

Determining the fair market price for capital is a complicated process. This is because its price depends on the specific use to which it will be put, and especially the risk related to it. In general, the *higher the risk (the higher the possibility of incurring losses), the higher the returns* or rewards an owner of capital expects to receive for lend-

interest rate The price at which capital will be loaned.

risk The possibility of incurring future financial losses because of one's investment decisions.

ing that capital. Frequently, this return amounts to the interest rate the borrower will have to pay. The higher a project's risk, the higher the interest rate lenders will demand for funding it.

But it's not just interest lenders are interested in. In high-risk ventures, the owners of capital run the risk of losing their money altogether. They therefore demand an even higher fee, or "rent," for their capital. Frequently, this rent amounts to a large portion of the venture firm's stock and/or profits it generates. When capital is lent and a profit is generated from it, "money starts to make money" (instead of land and labor making money). A highly profitable investment is one that results in a high rate of future return on capital invested.

Mercantilism: Trade and Enterprise

mercantilism The business system in which a product's price differences are exploited by trading the product across markets and countries.

merchant A trader who uses the discrepancy between the value and price of a product in one market and another to trade goods for profit.

From early times, one of the most important uses for borrowed capital was to fund business trading. Mercantilism is the business system in which products are traded across markets and countries until they are put to their most highly valued use, that is, invested or consumed where they create the most utility.(See Figure 2.4.) Merchants are traders who notice a discrepancy (difference) between the value and price of a product in one market and its value and price in another. They recognize an opportunity to profit from the price difference. The higher price can be obtained when a product has a higher utility (is more highly valued) in one market because it is more scarce and thus in higher demand. Merchants borrow capital and use it to purchase products in the market where they are plentiful, and then transport them to another market where they can be sold at a higher price.

Most commonly such price discrepancies are found in international trading arenas. This is because countries differ widely in the nature of their productive resources. Some countries have better quality land or a better climate, for example, which allows them to produce large quantities of a particular product such as wool, wheat, or grapes. Or some countries may have made advances in a certain technology like computer-chip making and people skilled in certain occupations. India and France, for example, are known for their high quality of engineers. Countries also differ with regard to their natural resources. Oil is abundant in the Middle East, but scarce in many Asian countries, where much of it must be imported. When a product is in plentiful supply its price drops sharply so suppliers are happy to have their products bought by merchants and shipped to other markets and countries where they are in short supply.

From the time of the Phoenician traders onwards, there was a great deal of mercantilism between countries in the Middle East and Europe. Even in Egyptian times this trade was huge. Papyrus records exist that describe vast quantities of grain and olive oil being stored in warehouses that extended over many playing fields in Alexandria, Egypt for sale abroad.

Merchants could, and still can, make enormous profits by taking advantage of differences in the prices of products in different markets. In the seventeenth century, tea imported from India into Britain cost the equivalent of $100 a pound in today's money. Tea was so expensive it was kept locked up in sterling silver tea caddies and was carefully spooned out as needed. The same was true of many spices such as nutmeg and cloves. The attempt by the British to maintain the artificially high price of tea in North America helped bring about the American Revolution.

The attempt by the British to artificially control the price of tea led to the Boston Tea Party, which proved to be a rallying cry for the American Revolution.

Another commonly traded commodity was wine which, while cheap and readily available in hot climates, is in great demand in countries where grapes cannot be grown, such as in Northern Europe. In the fifteenth century silk from China, in the seventeenth century wool from Britain, and in the nineteenth century furs and eventually cotton from the U.S., became the products that made vast fortunes for those who controlled their distribution and trade.

As the wealth of a country came to increasingly depend on the success of its merchants, European kingdoms raced to become centers of trade. The wealth of cities like Venice, Florence, Amsterdam, and London can be traced to successful mercantilism. Monarchs and their aristocratic families were the leaders of these country- or city-based trading empires. These families frequently attempted to "corner" the market, that is, create a monopoly to control the supply and price of a product in which it was sold. Moreover, these monarchs had the power to grant to a person or company the exclusive right to control a product being traded within their countries. They could even grant to one person or company the sole right to trade with a particular country, such as India. In return, the monarch received a large payment for granting the monopoly and often a percentage of the profits of the trading venture.

The Growth of Enterprise

The growing supply of profits and capital brought about by combining land, labor, and trade led to a rapid increase in the fourth productive resource, enterprise. Traders and merchants increasingly functioned as the agents of wealthy people who sought to increase their capital and wealth in ways that were unobtainable just by focusing on their landed estates. Great banking families, with close ties to rich propertied families, became the intermediaries between the merchants and owners of capital.

bankers The people who estimate the risks associated with a new venture and determine the way profits from a venture should be shared.

Bankers are the people who estimate the risks associated with a new venture and determine the way profits from a venture should be shared. Bankers therefore promote enterprise because they help capital to flow to its most highly valued use. Not only do they receive payment for this service, they also receive a percentage of the profits earned by the owners of capital. Thus, if they are skilled, bankers can quickly build up vast amounts of capital in their own right that they, themselves, can then invest in business ventures. Over the centuries the names of bankers such as the Medicis, Rothschilds, and later the Morgans became famous, often because their fabulous wealth allowed them to live like aristocrats.

Indeed, many of the most successful merchants and bankers actually became aristocrats, often by purchasing their titles from monarchs determined to share in the profits being made. Many English dukes and earls were originally successful merchants and bankers, as well as being brewers or soap makers. Sometimes it was very dangerous for newly rich merchants and bankers to become too successful. Some would build themselves large palaces and act in ways that challenged the prominence of the monarch. This frequently proved dangerous, as described in Business in Action, which also highlights the intimate relationship between profit, capital, and power.

Business in Action

Power Plays and Medieval Banking

By the sixteenth century, rich merchants and bankers throughout Europe began buying themselves titles and estates and joining the ranks of the aristocracy. They used their huge trading fortunes to gain political power, often by lending large sums of money to the European kings to help finance wars. Two of these merchant bankers, the Italian Medici and Gonda families, had developed the best economic and political intelligence organizations in Europe. They were utterly ruthless in using their wealth to squash potential competition and protect their monopolies. Their power, in fact, influenced the course of European history.

Catherine de Medici, who was Italian but became the queen of France by marriage, used her family's money and power to help take control of France's economic and political system in the sixteenth century.

In France, for example, the Protestant Reformation had led to the rise of the Huguenots, a Protestant sect. The Huguenots were enterprising and thrifty and fast becoming a dominant force in France's trading and banking system. The Medici and Gonda families feared the Huguenots continuing commercial success might give them the political power necessary to turn Catholic France into a Protestant country like England. Worse yet, they feared the Huguenots would threaten their control over European trade.

To prevent this from happening, Catherine de Medici took advantage of the weakness of the French king to use the Medici's money and power to crush the Huguenots and effectively take control of France's economic and political system. The Italian banking families began buying up titles and estates throughout France. This gave them direct access to the French king. Convincing the king of the danger posed by the Huguenots to his throne, the king agreed to allow the Italian banking families to fund a campaign to destroy the Huguenots by force. At the infamous "Massacre of St. Bartholomew," foreign mercenary troops, paid for by the Italian bankers, massacred many thousands of the leading Huguenots. This effectively destroyed them as an economic and political force in France and set back that country's economic development for a century.

By the seventeenth century, the kings of France had gradually reasserted their control over the aristocracy. The Sun King, Louis XIV, was fast becoming the most spendthrift of Europe, dazzling the world with expensive pageantry designed to show off his power. He had a rival, however—a French banker named Fouquet, who was the richest man in France and routinely lent money to the king. Fouquet lived in grand style, and one year he invited Louis XIV to stay with him at his chateau, La Fontaine. There Fouquet entertained the Sun-King with a feast. Six thousand aristocrats were invited to the dinner where, among other things, Fouquet gave away fine jewels and horses to the guests as prizes. His guests admired the hundreds of pieces of his gold and silver collection made by the finest Italian craftsmen; the hundreds of rooms of his palace decorated with works of art and ceilings painted by great artists; and the incredible outdoor gardens and fountains that made La Fontaine so famous.

Louis XIV was furious at this banker who dared to live in a richer state than a king. The king was so jealous he trumped up charges against Fouquet for treason, confiscated his property and wealth, and threw him into jail. After nineteen terrible years in prison, he died.

Fouquet is said to have inspired the tale of the "Man in the Iron Mask." Louis himself was now inspired to imitate La Fontaine; he decided to build himself a splendid new palace, Versailles, which was to be big enough to house the entire French aristocracy in great style. His motivation to do so, however, was to keep the aristocracy under his close control so they would not be able to conspire against him! His strategy worked. He and his successors were in total control of the country until the French Revolution in 1789.[4]

European rulers like Louis XIV had the "absolute power" they needed to crush their opponents and control the path of economic development in their countries. In England, however, the king could not act in such a high-handed way because in that country, aristocrats had forced King John to sign the Magna Carta in 1215. King John was in a very weak position, bankrupt and deeply in debt. He lacked a strong army to protect his throne. As a result, he was forced to sign the Magna Carta, an event that changed the balance of power between English rulers and their aristocratic families forever.

In a nutshell, the Magna Carta granted aristocratic families the right to hold property in their *own* names, not just in the name of the king—it granted them *private property rights,* in other words. Henceforth, although the aristocrats had a duty to obey the king, they nevertheless claimed the rights to do with their property as they saw fit. The Magna Carta was a turning point in business history for the now-propertied English class. Secure in their claim to land and capital, they became much more willing to use and risk that capital in business ventures to increase it.

Craft Guilds and Occupational Specialization

craftspeople Workers or artisans with the skills to produce higher-quality goods and services.

Around the same time the Magna Carta was signed, major changes were also taking place in other areas of business. In every country, a skilled class of artisans or **craftspeople** existed. These people were valued by society because they had the skills to produce higher-quality goods and services people wanted. In addition, as the wealth of a society increased, the demand for these products increased, and craftspeople prospered.

craft guild A group of skilled artisans organized to control and govern different aspects of its trade.

Just like the aristocrats, this rising class of affluent people also recognized the need to protect their property and wealth. They did this by banding together into **craft guilds.** Guilds of goldsmiths, silversmiths, metal workers, clothing makers, coach makers, barrel makers, builders, masons, and carpenters were organized to control and govern different business trades in different cities or regions. These craft guilds acted like monopolies. They were able to dictate the quality and quantity of the goods made and the prices charged for them. They were a form of business organization, with task and authority relationships, rules, and procedures necessary to control and regulate all aspects of their trades. Formal, seven-year apprenticeships were established for new craftspeople, for example, and the number of new apprentices admitted into a guild strictly limited. This, of course, also limited competition.

Nonetheless, craft guilds helped increase the occupational specialization of society, thereby increasing its wealth. Rulers allowed the guild system to operate because they benefited from the taxes levied on the sale of the guilds' products.

The Industrial Revolution

Industrial Revolution An era in the eighteenth and nineteenth centuries that marked improved production and trade brought about by advances in technology.

In all aspects of business—commerce, occupations, and organizations—the pace of change was accelerating. More and more people found opportunities to share in the wealth being generated by the combination of all four productive resources—land, labor, capital, and enterprise. Eventually, technological progress led to the next major change in business system:the Industrial Revolution. The **Industrial Revolution,** which burgeoned in the late eighteenth and early nineteenth centuries, marked a major shift in the production and trade brought about by advances in technology. It first began in Britain and then spread to the continent of Europe and the United States. As we discussed in the opening case, Andrew Carnegie suffered from its effects—the transition from handloom to steam-powered weaving—but then took advantage of improvements in steel production methods and made a fortune.

Although scholars dispute the exact cause of the Industrial Revolution, many agree that the emergence of the steam engine was a crucial event. The steam engine provided the power needed to work the new spinning and weaving machines that produced the wool and cotton cloth that had become a major part of world trade. It also allowed production to be centralized in huge new factories where thousands of people labored together to make low-cost products. The steam engine also led to the development of steam trains and railways that sped communication and travel and spurred trade both inside of and between countries.

Because the steam engine required huge amounts of coal to power it, this ignited the development of coal mining, an industry that soon employed millions of people. High-quality steel was also needed to make the engines, and this led to the search for improved methods of making steel, such as Bessemer's process. In turn, improved technology resulted in the rapid growth of the steel industry. The ability to produce low-cost steel led to growing demand for steel products such as rail track, an opportunity Carnegie was quick to notice and act upon. Finally, as steam engines became more powerful, steamships quickly replaced wooden ships because they were cheaper to operate. This lowered the cost of global trade as well as sped it up.

A Revolution in Farming and Manufacturing

The Industrial Revolution affected both farming and manufacturing and led to a dramatic increase in the wealth and prosperity of the countries in which it occurred. Three factors transformed farming and increased the productivity of land. First, new and improved methods of planting and harvesting crops, breeding and rearing animals, and fertilizing the land increased productivity. Second, mechanization and the arrival of steam-powered farm machinery meant that far fewer farm laborers were needed to work the land. Third, during the Middle Ages, a significant amount of land had been set aside as "common land" for peasants, serfs, and farm laborers to use on their own time, once their obligations to their owner or landlord were fulfilled. Now, throughout Europe this common land was being fenced in and enclosed by people who claimed property rights over it. The result was that a multitude of people were being displaced from the land.

Without jobs or income, millions of people throughout Europe starved to death. To survive, millions of other people began to emigrate to countries such as the United States, which needed immigrants to propel their own economic development. Other people were saved from starvation by going to work in new industrial enterprises— manufacturing companies brought about by the Industrial Revolution.

Why Did the Industrial Revolution Occur So Late?

innovation The development of new and improved products and new and improved methods to create them.

Why did it take so many centuries for people to discover and utilize the physical and engineering principles that made the invention of machinery, such as the steam engine, possible? The answer cited by most scholars is that the constant wars that had raged throughout the world for centuries isolated people, making it difficult for them to learn about new innovations from one another. Innovation is the development of new and improved products and the discovery of new and improved methods to create or produce them. Because people were relatively isolated, there was little dissemination of new ideas and innovations. Cooperation was needed to advance science and speed up the process of innovation.

The Greeks, for example had acquired great knowledge of mathematics and science. The Romans capitalized on this knowledge to advance their road building and engineering skills. But the wars that led to the fall of the Roman Empire resulted in the loss of much of this knowledge. For many centuries, scientific advances in different countries were unknown to scientists elsewhere,

Until the Industrial Revolution, inventions such as the steam engine were not possible, in part, because of wars that raged for years. These wars isolated people and hampered the dissemination of knowledge among them.

as lone thinkers tried their best to piece together available information and advance it. With growing commercial trade, however, knowledge and new ideas also spread as people came into more contact with one another.

Recognizing that technological advances were economically and politically important, rulers in many countries established colleges and universities where talented people could pursue knowledge for its own sake. Many propertied people, Sir Isaac Newton and Louis Pasteur among them, also began to pursue scientific research. Churches and chapels, especially Protestant ones, established schools and advanced the education of ordinary people. Eventually, this made it possible for the Industrial Revolution to occur and societies to prosper like they never had before.

Even though the Industrial Revolution rendered obsolete many old-style monopolies (those operated by aristocrats and craftspeople), people like John D. Rockefeller found ways to create new monopolies. History repeats itself, as Business in Action describes.

Business in Action

Rockefeller Plays Monopoly

By the 1880s, people understood that monopolies raised prices artificially and hurt consumers. Nonetheless, laws in the United States preventing monopolies were quite weak at the time. There was little to prevent clever, unethical people from finding ways to control the supply and prices of products. One such person was John D. Rockefeller.

Rockefeller started life as bookkeeper in Columbus, Ohio. Always an enterprising man, he had a knack for finding profitable business opportunities and was a genius at raising capital to fund his ventures. In 1884 an engineer named Walker, who was an expert in the design of oil refineries, approached Rockefeller. Many different uses for oil had been discovered, and refineries were springing up in growing numbers in the United States. Walker had designed a new kind of oil refinery that could extract many times the amount of saleable oil from a gallon of crude oil than was possible using the old technology. The huge potential profits from this new process attracted Rockefeller. He began to invest heavily in Walker's refinery and eventually bought it from him.

Rockefeller realized, however, that oil would soon be in plentiful supply. New oil fields were being discovered quickly in response to the growing demand for oil. He knew the price of oil would tumble as its supply grew to match demand. Rockefeller needed a plan to control the supply of oil and its price. The problem was how could he create a monopoly and keep it hidden from public view? If the public realized what he was doing the ensuing outcry would lead to laws that made such unethical anticompetitive tactics illegal.

Rockefeller's solution was to use the profits from his efficient oil refineries, and capital he raised from friends, to secretly buy up every small refining company he could get his hands on. These companies became, for all intents and purposes, a part of the main company he created, The Standard Oil Company. But from the outside, these companies still appeared to be *separate* and *independent* companies. Each had its own stock and management teams. Yet Rockefeller had created a trust, a combination of companies, linked by legal titles and property rights, which allowed them to function as a single corporation. From a legal point of view, however, they were still separate entities.

The trust was effective. Although it appeared Rockefeller was only producing about 30% of U.S. oil, he actually controlled about 90% of the oil coming from the wells and going into U.S. refineries. This allowed him to set the price of oil, and he set it high. Standard Oil was making profits of between 35-50%, and by 1900, Rockefeller had become the richest man in the world, with a fortune of over $900 million.

trust A combination of companies linked by legal titles and property rights that allow them to function like one large company.

By 1900, John D. Rockefeller had become the world's richest man. He did so by finding ways to covertly control the supply and price of oil in the United States.

In the early 1900s the public finally woke up to fact that something "illegal" must be going on if huge profits could be made from a cheap commodity like oil. The nature of Rockefeller's trust system was gradually exposed, as were the many other unethical business practices Rockefeller had used to control the oil supply. He became the target of intense public criticism and the most hated and despised man in America.

One reason for the intense public dislike was that Rockefeller's actions inspired other bankers and industrialists to do the same, including the investors who had bought out Carnegie. By 1900 there were over 198 trusts in the United States. Eventually comprehensive *antitrust laws* were passed that made Rockefeller's unethical tactics illegal. His trust and the others were broken up, and many new companies that were truly independent were created. However, by this time the car and its internal combustion engine had been invented. Demand for oil was so great that the oil industry remained highly profitable.

Shocked by the hostility he had inspired, Rockefeller spent the last part of his life competing with Andrew Carnegie to give away the greatest portion of their fortunes. He established the Rockefeller Foundation with over $100 million of his money and is estimated to have given away over half his fortune by the time of his death. Nevertheless, the U.S. public never responded positively to his benevolence, and he died a hated man. The next generation of Rockefellers who, of course, were still fabulously wealthy, continued to give away a large part of their family fortune. Eventually, the Rockefellers did reestablish their good family name, and today their philanthropy is widely recognized.[5]

Capitalism, Unionization, and the Modern Class System

capitalism The economic or business system in which the private ownership of resources becomes the basis for the production and distribution of goods and services.

capitalists People who personally own or control the physical capital of industrial production such as machinery, factories, distribution networks, raw materials, and technology.

Capitalism is the economic, business, and political system that allows people to own resources and use them to engage in production, trade, and the distribution of goods and services. (See Figure 2.4.) Capitalists are people, like Carnegie and Rockefeller, who personally own and/or control the physical capital of industrial production—machinery, factories, distribution networks, raw materials and inputs, research and development and technology. Today, the word "capitalist" has many negative overtones because of the actions of industrialists like Rockefeller and Carnegie who ruthlessly pursued their own self-interest at the expense of others. It was not only for their ability to control product prices that capitalists came to be so feared and disliked, however. It was also because of the way they treated one particular resource: labor.

As we discussed, capitalists like Carnegie and Rockefeller built the factories needed to manufacture large quantities of low-cost products—products that could be sold profitably at prices much lower than competing products made by skilled workers. In many manufacturing settings, little skill was required of most workers;

Capitalists like Carnegie and Rockefeller employed children as young as six because they could be paid much less than adults.

complex tasks could be done by machines. As a result, skilled workers were now competing for unskilled jobs just to survive—as in Carnegie's father's case.

Capitalists and factory owners began to take advantage of their economic power by putting greater demands on labor. The average worker's wage fell rapidly, and workers were forced to work longer hours. (Twelve-hour days and six-day workweeks were common.) Conditions were often difficult and downright dangerous. Women, and children as young as six, were increasingly being employed in factories and mines because they could be paid much less than men. This new working class came to be called the proletariat, the vast, faceless mass of laborers who worked for subsistence wages. The rise of the new capitalist class, and the conversion of both skilled and farm labor into the proletariat, changed the world forever.

proletariat The class of unskilled workers who have no capital and only possess the rights to sell their own labor.

Take conditions at Henry Ford's Dearborn, Michigan, car plant, which manufactured the "Model T." Ford's workers were actually paid 25% more than a typical factory worker could expect in 1914. Yet to keep Ford's assembly lines up and running, 500 workers had to be hired each day to replace those who had quit. Why? Because of the horrendous work conditions. Workers toiled continuously for 12 hours a day, with hardly a break. To keep up with the speed of the assembly lines, they were forced to perform thousands of repetitive actions as quickly as they could. Moreover, they were barred from joking around or even *talking.* If they broke any rules, they were instantly fired, Now do you understand why 500 new workers were needed on a daily basis?

trade union An organization that lobbies on behalf of its members (workers) to increase their bargaining power in work-related negotiations.

In most newly industrialized countries, the response of workers to these conditions is to band together into trade unions. A trade union is a business organization that lobbies on behalf of its members to increase their wages and working conditions. In fact, the craft guilds were the original breeding grounds of the trade unions. Throughout the twentieth century hundreds of millions of workers in countries around the world became unionized, often after bloody battles with companies like Carnegie Steel, Standard Oil, and Ford, which refused to negotiate with them and tried to "break" them.

Eventually most countries enacted labor laws upholding the rights of workers to unionize and bargain with their employers. Laws were also passed to regulate the negotiation, or collective bargaining, process to ensure fair play. The goal was to create a more level playing field with industrial companies to prevent violence, strikes, and general economic problems. We discuss the issue of labor relations in detail in Chapter 13.

class system A social ranking of people based upon the amount of their capital and wealth, and because of factors such as heredity, kinship, fame, and occupation.

In most industrialized countries, the Industrial Revolution also led to the development of the modern class system. A class system is a ranking of people in a social hierarchy based upon the amount of their capital, wealth and other factors such as their heredity, kinship, fame, occupations, and connections. At the top are the *upper class,* the owners of capital—industrialists, merchants, bankers, and lawyers—who control a significant amount of a nation's private financial wealth.

At the bottom is the *working class,* people who own their own labor and often very little else. In the center developed the "great middle class," people who through education, training, enterprise, luck, marriage, thrift, and so on, are able to accumulate enough capital to purchase their own homes and/or make the investments necessary to provide a secure future for themselves and their families. The relationship between the classes is shown in Figure 2.6.

Today, sociologists divide the middle class into at least two different layers. The "lower middle class," for example, is com-

Did You Know?

In medieval Italian city-states, maritime firms began to call themselves *compagnie* because their members took bread together (*cum-panis*).[6]

**Figure 2.6
The Class System
in Capitalism**

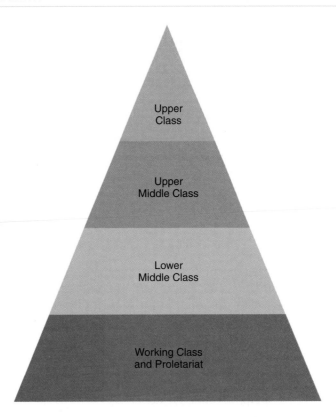

posed of people who still must possess a regular job to maintain their standard of living. They are people, for example, who might own modest homes and have three- to six-months' savings to carry them through the times they are unemployed. Once their capital is exhausted, they face the prospect of joining the working class. On the other hand, if their fortunes improve they might be able to join the "upper middle class."

The upper middle class is composed of people like successful small-business owners and entrepreneurs, medical doctors, senior corporate executives, and so on. These people have high incomes and are able to invest a significant proportion of their income to increase their capital, which is held in the form of property, stock, bonds, and so on. Eventually, their rising wealth makes them impervious to a loss of job or some other economic misfortune. Since these people might possess millions or tens of million of dollars, the gap between the upper middle class and upper class often becomes a matter of social factors. These factors include their family ties and connections through marriage, and the social status they have achieved by virtue of their fame, philanthropy, and expertise.

The Industrial Revolution Continues

Finally, we should note that this chapter only describes some of the main events that took place in Western countries. Most developed countries around the world have experienced at least some of the aspects of the Industrial Revolution, and this has had a lasting effect on their business and social systems. We should also note that the Industrial Revolution is still going on. Many third-world nations are just now beginning to mechanize, and companies are increasingly locating their facilities in these countries such as in China, India, Malaysia, Mexico, and Brazil. In developed countries, vastly improved communications, digital information technology, the Internet, and the globalization of business are continuing the transformation. In fact, some would say that the pace of change is quickening because of the Internet. It has spawned the emergence of millions of small new businesses around the world and changed the way people do business.

The Changing Forms of Business Organization

Side by side with these major changes taking place in business commerce and occupations, the form of business organization was also changing. At each stage in the history of business discussed above, new forms of organization came into being to put the four productive resources to their most profitable use. Recall from Chapter 1 that a business organization is a tool created to give owners and managers the power they need to shape and control the behavior of workers or employees to produce goods and services. Choosing the right form of organization is important because this determines how productively and profitably resources will be used to create the most wealth for their owners.

Early Forms of Business Organization

Perhaps the first type of business organization was the tribe or clan discussed earlier (Figure 2.7). Composed of family groups united by ties of blood and kinship, it was usually organized into some kind of hierarchy, as with the Kwakiutl. Tribal leaders owed their positions to their membership of a particular family, or to particular qualities such as prowess in hunting or the ability to settle disputes and negotiate exchanges between families and maintain the tribal organization as an effective unit.

The tribal organization can function effectively when the property rights and obligations of all its individual members—and the rights of different tribes—are recognized and protected. Problems start to arise when tribes compete for resources, such as the land of their neighbors, herds of wild animals, fishing streams, or good harbors. Competition over property rights has been the cause of most wars.

Throughout history slavery and serfdom was the norm in most societies. Slavery is a form of business organization because it is based on ownership of a resource (people) that builds capital and wealth. For example the conquests of the Pharaohs brought hundreds of thousands of slaves to Egypt. There the slaves tilled the fields to grow corn and build the cities and monuments for which the country is famous. The growth and prosperity of the Greek and Roman Empires was based on the use of slaves for agricultural and building purposes.

Although obviously unethical (and illegal) by today's standards, the problem with slavery as a form of business organization is that the costs related to managing slaves are enormous. Lacking any right to accumulate capital of their own, and being a principal source of wealth of their owners, slaves have little or no motivation beyond fear to work hard. Slavery does not provide any incentive for people to be enterprising and develop the skills and abilities that spur economic growth. Another major problem with slavery is that it reduces the enterprise of slave owners. What motivation do they have to learn new skills and engage in new ventures when they can simply live comfortably and prosper off the labor of others? Thus, slavery not only brutalizes those who are owned, it also corrupts their owners. As a result, forms of business organization like slavery tend to wither and die because they do not provide a platform on which a people and society can advance economically, socially, and morally.

The Joint-Stock Company

Labor and land are normally used in conjunction with capital and enterprise to promote trade and commerce. The trick is to create a form of business organization that provides a way to employ all four productive factors to create profit and wealth. A major obstacle to being able to do this effectively is aligning the interests of people who want to borrow capital with the interests of people who own it. One of the problems with mercantilism, for example, was being able to attract investors. We mentioned earlier how trading ventures were risky. Ships might sink or be robbed of their valuable cargoes, for example.

Figure 2.7
Changing Forms of Business Organization

To overcome this problem, people invented a form of business organization known as the *joint-stock company*. In a joint-stock company an entrepreneur raises capital by issuing stock certificates of its ownership. This involves selling shares of the stock to investors that guarantee them the right to a certain percentage of the company's profits. For example, a group of merchants might retain a 30% share of a venture's stock as their reward for organizing and managing the venture; its investors would then share the other 70%. To minimize their risk, wealthy investors would spread their money around. They would invest in many ventures, just as today people are advised to buy an assortment of stocks and bonds to reduce their investment risks. That way, they didn't have "all of their eggs in one basket" should any single venture fail.

The joint-stock form of business organization allowed many people to share, and hence reduce, the risks of investing in individual trading ventures. As such, this form of business organization facilitated the funding of many business ventures, and this, in turn, expanded global trade. However, one significant risk still existed when a person decided to invest in a joint-stock company. If it failed—and many did because of poor management, economic downturns, and fraud—the people to whom the business owed money such as its suppliers or creditors could sue all of the company's stockholders to recover their money. Stockholders in these companies had unlimited liability meaning that *all* of a stockholder's capital and wealth, right down to his or her house, furniture, and clothes could be seized to pay the company's debts. Stockholders could also be thrown into debtors' prison. This was still too much for most investors to bear.

unlimited liability
A legal system in which the personal capital and wealth of all of a company's stockholders can be seized to pay its debts.

Video
Small
Business
in Action

Joe To Go

Summary: Seven short years ago, Jerry Andrews was a soccer dad who promised to bring coffee to the field for a large group of parents as shown in this original video on your Student DVD. Jerry was faced with several vexing issues—how to transport that much coffee, keep it hot, and contain it from spilling all over the car. The soccer dad's dilemma was the catalyst that launched the now nationally distributed "Joe-To-Go" coffee "box." The evolution of this business was fraught with challenges. Without much capital, and virtually no distribution expertise, Andrews had difficulty bringing his product to a large market. Today, however, the "Joe To Go" coffee box has been adopted by all major chains including Dunkin Donuts and Starbucks.

The story demonstrates the struggles involved in taking a new business idea from the development and patent stages through successful marketing, licensing and distribution. The evolution of this new business demonstrates several important characteristics leading to Andrews's success. Personal characteristics such as self-direction, self-nurturing, action orientation and a high energy level are the essential elements in a successful business evolution.

The "Joe To Go" success story is even more impressive when one considers that statistics suggest that more than 50% of all small business start-ups fail within the first four years.

Discussion Questions

1. Identify the impediments that interfere with the successful evolution of the "Joe To Go" concept.
2. What type of business organization would characterize Jerry Andrews's "Joe To Go?"
3. The video notes that more than 56% of all college students indicate an interest in becoming entrepreneurs. What are the potential barriers and risks associated with entrepreneurship?

The Limited Liability Company

The burden associated with unlimited liability was choking off the supply of capital necessary to fund businesses growing rapidly as a result of the Industrial Revolution. This threatened to derail economic progress. Consequently, capitalists and industrialists lobbied for laws to create a new form of business organization, called the limited liability company. With **limited liability**, if a company goes bankrupt, its creditors cannot seek the personal wealth of its stockholders for reimbursement. Only the money stockholders have initially invested in the business is at risk.

limited liability A legal system that prevents creditors from seizing the personal wealth of a company's stockholders to pay a company's debts.

This was a major change in the form of business organization. One reason the unlimited liability law had been implemented in the first place was to discourage corruption and fraud. It was thought that investors would think very carefully about where to invest their money if they were personally liable for the actions of the venture they funded. However, the world is a very uncertain place, there are enormous risks involved in starting *any* new business venture, and many new businesses do fail. The new limited liability law was passed because people believed that more wealth would be created–if people were encouraged to risk their capital to promote enterprise–than would be lost because of fraud.

In the event, the new form of organization did achieve its goal. It led to the founding of thousands of new businesses that further spurred specialization and the division of labor and led to unprecedented economic growth. The new limited liability model became the standard way of organizing a company. Today, even a single entrepreneur can set up a business as a limited liability company to protect his or her personal assets should the business fail. Once again, the upper class were the big investors in these new, limited liability enterprises. Via an emerging international banking system, they were able to invest worldwide. So, for example, propertied British, German, and French families invested heavily in U.S. commerce and business. Some like the DuPont family also owned and managed companies. The outcome of all this early investment has been the emergence of the giant multinational companies that dominate the global business system today. Multinationals are the most recent development in the history of business organization and are discussed in Chapter 4.

The Partnership and the Sole Proprietorship

partnership Two or more skilled professionals who agree to pool their talents and capital to establish a company in which they are the stockholders and owners.

Throughout history, another way to pool risks and returns on a smaller scale has been to use a business organization known as a partnership. In a **partnership**, skilled professionals such as bankers, merchants, doctors, lawyers, and accountants agree to pool their talent and resources by establishing a company in which they are the only stockholders and owners. Each founding partner receives an agreed-upon percentage of the stock of the business based upon the money the partner initially puts into it, the value of his or her skills, experience, and so on. The profits of the business are then divided according to the percentage of stock each partner owns. If the business grows and prospers, new professional employees are commonly added. If these employees perform well, they are sometimes selected to become new partners. In this case they are given the right to purchase stock in the company and also become an owner.

It's common for a law firm to be created by a partnership and then eventually expand by hiring new employees who often then become partners.

Many prestigious and profitable companies, including a number of New York law firms and investment banks, began as limited liability partnerships. In the 1990s when the stock market was going gangbusters, a number of them decided to "go public," that is, to sell their stock to outside investors. Salomon Smith Barney, an investment banking company, and Accenture, a consulting company, are two notable examples.

The advantage of going public for partners is that this establishes a free market for their company's stock. This allows the stock's value (price) to be competitively determined in the marketplace. If the public thinks the business is valued more highly than the price the stock is being offered at, the partners will receive a premium for the shares they sell. This money could not be realized if the business remained private.

The owners of a limited liability business can take it public at any time. In this way, its owners can realize the value they created by launching the company. The money raised from the sale of the stock can be used to fund the company's future growth. Or the owners can use the proceeds from the sale and invest it in other companies, land, and so on to diversify their investments and lower their risk. (This is not a bad idea when you consider the fact that few companies perform successfully forever.)

Bill Gates is a case in point. Gates, who took Microsoft public in the 1980s, has seen the value of his personal Microsoft stock exceed $50 billion. At the same time, however, he has sold hundreds of thousands of Microsoft shares and used the billions of dollars generated from the sale to buy stock in many other companies. He has also used some of this money to establish a charitable foundation to which he and his wife have given over $25 billion, making it the largest charitable foundation in the world.

sole proprietorship
A nonincorporated business entirely owned by one person.

Finally, a sole proprietorship is a nonincorporated business entirely owned by one person. A sole proprietorship is the simplest form of business organization to start and maintain. The business has no existence apart from its owner, and its liabilities are the owner's personal liabilities. The owner undertakes all of the financial risks associated with the business, and the rewards, or income, are included on the owner's personal tax return. Frequently, highly skilled people such as dentists, lawyers, or plumbers choose this route to avoid the disputes that often arise in partnerships. Also, they are often the form of organizing chosen by entrepreneurs, who are discussed in the next chapter.

Summary of the Chapter

This chapter described the way business systems have evolved from earliest times to feudalism, mercantilism, and then to capitalism. It also described how people organized themselves into business systems to take control of productive resources and use them to create capital and wealth. How business organization forms have changed over time was also discussed. This short account of the evolution of business has enriched our discussion of business in Chapter 1. It charts the way business as commerce, occupation, and organization evolved to allow land, labor, capital, and enterprise to be used most productively and profitably.

The chapter made the following main points:

1. The hierarchy of authority is a ranking of people according to their relative rights and responsibilities to control and utilize resources.

2. Property rights are the claims by people to own, use, or sell the rights to valuable resources. In earliest times, the claim to property rights was a matter of brute force. Today laws provide people with the legitimate claim to own and use resources.

3. Feudalism is the system in which one class of people, aristocrats, control the property rights to all valuable resources, including people.

4. Much of the bargaining and negotiating that goes on in society, like that between landowners and tenants under feudalism, for example, results in land, labor, and capital being put to its best use.

5. The need to overcome problems associated with the double coincidence of wants led to the development of money. Money acts as a standard of value, a store of value, and is a source of capital in its own right. The use of money creates many new kinds of profitable business opportunities. When it is loaned out and a profit is generated from it, "money starts to make money." Money then becomes a desirable productive resource in and of itself.

6. Mercantilism is the business system in which products are traded across markets and countries until they are put to their most highly valued use. Merchants and bankers are traders who notice a difference between the value and price of commodities—resources and products—in one market and its value and price in another. They recognize an opportunity to profit from the difference in prices by trading commodities between one market and the next.

7. Increased trade led to the development of finance and banking institutions. It also led to a general increase in specialization and the division of labor, thereby increasing the capital and wealth of society.

8. The Industrial Revolution provided new opportunities for capital to be put to work. It represented a major shift in production and trade brought about by advances in technology. This technology transformed the production process and increased the profitability of all kinds of business activities.

9. Capitalism is the economic or business system in which the private ownership of productive resources becomes the basis for the production, trade, and distribution of goods and services. Capitalists personally own and/or control the physical capital of industrial production—the

machinery, factories, distribution networks, raw materials and inputs, research and development and technology.

10. Capitalism gave rise to increasing conflicts between capitalists and workers. This led to the formation of trade unions that lobby on behalf of their members to increase their wages and working conditions. Capitalism also gave rise to a more complicated class system: a social hierarchy based upon people's capital and wealth, heredity, kinship, fame, occupations, and connections.

11. As business commerce evolved so did the forms of business organizations used to increase the productivity and profitability of productive resources. The hierarchy of authority evolved early to reduce the transaction costs surrounding business activity. The joint-stock corporation evolved to make it easier for enterprising people to borrow capital to pursue new ventures, and for wealthy people to find new ways in which they could build their capital and increase their wealth.

12. Joint-stock companies evolved into limited liability companies to encourage people to risk their capital to promote enterprise. Today, the limited liability model is the standard way to organize a business.

Developing Business Skills

QUESTIONS FOR DISCUSSION AND ACTION

1. What are property rights and how do they affect the use of productive resources?

2. In what ways can the use of money lead (1) to a more productive use of resources, and (2) to a more profitable use of resources?

3. What is the difference between feudalism and mercantilism? How are the two connected?

4. What is the relationship between capital and enterprise? How did capitalism affect the use of productive resources?

5. What caused the Industrial Revolution, and why did it take so long?

6. How did the emergence of business organization forms based on (1) the hierarchy of authority (2) the joint-stock arrangement and (3) limited liability help to further business commerce and occupations?

ETHICS IN ACTION

Ethics and History

Each of the three main kinds of business systems—feudalism, mercantilism, and capitalism—is associated with a particular kind of ethical or moral position: for example, different views about the rights workers should have relative to the owners of land or capital.

- Identify differences in the ethical or moral positions that explain how labor is treated in each of these three business systems.

- Do you see any themes going through them? Would you say the treatment of workers improved over time from an ethical point of view or did it get worse? Why?

- What basic kinds of rights do you think workers should have in business organizations today? For example, do you think rights, such as the rights to unionize, or to receive fair and equitable treatment are appropriate? What about workers' rights to privacy? Do employers have a right to monitor workers' e-mail and telephone conversations, for example?

- What ethical principles do you think multinational companies should abide by when deciding where to locate their operations or how to treat their workforces in the countries in which they operate?

SMALL GROUP EXERCISE

The Landscape Architecture Business

After reading the following scenario break up into groups of three or four people and discuss the issues involved. Be prepared to share your thinking with the rest of the class.

Imagine you and some of your college friends have decided to start your own business doing landscape architecture, the subject each of you majored in. One of you has the capital to start the new venture. The rest of you are bringing your skills and experience to the business. You know that many new businesses fail because their owners frequently have a falling out as their businesses grow. Owners frequently disagree on the right way to operate the business. They also disagree on how to share the profits, and conflict between owners is a very common occurrence.

What form of business organization will you choose? Should the person supplying the capital have more rights or a greater say in the way the business operates? Who will be in charge of the business? What criteria should you use to allocate future profits among yourselves?

DEVELOPING GOOD BUSINESS SENSE

The Lessons of History

Using the material in the chapter, what does the history of business teach you about the general issues that underlie the way modern companies operate? To answer this question, think about the following.

1. What kind of skills and qualities does an enterprising person need to succeed in business?

2. As you consider what your personal role in the business world will be, what do the lessons about the way businesses are organized teach you?

3. What general business principles do you think modern multinational companies follow today?

EXPLORING THE WEB

The Evolution of Union Pacific

Go the Web site of Union Pacific Railroad (www.up.com), click on the "General Public" tab, and then the "History of the Company" tab (http://www.uprr.com/aboutup/history/index.shtml).

Read the material in this section, including the historical overview, the chronological history, and past and present railroad job descriptions. Then answer the following questions. **For more Web activities, log on to www.mhhe.com/jonesintro**

1. Why did the growth of national railroads like Union Pacific transform the nature of business activity in the United States?

2. In what ways have the occupations of railroad employees changed over time?

3. Why did gas-driven vehicles and then the jet aircraft come to replace the railroad as the principal method of passenger transportation?

BusinessWeek   CASE FOR DISCUSSION

The New Nike: No Longer the Brat of Sports Marketing, It Has a Higher Level of Discipline and Performance

In many ways, the sleek, four-story building that houses Nike Inc.'s Innovation Kitchen is a throwback to the company's earliest days. Located on the ground floor of the Mia Hamm building on Nike's 175-acre headquarters campus in Beaverton, Oregon, the Kitchen is where Nike cooked up the shoes that made it the star of the $35 billion athletic footwear industry. In this think tank for sneakers, designers find inspiration in everything from Irish architecture to the curving lines of a Stradivarius violin. One wall displays models of every Air Jordan ever made, while low-rise cubicles are littered with sketches of new shoes. The Kitchen is off limits to most visitors and even to most Nike employees. The sign on the door says, only half in jest: "Nobody gets in to see the cooks. Not nobody. Not no how."

This is where, nearly 20 years ago, Nike star designer Tinker Hatfield came up with the Air Jordan—the best-selling sports shoe of all time. Right now, Hatfield and his team are tallying the results of the Athens 2004 Olympic Games. Hatfield and his design geeks produced an array of superfast sneakers for the Games, including the sleek track spike called Monsterfly for sprinters and the Air Zoom Miler for distance runners. As befits a global company, Nike's sponsored athletes hailed from all over the world. They took home a lot of hardware from Athens, including 50 gold medals and dozens more silver and bronze. And Nike apparel had its day in the sun, too. The top four finishers in the men's 100-meter race all wore the sign of the Swoosh.

GOING ESTABLISHMENT. The most telling events for Nike didn't take place on the track, however. The brash guerrilla marketer, famous for thumbing its nose at big-time sporting events, was showing a new restraint. Eight years ago in Atlanta, Nike ambushed basketball sponsor Champion (a brand of Sara Lee Corporation) by sneaking giant Swoosh signs into the arena. When the cameras panned the stands, TV audiences saw the Nike logo loud and clear, while Champion had nothing. Nike has even signed up to become an official U.S. Olympic sponsor in four years in Beijing, and it has toned down its anti-Establishment attitude. For good reason: These days, Nike is the Establishment when it comes to global sports marketing. With revenues exceeding $12 billion in fiscal 2004, the company that Philip H. Knight started three decades ago by selling sneakers out of the back of a car at track meets has finally grown up.

The kind of creativity that led Bill Bowerman, the University of Oregon track coach who co-founded the company with Knight, to dream up a new kind of sneaker tread after studying the pattern on his wife's waffle iron, is still revered at Nike. When it comes to the rest of the business, however, it's a whole new ball game. Gone are the days when Nike execs, working on little more than hunches, would do just about anything and spend just about any amount in the quest for publicity and market share.

But in the past few years, the company has devoted as much energy to the mundane details of running a business—such as developing top-flight information systems, logistics, and (yawn) supply-chain management—as it does to marketing coups and cutting-edge sneaker design. More and more,

Nike is searching for the right balance between its creative and its business sides, relying on a newfound financial and managerial discipline to drive growth. "Senior management now has a clear understanding of managing the creative process and bringing it to the bottom line. That's the big difference compared to the past," says Robert Toomey, an equity analyst at RBC Dain Rauscher Inc. in Seattle.

BUSINESSLIKE–AND UNCOOL? In the old days, Nike operated pretty much on instinct. It took a guess as to how many pairs of shoes to churn out and hoped it could cram them all onto retailers' shelves. Not anymore. Nike has overhauled its computer systems to get the right number of sneakers to more places in the world more quickly. By methodically studying new markets, it has become a powerhouse overseas–and in new market segments that it once scorned, such as soccer and fashion. It has also beefed up its management team. And after stumbling with its acquisitions, Nike has learned to manage those brands–Cole Haan dress shoes, Converse retro-style sneakers, Hurley International skateboard gear, and Bauer in-line and hockey skates–more efficiently. Indeed, part of Nike's growth strategy is to add to its portfolio of brands.

To many of the Nike faithful, those sorts of changes smacked of heresy. Lebron James is cool. Matrix organization and corporate acquisitions aren't. But cool or not, the new approach is working. In fiscal 2004, ended May 31, Nike showed just how far it had elevated its financial game. It turned in a record year, earning almost $1 billion, 27% more than the year before, on sales that climbed 15%, to $12.3 billion. What's more, orders worldwide were up a healthy 10.7%. In North America orders rose 10% following eight stagnant quarters.

Nike believes its newfound discipline will enable it to meet its targets of 15% average annual profit growth and revenue growth in the high single digits. Wall Street shares that optimism. Says John J. Shanley, an analyst at Susquehanna Financial Group, an institutional broker in Bala Cynwyd, Pennsylvania: "Nike is probably in the best financial position it has been in a decade." In fact, some analysts believe Nike is poised to become a $20 billion company by the end of the decade.

That would have seemed laughable just a few years ago–sales started falling after hitting the $9.6 billion mark in 1998. Even before Nike's superstar endorser and basketball great Michael Jordan retired from the game in 2003, Nike's creative juices seemed to have run dry. Air Jordans at $200 were collecting dust on store shelves as buyers seeking a different look began switching to Skechers, K-Swiss, and New Balance shoes. Nike wrestled with accusations that it exploited Asian factory workers. Ho-hum new sneakers and troubled acquisitions didn't help. Nike, eager to regain its old momentum, bumped up production–only to end up pushing more sneakers into the market than the customers wanted to buy. As for financial discipline? Well, just consider this: From 1997 to 1999, Nike didn't even have a chief financial officer.

It was during those tough times that Phil Knight, who had disengaged from Nike in order to travel and pursue other interests, came back to the company. The year was 1999. Co-founder Bowerman had died, and Nike was floundering. Knight, now 66, needed to set things straight. Standing before thousands of employees at a company meeting, he admitted that the managers who were running the place had failed. And he went on to blame himself. "He said he wasn't as engaged as he should be, and he said there were things he could do better," recalls Steve Miller, Nike's former global sports marketing director, who was there. "I was personally stunned he would be so open about his failings."

Still, when his iconoclastic company faltered, Knight looked beyond the technology and marketing antics that had served it well in the past. Upon his return to the company five years ago, his first order of business was to put together a new executive team. Knight drew on some Nike veterans, executives who carry the heritage and culture of Nike's early years. But he also recruited some key players from far outside Nike and its industry. CFO Donald W. Blair, who came aboard in 1999, was lured from Pepsi, while Mindy F. Grossman was plucked from Polo Ralph Lauren Corporation the next year with the mission of redefining Nike's $3.5 billion global apparel business. The-day-to-day boss, Chief Operating Officer Thomas E. Clarke, now runs Nike's new business ventures division.

Knight made his boldest management move in 2001, when he named two longtime Nike insiders, creative brand and design wonk Mark G. Parker and operations maven Charles D. Denson, as co-presidents. With Grossman and Blair providing an outsider's perspective and with Parker and Denson steeped in the company's culture, Knight hoped to achieve a balance between the old and the new, the creative and the financially responsible. The unusual co-president structure was hardly Business 101, and many observers figured the new team wouldn't last. Few believed co-presidents could survive the inevitable political maneuvering and clash of egos.

Possibly because there was little time for politicking or backstabbing, given Nike's plight, Parker, Denson, and the rest have mostly steered clear of those pitfalls and focused on shoring up Nike's weaknesses. In the old days at Nike, the culture encouraged local managers to spend big and to go flat-out for market share instead of profitability. In Paris, for instance, the company spent lavishly for a soccer park at the 1998 World Cup to promote itself. Analysts estimate, conservatively, that it was more than $10 million over budget. The cost, which Nike never disclosed, caused Wall Street to start asking whether anyone was in charge.

So Parker and Denson engineered a matrix structure that breaks down managerial responsibility both by region and product. Because the company pumps out 120,000 products every year in four different launch cycles, local managers always had plenty of choice—but also plenty of ways to screw up. Under the matrix, Nike headquarters establishes which products to push and how to do it, but regional managers are allowed some leeway to modify those edicts. The matrix won't guarantee that another fiasco like the Paris soccer park cannot occur, but it makes it a lot less likely.

FILLING THE ORDERS. Nike also overhauled its supply-chain system, which often left retailers either desperately awaiting delivery of hot shoes or struggling to get rid of the duds. The old jerry-built compilation strung together 27 different computer systems worldwide, most of which couldn't talk with the others. Under Denson's direction, Nike has spent $500 million to build a new system.

Nike has also had to grapple with the touchy topic of sweatshop labor at the 900-odd independent overseas factories that make its clothes and sneakers. When Nike was getting pummeled on the subject in the 1990s, it typically had only two responses:anger and panic. Executives would issue denials, lash out at critics, and then rush someone to the offending supplier to put out the fire. But since 2002, Nike has built an elaborate program to deal with charges of labor exploitation. It allows random factory inspections by the Fair Labor Assn., a monitoring outfit it founded with human rights groups and other big companies, such as Reebok International Ltd. and Liz Claiborne Inc., that use overseas contractors. Nike also has an in-house staff of 97 which has inspected 600 factories in the past two years, grading them on labor standards.

It's overseas, in fact, where most of Nike's sales now come from. Last year, for the first time, international sales exceeded U.S. sales—still the company's single largest market. Under Grossman, Nike is making sports fashion a core business, something unthinkable until recently inside Nike's male-dominated culture. Thanks to stylish athletic wear—think tennis star Serena Williams at the U.S. Open—Nike's worldwide apparel sales climbed 30% in three years, to $3.5 billion in fiscal 2004.

SWIFTEST KICK. Just before this summer's European soccer championships, Nike launched its Total 90 III, a sleek shoe that draws inspiration from cars used in the Le Mans 24-hour road race. Nike realized that millions of kids around the globe play casual pickup soccer games in the street and developed the shoe especially for them. That insight does not impress soccer purists. "Nike is selling a lot of the Total 90 street shoes and is including them in the soccer category," huffs Adidas CEO Herbert Hainer. "They are trying to turn the business model into a lifestyle." He's right, of course. Just as Nike made basketball shoes into an off-the-court fashion statement, its Total 90s have become fashion accessories for folks who may never get closer to a soccer pitch than the stands.

What's the lesson? Let other companies worry about the traditional boundaries between sport and fashion. Nike has built its empire by transforming the technology and design of its high performance sports gear into high fashion, vastly expanding its pool of potential customers. If competitors want to get hung up on what exactly Nike's selling, that's O.K. with the folks in Beaverton. It's all Nike to them.

Source: Stanley Holmes and Aaron Bernstein, "The New Nike:No Longer the Brat of Sports Marketing, It Has a Higher Level of Discipline and Performance," *BusinessWeek Online,* September 20, 2004.

QUESTIONS

1. What was Nike's original approach to business commerce? What kinds of business occupations and organization did Nike adopt to pursue its business model?

2. What kinds of business problems did Nike encounter as it evolved over time?

3. In what ways has Nike been changing its business operations and processes, especially its functions, to improve its performance as it has grown and matured over time?

BUILDING YOUR MANAGEMENT SKILLS
Know Thyself

Computers and cell phones are considered "old" after a year or two. Change is occurring at an increasingly rapid pace in our technology, business, social, and political systems. Conditions in the world are constantly in flux and affect the way we do business and with whom. U.S. government surveys tell us that employers value flexibility, the ability to adapt to change, very highly. The self-assessment exercise on your Student DVD called "Assessing Your Flexibility" will help you determine how easily you adapt to change and give you some tips to becoming more flexible.

CHAPTER VIDEO
Denim Blues

Levi Strauss is a name that most Americans recognize. They usually relate the brand to "jeans" or levis. Changes in trends and consumer preferences forced Levi Strauss to diversify its product lines over many years. In fact, at one time the company had over 65,000 different products on the market. Over the past six years, Levi's has seen it sales volume decrease by 40%. With the first three months after 9/11/2001, Levi's was down a whopping 12% in sales. Further, Levi's management perceives its marketing plan as consistent with the research data. Outside industry experts disagree, however. There was a time not long ago when Levi's would introduce mass produced trendy jean wear (at around $30) and simultaneously attempt to market high-end products to an entirely different market segment. In a sense, Levi's was trying to be all things to all consumers at the same time. Based on this and other examples, industry experts suggest that Levi's must segment the market and target their segments more directly and carefully if they are to return to profitability.

High labor and production costs and the need to respond rapidly to changes in the marketplace have forced Levis' to locate all of its manufacturing facilities outside of the U.S. The company has reduced the number of products it sells from 65,000 to 20,000. While Levi Strauss is a 4.2 billion dollar firm, it needs to find a way to define its customer more clearly, target that market, and continue reducing costs as it has recently. While Levis may no longer be manufactured in the United States, it may remain an American icon nevertheless.

1. The chapter discusses the hierarchy of authority. How does this concept relate to Levi Strauss?

2. What qualities does Levi Strauss have that may ensure continued success in business?

3. How does the video segment relate to the evolution of capitalism as discussed in the text?

3 Entrepreneurs, Managers, and Employees

Learning Objectives

After studying this chapter you should be able to:

1. Describe the nature of entrepreneurship and the kinds of entrepreneurial opportunities that can increase the profitability of business commerce, occupations, and organizations.

2. Identify how the process of creative destruction leads to the emergence of new companies, the decline of established companies, and raises a society's standard of living.

3. Appreciate the problems involved in aligning the interests of a manager with those of a company's owners.

4. Distinguish between the three different levels of managers and understand the different roles they perform to increase efficiency, effectiveness, and profitability.

5. Differentiate between two main approaches employees can take to their jobs and the way their performance affects their long-term career prospects.

WHY IS THIS IMPORTANT ❓

Do you want to start a new business and be your own boss? Maybe you picture yourself working on a product development team at Xerox to bring a new printer to market. How are entrepreneurs different from managers? Think of yourself as a product that you will bring to the labor market. Whether your goal is to be your own boss or to be a CEO, how will you develop a competitive advantage and maintain it through different stages in your career? How will your career opportunities be affected by environmental factors such as changes in technology and globalization?

This chapter will explain how people create value in organizations through the functions of planning, organizing, leading, and controlling. Although there may be differences depending on the size, nature, and your position in a business, you will need to know how to increase an organization's effectiveness and efficiency in order to advance your own goals.

A Question of Business
Yahoo!'s Rough Ride

Why did Yahoo!'s founders recruit a new CEO to plan its business model?

Yahoo!, an acronym for "Yet Another Hierarchical Officious Oracle," is the best-known Web site directory on the Internet. The directory originated as a hobby of Yahoo!'s founders, David Filo and Jerry Yang. Filo and Yang, two Ph.D. candidates in electrical engineering at Stanford University, simply wanted a quick and easy way to revisit the Web sites they liked best. They realized that as the list of their favorite Web sites grew longer and longer, the Internet began to lose its usefulness. It was cumbersome to have to look through a long list of URLs each time they wanted to find something.

To reduce their search time Filo and Yang subsequently found a way to break up their list of Web sites into smaller, more manageable categories. Sites were grouped by their subject matter, such as sports or business. Eventually, each of these subject categories also became large and unwieldy, so Filo and Yang further divided them into subcategories. Thus, Yahoo! was born.

Filo and Yang posted Yahoo! online for their friends to use, and soon hundreds of people were clicking on the site. By 1994 hundreds of thousands of users were visiting the site every day.

When they first created their directory, Filo and Yang had no idea they had a potential moneymaking business on their hands. They enjoyed surfing the Internet, and they just wanted to make it easier for others to do so, too. By 1994, however, it had become clear to Yahoo!'s creators that they could make money from their

directory if they allowed companies to advertise their products on the site.

Because the Internet was rapidly expanding, Filo and Yang realized they had to move quickly to capitalize on Yahoo!'s popularity. Although their directory was the first of its kind to be up and running, they knew it could be imitated by other entrepreneurs. Indeed, competitive search-engines like Altavista had already emerged. The virtue of Yahoo!, however, was that unlike having just a search engine, sites were handpicked for their usefulness. In other words, Filo and Yang had already done the legwork for ordinary Internet users.

The problem facing Filo and Yang was getting the funding they needed. Because they were students, they had little or no capital. However, they were able to find a venture capitalist, called Sequoia Capital, which was willing to put up the money. Sequoia had funded such well-known startups as Apple, Oracle, and Cisco Systems. It agreed to provide Filo and Yang with $2 million if they not only agreed to give Sequoia a major equity stake in their venture, but also agreed to hire experienced managers to head their company and develop its business model.

Sequoia's partners had learned from experience that entrepreneurs often do not make good managers when they become responsible for running a company. The skills needed to be a successful manager often diverge from those necessary to notice entrepreneurial opportunities. This is particularly true if entrepreneurs have technical or scientific backgrounds and no exposure to how business operates.

Filo and Yang realized they did lack business experience and agreed to recruit a new management team. To be their chief executive officer (CEO), they hired Tim Koogle, an experienced ex-Motorola executive with an engineering background. Jeffrey Mallett, an ex-Novell software manager with a marketing background, was hired as chief operating officer (COO). Filo and Yang became joint co-chairmen of Yahoo!, and under the control of Koogle and Mallett, who also received a significant share of the company's stock, the four executives created Yahoo!'s business model.

The success of the business model became clear with Yahoo!'s explosive growth. By the end of the 1990s, 15 million people a day were visiting Yahoo!, and it had become the leading portal on the Web. In the meantime, the amount of information and services Yahoo! provided customers also multiplied. The Web site began offering personals, online stock brokerage and banking services, instant messaging, chatrooms, and a host of other offerings. Its business model was based on the idea that the more services it offered, the greater the number of Internet users it would attract, and so the greater would be the advertising fees it could charge. (The cost of advertising is a function of the number of people that an advertising medium, such as radio, TV, or a Web site, can potentially reach.)

In 1996, Yahoo! went public, and in 2000, its stock price reached an astronomical height of $237.50 per share, giving the company a value of $220 billion. That's not bad for a business started by a couple of college students. But just two years later, Yahoo!'s stock plummeted to just $9 a share, and at that point the company was worth less than $10 billion. Why? Because of a series of managerial mistakes at the top of the company combined with the dot.com bust. The nature of these mistakes is discussed later in the chapter.[1] •

Overview

This chapter explains the roles entrepreneurs, managers, and employees play as a company goes about developing its business model and putting it into operation. First, we discuss how entrepreneurs sense opportunities both in the environment and within their organizations. Second, we consider how managers use resources in order to profit from these opportunities. Third, we look at employees and how, by using an entrepreneurial mindset like that of their companies' founders, they can contribute to this endeavor and their own personal success.

To help you develop an appreciation of the challenges you will face once you begin your career, we then examine the issue of what is appropriate employee behavior. Finally, we relate employee behavior to career opportunities over the course of a person's work life and offer guidance about how to obtain a job and get promoted in a company. By the end of this chapter you will understand how the different players in a business—entrepreneurs, managers, and employees—working together can create a successful business model—one that leads to profit for stockholders and for themselves.

The Role of the Entrepreneur

entrepreneur A person ready to supply the enterprise—energy, boldness, courage, spirit, expertise—necessary to start and grow a business.

The discussion of the history of business in the last chapter highlights how aristocrats, merchants, and capitalists acquired and utilized productive resources to create capital and wealth. Their business activities suggest the crucial role entrepreneurs play in starting and growing a business. An **entrepreneur** is the person ready to supply the *enterprise,* that is, the hard-to-define mixture of energy, boldness, courage, expertise, insight, and often ruthlessness, necessary to:

- acquire productive resources; and
- combine and use them efficiently and effectively; to
- take advantage of business opportunities to create goods and services; that
- customers want to buy and which creates profit.

Forms of Entrepreneurial Opportunities

There are many different forms of opportunity in the environment that entrepreneurs can seize upon. They can then establish a business organization to take advantage of them. It is useful to examine the kinds of opportunities open to entrepreneurs in terms of the three main dimensions of business: commerce, occupation, and organization. (See Figure 3.1.)

COMMERCIAL OPPORTUNITIES The first kind of opportunity comes from business as commerce, that is, from new kinds of commercial opportunities in production and trade. The last chapter discussed how discrepancies in the price of raw materials, labor, or finished products in different cities or countries can lead to commercial opportunities. Today, for example, the presence of plentiful inexpensive labor in developing countries around the world has led many U.S. companies to shift their manufacturing activities abroad to take advantage of this commercial opportunity. A shirt that might have cost $5 to make in a U.S. factory now costs only 50 cents to produce abroad in a country like Indonesia or Malaysia. Entrepreneurs who import these shirts can sell them to U.S. stores for around $2 and they can then be sold to customers for $4.99–a price less than what it used to cost to make a shirt in the United States.

Levi-Strauss, the famous jeans maker, has suffered badly because it was late to take advantage of this global opportunity. Many of its competitors had no ties to workers in U.S. factories and quickly moved their production abroad. Levi's, however, employed thousands of U.S. workers in its clothing factories and was reluctant to lay them off. When its competitors proceeded to undercut the price of Levi's jeans, the company's sales plummeted, and it lost billions of dollars in the late 1990s. Today, all of Levi's U.S. clothing factories have been shut down, and its workers have experienced the fate of millions of other U.S. factory workers–a loss of jobs because of low-cost global competition.

Another form of commercial opportunity is when entrepreneurs recognize the opportunities offered by advances in technology to find a new way to *make or supply* a product more cheaply. For example, Toyota was the first car company to develop low-cost, or "lean," manufacturing technology in the 1980s. This allowed the Japanese automaker to charge lower prices for high-quality cars than its U.S. competitors could. In addition, companies that are the first to introduce new IT can often lower their prices and lure away their competitors' customers. Wal-Mart has done this. By installing sophisticated new IT systems to track its inventory, for example, Wal-Mart has been able to lower its prices beyond those of its competitors.

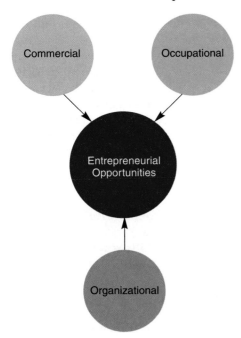

Figure 3.1
Forms of Entrepreneurial Opportunities

The growth of e-business provides a recent example of the way in which entrepreneurs can find new ways to supply products to customers that bypass established distribution channels and break existing companies' hold on their customers. Amazon.com, for example, bypasses "bricks and mortar" bookstores to reach customers directly and offer them a customized shopping experience. As discussed in the opening case, Yahoo! rapidly expanded its online service to include bill paying and banking and in doing so, it bypassed bricks-and-mortar financial institutions.

Yet a third form of commercial opportunity arises when a company creates a new or improved product that better satisfies customer needs—*even though the new product's price may not be lower.* Many people, for example, are willing to pay a higher price for a car with the latest features, or for the best new video games, or for the latest clothing fashions. When Porsche introduced its new Cayenne SUV it boasted that the Cayenne's advanced engine and transmission drives as well as its famous sports cars. Is it any surprise, then, that its Cayenne sold well, even though it costs between $65,000-90,000? As you can see, if a company can find a better way to satisfy its customers, it can often charge a premium for its products.

From a commercial point of view, entrepreneurship is about *creating price discrepancies* by producing or providing something that customers just have to have—such as a Porsche SUV or a tablet computer or PDA with a color screen, built-in cell phone, digital camera, and web-browsing capability. Companies that are first to enter the market with a product that offers customers increased utility often obtain a first mover advantage. A first mover advantage is the acknowledgment, fame, or brand-name reputation gained from being first to innovate a new product. Competitors often rush to copy and imitate the first mover's product to stop their customers from switching to it.

first mover advantage
The competitive advantage gained by being first to develop a new product or process.

OCCUPATIONAL OPPORTUNITIES
Many opportunities for entrepreneurship also exist when it comes to choosing a business occupation. A person who decides to invest ten years of his or her life to learn the complex and demanding skills necessary to become highly specialized in an occupation is acting like an entrepreneur. Would-be surgeons, musicians, teachers, artists, scientists and engineers are banking on their ability to succeed in their chosen line of work. They do not know in advance if they will be able to become an expert in their field of work so that they can command high prices for their services. They also have no idea if they will be able to invent or come up with new products that will make them a fortune. Nonetheless, *prospective* profits motivate these people to devote enormous time and effort to learning a set of work skills. Short-term pleasure is sacrificed for long-term gain.

Alert people who notice changes in the business environment having an impact on occupational opportunities are frequently the first to develop new skills. These people are behaving entrepreneurially as it relates to their own careers. They know that the first people with the skills needed to perform these new jobs will be in scarce supply and that because of this, they will be able to command a high price, or wage. Over the last twenty years, for example, millions of new IT jobs have emerged—everything from creating moving animations or "rich media" for Web sites; to developing new security programs to protect computer systems from viruses and hackers; to building, hosting, and managing Web sites.

The people who develop and learn these new kinds of skills will not be able to charge a high price for them forever, though. Other people will move quickly to develop similar skills. As the supply of people with a specific kind of skill increases, the wages paid for these skills falls. If the skills they develop are unique or hard to imitate, however, people can expect to earn a premium from them for longer periods of time—such as famous architects, musicians, and CEOs. Business in Action profiles the way the Rolling Stones developed a set of unique skills and a business model that over the course of many years, have made them the wealthiest rock band in the world.

**Business
in Action**

The Rolling Stones Are Not Gathering Moss

The Rolling Stones have been one of the world's leading rock bands since the early 1960s when they burst onto the music scene as the "bad boys" of rock and roll. Like most rock groups, in their early days, the Stones were an unproven product with no track record. Desperate to sign recording contracts, they were in a weak bargaining position compared to the record companies they were dealing with. As a result, despite their enormous initial success, the Stones received a relatively small percentage of the profits their best-selling records were generating. Later, after the Stones had become world famous, they were able to renegotiate their contracts on their own terms. But the Stones didn't stop there. They continued to find new avenues for entrepreneurship.

Under the leadership of Mick Jagger (the CEO of Rolling Stones Inc.), the Stones have continually found new ways to generate profits. Since 1989 they have earned more than $1.5 billion, but only about $500 million of it has come from royalties earned on their records. Incredibly, the rest of it has been generated from concert ticket sales, merchandising, and company sponsorships associated with their tours.

The way the Stones "create" their world tours shows how entrepreneurial they are. It all began with the band's "Steel Wheels" tour in 1989 when, for the first time, working with a Canadian promoter named Michael Cohl, the Stones took total control over all aspects of their tour. Before this, like most rock bands, they had put together a schedule of cities to tour and then contacted well-known promoters in those cities to stage the concert and sell tickets. The Stones would then receive a percentage of total concert revenues as their payment. Under this business model the promoters were walking away with over 60% of the revenues.

Cohl proposed a new model whereby he would assume responsibility for all 40 concert venues on the Steel Wheels tour and guarantee to pay the Stones $1 million per concert–a much higher amount than they had ever received before. Cohl felt he could do this because his approach cut out the profits earned by the promoters. He also agreed to personally negotiate the merchandising contracts for Stones T-shirts, posters, and so on and to get corporate sponsorship for the tour.

However, after the Stones had played in their first few venues, Cohl realized he was losing money on each one. To make the tour a success, he and the members of the band would *all* have to find new ways to cut costs and increase revenues. From this point on the Stones became directly involved in every decision concerning staging, music, advertising, and promotion, and even the price of concert tickets– which have continued to climb with each new tour. The Stones, and particularly Jagger, faced a huge task to learn how to improve the concert tour business model, but the band persevered, and step-by-step have continued to refine and develop their approach in every subsequent tour.

In the end, the Steel Wheels tour made over $260 million, and the Stones made far more than the $40 million they were promised. In later tours, from "Packing Them In" to the huge "Voodoo" tour in 1995, world revenues from Stones concerts surged. When Mick Jagger and Keith Richard, who are both now in their 60s, were asked how long they planned to go on touring, their answer was "until we drop." Indeed, in May 2005 they announced the Stones would begin yet a new multi-city tour kicking off in Boston in the fall.[2]

After years of paying promoters nearly 60% of the revenues from their concert tours, the Rolling Stones decided to take control of their business and become directly involved in every financial decision.

People who act like entrepreneurs and take advantage of occupational opportunities notice the changing trends in business and keep track of advances in their own occupations. The Stones, for example, have spent considerable time and money discovering exciting new ways to stage and present their concerts. Similarly, given one's personal interests and talents, people who think the Internet will become more important in the future would be wise to develop skills that match the different kinds of occupational opportunities it offers. Likewise, people whose interests move towards the personal assistant direction, would be wise to enroll in courses to learn how to use new kinds of business software.

It is important to realize that, just as in any other area of business, a competitive market is operating in the occupational or job market. In most industries, dozens, if not hundreds, of people are competing for the same jobs. Having some kind of unique or scarce skill, or the willingness to acquire it, is a selection criterion that potential employers use to evaluate job candidates. But being able to think and act like an entrepreneur like the Stones did is something that will help you not only in your job search but also with the opportunities you will face during the rest of your life. It will affect your long-term ability to build human capital and personal wealth.

In order to compete successfully against Japanese carmakers, Chrysler grouped its employees into teams of people from all of the company's different functional groups. This lowered Chrysler's operating costs and increased vehicle quality.

ORGANIZATIONAL OPPORTUNITIES The third main form of opportunity for entrepreneurs is to create new business organization forms and find new ways to design and control a business's organizational structure to increase its profitability. Perhaps, for example, a new way of grouping employees through the use of web-based IT will allow them to communicate and cooperate better with each other and with customers. For a company, the result of finding better ways to organize is lower operating costs and the ability to make better products that command higher prices in the marketplace.

In the last decade, new forms of global business organization, using new kinds of IT, have changed the way companies make and sell their products and increased company profitability. In the 1990s, for example, Chrysler regrouped its employees into teams comprised of people from all the different occupational functions such as marketing, research and development, and manufacturing. The result was that Chrysler was able to reduce its operating costs and increase its vehicle quality dramatically. This has helped the company compete more successfully against Japanese carmakers. Similarly, Citicorp developed software giving its employees a better understanding of the needs of its customers, which improved customer-service quality. By 2003 the marketplace had rewarded Citicorp with millions of new global customer accounts.

Finding new, more profitable ways to run a business, large or small, is as entrepreneurial an activity as creating better products. Whenever employees take even small, incremental steps to improve the quality of a particular product or operation in a firm, they are behaving entrepreneurially. If all employees are on the lookout for ways to improve the firm's processes and products, the firm will be more competitive.

Countless opportunities exist for entrepreneurs to found new companies with viable business models. Often, it is small companies, founded by one or a group of entrepreneurs such as Dell, Apple, and Microsoft, which introduce the new products that change the business and social world. At the same time, a substantial amount of entrepreneurship takes place in large companies that invest huge amounts in new research and development to advance technology and create new and improved goods and services. Intrapreneurship is the entrepreneurial activity that takes place *inside* an established company. Often, it is the capital spent by large global companies on Intrapreneurship that fires the advances in technology that can, and have, revolutionized business in the last decades.

intrapreneurship
Entrepreneurial activity that takes place inside of an established company.

Why Be an Entrepreneur?

The reason established companies, individual entrepreneurs, and other investors like venture capitalists, are willing to risk or lend their capital to pursue new ventures is that the potential profits are enormous. In the last chapter we discussed how merchants and companies could charge premium or above-average prices when they had a monopoly. Entrepreneurs and companies that create products customers perceive as valuable also can charge premium prices that lead to high profits. Michael Dell, for example, created a highly profitable small business by selling low-priced computers over the telephone. Today Dell Computer is the leading PC maker and its founder is a rich man. The same is true for Filo and Yang (and for Sequoia capital), who profited handsomely by launching Yahoo!

Of course, entrepreneurship is also fraught with great risks. Many entrepreneurs make mistakes, their businesses collapse, and their companies go bankrupt. There are several reasons for this.

First, entrepreneurs frequently overestimate their ability to create new products customers desire and are willing to pay a high price for.

Second, they underestimate how difficult it is to actually reach prospective customers and get them to try their products—even when they are excellent. The importance of marketing and advertising—and its high cost—is often not given enough weight in a new company's business model.

Third, entrepreneurs may not realize how much ready cash is needed to see a small business through its critical, initial "birth" period, which can sometimes take up to two years. This is the time period in which most new businesses fail because they lack cash flow—the money that must be constantly available to pay the cost of the business's everyday operations.

Given the potential risks and returns of entrepreneurship, most scholars agree that although capital and wealth may be the ultimate reward, many entrepreneurs are *not* driven by money. Rather, they are driven by the challenge of creating valuable new goods and services. The profit they receive is essentially the *by-product* of their drive to bring their new products to market and watch them succeed.

The point here is that many entrepreneurs are *intrinsically motivated,* meaning they are driven by personal or inner motives, such as the need for achievement or the need to create new and better things for themselves and others to use. They are not always *extrinsically motivated,* meaning that they are not driven solely by the desire for money and personal wealth. When Michael Dell started his PC business from his dorm room when he was a student at the University of Texas in Austin, he had no idea he would end up becoming a multibillionaire. He was driven by his vision of competing with, and beating, companies like IBM and Compaq at the business of delivering less expensive PCs to computer users. The inventors of the earliest video games were driven by their own enjoyment of playing their games, not by the prospect of making a fortune. Many successful high-fashion clothes designers are driven by the vision of themselves in their own creations. Successful chefs are motivated by their desire to produce food dishes with flavors unlike any other. Figure 3.2 outlines the different types of entrepreneurship people engage in and their motivation.

Enterprise, and the number of new small business startups that result from it, are commonly seen as one of the major indicators of a particular society's present and future prosperity. If entrepreneurs do not rise to the challenges of succeeding in a changing global environment,

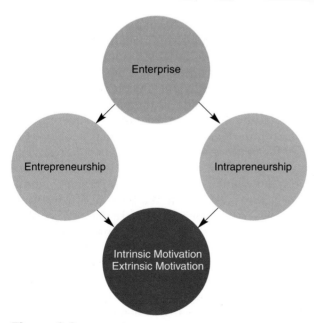

Figure 3.2
Types and Motives for Enterprise

a nation's economic growth may be stifled. To encourage entrepreneurship, many countries provide education, training, and "seed money," or startup capital, to foster the establishment of small businesses and nurture the entrepreneurial spirit of their citizens. Nowhere is this truer than in the United States. It has been said that the "business of America is business." Perhaps in part due to its "frontier" heritage, people around the world see the United States as a place where ordinary people can succeed.

Entrepreneurship as "Creative Destruction"

Economists refer to the widespread changes brought about by increasing global competition and advancing technology as the process of "creative destruction." This process drives old, inefficient companies out of business as they are replaced by new, more efficient ones. When small companies, like Dell, Apple, and Microsoft, launched by a single entrepreneur or group of entrepreneurs, introduce new products that change our lives, larger established companies that fail to invest in new technologies can find themselves driven out of business. And its not just companies but entire industries that get driven out of business. The Industrial Revolution, discussed in the last chapter, is an example of how creative destruction works. The old agricultural age where wealth depended on land and physical labor gave way to the age of steam-powered machinery and transportation; capitalists created new low-cost industries and products making craftspeople largely a thing of the past.

It is not surprising, then, that smaller companies with cutting-edge products often become the takeover targets of larger, more-established companies that want their products, technology, or expertise. The larger companies know it's a matter of their survival. Even Google, which is presently enjoying great success, knows it has to evolve to stay at the top of its game. In May 2005, for example, Google purchased a small networking company called Dodgeball.com. Dodgeball.com has developed software that, through cell phones, signals people when they are in close proximity to one another—so they can meet for coffee and such.

Nonetheless, a substantial amount of entrepreneurship definitely takes place in large companies. Most large companies invest huge amounts of capital in their own research and development endeavors. Often, it has been this capital that has fueled the advances in technology revolutionizing business and our lives in the last century.

Today, of course, the emergence of new industries, such as the computer hardware and software, biotechnology, robotics, fuel cell, and home videogame industries, have created massive disruptions in the business world. The experience of the Levi-Strauss's workers has been repeated across most industries including the industries for steel, cars, clothing, footwear, electronics, and so forth. As you can see, the creative destruction process affects not just companies and industries, but individual people and workers too.

But there is a flipside to the creative destruction process. Although improved communications and information technology destroyed many jobs in the United States in the last decade (particularly manufacturing jobs), it has created many millions more, including jobs in research, engineering, design, sales, consultancy, health and human services to provide new goods and services such as wireless phones, physical rehabilitation, home videogames, and heath care to businesses and ordinary people. Many of these jobs are higher paying jobs than the manufacturing jobs that have been lost to workers in countries abroad. Some people believe that this new wave of disruptive change will ultimately lead to a higher standard of living and better quality of life for the average U.S. worker.

Rapid enhancement in IT has spawned the growth of employment in many industries related to digital and electronic-based computing, such as wireless phones, personal digital assistants (PDAs), and home video games.

Another trend occurring alongside the loss of former high-paying manufacturing jobs has been the growth of low-paying jobs in the service sector in the United States. This has once again created a large class of workers being paid at, or just above, the minimum wage. Many U.S. workers who lack the skills needed in the new IT age have been forced into low-paying jobs in retail stores and fast-food restaurants. Wal-Mart, for example, is currently the largest U.S. employer. In 2005 the company employed over 1,000,000 workers who earn at or just above the minimum wage and receive little or no health insurance benefits. Of course, low wages are one reason Wal-Mart is able to charge lower prices.

It is still not clear how the new business system that is emerging will affect the prosperity of the average person. However, Adam Smith's invisible hand of the market offers hope that most people and classes in the United States and all countries will benefit from changes in technology and competition. Once again, however, there is no rule that says everyone is made better off by capitalism. In many instances, government intervention and international agreements are needed for this to happen. For example, governments can help people adapt to changing conditions in the marketplace by providing them with the training and education programs needed to learn new skills.

The lesson to be learned from the process of creative destruction is that it is always occurring. Most experts now predict that the average worker should expect to make at least three occupational changes in his or her lifetime. It is therefore vital that you continue to acquire and hone new skills. This can help lessen the challenging and sometimes adverse human effects of the changes that constantly occur as the process of creative destruction unfolds.

The Role of Management

It is one thing to have a good business idea; it is quite another to get that business up and running. Just as the survival of a clan or tribe depended on cooperation of its members, entrepreneurs need help to operate a business of any size. The work and cooperation of many people is always needed in business. But getting people to work together to achieve a common goal is not an easy thing to do.

To continue to grow a business, entrepreneurs have to recruit people to take over the various functional tasks that must be performed to get products to customers. Recruiting skilled, honest, and reliable people is a difficult and time-consuming process. The information provided by job applicants must be scrutinized, for example, and new recruits may require considerable training in their new tasks. All the other aspects of employing people, such as monitoring and evaluating their performance and deciding how to reward them, also have to be managed.

The Agency Problem: The Separation of Ownership from Control

delegate Giving up decision-making authority to other people.

Clearly, to run a business of any size, an entrepreneur will have to **delegate**, or give up, some decision-making authority. Delegating is difficult for entrepreneurs. Many of them are used to having total control of their businesses and making all of the important decisions. Hopefully the people an entrepreneur hires will act entrepreneurially as well and take responsibility for sensing new opportunities both in the marketplace and within the organization. The question is, will they? Why would these people want to work as hard as the firm's

Did You Know?

"It was not until the mid-nineteenth century that the concept of the business manager began to appear as an agent, operating between the owners and the workers." –Anthony Sampson[3]

owner? How can they be trusted to make good decisions about how to use the firm's resources when it is not their money at stake? Even if the owner hires good employees, these employees can always leave the company should a better opportunity come along. How can the owner prevent this from happening?

agency problem
The problem that arises because of the separation of the ownership and control of a business. It occurs when the firm's owner delegates authority to managers.

This problem is called the agency problem. It is inevitable whenever there is a separation between the ownership and control of a business. The aristocrat who delegated control over his estates to *land agents* had to rely on them to monitor the performance of tenant farmers and make sure they made good use of the land. The merchants who equipped and manned their ships had to watch them sail away under the control of a captain (an agent) upon whose skills the success of the voyage depended. The problem facing owners is to find people skilled in running a business—*managers*—who can be trusted and motivated to work hard in their interests. Managers are the employees to whom a company's owners delegate responsibility for creating profitable goods and services. Managers control and develop a company's business operations, such as manufacturing, marketing, accounting, and so on. They are also responsible for designing a company's organizational structure. The success of the firm lies in their hands.

managers Employees to whom a company's owners delegate responsibility for using its resources to create profitable goods and services.

To motivate managers to perform at a high level the owners or stockholders of companies provide managers, and particularly top managers, with extremely high financial rewards. These rewards are directly linked to a company's profitability so that managers' interests become *aligned* or consistent with its owners' interests. (Remember, stockholders benefit when a company's increasing profitability causes the value of its shares to increase.)

stock options The right to buy a stock at a certain price and to benefit from increases in the stock's value in the future by selling it.

These rewards can take several different forms. First, managers can be paid a high salary. Second, they can be paid on a bonus system contingent upon the firm meeting certain revenue and profitability goals. Such a bonus might consist of an extra percentage of the manager's salary, say, 30%, as a bonus. Third, many large companies motivate their managers by granting them stock options. Stock options give managers the right to buy a stock at a certain price, say $10 a share. If in the future the company's share price increases to, say, $25 a share, then the managers can exercise their options to buy the stock at $10. They will therefore receive a $15 profit on each share they own if they choose to sell the stock at $25. Since top managers often receive tens of thousands of stock options, they stand to profit to the tune of millions of dollars. Over one thousand of Microsoft's managers have become millionaires as a result of that company's stock option program. Its top executive, Steve Balmer, has received stock options that today are worth more than $500 million. Such a reward structure will motivate a manager to work hard to make the company succeed and the stock price climb. Figure 3.3 outlines the steps owners can take to overcome the agency problem.

Levels of Managers

board of directors
Experienced business executives from inside and outside of a company who are elected by a company's shareholders to act as their representatives.

Creating a reward structure is not the only way the owners of a company try to ensure managers work towards increasing its profitability, however. Owners or shareholders also create a *monitoring and control system* enabling them to scrutinize managers' business decisions and actions. The first step involved with this process is to create a board of directors. A firm's board of directors consists of experienced business executives from inside and outside of the company who are elected by a company's shareholders to act as their representatives. These people oversee the company's business dealings to ensure its resources are being put to their best use. The board also has the authority to recruit, oversee, reward, and fire the

Did You Know?

Some nations are more entrepreneurial than others. Ecuador's total entrepreneurial activity, for example, is nearly twice that of the United States and Canada. Uganda has nearly three times the entrepreneurship per capita as North America, and Peru has nearly four times. Singapore, Denmark, and South Africa, however, have about half as many entrepreneurs per capita as exist in North America.[4]

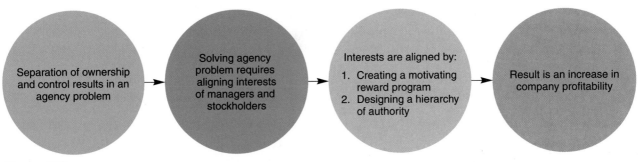

Figure 3.3
The Agency Theory Problem

chief executive officer A company's top manager. The CEO is responsible for overseeing the operations of the company and ensuring its capital is used to create the most profit possible.

company's chief executive officer (CEO). The CEO is the company's top manager—the person ultimately responsible for operating the company and using its capital in a way that makes a profit.

The task of the CEO is then to create a hierarchy of managers in which managers at higher levels scrutinize managers at lower levels—much as the board of directors scrutinizes the CEO's performance. In most companies, it is possible to distinguish between three main levels of managers: top managers, middle managers, and first-line managers (as shown in Figure 3.4).

top managers
Employees who are responsible for developing a company's business model and who, along with the CEO, are ultimately responsible for its success or failure.

TOP MANAGERS   Top managers report to the CEO. Or sometimes they report to the *president* of the organization—the firm's second-in-command. The CEO and president are responsible for developing good working relationships among the top managers, who usually head up the firm's various major functions, manufacturing and marketing, for example. (These managers are often given the title of *vice president*.) Top managers establish the company's major goals, such as its revenue and profit targets, and they decide how the company's different functions should work together to achieve those goals. In particular, they are responsible for monitoring and controlling the actions of middle managers (discussed next).

One example of a CEO who has had great success is Ann Mulcahy, who became the CEO of struggling Xerox Corp in 2001. At the time, Xerox was in terrible shape. Its revenues were falling because its sales managers were fighting with its product development and manufacturing managers. The company was also involved in a scandal over illegal accounting practices. Mulcahy proved relentless in finding solutions to Xerox's problems. She terminated a large number of top and middle managers in business lines she felt were the source of Xerox's problems, and she demanded strict financial accountability. She also focused on finding a range of new products that would "re-attract" Xerox's customers. By 2005, Mulcahy had returned the company to profitability. (Mulcahy is the subject of the "Exploring the Web" exercise at the end of the chapter.)

middle managers
Employees in charge of a company's various functions and who are responsible for using the company's functional resources productively to increase its profitability.

MIDDLE MANAGERS   Middle managers are in charge of the nuts and bolts of running the company's various functions. These people make the thousands of daily decisions that go into the production of goods and services: Which first-line supervisors should be chosen to control a particular project? Where can the most highly skilled scientists and the highest-quality inputs or parts be found? How should employees be organized? Should they work as individuals or in teams? Very often, the suggestions that middle managers make to top managers help promote the level of entrepreneurship inside a company and spur it toward greater success.

A major part of the middle manager's job is to develop a function's occupational skills and know-how, such as manufacturing, human resource, or marketing expertise. Within the sales force, middle managers are responsible for training, motivating,

**Figure 3.4
Levels of
Management**

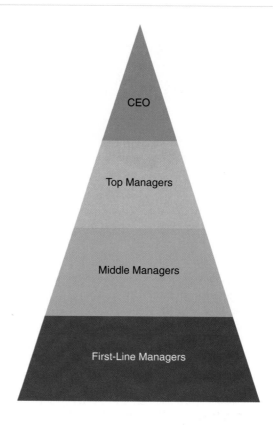

and rewarding individual salespeople. Behind a team that develops a new life-saving drug, for example, look for the team leader—the middle manager responsible for steering the project past the many obstacles it will face.

Middle managers also monitor the performance of the managers lower in the company's hierarchy. Business in Action explains the way in which Deborah Kent, the most senior African-American middle manager in charge of an important Ford production plant, performs her job of managing the production of Ford's minivans.

Business in Action

How to Be an Effective Plant Manager

When Deborah Kent took control of Ford Motor Company's manufacturing plant in Avon Lake, Ohio, the first thing she did was walk the production line. Kent believed that the only way to know how goods are produced is to watch it happen and learn from the employees who actually perform the tasks necessary to get the job done. Kent's hands-on approach is the result of a 17-year career in the automobile industry, first with General Motors and then with Ford. The experience she gained in manufacturing, quality control, and customer relations has given her the know-how she needs to manage these crucial areas of the manufacturing process and rise up through the ranks.

An industrial psychologist with a degree from Washington University in St. Louis, Kent is known for her open, accessible management style and for her insistence that both managers and employees below her feel free to approach her with their opinions and suggestions about how to alter work procedures to improve quality in the car plant. She continually looks for feedback from her subordinates and nurtures, develops, and motivates them to find new ways to be more efficient.

Kent's hardworking, no-nonsense style also sits well with officials from the United Auto Workers (UAW) union. The UAW is cooperating with Ford's managers to increase quality in order to protect their members' jobs at a time of intense competition from other makers of minivans, especially Chrysler, the minivan industry leader. Kent knows that the quality and reliability of the minivans are the result of her managerial abilities and her plant's performance. She often asks owners what they think of their vehicles, and on the rare occasions when she sees one broken down, she stops to find out the cause and to offer assistance. Kent believes that this type of involvement is part of her responsibility.

To perform her job effectively, Kent begins each workday with a walk through the plant to get a feel for the problems and issues at hand. Responsible for managing two shifts–including 3,746 employees and 420 robots–and for the quality and performance of the over 400,000 vehicles that her plant produces every year, she finds it hard to leave her responsibilities behind. Deborah Kent works long hours to make her plant one of Ford's highest-performing operations; she is a good example of a committed middle manager.[5]

first-line managers Employees at the base of the managerial hierarchy. They are often called *supervisors.*

FIRST-LINE MANAGERS   At the base of the managerial hierarchy, first-line managers (often called *supervisors*) are found in all functions and departments of an organization. They are responsible for the daily supervision of nonmanagerial employees–the people whose job it is to perform the different work activities necessary to get the product to the customer. Examples of first-line managers include the supervisor of a work team in the manufacturing department of a food product plant, the head nurse in the emergency room of a hospital, and the chief mechanic overseeing a crew of mechanics in the service department of a car dealership.

Types of Managers

Because so much of managers' responsibility is to acquire and develop productive resources, they are typically a member of one of a company's functions. Managers inside a function possess a certain type of occupational or job-specific skill and are known as, for example, marketing managers or manufacturing managers. As Figure 3.5 indicates, first-line, middle, and top managers, who differ from one another by virtue of their job-specific knowledge and responsibilities, are found in each of a company's major functions. Inside each function, the three main levels of management emerge.

One of the major reasons managers are divided into functions is to obtain the advantages of specialization and the division of labor discussed in the last chapter. These advantages arise for several reasons. First, inside each function, people further up the managerial hierarchy can mentor those below and help them improve their ability to create better products. Second, when people are grouped together because they share similar knowledge or use the same skills, it is easier for managers to scrutinize their performance. Third, the highest performing employees in every function can expect to be promoted to a higher level of management and receive a higher salary and bonuses. This also encourages individual employees to behave entrepreneurially.

Profitability: Efficiency and Effectiveness

As we discussed earlier, a company's owners expect its managers to behave entrepreneurially, that is, to search for opportunities to develop better, more profitable goods and services. At a managerial level profitability is often viewed from two related perspectives–in terms of efficiency and effectiveness.

efficiency A cost-focused measure of how productively a company's resources are being used to produce goods and services.

Efficiency is a measure of how well or how *productively* a company's resources are being used to produce goods and services. Companies are efficient when managers minimize the *amount* of resources (such as labor, raw materials, and component parts) or the amount of *time* needed to produce a given output of goods or services. For example, McDonald's recently developed a more efficient fat fryer that not only reduces (by 30%) the amount of oil used in cooking, but also speeds up the cooking of French fries.

**Figure 3.5
Levels and Types
of Managers**

Efficiency is directed at the *cost side* of the profit equation. By becoming more efficient and increasing productivity, a company can become more profitable over time.

By contrast, **effectiveness** is attention directed at the *revenue side* of the profit equation. Effectiveness is a measure of the competitiveness of the firm's business model and its ability to meet its sales goals. By becoming more effective, a company can also increase its profitability.

Some years ago managers at McDonald's changed the restaurant's business model to include selling breakfast food. The goal of this change was to increase McDonald's revenues by 15%. The new model proved successful. Breakfast food now accounts for not just 15% of McDonald's revenues but a full 30% of its revenues.

One simple way to differentiate between these two concepts is to view effectiveness as "doing the right things," and efficiency as "doing things right." Profitable organizations like Campbell Soup, McDonald's, Wal-Mart, Intel, and Home Depot, are simultaneously efficient and effective, as shown in Figure 3.6.

Thus, a company's owners want managers and employees to be enterprising in two ways: to "do the right things" (be effective) and to "do things right" (be efficient). One of the most important determinants of managers' ability to do this is the way they perform the four main functions of a manager, discussed next.

effectiveness

A revenue-focused measure of how competitive the firm's business model is.

Managerial Functions

Managers perform four essential functions: *planning, organizing, leading,* and *controlling.* (See Figure 3.7.) French manager Henri Fayol first outlined the nature of these managerial activities around the turn of the century. Managers at all levels and in all functions—whether they work in small or large companies, for-profit or not-for-profit companies, or domestic or international companies—are responsible for performing these four functions, and we will look at each in turn. How well managers perform them determines how efficient and effective their companies are.

Figure 3.6
The Relationship Between Efficiency, Effectiveness, and Profitability

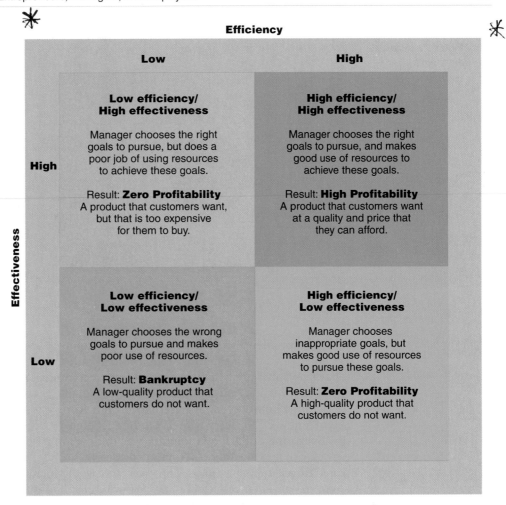

PLANNING Planning is a process that managers use to identify and select the appropriate business model and goals for their company. Recall from Chapter 1 that a business model is a plan of action that describes which goods and services a company intends to develop and how a company intends to use its productive resources to make a profit. There are three stages in the planning process; managers must:

1.   Choose which business model to pursue.
2.   Decide how to allocate the organization's resources to pursue the business model.
3.   Select the goals or targets that will be used to measure how efficiently and effectively the business model is working.

planning A process that managers use to select the best business model and goals for their company.

How well managers plan often determines how profitable their companies are. Planning is a difficult activity because the future success of a particular business model is not known. Committing an organization's resources to pursue a particular business model is risky. Managers have to make these decisions based on their knowledge and hunches. Both success and failure are possible outcomes of the planning process.

Consider Yahoo!'s planning mistakes discussed in the opening case to this chapter. Under CEO Tim Koogle, Yahoo!'s business model was to develop more Web content, become the number one portal on the Web, and buy other dot.com companies to expand its range of services. This, in turn, would attract more people to Yahoo!, generate even greater advertising revenues, and the process would begin all over again. Yahoo! would continue to grow as a result. The problem with the model was that it made Yahoo!'s profitability (and therefore its stock price) totally dependent on the size of its advertising revenues. And, after the dot.com bust of the early 2000s, Yahoo!'s advertising revenues (and stock price) plummeted. Critics said that when Yahoo!'s stock price was high, it should have purchased a company that was generating revenue by some other

Figure 3.7
The Four Functions of Managers

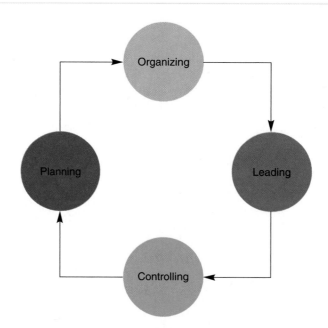

means than advertising. That way, if ad revenues tanked (which they did), Yahoo! wouldn't have been so vulnerable. In fact, Yahoo! had considered purchasing eBay. (eBay's revenues are largely generated from a commission on the sale of products on its site.) However, infighting among Yahoo!'s top managers prevented that from occurring.

Yahoo!'s board eventually replaced both Koogle and Mallett with new top managers. A new CEO, Terry Semel, was hired. Semel decided Yahoo! could not rely solely on advertising dollars. His solution was to develop a new business model based on a new goal of making Yahoo's content and services so useful and attractive that customers would be willing to pay for it. These services would include things like personal ads and ads to sell or rent merchandise like cars or homes. This new business model has worked much better for Yahoo! Over 40% of its revenues now come from this source.

organizing A process managers use to create a company's organizational structure.

ORGANIZING   Organizing is the process managers follow to create a company's organizational structure. Recall, that the organizational structure is the formal system of task and reporting relationships that coordinates and motivates members so that they work together to achieve the organization's goals. Organizing involves grouping people into functions according to the kinds of job-specific tasks they perform. Managers also lay out the lines of authority and responsibility between different individuals and groups, and they decide how best to coordinate across functions.

organizational culture The set of values, norms, and beliefs shared by members of an organization that determine how well they work together to further the company's goals.

A second outcome of organizing is a business's **organizational culture,** the shared set of values, norms, beliefs, and feelings that determine how people in the organization behave and work together—for example whether or not they feel loyal to their company and are willing to work hard to further its interests—or, whether they resent their co-workers and bosses and put their own interests above those of the company. To a large degree, a company's efficiency and effectiveness is a result of the choices managers make about the design of its organizational structure and culture. These issues are discussed in greater depth in Chapter 8, but consider how CEO Paul Pressler (profiled in Business in Action) has performed the organizing and planning functions at Gap Inc.

A Turnaround at The Gap

Business in Action

During the 1990s, Mickey Drexler, then the CEO of Gap Inc., revolutionized the U.S. apparel retailing industry by adding two chains—Banana Republic and Old Navy—to the company's lineup. By 2002 Gap had opened over 3,000 new stores, and its profits and revenues had increased through much of that time period. But in 2001, although its revenues totaled nearly $14 billion, The Gap failed to make a profit. In 2002, its sales actually dropped by more than 10%, and its losses widened.

Paul Pressler brought a little of Disney magic with him when he became the CEO of Gap Inc. Pressler managed to increase sales by reorganizing the company's retail chains and putting the needs of customers first.

Analysts wondered what had happened at The Gap. It seemed that Mickey Drexler had lost his magic touch.

The Gap's board decided that it was time to bring in a new CEO with a fresh perspective to fashion a new strategy and structure for the ailing company. But what kind of background should the new CEO have and what kinds of changes were necessary? All of The Gap's top managers were highly experienced in the apparel industry, but they had been unable to figure out a way to turn around the company's performance. Gap's board decided on a radical move. It chose to hire Paul Pressler, then the head of Walt Disney's global theme parks and resorts, as The Gap's new CEO.

Pressler had no experience in the apparel industry and no background in clothing fashion or design. Some analysts were wondering how he could help The Gap. What did he bring to the table that retail insiders couldn't? But the fact is that Pressler had been in charge of Disney's retail stores for three years. Moreover, from a management perspective, each of Disney's theme parks could be viewed as a giant retail location: Once visitors entered the park, the goal was to get them to spend as much as possible on food, souvenirs, rides, and so forth. What The Gap's board wanted from Pressler were his retail planning and marketing skills —skills he could use to develop a new marketing approach the company could take.

Before Pressler became CEO, The Gap, Banana Republic, and Old Navy were led by different management teams, and each team made decisions based on its own brand. Pressler saw that there were many opportunities for managers in one chain to learn from managers in the other chains how to better position each brand. He subsequently hired a top advertising agency, Leo Burnett USA, to research each of the chain's consumers, brand positioning, and business models. Based on Leo Burnett's advice Pressler decided to reorganize the marketing and operations of the three chains to better position the brands and reduce the operating costs of each.

Pressler also decided that The Gap had lost contact with its customers. Its clothing and accessories were being designed without an understanding of their needs. He then conducted extensive market research to better position Gap's three brands to fit these needs. He decided clothing would be selected and designed knowing what customers wanted–not what The Gap's designers *thought* they wanted. This was a radically different approach to planning, one that caused quite a stir.

Nonetheless, by 2003 sales at Gap Inc.'s stores were up by 5%, compared to the drop of 11% in the previous year. In 2004–2005 the company's performance continued to improve, and the value of its stock increased by 50%. Pressler credited this to a change in the product mix each store offered it customers as a result of Gap's better understanding of their needs. Analysts who had questioned his appointment were now "on board" and acknowledged that, so far, Pressler has reenergized The Gap and led it back to profitability.[6]

leading The ability to develop a plan and motivate others to pursue it.

LEADING   Leading involves being able to articulate a clear vision for a company's members and motivate them to pursue it. This requires power, influence, vision, persuasion, and communication skills. Although The Gap felt it had to bring in new leadership to reenergize the company, J. Crew, another major clothing store chain, decided that Mickey Drexler, with his vast retailing expertise was just the right person for them. In 2003, J. Crew named Drexler chairman and CEO, hoping he could turn the company around. He succeeded. By 2005 J. Crew was once again highly profitable, and Drexler, who owns 22% of its stock was proud of the way he had handled his new challenge.

cross-functional team A group of people from the different functions who work together on a particular project.

controlling The process of evaluating whether or not a company is achieving its goals and taking action if it is not.

Leadership is not just a trait exhibited by individual managers, however. It also occurs when groups of managers pool their talents to achieve cooperation via cross-functional teams. Cross-functional teams consist of groups of people from a firm's different functions working together on a particular project. These teams are often vital when it comes to developing new and improved products that can be launched quickly. Whether it occurs at the individual or the group level, the outcome of effective leadership is a high level of motivation and commitment among an organization's members. These issue of motivation, leadership, and teams are discussed in detail in Chapter 6.

After winning their fourth consecutive World Series in 2000, the New York Yankees served as a benchmark for all other baseball organizations. (Could it be because the Yankees' owner, George Steinbrenner, is controlling?)

CONTROLLING   Controlling is the process of evaluating whether or not a company is achieving its goals and taking action if it is not. As noted earlier in the chapter, to evaluate the success of its business model, managers monitor and measure how efficiently and effectively employees, individual functions, and the company as a whole are operating. These measures are frequently reflected on the organization's balance sheet in terms of its revenues, costs, and profitability. If the measures indicate efficiency or effectiveness is dropping, or if there is evidence that the company's competitors are operating more efficiently and effectively, managers need to take action.

The practice of comparing a business's strengths and weaknesses to those of its competitors is called benchmarking. Benchmarking is a technique widely used to increase profitability. Managers first choose a company that they believe is operating more efficiently than a functional area in their own company. The functional area might be related to customer service or new product development, for example. Second, they study it to try to determine the sources of their competitor's superior performance. Third, they change the way their company operates to match, or benchmark, the way the other company operates.

The relative importance of planning, organizing, leading, and controlling—the four managerial functions—and how much time a particular manager spends on any one of them—depends on the manager's position in the hierarchy. Top managers devote most of their time to planning and organizing as it relates to the firm's business model, long-term goals, and profitability. Lower-level managers spend more time leading and controlling first-line managers or nonmanagerial employees to meet those goals.

The Role of the Employee

benchmarking The practice of comparing a business's strengths and weaknesses to those of its competitors.

Although managers are employees—they work for a company's owners—we typically think of them as being different from "ordinary" employees because they have decision-making authority over the organization's resources. What is the role of nonmanagerial employees—the people who actually perform the many jobs and tasks necessary to make and sell a product? What kind of expectations does a company have of its employees—and what can employees reasonably expect from a company in return for their labor? Moreover, how does a person get a job and become an employee, keep that job over time, and get promoted?

What Is Appropriate Employee Behavior?

When people accept jobs in organizations they typically sign some kind of written agreement, a legal contract, that specifies the nature of their job responsibilities and employment conditions concerning pay, benefits, and so on. Managers now have the

Being a proactive employee often results in career progress in a company and generates greater rewards. In what ways can an employee be proactive?

role The set of tasks a person is expected to perform because of the position he or she holds in an organization.

legal right to direct and supervise these new employees. Employees have also accepted the legal obligation to follow orders and to perform the work they were hired to do. Contracts can never be written to specify everything an employee should or should not do, however. Indeed, a company would not want such contracts because factors such as changing technology might require employees to perform new or different job-related activities at any time. Employees might then argue, "But that's not in our contract." Also, writing such contracts would be very time consuming and result in high and unnecessary transaction costs.

Because of the many "gray" or unspecified areas in a job contract, employees have some freedom to decide how to perform their company roles. A role is the set of tasks a person is expected to perform because of his or her job or position in an organization. On the one hand, an employee could decide to perform at some "minimum" level and just do what is required and no more. At the other extreme, an employee could choose to perform at a high level and work efficiently throughout the day. They might even decide to come into work early and leave late if an unusually large amount of work needs to be completed. An employee could also pull apart the various tasks involved in a job to figure out how it could be done more efficiently. Companies also differ with regard to what they expect from their employees. Some companies simply expect employees to follow their job descriptions and perform a "fair day's work for a fair day's pay." Other companies demand people who will work long hours and strive to find better ways to do their jobs.

In general, however, employees will increase their chances of being promoted within their companies if they are *proactive*–if they take an enterprising approach to their jobs and are on the lookout for ways to improve their work performance. The problem is that managers usually do not "spell this out" for employees. Astute employees, however, understand this and behave proactively rather than simply doing what they are told. These employees eventually are promoted because their supervisors see them as people who demonstrate initiative, commitment, and loyalty. The employees become more trusted and are given more interesting tasks to perform and more responsibility over company resources.

At the same time, continually trying to discover better ways to work helps an employee build his or her own personal or human capital. Recall from Chapter 1 that *human capital* is the set of skills, knowledge, and expertise that a person develops from pursuing a specialized job over time. People who develop human capital are investing in themselves. Moreover, this capital is their own: It goes with them when they take a job in a new company or start their own business. For most people, human capital is what gives them their best opportunity to accumulate wealth. If employees take a short-term view and believe the extra effort necessary to be proactive "isn't worth it," their careers are likely to be hampered. The fact is the extra effort simply is *not* rewarded with more money *now*.

Did You Know?

Companies and the capital that launched them:

$1,300–Apple Computer
$1,000–Dell
$175–Raging Bull (financial information company)
$50–Water Wonders (decorative water fountain manufacturer)
$15–DataMark (college and university marketing)
Paper, envelopes, and stamps–Jasc Software (originator of PaintShop Pro)[7]

Successful people take a long-term time perspective. They know that the extra work they do now will pay off in the future in the form of the building of a reputation for being competent and trustworthy, acquiring the respect of one's superiors and co-workers, and receiving excellent letters of recommendation if they choose to change jobs and companies. It is also important to recognize that companies spend enormous amounts of money training and educating their employees.

High performance ratings and the recommendations of the boss are the selection criteria used to determine which employees receive this training–advanced skills-based training and even financial support to obtain a bachelor's or master's degree. Because this training builds human capital, it is an important source of future career success and the rewards that go with it.

Career Management

After you graduate your goal will likely be to land a satisfying, well-paying job in a business organization. Or perhaps you plan to start your own business. If either is the case, it will be worth your while to examine the path of your career development in some depth. A model that illustrates the different stages in a person's career, and the work issues related to them, is presented in Figure 3.8.

Stage 1: Preparing for Work

The single most important thing you can to do to prepare for work is to obtain some kind of advanced certification or degree because it *unlocks* the door into better-paying jobs in companies known to be good employers. Some people find it hard to get that degree and put it off. This is a serious mistake.

Studying is a state of mind. It is never easy, but it gets much more difficult if a person takes a break. The focus and concentration needed to study efficiently is lost–and it takes much more time and effort to get back into it later. Then, when people do start school again, they sometimes find getting back up to speed is too much to bear. This is why people end up dropping out during the semester or getting poorer grades than if they had stayed the course all along. Starting afresh several times over, especially when this involves changing subject areas mid-course and additional course work can significantly stretch out the time it takes to complete a degree–and time is money. In the long run, every "unnecessary" year spent on education reduces a person's future income stream by a substantial amount.

Once again, if people do not think carefully about career issues they may benefit in the short run but this may cost them dearly in the long-run. Research shows that the size of a person's lifetime income stream is closely related to the number of years he or she spends in school and the highest degree he or she obtains. The difference in the lifetime income of a high school graduate versus someone with a bachelor's degree, master's degree, or PhD can run into hundreds of thousands and even millions of dollars.

But what degree should you get? In the preparing-for-work stage of their lives, people are considering the kinds of jobs and occupations they seem most suited for and would enjoy doing the most. They must also find out what abilities and qualifications are needed to pursue these jobs and occupations. In this way they can assess whether there is a "fit" between their personal talents and desires and the kinds of careers they are considering. Utilizing resources such as career centers, the Internet and company Web sites can help people find out about different careers and companies.

Although searching for career information is an important first step, in practice most people do not end up pursuing exactly the kind of occupation or job that they originally anticipated they would. Someone once said, "Life is what happens to us while we are making other plans." The fact is that unexpected events occur during one's career. If you're not absolutely certain about what you want to do, and you become too specialized in your career, too early, it's possible you could end up locked into a career path that might prove to be a dead end or a poor match for your talents. This is why people pursue general degrees in, for example, liberal arts and business. It gives them

Did You Know?

Over 1,000 franchises are available in the United States–everything from A to Z including asphalt sealing, home storage, fitness centers, alloy wheel repair, pet boarding, and ice cream shops. Interested? Check out the International Franchise Association (www.franchise.org).[8]

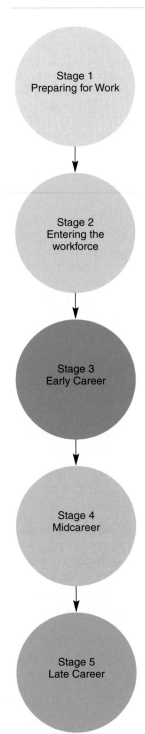

Stage 1
Preparing for Work

Stage 2
Entering the
workforce

Stage 3
Early Career

Stage 4
Midcareer

Stage 5
Late Career

Figure 3.8
Stages and Career
Management

time to assess their skills and future opportunities. Working part-time in several different jobs, or as an intern, also helps expose people to different occupations. Sometimes they find that the occupation is not what they expected or that they are not suited to it.

Stage 2: Entering the Workforce

Choosing the right kind of company to join is, in many cases, as important as choosing the right occupation. For example, does the company offer good on-the-job experience, skills training, or educational opportunities? Or does it simply require employees to perform routine tasks? This will necessitate collecting information from job advertisements, job fairs, and of course, the Internet. Don't, however, discount "word of mouth" information about jobs. The fact is that most jobs are filled via the "grapevine"—when someone who knows about a job opening tells someone else who is looking for a job. It is also common to receive many letters of rejection after submitting an application or no letter at all from companies. For every one hundred resumes sent out, a person might get 10 responses, five interviews, and one job offer if lucky. Once again it takes enormous time and effort to find the right job, but the fact is that almost all people do find jobs. The crucial thing is to get one's foot in the door. Then as you gain experience, establish a track record, and get to know other people in your industry, you will find it easier to move into other positions and companies.

However, before a company makes a job offer in the first place, it will consider the following: First, does the candidate possess the level of functional and job-specific knowledge needed to do the job? Or can he or she be trained to do it? Second, will the candidate "fit into" their organization? Does he or she have the right attitude for the job? Does the candidate seem enthusiastic, agreeable, and able to work well with the other people in the company?

One model of how the recruitment process works is as follows: Over time, employees in a particular company develop a set of characteristic work styles and company-specific values, norms, and work attitudes. Very often these work styles and values and norms are those of the company's founder, who tends to recruit people who have similar values and norms. In turn, these employees hire people who are similar to them, and so on. Over time a definite kind of work culture, or "climate," develops in the company. Prospective employees may be attracted to a particular company because of its particular work styles, values, and norms. But if they are to be "selected" by this company they must possess the kinds of values and attitudes it desires, or be able to quickly develop them.

There are some important steps you can take to make yourself more attractive to a company you are interested in working for. Even getting an interview is not easy. Most people are eliminated during the resume screening process. Thus, it pays to do a good job designing and writing your resume. Think about what kind of skills, attitudes, abilities, a company is likely to want from a prospective employee. Then, tailor your resume to match those strengths whenever possible.

Prior to the interview (assuming you are granted one) think about what you think the company expects from its employees. Those attributes are likely to be loyalty, commitment, enthusiasm, respectfulness, open-mindedness, and the willingness to work with others. Bear in mind that everything you say during your interview, how you talk about your family, hobbies, likes and dislikes, or personal strengths and weaknesses are being thought of from this perspective. Suppose you are interviewing for a job with a major bank or hotel chain for a position as a bank teller, desk clerk, or managerial trainee. What kinds of personal characteristics, skills, and attitudes are these companies likely to be looking for? How do they expect their employees to dress and act? Imagine you went to the bank job interview wearing a brightly patterned shirt or blouse, or if you had forgotten to shave or make sure your nails were clean. Would you make a good impression? Suppose you were then asked about your hobbies and you said you liked mainly to read books, collect stamps, and play Yahoo!'s online games and didn't like to go out much. What impression have you made on the interviewer?

Video Small Business in Action

Switching Careers

Summary: The federal government's data indicate that the average adult will change careers three times during their work life as shown in this *BusinessWeek* TV segment on your Student DVD. People in their 30's and 40's are most likely to switch careers. These people most often have advanced degrees and therefore, more opportunity. There are several reasons for switching from successful careers. These include seeking higher levels of job satisfaction and job status.

Often times, switching careers involves significant reductions in pay. Two examples are featured in the segment. The first, Nicole, is a mother who returned to College to work on a degree in environmental science. She was formerly a dental hygienist. After the birth of her child, it appears that her "career" was no longer fulfilling. The second example focuses on Jimmy who left the successful law practice. He moved into a substantially different career working in the marketing and sale of real estate projects. While he experienced a 50% reduction in pay, the level of responsibility, interest and challenge are all significantly more rewarding. He couldn't see himself practicing law and litigating for the rest of his adult life. His career change was a "leap of faith." However, he is far more satisfied in his new career. In order to make the transition successful and rewarding, Jimmy tells us that "you have to have confidence in yourself that it will work out."

Discussion Questions

1. What is organizational culture and how might it have had an impact on Jimmy's decision to leave the successful law practice?
2. Why did Nicole leave the career that she had gone to school for and return to college to study environmental science?
3. For both Nicole and Jimmy, what stage of their career would you place them in?

Bank tellers and hotel clerks are constantly meeting different kinds of people during the workday. They are expected to be polite, helpful, tactful, and professional and do their best to satisfy customers. A recruiter from these companies would be looking for someone who likes to meet people and interact with them. An interviewee who smiles often, asks intelligent questions, is courteous, agreeable, clean, neat, and dresses smartly is likely to be well received. It is unlikely that the company would hire an interviewee who is rude or arrogant, talks too much and doesn't seem to listen, who never laughs except at his or her own jokes, and who dresses garishly or is unkempt. All too often people go into an job interview not understanding the importance of just being clean and neat and wearing well-pressed clothes.

Also, given the fact that companies usually want to hire people who are enthusiastic, enterprising, and work well with others, it is important that people develop these

An interviewee needs to keep in mind that throughout the interview, the employer is looking for people with qualities such as loyalty, commitment, and agreeableness.

social skills. Although much of this development occurs naturally as a person progresses through school, joins clubs, and makes friends in life, good social skills can also be deliberately learned and practiced. People join toastmasters to hone their public speaking skills, for example. Likewise, volunteering in one's community or serving on a committee can help a person become a better negotiator and team player.

Prospective employees need to act like detectives. First, they need to think about what kinds of work values and attitudes companies, in general, expect. Second, to get an impression of what is unique or different about a company they should also visit a company's Web site, or visit its stores or offices, or talk to people who work for it to find out. Then, in the job interview, it is always important that the interviewee demonstrates that they understand that company's business model.

At the same time, however, it is important to ask the company's recruiters questions abut the firm, for example, how it operates and even how the interviewers came to be hired. After all, the recruitment process is a *two-way street*. You are gathering information about the company and gauging whether it seems like a good match for you, just as the company is gathering information about you. Recruiters therefore *expect* you to ask questions. In fact, asking the recruiters no questions about what they do is often taken as a sign that interviewees are not really interested in the job or that you are unlikely to be good future colleague. Think about the kinds of people you would like to work with on a day-to-day basis and be around 40 hours or more a week. This is more time than most people spend with their partners or children in today's world!

Stage 3: Early Career

Once a person has found a job, he or she enters the early career stage. At this stage, it is vital for people to quickly learn the task specific skills necessary to do their jobs. Frequently, the early career stage also involves a change of jobs Proactive employees are often offered new, more challenging job assignments after a few months or years. Sometimes they are transferred to new locations. Other people change companies entirely to find better-paying or more challenging jobs. Still other people realize they have made the wrong career choice. They then begin to search for different kinds of jobs or companies, or they go back to school to learn a new occupation.

It is important to be open to the idea of changing jobs early in one's career. Most experts recommend that a person should change companies in the early career stage to learn a variety of skills and to learn how different companies operate. This will make you more marketable, and you are less likely to get "pigeon-holed" in a position. Pigeonholing occurs when people have been in their jobs for so long that their managers can't envision them doing anything else.

Although many companies offer a variety of jobs and career opportunities worth pursuing, others do not. What you want to avoid is ending up in the proverbial "dead end" job. Remember, you are not working for a firm to be just a good employee. You are in business for yourself—to build your own human capital and personal wealth. Therefore, it is important to have an entrepreneurial outlook and remain alert for better opportunities.

Indeed, building one's human capital isn't just a good idea these days. It's becoming a matter of financial survival. Layoffs and the offshoring and outsourcing of jobs are now widespread. What this means is that the relationship between companies and their employees is changing. In the past, employees believed that if they worked hard for a particular company, they could expect to receive a long-term career and benefits from it. As they watch their companies routinely lay off employees and employ temporary or contract workers, many employees now view their jobs as short term rather than long term.

As result, it is especially important that employees in the early career stage evaluate their companies in terms of what they have to offer now and in the future. It is a sad fact of life that many jobs do not stretch employees skill-wise: Employees learn what they

Did You Know?

Small businesses in the United States[9]:

- Represent 99.7% of all employer firms
- Generated 60 to 80% of net new jobs annually over the past decade
- Produce 13 to 14 times more patents per employee than large patenting firms
- Make up 97% of all identified exporters

In efforts to remain afloat, many companies are laying off employees. As a result, employees increasingly view their jobs as short term rather than as long term.

need to do and then just repeat daily the same activities over and over again. This is why it is important for employees to be alert to opportunities, be enthusiastic, and develop the human capital that will help them get more interesting, better-paying jobs.

Stage 4: Midcareer

By the midcareer stage employees have often settled into a particular company. It might be the fourth or fifth company they have worked for. At this stage, they are focused on achieving success in that company and are working hard to be promoted. Keep in mind, however, that the higher a person rises in a company's hierarchy, the fewer and fewer opportunities there are to rise further. An organization is shaped like a pyramid, top jobs are few, and competition to get them is fierce. In this competitive job market, employees must continually work at developing new company-specific skills that will allow them to perform at a higher level. The people who rise to the top are those who have work achievements that are directly attributable to their personal actions and qualities.

Of course, many people are perfectly happy with the position in the hierarchy they occupy and feel no desire to compete for these top jobs. However, this can be a mistake. At *any* level in the hierarchy, people who are content to stay in one position can lose their edge when their familiarity with a job blinds them to new opportunities arising around them. For example, a person who has headed a marketing department for 20 years might not recognize the growing importance of the Internet and new customer relationship management (CRM) software for reaching consumers. If a person stays in the same job and company, he or she must do all they can to keep informed about changes affecting their department, the company as a whole, and their industry in general. They can do this by attending job-related seminars and learning programs, for example.

Stage 5: Late Career

Finally, in the late career stage employees, no matter what their position or level in a company, are anticipating their retirement. Given all the years of experience these people possess, companies need to ensure what they know is passed on to other employees in their early and midcareer stages. For example, an experienced marketing manager might be encouraged to conduct training classes for new and established employees. Often, managers can help their companies and younger employees by acting as **mentors**, people who provide advice, guidance, and technical expertise to help others advance in their careers. Sometimes this is a formal relationship established between employees by the company. Other times mentors and mentees develop a relationship informally just by working together. Mentors and mentees also change as people switch jobs and move around in their careers.

Mentorship is important because so much of a company's knowledge is not written down. It is held in the heads of experienced employees. A close personal relationship between mentors and their mentees is an excellent vehicle for transferring this knowledge. Note that mentorship takes place at every level in a company. Even a company's CEO is responsible for mentoring the managers who are next in line for the top job and for deciding which subordinate seems to have the skills that make them best suited to become the next CEO.

mentor A person who provides advice, guidance, and technical knowledge to other people *(mentees)* in order to help them advance their careers.

Summary of the Chapter

Companies operate in a competitive environment where the search for ways to increase efficiency and effectiveness often determines their very survival. This chapter discussed how entrepreneurs, managers, and employees, using their ingenuity and enterprise, each contribute to this effort. Harmonizing the interests of these groups so they work together toward that goal is crucial to a business's success. This chapter made the following major points:

1. An entrepreneur is the person who supplies the mixture of energy, boldness, courage, spirit, expertise, insight, and often ruthlessness necessary to create or develop new or improved products.

2. Entrepreneurship is the process of acquiring and combining productive resources to create goods and services customers want to buy and that create profit.

3. Opportunities for entrepreneurs arise as business commerce, occupations, and organizations change.

4. The reason entrepreneurs are willing to risk their capital to pursue new ventures is that the potential profits are enormous. Many entrepreneurs do make mistakes, however. Three common ones are overestimating the value of a new product to potential customers, failing to realize the difficulty of reaching these customers, and underestimating the amount of cash needed to sustain a business until it is profitable.

5. The widespread changes brought about by increasing global competition and advancing technology is known as the process of "creative destruction." This process leads old, inefficient companies, and even entire industries, to be driven out of business by new, more efficient ones.

6. It is one thing to have a good business idea; it is quite another to get a business off the ground. For a business to prosper and grow, its founder needs to recruit managers to oversee the functions needed to get the product to the customer.

7. The agency problem—the misalignment of the interests of managers and owners—occurs whenever there is a separation of a business's control and ownership. The agency problem can be solved by creating a motivating reward structure for managers and developing a hierarchy of authority that allows stockholders to scrutinize managers' business decisions.

8. Managers are the employees to whom a company's owners delegate the responsibility of using its resources to create profitable goods and services. Managers are responsible for developing the company's business model and controlling its operations and functions (manufacturing, marketing, accounting, and so on).

9. There are three main levels of managers: top managers, middle managers, and first-line managers. Managers typically are also members of a business function who possess a certain type of occupational or job-specific skill.

10. Managers measure companies in terms of their efficiency and effectiveness. Efficiency is a measure of how well or how *productively* a company's resources are used to produce goods and services. Effectiveness is a measure of the competitiveness of the business model that managers have selected for the organization to pursue. Profitable organizations are simultaneously efficient and effective.

11. Four essential managerial functions are planning, organizing, leading, and controlling a company's productive resources. How well managers perform these functions determines the profitability of a company's business model.

12. Employees have some freedom to decide how to perform their company roles. They can perform at some "minimum" level—do just what is required of them and no more—or they can perform in an enterprising way that improves the company's efficiency and effectiveness as well as their own success.

13. People experience several different stages in their careers. The stages are as follows: the preparing-for-work and entering-the-workforce stages, and the early-career, midcareer, and late-career stages. How well people manage the challenges involved at each stage determines their long-term prosperity and well-being.

Developing Business Skills

QUESTIONS FOR DISCUSSION AND ACTION

1. What are the main differences between the roles played by entrepreneurs and managers?

2. Give an example of an entrepreneurial opportunity that arises from changes in business (a) commerce, (b) occupations, and (c) organizations. Describe how these changes can lead to entrepreneurship and increased profitability.

3. *Action.* Find someone in your city who has recently opened a new business. Try to discern what opportunity he or she noticed and what business model he or she used to take advantage of the opportunity.

4. What is the agency problem that arises between owners and managers? How can it be solved?

5. How can managers of (a) a large computer maker, (b) a department store, and (c) a hospital measure how efficiently and effectively they are operating?

6. Why is planning such a difficult function to perform? Find a manager responsible for some kind of planning activity and discuss the obstacles to creating an effective plan.

7. What opportunities and problems are likely to arise at each of the different stages of a person's career?

ETHICS IN ACTION

Why Do Businesses Experience Agency Problems?

Agency problems can sometimes lead to major ethical problems for firms. With this issue in mind think about the following issues:

- Why would there be a conflict of interest between managers and stockholders? Why is this an ethical issue?

- Give some examples of the ethical issues that can arise as managers perform their functions.

- What are some of the ethical issues involved when it comes to aligning the interests of managers and employees?

SMALL GROUP EXERCISE

We're in the Restaurant Business Now

Read the following then break up into groups of three or four people and answer the discussion questions. Be prepared to share your discussion with the class.

You are the founding partners of a new sandwich and snack restaurant opening in your city to take advantage of people's desire to eat healthier food. You know you will have to hire at least 50 waiters, 20 cooks, and 20 busboys to operate the restaurant. You have to decide how to design an organizational structure and create a set of task and authority relationships that will give your business the best chance in the competitive restaurant market. You know most new restaurants fail within three years of opening.

1. What kinds of managerial roles will each of you play and what functions will you perform once the restaurant is up and running? To increase the restaurant's efficiency and effectiveness, what authority will each of you have over the restaurant's operations?

2. What other kinds of managers will you need to employ? Draw a picture of the hierarchy of authority that will best suit your restaurant. For example, how many levels will the hierarchy have, and what kinds of functions will each of them perform?

3. How will you try to align the interests of your managers and employees with your own interests to increase efficiency, effectiveness, and profitability?

DEVELOPING GOOD BUSINESS SENSE

Managing Your Career

All too often people do not think carefully enough about what it takes to manage their own careers. Imagine you have been hired by a major electronics retailer in an entry-level sales position. You have been told that you are viewed as a likely candidate for assuming a supervisory, or management, position once you have hands-on experience.

1. What important things should you need to initially learn about your tasks, job responsibilities, and the company? What is the best way to gather this information?

2. What kinds of behaviors and attitudes should you try to cultivate to increase your chances of being selected for management training?

3. What kinds of new skills and human capital should you try to develop that you will be able to use in any job in sales and marketing?

EXPLORING THE WEB

Anne Mulcahy
Transforms Xerox

Go the Xerox's Web site, and click on the "About Xerox" tab. Then look through the information in Xerox's "Online Fact Book." Type Anne Mulcahy in the search box to bring up a list of articles about her. Then answer the following questions. **For more Web activities, log on to www.mhhe.com/jonesintro.**

1. What skills and qualities does Anne Mulcahy bring to her job as CEO of Xerox?

2. What kinds of managerial functions and roles did she adopt as the head of Xerox to turn around the company's performance?

3. What kind of attitudes and behaviors does Mulcahy expect from Xerox's managers and employees to help it succeed?

BusinessWeek CASE FOR DISCUSSION

Want to Be an Instant Enrepreneur?

You're a student on a college campus, and you have entrepreneurial dreams. Before you forge ahead, listen up: This is your professor speaking. As a chaired entrepreneurship professor at the Kellogg School of Management at Northwestern University, I teach students like you. And my message is that it's OK—in fact, it's probably preferable—to slow down and delay your entrepreneurial pursuits for a year or two after graduation.

I speak also from the perspective of having run my own company, Akar Corporation., a collection of two manufacturers and a retail concern in the lampshade industry, for seven years in the 1990s. In fact, as a student at the Harvard Business School in the 1980s, I had attended for one reason: to acquire the skills necessary to launch a company. A classmate and I were rather cocky about this objective, foolishly ridiculing classmates as "sellouts" for pursuing jobs.

Flash forward to today. Having learned from the toughest teacher of all, namely experience, that building a business is grueling work, I now advise students that it's perfectly acceptable to put on a suit and go to work for a company that isn't their own. I tell them that it's a good idea to learn the ropes on someone else's time and someone else's dime.

VOICE OF EXPERIENCE. Most students lack experience in one or more of the critical disciplines, such as management, sales, marketing, and finance, necessary to build companies. Moreover, they generally aren't adept at dealing with the continual vagaries of entrepreneurial life in the real world.

In my case, shortly after graduating from business school in 1985, I rejected an offer to buy a McDonald's franchise in Boston, because I felt the purchase price was too high. I had participated in the formal owner/operator training program for two years, learning everything about running a restaurant and franchising. Instead, I went to work for Bain & Company, the Boston-based consulting firm, to build a financial cushion and learn the applied science of problem-solving.

Then my wife and I moved to the Midwest, where we wanted to raise our family, and I launched my entrepreneurial dream by purchasing Fenchel Lampshade, a family-owned manufacturer. With two subsequent company purchases, I had formed Akar.

In my view, business is about being a generalist, with a wide range of experience, confidence, and competence, rather than pursuing a specific idea. I agree with most business specialists who argue that entrepreneurship is about being able to execute on a plan. My four years at Cummins Engine, supervising union employees and negotiating contracts for diesel-engine parts, along with the two years each at McDonald's and Bain, had given me the confidence that I could operate a company.

ON-THE-JOB TRAINING. At Akar, however, I soon learned that building a business was tougher than I had expected–so tough that the Akar story has become a Harvard Business School case study. In an industry that was no more than $100 million, I wasn't able, as I had planned, to increase revenue through organic growth. It was hard taking business from competitors, and the number of potential retailers was declining.

Managing cash flow proved to be a monthly crisis. Collecting from customers was tougher by a factor of 10 than the discussions we had had in finance classes. Instead, I learned that collecting was related to the vagaries of getting and keeping customers, and the entrepreneur's expectations for those accounts. You may think you are assured an account, for example, only to get a call saying the customer is dropping you.

Businesses, in short, rarely operate according to plan. They are living and breathing organisms that change frequently. After seven years in business, my sales had reached a little less than $5 million and profits were solid, but I concluded that I wouldn't be able to reach my goal of building a $50 million company in an industry that wasn't expanding. Those years, however, had allowed me to live and learn the countless realities of entrepreneurship.

LESSONS FROM THE TRENCHES. So, with the entrepreneurial experience under my belt and a Kellogg offer in hand, I sold my company and turned to full-time teaching, which I expected to do for a couple of years while I looked for another, larger business to purchase. This enabled me to find my true passion in life–teaching entrepreneurship!

Therefore, as a professor and former experienced entrepreneur, I am not a sideline cheerleader for entrepreneurship. Please don't get me wrong. I absolutely love it. I understand that our country (and, indeed, our global village) desperately needs high-growth entrepreneurs, because they create jobs. I have said repeatedly that these people are my personal heroes and she-roes.

It's just that, as a professor, it would be something akin to malpractice if I were not completely honest about the difficulties involved. It is also my duty to downplay the romanticism of it. Rather than prodding students to become immediate entrepreneurs, I want them to be successful when they decide to pursue it.

From my own entrepreneurial experience, I've compiled six lessons that fledgling campus entrepreneurs might want to consider before taking the plunge:

The Odds.

Your chances of success with a campus-launched business are very, very slim. To let megafounders, such as Gates, Jobs, and Dell, persuade you otherwise would be like attempting to become an NBA player straight out of high school because of the success that Kevin Garnett has had. As my colleague, Professor Lloyd Shefsky, says: "Open a business as a student only if you think you are the next Bill Gates or Michael Dell. Otherwise, get more business experience first." For every Microsoft, there are at least 10,000 entrepreneurial failures.

The Cash.

From my experience at Akar, I cannot say enough about the difficulty of managing cash flow. When accounts are unpaid, your company takes a hit. Moreover, accounts are usually pulled unexpectedly, meaning you can't easily recover. That's the real world thumbing its nose at your plans. Cash management is the difference between a company's life and death; it is a skill especially worth honing at a company other than your own.

The Expectations.

As I've mentioned, businesses are messy; there hasn't ever been one that met expectations. That's because the real world gets in the way. You want to sell sweaters, for example, and you've designed the sweater to die for. Only the weather turns hot, and no one is buying sweaters. So much for your business "plan."

The Ethics.

Students might be familiar with the professorial admonishments to avoid lying, stealing, and cheating.

The Philosophy.

Did you know that it's you and not your idea–even if yours is the ultimate better mousetrap–that gets companies off the ground. An "A" entrepreneur with a "C" idea stands a better chance than the reverse. There is an old adage in entrepreneurial circles "that the investment is in the jockey, not the horse."

The Salesmanship.

This one is a killer. Many of the nation's best business schools don't teach salesmanship, perhaps because the skill smacks of "trade school" training. Don't be fooled. Sales are central to your business. An entrepreneur must learn, even if the first experience is at a flea market, how to sell to customers at a profit. Selling isn't hanging up a corporate shingle, nor is it developing, marketing, or shipping a product–that thinking was the downfall of many a dot.com dream.

DREAMS AND REALITIES. Campuses are wonderful places. Colleges and business schools alike offer environments that nurture impressionable students with entrepreneurial dreams. All around are eager peers, supportive professors, and an aura of excitement about the possibilities.

What they don't offer, however, is entrepreneurial reality: that the odds are heavily against the student founder succeeding. To beat those odds, you need to take a different route, or at least understand what you will encounter if you nonetheless persist. As a student, how can you best prepare for your future entrepreneurial endeavor? Consider the following steps:

- Take as many courses in entrepreneurship that are offered by your school. Primary consideration should be given to courses in finance, sales, and organizational behavior.

- Participate in your school's entrepreneurial internship program. Instead of taking a summer job with an investment-banking firm, become an intern with an entrepreneurial firm. It is well worth sacrificing compensation for the great experiential learning experience.

- Participate in your school's entrepreneurship clubs and programs, including attending conferences, panel discussions, and guest speaker presentations.

- Pursue jobs that will allow flexibility in job assignments. If you have no experience in finance, go to a company where you can get a job in that area to strengthen that weakness.

- Continue to improve your management, interpersonal, and leadership skills. If you have never managed people before, become a coach of a little league baseball or basketball team. Learn how to manage people toward a common goal.

ONE STEP AT A TIME. So, students, let me release you from any feeling of obligation to become an entrepreneur during, or immediately after, your school years. A survey of entrepreneurs who did not succeed found that they attributed their failure to "lack of training and too much on-the-job training," which is quite expensive due to the common occurrence of mistakes.

Be wise and slow down. Believe it or not, you are much younger than you think. The entrepreneurial opportunity and your interest, if you are sincerely committed to becoming an entrepreneur, will be there when you are truly ready.

QUESTIONS

1. What are some of the key skills a person needs to acquire to be a successful entrepreneur?

2. What practical real-time activities could you engage in now to promote your chances of being a successful entrepreneur?

3. Would you rather be an entrepreneur or a manager?

Source: Steven Rogers, "Want to Be an Instant Entrepreneur?" *BusinessWeek Online,* October 6, 2004.

BusinessWeek CASE FOR DISCUSSION

Family Business: A Clan on the Cutting Edge

At Buck family dinners every night, C.J. Buck always sits down with his five adolescent kids to discuss the day's happenings. But the subject matter is far from the school updates and allowance requests one would expect. Instead, issues like globalization, outsourcing, entrepreneurship, and supply-chain management often come up—with heated debates ensuing. And for C.J., president and CEO of Buck Knives, his family wouldn't have it any other way. "They all have something to say," C.J. says. "It's good for them to discuss the business."

C.J. Buck is the fourth-generation CEO of Buck Knives, a century-old knife-maker based in San Diego. His father, Chuck Buck, is chairman of the board, his brother-in-law, Joe Houser, is head of customer service, and his eldest daughter, Sarah, works in the company store giving weekend tours of the manufacturing plant.

Having made multi-use pocket and hunting knives since 1902, Buck Knives enjoys all the benefits of a successful and storied family business: a tradition of customer service, a loyal following, and an impeccable reputation for quality. It also has experienced some of the drawbacks of family businesses.

"I would say that the biggest challenge is being the boss's kid," says C.J. who graduated from college but has never worked for anyone but his father. "We did have a rough patch there for a while."

RESTRUCTURED TEAM. When C.J. took over as CEO in 1999, at just 39, he admits there was some "floundering." He wasn't ready to fill his father's shoes, but 63-year-old Chuck Buck was more than ready to retire. Struggling with the transition, Buck Knives experienced its first losses in decades, a tough pill to swallow for a company that had been a rousing success story from day one.

By transforming Buck Knives and its operation gradually, and growing increasingly comfortable being at the helm, C.J. has turned a seven-figure loss into a six-figure profit in five years. "Life is looking much better now," says C.J., who recently decided to relocate the business from San Diego to Post Falls, Idaho, to help trim operating costs and overhead.

The recovery wasn't easy. In 1999, C.J. had to go outside the family for help. He completely restructured the executive team to incorporate three outside members on the board of directors and only two company insiders—he and his dad. The previous setup always had three Bucks and two outsiders.

LEAN MODEL. "My approach was to be as transparent as possible and realize that I needed help to take this business and grow it," says C.J. Together, the team developed a new three-year business plan to help salvage the company and keep manufacturing in the United States, because all the Bucks agree, "we've always been a great American brand."

The plan's immediate provisions called for a revamping of the production line to a "lean cellular manufacturing" model. Where it once took six weeks to make a product from start to finish, Buck reorganized workers into pods, or "cells," and can now crank out a Hunter folding-blade knife in about 20 minutes. The ability to make a knife quickly eliminates the need to have huge inventories. Buck says the company has also cut scrap numbers in half since implementing the new plan in 2001.

Relocating to Idaho was the next part. Buck estimates he'll save $3 million annually in the new location because of lower costs for energy, salaries, and worker's compensation insurance. "California is not a good place to have a manufacturing business," he says.

MOVING SHOP. That Buck Knives was able to absorb the hiccup of the past few years and go on to prosper again is an accomplishment, says Daniel Van Der Vliet, director of the Vermont Family Business Initiative at the University of Vermont. "To keep the business in the family for three or four generations is becoming very rare," he says, estimating that only about 3% of family-owned businesses now reach their fourth generation.

Buck Knives is back in the black—and on the road to the Gem State. In November, it officially shut down its Southern California operations and started the move up north, laying off about 80 of its 270 employees and relocating 50. Once things are settled in the new Idaho plant, C.J. plans to hire about 100 more employees there, with the goal of getting back up to the 250 level. While the restaffing effort is under way, Buck will import some products from overseas manufacturers to help ease the move.

Now, C.J. is busy taking what he learned in the past five years and grooming the next generation—two of his five kids are interested in the knife business—to take over. As C.J. is discovering, succession is a perennial thorn for many family businesses. The most valuable lesson he plans to impart on his kids when passing on the family trade? Get input from outside experts. C.J. calls bringing in an additional outside board member one of his "key victories" when making the transition to CEO.

MADE IN USA. In the years ahead, both C.J. and his father agree that the new digs in Idaho may also quell some of those heated dinner conversations with their kids about outsourcing by keeping the manufacturing jobs in the United States.

QUESTIONS

1. Why is entrepreneurship and succession planning so important in a family business?

2. What kinds of management challenges do the owners of small businesses face?

3. How did this small business alter the way it operated to remain competitive?

Source: Erin Chambers, "A Clan on the Cutting Edge," *BusinessWeek Online,* January 27, 2005.

BUILDING YOUR MANAGEMENT SKILLS
Know Thyself

Developing the skills and knowledge for the career you want by taking courses and getting degrees will not be enough. The difference between those who succeed and those who get stuck is often the factor known as Emotional Intelligence (EI). It differs from mental intelligence (IQ), because it involves your ability to understand and manage your emotions and interpersonal relationships. It is helpful to assess your EI because these skills can also be learned. You can begin to manage your emotions and relationships better by assessing where you are now. To do so, go to the exercise titled "Assessing Your Emotional Intelligence" on your Student DVD.

CHAPTER VIDEO
The Syl Tang Story

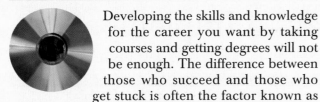

Syl Tang is a Chinese American woman living and working in New York City. She also happens to be the CEO of HipGuide.com, an entrepreneurial business pioneered by Tang.

Tang is the true entrepreneur. She is very passionate about her business. She sees herself as waking each day with a belief in her business, its mission, and the need for constant enthusiasm. Being an entrepreneur is a very rewarding experience; however, it can be quite lonely as well.

Tang recommends that a business plan be carefully articulated as it is the most important document for those in financial roles for the business. This group includes bankers, accountants, and potential investors. She is firm about starting out by having a destination in mind, a roadmap. But, she says, one must remain flexible as there are events that occur that cannot be anticipated by even the best business plan.

To be a successful CEO, Tang believes that you must realize that one cannot know everything. The goal is to surround yourself with people who are experts in those areas that are critical to your business. Finally, she advises that one must "listen" first and be a cheerleader for your people and the business.

1. If HipGuide.com founder and owner Syl Tang were to choose the right goals to pursue for the business model but does a poor job in the area of efficiency, what is the likely result?

2. What qualities does Tang have that ensure her success as an entrepreneur?

3. Syl Tang is an independent owner of her business. How might she differentiate between efficiency and effectiveness?

Appendix to Chapter 3

Creating a Business Plan to Implement a New Venture

As we discuss in Chapter 1, a company's *business model* outlines the way it will use its resources to create products that give it a competitive advantage. Recall, a company has a *competitive advantage* when it can make and sell products that have more value to customers than similar products offered by other companies. The business plan is a highly-detailed, written statement that explains the purpose of creating a new venture–either a new company or a new project in an existing company–to provide products to customers. A business plan contains several important kinds of information: (1) It explains the new venture or company's business model describing what kinds of product it will make and sell and why they will appeal to customers; (2) it explains why and how the new venture will be able to compete successfully against established competitors; and (3) it explains how the entrepreneur, business owner, or manager intends to obtain, use, and organize the resources the company will need to make and sell these products.

If the assumptions in the business plan work out as intended, a company will have created a competitive business model that attracts customers and generates sales revenues that exceed expenses and lead to a profit. If the business plan does not work out because entrepreneurs and managers have chosen the wrong business model and made mistaken assumptions about customers' needs, or underestimated how much it will cost to make and sell the product, expenses will exceed revenues, and the new venture will be unprofitable. It will likely go out of business and people will lose the capital they invested in it.

To avoid this financial disaster, it is therefore vital that the entrepreneur or managers planning the new venture, and the banks or venture capitalists who loan their money to fund it, do an accurate and thorough job of developing and testing the business model to increase their chances of success. Given that new ventures are highly risky and many fail, this planning process is crucial.

Developing a Business Plan

Planning for a new business venture begins when an entrepreneur notices an opportunity to develop a new or improved good or service for the entire market or for a specific market segment (see Chapter 10). Similarly, planning for a new business venture or project *inside of* an established company begins when an intrapreneur notices an opportunity. On the one hand, an entrepreneur might notice an opportunity in the fast-food market to provide customers with healthy fast food such as rotisserie chicken served with fresh vegetables. This is what the founders of the Boston Market restaurant chain did. On the other hand, an intrapreneur at McDonald's might notice an opportunity to create a new kind of hamburger or fast-food product to attract more customers. And, in fact, the idea for the Big Mac and Egg McMuffin came from two of McDonald's franchisees who independently developed and tested these new products and then shared them with the whole McDonald's Company.

There is no formalized way in which a person can "come up" with a new idea for an attractive new product. Many successful new products result from continuous hard thinking and from intuition and luck. They can also result from a formal, in-house strategic planning process whereby product development and marketing managers brainstorm ideas for new products or new ways to package and deliver them to customers. Once a new product idea has been generated, the crucial next step in creating a business plan is to test the feasibility of the new idea and the business model behind it.

To accomplish this, an entrepreneur or functional experts perform a detailed SWOT analysis, which is a kind of strategic planning exercise. SWOT analysis is a technique that focuses on identifying the *internal Strengths and Weaknesses* of the proposed new venture–such as the financial resources available for the project and the skills and experience of the entrepreneur and functional experts in marketing or manufacturing responsible for launching the new product. SWOT analysis also focuses on assessing *external Opportunities and Threats* in the competitive environment that will promote or impede the success of the new venture (hence, the term *SWOT analysis*). Figure 1 outlines some of the essential questions to ask when conducting a SWOT analysis.

Take the fast-food example earlier. To assess the viability of selling rotisserie chicken served with fresh vegetables, the entrepreneur needs to analyze

Strengths	Opportunities
Does the venture have experienced, creative leaders and researchers?	Is customer demand in the targeted market segments increasing?
Does it have a well-developed and researched business model?	Can the existing product range be widened to target new market segments?
Does it have a well-designed product that better satisfies customers' needs?	Can the company's R&D skills be used to create new and improved products?
Are market segments accurately targeted?	Are there opportunities to develop new distribution channels and be more responsive to customers?
Does its personnel have good marketing skills and the product, the right marketing mix?	Will it be possible to improve employees' value-creation skills to increase efficiency, lower costs, and improve product quality?
Does it have an efficient operations and materials management system?	Are there opportunities to enter new product markets or expand globally?
Are the distribution channels chosen and the sales force trained?	
Does it have human resource competencies in recruitment and compensation areas?	
Does it have an appropriate leadership and management style?	
Does it have a well-designed organizational structure and culture?	
Does it have sufficient capital in reserve to make and sell the product for six months to a year?	

Weakness	Threats
Does the venture have a poorly thought-out business model?	Has the venture failed to anticipate the reactions of competitors?
Have customer needs been defined inaccurately and market segments incorrectly identified?	Are changes in customer tastes occurring rapidly?
Does the venture have an inappropriate or poorly designed marketing plan and mix?	Are new or substitute products from competitors under development?
Are operations and materials management systems not developed or in place?	Is competition in the industry increasing?
Is the choice of distribution channels poor?	Are changes in demographic factors affecting customer tastes?
Is the sales force training program poorly designed?	Is the market experiencing changes in economic and global factors such as the rise of low-cost competitors?
Are human resources and competencies poor?	How quickly will rivals be able to develop competing products?
Do managers have an inappropriate leadership style?	Are there ways competitors can reduce the cost of value-creating functional activities chosen by the venture?
Does the venture have a poorly thought out organizational structure and culture?	
Is there insufficient capital to keep the business in operation for six months to a year?	

Figure 1
Testing the Business Plan Using SWOT Analysis

opportunities and threats. One potential threat might be that if the new idea succeeds, McDonald's or KFC might decide to imitate the idea and rush to do so. If this happens, whatever competitive advantage the entrepreneur may have had will be short-lived. (KFC actually did this after Boston Market was suc-cessfully launched.) As the entrepreneur conducts a thorough analysis of the competitive environment, he or she must be willing to abandon an idea if it seems likely that the threats and risks are too great for an acceptable profit to be earned. Entrepreneurs must not become so committed to their ideas that they discount potential threats and forge ahead—only to lose all of their capital.

If the environmental analysis suggests that the product idea is feasible, the next step is to examine the strengths and weaknesses of the idea. For a new company venture the main strength is likely to be the resources possessed by the entrepreneur. Does the entrepreneur have access to an adequate source of funds? Does the entrepreneur have any experience in the fast-food industry such as having been a chef or managed a restaurant?

To identify weaknesses, the entrepreneur needs to assess what kinds of functional resources will be necessary to establish a viable new venture—such as a chain of chicken restaurants—and how much capital will be required. This analysis might reveal that the new product idea might make a *profit*, but it will not generate a sufficient return on investment, that is, be *profitable* enough to justify risking the capital that will be needed to fund the venture. Thus the first three steps in creating a business plan for a new venture are as follows:

- Notice a product opportunity, and develop a basic business model that focuses on the product, customer needs, and potential markets. (Chapters 10 and 11 discuss different marketing and product development techniques to use for this purpose.)
- Conduct a strategic (SWOT) analysis to identify opportunities, threats, strengths, and weaknesses.
- Make an initial assessment of whether the business model is feasible. If it is, then it is time to write the detailed business plan.

Writing a Detailed Business Plan

Once these steps are completed, the hard work of writing up the detailed business plan begins. The business plan will be used to (1) continue the process of testing, assessing, and fine-tuning the proposed business model, and (2) attract the banks or investors who will provide the capital needed to launch the venture (or, in the case of an existing company, get the buy-in of top managers). Business plans are formatted in many ways, but a typical format is as follows:

The Executive Summary

The executive summary is an opening, two-page executive summary that contains a statement of the organization's business model, mission, goals, and financial objectives. The summary also contains a statement of the organization's strategic objectives, including an in-depth analysis of a new product's market potential based on the SWOT analysis that has already been conducted. Finally, it outlines the strategies needed to use an organization's resources and core competencies to compete effectively in the market or industry. In particular, these strategies should explain how the new venture will obtain a *sustainable competitive advantage,* one that will allow it to perform effectively over time and adapt to changing competitive conditions as needed.

Company Background Information

The second part of the business plan provides a short history of the entrepreneur and the new venture company that has been founded, or, in the case of a venture within an established company, specific details about a new project team's history. This should include:

- The age of the new venture, or company, and time of its founding.
- The number people involved in the venture, including its owners, senior managers, scientists, researchers, and other functional experts, and what their background, experience, and competencies are.
- Existing and projected annual sales figures.
- The current and future location of the facilities that will be used to make and sell the product.
- The current and future form of the legal ownership structure of the business, for example, whether it will be organized as a sole proprietorship, partnership, entrepreneurial startup, private corporate startup, publicly traded corporation, or not-for-profit organization.

Functional and Organizational Strategies and Resources

The third and very important section of a business plan contains a detailed account of the set of functional subplans and strategies that will be required to implement the business model and organize the new venture. Some of these subplans are a marketing plan, operations and materials management plan, financial plan, and human resource plan. A short description of each is as follows:

1. Marketing Plan *describes*
- The competitive industry environment.
- Customers' needs, priorities, and location.
- The product strategy.
- The pricing strategy.
- The promotion and advertising strategy.
- The distribution strategy.

2. Operations and Material Management Plan *describes*
- All production and manufacturing processes.
- The requirements of the production facility, including its size, layout, capacity, and location.
- The inventory and supply chain management plan for raw materials and finished goods inventory, and the warehouse space needed for each.
- Production and computer equipment requirements.

3. Financial Plan *describes*
- The size, source, and amount of initial equity capital needed.
- The monthly operating budget for the first year.
- Three years of projected quarterly balance sheets and profit/loss statements.
- The expected and potential financial return (profitability) of the project.
- A breakeven analysis of the project, that is, the minimum amount of revenue it will need to earn to just "break even," (earn) zero profit but not suffer a loss.
- The monthly estimated cash flow.
- Existing loans and liabilities.

4. Human Resource Plan *describes*
- The allocation of authority and responsibility.
- The skills and training requirements personnel will need.
- The venture's recruitment and employee selection policies.
- The performance evaluation and compensation plans for the venture's members.

Time Line and Major Milestones

Finally, a business plan contains a detailed description and roadmap of how and when a new venture intends to meet the overall goals and objectives set out in the other sections of the business plan. In particular, it contains a detailed timeline for purchasing resources, hiring new personnel, and creating the functional and organizational infrastructure that will be needed to implement the business model. Examples include the target dates for the final design, construction, and opening of the first chicken restaurant. Such a roadmap allows the entrepreneur, employees, and investors to assess how much progress has been made in getting the new product to market. It also provides a way of assessing how new issues and problems may have emerged because of changing internal strengths and weaknesses and external opportunities, and threats.

Developing Your *Own* Business Plan

As you can see developing a detailed business plan that provides an in-depth explanation of how entrepreneurs or intrapreneurs will implement a business model is a complex, time-consuming, and extremely creative task. Yet it must be done to more accurately assess the potential risks and returns of the new venture. And, as we discuss in Chapter 15, the higher the risk, the higher the potential returns investors will require, so a breakeven analysis and assessment of a new product's potential profitability is an important part of this analysis.

Unlike intrapreneurs in established companies, many individual entrepreneurs do not have a team of expert functional managers to help them develop a detailed business plan. Also, they typically lack the in-house financial resources intrapreneurs can draw upon. This is one reason why franchising has become such a popular method of starting a new business in the United States. A prospective entrepreneur can purchase and draw upon the proven business plan of an already existing company, and, in this way, reduce the problems and risks associated with opening a new business. Of course, in return, a franchisee often pays a significant percentage of the franchise's revenues and profits to the franchising company. The founders of chains like Subway Sandwiches and Stanley Steamer have made a fortune by selling the rights to use their business model.

A useful exercise to help you appreciate the amount of thought and effort that goes into opening a new business is to prepare a *simplified* business plan along the lines suggested above. (Some instructors make this a required part of a semester-long course.) But a good place to start—either by yourself or with others as a team—is to "brainstorm" about a novel product idea that you think might have commercial possibilities. Then test the idea by performing a SWOT analysis using some of the questions in Figure 1. Write down your responses to these questions, and after you have examined the strengths, weakness, opportunities, and threats associated with your new business idea, you can assess how viable it is. You may decide it is not, so then start another round of brainstorming.

Once you have found a viable new product idea, write a simplified business plan. Start by describing your business model. Then, utilize the concepts, techniques, and tools contained in the chapters in Part 3 of this book, which discuss the main value-creation functions needed to develop and implement your idea. Be sure to describe the series of subplans for marketing, operations and materials management, HRM, finance, and so on.

A good way to test your detailed business plan is then to give copies of it to classmates or friends and have them assess its viability. Also, develop a slide-show presentation of your business model and plan, and then allow other people or teams to question and probe its details and assumptions. In this way you will gain an appreciation of the many complex issues involved in the "great game of business." You will get a much better understanding of how much hard work and effort it takes for people to found, organize, and manage companies that provide customers with valuable goods and services.

4 Multinationals and the Global Environment of Business

Learning Objectives

After studying this chapter you should be able to:

1. Describe the role of multinational companies in global production and trade today and the way they affect the countries in which they operate.

2. Discuss how multinationals are affected by the political systems of the countries in which they operate, and especially by the desire of countries around the world to pursue free trade and reduce or abolish tariff barriers.

3. Describe the nature of the specific forces in the global environment and appreciate why they present so many challenges for multinational companies today.

4. Describe the nature of the general forces in the global environment that affect all companies as they compete in industries and countries around the world.

5. Identify the main challenges facing multinationals in terms of managing global business commerce and business occupations and choosing a method of global organizing.

WHY IS THIS IMPORTANT ?

Where do you think you will be working when you complete your education? If you travel to another country, or even a new part of the United States, would you understand how to deal with the customers, suppliers, and government agencies?

This chapter looks at the forces in the global environment that affect whether a company is able to create a profitable, sustainable business model or not. General forces in the environment such as a nation's culture, political, and economic systems will shape an organization and how it competes there. The more specific forces affecting an industry, such as a nation's supply and distribution systems, also affect whether or not a company will achieve success. Learning to understand and appreciate differences between nations and their cultures is vital to anyone in business today.

A Question of Business

Nestlé's Global Food Empire

What challenges is Nestlé facing in the global environment?

In 1886 Henri Nestlé, a pharmacist living in Vevey, Switzerland, invented an infant formula made from cow's milk and wheat flour that could be used as a substitute for mother's milk. Today, Nestlé S.A., the company Henri founded, is the world's largest food company. Its sales are over $75 billion annually, and it has 250,000 employees and 500 factories in 80 countries worldwide. In 2004, Nestlé made and sold over 8,000 food products, including popular brand-name products such as Kit-Kat chocolate bars, Taster's Choice coffee, Carnation Instant Milk, and Stouffer's foods.

At Nestlé's corporate headquarters in Vevey, CEO Peter Brabeck-Latmathe (who has been in charge of the company since 1997) is responsible for boosting the company's profitability. Brabeck has faced many challenges. He has been working to increase Nestlé's global revenues by entering attractive markets in both developed and emerging countries. He is continuing the global expansion that Nestlé began in the 1990s when, for example, it bought the U.S. food companies Carnation and Buitoni Pasta, the British chocolate maker Rowntree, the French bottled-water company Perrier, and the Mexican food maker Ortega. Under Brabeck, Nestlé has spent $18 billion to acquire U.S. companies Ralston Purina, Dreyer's Grand Ice Cream, and Chef America. Brabeck intends not only to continue selling these

food brands in the United States but also to modify them to suit the tastes of customers in countries around the globe. He is particularly anxious to enter emerging markets, such as those in Eastern Europe and Asia, where there are an enormous number of potential new customers.

But increasing global revenues by improving product sales is only the first part of Brabeck's global business plan. He is also anxious to increase Nestlé's operating efficiency and reduce the costs of running its global operations. As you can imagine, with 250,000 employees and 500 factories, the costs of organizing Nestlé's global activities are enormous. Brabeck benchmarked the company's operating costs to those of its competitors, including Kraft Foods and Unilever, and found Nestlé's costs were significantly higher. So, he then cut Nestlé's global workforce by 15%, closed 114 of it factories, and reduced its operating costs by over 10%. And he plans to make more sizable cuts over the next five years.

In another move to reduce operating costs, Nestlé is investing $1.8 billion to install a global information system to link all of its companies *and* their global suppliers to corporate headquarters in Vevey. Brabeck's goal is to automate and integrate all of Nestlé's operations from purchasing through manufacturing, distribution, and marketing. Nestlé began this overhaul by signing a $200 million contract with SAP, the world's leading enterprise management software supplier. It will use SAP's information technology to monitor its purchasing activities around the globe. This will help ensure Nestlé is getting the lowest-priced and highest-quality inputs possible. Nestlé is also using SAP's technology both to reduce the number of its global suppliers and to negotiate more favorable supply contracts with them— moves that should result in a significant drop in purchasing costs. To improve the efficiency of its purchasing and retailing functions, it has also developed e-business Web sites where it lists the detailed specifications of the inputs it requires from suppliers.

Brabeck hopes that the new IT system will result in an increased flow of information allowing Nestlé to capitalize on what has always been its main source of competitive advantage—superior innovation. His goal is to use Nestlé's new IT system to share information between its global food divisions, which he believes will enhance their ability to create a flow of new and improved products for Nestlé's markets around the world. If his plan works, Brabeck will be well on the way to making Nestlé not only the largest but also the most profitable global food company.[1] •

Overview

Multinational companies like Nestlé compete with other multinationals in the global environment for scarce and valuable resources, such as customers and raw materials. In this chapter we first describe the nature of the multinational company and the way it affects, and is affected by, the countries in which it operates. Second, we discuss the forces in the specific global environment that affect the way these companies operate. Third, we describe the forces in the general global environment that affect the activities of multinationals as they compete around the globe. Lastly, we examine the challenges that confront all businesses today in a changing global environment. By the end of the chapter you will appreciate why conditions in the global environment are a major determinant of a multinational company's profitability.

The Multinational Company

multinational companies Companies that operate and trade in many different countries around the world.

Today, in most industries, giant **multinational companies** have come to dominate the global business system. The largest multinational companies, such as General Motors, Exxon Mobil, Pfizer, and Wal-Mart, generate sales and revenues greater than those of many countries in the world. Many of the millions of small businesses around the world also operate as multinationals, however. They also buy their inputs from companies located around the world and sell their products internationally. For example, automakers like Porsche and Ferrari make their cars from the finest components available globally; similarly, fashion designers like Dior and Armani buy their fabrics, leathers, and accessories from small specialist suppliers around the world. In turn, all of these companies— Porsche, Ferrari, Dior, and Armani—sell the products they produce to people around the world.

Multinationals and the Global Business System

In terms of business commerce, multinationals control the global production and distribution networks that handle the majority of world trade. In industries such as the car or computer industry, for example, a handful of multinationals compete for the same customers everywhere. In many cases, the products these companies create are designed for global consumption: For example, the same car (with perhaps just a few modifications for local markets) can be produced and traded around the world.

In terms of global occupations, multinationals locate in, and purchase inputs from, countries where the costs of productive resources are favorable. They are attracted to countries where labor costs are relatively low and occupational skills are relatively high. Capital thus moves to those countries where the labor characteristics seem to offer the greatest prospect for increasing companies' productivity and profitability. The demand by these companies for skilled employees typically increases the division of labor in the countries in which they locate, speeding the economic growth of these nations. In fact, countries compete to be the places where multinationals operate for this very reason: They increase a country's prosperity.

Designing a global business organization to operate across countries is a very critical issue for multinational companies, as we discuss later in the chapter. Ford is a good example of a company that has confronted these issues. Following World War II, Ford realized that it could increase its profitability by taking its car making skills abroad. It established operating units in different countries in Europe, the Far East, and Australia. Each of these units was allowed to control its own activities and develop cars suited to its local market. The result was that each unit operated more or less independently from Ford in the United States. Ford of Europe, for example, became the largest carmaker in Europe and produced many kinds of small cars suited to European roads and budgets.

Japanese car manufacturers began their big push to export reliable, low priced, small cars to the rest of the world in the 1970s and 1980s. To counter the growing success of the Japanese, Ford tried to draw upon the skills of its European operations to help it build smaller, more fuel-efficient cars for the U.S. market. However, because Ford had never before tried to get its U.S. and European design and manufacturing units to cooperate with one another, it took a decade for them to do so. In the meantime the Japanese continued to gain market share.

Despite being one of the first companies to establish foreign operating units, Ford experienced many organizational problems getting its world structure to work. What could Ford have done differently?

Ford realized that task and authority problems in its organizational structure were preventing it from utilizing its global resources productively. It decided to change its global organizational structure. It moved to a "world structure" in which one set of managers was given authority over the whole of a specific global operation such as manufacturing or car design. Then it began to design cars for the global market. However, it took a decade before Ford was able to produce its first fuel-efficient small car that could be sold to customers throughout the world.

Ford has encountered many organizational problems in getting its world structure to work. The company is constantly changing its lines of authority and the locations in which it operates to increase profitability. But all multinationals—not just Ford—face significant challenges when they organize their business activities on a global basis.

Political Systems and National Governments

We mentioned earlier that some multinationals are so large they can affect the well-being of the countries in which they operate. One important role of a nation is to control the relationship between the business system and society. The government is the political system chosen to create and manage the set of laws, rules, and regulations this involves, including the activities of both domestic companies and multinationals. Recall from Chapter 2 that one of the most important kinds of laws are those that protect the rights of people and companies to own, use, protect, and benefit from their property. The nature of a country's property rights, and the specific kinds of rules and regulations that enforce them, determine which kind of activities and behaviors are acceptable or unacceptable in the course of business. Moreover, a country's choice of property rights is a main determinant of its political system. Figure 4.1 outlines the relationship between a business, the government, and the society in which it operates.

Today, representative democracy and totalitarianism are regarded as the two principal, and opposite, kinds of political systems. In a representative democracy, citizens have the legal right to periodically elect individuals to represent their interests, and to pass the laws and regulations that protect and modify private property rights to suit changing conditions. A *democratic government* therefore reflects the desire and wishes of people and groups in its society.

As you might expect, *capitalism* is the most common form of business system found in representative democracies. (Recall from Chapter 2 that capitalism is the political system in which the private ownership of productive resources is the basis for the production and distribution of goods and services.) However, many varieties of capitalism have been adopted by different countries around the world. The United States, for example, is commonly regarded as practicing the "strong" form of capitalism because it makes individuals ultimately responsible for their own future success–their ability to accumulate property and wealth–the ultimate goal of a capitalist system. U.S. law is designed to promote the free flow of resources to the people and companies that can make the best use of them.

On the other hand, many other countries such as Canada, Germany, Sweden, New Zealand, and to a lesser extent the United Kingdom and France, practice a "weaker" form of capitalism, known as *welfare capitalism* which, while encouraging and rewarding enterprise, also establishes a social support framework to aid citizens who, for whatever reason, lack the ability or resources to support themselves. In these countries, guaranteeing some degree of equity in the social or class system is an important political objective–perhaps a more important objective than encouraging people to act in a self-interested and enterprising way. All these countries have strong private property rights systems, however.

A totalitarian government is one in which one person or political party attempts to exercise absolute control over all forms of business and social activity. Such a government commonly bars or outlaws any other political party. Normally, a *dictatorship* exists in which one political or social group or family has gained the power to impose their will on a society and decide which rules and regulations should govern business and other aspects of life.

government The political system chosen to create and manage the set of laws, rules, and regulations that control the actions of people and companies that operate in a society.

representative democracy A form of government in which citizens periodically elect individuals to represent their interests.

totalitarian government A form of government in which a person or group of people attempt to exercise absolute control over all forms of business activity.

Figure 4.1

The Relationship between Business, Government and Society

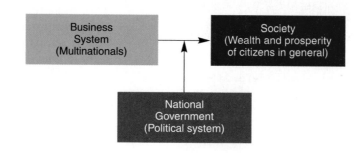

communism A one-party totalitarian system based on the dogma that all property should be owned by the state and that no individual should have the right to own private property.

The relationship between property rights and totalitarianism is complex. Communism, for example, is a one-party totalitarian system based on the dogma that all property should be owned by the state and not by private individuals. The communist belief is that no individual should have the right to own private property because this does not result in wealth being created and distributed in a way that benefits the most people—it only benefits the wealthy owners of capital. "To each according to their needs and from each according to their abilities" is one well-known communist adage used to defend the lack of any private property rights. The failure of communism as a political system is most commonly attributed to the fact that it does *not* lead to much wealth being produced because people have little motivation to work hard if they cannot claim "ownership" of the results of their hard work. So people and society do not prosper over time under a communist system.

Many totalitarian states exist in the Middle East, Africa, and Asia today. In these countries the political party or ruling family that controls the government decides how to allocate property rights among different kinds of social groups and therefore determine which groups gain at the expense of others. Commonly, laws and regulations are drawn up that benefit the social group that is in power. In essence, in this kind of totalitarian system a few people prosper but most do not, and freedom, equity, and justice are lacking in the system.

Almost all countries that are home to multinational companies have developed representative democracies or are in the process of doing so. Many dictatorships and totalitarian regimes have collapsed around the world because their business systems do not provide the political and economic security necessary to attract multinationals and their vital foreign capital to stimulate the growth of their economies. In general, the richer a society, the more stable tend to be its political institutions, and the more democratic is its government. A stable and democratic society, in turn, continues to attract more business investment from multinationals whose activities result in a country becoming richer over time. Where totalitarian regimes still exist, they do so because their complete control of the armed forces allows them to suppress their people and fend off attempts to reform their economic and political practices.

National Governments and Free Trade

free-trade agreements Joint decisions by countries to reduce or eliminate trade barriers that impede the flow of products between nations.

tariffs Taxes or duties on imported products that raise the price at which they must be sold in foreign markets.

quotas Restrictions on the amount of a good or service than can be imported into a country.

One important way countries can increase their living standards is by eliminating their barriers to trade. Free-trade agreements are joint decisions made by countries to reduce or eliminate price- and quantity-restricting barriers that impede the flow of products between nations. For example, tariffs are one main form of trade barrier. Tariffs are taxes or duties on imported products that raise the price at which they must be sold in a country abroad; this often makes them uncompetitive with locally produced products. Competition is hampered by tariffs, so consumers pay higher prices than they might otherwise have to had free trade been allowed. Quotas are restrictions that limit the *amount* of a product that can be imported into a country. The effect of a quota is much like a tariff. Competition is hampered, so consumers end up paying higher prices. As a result, some of the benefits that could be derived by both buyers and sellers are lost because many exchanges don't come to pass. They simply cost too much to execute.

Lower trade barriers have created many new opportunities for multinationals to expand the markets for their goods and services by exporting and investing in foreign countries. And, of course, the shift toward a more open global economy has created more opportunities to buy foreign goods and services, too. Land's End, was one of the first U.S. multinationals to enjoy increasing success because of its decision to

Did You Know?

Percent of world population who speak these as first languages[2]:

1.5%–German	2.8%–Hindi
2.0%–Japanese	4.8%–English
2.3%–Russian	5.1%–Spanish
2.7%–Bengali	14.9%–Chinese
2.8%–Portuguese	

import low-cost clothes and bedding from overseas manufacturers. Land's End purchases clothing from manufacturers in Hong Kong, Malaysia, Taiwan, and China because U.S. textile makers often do not offer the same quality, styling, flexibility, or price. Today, most big retailers of clothing, including Levi Strauss, Wal-Mart, and Target, are major players in the global environment by virtue of their purchasing activities.

GLOBAL AND REGIONAL TRADE AGREEMENTS   Tariff barriers designed to prevent the import of inexpensive products from abroad have been greatly reduced by agreements such as the General Agreement on Tariffs and Trade (GATT), a worldwide international treaty forged following World War II. GATT led to a massive reduction in tariffs and the creation of the World Trade organization (WTO). Since its passage, the amount of world trade has multiplied like never before. The WTO continues today to fight to lower trade barriers. In this way, resources move to the countries that possess the skills, technology, and know-how to put them to best use to create the most value and profit.

> **GATT** An international treaty between nations following WWII, dramatically fueling free trade.

A free-trade area is a group of countries that have committed themselves to removing all barriers to the free flow of goods and services between them. More free-trade agreements are being negotiated and agreed upon on a regular basis than ever before. Notable examples include the North American Free Trade Agreement (NAFTA), the European Union (EU), and the Association of Southeast Asian Nations (ASEAN). But there are many more.

> **free-trade area** A group of countries that agree to promote the free flow of goods and services between them.

The growth of these regional trade agreements also presents opportunities and threats for multinationals. NAFTA, which became effective on January 1, 1994, for example, abolished the tariffs on 99% of the goods traded between Mexico, Canada, and the United States by 2004. NAFTA also removed most barriers on the cross-border flow of resources, giving, for example, financial institutions and retail businesses in Canada and the United States unrestricted access to the Mexican marketplace. After NAFTA was signed there was a flood of investment into Mexico from the United States and many other countries such as Japan. Wal-Mart, Price Club, Radio Shack, and other major U.S. retail chains also expanded their operations in Mexico.

Some multinationals see regional free-trade agreements as a threat because the agreements expose them to increased competition from companies abroad. Indeed, companies in Mexico, the United States, and Canada have all experienced this since NAFTA's passage. For the first time, for example, many Mexican companies faced head-to-head competition with more efficient U.S. and Canadian companies. But the opposite is true as well: U.S. and Canadian companies operating in labor-intensive industries, such as the tile and textile industries, faced new competition from Mexican businesses that have a cost advantage in these industries.

Land's End is one company that has benefited from free trade. The company purchases clothing from manufacturers in Hong Kong, Malaysia, Taiwan, and China because U.S. textile manufacturers often do not offer the same quality, styling, flexibility, and price advantages. Do you think there are negative aspects to free trade? If so, what are they?

In 2005, the United States, Costa Rica, El Salvador, Nicaragua, Guatemala, Honduras, and the Dominican Republic were negotiating to establish a new agreement called the Central American Free Trade Agreement (CAFTA). CAFTA would eliminate tariffs between the countries and give them duty-free access to the U.S. market. Because wages in countries like Honduras are only $1 hour, compared to $3 an hour in Mexico, if CAFTA is implemented, opponents of the agreement argue that in addition to the United States, even Mexico would lose jobs—despite the fact that wages are already relatively low there.

Clearly, the establishment of free-trade areas creates an opportunity for global manufacturing companies because it allows them to reduce their costs. They can do this either by shifting production to the lowest-cost locations within the free-trade area or by serving the whole region from one location, rather than establishing separate operations in each country.

Video Small Business in Action

Your Own Boss: Vineyard Vines

Summary: Each year in the United States there are about 600,000 new start-up small businesses and nearly an equal number of failures as shown in the video from *BusinessWeek TV* on your Student DVD. This segment introduces brothers Shep and Ian Murray who are the successful owners of Vineyard Vines. The Murrays started their business a few years ago by maxing out their credit cards to fund their business start-up—manufacturing ties.

Originally, there was no store front and sales were generated by going door to door. During this formative stage, the business was struggling. The struggle is over, however. Today, gross sales will reach 20 million dollars. The Murrays initially had only one product—neckties. Today, however, their product lines include the original neckties and totes, shirts, and belts. Their products are sold in a variety of department and specialty stores. The importance of "passion" for the enterprise is emphasized as the key element in their tremendous success. They don't see themselves as selling ties and other products. Rather, they focus on building relationships as the central activity in growing their business.

The video segment concludes with a feature on Columbia University's innovative Business School's program. The "Entrepreneur-in-Residence" provides students with direct exposure to a successful entrepreneur and classes on how to be successful. The professor notes that between 2001 and 2004 the most frequent new business start-ups have been service enterprises such as convenience stores. He concurs with the observations of the Murray brothers that "passion" for what you do is the most important factor in being successful.

Discussion Questions:

1. If Vineyard Vines was interested in expanding to global markets, what factors should it take into consideration as it developed its growth strategy?
2. What "general forces" in the global market would Vineyard Vines have to consider if they were seeking to expand globally?
3. The Murrays emphasize "relationship building" rather than "sales" as the principal element in the successful growth of Vineyard Vines. What issues and/or concerns should be explored by the Murrays if they were to consider expanding globally?

The Global Environment of Business

Like Nestlé, multinationals have to take into account many different factors when they develop a business model to compete on a global level. The existence of vast markets and billions of potential new customers is a major opportunity; there are potentially 1.2 billion customers in China for cell phones and cars, for example. Also, the possibility of gaining global access to lower-cost resources like raw materials and labor can help a company increase its profits.

global environment
The set of forces surrounding a company that determine its ability to obtain productive resources—land, labor, capital and enterprise.

The global environment a company operates in is the set of forces surrounding it that determine the ease with which it can obtain these resources—land, labor, capital and enterprise. A multinational depends on the global environment for the resources it needs to make and sell goods and services to customers worldwide. Because resources are often scarce, and because many companies compete for the same resources, obtaining them is a challenging task.

To understand how the global environment can affect a company, it is useful to distinguish between three stages in the process of making and selling goods and services—the input, conversion, and output stages. Business commerce begins at the input stage when an entrepreneur searches out and purchases the resources necessary to produce a particular product. At stage 2 it uses its technical skills and knowledge to change or transform these inputs into finished goods and services. At the output stage, products

**Figure 4.2
Forces in
the Global
Environment**

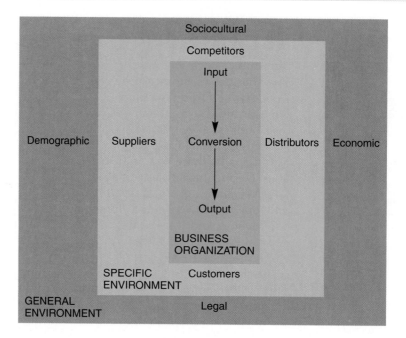

are ready to be sold to customers. Figure 4.2 illustrates these three stages, it also shows two kinds of forces in the environment that affect a company's profitability: *specific forces* that directly affect a company's business model, and *general forces* that affect all types of multinationals across different industries. These types of forces are discussed in depth in the next two sections of this chapter.

Specific Forces in the Global Environment

Specific forces in the global environment are those that directly increase or decrease a multinational company's sales revenues or operating costs, and thus its profitability. Below we examine the four main specific forces—suppliers, distributors, competitors, and customers.

Suppliers

specific forces Forces in the global environment that directly increase or decrease a company's sales revenues or operating costs, and thus its profitability.

suppliers The individuals and companies that provide a company with the resources that it needs to produce goods and services.

Suppliers are the individuals and companies that provide a company with the inputs (raw materials, component parts, employees, and so on) that it needs to produce goods and services. Obviously, a company prefers lower-priced inputs because this reduces what it costs to make products. The price the company ultimately pays for its resources, however, depends on its *relative bargaining power* versus its suppliers.

In general, suppliers will have more power to raise the price of a particular resource if they are few in number or they are prominent in their industry. Intel, for example, is the world's leading supplier of computer chips. As such, Intel has the power to demand high prices for the chips its sells to PC makers. Buyers, if they are large enough, also have more bargaining power: A company that buys a large amount of a certain input will have more power over the price—especially if there are many suppliers competing for its business. For example, there are hundreds of global companies that make car parts like light bulbs, door handles, and hub caps. These companies compete fiercely for the business of large buyers like Ford and GM, which need these parts to make their cars. This gives Ford and GM more bargaining power to demand lower overall input prices.

Other forces that affect the prices companies have to pay for their inputs include the availability of natural resources. Presently the demand for oil is extremely high, so gasoline prices are, too. This is driving up the prices companies around the world are having to pay to ship their products.

Companies everywhere have experienced a massive rise in fuel prices. The world's demand for oil is increasing, but the supply of it is not.

global outsourcing
The process of purchasing inputs from throughout the world to take advantage of differences in the cost and quality of resources.

GLOBAL OUTSOURCING The purchasing managers of multinationals like Ford, Procter & Gamble, and IBM are responsible for searching out the lowest cost, best-quality inputs no matter where they are located. This task is called global outsourcing. Consider how Boeing's newest jet airliner, the 777 was built. The 777 required 132,500 engineered parts produced around the world by 545 suppliers. Although Boeing makes the majority of these parts, eight Japanese suppliers make parts for the 777's fuselage, doors, and wings. A Singapore supplier makes the doors for the plane's forward landing gear, and three Italian suppliers manufacture wing flaps. Boeing's rationale for buying so many inputs from suppliers abroad is that these suppliers are the best in the world at what they do. In order for Boeing to produce a high-quality final product—a safe and reliable commercial aircraft—it is vital. (An interesting article on the growing supply of chips made in China appears at the end of the chapter.) But again, it's not just multinationals like Boeing that engage in global outsourcing. The Internet has made it much easier for companies both large and small to purchase inputs and sell outputs around the world.

Distributors

distributors Firms that link the companies that *make* products with the customers who *buy* them.

At the output stage are distributors. Distributors link the companies that *make* products with the customers who *buy* them. Wholesalers and merchants are examples. Once again, bargaining and negotiation takes place over the price a company can obtain for its products. The more powerful a company's bargaining position relative to its distributors, the higher the price it will receive. For example, major U.S. film studios have the bargaining power to control the price of the videotapes they sell to distributors like Blockbuster and Best Buy. This is because the movie studios control most of the hit movies on which the success of these distributors depend. On the other hand, Wal-Mart is a very powerful global distributor of consumer products to customers worldwide. Wal-Mart uses its buying power to negotiate large price discounts from the thousands of companies around the world competing to supply it with detergent, clothing, hardware, and so on.

intermediary A company such as a merchant, broker, or wholesaler that buys the products of one company and sells them to another.

THE ROLE OF INTERMEDIARIES Sometimes companies called intermediaries act as a "go-between" to manage the sales of products between sellers and buyers. An intermediary is a company such as a broker, merchant, or wholesaler that does not make a product but acts as a supplier or distributor, buying the products of some companies and selling them to others, often across countries. Figure 4.3 illustrates the role of the intermediary.

For example, hundreds of companies worldwide make lighting products. For a small, privately owned lighting store, the transaction costs related to finding and negotiating with each of these manufacturers would be enormous. So, a wholesaler takes advantage of a commercial opportunity to act as a go-between, linking lighting manufacturers and individual stores. The wholesaler selects a range of lighting products to buy from a set of global manufacturers. It then sells these products to thousands of individual lighting stores, using a product catalogue, online store, or skilled sales force. Store owners, in turn, select and stock those lighting products they think will be the most profitable to sell to customers in their cities.

The intermediary's profit is the difference between the price at which they buy products from lighting manufacturers and the price they can sell those products to individual stores. Stores are willing to pay the wholesaler's

```
┌─────────┐     ┌──────────────┐     ┌─────────┐
│ Company │ ──> │ Intermediary:│ ──> │ Company │
│    A    │     │ • Merchant   │     │    B    │
│         │     │ • Broker     │     │         │
│         │     │ • Wholesaler │     │         │
└─────────┘     └──────────────┘     └─────────┘
```

Figure 4.3
The Role of the Intermediary

higher prices to avoid the transaction costs involved in searching out lighting products for themselves. Today, the Internet is making it much easier for individual stores to deal directly with manufacturers and "cut-out" the intermediary. This increases their profitability because they keep the profit the intermediary would otherwise have earned. We discuss the issues of managing the flow of resources into and out of the production process later in the book.

Customers

To increase its profitability a company must make sure its products meet the needs of customers. One way of doing this is by grouping customers according to what they are seeking from a product. For example, Dell groups customers according to whether they are (1) individuals purchasing PCs for home use, (2) small companies, (3) large companies, (4) government agencies, or (5) educational institutions. Each of these groups wants something different from its PCs: Individual people might want PCs with many multimedia applications; large companies might want very powerful PCs called workstations; and educational customers with limited budgets might want low-priced PCs. Dell then sells PCs with different features and prices to each of these groups of customers.

A company must be prepared to quickly alter its business model to changing trends in the global environment, such as changes in customers' tastes and needs, for example. A vital role played by the marketing function is to provide a company, such as Nestlé, with exactly this kind of information. For example, Nestlé makes dehydrated soup. It is not a popular product in the United States, but it is a best-selling product in some countries in Europe and Asia. If dehydrated soup becomes more popular in certain countries, Nestlé's marketing group needs to be aware of this so the company can meet this new demand before its competitors do. Global marketing and sales issues are discussed in detail in Chapters 10 and 11.

Competitors

market share The total percentage of a product a company sells in a particular market.

One of the most important forces that a company confronts in the global environment is, of course, competitors. Competitors vie to obtain a larger share of the market. A company's **market share** is the percentage of the total quantity of a particular product that it sells in a market. The relative market share of different companies in an industry can be illustrated by the size of the piece of the "pie" it occupies, as shown in Figure 4.4. Toyota has a 20% share of the U.S. national market in SUVs, for example, and over a 40% share of the global market.

Figure 4.4
Market Share of Three Largest Companies

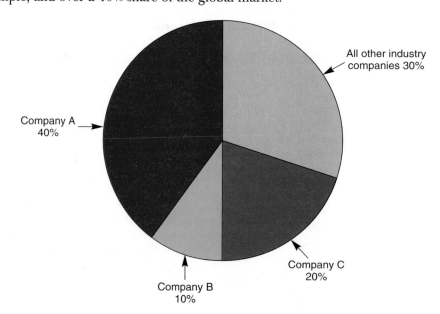

All other industry companies 30%

Company A 40%

Company C 20%

Company B 10%

The greater the number of competitors there are in a particular market, the lower will be the prices they can charge. Competitors directly affect each other's sales and revenues. More competition means lower profitability. As a result, a company must carefully consider how its competitors will respond to its business decisions—especially pricing decisions.

For example, a small German PC maker might think it can increase its profitability if it reduces its prices to attract more customers. The company might forecast that it can sell 10,000 PCs priced at $1,000 each (resulting in $10 million in revenues) but that it can sell 30,000 PCs if it reduces the price to $600 (resulting in $18 million in revenues). This seems like a clever competitive move because it would result in a large increase in profitability. But the company may not have considered how competitors like Dell, which also operates in Germany, will respond.

Competitors will do all they can to avoid losing customers because this will reduce their market share. They know that if a competitor cuts its prices, they will also have to do so, too, or lose customers. The result will be that Dell and other PC makers will also cut the prices of their PCs to $600 apiece.

The German company that initially cut its price will sell more computers—for a time. But once its competitors lower their prices, its sales will taper off. In six months' time, it might sell only 15,000 computers versus the 30,000 it had projected. At $600 per PC, this will generate only $9 million in revenues. So, even though the company has increased its market share, it has actually become less profitable! (Remember, before the price cut, it was earning $10 million in revenues.)

Rather than engaging in a price war, companies develop different strategies to compete for customers. These strategies include competing on the basis of better product design, quality, or better customer service. By differentiating their products this way, companies can charge higher prices and not get caught in a price war. A striking example of the way a multinational company can achieve this feat is the meteoric rise of Samsung, discussed in Business in Action.

Business in Action

Samsung's New Global Business Model

In the last five years Samsung, based in Seoul, Korea, has risen to become the most profitable consumer-electronics company in the world. Since 1999 Samsung's revenues have doubled, and in 2004 it made a record $12 billion profit, which made it the second most profitable global technology company after Microsoft. The way Samsung's global business model has changed over time explains how the company has reached its enviable position.

In the 1980s, Samsung could only watch as Japanese companies like Sony and Matsushita (the maker of Panasonic and JVC products) turned out hundreds and thousands of innovative new consumer electronic products such as the Walkman, VCRs, high-quality televisions, and CD players. Samsung's strategy was to watch which of these products, and which of their specific features, customers liked best. Samsung would then make a low-cost copy of these products and sell them at lower prices. However, although it was profitable, Samsung was not in the same league as companies like Sony. Sony, for example, plowed back the huge profits it made from its products into research to make even more advanced, better electronic products—thus sustaining its increasing profitability.

Samsung continued to pursue its low-cost strategy until the mid-1990s when its chairman, Lee Kun Hee, made a major decision. Sensing the emerging threat posed by China and other Asian countries whose cheap labor would rob Samsung of its low-cost advantage, Lee realized that Samsung needed to find a way to enter the big leagues and compete directly against the Japanese giants. The question was how.

Lee began his new strategy by closing down 32 unprofitable product divisions and laying off 40% of Samsung's workforce. With its costs lower, Samsung was able to invest much more of its capital in research and development. Lee decided

to spend much of Samsung's research money developing new components like microprocessors and LCD screens, which he sensed would eventually be in great demand by companies producing new digital products.

Today, Samsung supplies chips and LCD screens to electronics makers all over the globe.

But at the center of Lee's new business model for Samsung, was his intent to develop the company's engineering skills to improve on the technology being innovated by Sony, Matsushita, Phillips, and Nokia. In addition Lee's strategy called for Samsung to pump out a wider *variety* of these products *faster* than its competitors. He believed this would continually increase its market share.

By making the speed of new product development the centerpiece of its business model, Samsung was able to sprint ahead of Sony and Nokia. Both companies, because of the slow speed of their decision making, have been hard hit by Samsung's success. As a result, their profitability has declined sharply.

Today, Samsung is in the first tier of electronic makers and regarded by many as one of the most innovative companies in the world. One indication of how far it has come came in 2004 when Sony and Samsung announced a major agreement to share the costs of basic research related to improving LCDs, which can run into many billions of dollars.

For years Samsung's business strategy revolved around imitating other companies' products and selling them at a lower cost. But in the mid-1990s, Samsung Chairman Lee Kun Hee decided the company needed to step up to the plate and develop its own cutting-edge products in order to stay competitive.

However, we should not forget that Samsung's competitive advantage was originally built upon its ability to make many kinds of electronic components at a low cost. As Lee predicted, many low-cost Chinese producers are now doing to Samsung what Samsung did to Sony! The question is, will they be able to eventually set themselves apart from their competitors like Samsung did?[3]

General Forces in the Global Environment

Four general forces in the global environment—political-economic, sociocultural, demographic, and legal forces—affect multinationals' access to resources and determine worldwide demand for their products. These forces are general because they affect *all* multinationals and their suppliers, distributors, and customers.

Political-Economic Forces

political-economic forces Changes that occur in the form of a country's social and political systems.

Political-economic forces are caused by changes in the form and nature of a country's social and political systems. Around the globe, political-economic systems range widely and change over time. Managers must learn how different economic systems work in order to understand the opportunities and threats associated with them. This is especially true when they are changing.

free-market economy Economic system in which the production of goods and services is left in the hands of private enterprise.

In a free-market economy, the production of goods and services is left in the hands of *private* (as opposed to *government*) enterprise. The goods and services that are produced, and the quantities that are produced, are not specified by any central authority. Rather, production is determined by the interaction of the forces of supply and demand. If demand for a product exceeds supply, the price of the product will rise, prompting managers and organizations to produce more. If supply exceeds demand, prices will fall, causing managers and organizations to produce less. In a free-market economy the purchasing patterns of consumers, as signaled to managers by changes in demand, determine what and how much is produced.

In a **command economy**, the goods and services that a country produces, the quantity in which they are produced, and the prices at which they are sold are all planned by the government. In a pure command economy, all businesses are government owned and private enterprise is forbidden. As recently as 1990, the communist countries of Eastern Europe and the Soviet Union had command economies. Other communist countries such as China and Vietnam still do.

The failure of these economies to improve the well-being of their citizens relative to free-market countries like Germany, Japan, and the United States helped precipitate the collapse of communism in many countries (along with their command economies). People began to figure out that when the government gets involved in economic activity, economic growth is often impeded. Although China and Vietnam remain communist controlled, they are moving away from command economies and becoming more free-trade oriented. Figure 4.5 shows the changes in the political and economic freedom of select countries during the last decade.

Between free-market economies, on the one hand, and command economies, on the other, are mixed economies. In a **mixed economy**, certain sectors of the economy are characterized by private ownership and free-market mechanisms, and other sectors are characterized by significant government ownership and government planning. Mixed economies are most commonly found in the democratic countries of Western Europe, but the size of the government component is falling as these countries shift more toward the free-market model. For example, many European and Asian countries are selling off what once were government-run industries—including airlines, rail, health care, steel, and telecommunications operations—to private investors.

Multinationals generally prefer a free-market system for two reasons. First, because much of the economy is in private hands, there tend to be few restrictions on companies that decide to invest in countries with free-market economies. For example, U.S. companies face fewer impediments to investing in Britain, with its largely free-market system, than they do in China, where a free market is allowed in only certain sectors of the economy. Second, free-market economies tend to be more economically developed and have higher rates of economic growth than command or mixed economies, so their citizens tend to have higher per-capita incomes and more buying power.

A decade ago, few Western companies exported to or invested in Eastern Europe because the combination of totalitarian political regimes and command economies created a hostile environment for Western businesses. Since 1990, however, the

command economy
Economic system in which the quantity and price of goods and services that a country produces is planned by the government.

mixed economy
Economic system in which certain goods and services are produced by private enterprise and others are provided via centralized government planning.

Figure 4.5
Changes in Political and Economic Forces

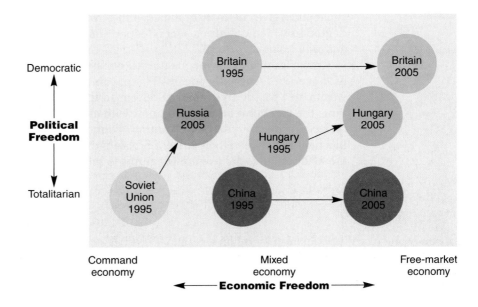

environment in Eastern Europe has become far more favorable for Western businesses; from 1990 to 2005, Western businesses have invested more than $250 billion in Eastern Europe.

A similar story has unfolded in China, where despite the continued presence of a totalitarian communist regime, a move toward greater economic freedom has produced a surge of Western and Japanese business. By 2005, multinationals had invested over $800 billion in China.

Sociocultural Forces

sociocultural forces
Changes in the social structure of a country and in its class structure, culture, customs, and beliefs.

values General standards and guiding principles that people in a society use to determine which kinds of behaviors are right or wrong.

norms Unwritten codes of conduct that prescribe how people in a particular culture should act in certain situations.

national culture The particular set of economic, political, and social values and norms that exist in a particular country.

Sociocultural forces relate to changes in a country's class structure, culture, customs, beliefs, and so on. A country's culture is a product of the values and norms its citizens hold. **Values** are general standards and guiding principles that people in a society use to determine which kinds of behaviors and outcomes are desirable or undesirable, that is, which are good or bad. **Norms** are unwritten codes of conduct that prescribe how people should act in particular social situations.

National culture is the particular set of economic, political, and social values and norms that exist in a particular country, and members of a particular national culture are socialized with these values as they grow up. U.S. national culture, for example, is based on capitalistic economic values, democratic political values, and individualistic, competitive social values—all of which characterize the way people in the United States live and work. The culture of U.S. organizations is therefore distinct from the culture of Japanese, French, or German companies because the values of these countries differ in significant ways.

Not tested on unit read

HOFSTEDE'S MODEL OF NATIONAL CULTURE Researchers have spent considerable time and effort identifying similarities and differences between the cultural values and norms of different countries. A model of national culture developed by researcher Geert Hofstede in the 1970s and 80s argues that differences in the values and norms of different countries are captured by five cultural dimensions:

The first dimension, which Hofstede called *individualism versus collectivism,* focuses on the values that govern the relationship between individuals and groups. In countries where individualism prevails, individual achievement, freedom, and competition are values that are stressed. In countries where collectivism prevails, group harmony, cohesiveness, consensus, and cooperation are stressed. Japan epitomizes a country dominated by collectivism, whereas the United States epitomizes a country dominated by individualism.

Hofstede used *power distance,* the second dimension, to refer to the degree to which a country accepts the fact that differences in its citizens' physical and intellectual capabilities give rise to inequalities in their well-being. This concept also measures the degree to which countries accept economic and social differences in wealth, status, and well-being as natural.

Countries that allow inequalities to persist or increase are said to have high power distance. Professionally successful workers in high-power-distance countries amass wealth and pass it on to their children. In these countries, inequalities increase over time; the gap between rich and poor, with all the attendant political and social consequences, grows very large. In contrast, countries that dislike the development of large inequalities between their citizens are said to have low power distance. Such countries use taxation or social welfare programs to reduce inequality and improve the lot of the least fortunate members of society. Low-power-distance countries are more interested in preventing a wide gap between rich and poor and discord between classes.

Advanced Western countries such as the United States, Germany, the

Did You Know?

The portion of the world's population living on less than $2 per day: 2.8 billion or 44% of the world.[4]

The United States is considered a low-power-distance country because even though the nation still has numerous levels of social classes, programs are available to reduce inequality and improve the lives of the poorest members of society.

Netherlands, and the United Kingdom score relatively low on power distance and are high on individualism. Poor Latin American countries such as Guatemala and Panama and Asian countries such as Malaysia and the Philippines score high on power distance and low on individualism. These findings suggest that the cultural values of richer countries emphasize protecting the rights of individuals and, at the same time, providing a fair chance of success to every member of society. But even among Western countries there are differences, as noted earlier. Both the Dutch and the British see their countries as more protective of the poor and disadvantaged than do Americans, who believe that people have the right to be rich as well as the right to be poor.

Hofstede's third dimension is an *achievement-oriented versus a nurturing* country orientation. Countries that are achievement oriented value assertiveness, performance, success, and competition and are results oriented. Countries that are nurturing oriented value the quality of life, warm personal relationships, and service and care for the weak. Japan and the United States tend to be achievement oriented. The Netherlands, Sweden, and Denmark tend to be nurturing oriented.

Just as people differ in their tolerance for uncertainty and willingness to take risks, so do countries. Hofstede refers to this as the dimension of *uncertainty avoidance*. Countries lows on uncertainty avoidance (such as the United States and Hong Kong) are easygoing, value diversity, and are tolerant of differences in what people believe and do. Countries high on uncertainty avoidance (such as Japan and France) tend to be rigid and intolerant. In high-uncertainty-avoidance cultures, conforming to the values of the social and work groups to which a person belongs is the norm, and structured situations are preferred because they provide a sense of security.

The last dimension that Hofstede identified concerns whether citizens of a country have a long- or a short-term orientation toward life and work. A long-term orientation derives from values that include thrift (saving) and persistence in achieving goals. A short-term orientation derives from values that express a concern for maintaining personal stability or happiness and for living in the present. Countries with long-term orientations include Japan and Hong Kong, which are well known for their high per-capita savings rates. The United States and France, which tend to spend more and save less, have a short-term orientation.

Differences in national culture help to explain why the cultures of multinationals based in one country tend to be different from those based in another. More generally, sociocultural forces affect the way multinationals can and should operate in different countries. For example, in some countries night shifts are taboo. In other countries employers are expected to provide employees with meals and transportation to and from their homes and workplaces.

Sociocultural forces also affect what kinds of products companies should offer customers in different societies. During the 1980s and 1990s, for example, people in Western countries became increasingly concerned about their personal health, fitness, and safety. Global companies that recognized this trend early were able to reap significant gains. PepsiCo, for example, used the opportunity presented by the fitness trend to take market share from rival Coca-Cola by being the first to introduce diet colas whose sales have soared worldwide. Similarly, the rising price of oil and global warming have led to greater environmental consciousness in many countries. People in the United States, for example, are beginning to question how socially responsible it is to drive a gas-guzzling SUV. Many customers are demanding more fuel-saving hybrid vehicles and automakers are now rushing to meet this demand.

Demographic Forces

demographic forces
Changes in the characteristics of a country's population, such as its age, gender, ethnic origin, race, and sexual orientation.

Demographic forces are outcomes of changes in the characteristics of a country's population such as age, gender, origin, race, and sexual orientation. Changing demographic forces affect the way companies operate and the kinds of products that customers want. For example, most industrialized nations are experiencing the aging of their populations. As the number of older people increases, companies that cater to older people such as the pharmaceutical and home health-care industries are seeing an increase in demand for their products and are becoming more profitable as a result. (An interesting *BusinessWeek* article that discusses these issues appears at the end of the chapter.) Similarly, the rising numbers of Hispanic consumers in the United States is changing the ways companies do business. For example, Minyards, a Texas-based grocery store chain, recently decided to convert many of its regular stores into supermarkets with a distinctly Hispanic flair.

Legal Forces

legal forces Changes in a country's laws and regulations that often occur because of changes in the political and ethical attitudes within a society.

Legal forces are outcomes of changes in a country's laws and regulations that occur because of changes in political and ethical attitudes within a society. Important legal forces include changes in laws on environmental protection and the preservation of endangered species; an increased emphasis on safety in the workplace; and legal constraints against discrimination on the basis of race, gender, or age. Laws differ from country to country and change over time, and this can also pose complications for multinationals. For example, in many countries (those with command economies, in particular), bribes and kickbacks are commonly accepted business practices. But U.S. anti-bribery laws prohibit this sort of activity, and the enforcement of these laws has become stricter in recent years. As a result, U.S. firms lose millions, if not billions, of dollars in business each year to foreign companies glad to offer kickbacks to customers and government officials abroad if it means closing a deal.

Another important change throughout the world that goes hand in hand with increasing free trade has been a strong trend toward industry deregulation so that industries once heavily regulated by the government are now allowed to compete freely with fewer restrictions. In the United States, deregulation of the airline industry allowed 29 new airlines to enter the industry. This has led to intense competition, fare wars, and the bankruptcy of numerous airlines. The same pattern has been seen in Europe. High-cost national airlines that used to have a monopoly in their own countries are being threatened by new low-cost airlines that are now allowed to carry passengers between any countries they choose as Business in Action illustrates.

Business in Action

A Battle for Control of European Skies

Ryanair, based in Dublin, Ireland, imitated and improved upon the low-cost business model pioneered by Southwest Airlines in the United States and used it to become a leading player in the European air market. Ryanair's CEO, the flamboyant Michael O'Leary, saw how he could use the specific strategies Southwest had developed to cut costs. Today, Ryanair is positioned as the lowest-cost, lowest-priced airline in Europe.

The average cost of a Ryanair ticket within Europe is $48, compared to $330 on British Airways, and $277 on Lufthansa, which have long dominated the European air travel market. The result is that Ryanair now flies more passengers inside Britain than British Airways, and its share of the European market is growing as fast as it can gain access to new landing spots and buy the new planes needed to service its expanding route structure.

How has O'Leary managed to improve on Southwest's low-cost business model? By using every trick in the book to squeeze every cent out of Ryanair's cost

Ryanair CEO Michael O'Leary saw how he could use the cost-cutting strategies developed by Southwest Airlines to similarly position Ryanair in Europe.

structure. Ryanair imitated the main elements of Southwest's model such as using only one type of plane (the 737) to reduce maintenance costs, selling tickets directly to customers, and eliminating seat assignments and free in-flight meals. Ryanair also avoids high-cost airports like London's Heathrow airport, opting for smaller ones outside of big cities, such as Luton, its London hub.

This was just the beginning for O'Leary, however. To reduce cleanup costs, he eliminated the seat-back pockets in which passengers would throw trash. He also eliminated blankets, pillows, free sodas, snacks, and even "sick" bags—virtually everything passengers had come to expect on regular airlines. "You get what you pay for," is Ryanair's philosophy.

To implement his business model, O'Leary expects all Ryanair employees to also find ways to wipe out the small, incremental expenses associated with performing the tens of thousands of specific operations needed to run the airline. Using all of these tactics, Ryanair has been able to lower its costs to such an extent that no other European Airline can come close to touching its fares and still break even, let alone make a profit.

How have global competitors reacted to Ryanair's low-cost strategy? Some airlines, like British Airways, are not suffering because their strengths lie in the lucrative, higher-fare business segment of the market. However, other airlines like Italy's flagship airline, Alitalia, are close to bankruptcy; the Irish carrier Aer Lingus has had to cut its costs by 50% just to survive. Still other airlines have launched their own low-priced, low-cost subsidiaries, like United Airlines did when it created Ted to compete with Southwest Airlines in the United States. O'Leary says he expects other airlines to do the same in Europe, in which case the brutal price wars will continue.[5]

Challenges in the Global Environment

The challenge facing a multinational today is to develop a business model that results in superior profitability—one that allows it to extract the most profit it can by operating on a global scale. Figure 4.6 summarizes the process by which a company can take advantage of operating globally.

A company usually begins operating globally by transferring its domestic or domestically developed skills and know-how to a foreign market. Microsoft, for example, with its competence in the development of state-of-the-art software, has taken its expertise to countries around the world. Its foreign units or divisions then sell customers in those countries software specifically tailored to their local needs. In 2004, for example, Microsoft introduced a stripped-down version of Windows that could be sold at prices low enough to attract customers in India. Today, over 50% of Microsoft's revenue comes from its sales abroad. Similarly, McDonald's has established restaurants in most countries; its German stores sell beer, for example. Virtually all of Coca-Cola's sales growth is occurring in countries abroad because the company has already captured much of the U.S. market.

Usually, when a company decides to expand globally it locates in countries where economic and sociocultural forces create favorable conditions in which to make and sell its products. It then establishes a global network—a set of task and reporting relationships among its employees, managers, and operating units around the world to take advantage of those conditions.

global network A set of task and reporting relationships among managers, functions, and operating units around the world.

For example, to increase its efficiency a videogame maker like Sony might perform its assembly operations in Malaysia, which has low labor costs, locate its game design operations in the United States, which has skilled game designers, have its corporate

Figure 4.6
Profiting from
Global Expansion

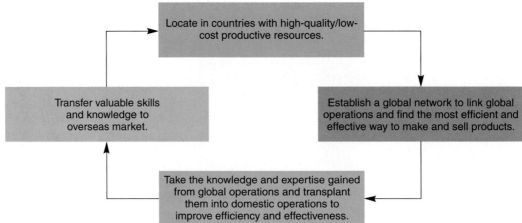

headquarters in Japan, where its top managers plan its business model, and buy the component parts and services it requires from whichever country is the lowest-cost source. Similarly, India has a plentiful supply of skilled IT workers, many of whom are employed as customer service reps by large multinationals like Sony, Dell and Microsoft. Dell, for example, recently moved over half of its customer service operations to India. In fact, Dell employs more people outside of the United States than within it.

Moreover, sometimes companies in one country have a certain kind of technological or manufacturing competency that gives them a competitive advantage. For example, Japan is known for its efficient manufacturing practices. So, a company can potentially benefit by establishing an operating unit in Japan in order to learn better manufacturing techniques. Many U.S. companies have done exactly this. Ford and GM have both purchased large stakes in various Japanese carmakers to get access to their skills and expertise.

After a company masters these new skills it can then transfer them to its domestic operations. By capitalizing on the strengths of its different plants around the world, it can continuously improve its overall operations. Having a global network in place also constantly exposes a company to new entrepreneurial opportunities it can seize upon. Next, we discuss these opportunities in light of the business-as-commerce, business-as-an occupation, and business-as-an organization framework introduced in Chapter 1.

Global Commerce Challenges

There are many ways in which a multinational company can profit from global expansion. Table 4.1 lists the 100 biggest multinationals by the size of their sales revenues. Four challenges that these, and all other, companies competing globally face are (1) building a global competitive advantage, (2) integrating the Internet into their business models, (3) managing ethically, and (3) incorporating the effects of differences in national cultures into their global planning and organizing.

BUILDING A GLOBAL COMPETITIVE ADVANTAGE   A multinational gains a competitive advantage by more efficiently and effectively producing goods or services customers around the world desire. The four main ways to increase efficiency and effectiveness are to improve a company's *productivity, quality, innovation,* and *responsiveness to customers* as shown in Figure 4.7.

Productivity, as discussed in Chapter 3, measures how efficiently a company is using its resources to make a product. This is measured by the company's *average cost* of production—the cost of making one unit of a particular kind of product. Suppose all companies charge a similar price for a particular product, say an entry-level car. The company that has the highest productivity and therefore the lowest costs has a competitive advantage. Toyota, for example, is the most productive carmaker in the world. None of its competitors can match its low costs, so this gives it a competitive

Table 4.1
Top 100 Multinational Companies

Rank	Company	Revenues ($ millions)	Profits ($ millions)
1	Wal-Mart Stores	287,989.0	10,267.0
2	BP	285,059.0	15,371.0
3	Exxon Mobil	270,772.0	25,330.0
4	Royal Dutch/Shell Group	268,690.0	18,183.0
5	General Motors	193,517.0	2,805.0
6	DaimlerChrysler	176,687.5	3,067.1
7	Toyota Motor	172,616.3	10,898.2
8	Ford Motor	172,233.0	3,487.0
9	General Electric	152,866.0	16,819.0
10	Total	152,609.5	11,955.0
11	Chevron	147,967.0	13,328.0
12	ConocoPhillips	121,663.0	8,129.0
13	AXA	121,606.3	3,133.0
14	Allianz	118,937.2	2,735.0
15	Volkswagen	110,648.7	842.0
16	Citigroup	108,276.0	17,046.0
17	ING Group	105,886.4	7,422.8
18	Nippon Telegraph & Telephone	100,545.3	6,608.0
19	American Intl. Group	97,987.0	9,731.0
20	Intl. Business Machines	96,293.0	8,430.0
21	Siemens	91,493.2	4,144.6
22	Carrefour	90,381.7	1,724.8
23	Hitachi	83,993.9	479.2
24	Assicurazioni Generali	83,267.6	1,635.1
25	Matsushita Electric Industrial	81,077.7	544.1
26	McKesson	80,514.6	−156.7
27	Honda Motor	80,486.6	4,523.9
28	Hewlett-Packard	79,905.0	3,497.0
29	Nissan Motor	79,799.6	4,766.6
30	Fortis	75,518.1	4,177.2
31	Sinopec	75,076.7	1,268.9
32	Berkshire Hathaway	74,382.0	7,308.0
33	ENI	74,227.7	9,047.1
34	Home Depot	73,094.0	5,001.0
35	Aviva	73,025.2	1,936.8
36	HSBC Holdings	72,550.0	11,840.0
37	Deutsche Telekom	71,988.9	5,763.6
38	Verizon Communications	71,563.3	7,830.7
39	Samsung Electronics	71,555.9	9,419.5
40	State Grid	71,290.2	694.0
41	Peugeot	70,641.9	1,687.8
42	Metro	70,159.3	1,028.6
43	Nestlé	69,825.7	5,405.4
44	U.S. Postal Service	68,996.0	3,065.0
45	BNP Paribas	68,654.4	5,805.9
46	China National Petroleum	67,723.8	8,757.1
47	Sony	66,618.0	1,524.5
48	Cardinal Health	65,130.6	1,474.5
49	Royal Ahold	64,675.6	−542.3
50	Altria Group	64,440.0	9,416.0

(continued)

Table 4.1 (continued)
Top 100 Multinational Companies

Rank	Company	Revenues ($ millions)	Profits ($ millions)
51	Pemex	63,690.5	−2,258.9
52	Bank of America Corp.	63,324.0	14,143.0
53	Vodafone	62,971.4	−13,910.4
54	Tesco	62,458.7	2,511.3
55	Munich Re Group	60,705.5	2,279.8
56	Nippon Life Insurance	60,520.8	1,886.3
57	Fiat	59,972.9	−1,972.6
58	Royal Bank of Scotland	59,750.0	8,267.4
59	Zurich Financial Services	59,678.0	2,587.0
60	Crédit Agricole	59,053.8	4,936.5
61	Credit Suisse	58,825.0	4,529.0
62	State Farm Insurance Cos	58,818.9	5,308.6
63	France Télécom	58,652.1	3,462.6
64	Électricité De France	58,367.2	1,667.9
65	J.P. Morgan Chase & Co.	56,931.0	4,466.0
66	UBS	56,917.8	6,509.5
67	Kroger	56,434.4	−100.0
68	Deutsche Bank	55,669.5	3,074.6
69	E.ON	55,652.1	5,396.7
70	Deutsche Post	55,388.4	1,975.1
71	BMW	55,142.2	2,763.6
72	Toshiba	54,303.5	428.4
73	Valero Energy	53,918.6	1,803.8
74	AmerisourceBergen	53,179.0	468.4
75	Pfizer	52,921.0	11,361.0
76	Boeing	52,553.0	1,872.0
77	Procter & Gamble	51,407.0	6,481.0
78	RWE	50,951.9	2,657.9
79	Suez	50,670.1	2,244.2
80	Renault	50,639.7	4,416.6
81	Unilever	49,960.7	2,333.3
82	Target	49,934.0	3,198.0
83	Robert Bosch	49,759.2	1,950.2
84	Dell	49,205.0	3,043.0
85	ThyssenKrupp	48,756.1	1,100.3
86	Costco Wholesale	48,107.0	882.4
87	HBOS	47,755.7	5,601.4
88	Johnson & Johnson	47,348.0	8,509.0
89	Prudential	47,055.8	765.9
90	Tokyo Electric Power	46,962.7	2,104.5
91	BASF	46,686.6	2,342.0
92	Hyundai Motor	46,358.2	1,472.6
93	Enel	45,530.4	3,522.3
94	Marathon Oil	45,444.0	1,261.0
95	Statoil	45,440.0	3,697.3
96	NEC	45,175.5	631.5
97	Repsol YPF	44,857.5	2,425.3
98	Dai-ichi Mutual Life Insurance	44,468.8	1,301.7
99	Fujitsu	44,316.0	296.9
100	Time Warner	42,869.0	3,364.0

Source: "The Global 500," *Fortune,* July 25, 2005.

**Figure 4.7
Building Global
Competitive
Advantage**

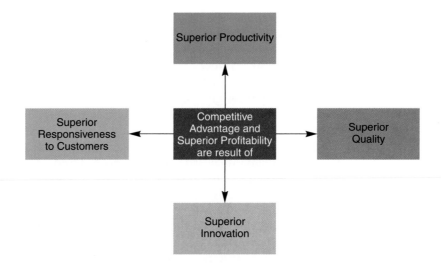

advantage that leads to superior profitability. To increase productivity companies need to find lower cost resources, and they must find new ways to perform global business activities at a lower cost.

Quality is a function of how well a product performs when it is put to use and is measured by such things as durability and reliability (how well the product works and how often it breaks down), and customer satisfaction (the consumer's perception of a product's value, given its price). Multinationals that can make higher-quality products relative to the average cost of producing them are effective because these products command higher prices and lead to higher profit margins. Also, over time higher-quality products attract more customers. This happened to Toyota after it entered the U.S. car market in the 1960s. Toyota began by selling a small, ugly, entry-level car at a low price. But as the quality of the car became apparent, demand for it soared. Toyota used its growing profits to continually improve its car design and quality, and its sales have continued to climb. Today, as Table 4.1 shows, its sales revenues are not much less than GM and Ford's, but its profitability is much higher.

Innovation, as you have learned, is a function of a company's ability to develop new and improved products that better satisfy customers' needs. This also increases a firm's effectiveness because when a product better meets the needs of customers, the demand for it increases. For example, Toyota, has consistently used its growing profits to create new kinds of vehicles to appeal to existing and new groups of customers. In the last decade it has introduced over 20 different kinds of vehicles in the SUV, family sedan, economy, and sports segments of the market. The automaker's new Matrix hatchback and Scion hybrid models designed to appeal to students and young people, for example, have become extremely popular. This was a market segment previously overlooked by other automakers. Innovation also involves finding ways to make products faster or at a lower cost. This leads to higher productivity and efficiency. Toyota also constantly searches for ways to improve the quality and reduce the cost of making its cars—which is why it locates its manufacturing plants in many different countries around the world.

responsiveness to customers A measure of a company's ability to anticipate changing customer needs, resolve problems customers have with a product, and provide fast after-sales service.

A company's responsiveness to customers is a function of its ability to better anticipate the changing needs of customers, resolve any problems they have with a product, and provide fast after-sales service. The greater a company's ability to respond to its customers' needs, the higher is its effectiveness. This increases the loyalty of existing customers and attracts new customers. Once again, Toyota is very responsive to customers. Even though the Toyota Camry is the best-selling family sedan in the market, Toyota has continued to improve its performance and reliability. Likewise, Subaru has excelled in the customer satisfaction area for many years. Its customer satisfaction levels rival those of Mercedes-Benz.

GLOBAL E-COMMERCE AND ELECTRONIC MARKETS   Today, most multinationals are finding ways to increase their efficiency and effectiveness by integrating

business-to-business (B2B) networks
Electronic markets that link suppliers to companies that assemble or manufacture products.

business-to-customer (B2C) networks
Electronic systems that connect companies that make finished products directly to the final customers who use them.

e-commerce into their global business models. Business-to-business (B2B) networks link suppliers (for example, suppliers of car parts or electronic components), to companies (automakers) that use them to make finished products. By contrast, business-to-customer (B2C) networks link "selling" companies, for example, the manufacturers of finished products such as cars or PCs, directly to the final customer.

B2B networks give multinationals better global access to low-cost raw materials, components, and labor. B2C networks help companies find new national markets and customers for their products. By making product information directly available to customers, the Internet has also expanded the size of the global marketplace for sellers. Companies like Amazon.com, eBay, Land's End, and E*Trade moved quickly to take advantage of the Internet to do just this, as described in Business in Action.

Additionally, by using the Internet, many companies have been able to bypass intermediaries like wholesalers or brokers and deal directly with companies abroad. As noted earlier, when buyers and sellers deal directly with each other they can buy and sell products at a lower price. Moreover, buyers who are able to choose from among a large number of global suppliers are also able to use their bargaining power to negotiate price discounts.

Business in Action

E-Commerce and Customer Responsiveness

The founders of U.S. dot.com companies like Amazon.com and eBay were quick to understand the potential of the Internet as a new way to reach customers and create a competitive advantage. These companies quickly built their virtual storefronts and began to offer their products to U.S. customers first. Amazon.com, for example, is the acknowledged leader in terms of designing an online storefront that offers customers an easy-to use, personalized shopping experience. The company's ability to provide customers with every book in publication at a low price wiped out thousands of small bookstores throughout the United States. Similarly, eBay's ability to create a place where buyers and sellers around the globe could exchange virtually any type of product (even bottled air) revolutionized the $300 billion-a-year auction business.

Given their appeal in the United States it seemed natural to dot.com managers that they should expand their companies globally. Because their U.S. storefronts were already up and running, they also believed they could do it quite inexpensively. All they would have to do is tweak these sites by making a few country-specific adjustments.

Amazon.com was particularly aggressive with its expansion plans. In 1996 it established an online bookstore in the United Kingdom, and in 1998, it entered the German market. Since then, it has entered countries such as Japan, France, and Australia. Similarly, E*Trade, the stock brokerage and banking company, entered the Japanese market and expanded into Europe.

But developing a successful global business model was much more difficult and expensive than the dot.coms anticipated. As Amazon.com discovered in the United States, having a successful virtual store is only one of many pieces of the puzzle. The need to create a sophisticated global purchasing and distribution network to get the product to the customer was also vital—and very expensive. Indeed, the enormous investment needed to establish its overseas operations drained Amazon.com's profits for several years. Similarly, E*Trade found that the need to customize its brokerage and banking services to the legal and tax regulations that

Amazon.com found that in order to be successful in the global marketplace, it not only needed a successful virtual store but also a global distribution network to get its products to customers.

differ from country to country was much more time consuming and costly than it expected.

The dot.coms that performed the best on a global level turned out to be catalogue-based sellers like Lands' End and Avon. These companies already had well-established overseas sales and distribution networks and were in a strong position to profit from them when they took their catalogues online. Other companies that also performed well were those whose products did not require a high investment in a physical business infrastructure. eBay, for example, merely provides an electronic platform that links buyers and sellers around the world. All the actual time and cost involved in shipping products globally is borne by the buyers and sellers.[6]

GLOBAL ETHICS Ethics are discussed in depth in the next chapter. It is important to note here, however, that most global business decisions have ethical and legal consequences. People in countries throughout the world are affected by multinationals whose headquarters are most commonly in the world's richest and most prosperous countries. The way that multinationals buy from and deal with overseas companies, and treat resources such as land and labor in different countries cannot be ignored. Their business practices can benefit or harm millions of people and whole nations.

As we have discussed, U.S. companies often obtain lower-cost raw materials or finished products by buying or making them in countries where labor costs are low. Low labor costs often mean, however, that people abroad, commonly women and children, are paid subsistence wages and work in "sweatshop" conditions. In countries with totalitarian governments, many of which are located in Central and South America, the Caribbean, Africa, Asia, the Middle East, and Eastern Europe, workers often have few or no rights and are mistreated. Is it ethical for multinationals and other U.S. companies to do business with such countries? At the same time, jobs at home, such as those in the U.S. clothing industry, are lost and people there suffer too. How should U.S. businesses behave when their actions can either help or harm different people and societies?

The environment is another ethical hotbed. Manufacturing costs may be low in other countries because no environmental laws exist to protect the environment. In the United States it is illegal to pollute the environment, and the safe disposal of toxic waste is a major expense for companies. If multinationals choose to operate in countries where few or no antipollution laws exist, they can avoid this expense. Some companies do pursue this course of action, polluting rivers, contaminating drinking water and the air, and dumping toxic waste near populated areas.

But it's not just undeveloped countries that are being polluted. Because few antipollution laws exist in Mexico, some U.S. companies ship their waste across the border to Mexico and simply dump it into the Rio Grande. But the waste sweeps out into the Gulf of Mexico and is currently destroying the rich shrimp beds off the U.S. Gulf coast and polluting U.S. beaches. Is this the right way to behave?

The way multinationals and we, as customers, behave determines the way global commerce takes place and the rules under which it operates. Every time you buy clothing, a new cell phone, or a CD take a look at where it is made. You will recognize how much the quality of your life, in terms of how much you can purchase, depends on the actions of people in other countries. What is your responsibility for these people? What is a multinational's responsibility toward them?

Moreover what is our responsibility to people in the United States? After all, pollution, sweatshops, and

Companies worldwide are looking for ways to capitalize on the global labor market in order to keep their costs down.

subsistence conditions also exist here. In fact, in 2005, almost 12% of U.S. citizens or 13.7 million people lived below the official U.S. poverty line, a line that is higher than that found in many other countries.

Increasingly, however, companies are realizing that corporate social responsibility isn't just a good idea; it also affects their profits. A few years ago, Nike generated a lot of bad press after it was revealed that the people who manufacture its expensive shoes work in sweatshops and earn just pennies on the dollar daily. Nike had to hire a public relations company to deal with allegations, and is still, to some extent, suffering from the fallout. Today, Nike polices its overseas manufacturers much more carefully and tries to ensure they are treated fairly.

Global Occupational Challenges

The expansion of international business has had many far-reaching effects on business occupations. The pace of occupational specialization and the division of labor has quickened as a result. In the computer sector, for example, globalization has led to the development of large pools of skilled IT workers in countries like India, China, and Russia, who are employed by multinationals. These workers are linked to their multinational employers via the Internet. Many software companies like Microsoft and Oracle employ programmers in the United States to write computer code during the normal eight-hour workday. After the workday is over, these programmers send their work via the Web to India where programmers there spend the next eight hours continuing work on the code. Workers in India then hand-off their work to programmers in Russia who work the next eight-hour shift. The result is around-the-clock computer code writing. This obviously speeds product development, but it also reduces costs because programmers in India and Russia are paid far less than programmers in the United States.

GLOBAL WORKFORCE CHALLENGES   The United States is the most diverse country in the world in terms of its ethnic, social, and religious makeup. But its diversity pales in comparison to the diversity of the global workforce. As a result, even a U.S. multinational can find itself overwhelmed by the challenge of managing people far and wide with very different backgrounds.

When a company expands globally a major occupational challenge is for its managers to learn to understand how the cultures of different nations vary from one another. As noted earlier, national culture is a product of the values and norms that people use to guide and control their behavior. To trade with companies in other countries it is vital that managers understand how the cultures of different countries differ. This allows them to better manage the global exchanges necessary to conduct business successfully.

Gaining such understanding is often difficult and complex. There are countless ways in which the perceptions, attitudes, beliefs, and values of managers vary from country to country. Effective global managers go to great lengths to learn about the particular countries in which they do business and often immerse themselves in their cultures to better understand their citizens. Languages differences, for example, pose some of the biggest hurdles. After exploring opportunities in China, U.S.-based ARCO Products, set up a language training to teach its managers Mandarin Chinese.

To help their managers understand how differences in national cultures affect business, multinationals are increasingly training and developing their U.S. managers to work and manage their business operations abroad. Expatriate managers are managers who both live and work for their companies abroad on assignments that can last for months or years. Expatriate managers are vital to multinationals. Frequently, these managers are responsible for transferring the multinational's

expatriate managers
Domestic managers who work for their companies abroad.

Did You Know?

"Even George Bush's (Made in America) baseball cap, the one only the commander in chief wears, [is] NOT made in America."[7]
–Caitlin Kiernan

MTV, based in New York, has benefited from the sharing of knowledge that goes on between its divisions around the world.

competencies to its worldwide divisions as well as recruiting and training foreign employees and setting up entirely new divisions. To do this well they have to understand the local economic, political, and cultural conditions of the countries in which they are doing business. In some sense, an expatriate manager is the multinational's "ambassador" in the country in which he or she works. He or she is the company's representative abroad, in other words.

In addition, expatriate managers in functions such as research and development and manufacturing are responsible for learning about the special skills and techniques developed by companies in the countries to which they are assigned. They are then expected to convey this knowledge to both the firm's foreign and domestic employees. GM, Motorola, Kodak, Xerox and many other U.S. companies sent thousands of their managers to Japan in the 1980s and 1990s to learn about the country's new low-cost manufacturing techniques. These companies then incorporated the Japanese techniques into their manufacturing operations, often improving them in the process. Expatriate managers are also frequently responsible for locating the lowest-cost inputs and places to assemble products throughout the world.

host-country nationals Natives of a foreign country hired to manage a multinational's divisions there.

In addition to hiring expatriates, multinationals, sometimes also hire host-country nationals (natives of the foreign country in which they are doing business) to manage their foreign divisions. Many companies will initially send expatriates abroad to set up an operation but then eventually turn it over to a host-country national to manage. This is generally far less expensive than relocating an expatriate to a foreign country, and it gives the firm a greater "local" presence, which local consumers like. Third-country nationals, managers who are neither native to the country the multinational is headquartered in nor the foreign countries in which it operates, are also sometimes hired. These people often live in nearby countries and can relocate more easily to the firm's foreign divisions. Usually a third-country national has previously worked in the foreign country to which he or she is assigned and is familiar with its culture, language, and business customs.

third-country nationals Managers who are neither native to the country the multinational is headquartered in nor the foreign country in which it operates.

Finally, many companies try to develop a better understanding of the countries in which they operate by recruiting and training people from those countries to work in their U.S. divisions. This allows them to create products that better fit the needs of their customers abroad. Products specifically designed by a multinational's employees abroad for its customers abroad are also being increasingly accepted by domestic customers. For example, MTV operates in countries like India, Germany, and so on. Many of the MTV shows developed in these countries have been slightly modified and successfully introduced in the United States. Often, fresh ideas arise because people in different countries look at things differently. This can be a source of many opportunities.

OCCUPATIONAL-SHIFT CHALLENGES As we discussed earlier, the expansion of global business is changing the supply and demand for different occupational groups both in the United States and abroad. In the United States the decline in manufacturing jobs because of global outsourcing, and the growth in jobs in IT and service occupations, has changed the makeup of the U.S. workforce. The changing nature of the occupational skills U.S. companies require because of globalization pose challenges for both companies and employees. In some sectors, companies are having an extremely hard time hiring employees with the skills they need. Boeing, for example, needs skilled engineers so badly it now recruits in most major countries around the world. Likewise, a nursing shortage in the United States has motivated many hospitals to begin recruiting medical employees in Mexico.

In terms of employees, as was mentioned, a huge number of U.S. manufacturing workers have been forced to change careers due to outsourcing, and many workers have been forced into lower-paying jobs in the service sector. The effects of global business on occupations have been far reaching and will continue to affect the kinds of skills required by workers the world over in the coming years.

Global Organization Challenges

As the discussion above suggests, the rise of multinationals and the growing use of new IT has changed the form of the business organization used to manage global business. In general, a company's method of organizing its global operations depends on the way it chooses to do business abroad, of which four forms are discussed next: exporting and licensing, using a global network, joint ventures, and creating wholly owned overseas subsidiaries.

exporting Selling domestically produced goods and services to customers in countries abroad.

licensing Contracting with companies in other countries in order to give them the right to use a company's brand name and business model.

network structure A system of task and reporting relationships based on the use of electronic ties that links suppliers, manufacturers, and distributors.

EXPORTING AND LICENSING   Many manufacturing companies simply choose exporting and sell domestically produced goods and services to customers in countries abroad. Service companies, on the other hand, often employ licensing: For a fee, they contract with companies located in other countries and grant them the right to use their brand names and business model. For example, a company like the Hilton or McDonald's might license the right to use its business name and operating expertise to a hotel or fast-food restaurant in India. In return the Indian company pays McDonald's or the Hilton a fee, often based on product sales in these countries.

NETWORK STRUCTURE   To avoid the high costs of operating abroad, some companies use a network structure, a system of task and reporting relationships based on the use of global outsourcing and B2B network. The network links a company's suppliers, manufacturers, *and* distributors to the final customer. Nike, for example, uses a network structure. Although its shoe design operations are performed at its headquarters in Beaverton, Oregon, other companies around the world perform other functional activities such as advertising, manufacturing, and distribution. Companies in Malaysia make shoe components, which are then shipped to India and other countries where the shoes are made. The finished shoes are then collected by global distributors who arrange for them to be shipped to countries around the world. A Madison Avenue advertising agency is in charge of Nike's global marketing campaign.

joint venture An alliance in which companies from different countries agree to pool their skills and resources to make and distribute a product together.

wholly owned subsidiaries Business units established in countries abroad to manufacture and distribute a multinational's products.

JOINT VENTURE   An increasingly popular way for companies to distribute and sell their products abroad is by entering into joint ventures with companies overseas. A joint venture is an alliance in which companies from different countries agree to pool their skills and resources to produce and distribute a product together. A company enters into a global joint venture to take advantage of an overseas company's knowledge of local customer tastes, sources of low-cost inputs, and the best channels of distribution for a product. In return, the overseas company can take advantage of the other company's advanced technology, or its skills in designing and making a product, such as Microsoft's world-class software development skills or Toyota's low-cost car manufacturing skills. By pooling their skills in a joint venture, each organization offers the other something that would otherwise be very expensive to obtain, and both companies gain. For example, in the 1990s Kodak and Chinon teamed up to manufacture digital cameras that are made in Japan and sold in the United States under the Kodak brand name.

Did You Know?

YKK on the zipper of Levi's jeans stands for YKK Corporation, the world's largest zipper manufacturer headquartered in Tokyo, Japan. Their expertise for understanding fasteners extends to architecture as well as fabric–they also make windows and doors.[8]

WHOLLY OWNED SUBSIDIARIES
When multinationals want to retain complete control over their activities, they establish wholly owned subsidiaries to manufacture and distribute their products in countries abroad. Wholly owned subsidiaries are most commonly created when a multinational wants to protect its

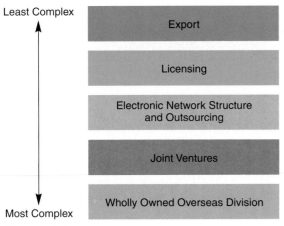

Least Complex

Most Complex

Figure 4.8
Forms of Global Organizing

product quality, manufacturing methods, and trade secrets. In a joint venture, a company must share its skills with the company overseas, so there is a danger that the partner might take this knowledge and "go it alone" in the future. In fact, to avoid this problem Kodak took full control over Chinon in 2001, and it is now one of Kodak's wholly owned subsidiaries.

To protect their technology or their product's reputation, many companies such as IBM and Daimler-Benz establish their own foreign divisions so that they have complete control over the distribution, sale, and after-sale service of their products in foreign countries. The biggest problem with establishing operating divisions in foreign countries is that the more manufacturing plants a company has, the more it costs to operate them—something Nestlé found out the hard way. Nevertheless, these high costs are often offset by the lower labor costs and the huge revenues companies can earn by selling their products in these markets. Managing a multinational company is a complicated process. Companies frequently change their organizing methods in search of methods that give them the biggest advantage and lead to the most profits. Figure 4.8 outlines the various methods and relative complexity of each.

Summary of the Chapter

The global environment of business today is characterized by forces of all kind—economic, demographic, and so on—that affect the profitability of companies and industries and the prosperity of the countries and world regions in which they operate. From the perspective of commerce, occupation, or organization, the business system evolves to take advantage of the new opportunities that arise in the global environment as a result of these changes. This chapter made the following major points:

1. Multinational companies are companies that operate and trade in many different countries around the world. Some multinationals have grown so large they can affect the well-being of the countries in which they do business. A country's government controls the political system that determines the set of laws, rules, and regulations that control the actions of people and businesses in a society. Almost all countries that are home to multinational companies have developed representative democracies.

2. The global environment is the set of forces surrounding a company that determine its ability to obtain productive resources—land, labor, capital, and enterprise.

3. Two kinds of forces in the environment that affect a company's profitability are the specific forces that directly affect a company's business model and the general forces that affect all types of companies engaged in global business.

4. Specific forces in the global environment are those that directly increase or decrease a company's sales revenues or operating costs, and thus its profitability. Four main specific forces are suppliers, distributors, competitors, and customers.

5. Four general forces affect multinationals' access to global resources and determine worldwide demand for their goods and services: political-economic, sociocultural, demographic, and legal forces.

6. The challenge facing a multinational is to develop a global business model giving it a competitive advantage over its rivals so it can achieve superior profitability.

7. Multinationals face three main challenges in managing global business commerce: (1) building global competitive advantage, (2) integrating the Internet into their business models, and (3) managing ethically.

8. Two principal occupational challenges facing global business are managing a diverse workforce and recruiting employees with the skills they need when the occupational mix changes.

9. Four principal methods of global organizing are exporting and licensing, using a network structure, joint ventures, and establishing wholly owned subsidiaries.

Developing Business Skills

QUESTIONS FOR DISCUSSION AND ACTION

1. Go the Web site of a large multinational company (see the list in Table 4.1). Search for information about the way that the company describes its global operations and activities.

2. What are the different specific and general forces in the global environment the company is facing?

3. What role do intermediaries play in business commerce and how is that role changing?

4. Think of three kinds of changing global sociocultural forces affecting the way companies in the United States and abroad do business.

5. What is a global network and how does it help a company to build global competitive advantage?

6. Discuss three ways in which information technology and global e-commerce affect the way multinationals operate.

7. Why would a company prefer to use a wholly owned subsidiary, rather than joint venture to organize its global business activities?

ETHICS IN ACTION

Protecting People and Their Jobs

There are many laws governing the way companies in the United States should act to protect their employees and to treat them in a fair and equitable manner. These laws make many kinds of unethical behaviors illegal, yet many countries abroad do not have similar laws and treat employees in ways that would be unacceptable in the United States. Using the information in the chapter, what is your view of the following issues?

- In Pakistan and India it is common for children as young as eight years old to weave the handmade carpets and rugs that are exported to Western countries. Many of these children work for a pittance and are losing their eyesight because of the close attention they have to devote to their task, often for twelve hours a day. Do you think these children should be employed in such occupations? Do you think it is ethical to buy these rugs?

- Millions of U.S. workers in manufacturing industries have lost their jobs because companies have moved their operations to low-cost countries abroad. Many women and children now do these jobs and work long hours for low wages. Do you think it is ethical for multinationals to operate just on the basis of where they can obtain low-cost resources?

- Debate the advantages and disadvantages of passing laws to prevent multinationals from locating abroad.

SMALL GROUP EXERCISE

How to Make a Snowboard?

Read the following, then break up into groups of three to four people and answer the questions below. Be prepared to share your answers with the entire class.

You are the owners of a small sporting goods company that has obtained a patent on a revolutionary new kind of snowboard that is easier and much safer to use than those currently on the market. You have had great success in selling your new snowboard to ski shops in the United States, but you want to take advantage of the large potential market for your product in Europe. You have to decide which global business model will best allow you to profit from your invention. You are debating two possible alternatives. The first is to export your product to Europe and enter into joint ventures with European sporting companies to handle the overseas distribution, marketing, and sale of your product. The second alternative is to take the plunge and invest your U.S. profits to create a wholly owned subsidiary in Europe. You would then create your own distribution and sales operations in each European country. This alternative might result in the highest potential profits, but it is an expensive proposition.

1. What kinds of information do you need to collect about the specific forces in the European snowboarding environment to help you to make your decision?

2. What are the pros and cons associated with each of the two alternatives proposed, given the nature of the environment and the nature of your product?

3. Which alternative is the one you will pursue? Why?

DEVELOPING GOOD BUSINESS SENSE

Selling in Southeastern Asia

Imagine that you are an experienced salesperson who works for a multinational pharmaceuticals company. Your company wants to promote you and has offered you a position as an expatriate manager in charge of its sales operations in South-Eastern Asia. This job will require frequent travel between the many different countries in this world region as you oversee its local sales operations, build an effective sales model, and help train the local salesforce.

1. What kinds of information do you need to collect about the specific environment in Southeastern Asia to help you perform effectively in your job?

2. What kinds of information do you need to collect about the general environment in Southeastern Asia to help you perform effectively in your job?

3. Now that you have this information, how will you use it to (1) decide on the most effective approach to selling your products to Asian customers; (2) decide on the most effective way to motivate and reward the local salesforce who are almost all nationals from countries within your region.

EXPLORING THE WORLD WIDE WEB

Fuji's Global Film Empire

Go to Fuji Films Web site (http://home.fujifilm.com)and then click on corporate, profile, and global operations and read about Fuji's global activities. **For more Web activities, log on to www.mhhe.com/jonesintro.**

1. How would you characterize the way Fuji manages the global environment? For example, how has Fuji responded to the needs of customers in different countries?

2. How has increasing global competition and declining barriers of distance and culture been affecting Fuji's operations?

BusinessWeek   CASE FOR DISCUSSION

Global Aging

Jenny François doesn't have the world's most glamorous job. For 20 years she has commuted 45 minutes to the office of insurer Macif in Agen, France, where she punches data from insurance forms into a computer. But in the not-too-distant future, François and hundreds of millions of people like her in the industrialized world could look back at the early twenty-first century as the beginning of the end of a wonderful era, when even average workers could retire in reasonable comfort in their still-vigorous 50s. Thanks to France's generous pension system, François, 58, is in "pre-retirement." For the past three years she has worked just two days a week and still collects $1,500 a month—more than 70% of her old full-time salary. Her pay will decline only slightly when she reaches 60. "The system is great for me," François says, "and I think it should be every worker's right."

Lower Living Standards

It's already clear that the system will be far less generous to future retirees in France and elsewhere. And the message isn't going down easy. To avert a looming fiscal crunch, President Jacques Chirac's government in 2003 enacted new rules requiring people to work longer to qualify for benefits. The government endured a national wave of strikes. Italy and Germany also witnessed massive protests after their governments proposed similar measures. Despite electoral setbacks, Japanese Prime Minister Junichiro Koizumi still vows to ram through proposals to hike pension taxes from around 14% of pay to 18% by 2017 and to slash benefits from 59% of average wages now to 50%. In the United States, the political debate is just starting to heat up over President George W. Bush's proposal to let workers park some of their Social Security contributions in personal investment accounts. Finland, South Korea, Brazil, and Greece all have recently moved or proposed to trim benefits, extend retirement ages, and hike workers' pension contributions.

The rollback of pension promises is just one symptom of one of the greatest sociological shifts in history: The graying of the baby-boom generation. The ranks of 60-year-olds and older are growing 1.9% a year—60% faster than the overall world population. In 1950 there were 12 people aged 15 to 64 to support each one of retirement age. Now the global average is nine. It will be only four-to-one by mid-century, predicts the UN Population Div. By then the elderly will outnumber children for the first time. Some economists fear this will lead to bankrupt pensions and lower living standards.

That's why even more cutbacks in retirement benefits are likely. "I don't even want to think about my children's pensions," says Lina Iulita, 72, referring to Italy's hugely underfunded system. "There won't be enough money coming in." In Iulita's town of Dormeletto, on the shore of Lake Maggiore, coffee bars are jammed with seniors. The town's over-75 population has doubled since 1971, and there are one-third fewer children under 6. Local schools and gyms have closed, while senior citizens' clubs are flourishing.

The trend has drawn the most attention in Europe and in Japan, where the working-age population will decline by 0.6% this year. By 2025 the number of people aged 15 to 64 is projected to dwindle by 10.4% in Spain, 10.7% in Germany, 14.8% in Italy, and 15.7% in Japan. But aging is just as dramatic in such emerging markets as China—which is expected to have 265 million 65-year-olds by 2020—and Russia and Ukraine. Western European employers won't be able to count on the Czech Republic, Hungary, and Poland for big pools of low-cost workers forever: They're aging just as quickly. Within 20 years, East Asia's dynamic tigers will be youthful no longer. South Korea, Thailand, Taiwan, Singapore, and Hong Kong will have a median age of 40. Indonesia, India, Brazil, Mexico, the Philippines, Iran, and

Egypt will still boast big, growing pools of workers for two decades. But they're on the same demographic curve and will show the effects of an aging population a generation or two later. "The aging workforce is the biggest economic challenge policymakers will face over the next 20 years," says Monika Queisser, a pension expert at the Organization for Economic Cooperation & Development.

The same basic factors are driving this shift: declining fertility and longer lifespans. Both are signs of enormous progress in the twentieth century. With rare exceptions—such as impoverished Sub-Saharan Africa—birth control and better opportunities for women have lowered birth rates from five or six children per female in the 1950s to as few as one or two today. A fertility rate of 2.1 is seen as the population breakeven point. Over the same period, great advances in health care have added two full decades to the world's average life span, to age 66 now.

For most of the postwar era, the combination of baby booms, healthier populations, and smaller families amounted to what economists call the "demographic dividend," a tremendous, once-only chance to spur rapid development in nations with the right pro-growth policies. As boomers flooded into the workforce—first in the West and Japan, then Latin America and East Asia—they provided the labor for economic takeoffs. Then, as they became parents, boomers had fewer children. So adults had more money to spend on goods and services and invest in their families' education.

But analysts and policymakers are starting to obsess over the flip side of the story: What happens when the baby boom becomes the geezer glut? How successfully this transition is managed around the world could determine the rise and fall of nations and reshape the global economy. Two key ingredients of growth are increases in the labor force and productivity. If countries can't maintain the size of their labor forces—say, by persuading older workers to retire later, getting stay-at-home wives to find jobs, or taking in more immigrants—they must boost productivity to maintain current growth levels. That will be a particular challenge in Europe, where productivity growth has averaged just 1.3% since 1995.

By these measures the United States is in relatively healthy shape despite the hand-wringing over Social Security and Medicare. Because of a slightly higher fertility rate and an annual intake of 900,000 legal immigrants, America's population should grow from 285 million now to 358 million in 2025. And the U.S. median age will rise just three years, to 39, over the next quarter-century, before the aging of America really starts to accelerate. The U.S. also has one of the world's most diversified retirement systems, including Social Security, company pensions,

401(k) savings plans that are largely invested in stocks, and private retirement insurance policies.

Nations with insolvent pension systems or insufficient private nest eggs, meanwhile, could face "an unprecedented societal crisis," warns OECD Secretary General Donald J. Johnston. Analysts say pension systems in Europe, Asia, and Latin America will start running into serious funding problems in a decade or two. Further down the road, some economists fear inadequate retiree savings will lead to lower consumption and asset values. The McKinsey Global Institute predicts that by 2024, growth in household financial wealth in the United States, Europe, and Japan will slow from a combined 4.5% annual clip now to 1.3%. That will translate into $31 trillion less wealth than if the average age were to remain the same. Higher productivity would help, says McKinsey Global Director Diana Farrell. But without radical changes in labor and pensions, U.S. output per worker would have to be at least twice as high as the 2.6% McKinsey projects for the next decade, in part because workers will be a smaller portion of the population. "You would need numbers way north of what we can reasonably expect," says Farrell.

The Future Is Now

From Stockholm to Seoul to Santiago, policymakers are seeking to boost private savings in stock and bond funds, lure young immigrant workers, find cheaper ways to provide elder care, and persuade companies to hire or retain older workers. On their own, none of these approaches is seen as a practical solution: Germany would have to more than double its annual intake of 185,000 foreigners to make up for fewer births, while immigration to Japan, now just 56,000 a year, would have to leap elevenfold. And slashing pensions enough to guarantee long-term solvency would mean political suicide. But a combination of sensible changes might make a big difference.

Developing nations with young and growing populations, meanwhile, face other issues. India is on pace to catch up and pass China's 1.4 billion population in three decades, for example. The trouble is, 40% of Indians drop out of school by age 10. Efforts to greatly expand education could determine whether India is a future economic superpower or if it will be burdened with the world's biggest population of poor illiterates. In Iran, an explosion of educated youth now joining the workforce could fuel a takeoff—or foment political strife if there are no jobs.

Why the sudden attention to a demographic trend that has been obvious for decades? In part, it's because the future is already dawning in many nations. In South Korea and Japan, which have strong cultural aversions to immigration, small factories, construction companies, and health clinics are relying more on "temporary" workers from the Philippines, Bangladesh, and Vietnam. In reality they are becoming permanent second-class citizens. In China's northern industrial belt, state industries are struggling over how to lay off unneeded middle-age workers when there is no social safety net to support them.

Across Europe, meanwhile, baby boomers such as Jenny François in France are retiring in droves— even though the first of this generation won't reach 65 until 2011. Most of Europe's state-funded pension systems encourage early retirement. Now, 85.5% of adults in France quit work by age 60, and only 1.3% work beyond 65. In Italy, 62% of adults call it quits by age 55. That compares with 47% of people who earn wages or salaries until they are 65 in the United States and 55% in Japan. With jobless rates still high, there's been little urgency to change. "I feel like I am in good enough shape to work, but there isn't enough work to go around," says Uwe Bohn, pouring a cup of coffee in his 12th-floor apartment in a drab Berlin high-rise. Bohn, 61, retired four years ago after losing his civil-engineering job and failing for years to find steady work.

Dire Math

Some European countries are making progress. In Finland, new government and corporate policies are boosting the average retirement age. No longer is Italian home-appliance maker Indesit coaxing older workers to retire early to make room for younger recruits. Instead, it's teaching its over-50 staff in its seven Italian factories new skills, such as factory and supply-chain management. So far the program is going smoothly, says Indesit human-resource director Cesare Ranieri. Luxembourg-based steelmaker Arcelor, which until 1991 offered early retirement at 92% of pay at age 50, says it has more than doubled productivity since raising the age to 60. Among other things, it hiked salaries for veterans who agreed to extra training and made it easier for them to work part time. "The policy proved very successful," says Arcelor human-resources manager director Daniel Atlan.

What really has pushed aging to the top of the global agenda, though, are ballooning fiscal gaps in the United States, Europe, Japan, and elsewhere that could worsen as boomers retire. While U.S. Social Security is projected to remain solvent until at least 2042, the picture is more dire in Europe. Unlike the United States, where most citizens also have private savings plans, in much of Europe up to 90% of workers rely almost entirely on public pensions. Benefits also are generous. Austria guarantees 93% of pay at retirement, for example, and Spain offers 94.7%. Without radical change, pensions and elder-care costs will jump from 14% of industrial nations' gross domestic product to 18% in 35 years, warns Washington's Center for Strategic & International Studies.

Fortunately, the global public appears to be bracing itself for rollbacks. Polling agency Allensbach reports that 89% of Germans don't believe their pensions are safe, up from 63% a decade ago. Surveys of workers 25 and over by Des Moines financial-services provider Principal Financial Group found that just 26% of French and 18% of Japanese are confident that their old-age system will pay the same benefits in the future as today.

Japanese workers such as Yumiko Wada certainly aren't in denial. "Old people today get a quite a good pension, so they don't have a problem," says Wada, 30, an office employee in Tochigi. "But I wonder who will support us when we get old." Shunichi Kudo, 35, a salesman at a Fukuoka map-publishing house, says he agrees with Koizumi's plan to raise premiums and lower retiree benefits. "It's going to be difficult, and I don't like it, but I understand why it's happening," Kudo says.

The basic math of Japan's demographic profile is dire. Already, 17 of every 100 of its people are over 65, and this ratio will near 30 in 15 years. From 2005 to 2012, Japan's workforce is projected to shrink by around 1% each year—a pace that will accelerate after that. Economists fear that, besides blowing an even bigger hole in Japan's underfunded pension system, the decline of workers and young families will make it harder for the nation to generate new wealth: Its potential annual growth rate will drop below 1%, estimates Japan Research Institute Ltd. chief economist Kenji Yumoto, unless productivity spikes.

Shoring up public pensions is hardly the only avenue nations are exploring. In developing countries, privately managed savings accounts have been the rage. Two decades ago, nearly every Latin American nation had pay-as-you-go systems like Social Security, but more generous. Some granted civil servants retiring in their 50s full salaries for life. Widening budget deficits changed that. In 1981, Chile replaced its public system with retirement accounts funded by worker contributions and managed by private firms. Urged to follow suit by the World Bank, 11 other Latin nations introduced similar features. The movement also spread through Eastern Europe. The upsides have been enormous: Chile helped plug a big fiscal budget deficit, has mobilized $49 billion of pension-fund assets that make it easier for companies and governments to fund investments in the local currency with bond offerings, and most workers have some retirement benefits. Mexico and other Latin nations have seen similar payoffs.

Privatization alone is no panacea, however. For starters, private managers charge fees that often devour one quarter of workers' funds—prompting calls for fee limits and greater regulation. Also, private funds are leaving many workers virtually uncovered, either because they don't contribute much or work in the so-called informal sector of small, unregistered businesses. In Mexico, only 38% of the 32.6 million accounts are active, receiving monthly deposits from workers, employers, and the government. Of Brazil's 68 million workers, meanwhile, 56% are in the informal economy and get no pensions beyond their own savings. What's more, the pension system for private-sector workers already runs $9 billion in the red each year. As for Brazil's 1.2 million civil servants, they still collect generous benefits and retire early. Yet the public system runs $10 billion deficits, and civil servants have thwarted attempts to scale back.

The challenge of providing for the elderly is especially urgent in the world's two biggest nations—India and China. Only 11% of Indians have pensions, and they tend to be civil servants and the affluent. With a young population and relatively big families, many of the elderly can still count on their children for support. That's not the case in China. By 2030, there will be only two working-age people to support every retiree. Yet only 20% of workers have government- or company-funded pensions or medical coverage.

Pension and medical reform. Later retirement. Higher productivity. More liberal immigration. Around the world, governments and businesses are searching for creative policies in each of these areas as they come to grips with one of the most profound social transformations in history. "Right now all of these issues are being dealt with piecemeal," says Ladan Manteghi, international affairs director for the Association for the Advancement of Retired Persons' global aging center. It all adds up to a big agenda—one that will determine whether the global economy that achieved such astounding progress in the youthful twentieth century will continue to prosper as it matures in the twenty-first.

QUESTIONS

1. Why is aging becoming a major demographic force, and how will it affect the future prosperity of countries around the world?

2. In what kinds of ways could multinationals help countries solve some of these problems?

3. How is the United States responding to these problems?

Pete Engardio and Carol Matlack, "Global Aging," *BusinessWeek Online*, January 31, 2005.

BusinessWeek   CASE FOR DISCUSSION

Here Comes China, the Chipmaker

Three years ago, semiconductor giant Texas Instruments seemed to have run out of options. As chip technology took another leap, it needed to spend $300 million to $400 million to upgrade its factories. An alternative: Look for a contract chip manufacturer willing to spend on a new production line to finish TI's semiconductors.

But it found no takers. Established manufacturers such as Taiwan Semiconductor, United Micro Electronics, and Chartered turned up their noses because TI had an unusual request. It wanted to half-finish the chips in its Dallas plant, then complete them at another company's foundry, says Tom Thorpe, TI's vice-president for external manufacturing. Foundries typically do only whole-chip production because it means fatter profits.

But a Chinese newcomer, Shanghai-based Semiconductor Manufacturing International, was willing to take the risk. Like most Chinese chipmakers, it was "young and hungry," says Thorpe. Now, the two companies are inseparable. In future years, SMIC is likely to reap a bigger slice of TI's business.

LOOKING HOMEWARD. It's also likely to cut into the business of other big-name chipmakers. The Chinese are flexing their youthful muscles due to many factors, both global and local. For one, domestic demand is skyrocketing. This year, China is expected to use $34.3 billion worth of semiconductors, making it the world's largest chip market, according to chip consultancy IC Insights in Scottsdale, Arizona.

Today, most of those chips are imported. But it's financial common sense for companies catering to China to produce semiconductors locally. Since TI's aggressive effort paid off, expect other companies to be a lot more willing to couple with a Chinese manufacturing partner.

China's chip industry has come of age very fast. Its first semiconductor-only foundries went online four to five years ago. Local makers seemed doomed from the start because various international laws prohibit companies from sending their advanced chip-manufacturing technologies to China. The new industry appeared destined to produce nearly obsolete chips, essentially, to pick up low-end crumbs falling from the table of chipmaking heavyweights like Taiwan Semiconductor.

"MAINSTREAM CHOICE." Four years later, Chinese chipmakers are at the back of no one's line. Their prices are cheaper, typically 10% to 20% below competitors. Often subsidized by the Chinese government and able to take massive losses, these "foundries are willing to sell stuff just as long as they cover their variable costs," says Len Jelinek, an analyst with the electronics industry consulting firm iSuppli in El Segundo, California.

That's allowing Chinese foundries such as SMIC, Shanghai SIM-BCD, Jilin Sino-Microelectronics, and CSMC Technologies to gain prominence and market share. Already, SMIC "is emerging as a mainstream choice," says Jelinek. "In the past, customers went to UMC and Taiwan Semiconductor."

China produced about $2.4 billion worth of chips last year. In 2003, it accounted for 4% of world production. But by 2007, it should more than double that, to 9%, Jelinek estimates. And this could be conservative. China's market-share gains are expected to increase this year, with global demand for chipmaking capacity growing a lot more slowly than in 2004. As that happens, foundries will compete even more on price, where the Chinese, with lower labor costs and government subsidies, have an advantage.

PROFIT SQUEEZE. Already, many major semiconductor manufacturers are building plants in China as well as placing orders with local foundries. Taiwan Semiconductor opened a Chinese plant in October. STMicroelectronics, together with joint-venture partner Hynix, hopes to launch a China plant by the second half of this year. "You have to produce where your customers are," says Laurent Bosson, corporate vice-president for manufacturing at Geneva-based STMicro. "China is becoming the manufacturing workshop of the whole world."

China's lower prices could pressure the entire chip industry. Chipmakers that don't produce there will suffer as their rivals come out with lower-cost products, says Joanne Itow, an analyst at chip consultancy Semico Research in Phoenix.

Of course, the Chinese won't be able to offer dirt-cheap prices for too long. Many local chipmakers would like to go public, and investors won't accept massive losses as the government does. Customers also look for more than low cost: "Price is just one of the factors," says Chuck Byers, director of worldwide brand management for Taiwan Semiconductor in San Jose, California. "Customers come to us for quality and reliability." By going to China, companies still face an increased risk of delays and glitches.

Still, with glitches less common, what was a small slice of business could multiply many times.

QUESTIONS

1. In what ways are Chinese chipmakers altering the specific forces in the global environment?

2. How are multinational chipmakers responding to the threat of Chinese competition?

Olga Kharif, "Here Comes China, the Chipmaker," *BusinessWeek Online*, January 11, 2005.

BusinessWeek CASE FOR DISCUSSION

The High-Tech Threat from China

The news is full of headlines about China—its rising trade surplus, ballooning currency reserves, relentless search for oil, and its tensions with the United States over textiles and intellectual property rights. But one development has been seriously underreported: China's emergence as a technological superstate. Could Beijing pose a threat in the one area where the United States has assumed it would always retain supremacy?

Since 1985, China has repeatedly declared its resolve to reach technological parity with the West. Between 1992 and 2002, the latest period for which figures are available, Beijing has more than doubled the proportion of gross domestic product it spent on research and development, while the level stagnated in America. China boosted its output of PhDs in science and engineering by 14% a year, while the number of U.S. grads fell. Its technology-intensive exports grew by 22% annually, while exports of U.S. high-tech goods have declined. Today, moreover, while American universities award 25% of all their PhDs in science and engineering to Chinese citizens, Beijing is sparing no effort to lure many back. Among China's research and development priorities are superscale integrated circuits, computer software, and information security systems.

Western companies are speeding up China's advancement by establishing huge research and development facilities there. General Electric has 27 labs in China working on projects from composite-materials design to molecular modeling. Microsoft has nearly 200 researchers in the country. Cisco, DaimlerChrysler, IBM, Intel, and many others are following suit.

Experts are split on the implications of the globalization of research and development. In a forthcoming report, for example, Nicholas Lardy of the Institute for International Economics downplays China's technological position by pointing to the relatively low sophistication of even its high-tech exports, its heavy dependence on imported technology, and the benefits that accrue to U.S. companies investing there. On the other hand, in an upcoming book, Ernest Preeg of the Manufacturers Alliance/MAPI is sounding alarms because of China's steep upward technological trajectory. In a recent study, Kathleen Walsh of the Henry L. Stimson Center calls for Washington to wake up to the economic and national security implications of China's growing research and development capabilities. And the National Science Foundation is upset by the decline in research funding and scientific education in America.

I fear that the U.S. hasn't come to grips with the implications of corporations doing so much research and development in China. U.S. companies are understandably seeking the best talent and lowest cost of operations anywhere. But in the process they are sharing America's intellectual treasures with a foreign rival in unprecedented ways. They are training foreign scientists and engineers and giving them and the omnipresent Chinese government access to their proprietary research programs.

To keep its undisputed technology lead, the United States must go beyond larger government-sponsored research budgets, better K-12 education, and closer government-business cooperation, all prescriptions made in the 1980s, when the United States last had a competitiveness debate. Now Washington must also figure out how to deepen basic research and development in America when so much is dispersed abroad. And it must adapt to the reality that U.S. multinationals' goals may no longer dovetail with national interests. I've not seen a way to achieve all the goals at the same time.

Intel Corporation. is illustrative. CEO Craig Barrett advocates more federally funded research, which would eventually benefit the country and the company. But Congress and the public have to wonder whether Intel should receive, in effect, subsidies if it then shares its know-how with Chinese partners. At the very least, a quid pro quo should be established. Intel's sharing of technology could enrich its shareholders, China's economy, and to some extent the United States. But unlike in the past, its goals no longer center on creating industries and jobs in the United States, which is what American taxpayers deservedly expect.

In the 1960s, Americans were galvanized by Sputnik, and in the 1980s they were spurred on by Japan Inc. As the challenge of remaining technologically superior becomes more complex, United States needs another shot of adrenaline. The perceived threat of China could supply it, but I worry that it won't be strong enough or soon enough.

QUESTIONS

1. In what ways does China's growing strength in basic research and development threaten the United States and other countries?

2. Do you think U.S. companies should continue to establish basic research facilities in China? Why or why not?

Jeffrey E. Garten, "The High-Tech Threat From China," *BusinessWeek Online*, January 31, 2005.

BUILDING YOUR MANAGEMENT SKILLS
Know Thyself

How often do you eat Italian, Mexican, Asian, or Indian food? Do you speak more than one language? Working in a global economy requires understanding and appreciation of other cultures and their systems. Do you like to learn different ways of doing things? Whether you find yourself in a different region of the U.S. or another country, it will help to know more about your attitudes and beliefs about others. The Student DVD has an exercise called "Appreciating and Valuing Diversity" to help you assess your thoughts, feelings, and actions toward those who are different than you are.

CHAPTER VIDEO
Peace Corps

In 1961, President John F. Kennedy, through Executive Order, established the United States Peace Corps. Forty three years later, the Peace Corps remains a strong organization that promotes cross cultural understanding through volunteerism. More than 170,000 volunteers have participated in the program serving over 135 countries.

The Peace Corps provides significant experience for individuals in preparing them for life and work in a global business environment. Business problems ranging from complex business strategy to bringing products to market, economics, productivity, and visibility are areas addressed by the volunteers as they provide assistance to people in other countries. Volunteers are provided training and development in key areas including language and socio-cultural components of different countries including aesthetics, attitudes and beliefs, religion, education, and legal and political elements.

Volunteers are given intensive training lasting from 9-12 weeks in the host country covering language through local cultural customs. The benefits of participation flow both ways, however. In addition to exposing American volunteers to different cultures, the diversity of volunteers helps to shape outsiders' perspectives of Americans.

The current director of the Peace Corps is the son of immigrant migrant workers from Mexico. His parents did not attend school beyond the seventh grade. Today, Gaddi H. Vasquez is the director of the Peace Corps, appointed by the President of the U.S. Vasquez is an example of the diversity that is America as we enter the 21st century.

1. What are the forces in the global environment that impact volunteers in the Peace Corps?

2. Of the broad forces in the global environment, which area does the Peace Corps have the most impact?

3. How would Hofstede's model assist the Peace Corp volunteer?

5 Business Ethics and the Legal Environment of Business

Learning Objectives

After studying this chapter you should be able to:

1. Understand the relationship between ethics and the law and appreciate why it is important to behave ethically.

2. Differentiate between the claims of the different stakeholder groups affected by a company's actions.

3. Identify the four main sources of business ethics, and describe four rules that can be used to help companies and their employees behave ethically.

4. Describe some methods companies can use to strengthen their ethical rules and positions.

5. Appreciate the important ways in which a nation's business laws and regulations affect business commerce, occupations, and organizations.

WHY IS THIS IMPORTANT ?

A friend who is an A-student has offered to write your paper, which is worth 25% of your grade, for $50. You need the course to graduate because you only have a low C average. You hate writing, do it very poorly, and know others have had good results submitting this student's papers as their own. Will you pay the money and submit the paper or submit your own paper and pray for a good result?

This chapter will help you learn how to act ethically when facing dilemmas in your business and personal life. This is important because the decisions you make will affect your own future and those of stakeholders of the organizations that employ you.

A Question of Business
How Different Ethical Stances Can Help or Harm a Company

How can companies ensure their managers and employees follow their ethical codes of conduct?

In 1982, managers at Johnson & Johnson (J&J), the well-known medical products company experienced a crisis. Seven people in the Chicago area had died after taking Tylenol capsules that had been laced with cyanide. J&J's top managers needed to decide what to do. The FBI advised them to take no action because the likelihood that supplies of Tylenol outside the Chicago area were contaminated was very low. Moreover, withdrawing the drug from the market would cost the company millions of dollars. J&J's managers were of a different mind, however. They immediately ordered that supplies of all Tylenol capsules in the U.S. market be withdrawn and sent back to the company, a move that eventually cost J&J more than $150 million.

In 1992, managers at Dow Corning (DC), a large pharmaceutical company that had pioneered the development of silicon breast implants, received disturbing news. An increasing number of reports from doctors throughout the United States indicated that many women who had received DC's silicon implants were experiencing health problems ranging from fatigue to cancer and arthritis due to ruptured implants. DC's managers believed that the available evidence did not prove that fluid leaking from the implants was the cause of these health

problems. Nevertheless, a few months later, DC's chairman, Keith McKennon, announced that the company was discontinuing its breast

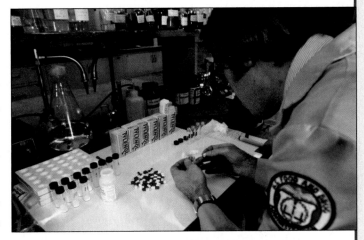

implant business and closing the factories that produced them.

Soon after DC's withdrawal from the implant business, it became known that a DC engineer had questioned the safety of silicon breast implants as early as 1976. In 1977, the engineer had sent top managers a memo summarizing the results of a study by four doctors who reported that 52 out of 400 implant procedures had resulted in ruptures. In response to a court order, the company eventually released this memo, along with hundreds of other pages of internal documents. Women filed hundreds of lawsuits against DC for knowingly selling a product that may have been defective. Lawyers accused DC of deliberately misleading the public and of giving women whose implants had caused medical problems false information to protect the interests of the company.

Dow Corning's ethical stance eventually cost the company billions in product liability claims. In fact, the size of these claims pushed the company into Chapter 11 bankruptcy, and it remained there for eight unprofitable years until 2004 when a judge accepted its plan to pay future damages to settle all the lawsuits against it and allowed it to resume full control of its business. Its managers' unethical behavior almost destroyed the company.

In 2002 the accounting giant, Arthur Andersen (AA) was found guilty of obstruction of justice for shredding documents related to its audits of the Enron Corp. Apparently, senior partners at AA, to hide evidence of its fraudulent auditing of Enron's accounts, ordered AA's middle managers to shred thousands of pages of accounting documents in an effort to hide AA's role in the Enron scandal.

When knowledge of AA's illegal actions became public in 2001, however, the company's reputation had already collapsed. Most of the companies it audited, such as Merck, Freddie Mac, and Delta Airlines had terminated their contracts with the company. After AA was convicted of obstruction of justice it lost its auditing license to practice accounting in the United States. With the collapse of their company, its partners and employees found themselves without jobs. They also lost much of the personal capital they had invested in the company. In this case, the unethical and illegal behavior of its managers and employees destroyed their company.

The behavior of DC and AA managers seemed out of character to many people. Both companies had widely publicized and well-developed internal ethics rules that were supposed to reign in and prevent unethical behavior. When confronted with a crisis, their ethics systems did not prevent either company's managers behaving unethically and illegally. J&J also had a system of ethical rules in place. At its center is a credo describing its ethical stance toward customers, employees, and other groups (see Table 5.2, p. 156). Why did J&J's credo lead its managers to act ethically while DC's and AA's did not?

One reason appears to be that J&J's managers believed in their company's ethical values, so that when confronted with an ethical dilemma as in 1982, they consistently followed the credo's rules when making business decisions. At DC and AA, in contrast, managers had been just "going through the motions." When push came to shove, they protected their own interests and those of their companies in illegal ways. Both companies paid the price. Within months of its decision to pull Tylenol from store shelves, however, J&J regained its status as leader in the painkiller market and has since increased its market share because of its enhanced reputation for being a highly ethical company.[1] •

Overview

As the behavior of Johnson & Johnson's, Dow Corning's, and Arthur Andersen's managers suggests, managers may interpret their responsibilities to their customers and to their organizations in very different ways. Johnson & Johnson moved immediately to protect the public even though there was little chance that any other supplies of Tylenol were contaminated. Dow Corning's managers postponed action and, to safeguard the profits of their company, did not confront the fact that their product was defective and dangerous. As a result, women continued to receive silicon breast implants, and the potential for harm increased. Arthur Andersen's managers intentionally committed illegal actions to protect their own interests. Their sole goal was to hide evidence of their wrongdoing at the expense of the public.

As the story of these companies suggests, an important ethical dimension is present in most kinds of business decision making. In this chapter, we examine the nature of the obligations and responsibilities a business has to the people and society affected by the way it operates. First, we examine the nature of ethics and the sources of ethical problems. Second, we discuss the major groups of people, called *stakeholders,* who are affected by business. Third, we look at four rules or guidelines that companies can use to decide whether a specific business decision is ethical or unethical. Fourth, we consider the sources of business ethics and the way companies can promote ethical behavior. Finally, we examine the legal environment of business and describe the many kinds of laws, rules and regulations that must be followed, both at home and abroad, if a company is to do business in an honest and ethical way. By the end of this chapter you will understand the central role that ethics plays in shaping the practice of business and the life of a people, society, and nation.

The Nature of Ethics

Suppose you see a person being mugged in the street. How will you behave? Will you act in some way to help even though you risk being hurt? Will you walk away? Perhaps you might adopt a "middle-of-the-road approach" and not intervene but call the police instead? Does the way you act depend on whether the person being mugged is a fit male, an elderly person, or even a street person? Does it depend on whether there are other people around, so you can tell yourself, "Oh well, someone else will help or call the police. I don't need to"?

Ethical Dilemmas

ethical dilemma
The quandary people experience when they must decide whether or not they should act in a way that benefits someone else even if it harms others and isn't in their own self-interest.

ethics The inner-guiding moral principles and values people use to analyze a situation and decide what is "right."

The situation described above is an example of an **ethical dilemma,** the quandary people find themselves in when they have to decide if they should act in a way that might help another person or group, and is the "right" thing to do, even though doing so might not be in their own self-interest. A dilemma may also arise when a person has to decide between two different courses of action, knowing that whichever course he or she chooses will result in harm to one person or group even though it may benefit another. The ethical dilemma here is to decide which course of action is the "lesser of two evils."

People often know they are confronting an ethical dilemma when their moral scruples come into play and cause them to hesitate, debate, and reflect upon the "rightness" or "goodness" of a course of action. Moral scruples are thoughts and feelings that tell a person what is right or wrong; they are a part of a person's ethics. Ethics are the inner-guiding moral principles, values, and beliefs people use to analyze a situation and decide what is "right." At the same time, ethics also indicate what inappropriate behavior is and how a person should behave to avoid doing harm to another person.

The essential problem in dealing with ethical issues, and thus solving moral dilemmas, is that there are no absolute or indisputable rules or principles that can be developed to decide if an action is ethical or unethical. Put simply, different people or groups may dispute which actions are ethical or unethical depending on their own personal self-interest and specific attitudes, beliefs, and values. How, therefore, are we and companies and their managers to decide what is ethical and act accordingly?

What would you do if you witnessed a mugging?

Ethics and the Law

The first answer to this question is that society as a whole, using the political and legal process, can lobby for and pass laws that specify what people can and cannot do. In the last chapter, for example, we examined the many different kinds of laws that exist to govern business. Laws also specify what sanctions or punishments will follow if those laws are broken.

Different groups in society lobby for laws to be passed based on what they believe is right or wrong. Once a law is passed, the decision about how to behave in a certain situation moves from the personally determined ethical realm to the socially determined legal realm. If you do not conform to the law, you can be prosecuted and punished.

Changes in Ethics over Time

Neither laws nor ethics are fixed principles cast in stone, however. Both change over time. As a society's ethical beliefs change, its laws change to reflect them. As we saw in Chapter 2, it was considered both ethical and legal to own slaves in ancient Rome and Greece and in the United States until the nineteenth century. Ethical views regarding whether slavery was morally right subsequently changed, however, and slavery was later outlawed.

In most societies today behaviors like murder, theft, slavery, and rape are considered unacceptable and prohibited. But many other kinds of behaviors are open to dispute when it comes to whether they are ethical or should be made illegal or not. Some people might believe that a particular behavior such as smoking tobacco or possessing guns is unethical and should be made illegal. Others might argue that it is up to individual people if they want to own guns or smoke. In the United States it is, of course, illegal to possess or use marijuana even though it has been shown to have many medical uses. Some cancer sufferers and AIDS patients find that marijuana relieves many of the side effects of medical treatment, like nausea and lack of appetite. Yet, in the United States, the Supreme Court has held that the federal government can prohibit doctors from prescribing marijuana to these patients, so their suffering goes on. By contrast in Canada there has been a widespread movement to decriminalize marijuana, and in other countries, marijuana is perfectly legal.

The point is laws can and do change as people's ethical beliefs change. For example, in Britain in 1830, there were over 350 different crimes for which a person could be executed, including sheep stealing. Today there are none. Capital punishment has been abolished. As you can see, both ethical and legal rules are *relative*: No absolute standards exist to determine how we should behave. Consequently, we frequently get caught in moral dilemmas and are continually faced with ethical choices. It is a part of life.

Companies and their managers are no different. Some make the right choices, while others do not. In the early 2000s, a rash of scandals occurred at major U.S. companies, including Enron, WorldCom, Tyco, Merrill Lynch, and others. Managers in some of these companies clearly broke the law and defrauded investors. In other cases, managers used legal loopholes to divert hundreds of millions of dollars in corporate money for their own use. At WorldCom, for example, former CEO Bernie Ebbers used his position to place six of his friends on WorldCom's 13-member board of directors. Obviously these six people voted in favor of Ebbers's recommendations to the board. As a result, Ebbers received huge stock options and a personal loan of over $150 million from WorldCom. In return, his supporters were well rewarded for being directors. Among other perks, Ebbers allowed them to use WorldCom's corporate jets for a minimal fee—something that saved them hundreds of thousands of dollars each year.

Although not all of the activities Ebbers and other corporate wrongdoers engaged in were illegal, this does *not* make these behaviors ethical. In many cases societies later pass laws to close the loopholes used by unethical people, such as Ebbers and Rockefeller, discussed in Chapter 2, who gain at the expense of others. But ordinary people, not just corporate executives make everyday decisions in the course of business about what is ethical and what is not. A case in point is the pirating of digital products using the Internet, as Business in Action discusses.

Do you think marijuana should be legalized, and, if so, under what circumstances? Do you think U.S. laws will eventually change to allow marijuana to be used more freely?

Business in Action

Is Digital Piracy Unethical? Or Just Illegal?

Today, almost all written text, music, movies, and software are recorded digitally and can be easily copied and sent between PCs via the Internet. Millions of people and companies have taken advantage of this to make illegal copies of music CDs, software programs, and DVDs. In 2003, for example, it was estimated that more than one-third of all CDs and cassettes around the world were recorded illegally. This is costing the music industry billion of dollars in sales revenues. As you can imagine, media industries have been doing everything they can to crack down on this practice, including shutting down Napster.

Shawn Fanning created Napster.com while he was an undergraduate student at Northeastern University. His roommate had got into the habit of downloading music from Internet sites using the MP3 format, which compresses digital files, making them faster to transmit and easier to store. Fanning watched his roommate search the Internet for new material, and he realized that there was an opportunity to create a software platform that would allow people to more easily locate and download digital music files. Fanning created the software needed to do this, and word about Napster and the enormous volume of music available for free on the site, quickly spread. Soon, hundreds of thousands of people were swapping and downloading music. Computer servers at a number of colleges actually shut down, overwhelmed by people downloading songs from Napster.

Obviously, companies in the music industry became desperate to stop this practice. Collectively, they sought a legal injunction to shut Napster down. Since it was clear that Napster was violating copyright laws, the courts stopped Napster from providing the free service. However, many other Internet sites quickly sprang up to fill the void. The music industry then successfully sought to have individual downloaders prosecuted.

Is swapping songs on the Internet really unethical? Why are so many people doing it if it is illegal? The obvious answer is that people are doing it for their own personal gain. Who, goes the argument, suffers anyway? Music companies have been making billions of dollars from music sales for decades. True, the songs might be the property of music stars like the Rolling Stones and Eminem, but these people are fabulously wealthy. Why, then, shouldn't the average person benefit from the new technology? After all, the pleasure gained by hundreds of millions of people is more important than the harm done to only a few thousand rich musicians and a handful of wealthy music companies. Therefore, copying is not *really* unethical. It may be illegal, but it's not actually such a bad thing to do—or is it?

Arguments like these may make people feel that their copying is doing no real harm to others, but the other side of this ethical dilemma also needs to be taken into consideration. What about the rights of artists and companies to profit from their own property—the songs, books, and movies that result from their creative endeavors? Those who claim the practice should be made illegal say that copiers should think about how they would react if someone tried to take *their* property away. Would they like it if a "poorer" person came along who believed, "They don't need all those appliances, cars, and jewelry? I'll just help myself; they'll never miss it"?

The fact is that those who steal digital media not only are weakening the rights of musicians and

One enterprise that music companies went after with a vengeance for digital piracy was Napster. Why do you think digital piracy is considered unethical?

writers to own property, they are also weakening *their* own personal rights to own property. Digital piracy is neither fair nor equitable. And, although each person that engages in it might argue that the pilferage doesn't have much of an effect because he or she is "only one person," if many people do it, it's clearly a problem. And that's exactly what's happening.

To illustrate the problem, suppose that by 2010, 75% of all music and movies are illegally copied rather than bought. What will musicians, music companies, movie stars, and movie studios do? If these people and companies cannot protect their property and profit from it, then they are not going to make or sell digital products. Over time, music and movie companies will cease to operate. Creative people will find new ways to make money. Musicians will make music only for their own pleasure or perform only in live concerts (where recording devices are not permitted). Fewer new songs and movies will be recorded, and the world will become a less interesting place to live in.[2]

Stakeholders and Business Ethics

Just as people have to work out the right and wrong ways to act, so do companies. When the law does not specify how companies should behave, their managers must make these decisions. Who are the people or groups affected by a company's business decisions? If a company behaves in an ethical way, how does this benefit people and society? Conversely, how are people harmed by a company's unethical actions?

The people and groups affected by the way a company does business are called its stakeholders. Stakeholders supply a company with its productive resources. As a result, they have a claim on and stake in the company. Because stakeholders can directly benefit or be harmed by its actions, the business ethics of a company and its managers are important to them. Who are a company's major stakeholders? What do they contribute to a company, and what do they claim in return? Next we examine the claims of these stakeholders–stockholders, managers, employees, suppliers and distributors, customers, the community, and the nation-state. These various stakeholders are shown in Figure 5.1.

stakeholders People or groups of people who supply a company with its productive resources and thereby have an interest in how the company behaves.

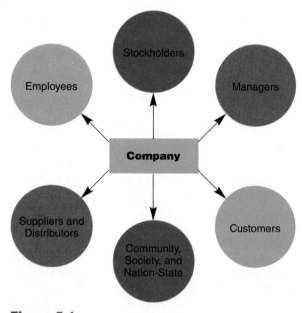

Figure 5.1
Types of Company Stakeholders

Stockholders

Stockholders have a claim on a company because when they buy its stock, or shares, they become its owners. This stock grants them the right to receive some of the company's profits in the form of dividends. And they expect to get these dividends. In 2003, for example, Microsoft had over $46 billion in cash on hand to fund its future operations. Under pressure from its shareholders, Microsoft declared a dividend of 31 cents per share be paid to the owners of its 5 billion shares. (Bill Gates received $100 million in dividends based on his own personal stockholdings.) Stockholders are interested in the way a company operates because they want to maximize their return on their investment. Thus, they watch the company and its managers closely to ensure they are working diligently to increase the company's profitability. Stockholders also want to ensure that managers are behaving ethically and not risking investors' capital by engaging in actions that could hurt the company's reputation and quickly bankrupt it. Once-mighty Enron took less than one year to fall after the covert actions of its top managers came to light. The Enron tragedy was brought about by a handful of greedy top managers who abused the trust of stakeholders. A number of pension funds that had invested heavily in Enron stock were especially hard hit, adversely affecting thousands of retirees. The collapse of Enron is also said to have precipitated the crash of the entire stock market in 2001, wiping out the savings of millions of Americans.

Managers

Managers are a vital stakeholder group because they are responsible for using a company's financial capital and human resources to increase its profitability and stock price. Managers have a claim on an organization because they bring to it their skills, expertise, and experience. They have the right to expect a good return or reward by investing their human capital to improve a company's performance. Such rewards include good salaries and benefits, the prospect of promotion and a career, and stock options and bonuses tied to the company's performance.

As we discussed in Chapter 3, managers must be motivated and given incentives to work hard in the interests of stockholders. Their behavior must also be scrutinized to ensure they do not behave illegally or unethically and pursue goals that threaten stockholders' (and employees') interests. Unfortunately, we have seen in the 2000s how easy it is for top managers to find ways to ruthlessly pursue their self-interest at the expense of stockholders and employees because laws and regulations were not strong enough to force them to behave ethically.

In a nutshell, the problem has been that in many companies, corrupt managers focus not on building the company's capital and stockholders' wealth but on maximizing their own. In an effort to prevent future scandals the Securities and Exchange Commission (SEC), the government's top business watchdog, began in 2003 to rework the rules governing a company's relationship with its auditor, as well as regulations concerning stock options, and to increase the power of outside directors to

Video Small Business in Action

Small Biz Power

Summary: As shown in this segment from *BusinessWeek TV* on your Student DVD, 99% of all US companies are considered small businesses. These small businesses are responsible for employing over 50% of the nation's employees. The segment features small businesses such as Oki Ton Restaurant in California. The restaurant has experienced tremendous success. The emphasis on "service" to the customer is seen as a key success factor.

The report shows that small business is thriving in a "down" economy while larger companies are not performing well. In recessionary economies, it appears that small businesses are most prevalent in the fastest growing segments of the economy and are virtually nonexistent in the declining segments. Service such as restaurants, convenience stores, and health care are seen as expanding areas where manufacturing characterizes the declining economic segments.

A recent survey found that small business owners are feeling optimistic about their future even in a less than robust economy. There are some states in the U.S. where that enthusiasm is not as robust. In California, for example, small business owners are not as positive as in other areas of the country. The state ranks as the 6th worst in the U.S. for small business. The principal reasons for this ranking are due to high property, income, and sales taxes as well as high energy costs.

Discussion Questions

1. Generally, who represent the significant stakeholder groups for small businesses?
2. What are the rules for ethical decision making for the small business owner/manager?
3. What are two types of law that are particularly relevant to a company's form of business organization?

scrutinize a CEO. The SEC's goal is to turn many acts that were only unethical behavior in 2003 into illegal behavior in the near future. Managers could then be prosecuted if they engage in these acts.

Many experts are also arguing that the rewards given to top managers, particularly the CEO and COO (chief operating officer), grew out of control in the 1990s. Top managers are the new "aristocrats" today. Via their ability to influence corporate boards and raise their own pay, they have amassed personal fortunes worth hundreds of millions of dollars. For example, in 1982 a typical CEO earned about 18 times as much as the average worker. By 2002 that number had risen to 2,600 times as much–a staggering increase. Michael Eisner, the CEO of Disney, has received over $800 million in Disney stock options. Jack Welch, the former CEO of General Electric and one of the most admired managers in the United States, received more than $500 million in GE stock options as a reward for his services. Upon his retirement he was also awarded $2.5 million in annual perks ranging from round-the-clock access to a corporate jet to free dry cleaning service. When this information was revealed to the press, Welch quickly agreed to pay GE $2 million for these services.

Is it ethical for top managers to receive such vast amounts of money from their companies? Do they really earn it? Remember, this money could have gone to shareholders in the form of dividends. It could also have gone to reduce the huge salary gap between those at the top and those at the bottom of the hierarchy. Many people argue that the growing disparity between the rewards given to CEOs and those given to other employees is unethical and should be regulated. CEO pay has become too high because CEOs are the people who set and control one another's salaries and bonuses! They can do this because they sit on the boards of other companies, as outside directors, and thus can control the salaries and stock options paid to other CEOs. As the example of Bernie Ebbers at WorldCom suggests, when a CEO can control and select many of the outside directors, the CEO can abuse his or her power.

Others argue that because top managers play an important role in building a company's capital and wealth, they deserve a significant share of its profits. Jack Welch, for example, deserved his $500 million because he created hundreds of billions of dollars in stockholder wealth. The debate over how much money CEOs and other top managers should be paid is currently raging. The recent changes at Walt Disney illustrate many of these issues, as discussed in Business in Action.

Business in Action

All Change at Walt Disney

In the early 2000s, the performance of the Walt Disney Company fell precipitously. By 2003, many analysts were wondering if Michael Eisner, who had been its CEO for the last 18 years, was still the right person for the job. Eisner had a hands-on approach to running the business: He wanted to be involved in every major business decision, and he kept a tight reign on his managers. He was also criticized because although he was 60 and due to retire in 2006, he had not laid out a succession plan that indicated which managers would assume the top roles at Disney after he stepped down. Such a plan is important because many companies flounder if a new CEO has not been groomed to take over the top job.

In addition, Eisner was criticized for creating a weak, captive board of directors that was unwilling to scrutinize and question his business decisions, some of which were major errors. Over the years, Eisner created a 16-member board of directors in the company, at least 8 of whom had personal ties to him. This did not serve Disney's stockholders well because Eisner's decisions often hurt the company's performance. For example, Eisner pushed through the merger between Disney and Capital/ABC. But since the acquisition, the poorly performing ABC network has dragged down Disney's stock price. Neither was it lost on Disney's shareholders that Eisner had received more than $800 million in stock options during his 19 years as CEO, along with lavish perks, including the use of Disney's corporate jets, penthouse suites, and all-expenses paid trips.

Upset by Disney's poor performance and CEO Michael Eisner's lavish perks, stockholders ousted him as chairman of the board. But he remained Disney's CEO until 2005.

With its performance falling, Eisner came under increasing criticism for his autocratic management style, his lack of a succession plan for the company, and his creation of a weak board of directors, as well as the fact that he is still paid vast sums of money despite his company's declining performance. Indeed, many analysts began to wonder if Eisner was behaving ethically as CEO or whether his behavior was a prime example of the agency problem (see Chapter 4). So, in 2003 Disney reorganized its board of directors. Two new special outside directors were appointed, one of whom chairs two board meetings a year that Eisner— who normally chairs these meetings—was not permitted to attend. The board now had more freedom to assess Eisner's performance.

Many analysts claimed these changes were not enough because the majority of Disney's board members were still beholden to Eisner. In 2004, Roy Disney, Walt Disney's nephew and a major stockholder began a campaign to remove Eisner from his position as CEO and he lobbied board members for a change in leadership. Although unsuccessful in removing Eisner, in the fall of 2004, Eisner announced that he would not seek another term as CEO when his contract expired in 2006. The board then began an immediate search for Disney's next CEO, and in 2005, named Robert Iger, Eisner's second in command, to be its next CEO when Eisner stepped down in September 2005, one year early. However, it appeared likely that Eisner would become Disney's new chairman of the board. This means he would still retain substantial control of the company. Once again analysts wondered, is this the ethical thing to do? Wouldn't Disney's shareholders be better served if the company had an all-new team at the top?[3]

Employees

A company's employees are the hundreds of thousands of people who work in its various functions, like research, sales, and manufacturing. Employees expect that they will receive rewards consistent with their performance. One principal way a company acts ethically toward employees and meets their expectations is by creating an occupational structure that fairly and equitably rewards them for their contributions. Companies, for example, need to develop recruitment, training, performance appraisal, and reward systems that do not discriminate between employees and that employees believe are fair.

Suppliers and Distributors

No company operates alone. Every company relies on a network of other companies that supply it with the inputs it needs to operate. Companies also depend on intermediaries such as wholesalers and retailers to distribute its products to the final customer. Suppliers expect to be paid fairly and promptly for their inputs; distributors expect to receive quality products at agreed-upon prices.

Once again, many ethical issues arise in the way companies contract and interact with their suppliers and distributors. Important issues concerning how and when payments are to be made or product quality specifications are governed by the terms of the legal contracts a company signs with its suppliers and distributors. Many other

Table 5.1
Select Principles from Gap Inc.'s Code of Vendor Conduct

As a condition of doing business with Gap Inc., each and every factory must comply with this Code of Vendor Conduct. Gap Inc. will continue to develop monitoring systems to assess and ensure compliance. If Gap Inc. determines that any factory has violated this Code, Gap Inc. may either terminate its business relationship or require the factory to implement a corrective action plan. If corrective action is advised but not taken, Gap Inc. will suspend placement of future orders and may terminate current production.

I. General Principles

Factories that produce goods for Gap Inc. shall operate in full compliance with the laws of their respective countries and with all other applicable laws, rules, and regulations.

II. Environment

Factories must comply with all applicable environmental laws and regulations. Where such requirements are less stringent than Gap Inc.'s own, factories are encouraged to meet the standards outlined in Gap Inc.'s statement of environmental principles.

III. Discrimination

Factories shall employ workers on the basis of their ability to do the job, without regard to race, color, gender, nationality, religion, age, maternity, or marital status.

IV. Forced Labor

Factories shall not use any prison, indentured, or forced labor.

V. Child Labor

Factories shall employ only workers who meet the applicable minimum legal age requirement or are at least 14 years of age, whichever is greater. Factories must also comply with all other applicable child labor laws. Factories are encouraged to develop lawful workplace apprenticeship programs for the educational benefit of their workers, provided that all participants meet both Gap Inc.'s minimum age standard of 14 and the minimum legal age requirement.

VI. Wages & Hours

Factories shall set working hours, wages and overtime pay in compliance with all applicable laws. Workers shall be paid at least the minimum legal wage or a wage that meets local industry standards, whichever is greater. While it is understood that overtime is often required in garment production, factories shall carry out operations in ways that limit overtime to a level that ensures humane and productive working conditions.

issues are dependent on business ethics. For example, numerous products sold in U.S. stores are produced in countries that do not have U.S.-style regulations and laws to protect the workers who make these products. All companies must take an ethical position on the way they obtain and make the products they sell. Commonly this stance is published on the company's Web site. Table 5.1 presents part of the The Gap's statement on global ethics.

Customers

Customers are often regarded as the most critical stakeholders: If a company cannot persuade them to buy its products, it cannot stay in business. Thus, managers and employees must work to increase efficiency and effectiveness in order to create loyal customers and attract new ones. They do so by selling customers quality products at a fair price and providing good after-sales service. They can also strive to improve their products over time.

Many laws exist that protect customers from companies that attempt to provide dangerous or shoddy products. Laws exist that allow customers to sue a company that produces a bad product, such as a defective tire or vehicle, causing them harm. Other laws force companies to clearly disclose the interest rates they charge on purchases—a cost that customers frequently do not factor into their purchase decisions. Every year thousands of companies are prosecuted for breaking these laws, so "buyer beware" is an important business rule customers must follow.

Community, Society, and Nation

community The physical society in which a company is located.

As we have seen in previous chapters, the effects of business activity permeate all aspects of the community, society, and nation in which it takes place. Community refers to the physical location in which a company is located, like a city, town, or neighborhood. A community provides a company with the physical and social infrastructure that allows it to do business; its utilities and labor force; the homes in which its managers and employees live; the schools, colleges, and hospitals that service their needs, and so on.

Through the salaries, wages, and taxes it pays, a company contributes to the economy of the town or region in which it operates and often determines whether the community prospers or suffers. Similarly, a company affects the prosperity of a society and a nation and, to the degree that a company is involved in global trade, all of the countries in which it operates.

Although the way an individual McDonald's restaurant operates might be of small consequence, the combined effects of the way *all* McDonald's (and other fast-food companies) do business are enormous. In the United States alone, over 500,000 people work in the fast-food industry, and many thousands of suppliers like farmers, paper cup manufacturers, builders, and so on, depend on it for their livelihood. Small wonder then, that the ethics of the fast-food business are scrutinized closely. The industry is the major lobbyer against attempts to raise the minimum wage, for example, because a higher minimum wage would substantially increase its operating costs. However, responding to protests about chickens raised in cages in which they cannot move their wings, McDonald's–the largest egg buyer in the United States–issued new ethical guidelines concerning cage sizes and related matters. Its egg suppliers must abide by these guidelines if they are to retain its business.

Business ethics are also important because the failure of companies can have catastrophic effects on the communities in which they operate, and, if the businesses are large enough, entire regions and evens nations. The decision of a large company to pull out of a community can seriously threaten its future. Some companies attempt to improve their profits by engaging in actions that, although not illegal, can hurt communities and nations. One of these actions is pollution. As we discussed in the last chapter, many U.S. companies reduce costs by trucking their waste to Mexico where it is legal to dump it in the Rio Grande. The dumping pollutes the river from the Mexican side, and the effects are increasingly being felt on the U.S. side, too.

Rules for Ethical Decision Making

When a stakeholder perspective is taken, questions of business ethics abound. What is the appropriate way to manage the claims of all stakeholders? Business decisions that favor one group of stakeholders, for example, are likely to harm the interests of others. High prices to customers might lead to high returns for shareholders and high salaries for managers in the short run. But if in the long run, customers turn to companies that offer lower-cost products, the result could be declining sales, laid-off employees, and the decline of the communities that support the high-priced company's business activity.

When companies act ethically, their stakeholders support them. For example, banks are willing to supply them with new capital, the companies attract highly qualified job applicants, and new customers are drawn to their products. Thus, ethical companies grow and expand over time, and all of their stakeholders benefit as a result. By contrast, unethical behavior will eventually result in the loss of a company's reputation and, ultimately, its resources–its shareholders, who will sell their shares, its managers and employees, who will leave the company to find better jobs, and its customers, who will turn to the products of more reputable companies.

When making business decisions, managers must consider all of the firm's stakeholders. The loss of any one of these groups can be very detrimental. Managers can

Figure 5.2
Four Ethical Rules

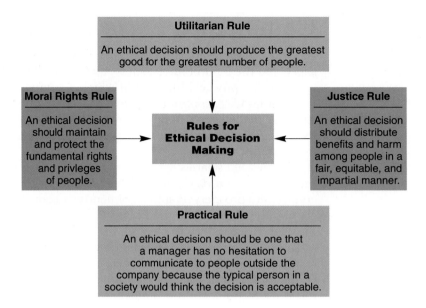

Utilitarian Rule

An ethical decision should produce the greatest good for the greatest number of people.

Moral Rights Rule

An ethical decision should maintain and protect the fundamental rights and privleges of people.

Rules for Ethical Decision Making

Justice Rule

An ethical decision should distribute benefits and harm among people in a fair, equitable, and impartial manner.

Practical Rule

An ethical decision should be one that a manager has no hesitation to communicate to people outside the company because the typical person in a society would think the decision is acceptable.

use four ethical rules or principles to analyze the effects of their business decisions on stakeholders: *utilitarian, moral rights, justice,* and *practical* rules, all of which are outlined in Figure 5.2. These rules are useful guidelines that can help managers decide what to do and how to balance the interests of different stakeholders. Remember, the right choices will result in resources being used to create the most value. If all companies make the right choices, all stakeholders will benefit in the long run.

The Utilitarian Rule

utilitarian rule A rule stating that an ethical decision is one that produces the greatest good for the greatest number of people.

The utilitarian rule is that an ethical decision is a decision that produces the greatest good for the greatest number of people. To decide which is the most ethical course of business action, managers should first consider how different possible courses of business action would benefit or harm different stakeholders. They should then choose the course of action that provides the most benefits, or conversely, the one that does the least harm, to stakeholders.

The ethical dilemma for managers is as follows: How do you measure the benefits and harms that will be done to each stakeholder group? Moreover, how do you evaluate the rights of different stakeholder groups and the relative importance of each? Because stockholders are the owners of the company, shouldn't their claims be held above those of employees? Consider a decision to outsource work globally: This decision can benefit shareholders and customers if it enhances the company's profits, but it will nonetheless result in layoffs affecting its domestic employees and the communities in which they live. Typically under capitalism, the interests of shareholders are put above those of employees, so production will move abroad. This is commonly regarded as being an ethical choice because in the long run, the alternative, domestic production, might cause the business to collapse and go bankrupt. If this happens, all of the company's stakeholders will suffer—not just its employees. According to the utilitarian view, the decision that produces the greatest good for the greatest number of people is best. In this case, that means outsourcing the jobs.

The Moral Rights Rule

moral rights rule A rule stating that an ethical decision is one that best maintains and protects the fundamental, inalienable rights and privileges of the people affected by it.

Using the moral rights rule, an ethical decision is a decision that best maintains and protects the fundamental or inalienable rights of the people affected by it. According to the moral rights rule, an ethical decision is one that protects people's rights to freedom, life and safety, property, privacy, free speech, and freedom of conscience. "Do unto others as you would have them do unto you" is the basis for the moral rights rule.

Even if someone benefits personally by ruthlessly pursuing his or her own self-interests, he or she will suffer. The adverse impact on society as a whole will make it a less desirable place for that person (and all of us) to live.

From a moral rights perspective, managers should compare and contrast different courses of business action on the basis of how each will affect the rights of the company's different stakeholders. Managers should then choose the course of action that best protects and upholds the rights of *all* the stakeholders. For example, decisions that might result in significant harm to the safety or health of employees or customers would clearly be unethical choices.

The ethical dilemma for managers is that business decisions that will protect the rights of some stakeholders often will hurt the rights of others. How should they choose which group to protect? For example, does an employee's right to privacy outweigh an organization's right to protect its property? Suppose your manager is having personal problems and is coming in late and leaving early. You are then forced to pick up the manager's workload. Do you tell your manager's supervisor, even though you know this will probably get that manager fired? How should the manager's supervisor deal with the problem? Is it morally right to fire someone who is already having personal problems?

The Justice Rule

justice rule An rule stating that an ethical decision is one that distributes benefit and harms among people in a fair or impartial way

According to the justice rule, a decision is ethical if it distributes benefit and harm among people and groups in a fair or impartial way. Managers should compare and contrast alternative courses of action based on the degree to which they will result in a fair or equitable distribution of outcomes for stakeholders. For example, employees who are similar in their levels of skill, performance, or responsibility should receive the same kind of pay. The allocation of outcomes should not be based on differences such as gender, race, or religion.

The ethical dilemma for managers is to determine the fair rules and procedures for distributing outcomes to stakeholders. Managers must not give people they like bigger raises than they give to people they do not like, for example, or bend the rules to help their favorites. On the other hand, if employees want managers to act fairly toward them, then employees need to act fairly toward their companies and work hard and be loyal. Similarly, customers need to act fairly toward a company if they expect it to be fair to them—something people who illegally copy digital media should consider.

The Practical Rule

practical rule A rule stating that an ethical decision is one that a manager can communicate to society because the typical person would think it is acceptable.

Each of the above rules offers a different and complementary way of determining whether a decision or behavior is ethical, and all three rules should be used to sort out the ethics of a particular course of action. Ethical issues, as we just discussed, are seldom clear-cut, however, because the rights, interests, goals, and incentives of different stakeholders often conflict. For this reason many experts on ethics add a fourth rule to determine whether a business decision is ethical: The practical rule is that an ethical decision is one that a manager has no hesitation about communicating to society because the typical person would think it is acceptable. Think of this as the *60 Minutes* rule. How will the public react if the decision were publicized (broadcast on the TV show *60 Minutes,* for example)? A business decision is probably acceptable on ethical grounds if a manager can answer *yes* to each of these questions:

1.   Does my decision fall within the accepted *values* or *standards* that typically apply in business activity today?
2.   Am I willing to see the decision *communicated* to all people and groups *affected* by it—for example, by having it reported in newspapers or on television?

3.   Would the people with whom I have a *significant* personal relationship, such as my family members, friends, or even managers in other organizations, *approve* of the decision?

If the answer to any of these questions is *no,* chances are the decision is not an ethical one.

Why Should Managers Behave Ethically?

Why is it so important for managers and people, in general, to act ethically? The answer was given in Chapter 2. The relentless pursuit of self-interest can lead to a collective disaster. When one or more people start to profit from being unethical, this encourages others to act in the same way. Quickly, more and more people jump onto the bandwagon, and soon everybody is trying to manipulate the situation in the way that best serves his or her personal ends with no regard for the effects of the action on others. The situation brought about by Napster is an example of how what is called the "tragedy of the commons" works.

Suppose that in an agricultural community there is common land that everybody has an equal right to use. Pursuing self-interest, each farmer acts to make the maximum use of the free resource by grazing his or her own cattle and sheep on the land. Collectively, all of the farmers overgraze the land, which quickly becomes worn out. Then a strong wind blows away the exposed topsoil, so the common land is destroyed. The pursuit of individual self-interest with no consideration for societal interests leads to disaster for each individual and for the whole society because scarce resources are destroyed. In the Napster case, the tragedy that would result if all people were to steal digital media would be that fewer records, movies, and books would be produced because there would be little incentive to do so.

Figure 5.3
Some Effects of Ethical and Unethical Behavior

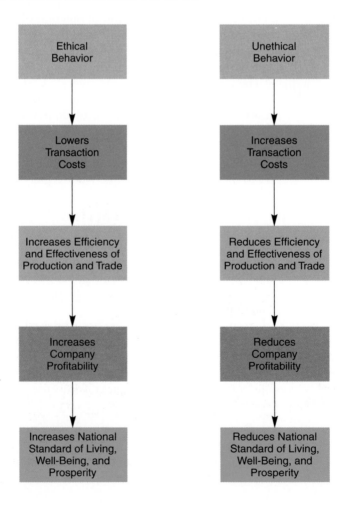

We can look at the effects of unethical behavior on business commerce and activity in another way. Go back to the example of people who are engaged in trading corn for sheep. Suppose this business activity takes place in an unethical society, meaning one in which people routinely try to cheat or defraud one another. If both parties expect the other to cheat, how long will it take them to negotiate an exchange? When they do not trust each other, stakeholders will probably spend hours bargaining over fair prices and looking to close any loopholes in a deal they can. This is a largely unproductive activity that reduces efficiency and effectiveness in an economy. All the time and effort that could be spent on improving the land and livestock is being lost because it is spent on negotiating and bargaining. Thus, unethical behavior and distrust hampers business commerce. Less capital and wealth are created in a society, so living standards are lower. Figure 5.3 illustrates this.

It has been said that there are two ways to acquire wealth: by plunder or productivity. In many African countries plunder is the order of the day. Theft, war, and lawlessness are widespread. As a result, few companies want to invest in these countries, productivity is very low, and most people are poverty stricken. Is this the type of society you would like to live in? Likewise, if corporate executives go unpunished for bilking shareholders, fewer people will be inclined to invest their money in the stock market. As a result, companies will have less money to invest in better products, new plants, and jobs for people. This will have an adverse effect on the economy as a whole and the quality of life for everyone.

Now suppose companies and their managers operate in an ethical society. Stakeholders believe they are dealing with others who are basically moral and honest. In this society stakeholders have a greater reason to trust others, which means they have more confidence and faith in the other person's goodwill. When trust exists, people are more likely to signal their good intentions by cooperating and providing information that makes it easier to trade and price goods and services. When one person does so, this encourages others to act in the same way. Over time greater trust between stakeholders allows them to work together more efficiently and effectively; transaction costs fall, and business commerce becomes more profitable (see Figure 5.3). When people can see that acting in an honest way yields positive results, ethical behavior becomes a valued social norm, and people in society become better off.

In summary, in a complex, diverse society, stakeholders and people, in general, need to recognize they are all part of a larger social group. The way in which we personally make decisions affects the lives of other people and the society around us. This, in turn, affects us.

trust A person's confidence and faith in another person's goodwill.

Business Ethics
Some companies, like Merck, Johnson & Johnson, Prudential Insurance, Fannie Mae, and Blue Cross-Blue Shield, are well known for their ethical business practices. Other companies, like Arthur Andersen, Enron, and WorldCom, are either out of business or struggling to survive. What explains such differences between the business ethics of these companies and their managers?

There are four main determinants of differences in business ethics between companies and countries: *societal* ethics, *occupational* ethics, *individual* ethics, and *organizational* ethics, as outlined in Figure 5.4.

Societal Ethics

societal ethics
Standards that govern how members of a society should deal with one another in matters involving issues such as fairness, justice, poverty, and the rights of the individual.

Societal ethics are standards that govern how members of a society should deal with one another in matters involving fairness, justice, poverty, and the rights of individuals. Societal ethics emanate from a society's laws, customs, and practices, and from the unwritten values and norms that influence how people interact with each other. Most people have *internalized* (made a part of their moral fabric) certain values, beliefs, and norms that specify how they should behave when confronted with an ethical dilemma. In other words, an "internal compass" of sorts guides their behavior.

Figure 5.4
Sources of
Business Ethics

Societal ethics vary among societies. Countries like Germany, Japan, Sweden, and Switzerland are well known as being some of the most ethical countries in the world, with strong values about social order and the need to create a society that protects the welfare of all people. In other countries the situation is very different. In many economically poor countries bribery is standard practice to get things done—such as getting a telephone installed or a contract awarded. As we learned in Chapter 4, in the United States and other economically advanced countries, bribery is considered unethical and is illegal.

IBM came under fire after managers in its Argentina division paid a $6 million bribe to land a $250 million contract servicing the computers of a large, state-owned bank. IBM won the contract, but the managers who arranged the bribe were fired. Although bribes such as these are not necessarily illegal under Argentine law, IBM's organizational rules forbid the practice. Moreover, the payment of bribes violates the U.S. *Foreign Corrupt Practices Act*, which prohibits U.S. companies from paying bribes in order to win contracts abroad. It also makes companies liable for the actions of their foreign managers, and allows companies found in violation to be prosecuted in the United States. By firing the managers, IBM signaled that it would not tolerate unethical behavior by any of its employees, and it continues today to take a rigorous stance toward ethical issues.

Countries also differ widely in their beliefs about appropriate treatment for their employees. In general, the poorer a country is, the more likely employees are to be treated with little regard. One issue of particular ethical concern that has set off protests around the world is the use of child labor, discussed in Business in Action.

Business in Action

Is It Right to Use Child Labor?

In recent years, the number of U.S. companies that buy their inputs from low-cost foreign suppliers has been growing, and concern about the ethics associated with employing young children in factories has been increasing. In Pakistan, children as young as age six work long hours in deplorable conditions to make rugs and carpets for export to Western countries. Children in poor countries throughout Africa, Asia, and South America work in similar conditions. Is it ethical to employ children in factories, and should U.S. companies buy and sell products made by these children?

Opinions about the ethics of child labor vary widely. The International Labor Organization and other labor activists believe that the practice is reprehensible and should be outlawed globally. Another view, championed by *The Economist* magazine, is that, although no one wants to see children employed in factories, in many poor countries, children must work to ensure their families' survival. Thus, denying children employment would cause entire families to suffer. Instead, *The Economist* favors regulating the conditions under which children are employed and hopes that over time, as poor countries become richer, the need for child employment will disappear.

Should child labor be outlawed worldwide? Some people feel the practice is reprehensible. Others see it as a matter of survival in many countries.

Many U.S. retailers that typically buy their clothing from low-cost foreign suppliers have had to take an ethical stance on the child labor issue. Managers in Wal-Mart, Target, J.C. Penney, and The Gap all have policies in place prohibiting their foreign suppliers from employing children. These companies vow to sever ties with any foreign supplier found to be in violation of these policies.

But retailers differ widely in the way they choose to enforce such policies. It has been estimated that more than 300,000 children under age 14 are being employed in garment factories in Guatemala, a popular low-cost location for clothing manufacturers that supply the U.S. market. These children frequently work more than 60 hours a week and often are paid less than $3 a day, close to the minimum wage in Guatemala. Many U.S. retailers do not check up on their foreign suppliers. Clearly, if U.S. retailers want to avoid the customer backlash that invariably results from the use of child labor, they must do more to regulate the conditions under which these children work.[4]

Occupational Ethics

occupational ethics
Standards that govern how members of a profession, trade, or craft, should conduct themselves when performing work-related activities.

Occupational ethics are standards that govern how members of a profession, trade, or craft should conduct themselves when performing work-related activities. For example, medical ethics govern the way doctors and nurses should treat their patients. Doctors are expected to perform only necessary medical procedures and to act in the patient's interest—not in their own. Most professional groups can punish their members for ethics violations. Doctors and lawyers can be prevented from practicing their professions if they disregard professional ethics and put their own interests first.

Likewise, within a business organization, occupational rules and norms often govern how employees such as lawyers, researchers, and accountants should behave to further the interests of its stakeholders. Employees internalize the rules and norms of their occupational groups (just as they do those of society) and often follow them automatically when deciding how to behave. Sometimes, however, a person's occupational ethics conflict with those of the firm in which they work. A scientist is surely aware of the fact that fabricating data goes against the grain of his or her profession. But what should he or she do if under corporate pressure to do so? In this case, the decision the scientist makes ultimately depends upon his or her own individual ethics. This is what we discuss next.

Individual and Organizational Ethics

individual ethics A person's standards and values that determine how he or she should act in situations when his or her own self-interest is at stake.

organizational ethics
The practices and beliefs that guide an organization's behavior towards its stakeholders.

Individual ethics are personal standards and values that determine how people should act towards others when their own self-interests are at stake. The influence of one's family, peers, and upbringing in general are the basis of a person's individual ethics. The individual ethics of a company's founders and top managers are especially important "shapers" of an organization's ethics. Organizational ethics are the values and beliefs that guide an organization's behavior toward its stakeholders. Organizations whose founders created highly ethical codes of organizational behavior include Merck, Hewlett-Packard,

Did You Know?

The gross domestic product of the poorest 30 nations is less than the wealth of the world's five richest people combined.[5]

Table 5.2
Johnson & Johnson's Credo

We believe our first responsibility is to the doctors, nurses, and patients, to mothers and fathers and all others who use our products and services.

In meeting their needs everything we do must be of high quality.

We must constantly strive to reduce our costs in order to maintain reasonable prices.

Customers' orders must be serviced promptly and accurately.

Our suppliers and distributors must have an opportunity to make a fair profit.

We are responsible to our employees, the men and women who work with us throughout the world.

Everyone must be considered as an individual.

We must respect their dignity and recognize their merit.

They must have a sense of security in their jobs.

Compensation must be fair and adequate, and working conditions clean, orderly and safe.

We must be mindful of ways to help our employees fulfill their family responsibilities.

Employees must feel free to make suggestions and complaints.

There must be equal opportunity for employment, development, and advancement for those qualified.

We must provide competent management, and their actions must be just and ethical.

We are responsible to the communities in which we live and work and to the world community as well.

We must be good citizens—support good works and charities and bear our fair share of taxes.

We must encourage civic improvements and better health and education.

We must maintain in good order the property we are privileged to use, protecting the environment and natural resources.

Our final responsibility is to our stockholders.

Business must make a sound profit.

We must experiment with new ideas.

Research must be carried on, innovative programs developed and mistakes paid for.

New equipment must be purchased, new facilities provided and new products launched.

Reserves must be created to provide for adverse times.

When we operate according to these principles, the stockholders should realize a fair return.

Johnson & Johnson, and the Prudential Insurance Company. Johnson & Johnson's code of ethics—that is, its credo, shown in Table 5.2—reflects a well-developed concern for the firm's stakeholders. Company credos, such as that of Johnson & Johnson, are meant to deter self-interested, unethical behavior—to demonstrate to managers and employees that a company will punish people who put their own interests above others and inflict harm on the organization's stakeholders.

Employees are much more likely to act unethically when a credo does not exist or is disregarded by a company's top managers. Arthur Andersen, for example, did not follow its credo at all. Its unscrupulous partners ordered the firm's middle managers to shred evidence of their wrongdoing. Although the middle managers knew this was wrong, they followed orders because the power of the firm's partners, not the company's code of ethics, dictated the firm's culture. The firm's middle managers were afraid they would lose their jobs if they didn't shred the documents. But they lost them anyway after the shredding came to light and the company's reputation was ruined.

Because they bear ultimate responsibility for setting policy, top managers establish the ethical values and norms of their organizations. A company's board of directors therefore needs to carefully scrutinize its top managers. It is the responsibility of the board to decide if a prospective CEO has the maturity, experience, and integrity needed to lead a company and be entrusted with its vast capital and wealth on which the well-being of its stakeholders depend. In 2003, the former CEO of Kmart was scrutinized for poor managerial decision making that ultimately led to the company's downfall. (Apparently, the scrutiny did not come soon enough.)

A financial track record of success is not enough to decide this issue because it could have been achieved by unethical or illegal means. Boards need to delve deeper than the bottom line and examine the other credentials of prospective top managers. In the early 2000s it was disclosed that the top managers of several major companies lacked the degrees or experience listed on their resumes–facts that should have been uncovered prior to their being hired. Often, the best predictor of future behavior is past behavior, but the board of directors needs to be on guard against unethical people who use unethical means to rise to the top of the organizational hierarchy.

These three sources of ethics collectively influence the ethics that develop inside of an organization. Each organization has a set of ethics. Some of these ethics are unique to an organization and are an important aspect of its organizational culture, a topic discussed in detail in Chapter 7. However, many ethical rules go beyond the boundaries of any individual company. Companies, collectively, are also expected to follow ethical and legal rules. If one company breaks the rules, others frequently follow.

The Advantages of Behaving Ethically

reputation The trust, goodwill, and confidence others have in a company that leads them to want to do business with it.

Several advantages result when companies and their managers behave in an ethical way. First, companies known for their ethical behavior enjoy a good reputation. Reputation is the trust, goodwill, and confidence others have in a company such that they want to do business with it. A company with a good reputation will find it easier to do more business and obtain resources from stakeholders. Behaving ethically is therefore the economically right thing to do because it increases a company's profits.

A second reason for companies to behave ethically is because when they don't, the government (and taxpayers) has to bear the costs of protecting their stakeholders–by providing laid-off employees with health care and unemployment benefits, bailing out pension plans gone bust, or seeking compensation for shareholders. If all companies in a society act socially responsibly the quality of life for people as a whole increases. Experts point to Japan, Sweden, Germany, the Netherlands, and Switzerland as examples. In these countries, organizations act in a highly ethical way towards their stakeholders. As a result, crime, poverty, and unemployment rates are relatively low, literacy rates are relatively high, and sociocultural values promote harmony between different groups of people. Business activity affects all aspects of people's lives, so the way business behaves toward stakeholders affects how stakeholders will behave toward businesses. You "reap what you sow," as the adage goes.

Creating an Ethical Organization

Although ethical values flow down from the top of the organization, they can be strengthened or weakened by the design of an organization's structure. Creating authority relationships and rules that promote ethical behavior and punish unethical acts is one way of strengthening this structure. The federal government, for example, continually tries to improve the set of standards governing the conduct of its 5 million federal employees. These standards govern activities such as gift giving and receiving, assigning government contracts on an impartial basis, and avoiding conflict of interest.

whistleblower A stakeholder who reveals an organization's misdeeds to the public.

Often, an organization uses its mission statement to guide employees in making ethical decisions. Policies regarding the treatment of whistleblowers can also be put into place. A whistleblower is a stakeholder (usually an employee) who reveals an organization's misdeeds to the public. Employees typically become whistleblowers when they feel powerless to prevent an organization from committing an unethical act or when they fear retribution if they voice their concerns. Whistle blowing, which is becoming more commonplace, can lead to steep fines and lawsuits levied against the firm and even prison time for its personnel. As a result, companies are now encouraging employees to come forward internally with

Did You Know?

Price of a medium Coca-Cola at a fast-food restaurant: $1.29
Price of the Coca-Cola syrup: $.09[6]

their concerns versus airing "their dirty laundry in public." Procedures are being put into place giving lower-level employees a forum in which to voice their concerns and access to air their grievances to the firm's upper-level managers.

In addition, many companies have installed "chief ethics officers." Chief ethics officers are managers employees can go to to report wrongdoing. After an alleged incident is investigated, the firm's ethics "committee" can make a formal judgment about whether wrongdoing has actually occurred, and, if so, what the consequences should be. Today, 20% of Fortune 500 companies have ethics officers. In addition to investigating unethical and illegal corporate conduct, these ethics officers are responsible for keeping employees informed about the firm's conduct codes and training them to make good ethical decisions.

There are many ways in which individual managers can, and should, personally influence the people in their companies to behave ethically. For example, as we mentioned earlier in the chapter, a manager acts as a figurehead and personifies the organization's ethical position. As such, he or she can promote moral values and norms that employees use to make decisions. He or she can demonstrate those values by behaving in a certain way—such as by being honest and acknowledging errors. Outside the organization, as a liaison or spokesperson, the manager can inform prospective customers and other stakeholders about the organization's ethical values and then unfailingly abide by them.

Homemaking maven Martha Stewart learned this the hard way—after she was found guilty of insider trading and the stock of Martha Stewart Living Omnimedia Inc. plummeted. Stewart was later sentenced to five months in prison and five months of house arrest. Many business analysts speculated that had Stewart "come clean" when charges against her were initially filed, both she and her company would have been better off.

The Legal Environment of Business

It is time to look at the U.S. laws and regulations that have been passed over the decades to curb unethical business activities. The most important laws, and the reasons why they were passed, are discussed below from the perspective of business as commerce, occupation, and organization. (See Figure 5.5.)

Laws Affecting Business Commerce

Four main types of laws affecting business commerce are antitrust laws, consumer protection laws, environmental laws, and laws protecting the public's general interest.

ANTITRUST LAWS   Perhaps the single most important reason U.S. laws governing trade and commerce were initially passed was to prevent the abuse of monopoly power. We discussed in Chapter 2 how throughout history merchants and traders have sought to monopolize their industries. U.S. capitalists such as John D. Rockefeller were well aware of the advantages a monopoly provided. They therefore developed "trusts," or groups of companies, to disguise the fact that they were really acting as one company (a monopolist) to limit supply and keep prices high. As this scheme became clear to the public, however, a number of powerful antitrust laws were passed making it illegal for one or more companies to conspire to limit supply and control a product's price. This was a huge blow to "big" business. Violators face severe penalties. It should be noted that we are referring here to U.S. antitrust laws, which cannot be universally enforced. OPEC, an international organization of oil producing countries, for example, controls the amount of crude oil produced worldwide. But there is nothing the U.S. government can do about OPEC.

The antitrust laws passed in the United States led to the creation of many other government agencies charged with overseeing corporate behavior and business commerce. The Securities and Exchange Commission (SEC) is the most important of these agencies. It has the power to investigate companies that seem to be behaving illegally. Microsoft is one of many companies investigated by the SEC. The SEC also

antitrust laws Laws passed to curb the power of big business and make it illegal for companies to conspire with one another to limit supply and keep prices high.

Figure 5.5

Types of Business Laws and Regulations

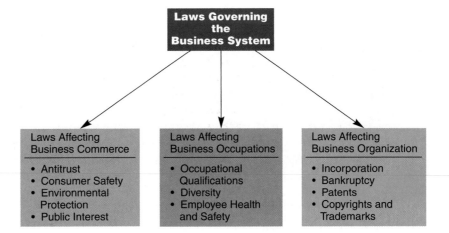

has the power to create new regulations that make emerging forms of unethical commercial behavior illegal. It can impose severe sanctions against people and companies who break those laws, including bringing lawsuits against them. In addition, the SEC is responsible for managing the agencies or committees that regulate specific kinds of business practices. For example, in 2002 the Arthur Andersen-Enron accounting scandal put accounting companies' audit procedures under the spotlight. Prior to the scandal, audits had been scrutinized only by the industry's regulatory committee. (After the scandal broke, however, it became clear that the industry had done a very poor job of policing itself.) Under pressure from Congress, the SEC moved to create a new, independent watchdog agency to oversee the auditing industry. One proposal was that the large accounting firms should not be allowed to audit a particular company's books for more than five consecutive years. The idea behind the proposal was that outside accountants, and a particular company's managers, would not break the law if they knew another accounting company would be reviewing the company's books in the future. Worried that if the proposal became law, it would cost them long-term clients, companies in the accounting industry lobbied Congress heavily to prevent that from happening. They succeeded. The new rules developed by the SEC to prevent illegal auditing practices are much weaker today as a result.

CONSUMER SAFETY LAWS "Snake oil" salesmen peddling their noxious tonics around the United Stated in the 1800s were an early warning of the need for consumer safety laws. Some of these tonics were probably safe to use in small quantities; others were pure poison and resulted in the deaths of hundreds of early settlers. Unfortunately, this type of behavior still goes on. In 2002, a Kansas City pharmacist pled guilty to diluting the chemotherapy drugs of 34 patients in an effort to pad his profits. Another example of this disregard for consumer safety became apparent in the early 2000s, as profiled in Business in Action.

Business in Action

How Metabolife Swept the Dangers of Ephedra under the Rug

In 2002, Metabolife International was one of largest companies that produced and sold ephedra, a supplement widely used for weight loss and body building. Fears about ephedra's safety had been around for years. Still, Metabolife resisted attempts by the U.S. Food and Drug Administration (FDA) to obtain a list of its customers' complaints. After the U.S. Justice Department opened a criminal investigation and the company was forced to turn over the list, it was revealed that over 16,000 customers had complained about the product. Nearly 2,000 adverse reactions, including 3 deaths, 20 heart attacks, 24 strokes, and 40 seizures had been reported.

Metabolife was not required by law to disclose the adverse effects its customers were experiencing, but should it have been? If you were a Metabolife stockholder, would you want the firm to disclose that information? What would this do to the price of your stock?

How was Metabolife able to get away with this behavior? Unlike prescription drugs, the FDA does not regulate over-the-counter supplements even though some of these supplements can have life-threatening effects. Because no laws existed to force Metabolife to disclose the adverse side effects—something all pharmaceutical companies are required to do by law—it chose to hide this information. Although Metabolife's actions were legal, they were anything but ethical.

Hundreds of personal injury lawsuits were later filed against Metabolife by consumers. In 2003 the company was ordered by an Alabama court to pay $4.1 million to four people who had suffered a stroke or seizure after using the product. If more of these consumers prevail in court, it seems likely that Metabolife will be put out of business. In the meantime a national campaign to ban ephedra was successful, and new laws governing supplements and the FDA's power to police their distribution have been proposed.[7]

ENVIRONMENTAL PROTECTION LAWS   A third class of commercial laws governs how companies treat the natural environment. This is one of the primary functions of government—to preserve the long-term health and prosperity of people when unregulated markets fail to do so. In the 2000s, the costs of disposing both toxic and nontoxic waste products increased substantially. Land has become more scarce and expensive. So to protect it, more laws are being passed to regulate the way products are disposed of. Stricter air pollution regulations have also been passed to, among other things, limit acid rain caused by the emissions of coal-fired power stations.(Whole forests around the world have been killed by acid rain.) Similarly, there is increasing realization that our seas are becoming overpolluted and overfished. Laws and regulations now govern the size of fish catches and oil drilling at sea throughout Canada, Alaska, the Gulf Coast, and elsewhere.

Unfettered by laws and regulations, unethical companies will simply maximize their own short-run returns at the expense of the environment and the people in it. Future generations will not only suffer physically because of pollution but also economically as the world's natural resources are depleted. The long-run consequences future generations face when these companies exploit the environment are not part of their business models.

Legal regulations can change this, however. When companies are forced to pay the real cost of obtaining valuable inputs and properly disposing of their waste products—costs they would otherwise impose on the rest of us in terms of the waste's cleanup, the higher health costs we experience, or the depleted resources we no longer have access to—their incentives change. These costs then become part of companies' total operating costs and must be considered in their business models. In the long run this motivates companies to pollute less and use their resources wisely. Society as a whole benefits.

The Clean Air Act passed by Congress in 1990 was a major step in this direction. Under this law, the U.S. Environmental Agency sets limits on how much of a pollutant can be in the air anywhere in the United States, and companies are responsible for bearing the cost of keeping this emission low (by installing cleaner burning equipment, and so forth). This ensures that all Americans, no matter what state they are living in, have the same basic health and environmental protections.

Of course, pollution isn't just limited to the United States. Recognizing this, countries worldwide are beginning to work together to reduce it. The Kyoto Protocol is an amendment to the United Nations' treaty on global warming. Countries that ratify the Kyoto Protocol pledge to reduce their emissions of carbon dioxide and other greenhouse gases. A total of 141 countries have ratified the agreement; however, notable exceptions include the United States and Australia.

LAWS RELATING TO THE PUBLIC INTEREST There are many other laws that also govern how a company should behave that further the public interest. The public interest is a country-specific set of standards or beliefs used by lawmakers and the courts to evaluate the appropriateness of certain actions—such as business actions. The private benefits that a person or company would receive from pursuing a certain course of action are weighed against the effects on the public at large. If lawmakers or judges decide that a particular course of action would significantly reduce the public's welfare even if private parties might benefit substantially, then the action might be made or deemed to be illegal.

public interest
Country-specific standards used to evaluate how a proposed course of action affects the welfare of society.

Public interest judgments are made about all kinds of business practices. These judgments determine which system of business law exists in a society such as the United States. In general, the more economically developed the country is, the better developed and stringent are its business laws regulating economic activity.

One kind of public interest judgments is made about the ethics involved in trade between a company and its suppliers and distributors. While driving a hard bargain is not necessarily unethical, sometimes a company that either buys in large quantities, like Wal-Mart, or controls the supply of a product, can force its suppliers or distributors to agree to business practices that could be considered uncompetitive under antitrust laws. Toys "R" Us, the most powerful toy buyer in the United States, was accused of this.

Faced with stiff competition from Wal-Mart and Target, Toys "R" Us told toy suppliers like Hasbro that it would not sell their toys in its stores if they sold the same toys to discount retailers who were undercutting its prices. This could be regarded as a use of "monopoly" power. It would threaten the public interest because it would limit competition, and consumers would pay higher toy prices. In a similar move, in 2002, Hasbro, the world's largest toymaker, attempted to artificially raise toy prices in the United Kingdom. Hasbro told U.K. toy retailers they could not discount the price of its toys—they had to be sold at *its* recommended price. Hasbro was later fined millions of pounds for *price-fixing,* a practice that is illegal in many countries.

Public interest judgments are also made to assess how a company should behave towards its stockholders to guarantee their welfare. Laws governing the rights of stockholders are particularly stringent. Strict rules and regulations exist that specify the way companies should report their financial results so that stockholders can understand how well they have performed. Among these requirements are that companies publish the salaries paid their top managers and the number of stock options awarded their employees. Of course, unethical managers can find many loopholes in these laws and many managers, such as those at Arthur Andersen and Enron, are driven by greed to act illegally and "cook the books."

To help prevent this, new laws and regulations have been enacted to force companies to more fully disclosure their financial results. In 2002, Congress passed the Sarbanes-Oxley Act, which requires CEOs and CFOs (chief financial officers) to personally vouch for the accounting numbers their firms report to Wall Street—and face jail time if those numbers are falsified. Stockholders rights become a prominent issue in the 2000s as company after company admitted it had broken business laws and regulations. In 2002, for example, Salomon Smith Barney agreed to pay a $5 million fine to settle charges that one of its star brokers was promoting a stock to investors—even though the company's internal e-mails suggested the stock was a dog. Brokers at Merrill Lynch were also found to have done a similar thing, privately laughing about the poor prospects of

In 2002, Hasbro was found guilty of using its power as the world's largest toymaker to artificially raise toy prices in the United Kingdom.

companies whose stocks they continued to recommend to thousands of investors. In 2004, many major mutual fund companies admitted they had allowed their fund managers and large investors to make stock market trades that made them millions of dollars for big investors but hurt millions of small investors. The companies have paid hundreds of millions in fines to settle these charges.

Laws Affecting Business Occupations

Many types of laws have been passed to prevent unethical practices related to business occupations: laws regulating occupational qualifications, laws governing business diversity, and laws promoting employee health and safety.

LAWS REGULATING OCCUPATIONS In many countries regulations exist that specify the skills, qualifications, and experience people must possess to be hired for government occupations. Air traffic controllers, tax auditors, schoolteachers, firefighters, and police officers, for example, all must have certain credentials. This serves the public interest because it ensures people have the skills they need to properly serve the public. It also prevents people from being hired for *whom* they knew versus *what* they know. Certainly, no person wants to feel he or she wasn't hired or promoted because the person who was went to the same school or belonged to the same club as the boss. Unethical hiring practices also mean that best people are *not* being hired. They are not being put to their most highly valued uses, so there is a loss in social welfare, and the public interest is threatened.

Many private-sector jobs also have occupational requirements designed to protect the well-being of society. Surely none of us would like to be treated by a doctor without a medical license or defended by an attorney who lacked a license to practice law. Most of us would also prefer to buy our medications from a licensed pharmacist rather than snake-oil salesman. Like the other laws in this chapter, occupational regulations are an attempt to prevent people from trying to unfairly profit at the expense of others.

LAWS GOVERNING DIVERSITY Laws governing diversity seek to create a level playing field for people in the job market. Once again, the goal of these laws is to foster the hiring, promotion, and retention of people based on their ability to do a job—not based on their ethnicity, religion, gender, age, and so on. If a company decides it needs to lay off workers, for example, the layoffs cannot unfairly affect a particular group of employees, such as workers over 50, or women or minorities. The procedures used to decide who should be hired, promoted, or laid off have to be defendable in court.

One reason such laws are necessary is to lessen the impact of the psychological bias called the "similar to me" effect, which research shows is a common tendency. As the name implies, people commonly tend to recruit, promote, and retain people from within their own religious, ethnic, or age groups because it's "easier" dealing with people who are more like themselves. Diversity laws help prevent this from happening by making it illegal to choose between people on nonjob-related grounds.

Of course, companies can be fined for discriminatory employment behavior and sued by people who feel they've been wronged. In 2003, female employees waged a class action suit against Wal-Mart claiming that the company systematically discriminated against women by unfairly promoting men to management positions. Also in 2003, FedEx was sued by a group of minority employees who, like the Wal-Mart employees, claimed they were unfairly passed over for promotions. In both cases, the companies paid hundreds of millions of dollars to settle these lawsuits.

Breaking antidiscrimination laws makes companies vulnerable to employees' lawsuits. In 2003 Fed Ex was sued by a group of its minority employees claiming the company overlooked them for managerial promotions.

Ultimately, companies do themselves a disservice by engaging in discrimination. In addition to facing fines and lawsuits, these companies do not take advantage of the best talent available to them when they discriminate. In addition, because the United States (and the world) is becoming a more diverse place, companies that fail to embrace minority employees often find themselves out-of-step with the marketplace. This puts them at a competitive disadvantage.

LAWS PROMOTING OCCUPATIONAL HEALTH AND SAFETY   A final set of laws governs how companies must protect the health and safety of their employees while on the job. The U.S. Department of Labor Occupational Safety and Health Organization (OSHA) is the government agency primarily responsible for enforcing these laws. Each year in the United States and other countries, thousands of employees are killed in work-related accidents, and hundreds of thousands more are injured in some way. The risks facing firefighters and police officers are clear, but the workers who build skyscrapers and cooling towers and are employed in industries like building and manufacturing must all be protected from harm.

Most companies make the need to protect their employees from harm a major priority. But because abiding by health and safety regulations can be expensive, other companies do not or they take shortcuts to save money. For example, in 2001 a huge power generator blew up in one of Ford's car plants killing several employees and inuring many others. Although Ford had generally followed U.S. health and safety laws, it became clear to investigators that Ford could have been more proactive. For instance, it could have better trained the workers responsible for repairing and servicing the generator. Instead, the workers had been allowed to take shortcuts that saved them time and Ford money, which indirectly may have contributed to the explosion.

One particularly horrid example of how an unethical company can cause harm by failing to follow basic health and safety procedures occurred in a chicken processing plant in 1991. Twenty-five employees were killed in a huge fire at a North Carolina plant because managers had illegally locked all of the plant exits. Why? To prevent employee theft. Although stealing chickens is not ethical behavior, there were other ways to prevent it, like putting alarms on doors or hiring security personnel. But that would have been more expensive.

The company chose to lock the doors, instead, and when the fire broke out employees could not escape and perished in the blaze. The plant's owner subsequently entered a plea bargain with the state of North Carolina and was sentenced to 15 years in prison. The company also was fined over $1 million, its plants in North Carolina and Georgia were shut down, and it went bankrupt as a result of the tragedy. Survivors of the blaze lobbied for the federal government and state of North Carolina to hire more inspectors to enforce laws that govern safe work practices so that such a tragedy will never happen again.

Laws Affecting Business Organization

In general most companies are free to group and organize their employees as they see fit. It is up to managers to design their company's organizational structure to make profitable use of its resources. To help promote the survival and increase the profitability of business enterprises, however, two types of law have been enacted: laws concerning a company's incorporation and bankruptcy and laws that help a company protect its resources.

LAWS OF INCORPORATION AND BANKRUPTCY   Companies are bound by laws that specify how they can incorporate. In addition, in order to "go public," or raise capital in the stock market, companies must provide detailed information about their business models and financial condition. This allows government agencies, such as the SEC, mutual fund companies, and individual investors to scrutinize a company's activities to ensure it is acting ethically and legally. All around the world business laws make it necessary for companies to issue periodic financial reports. These reports must discuss how well a company's business model is working, analyze the opportunities and threats a company is facing, and detail its current financial condition so investors can scrutinize the performance of its managers.

The directors and managers of a company are legally liable for the actions they take to manage a company's resources. They can be sued if they fail to carry out their duty to protect the assets of stockholders and the health and safety of employees. At the other end of the scale, companies that are performing poorly must abide by the laws that govern how they should restructure or dissolve their companies. Just as people in the United States can declare personal bankruptcy, so a company can declare **Chapter 7 bankruptcy,** in which case it is dissolved and its remaining assets go to its creditors and owners.

In the United States large companies typically declare **Chapter 11 bankruptcy,** in which case its creditors and owners cannot seize its assets while the company prepares a new business model. A judge decides if the new model will allow the company to survive and perform better. If so, it is approved, and the company is allowed to leave Chapter 11 and function normally. In 2004, for example, United Airlines, the fourth largest U.S. airline declared Chapter 11 bankruptcy for the second time after it continued to lose millions of dollars a month. The judge hearing the case is scrutinizing its managers' new business model that details how it will be able to reduce its operating costs. If the reorganization plan is not approved, the judge could order that United be dissolved and its assets sold to pay its creditors.

Chapter 7 bankruptcy
The dissolution of a business whereby its assets are sold to repay its creditors and owners.

Chapter 11 bankruptcy The dissolution of a company whereby it is legally protected from its creditors and allowed to develop a viable new business model.

LAWS PROTECTING A BUSINESS'S RESOURCES   When a company's managers use its resources in an enterprising way, the result is a stream of innovations that create new and improved products and increase its profitability. Companies invest enormous amounts of money in research and development to develop innovative new products. It also costs a great deal to build new manufacturing facilities to make the products and to pay for the nationwide marketing campaigns necessary to attract customers.

It would hardly be fair or equitable if, after a company spends hundreds of millions of dollars on these activities, a competitor could just come along and piggyback on the company's innovations and begin to produce a copycat product. If it were easy to do such a thing, few companies would make the investment necessary to develop new products. Technological progress would wane, and the standard of living in a society would advance little over time.

As Chapter 2 discusses, property rights give people the right to own and control productive resources and to profit from them. To motivate entrepreneurs and companies to take risks and invest in new ventures with unknown payoffs, laws have been enacted to protect the profits that result from successful efforts to innovate or create new products. People and companies are given the legal property rights to own and protect their creations by applying for and being granted, patents, copyrights, and trademarks.

Patents give their owners the property right to use, control, license, and otherwise profit from their creations for a period of 20 years from the date the patent is issued by the U.S. Patent Office. In other words, patents confer a monopoly right to their owners—the individual inventors or companies that conducted and paid for the research that led to the new products. One of the most profitable kinds of patent is that received by pharmaceutical companies that develop new drugs. Merck, the company that developed Prozac and Viagra, made billions from the sale of these drugs. Once a patent has expired, however (as the patent for Prozac

United Airlines has filed bankruptcy twice in recent years. The company was given an opportunity to fix its business model and reorganize after the first filing. Unfortunately, it did not work, and United was forced to file again. If the judge adjudicating the second filing doesn't believe a second reorganization will improve United's prospects, the company could be dissolved.

patents Legal documents that give their owners the right to use, control, license, and profit for a 20-year period from new products or processes they have created.

copyrights Legal documents that give their owners the right to own and profit from intellectual property such as written or visual media.

has), any company can manufacture a copy, or generic, version of the original drug. Generic drugs are sold at a much lower price because it's far easier to analyze and copy their chemical formulas than it is to develop the drugs in the first place.

Copyrights also confer a monopoly right on their owner. They are typically granted to people who create "intellectual property," such as written or visual works—books, videogames, poems, and songs produced by authors, software experts, poets and musicians. If they wish, the owners of the copyright can sell it to other people or companies—such as when a movie company buys the rights to turn a new book into a movie from its author. Copyrights last for much longer periods than patents, often the lifetime of the work's creator and beyond.

Currently, laws governing the length of copyrights are changing. There is a growing feeling that copyrights should be granted for much shorter periods, perhaps for just 20 years or for the life of their creator. Once a copyright expires, intellectual property enters the public domain and becomes a public good, meaning that anyone is free to make use of it at no cost.

trademarks Property rights to the name of a product or the company that produces it.

To increase the benefits from their creations, innovators of new products and services are also given the legal right to the trademarks that they use to identify their products to customers. Trademarks are property rights to the name of a product (such as Nescafé or Ivory soap), any symbols or logos associated with it, and the company that produces it (such as Nestlé or Procter & Gamble). Trademarks give their owner the sole legal right to use these names or symbols and control the use to which they are put, for example, advertising a product.

Since people and companies have to invest their creativity, time, and money to obtain copyrights and trademarks and develop a "brand name" it is only fair to allow them to benefit from the "identity" of their creations. Thus, J.K. Rowling, the creator of Harry Potter, holds the copyrights to her books, and she and her publishing company own the trademarks associated with the Harry Potter brand name. Nobody can issue Harry Potter toys or clothing without paying a licensing fee to them. Protecting property and resources of all kind is one of the principal purposes of the law.

In summary, a complex system of laws and regulations exists to govern business commerce, occupations, and organizations. They have been passed to protect the rights of companies, their stockholders, employees, and the public at large—all of whom are affected by their business activities. In essence, these laws have been passed to protect the public interest and ensure the continuing prosperity and well-being of a nation. A society's goal is to create a legal system that motivates entrepreneurs and companies to create goods and services that are profitable. At the same time, the purpose of law is to ensure that no person or group is able to ruthlessly profit at the expense of others.

Did You Know?

Descriptive terms—such as speedy, tasty, express, and sweet—cannot be trademarked unless they are so closely affiliated with one product that they would cause confusion among consumers if used to describe something else.[8]

Summary of the Chapter

Ethical issues permeate business decision making and affect the efficiency and effectiveness of a nation's business commerce. The result of ethical behavior is a general increase in a company's profitability and in a nation's standard of living, well-being, and prosperity. This chapter has made the following main points:

1. An ethical dilemma is the quandary people find themselves in when they have to decide if they should act in a way that might help one person or group (and is the "right" thing to do) even though it might hurt others or not be in their own self-interests.

2. Ethics are the inner-guiding moral principles, values, and beliefs that people use to analyze a situation and then decide the "right" way to behave.

3. Ethical beliefs alter and change as time passes, and, as they do so, laws change to reflect them.

4. Stakeholders are people and groups who have a claim on and a stake in a company. The main stakeholder groups are stockholders, managers, employees, suppliers and distributors, customers, and a community, society, and nation.

5. It is in the best interests of a company to behave ethically.

6. To determine if a business decision is right or wrong, companies can use four ethical rules to analyze it: the utilitarian, moral rights, justice, and practical rules.

7. When companies behave ethically, the tragedy of the commons can be averted. This lowers transaction costs and leads to a general increase in a company's profitability and benefits society as a whole.

8. Differences in a company's or a country's business ethics are based on societal, occupational, individual, and organizational factors.

9. The legal environment of business consists of the laws and regulations that have been passed to prevent unethical business activities from occurring when free markets cannot.

10. Four main types of laws affecting business commerce are antitrust laws, consumer protection laws, environmental laws, and laws relating to the public interest.

11. Several types of laws have been passed to prevent unethical practices related to business occupations: laws regulating occupational qualifications, laws governing business diversity, and laws promoting employee health and safety.

12. Two types of law that are especially relevant to a company's form of business organization are laws concerning incorporation and bankruptcy and laws that help it to protect its valuable resources. The granting of patents, copyrights, and trademarks are main ways of allowing people and companies to protect and profit from their creations.

Developing Business Skills

QUESTIONS FOR DISCUSSION AND ACTION

1. What is the relationship between ethics and the law?

2. Why do the claims and interests of stakeholders sometimes conflict?

3. Why should managers use ethical criteria to guide their decision making?

4. *Action.* Find a manager and ask about the most important ethical rules he or she follows to make the right decisions.

5. What are some of the most unethical business practices you have encountered as an employee?

6. What are main determinants of business ethics?

7. What purpose do laws and regulations governing business serve, and why is the public interest important?

ETHICS IN ACTION

Dealing with Ethical Dilemmas

Use the chapter material to decide how you should respond to each of the following three ethical dilemmas.

• You are planning to leave your job to go work for a competitor. Your boss invites you to an important meeting about the new products the company will be rolling out in the New Year. Do you go to the meeting?

• You sell expensive sports cars. A young manager who has just received a promotion comes in and really wants to buy one that you know is out of his or her price range. Do you encourage the manager to buy it so you can receive a big commission from the sale?

• You sign a contract with a young rock band, and they agree to let you produce their next seven records for which they will receive 5% of royalties. Their first record is a smash hit and sells millions. Do you automatically increase the band's royalty rate on their future records?

SMALL GROUP EXERCISE

Is Chewing Gum the "Right" Thing to Do?

Read the following. Then break up into groups or three or four people and answer the following discussion questions.

In the United States the right to chew gum is taken for granted. But if you chew gum on a street in Singapore and throw it on the ground you can be arrested. Chewing gum is strictly controlled in Singapore because those in power believe it creates a disgusting mess on pavements and people cannot be trusted to throw away their gum safely. Although in the United States you can generally chew gum anywhere you want, it is often against the rules to chew gum in a high school classroom, church, and so on.

1. What makes chewing gum acceptable in the United States and unacceptable in Singapore?

2. Why can you chew gum on the street but not in school or church in the United States?

3. How can you use ethical principles to decide whether gum chewing is ethical or unethical, or if its use should be strictly controlled by law?

DEVELOPING GOOD BUSINESS SENSE

Creating an Ethical Code

You are an entrepreneur who has decided to go into business and open a steak and chicken restaurant. Your business plan requires you to hire at least twenty people as chefs, waiters, and so on. As the owner, you are drawing up a list of ethical principles that each of these people will receive and must agree to when they accept your job offer. These principles outline your view of what behavior is acceptable both from you and from them.

1. Create a list of the five main ethical rules or principles you will use to govern the way your business operates. Be sure to spell out how these principles relate to your stakeholders. For example, specifically state the rules you intend to follow when dealing with your employees and customers.

EXPLORING THE WORLD WIDE WEB

3M's Code of Ethics

Go to 3M's Web site (www.3M.com), and click on About 3M tab. Then click on "Business Conduct Policies" tab and look at the chairman's statement. Finally, click on and read some of 3M's specific ethical policies. **For more Web activities, log on to www.mhhe.com/jonesintro.**

1. Why is reputation so important to 3M?

2. What kinds of laws and regulations most relate to 3M's businesses both at home and abroad?

3. How would you describe 3M's ethical stance?

BusinessWeek CASE FOR DISCUSSION

Putting Teeth in Corporate Ethics Codes

Clark Consulting, a compensation and benefit consulting firm, has had a corporate code of ethics in place for years. But following the 2002 passage of the Sarbanes-Oxley law reforming corporate governance, Chief Executive Tom Wamberg revised it, redistributed it, and started referring to it in weekly newsletters distributed to all employees. It wasn't long before the code was put to the test.

Earlier this year, Wamberg learned that one of his senior consultants was bragging to other employees about how he had "fired" a particularly demanding client. Wamberg was outraged. Rule No. 1 of the code is that clients come first. "For us, that was a cardinal sin," says Wamberg, who dismissed that consultant, citing the code.

Now he sees the benefits of having a public statement in place and sticking to it. "If you don't have something to stand up to and look to, you could easily give a slap on the wrist and say, 'Don't do it again,'" says Wamberg.

"SANCTIONS" SECTION. Well, not so easily anymore. In part due to new regulatory requirements (including a new Nasdaq rule requiring listed companies to distribute a code to all employees)— and also because of so many high-profile cases recently where corporate malfeasance has brought down major businesses—chief executives are doing their best to turn the code of ethics into a document with real teeth.

"There's a whole spectrum of activities that can make this thing come alive," says Dan DiFilippo, who leads PricewaterhouseCoopers' governance and compliance practice. Companies are rewriting the codes, making them much more detailed and specific. German software giant SAP has a 14-page code with sections that describe conduct with customers, vendors, and competitors, as well as stock-trading rules.

Businesses are adding enforcement measures, including guidelines for employees to follow if they see violations. A "sanctions" section in SAP's code explains that any act "in opposition to this Code of Conduct is subject to internal review, and can result in consequences that affect employment, and could possibly lead to external investigation, civil law proceedings, or criminal charges."

SIGNATURES REQUIRED. No longer just published in an employee handbook, the codes are being posted on corporate Web sites and around offices. Companies now want the statement to be visible to people outside, like regulators, vendors, and customers—as well as employees.

"It always was part of our DNA," says Harold Tinkler, chief ethics and compliance officer at accounting firm Deloitte & Touche, which is finalizing a new, more detailed code. "But in today's world, the public at large wants to see it demonstrated." According to a recent survey by New York-based research firm Governance Metrix, which rates companies on their compliance efforts, 51% of U.S. concerns disclose a code of ethics, although 32% allow a waiver in some cases.

Perhaps most notably, businesses are increasingly requiring all employees to read and sign the ethics statement. This measure is an apparent extension of the Sarbanes-Oxley rule that CEOs and CFOs certify the accuracy of company financials. "They're pushing that requirement down the ranks," says Kirk Jordan, a compliance attorney who's vice-president for research at Integrity Interactive, which provides Web-based ethics and compliance training programs. Usually the sign-off is a condition of employment—and sometimes a condition of getting a bonus or a raise.

TECH BACKUP. Another new trend: Companies are adding more training around their codes of ethics. Jordan says the new focus is on providing guidance for senior managers, rather than assuming they understand the issues. At software concern Hyperion Solutions, CEO Jeff Rodek trains managers to distinguish between employees who underperform—who should be given several chances to improve—and workers who violate the ethics code, where "it can be one strike, you're out," he says. "It's important that people know the difference."

One goal of the training is to bring ethics into play during key decision-making points. Some outfits are making research into ethical issues a part of the due diligence on another company during an acquisition, says PwC's DiFilippo. Deloitte & Touche will ask managers to explore ethical issues with the engagement team before starting each new audit, says Tinkler.

Technology is increasingly involved in all these pursuits. Integrity Interactive's code-of-ethics training course includes a testing component. All employees must continue training until they score 100% on a test.

HOW MUCH GOOD? Last November ACL Services, which makes software used in internal audits, launched a new "Continuous Controls Monitoring" solution, which flags possible code-of-conduct violations, like purchasing from a vendor that charges more than the standard price (that might mean the employee is getting some sort of kickback). "Actively testing for controls begins to create a culture of accountability and ethics," says Harald Will, ACL's president and CEO.

It's still unclear how much good a code of conduct can do in preventing ethical lapses. Even though accounting firm Arthur Andersen had a strong ethics program in place, it didn't survive the fallout of having signed off on failed energy giant Enron's books. The program clearly didn't do much good when the firm's Houston office should have raised questions about a major client's activities.

"It's during difficult decisions that someone's ethics are put to the test," says William Henrich, vice-chairman of turnaround consulting firm Getzler Henrich & Associates and a former partner at Arthur Andersen. "At that point, whether or not they signed a piece of paper doesn't make a difference."

FROM THE TOP. Many consultants on business-risk issues say a company needs to take more important measures than a statement to prevent ethical lapses from harming it. "A code of ethics is an easy thing to redo," says Michael Chagares, who leads consulting firm Marsh's business-risk practice. "The question is how you get a real change in behavior."

More important than emphasizing the code is making sure the board has independent members and that a system of checks and balances on management is in place throughout the company. It's also essential that the business has mechanisms in place that lets problems come to the surface, Chagares says.

Even if a code of ethics is just a starting point, it certainly doesn't hurt, consultants and chief executives agree. And it has the most power if it appears to come straight from the top. Wamberg says he worries that people at his company pay only lip service to standing by the corporate code of ethics. "That's why I just pound it in," he says. When it comes to ethics statements, employees can expect more pounding in the months to come.

Source: Amy Stone, "Putting Teeth in Corporate Ethics Codes," *BusinessWeek Online,* February 19, 2004.

QUESTIONS

1. In what ways are companies trying to strengthen their ethics codes?

2. One issue raised in the article and in the opening case of this chapter concerns instituting "real change" in the ethical behavior of companies and their employees. What more can a company do to make sure its code of ethics is followed?

BusinessWeek CASE FOR DISCUSSION

It Takes a Village—And a Consultant

Last summer, accounting-and-consulting giant PricewaterhouseCoopers (PwC) tapped partner Tahir Ayub for a consulting gig unlike anything he had done before. His job: helping village leaders in the Namibian outback grapple with their community's growing AIDS crisis. Faced with language barriers, cultural differences, and scant access to electricity, Ayub, 39, and two colleagues had to scrap their PowerPoint presentations in favor of a more low-tech approach: face-to-face discussion. The village chiefs learned that they needed to garner community support for programs to combat the disease, and Ayub learned an important lesson as well: Technology isn't always the answer. "You better put your beliefs and biases to one side and figure out new ways to look at things," he said.

Ayub may never encounter as extreme a cultural disconnect at PwC as he did in Namibia. But for the next generation of partners, overcoming barriers and forging a connection with clients the world over will be a crucial part of their jobs. It's those skills that PwC hopes to foster in partners who take part in the Ulysses Program, which sends top midcareer talent to the developing world for eight-week service projects. For a fairly modest investment of $15,000 per person, plus salaries, Ulysses both tests the talent and expands the worldview of the accounting firm's future leaders. Since the company started the program four years ago, it has attracted the attention of Johnson & Johnson, Cisco Systems, and other big companies considering their own programs.

While results are hard to quantify, PwC is convinced that the program works. All two dozen graduates are still working at the company. Half of them have been promoted, and most have new responsibilities. Just as important, all 24 people say they have a stronger commitment to PwC—in part because of the commitment the firm made to them and in part

because of their new vision of the firm's values. Says Global Managing Partner Willem Bröcker: "We get better partners from this exercise."

The Ulysses Program is PwC's answer to one of the biggest challenges confronting professional services companies: identifying and training up-and-coming leaders who can find unconventional answers to intractable problems. By tradition and necessity, new PwC leaders are nurtured from within. But with 8,000 partners, identifying those with the necessary business savvy and relationship-building skills isn't easy. Just as the program gives partners a new view of PwC, it also gives PwC a new view of them, particularly their ability to hold up under pressure.

For midcareer partners who were weaned on e-mail and the Blackberry, this was no walk in the park. They had become accustomed to a world of wireless phones, sleek offices, and Chinese take-out—so the rigors of the developing world came as quite a shock. Brian P. McCann, 37, a mergers and acquisitions expert from PwC's Boston office, had never been to a third-world country before his stint in Belize, where he encountered dirt-floored houses, sick children, and grinding poverty.

Ayub, having been born in Africa, considered himself worldly. Even so, long days spent among Africa's exploding HIV-positive population took their psychological toll. With his work confined to daylight hours—there was often no electricity—Dinu Bumbacea, a 37-year-old partner in PwC's Romanian office who spent time in Zambia working with an agricultural center, had plenty of time to dwell on the misery all around him. "Africa is poor, and we all know that," says Bumbacea. "But until you go there, you don't understand how poor it is. We take so much for granted."

For more than 15 years, companies have used social-responsibility initiatives to develop leaders. But PwC takes the concept to a new level. Participants spend eight weeks in developing countries lending their business skills to local aid groups–from an eco-tourism collective in Belize to small organic farmers in Zambia to AIDS groups in Namibia. Ulysses also presents participants with the challenge of collaborating across cultures with local clients as well as with PwC colleagues from other global regions. Ayub, for example, was paired with partners from Mexico and the Netherlands.

BEYOND ACCOUNTING

PWC says the program, now in its third cycle, gives participants a broad, international perspective that's crucial for a company that does business around the world. Traditional executive education programs turn out men and women who have specific job skills but little familiarity with issues outside their narrow specialty, according to Douglas Ready, director of the International Consortium for Executive Development Research. PwC says Ulysses helps prepare participants for challenges that go beyond the strict confines of accounting or consulting and instills values such as community involvement that are fundamental to its corporate culture.

Ulysses is also a chance for partners to learn what they can accomplish without their usual resources to lean on. The program forces them to take on projects well outside their expertise. In the summer of 2003, for example, McCann developed a business plan for an ecotourism group in Belize. The experience was an eye-opener. McCann's most lasting memory is a dinner he shared in the home of a Mayan farmer after they spent a day discussing their plan. "He didn't even have electricity," McCann recalls, "but he made do."

PwC partners say they've already adapted their experiences to the task of managing people and clients. Malaysian partner Jennifer Chang says her team noticed a shift in her managerial style after the Belize trip. She listened more and became more flexible. "Once you see how slowly decisions are made in other places, you gain patience for the people you work with," she says. Ayub, who was promoted in June, now manages 20 partners. He says he favors face-to-face conversations over e-mail because the low-tech approach builds trust. "It made the difference in Namibia," he says.

If insights like those ripple out across the firm, Ulysses will be more than a voyage of personal discovery for a handful of partners. It could help build leaders capable of confronting the challenges of an increasingly global business. And that, says PwC, is the whole point.

QUESTIONS

1. What does PwC's program of sending consultants to help people in developing countries say about its corporate ethics?

2. In what ways will the program benefit PwC and its consultants as well as the people the program is intended to help?

Source: Jessi Hempel and Seth Porges, "It Takes a Village—And a Consultant," *BusinessWeek Online,* September 2004.

BUILDING YOUR MANAGEMENT SKILLS
Know Thyself

Have you ever cheated on a test or seen another student do it? Watched another employee take something from your workplace without paying for it or play a computer game instead of working? How did you feel about the way you handled the situation? Lockheed Martin, the aerospace company, has devised a board game to help its employees develop their ethical and social responsibility decision-making skills. You can assess your own "Ethical Decision-Making Skills" by using a version of the game that is on your Student DVD.

CHAPTER VIDEO
New Belgium Brewery (NBB)

Business ethics and social responsibility are not equivalent concepts. Ethics guides behavior regarding appropriate business practices of individuals whereas social responsibility is organizational behavior that is directed toward the greater community.

At New Belgium Brewery, environmental ethics are part of the core value system of the company's corporate culture. Jeff Lebesch, owner of NBB, started the firm with very low capital investment, low volume production, and small margins. He and his company were forced to think outside the box. And think they did! Looking to cut costs, the company was able to reduce the amount of resources used as raw materials, invested in technology to achieve broader energy efficiency, re-uses resources, and recycles materials that cannot be immediately reused in the process. All of these goals are part of the core value system of social responsibility.

Social responsibility, environmentally safe production processes, and a corporate culture that is supportive, combine to create an organization where individuals forgo personal gain in order to achieve social responsibility for the firm. These values run so deep in fact that the employees voted to use part of their bonus pool to invest in longer-term solutions to achieve environmentally safer production methods.

The cost savings achieved by using a socially responsible approach have more than compensated for the investments made by Jeff and his employees.

1. What would be considered the basic "ethical dilemma" for New Belgium Brewery?

2. Is there a difference between ethics and values?

3. Theoretically, how did the decisions to be environmentally conscious and create a socially responsible corporate culture, evolve at NBB?

Part 2

The Human Side of Business

Part Two, *The Human Side of Business,* discusses the nature of the individual and group processes that must be managed when people work together in a business organization. Chapter 6 examines the role of leadership, influence, persuasion, communication, and politics in making a business organization function efficiently and effectively. Chapter 7 looks at the role of individual motivation and group processes including teamwork in the value creation process. It also examines how self-interest and competition lead to bargaining and negotiation. Both these chapters discuss basic processes that are at the heart of business commerce, and which frequently revolve around occupational issues, such as contests between people in the same function and between functions. Chapter 8 then discusses how organizational structure and culture motivate and coordinate people and reduce the bargaining and negotiation costs necessary to secure peoples' cooperation—the essential role of business organization.

CHAPTER

6

Leadership, Influence, and Communication in Business

Learning Objectives

After studying this chapter, you should be able to:

1. Appreciate the way a manager's ability to effectively lead, influence, and persuade other people influences a company's efficiency, effectiveness, and profitability.

2. Identify the five sources of a leader's power and understand how leadership involves the effective use of power to influence other people.

3. Differentiate between four main approaches to leadership and recognize that effective leadership involves matching a leadership approach to the characteristics of employees and the work situation.

4. Identify five characteristics of effective leaders.

5. Understand the vital role communication plays in influencing others in a business organization and describe a model of persuasive communication.

6. Define organizational politics and understand how political tactics are used to influence and persuade others.

WHY IS THIS IMPORTANT ❓

Have you ever found yourself watching a movie or eating at a restaurant when you hadn't wanted to go out? A friend, a parent, a brother or sister has persuaded you to do something you hadn't planned or thought about. How did that happen? Someone used influence or leadership skills to open your mind to a new possibility or change your direction.

Leaders understand how to use power and influence tactics to achieve their goals. These are skills that you can learn, as this chapter explains. Since it is an organization's people who create success or failure, good leadership and communication skills are vital in business.

A Question of Business
Tammy Savage and the "Threedegrees"

What is Tammy Savage's approach to leadership?

Tammy Savage joined Microsoft's New York City sales office straight out of Cal State, Fresno in 1993 when she was 22. A marketing whiz, Savage soon gained a reputation as an expert in understanding the needs of under-30 Internet users, the "Net Generation," or "Net-Gen." She became a central figure in the New York sales office's dealings with programmers back at Microsoft's Redmond, Washington, headquarters, and her NetGen knowledge earned her a promotion. Later, she became a manager in Microsoft's business development group and moved to Redmond.

Savage used her new, more senior, position to reevaluate the whole of Microsoft's business development efforts for the NetGen. Her conclusion was that Microsoft was missing the boat and risked losing the NetGen to rival companies such as AOL and Yahoo! whose instant messenger and entertainment services were already very popular. Savage's goal was to increase the popularity of Microsoft's own Internet services to regain the loyalty and business of the NetGen. Her problem was to devise new kinds of services that the NetGen would just have to have. Savage used the resources of her new position to begin a major research program to find out what needs NetGen's were trying to satisfy.

In the early 2000s, Savage presented her findings to Microsoft's top managers, including Bill Gates. She explained that the principal need

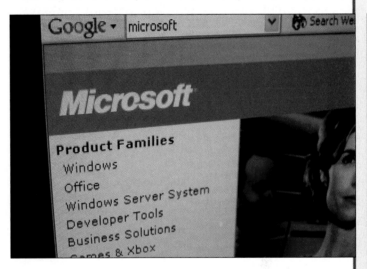

NetGenners were trying to satisfy was the need for online companionship, socialization, and building a "buddy" network. Microsoft's top brass listened to Savage's arguments but didn't find them persuasive: *Why* did the NetGen want to share their experiences and gain new friends on the Internet? Luckily for Savage, one top manager, Jim Allchin *did* understand what she was driving at. Allchin was persuaded that she had a new vision for how to develop Internet software that would attract young people. He saw to it that Savage was made the leader of a team assembled to develop the ideal NetGen Web software.

In 2001, Savage began recruiting new college graduates with software expertise to join her team. From the beginning, she adopted the leadership approach that Microsoft is well known for—a participative and achievement-oriented approach. Microsoft tries to hire the best new people it can and then gives them considerable freedom to find new and better ways to help the company achieve its mission. Just as Allchin had used this approach to encourage Savage to perform at a high level, now Savage, as a leader, was in the same situation. Because she was recruiting people who were highly competent and achievement driven, she had to master Microsoft's hands-off leadership approach. Savage made it clear to team members that they would all have to work together to develop the new NetGen Internet software as quickly as possible. It was up to them to find a way to create the new "relationship oriented" software that would allow Microsoft to take back the NetGen.

The result of Savage's team's efforts was software called *threedegrees* (3°), introduced in 2003. It provided a platform for the NetGen to develop online relationships. If you have used it yourself, you know that people can use 3° to build an online club of up to 10 friends who can jointly create a unique identity for their club using digital images, sounds, and animations called "winks." Whenever a club member wants to share something new with other members, he or she can inform all of the members of the club simultaneously using 3°'s instant messaging capabilities. The software also allows members to share their songs, music, feelings, and experiences, thereby building online "togetherness." When the 3° team rolled out its new software on Microsoft's internal Web site, thousands of Microsoft employees began to form clubs of their own to get to know each other better. The question in the 2000s was, would the software succeed with the NetGen?[1]

Overview

As we discussed in previous chapters, at the center of any business venture is the intent to create profit by finding ways to make and sell the goods and services that customers want to buy. In 2005, it was not clear if Tammy Savage's team's new product would be a success and if the NetGen would begin to use it. One of the most interested observers was Bill Gates who, having tried the new software, now understood the difference between using the Internet to "get something done" versus using it to "build relationships." According to Savage, Gates "totally gets it now." Whatever the eventual success of 3°, one thing is certain, the product was brought to market quickly because Tammy Savage proved to be an effective leader. She is an example of someone who is capable of developing a personal approach to leadership that results in a high-performing, committed team of employees.

In this chapter, we examine the issue of how to influence and persuade other people—managers and employees—to perform their jobs in ways that increase a company's efficiency, effectiveness, and profitability. First, we examine the nature of leadership and the sources of power available to managers to influence the work behaviors and attitudes of employees. Second, we describe four different kinds of approaches to leadership. Third,

Sir Richard Branson, the founder of Virgin Group, is an effective leader who is viewed as a "people person." Branson takes up notable challenges and encourages employees to achieve them.

we examine why, and under what conditions, these different approaches can be effective or ineffective and some general characteristics of effective leaders.

We then turn to the issue of influencing people through persuasive communication. We identify the different kinds of people and groups who need to be influenced and persuaded and describe a model of the communication process. We then examine how leaders use organizational politics to gain power over and influence other people. Several kinds of these political tactics are described. By the end of this chapter, you will understand the vital role leadership, communication, and politics play when it comes to influencing people in ways that increase the efficiency and effectiveness of business organizations.

Business Leadership

Once an entrepreneur has identified a business opportunity, to get the business off the ground, he or she then needs to engage in the four managerial functions discussed in Chapter 3: planning, organizing, leading, and controlling the business enterprise. Later chapters in this book discuss the thousands of specific operational decisions that must be made in order to do this. In this chapter, however, we discuss more generally what leaders do and how the way they lead can make or break a business.

Leadership involves much more than just possessing the formal power to tell employees what to do, however. Leadership is about using one's personality, beliefs, values, social skills, knowledge, and power to influence other peoples' thoughts, feelings, and behavior. In a business setting, leadership means influencing how people think about and do their jobs, as well as how they feel about the company they work for. An effective leader is a person who can influence, persuade, and engage their followers or employees to work hard and perform well. To approach the issue of leadership let's first examine the sources of power leaders have, which are outlined in Figure 6.1.

leadership The use of one's personality, beliefs, values, social skills, knowledge, and power to influence other peoples' thoughts, feelings, and behavior.

effective leader A person who can persuade his or her subordinates to work hard and perform at high levels.

power The ability of one person to make other people or groups do something that they would *not* have otherwise done.

legitimate power The rightful authority to direct and control employees' activities.

reward power A leader's ability to recognize and acknowledge employees who perform their jobs in a way that meets or exceeds the requirements of their job and company.

Sources of a Leader's Power

Power is often defined as the ability of one person to make other people or groups do something that they would *not* have otherwise done. In other words, power is the ability of a person to influence and control the way other people or groups can choose to act in a particular situation. In business, power ultimately derives from the possession of property rights to use resources. Once a person or company has bought the right to use people's labor, that is, has hired *employees,* they have the legal authority to direct and control these employees' activities. This source of power is known as legitimate power. Tammy Savage has legitimate power because she was appointed to her position by managers above her in Microsoft's hierarchy. She could simply instruct her subordinates to do as she tells them—but would this make her an effective leader?

When leaders possess legitimate power they gain access to two more kinds of power that are important sources of influence and control: reward power and coercive power. Reward power stems from a leader's ability to recognize and acknowledge employees who perform their jobs in a way that meets or exceeds the requirements of their job and company. *Job requirements* include things like achieving a certain level of performance or being courteous and cooperative to one's co-workers. *Company requirements* include things like following the company's rules regarding gift giving and receiving protocols and abiding by the company's health and safety procedures.

Figure 6.1
Sources of a Leader's Power

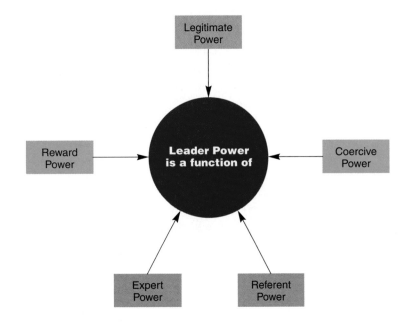

Leader like Tammy Savage selectively reward employees to influence their job performance. Employees who exceed the work performance standards set for them can be rewarded with pay raises and bonuses, more interesting job assignments, advanced training, promotions, and other forms of recognition. In her role as leader, Savage has had to decide how to distribute, or reward, Microsoft stock to her subordinates based on how well each of them performs.

coercive power A leader's ability to sanction or punish employees who fail to meet job and company requirements.

Coercive power, on the other hand, is the leader's ability to sanction or punish employees. When using coercive power, a leader like Savage withdraws rewards or selectively sanctions employees to encourage them to meet their work requirements. If they consistently fail to do so over time, this results in the termination of their employment. In short, leaders develop and use a system of rewards and sanctions, that is, an **incentive system,** to shape, influence, and control the way employees behave in the workplace.

incentive system A system of rewards and sanctions that shapes, influences, and controls the way employees behave at work.

A fourth source of a leader's power is expert power—something that Tammy Savage is widely acknowledged to possess. **Expert power** stems from a person's recognized expertise or superior skill in a particular functional area of business such as marketing or research and development. A marketing manager who has demonstrated an ability to forecast changing customer needs, like Tammy Savage has, or a research scientist with a track record of innovating successful new products, has expert power.

expert power A person's recognized expertise or superior skill in a particular functional area of business.

As leaders, these people are listened to and respected by employees because of their functional abilities and expertise. They attract followers who wish to learn from them in order to increase their own human capital. Expert power is frequently a potent source of influence at all levels. A supervisor who can quickly resolve a problem on a production line that saves a company thousands of dollars will have great influence over his or her employees and sometimes the boss, too.

referent power A leader's ability to influence and persuade other people because of personal qualities that make them attractive to others and effective in social situations.

A fifth source of power that some leaders possess is **referent power,** a leader's ability to influence and persuade other people because of personal qualities that make that person effective in social situations. Sometimes it might be a feature of a leader's personality—like Savage's ability to empathize with other people and make them feel good—that gives a leader influence. Or, it might be a leader's physical attributes such as stature or facial appearance that makes employees look up to and listen to them. Tammy Savage possesses a great stock of referent power. She is listened to and respected because of her ability to understand what the under-30 generation is looking for. She is also liked and respected by her subordinates.

Referent power can also stem from a person's social status, fame, or personal wealth. Many people are nervous or in awe when meeting the President of the United States, the Queen of England, or Bill Gates, for example. This makes these people receptive to what these leaders have to say and willing to follow their directives. Effective corporate leaders take advantage of their referent power to influence employees on a direct, personal level. Often employees want to help a leader succeed because they identify with the leader and his or her goals.

A **charismatic leader** is an exceptional leader whose referent and expert power result in the person being perceived as "larger than life." These people are often regarded as heroes who personify a company and what it stands for. Charismatic leaders seem to have the ability to "connect" with each employee at a personal level. They are also able to effectively communicate how important a company's goals are and how each employee is vital to achieving those goals. Charismatic leaders stir the imagination of their employees and give them the "big picture." They let

David Duncan, a former partner at Arthur Andersen, was a charismatic leader gone wrong. Under Duncan's leadership, Arthur Andersen employees obstructed justice by shredding thousands of Enron-related documents.

charismatic leader
An exceptionally effective leader whose referent and expert power results in followers perceiving them as someone who personifies a company and what it stands for.

employees know why the company they work for is great and what they can do to make it even better. Employees often believe they have a connection with the charismatic leader and want to help that person succeed.

In business, a charismatic leader's influence is often enhanced when they are also the founder or owner of a company. Bill Gates, the founder of Microsoft, has charismatic power not just because of his obvious referent power and acknowledged expertise, but because, as the company's largest shareholder, he has a huge amount of legitimate power. A charismatic leader also knows how to use reward and coercive power to mobilize employee support. Employees who are loyal and capable are promoted up the organizational hierarchy, while those who dissent are often driven from the organization. Here lies the "dark side" of charisma. Charismatic leaders whose intentions are *less* than noble are often able to persuade people to behave in ways that are unethical or illegal. Thus, charisma can be a double-edged sword: It can lead people down both the right and wrong paths.

Leader Power and Employee Behavior and Attitudes

Leaders use their power to influence and control the way employees perform their jobs and work to achieve a company's mission. Most commonly, leaders try to influence several specific kinds of employee work behaviors and work attitudes. These different behaviors and attitudes are outlined in Figure 6.2.

Effective leadership results when managers use their power in ways that improve these behaviors and attitudes. Research has shown, however, that obtaining such a positive outcome depends on the way leaders exercise the different kinds of power they have. It might appear, for example, that a leader who uses coercive power to punish employees who fail to meet their performance standards is using power in an effective way. Research shows, however, that punishing employees can actually lower their desire to work hard and perform at high levels. They are more likely to be inclined to come in late to work, take unnecessary sick days, and search for other jobs, for example. Recall from Chapter 2 how 500 workers a day left Henry Ford's Model-T factory despite being paid 25% above the going rate because they could not tolerate the harsh and abusive way in which supervisors enforced Ford's strict work rules. Punishment can also lower the self-esteem and confidence of employees. They can begin to feel that even if they work harder, they still won't measure up.

The same is true for the other types of power leaders can exercise. Take, for instance, reward power: Reward power can be a powerful motivator. However, leaders commonly fail to link rewards *directly* to the performance of their employees. When employees see no connection between how hard they work and the rewards they receive, they take the rewards for granted. When this happens, the rewards do not ultimately encourage high performance even though they are supposed to. Likewise, although leaders possess legitimate power, if they choose to behave in an overbearing and autocratic way, employees often respond in a negative way. Military personnel might respond well to this kind of power, but it isn't likely to motivate the types of employees who work for Tammy Savage.

As this discussion suggests, possessing power does not make a person an effective leader. *Leadership is the effective use of power in a particular work situation.* To be an effective leader a manager must first learn how to wield power wisely—in a way that that will result in higher performance levels—not employee backlash.

Work Behaviors	Work Attitudes
• Level of effort put into job	• Satisfaction with job
• Quantity, quality reliability of work performance	• Commitment and loyalty to company
• Unexplained absence from work	• Desire to cooperate with co-workers
• Intention to quit job and leave company	• Personal relationship with boss

Figure 6.2
Important Work Behaviors and Attitudes

Later in the chapter we discuss four different leadership approaches that combine the five sources of power in quite different ways. First, however, to help illustrate the complexity of business leadership, consider the following scenario. It describes the problems facing an entrepreneur setting up a new snack-food distribution company. We will use this scenario at many points in this chapter to clarify the leadership process.

Tony Knowles's Leadership Challenge

When, as the result of a graduation present from his parents, Tony Knowles visited New York City, he came across a just-introduced line of healthy new snack foods. The new snack foods were low fat and flavored with exotic herbs and spices that made them taste better than chocolate. They also went well with tea, coffee, and wine and had become popular with young, health-conscious New Yorkers. After tasting and enjoying the new snack foods, Knowles decided that if he could obtain the franchise to distribute and sell them to coffee shops, restaurants, and delicatessens in his home city of Tampa, Florida, he might have a profitable business on his hands.

Tony subsequently contacted the snack food manufacturer and used an inheritance from his aunt to pay the $25,000 franchisee fee giving Knowles the right to distribute and sell the snack foods in Tampa for one year. The contract requires that Knowles earn $1 million in snack-food revenues in the first year of the business's operation; otherwise the franchise will not be renewed. The snack-food manufacturer has informed Knowles that other new franchise holders will each earn between $100,000 and $250,000 in profit on $1 million in sales after paying their operating costs. It will cost $500,000 to purchase the snack-food franchise outright. This means that to make a profit of $250,000, a franchisee has to limit the business's other operating costs to $250,000. A franchisee's ability to control operating costs and run the business efficiently and effectively determines whether he or she can make $250,000 in profit.

Knowles decides he wants to earn $250,000 in profit, so he creates a budget to cover his operating costs. A **budget** is a set of financial constraints that limit how much money can be spent to purchase resources to meet a predetermined target, such as a profit goal. To make $250,000 in profit on $1 million in sales, Knowles cannot spend more than $250,000 to operate his business, or he will fail to meet that target. His budget is therefore $250,000.

budget A set of financial constraints limiting how much money can be spent to meet a predetermined target, such as a profit goal.

Knowles has calculated how much it will cost him to operate his new business for one year. He has leased five vans to distribute the product at a cost of $50,000 a year. He has interviewed and hired five drivers to distribute the snack foods; they will each receive a base pay of $30,000 a year. He forecasts that other operating expenses such as gas for vans, computers, telephones, insurance, and so on will come to $25,000 for the year. This means he has already reached his operating budget of $250,000. Luckily, on the Knowles family ranch just outside Tampa, is a large barn that will make a suitable warehouse. Knowles intends to operate the company from out of the barn to stay within his budget.

Knowles has negotiated agreements with 500 outlets in Tampa to stock and sell his snack food (although there are thousands more). After each outlet has been stocked, payment for the snack foods will be made based upon how much of it is subsequently restocked at each outlet. In this way, Knowles hopes to generate a constant cash flow that he can use to pay the snack-food manufacturer and his other operating costs. If he fails to sell a sufficient amount of the product in the first few months, he will have a negative cash flow. If this happens, however, he still has $25,000 of inheritance money that will allow him to operate for a few more months. After

Did You Know?

According to a survey of *Fortune*'s 1,000 top managers, the top two characteristics business leaders need for success are compassion and building teamwork.[2]

How can Tony Knowles make sure his drivers will perform their jobs reliably and consistently?

that, he will be unable to cover current operating costs. His capital will be gone, and that will be the end of his business venture. Knowles is excited and nervous, his five drivers are due to turn up at his warehouse today and he has 48 hours to teach them their jobs and routes. The snack-food supplier's truck is due in his barnyard shortly thereafter, and he will be in business.

As the owner and manager of a business, how should Knowles lead and motivate these five people so that they will work to make his business model profitable? How can he make sure his drivers will perform their jobs reliably and consistently and drive and stock their sales routes and outlets fast and efficiently? Given that he needs to increase snack-food sales quickly, how can he encourage his drivers to be enterprising and find better ways to perform their jobs—to locate potential new sales outlets as they are driving their routes, for example?

During college, Knowles worked several part-time jobs and had worked for several different managers with very different leadership approaches. Some of the managers created a work environment in which employees worked enthusiastically and diligently and cooperated with one another. Other managers created a work environment in which employees arrived late in the morning, called in sick a lot, and seemed to just "go through the motions." Knowles has been thinking about why and how these leadership approaches influenced employees to behave in such positive or negative ways.

Knowles knows that in addition to the right leadership approach, many other factors like rewards and job characteristics are important motivation factors. He is paying each of his drivers a salary of $30,000—about average for a local driving job in the Tampa Bay area. It is as much as he can presently afford to pay, although he could offer employees more incentives later if sales of the snack foods increase. But how should Knowles motivate his employees in the meantime? Should he have his drivers work separately or as a team, for example? Will he get the most effort from drivers if he creates five different routes and makes one driver solely responsible for servicing the sales outlets on that route? Or, should he design the jobs so that all drivers service all routes. If he does this, drivers can fill in for one another as needed and cooperate when business on one route gets particularly busy.

Knowles knows that the success of his business depends crucially on his drivers' motivation to work hard, to learn how to cover their sales routes quickly, and to be responsive to his customers (the sales outlets). What kind of personal approach to leadership should he adopt to promote these kinds of positive work behaviors? How does the nature of the drivers' job and their personal characteristics affect this decision? Moreover, what other kinds of incentives might Knowles need to use to encourage his drivers to be flexible and cooperative? We provide the answers to these crucial business leadership questions at many points in the rest of this chapter.

The Contingency Theory of Leadership

We just described four principal approaches to leadership. Research suggests that each of these different leadership approaches is best suited to a different kind of work setting. The contingency theory of leadership suggests that effective leadership results when managers adopt the leadership approach that *matches* the characteristics of their employees and the work setting. Figure 6.3 illustrates the main elements of the contingency approach.

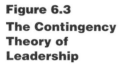

Figure 6.3
The Contingency
Theory of
Leadership

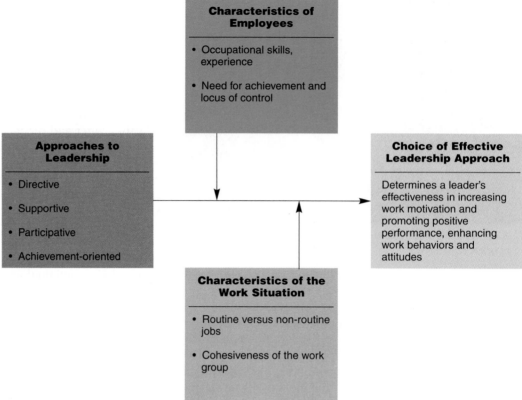

**contingency theory of
leadership** The theory
that effective leadership
occurs when managers
adopt a leadership
approach that matches the
characteristics of their
employees and the work
setting.

On the left side of the figure are four main approaches to leadership a manager like Knowles can adopt. These are discussed in detail below. Which approach will lead to effective leadership in a particular business setting depends (1) on the *characteristics of employees* such as their skill level, experience, qualifications, and their desire to succeed at work; and (2) on the *characteristics of the work situation,* such as the kind of jobs employees perform and the degree to which they need to work together to get things done.

The implication of Figure 6.3 is that a leader cannot simply adopt an approach to leadership that seems the easiest or most "comfortable" because it matches his or her own personality, beliefs, and so on. A leader must think carefully about which leadership approach to adopt because if it does not fit the work setting, unexpected kinds of negative employee reactions, such as those discussed earlier, may result. To see how contingency theory works, we need to first examine the differences between the four leadership approaches.

Four Types of Leadership Approaches

To appreciate the way these four approaches to leadership differ, the different ways Tony Knowles would function as a leader if he adopted each approach are described below. The main components of each approach are also summarized in Figure 6.4.

DIRECTIVE LEADERSHIP   The first approach that Knowles could adopt is called *directive leadership.* If he pursues this approach, he leads in the following way: When his drivers arrive for their first day at work, Knowles introduces himself, describes his company's business model, and issues each of them a company handbook. The handbook contains detailed rules and work procedures the drivers should follow—procedures that describe how they are to drive their routes and report on sales calls, for example. Knowles then takes the drivers through the handbook step by step. He asks the drivers to stop him if they don't understand something in the handbook or have questions. His goal is to ensure they understand every rule in the handbook and follow each of them to the letter.

Directive Approach	Supportive Approach	Participative Approach	Achievement-Oriented Approach
• Providing guidance and training	• Being friendly and approachable	• Involving employees in work scheduling	• Setting challenging goals
• Work scheduling	• Showing concern for well-being and needs of employees	• Encouraging suggestions and consulting with employees	• Emphasizing need to behave proactively and perform at highest level
• Maintaining clear work performance standards	• Treating workers as equals	• Putting employees' suggestions into action	• Demonstrating confidence in employees
• Linking incentives directly to performance	• Acting in a non-threatening way	• Encouraging proactive work behaviors	• Providing employees with autonomy and freedom to decide how to perform their job
• Developing clear work rules and procedures			

Figure 6.4
Four Approaches to Leadership

Knowles also instructs drivers about the specific goals he expects them to achieve, such as number of sales outlets they are expected to visit and stock each day, how to measure and report the quantity of snack foods sold, and how to conduct themselves at the outlets. He explains that they each need to make 25 sales visits a day and that he will accompany them on their routes for the first few weeks to determine if it is possible to increase the number of sales visits per day. He also tells them he will evaluate their performance based on their ability to meet this number-of-visits goal.

The benefit of the directive approach is that by the end of the first day, the drivers know exactly what is expected of them and how their performance will be evaluated. They know where they stand, although they may not be sure if Knowles is going to be an easy person to work for or if they will be able to perform up to his standards. Only time will tell.

SUPPORTIVE LEADERSHIP If Knowles adopts a *supportive leadership* approach, he behaves in the following way: After the drivers arrive, Knowles welcomes them warmly, sits with them in a circle, and describes his background, work history, family, and so on. He takes pains to show them he is a friendly and approachable person and that the drivers should come to talk to him right away should a personal or work problem arise. He recognizes that most new employees are anxious at first. Knowles then invites his drivers to share similar information about themselves, and he asks them questions in order to show he is interested in them as people. He makes it clear that he is genuinely concerned with their needs and well-being and that he believes in treating his employees as equals.

Knowles makes sure there is plenty of coffee and the new snack foods to go around. He tells the drivers about his business model and emphasizes how important they are to make it succeed. He distributes the handbook and informs them that he has prepared it to make it easier for them to learn their jobs, and that he is going to accompany them on their routes for the first few weeks to help them learn the ropes.

Around 11 a.m. he breaks off and invites them to play a game of softball in the field surrounding his barn. At noon he invites them to join him to try out their vans and uniforms. Then, after a buffet lunch he goes over the handbook with them. In a relaxed and humorous ways he clarifies the rules and procedures, patiently answers their questions, and emphasizes that he is sure they will understand everything they are required to do within a few weeks.

The benefit of a supportive approach is that Knowles's drivers feel comfortable and appreciated and know he will support their efforts. They feel confident that they can learn their jobs and will be able to live up to his expectations.

Employees at New Balance Athletic Shoes' five factories are competing effectively against low-wage factories abroad. They achieve this through self-directed work teams. Which leadership approach allows employees to work effectively without direct supervision?

PARTICIPATIVE LEADERSHIP   The third leadership approach is called *participative leadership.* If Knowles adopts this approach, then after first welcoming his new drivers, he passes out his handbook and goes through the work rules and procedures, asking them to speak up if they find anything unclear. He also requests their input and advice and asks them to think about how a rule could be changed to make the operation more efficient. Knowles seriously considers their ideas and acts upon their input, modifying the rules as they go along, and he writes down issues that will need to be discussed in the future. He indicates that his handbook is a "work in progress," and that the drivers should strive to improve upon it over the next few months.

Knowles then tells the drivers that he will be riding their routes with them to help them find the best ways to perform their jobs. He also makes clear that the 25-visits-a-day goal is subject to change. He will evaluate their performance based upon their ability to meet and exceed this goal, or he will help them find a way to do so. He makes it clear that they should never be afraid to make suggestions and that they have his support to act in a proactive way.

Knowles's decision to allow drivers to participate in the decision-making process will probably lead to differences in opinion. As a result, his drivers will not have a clear operating model to follow. The benefit of the participative approach is, however, that these differences can lead to better work procedures being developed over time. For example, by being able to experiment with their routes, the drivers will test out new ideas and see which ones lead to the most efficiency and effectiveness. Very likely different drivers will end up following the rules in different ways. Knowles will also have to deal with a greater variety of problems such as deciding whether or not a driver's approach is a good one and how to convince everyone else to follow that approach if it is.

ACHIEVEMENT-ORIENTED LEADERSHIP   If he adopts an *achievement-oriented leadership* approach, Knowles starts by sharing his future vision for his company with his drivers: to be the new snack-food distributor not only for Tampa but also for the entire state of Florida. He stirs their imagination about what they can achieve if they all work hard and cooperate with one another. Knowles gives out the company handbook and tells them he expects them to learn their new jobs as quickly as possible so that they get off to a running start.

After answering questions and clarifying what he wants his rules and procedures to achieve, Knowles makes it clear that this is just the first step for all of them. He tells them he chose to hire them because he is confident they can perform their jobs without supervision and accomplish challenging goals. He emphasizes that they are responsible for finding ways to improve the way they drive their routes so that they can fit in more sales visits as the business grows. He also tells them they need to talk to outlet employees to find out how customers are responding to the new snack foods. Finding ways to improve sales is also part of their job duties. As they drive their routes, they should be on the lookout for new sales outlets and report potential sales leads to him.

Knowles communicates to the drivers his need for them to perform at their highest level. Jointly he and his drivers will set challenging work goals. He will evaluate how well they meet these goals and reward each driver accordingly. He makes clear that if his company does well and grows, they can also expect to receive higher rewards. He also makes it clear that if they don't want to go the extra mile, then he won't be able to keep them on his team—he only has one year to prove his business model, after all.

The benefit of the achievement-oriented approach is that it focuses on the need to improve current *and* future operating efficiency and effectiveness. Some drivers might be energized by Knowles's leadership approach and see a bright future. Others might be worried they have bitten off more than they can chew and won't be able to meet his expectations. What kind of boss will Knowles turn out to be?

THE EFFECTS OF A LEADERSHIP APPROACH   As you can see, the same handbook of rules and procedures is used as a central part of each leadership approach. In six months' time, however, the specific rules and procedures in the handbook, and thus the way Knowles's company actually operates, is *likely to be very different depending on which leadership approach he chooses to adopt.*

If he chooses a directive approach, he will probably get a team of drivers who work efficiently to meet the goals he has set for them. The drivers will learn how to drive their routes to save time, and perhaps they will be able to serve more outlets too. However, drivers will not wish to explore other ways of doing their jobs or take on new job responsibilities (like talking to sales outlet employees). Doing so would slow them down and threaten their ability to achieve their goals. Thus, any operational improvements will mainly result from Knowles's efforts.

If Knowles follows a supportive approach, his employees will probably take a longer time to learn their jobs and may come to rely heavily on Knowles for help and guidance. He might find he is spending all of his time supervising his drivers and that he cannot perform his other crucial responsibility—like signing up potential new sales outlets. If Knowles adopts a supportive approach, it will take him far longer to get his business into full swing than if he adopts a directive approach.

A participative approach encourages steady, ongoing learning and a continuous improvement in job performance. Once again, however, it will take more time to get the business up and running because he and his drivers will need to discuss different work procedures and agree upon which are best. Conflicts might arise that Knowles will need to mediate. He might once again discover that he doesn't have the time to sign up new sales outlets.

If he adopts an achievement-oriented approach this might lead to sudden and significant improvements in the performance of his drivers as they find new ways to work their routes and increase sales revenues. Knowles will then face new challenges. He will need to change the work rules and communicate these changes to all his drivers so they can take advantage of improved procedures. He will also have to decide how to reward his most successful, high-performing drivers for their contributions. Over time, he will have to continually change the way his business operates, which creates new problems that have to be managed. He may, for example, have to work out how to alter the route structure to accommodate changes in the number or type of outlets they need to cover. If business picks up significantly, he will have to hire more drivers and create new routes.

On the surface, it seems that the achievement-oriented approach is superior to the others because it is most likely to lead to the largest gains in efficiency and effectiveness, particularly, increased snack-food sales. It also appears to be the leadership approach that will challenge employees to work at their peak level. By contrast, the supportive leadership approach, with its emphasis on putting people, rather than the job, first, seems least likely to result in swift gains in efficiency and increased snack-food sales. Should Knowles adopt the achievement approach?

Types of Contingencies

To answer this question, Knowles must identify and analyze the contingencies related to his particular leadership situation. As noted earlier, there are two main types of contingencies: employee and work-situation contingencies.

EMPLOYEE CONTINGENCIES   Two kinds of employee contingencies are discussed here. The first is the level of *occupational skills, knowledge,* and *experience* employees need to perform their jobs. In general, less-skilled employees are more likely to respond

Employees with advanced job qualifications tend to react negatively to being given direct orders. How might a leader try to motivate employees like this?

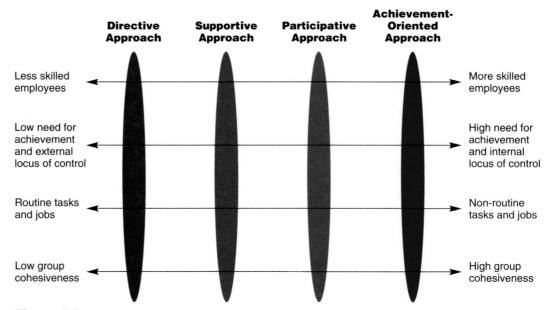

Figure 6.5
Contingency Factors and the Effective Approach to Leadership

favorably to either a directive or supportive type of leadership. (See Figure 6.5.) These employees will react positively to leaders who support them as they go about learning their new tasks, clarifying exactly what they need to do and how they will be evaluated.

Employees with advanced job qualifications who must rely on their experience to solve job problems are more likely to respond favorably to a participative or achievement-oriented approach. These employees are likely to react negatively to being given direct orders. They are also likely to be unresponsive to a supportive, people-centered approach. Instead, they are likely to view themselves as "professionals" and appreciate a leader who asks for their opinion and acts upon it. They also like it when a knowledgeable leader sets challenging goals and then gives them considerable freedom to decide how to go about achieving those goals.

The second employee contingency is a person's need for achievement and their locus of control. The *need for achievement* refers to a person's desire or drive to excel at a certain activity. People with high-achievement needs always try to "take it to the next level" and search out challenges to keep up to the mark. By contrast, people with low-achievement needs are content to stick with the tasks and activities they already do well.

People also tend to have either an internal or external locus of control. If they have an *internal locus of control,* then they believe they are in control of their situation, or destiny, and that good things will happen to them because of their own efforts—not because of the things other people do. By contrast, people with an *external locus of control* believe that how well they perform depends much more on the nature of the situation they are in and factors out of their control, such as luck, fortunate job assignments, or able co-workers.

Research has found that people with a high need for achievement and an internal locus of control are more likely to respond favorably to participative or achievement-oriented approaches. These approaches give them the most control and freedom to experiment with their jobs. People with a low need for achievement and an external locus of control are more likely to respond favorably to directive leaders who clarify the nature of their jobs and how their performance will be evaluated. They respond to a supportive leader who offers them guidance and makes them feel valued.

WORK-SITUATION CONTINGENCIES There are also two main work-situation contingencies. The first relates to the nature of the job. Some jobs require the employee

When employees work in a team, their ability to perform their tasks is directly affected by the performance of the other team members. How well will a team with low cohesiveness work together? Why?

to perform many different tasks, each requiring a different kind of skill. Considerable thought and decision making are needed on a continuing basis if the job is to be done well. Also, if they are to be performed successfully, these jobs require employees to assume a significant amount of responsibility. Jobs that have these characteristics are called *nonroutine* jobs. The job of a scientist engaged in genetic research is one example. The scientist might spend half the workday sitting at a computer involved in complex data analysis, and the other half in the lab setting up an experiment designed to test a new theory.

Research has found that when jobs are nonroutine, leaders who adopt a participative or achievement approach are more likely to be successful in influencing their employees and eliciting positive work behaviors and attitudes. These leadership styles give employees the freedom and autonomy they need to experiment and use their expertise to solve job problems.

On the other hand, workers in Ford's early car manufacturing plant performed the same simple, repetitive tasks all day long, and the moving conveyor belt controlled the pace of their work. Jobs that are based on the need to perform a small set of repetitive tasks controlled by machines or computers are called *routine jobs.* Research has found that the more routine the job, the more likely are employees to respond favorably to a directive or supportive leadership approach. When jobs are perceived as extremely boring by employees, a directive approach that keeps employees up to the mark and ensures they follow specified work procedures to perform it is often most suitable. Since employees are performing repetitive tasks, often at a fast pace, a supportive approach to leadership demonstrates a concern for employees' well-being even though leaders may be able to do little to make their jobs more interesting.

The second work situation contingency is the *level of cohesiveness* present in a work group or team. When employees work in a team, their ability to perform their tasks is directly affected by the behavior of the other team members. It is also affected by the quality of the relationships among team members. Group cohesiveness refers to the attractiveness of a team to its members; it affects their desire to cooperate with each other to get a job done quickly and reliably. Some teams have high group *cohesiveness:* Their members have similar attitudes and beliefs, like one another, and work well together. Some teams have low group cohesiveness: There is little personal liking or connection between members, and they have little desire to cooperate.

When people work in teams that are highly cohesive, research has found that they respond favorably to a participative or achievement-oriented approach. These approaches give them the freedom and responsibility to solve their own problems and work together to find better ways to do a task. By contrast, teams low on cohesiveness respond more favorably to a leader who adopts a directive or supportive approach. A leader who adopts a directive approach can monitor the performance of the team and direct its members to increase their cooperation. A leader who adopts a supportive approach can supply the missing social influence, or "glue," needed to persuade members to work together to meet their goals.

group cohesiveness
The attractiveness of a team to its members.

Choosing an Effective Leadership Approach

To identify and select the most effective leadership approach in a particular situation, a manager must examine each of these four contingencies and any others that might exist. Which leadership approach is appropriate for Tony Knowles given the contingencies he faces?

Because his budget was constrained, Knowles hired young, *inexperienced* drivers that he could pay less than more experienced ones. Also, when selecting his drivers, he tried to weed out those people who seemed to think they knew it all. Instead, he hired people with clean driving records who were polite, quiet spoken, and respectful—people he felt might have more of an *external locus* of control. The job of delivery drivers is also quite *routine;* they perform a narrow range of tasks, so rules and procedures related to those tasks can be easily developed and modified.

Knowles then made an important operating decision related to the work setting of his business. He decided that each of his drivers would operate a *separate* route. He knew that a lot more time and learning is necessary when drivers switch routes and that teams can be difficult to manage for the reasons just discussed.

Given these contingencies—inexperienced employees with an external locus of control doing routine tasks while working alone—Knowles chose to adopt a *directive leadership approach.* Knowles believes a directive approach will enable him to influence his drivers to meet the goals he wants them to. His directive approach will likely result in employee behaviors that are efficiency oriented and work attitudes that revolve around obeying the rules and using the business's time and resources frugally.

At the same time, Knowles understands the advantages of behaving in a supportive way. So, he plans to do all he can to build a good working relationship with his drivers as long as this does not hurt their ability to meet their work goals.

Knowles also designed a reward system to facilitate his directive approach. Drivers will receive a bonus for each sales lead they provide that results in a new sales-outlet account. They will also be paid a bonus if they find ways to do their jobs more efficiently. He also makes clear to each driver that as his company expands, he will be hiring more drivers and that those who perform the best will be the ones who will be promoted in the future.

Thus Knowles does not go with the "high-performing" achievement-oriented approach because he believes it is much too risky for his young company. Perhaps, later, when his company has achieved a solid foundation and he wants to expand his operations throughout Florida, he might change to this approach. His most pressing concern now is to get his business off to a quick start and he believes that the directive approach in combination with some social support will get him there fastest. Knowles believes directive leadership offers him the most chance of being able to survive and become a profitable company.

Tony Knowles's situation provides a good example of the way managers analyze contingencies in the work setting in order to choose an effective leadership approach. Managers must analyze these contingencies, understand the different leadership options available to them, examine the sources of power at their disposal, and put all this information together to choose the way in which they will function as a leader.

Characteristics of Effective Leaders

Contingency theory helps to determine the most effective leadership approach in a particular work setting. Research has also found that there are some personal characteristics or qualities that enhance the ability of *all* managers to function as effective leaders. Indeed, managers who possess one or more of these qualities to a high degree might be particularly adept at one of the four leadership approaches. On the other hand, managers who do not have these qualities might be unable to function effectively as leaders no matter which approach they adopt. We noted in Chapter 3, for example, that some entrepreneurs do not make good managers because they don't possess the right leadership qualities. For example, a brilliant scientist who invents a new product and starts a new

Did You Know?

Akito Morita created his company's name by consulting Latin: He combined the word *sonus,* meaning sound, with "sunny" to produce the name "Sony."[3]

Figure 6.6
Five Characteristics of Effective Leaders

company might lack the self-confidence or drive needed to function as a directive leader or the social skills necessary to develop a supportive leadership style.

Five important qualities or characteristics of effective leaders are described in Figure 6.6.

The first quality of an effective leader is *intuition, intelligence,* and the *cognitive ability* to process information and analyze a business problem–such as the need to identify the specific contingencies in a particular leadership situation. Employees are always "judging" their leaders. They respond favorably to leaders who demonstrate the ability to create viable business models and put them into action.

Effective leaders also display *energy, drive,* and a *need for achievement* to employees. These leaders show, through their own actions, their commitment to work hard and perform at a high level. They put in long hours and always seem to be in the right spot when problems arise, ready to put their cognitive, problem-solving abilities into action. Effective leaders never leave work before their employees on a regular basis.

Third, effective leaders tend to be *self-confident* and have an *internal locus of control.* The future success of a new company's business model, or of a new project in an established company, can never be predicted in advance. Effective leaders, demonstrate their confidence in their projects, however, and the ability of their subordinates to make them succeed. Effective leaders don't give up, complain, or blame other people when problems arise–actions that show employees that they lack control of the situation. Instead, they build commitment by taking control of the situation and making quick decisions to correct problems. They encourage employees to believe in themselves and perform to the best of their abilities to help solve problems, something that often leads to success.

A leader's *ethics and moral integrity* are also an important determinant of how effective he or she will be. Leadership is about influence and persuasion. The willingness of followers to be persuaded is a function of their beliefs that the leader is a fair and honest person who can be trusted. Effective leaders want to protect the rights of their employees, and their personal reputation for making fair decisions is an important indicator of their moral integrity. Leaders who play favorites, renege on their promises, or fail to reward good performance do *not* inspire confidence in their followers. They seldom can persuade employees to act in a proactive way.

A fifth characteristic of an effective leader is *emotional intelligence and empathy,* a person's ability to appreciate and understand the feelings and emotions of other people, as well as one's own, and to use this knowledge to guide one's behavior towards others. Some people seem to be "in control" of their own feelings and emotions and can use them in positive ways to build rapport with other people. Emotional intelligence helps a leader develop the social skills necessary to build good personal working relationships with individual employees and cohesiveness among people who work in groups and teams. Such leaders have a knack for smoothing over disputes, solving conflict, building cooperation,

Students who volunteer to work for and assist charities such as Habitat for Humanity gain many opportunities to learn valuable leadership skills.

and fostering shared feelings that help build a strong corporate culture. A high level of emotional intelligence is often a quality of a charismatic leader.

In sum, the more of these characteristics that managers possess, the more likely they are to function effectively as leaders. Moreover, as we mentioned earlier, a person who has one or more of these qualities might be able to pursue a particular leadership approach particularly effectively. A manager high in emotional intelligence and moral integrity seems particularly suited to a supportive or participative leadership approach. On the other hand, managers with great cognitive ability, drive, and need for achievement might be suited to a directive or achievement-oriented approach. Remember, however, a leadership approach most suited to a particular manager is *not* the most effective approach unless it is matched to the *contingencies of the leadership situation.* Tom Knowles's personal leadership style might be more achievement-oriented, for example. However, his business doesn't lend itself to that approach.

In a large company, leaders with different kinds of qualities might be selected to take charge of different kinds of leadership situations. A leader who might be effective as a CEO might have very different qualities than the leader required to build a motivated sales force, head up a team of senior research scientists, or control routine manufacturing activities on a factory floor. Note that a manager who rises to become a CEO has shown that he or she can be effective in many different leadership situations. For example, perhaps the CEO has performed well as the head of a work group, project team, or functional department as well as a foreign business unit.

To some degree the characteristics of an effective leader such as need for achievement, cognitive ability, self-confidence, or emotional intelligence are *personality characteristics* that people are born with. Nevertheless, most people can cultivate leadership qualities, and strengthen those they already possess, if they put their minds to it and take advantage of opportunities that arise. We discuss in Chapter 3 how employees can seek mentors (commonly managers who are proven effective leaders) and by observing how they behave, learn effective leadership skills. Employees can also seek out leadership opportunities by taking on new job projects. In high school and college, they can practice their leadership skills by assuming positions in sports or social clubs or by volunteering to take on projects for local charities, hospitals, and so on.

Influence, Persuasion, and Communication

communication The transmission and sharing of information between people or groups so that each party understands what the other is trying to achieve.

A leader's goal is to influence and persuade employees to develop work attitudes and behaviors that increase a company's efficiency and effectiveness. In fact, some experts view the four approaches to leadership discussed earlier as different *styles of persuasion.* They point out that leadership is a kind of "game" in which leaders seek to influence employees, but employees also seek to influence leaders in order to get what *they* want—like better performance evaluations or more interesting job assignments. Influence is a *two-way street,* in other words.

At the center of influence lies communication. Communication is the transmission and sharing of information between people or groups so that each party understands what the other is trying to achieve. If communication is effective, one person (or group) has an *accurate* perception of the other person's motives and intentions. Effective communication allows people to come to a common understanding, and it speeds up decision making. This reduces transaction costs so that resources can be used more efficiently to create products. Only when people understand what other people expect of them can they respond appropriately.

Video
Small
Business
in Action

Dale Gray Story

Summary: Gray Associates is featured in this original video on your Student DVD. In 1983, Dale Gray formed a small company called Gray Associates with nothing more than his vacation pay. In fact, there were no associates–only Gray himself. Today, the company is called Communication Services, Inc. It is one of the top companies in its field, has grown to 6 offices and currently employs over 100 people. The initial goal was to become a $1 million company. That was achieved and Gray became dissatisfied.

Early in the company's development, there was no need for a business plan. In fact, the company achieved the $1 million mark without a plan. Gray and his management team decided to re-examine the company. During an off-site three-day retreat, the team created a vision for the company and set a goal for $10 million. That goal has been achieved as well.

Gray discusses what he feels are the essential keys to the success of Communications Services, Inc. He emphasizes the need for the founder to become a part of a larger team; in other words, at some point the company outgrows the founder and he needs to know when to involve others. Significant investment in training is seen as a fundamental value at the firm. Personal characteristics of potential hires such as passion, drive, and high energy levels are also critically important. To be successful, Gray says, you need to have high levels of self-confidence and an unswerving belief in your self, goals, and abilities.

Discussion Questions:

1. What impact does Gray, as the leader of the business, have on employee attitudes and behavior?
2. Which of the five characteristics of effective leaders does Gray reflect (see Figure 6.6)?
3. How important was effective communication for the success of the company under Gray's leadership?

---

persuasive communication The attempt by a party to share information with another party in order to get them to understand their objectives and work toward them.

In a business context, however, achieving a common understanding is not the only objective. Leaders also want to *persuade* and get subordinates to agree with their wishes. **Persuasive communication** is the attempt by one person or group to transmit and share information with another person or group to get them to first *understand* their objectives, and second to *agree with* and *work to achieve* those objectives. For persuasive communication to be effective, it is necessary to frame or "package" the information in ways that influence other people to "buy into" it. Sometimes, people deliberately manipulate information to further their own personal interests. This is an issue of organizational politics discussed later in the chapter.

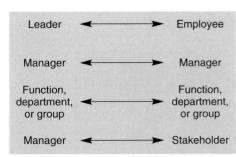

Figure 6.7
Types of Situations for Persuasive Communication

Situations for Persuasive Communication

There are many different types of situation in which communication, and particularly persuasive communication, is important. Figure 6.7 lists some of these situations. Persuasive communication is clearly important when leaders use their power to persuade their subordinates to behave in certain ways. However, it is also often needed in situations in which one party lacks any source of power to influence the other party. For example, managers in one functional department or group often need to influence managers in others. Because these managers have *no* power over one another, they must *persuade* the others to follow a certain course of action. Similarly, an employee who works in a group will often want to influence his or her co-workers even though the employee has no legitimate power over them. Finally, because managers have little or no legitimate power over stakeholders such as stockholders, suppliers, distributors, trade unions, and so on, they will need to use their powers of persuasion to get them to see their point of view. Some studies have found, in fact, that managers spend much of their time trying to elicit support for their ideas. Small wonder then, that people in almost any business setting need to become persuasive communicators.

Becoming a Persuasive Communicator

How does a person become a persuasive communicator? To learn what this involves, we need to first examine the different components of the persuasive communication process, which are shown in Figure 6.8. The two main parties involved in communication are known as the sender and the receiver. The sender is the party who is transmitting information or a "message" to influence the receiver. The receiver, in turn, transmits or feeds back information to the sender to communicate their understanding and reaction to the message received. This transfer of information between the receiver and sender goes on repeatedly for as long as there is a need to clarify the information or message, convince the receiver of its importance, and so on.

The sender's task is to influence the receiver's response to the message—to persuade the receiver to agree with and act on the message. Five factors determine how persuasive a message will be: the characteristics of the sender, active listening, the content of the message, the medium, or channel, through which it is sent, and finally, the characteristics of the receiver.

CHARACTERISTICS OF THE SENDER   As you might expect, messages are always more persuasive when they are sent by people who are *credible,* meaning that the receiver believes that the sender occupies a job position that gives them access to accurate information about work issues or objectives. Leaders, of course, are credible because they have legitimate power and use it to obtain the compliance of their employees. In addition, leaders with expert and/or referent power are also credible and use this power to influence others. Other factors that promote credibility are moral integrity and emotional intelligence. If the receiver believes the sender is an honest, trustworthy person, they are more likely to believe the information they receive is accurate or true. Empathetic people who can understand and appeal to the feelings and emotions of others are also able to use it to gain credibility and influence over them.

Often, people who are able to persuade others also possess good speaking and listening skills. When speaking they don't speak too quickly and they marshal their arguments logically—they know how to use every word to effect. Often, they will return to the same important points time and time again to ensure the key facts are not only being communicated but also emphasized and made significant. Good speakers invite questions to clarify issues and generate interest and support for their ideas. They use personal qualities such as their referent power or emotional intelligence to "emotionally charge" their words to convince their listeners that theirs is the *right* approach, that they *know* what they are doing, and that their plan will *succeed.*

sender The party that transmits a message or other information to a receiver.

receiver The party that receives the information transmitted by a sender.

Figure 6.8
A Model of Persuasive Communication

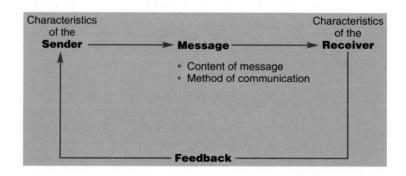

A competent sender knows that an active listener is always evaluating the implications of the information being conveyed and the motivations of the sender.

ACTIVE LISTENING   Effective senders and receivers also need to be good listeners and "active listening" is an important ingredient of persuasive communication. In Chapter 3 we discussed how job applicants, even though they are receivers, should ask questions of company interviewers. The same is true of persuasive senders. They need to actively listen to see how their arguments are being received, and then they can clarify issues and add information to get their points across.

People who are active listeners pay attention not only to the words that are being said but also to the many other things that are going on in the communication process. For example, they pay attention to the sender or receiver's tone of voice, and the nonverbal cues the person gives off, such as hesitation, laughter, or body posture. They know that all of this information sheds light on what is being said. Active listeners also avoid interrupting and maintain their interest in what the other party is saying. They give the other party time to frame their thoughts and get to the punch line. People who interrupt and finish other people's sentences often miss the real message being communicated. Active listeners also ask questions to elicit more information. For salespeople, this is one of their primary tasks. You might be under the impression that salespeople are great "talkers." But that fact is that some of the best salespeople are great "listeners." By rephrasing questions and picking up on casual statements, it is often possible to learn a great deal about a prospective buyer's intentions—much more than the buyer was planning to reveal. It is also an excellent way to learn about what one's competition is doing and saying to customers.

For the receiver, active listening is a way to find out how important the message they are receiving is to the sender. For the sender, actively listening to the receiver's response provides them with the same clues about the other's intentions. Often, for example, a busy employee given an order might say "Sure boss I'll get right on with that" but then does nothing because it would just slow their other work down. A boss who picks up on this by listening actively can take pains to reemphasize the point and ask probing questions to discover just how likely the employee is to follow orders.

CONTENT OF THE MESSAGE   The content of the message, that is, the information and arguments it contains, is also a crucial ingredient in the communication process. The receiver of the message, especially if he or she is an active listener, is always evaluating the implications of the information, examining its theme, and looking for ambiguities or inconsistencies in the arguments.

A competent sender knows this and is careful not to offer the receiver a one-sided message. To increase his or her credibility, the sender needs to present all sides of an argument, even those that seem contrary to his or her position. At the same time, the sender should always shift back to the major theme of the message, using a few strong arguments to persuade and win over the receiver. The content of a message can be made much more persuasive when it appeals to the receiver's feelings and emotions as well as to his or her intellect.

METHOD OF COMMUNICATION   In the discussion so far, we have not discussed how the message is communicated to the receiver. Everything said so far implies direct, face-to-face verbal communication, and indeed this method is the most effective for persuasive communication. There are many other methods of communication, however. Some are better suited to certain situations than others. Figure 6.9 shows five different methods of communication listed in terms of their ability to communicate a high volume and variety of information of both a logical and emotional nature.

**Figure 6.9
Methods of
Communication**

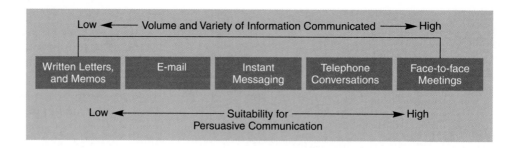

In general, face-to-face communication and telephone conversations are most appropriate for persuasive communication. Letters, memos, and e-mail are best suited to convey the detailed, factual information that requires time and effort to digest and act upon. In practice, written methods are more commonly used at the beginning of an "influence attempt." At this stage in the game, managers and employees are collecting the information they need to decide how to respond to some new development, such as a change in the competitive environment, for example, or a new product being proposed The sender and receiver share this information and use it to persuade the other about the best course of action to pursue. In the hours or days before a final decision is made, however, the sender and receiver resort to a more face-to-face persuasive approach. They begin to exchange fewer e-mails, and they increasingly pick up the telephone. Depending on the complexity of the issue they are dealing with, or the level of disagreement between them, face-to-face meetings now become the preferred method of communication because it allows for the processing of the most information, both logical and emotional, to make the optimum decision.

People who are persuasive have a good understanding of the strengths and weaknesses of different methods. They know when to send and when not to send an e-mail; when it is time to make a phone call; and, when it is vital to knock on the other person's door. Former President Lyndon Johnson was a master persuader. To influence senators to vote for his bills, he would first send his aids to persuade them and give them lots of written information. Later, he would call them on the telephone to discuss the issues and further his case. Then, in the days and hours before the final vote on a bill he would charge down to the Capitol building, locate the "swing-voters" and literally push them into a wall or corner. There he would put his hands on their shoulders, squeeze their arms, put his face close to theirs, and either cajole or threaten them until they were persuaded to do what he wanted! This physical approach is very common among powerful people, or people who know how to get their way. By contrast, the Space Shuttle Columbia disaster, discussed in Business in Action, shows how using the wrong communication methods can not only be unpersuasive, but even deadly.

Business in Action

A Fatal Failure to Communicate

One day before the breakup and crash of the Space Shuttle Columbia in the Spring of 2003, senior NASA engineers worried that the shuttle's left wing might burn off at reentry and cause the deaths of its crew. These engineers never sent their warnings to NASA's top managers. After intense debate via phone and e-mails, the engineers, supervisors, and the head of the space agency's Langley research facility in Hampton, Virginia, decided against taking the matter to top NASA managers.

One engineer suggested that NASA should ask the U.S. Strategic Command Center (a military-related facility) to use its sophisticated ground-based imaging equipment to inspect the shuttle for damage that might have been caused by debris striking the wing during launch. However, after asking for such help, a senior space agency official later withdrew the request before the NASA engineers had

After intense debate via phone and e-mail, engineers and supervisors at NASA's Langley research facility decided against insisting upon a face-to-face meeting with the space agency's top managers—a move that might have saved the Space Shuttle Columbia.

completed their analysis of how serious the damage to the shuttle's tiles was. Once again all this communication was handled by phone calls and e-mail.

Later, former NASA top administrator Sean O'Keefe commented that he probably should have taken part in the decision to cancel the survey. However, he had not been asked directly, face-to-face, to participate and had merely followed the debate through e-mail. Moreover, O'Keefe said he had not known for most of the mission about the shuttle's problems.

All these events point to the fact that the wrong method of persuasive communication was chosen during these discussions. All the people involved in the investigation were communicating by e-mail and phone calls. NASA's engineers knew all about the problems and had reported them through e-mails. However, at no point had they asked for a face-to-face meeting with top managers to lay out all of the issues. Their e-mail messages alone were unpersuasive—so the survey of the shuttle was not made. Likewise managers at all levels failed to request face-to-face meetings with the engineers who had voiced their concerns. This tragic event demonstrates how critical simply choosing the right mode of communication can be.[4]

CHARACTERISTICS OF THE RECEIVER   What about the receiver? In any communication attempt, a receiver, upon replying to a message, becomes a sender. Much of the information in the previous discussion therefore applies to receivers as well. Receivers, for example, can learn to develop their credibility, use their emotional intelligence, and select the best method to transmit a message back to the sender. In addition, however, there are certain characteristics of the receiver that are relevant when it comes to communicating persuasively.

First, receivers who are themselves highly competent and have high self-esteem are less likely to be taken in or swayed by emotional information and arguments they believe are flawed. They find it easier to "cut through the chaff" and go to the heart of an issue to determine if, for example, the sender is acting to further his or her own personal interests. People with high self-esteem are very useful to have around because they are frequently the ones who *will* challenge the ideas of a leader or manager when they sense they are flawed. Such a person plays the devil's advocate—the person willing to stand up and say "the emperor has no clothes," so to speak. This can be very helpful when someone is attempting to persuade others for his or her own personal benefit versus the benefit of an organization's stakeholders. When this happens, persuasive communication moves into the realm of organizational politics. This is the issue we turn to now.

devil's advocate
Someone who tries to convince others that an idea or plan is flawed.

The Political Process in Business Organizations

Figure 6.7 illustrates the many kinds of situations in which persuasive communication becomes important. These are the same situations in which organizational politics are often found. Organizational politics are the activities that managers and employees at all levels of a company engage in to increase their power and influence over others. Political tactics are the strategies managers and employees engage in to gain support and overcome the opposition of other people.

organizational politics The activities managers and employees engage in to increase their power and persuade others to achieve their personal goals and objectives.

political tactics The specific strategies managers and employees engage in to gain the support of an organization's members.

Organizational Politics

The term *politics* has a negative connotation for some people. Managers who are "political" are often viewed as people who have risen to the top not because of their own merit but because of "whom they know" and their ability to "work the system." These people believe political managers act in a self-interested way and wield power to benefit themselves and not their companies. There is some truth to this negative view. The scandals that plagued companies like Enron, Arthur Andersen, WorldCom, and others are warning about what can happen at the top of a company if corrupt managers are allowed to misuse their power.

Nevertheless, organizational politics can often be a positive force that helps a company pursue its business model profitably. This is because managers striving to improve the performance of a company often encounter resistance from other managers who feel threatened by their actions and want to maintain the status quo (and thus their personal benefits). To champion new products and increase profits, active, forceful managers often need to engage in politics to get the support they need to implement change. They often face resistance from other managers who, although they might not be resistant to change, disagree with the specifics of how the changes should be implemented. Indeed, in most business settings, politics is commonly used to influence and persuade others.

Political Tactics

When managers use political tactics to increase their power, they sometimes find it easier to persuade others. Some common tactics include attacking and blaming others versus making everyone a "winner"; reducing uncertainty and using objective information; being irreplaceable and in a central position; and building coalitions and alliances. (These tactics are shown in Figure 6.10.)

THE ATTACK-AND-BLAME TACTIC VERSUS MAKE-EVERYONE-A-WINNER TACTIC Two influential, but opposite, approaches can be effective in different situations. The first approach is to attack and blame others. When pursuing an attack-and-blame strategy, Manager "A" might spread the word to his or her colleagues and higher-level managers that Manager "B" is the source of all the firm's problems. The implication is that if these people would merely follow Manager's A's suggested course of action, everyone would be better off. Sometimes the attack-and-

Figure 6.10
Types of Political Tactics

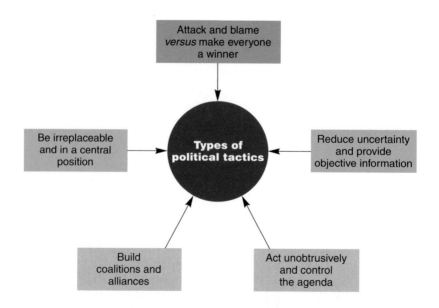

blame tactic occurs face-to-face in a meeting in which one manager comes under attack from others. If a manager cannot defend his or her position, the manager leading the attack will then find it easier to pursue his or her objectives. This tactic can be particularly useful when several managers are competing for an important position but only one will be chosen.

The second approach is to make everyone a "winner." When managers pursue the make-everyone-a-winner tactic, they try to find a way to make a proposed course of action benefit all the parties involved (or at least convince them that is the case). The idea is to build a consensus. This approach is particularly effective when the active cooperation of different functions or groups is needed to achieve a certain goal.

THE REDUCE-UNCERTAINTY AND USE-OBJECTIVE-INFORMATION TACTIC

Uncertainty is a threat for managers and their functions because it can cause their performance to suffer. Valuable time and resources can be wasted because people are uncertain about what must they do to achieve a particular goal. In the case of Microsoft, for example, the risk is that Tammy Savage's group and the other groups that work with it will develop software that the NetGen does not want. This uncertainty can cause the developers to suffer a sort of paralysis and flounder. But managers like Tammy Savage, who are able to understand the customer's needs and can clearly articulate them, can reduce uncertainty by providing these people with a vision and plan they can follow. This increases the power and influence a manager has. In general, managers gain power when they can eliminate uncertainty for other managers and groups.

Another way managers can reduce uncertainty and gain power is to collect and distribute accurate information supporting the course of action they are proposing. In many cases, the facts speak for themselves. This can lend a manager political credibility and put the person in a better position to influence others. Still, even the most accurate information has to be presented skillfully for a manager to gain support.

THE BE-IRREPLACEABLE OR OCCUPY-A-CENTRAL-POSITION TACTIC

Managers gain power when they are *irreplaceable,* that is, when they have valuable knowledge and expertise that that no one else has. The more influence a manager gains by being irreplaceable, the more power he or she has to persuade others. Managers also gain more influence when they are *central,* meaning that their activities are highly visible. These managers and the people who work with them must do a good job because if they don't, there is little chance the company will meet its goals. In most cases, managers such as these have access to important company information, and other members of the firm become dependent on them for their knowledge, advice, and political support. As such these, managers have a great deal of influence. People who are outstanding performers, have a great deal of knowledge, and have made important and visible contributions to their companies are likely to be offered central positions as managers. This works to increase their power.

THE BUILDING-COALITIONS-AND-ALLIANCES TACTIC

When managers build coalitions and alliances, they actively develop mutually beneficial relationships with other people and groups, both inside and outside of their companies. Unlike the make-everyone-a-winner strategy, this strategy is an ongoing activity. It involves finding other parties of equal power and allying with them to either achieve or sustain power. British Prime Minister Tony Blair and U.S. President George W. Bush are good examples. Bush and Blair know if they combined forces, they are more likely to influence people to follow the course of action they are proposing—such as fighting terrorism. The partners in an alliance support one another because they know they are far better off by cooperating versus competing with one another. In terms of business organizations, sometimes this leads to needed changes, but in other cases, this unity of power has an adverse effect on the firm. This is precisely what happened at Kodak, discussed in Business in Action.

Business in Action

Politics at Kodak

Eastman Kodak, with its little yellow film boxes, has long been a part of the global scene for decades. In more recent years, however, Kodak has experienced a serious decline in its performance. It was slow to react to the threat of global competition, and a series of political contests between its managers stifled any serious attempt to restructure its activities.

In the early 1990s, Kay Whitmore, a Kodak veteran, was appointed CEO. Whitmore gained the top job because he was the leader of a coalition of Kodak's most senior managers. However, he was reluctant to make the drastic changes Kodak needed to regain its competitiveness. To do so would have required massive job cuts in Kodak's film unit—cuts that would have hurt the members of his coalition.

Not surprising, in 1993, investors were delighted to hear that Christopher Steffen would be Kodak's new chief operating officer. Steffen had a reputation for turning around companies, including Chrysler and Honeywell. Investors thought that an outsider would be a breath of fresh air and bring new ideas to Kodak's inbred top-management team. Investors were therefore shocked when Steffen announced his resignation from the company less than a week after his appointment, citing "differences with the company's approach to problem solving." Apparently he, and the coalition of Kodak's top managers headed by CEO Whitmore, had very different ideas about how to restructure the company and the speed at which job cuts should be made. Also, Steffen felt that Kodak's operating costs could only be reduced significantly by closing several of its main businesses and laying off a large number of employees. Once again this threatened Whitmore's coalition, and, in the end, Steffen was fired.

Kodak's stock subsequently plunged. Within months, Whitmore was ousted by a concerned board of directors. In 1994, he was replaced by George Fisher, the first outsider ever to lead Kodak. Investors hoped that as an outsider, Fisher would be able to change the way organizational politics worked at Kodak. Fisher made many changes, but he, too, had to fight against the no-change tactics used by Kodak's top brass. He never gained their support.

In fact, behind the scenes, another Kodak veteran, Dan Carp, was waiting to become CEO. In 2000, supported by a coalition of Kodak's current top managers (all inbred), Kodak's board announced it had selected Carp to be the new CEO; Fisher was out. Carp pursued ambitious plans to try to boost Kodak's performance, but he did not close down any of Kodak's businesses until 2003 when it announced more poor operating results. Finally, in 2004, as its performance continued to plunge, Carp took the steps Kodak should have taken a decade earlier: He announced the closing of several of Kodak's businesses along with massive layoffs in its film division, and he vowed to speed digital-camera products to the marketplace.

Had Kodak's managers pursued this course of action a decade earlier, thousands of the company's employees might not have been laid off. Kodak might have been able to reduce its high operating costs and dedicate the savings toward producing digital products. Amid sharply lower profits, in May 2005, Carp announced he would step down as CEO that fall. His replacement is Antonio Perez, an executive with a deep understanding of the digital imaging business, hired by Kodak in 2003 to be its president.[5]

Despite laying off employees and exiting several businesses, Kodak CEO Dan Carp's efforts to turn Kodak around came a decade too late.

Summary of the Chapter

A company's profitability, and often its survival, is determined by how hard its employees are motivated to work toward its goals. Managers need to understand how to influence and persuade these employees using an effective leadership approach. This chapter has made the following major points:

1. Leadership involves using one's personality, beliefs, values, social skills, knowledge, and power to engage and persuade employees to do their jobs in a way that increases an organization's efficiency and effectiveness.

2. Power is the ability of one person to cause another person to do something that he or she would not have otherwise done. There are five sources of a leader's power: legitimate, reward, coercive, expert, and referent power. The possession of power does not create an effective leader. Leadership is the effective use of power in a particular work situation.

3. A charismatic leader is an exceptional leader who uses his or her referent or expert power to connect with and influence employees.

4. Leaders use their power to influence the work behaviors and attitudes of employees such that they further the interests of the company.

5. The contingency theory of leadership suggests that the most effective leadership approach is one that matches the characteristics of *employees* and their *work situation*.

6. There are four principal types of leadership approaches: directive, supportive, participative, and achievement-oriented.

7. The nature of the employee and work contingencies in a particular business setting determine which leadership approach will be most effective. The two most important employee contingencies are their (1) occupational skills and experience, and (2) their need for achievement and locus of control. The two most important work-setting contingencies are (1) the characteristics of the job (routine or nonroutine) and (2) the use of work groups and teams and the level of group cohesiveness.

8. Five important qualities all effective leaders possess are intuition, intelligence, and cognitive ability; drive and the need for achievement; self-confidence and an internal locus of control; good ethics and moral integrity; and emotional intelligence.

9. Persuasive communication is the attempt by one person or group to share information with another person or group in order to get them to understand their objectives and support them.

10. The different components of the persuasive communication process are the characteristics of the sender and receiver, the content of the message, active listening, and the method of communication.

11. Organizational politics are the activities that managers and employees engage in to increase their power and persuade others to pursue their goals. Political tactics are the strategies managers and employees use to gain support and overcome people's resistance.

12. Political tactics include attacking and blaming others versus making everyone a winner, reducing uncertainty and using objective information, being irreplaceable and in a central position, and building coalitions and alliances.

Developing Business Skills

QUESTIONS FOR DISCUSSION AND ACTION

1. Which sources of a leader's power would most be most effective for leading the activities of (a) the sales force of a large pharmaceutical company, and (b) the staff of a hospital emergency room?

2. What kinds of employee work behaviors and attitudes do leaders target to increase the firm's efficiency and effectiveness?

3. What are the main differences between a directive and achievement-oriented leadership approach? Which contingency factors determine the most effective approach in a particular business setting?

4. *Action.* Identify someone you think is an effective leader. Interview this person and find out what he or she thinks is the most important personal qualities a leader needs.

5. What are the main elements of persuasive communication? How do you identify a person who is an active listener?

6. What method of communication is most likely to persuade (a) a group of scientists working in a research laboratory; (b) the sales force of a large soft drink company.

7. How can organizational politics help or harm a company?

8. You are the manager of your company's sales department. You are trying to get managers in the manufacturing department to respond more quickly to the manufacturing needs of a major customer. They are resisting your suggestions for change. What political tactics could you use to overcome their opposition?

ETHICS IN ACTION

Influence at Work

Influence and persuasion are a central part of the business process. Managers routinely attempt to influence employees to work hard and perform at a high level by adopting a particular leadership approach. Managers routinely use persuasive communication and organizational politics to try to convince other managers to agree with their goals and follow the course of action they are championing.

Leadership can have a dark side if managers influence employees to behave in unethical ways or use politics to further their own interests at the expense of other stakeholders. Use the four ethical principles discussed in Chapter 5 to address the following leadership-related questions:

- What kinds of actions exhibited by a leader do you regard as unethical and why?

- At what point does persuasive communication become unethical in a business setting?

- Use the ethical principles in Chapter 5 to examine why and how organizational politics can harm a company and its stakeholders.

SMALL GROUP EXERCISE

A Leadership Problem at HighandTall

Break into groups of three or four people and discuss the following scenario. Be prepared to share your discussion with the entire class:

You are the founding entrepreneurs of HighandTall Company, a fast-growing digital software company that specializes in home-consumer electronics. Business has been booming. In just two years you have hired over 50 new software programmers to help develop a new range of software products. These people are young and inexperienced but are highly skilled and used to putting in long hours to make their ideas succeed. The growth of your company has been so swift that you still operate informally. As top managers, you have been so absorbed in your own work that you have paid little attention to the issue of leading your growing company. You have allowed your programmers to find solutions to problems as they go along. They have also been allowed to form their own work groups. Unfortunately, there are signs that problems are arising.

Employees have complained that good performance is going unrecognized and unrewarded. They have also expressed concern that you are either too busy or not willing to listen to their new ideas and act on them. A bad atmosphere seems to be developing, and several talented employees have already left the company.

You realize in hindsight that you have done a poor job of leading your employees and that you need to develop a common leadership approach to encourage them to perform well and stay with the company.

1. Analyze this leadership situation to uncover the contingency factors that will be important in choosing a leadership approach. Examine the four approaches to leadership using these factors.

2. Which is the most effective leadership approach that you should adopt?

3. In what other ways could you motivate your employees to perform well and stay with your company?

DEVELOPING GOOD BUSINESS SENSE

How to Lead Me

Each person has his or her own personality, values, beliefs, and way of viewing the world. To help you understand how different kinds of leadership approaches are likely to affect your *own* work behaviors and attitudes, use the chapter material to think about the following issues:

1. What kind of personal characteristics should a leader possess to encourage *you* to perform at the highest level you are capable of?

2. Which of the four leadership approaches described in the chapter would persuade you to perform at your highest level? Why?

3. Which of the four leadership approaches would be least likely to persuade you to perform at your highest level? Why?

4. Which approach would *you* be most likely to adopt as a leader?

EXPLORING THE WORLD WIDE WEB

GE's Jeffrey Immelt

Go to GE's Web site and click on the "Our Company" link. Under "Executive Bios," select Jeffrey Immelt, GE's CEO. Read the article that links to *Fortune* magazine (or another recent article there) and answer the following questions about Immelt. **For more Web activities, log on to www.mhhe.com/jonesintro.**

1. What is Immelt's approach to leadership? How effective as a leader is he?

2. In what kinds of ways does Immelt attempt to influence and persuade GE's members?

BusinessWeek CASE FOR DISCUSSION

Nissan's Boss: Carlos Ghosn Saved Japan's No.2 Automaker. Now He's Taking on the World

Carlos Ghosn is flat out the hottest automotive talent on the planet right now, and he enjoys the kind of street credentials that execs from Detroit to Stuttgart can only dream about. In Japan, a full five years after arriving from France's Renault to run Nissan Motor Co., CEO Ghosn is still feted in *manga* comic books, mobbed for autographs during plant tours, and generally heaped with national adulation for saving a car company once given up for dead. At glitzy auto shows from Paris to Beijing, his cosmopolitan air—Ghosn speaks five languages—and sterling track record for turnarounds make him a star attraction. He's as smooth as Thai silk in public, and his colleagues marvel at his personal magnetism, his 24/7 work ethic, and his rigorous attachment to benchmarks and targets. Heck, in Lebanon, where he is a citizen, Ghosn's name was floated a few weeks back as a potential candidate for president.

But Nissan insiders will also tell you there is another side to the 50-year-old car exec: If you miss a number or blindside the boss with a nasty development, watch out. "To people who don't accept that performance is what is at stake, he can be ruthless," says Dominique Thormann, a senior vice president with Nissan Europe. Just ask managers at Nissan's 16-month-old, $1.4 billion assembly plant in Canton, Mississippi, where sloppy craftsmanship marred the launch of the 2004 Quest minivan, the Titan full-sized pickup, and the Armada sport-utility vehicle. Car enthusiast Web sites are full of rants about loose moldings, water leaks, and noisy cabins. This spring, Nissan dropped from 6th to 11th in an annual quality survey by J.D. Power & Associates Inc. that tracks complaints in the first 90 days of ownership. Consumers quickly got wind of the troubles, and Nissan will have a tough time meeting its sales target of 80,000 Quests this year. In the first half, fewer than 26,000 moved off dealer lots. In July the company mailed recall letters offering to fix any defects for free. "We've been surprised by the level of degradation," concedes Ghosn, whose own stress on speedy execution contributed to the quality woes. "We recognize it is a problem, and we will fix it."

Ghosn is fixing the Canton debacle in his characteristic fashion—that is, with the subtlety of a chain saw. In May, he flew in 220 engineers from Japan and Nissan's older Smyrna (Tennessee) plant. The damage-control team searched every inch of the assembly line for flaws. Some were obvious: Factory hands, many of them newcomers to car making, wore rings and studded jeans that scratched freshly painted trucks. Other glitches were maddening: Power window switches and reading lights on the Quest often seemed possessed by gremlins, and its sliding doors didn't close quite right. So the team worked with suppliers to reengineer parts, while robots were reprogrammed to weld car bodies more tightly, and better insulation was added to the roof of the Armada. Then Ghosn shook up management, even raiding archrival Toyota to hire troubleshooter Douglas G. Betts as his new vice president for assembly quality. As the 2005 Nissans enter dealerships this fall, buyers will learn firsthand whether Ghosn's personal intervention has paid off.

LOFTY TARGETS

It's the Ghosn way: detailed planning, speedy execution, and a laser focus on what needs fixing. Since 1999, when Renault paid $5.4 billion for a controlling stake in Nissan and dispatched Ghosn to Tokyo to run it, he has set—and met—sales and profit targets that have stretched the automaker to the limit. That pattern appeared in 1990, when Ghosn turned around Michelin's North American division, and in 1996, when as chief operating officer of Renault he kicked off a program to cut $3.6 billion in annual expenses. Such acts earned Ghosn the overused sobriquet *le cost killer*. It is a name he loathes and hopes to banish for good by building an enduring car company based on product excellence, not painful restructuring.

The question is whether Ghosn is going too far, too fast. Today, he runs Nissan in Japan, where executives are battling for share in a soft market by launching six new models, and where preparations for a major expansion into China are under way. Since last spring, Ghosn has also taken charge of North America. And in April he starts his new job—replacing his mentor Louis Schweitzer as CEO of Renault, a $46 billion giant in its own right and the controlling shareholder in Nissan, with a 44% stake. Incredibly, Ghosn will continue to run Nissan from Tokyo headquarters even as he maintains oversight of U.S. operations.

Will this guy have to clone himself? Running two such complex organizations is a fiendishly difficult task, but Ghosn insists that he's ready—and that he needs to stay on at Nissan to keep the company headed in the right direction. "I won't be a part-timer, but one CEO with two hats," he says.

One CEO, as well, with an audacious plan to create what Daimler Benz and Chrysler Corp. could not—a successful global auto group from two very distinct companies. Renault and Nissan have been quietly cooperating on technology and parts buying for years. But this Franco-Japanese collaboration is set to expand significantly shortly after Ghosn arrives in Paris, in everything from parts purchasing to wholesale platform-sharing to engine design. Already, Nissan and Renault sell a combined 5.4 million vehicles a year and control 9.3% of the global market. If they were one company, it would be the fourth-largest automaker on earth, ahead of Daimler-Chrysler and right behind Ford. Ghosn says no full-fledged merger is coming—but his accession to the double thrones of Renault and Nissan signals that far deeper ties lie ahead.

TOP SPEED

At this crucial moment, when Ghosn can't afford a slipup, the Canton problems highlight the perils of his turbocharged management style. Carmakers know that doing too many new things at once is risky, so new plants typically make tried-and-true models, while fresh designs are usually built by seasoned workers at established factories. In Canton, though, Nissan launched five new models in less than eight months. "There was a need to get the products to market as soon as possible," says Dave Boyer, vice president in charge of Nissan's U.S. manufacturing operations and head of the Canton plant. Ghosn today acknowledges that he may have stretched too far. And one Nissan executive, who asked not to be named, grouses that the company's cost crackdown on suppliers may have aggravated the problems. "So much effort was spent getting costs down that the quality issue went unnoticed—until it was too late," this manager says.

Ghosn says he's starting to get a handle on the quality woes. Yet at the same time he's upping the ante for Nissan's U.S. operations, which continue to grow thanks to the revamped Altima sedan and Pathfinder SUV. "I can already commit that our [quality] scores will be much better," he says. He boosted his 2004 sales target for the United States to make up for soft results in Japan and Europe. Ambitious, yes, but necessary if Ghosn is to reach a goal he set two years ago of annually selling 1 million more cars—an increase of 38% over three years—by September, 2005. And forget about goosing sales with rebates. "We spent five years reining in incentives, and we're not going to give it back in five months," says Jed Connelly, chief of U.S. sales. Indeed, Nissan incentives in August averaged $1,559 a vehicle, compared with nearly $4,000 at Ford and General Motors Corp., according to auto data Web site Edmunds.com.

Can even a superstar such as Ghosn stay on top of industrial operations as vast as Nissan and Renault? Plenty in the industry would love to see the brash Ghosn stumble. The truth is, though, Ghosn has built a powerful machine. "It's tough to keep" a turn-around going, says GM boss G. Richard Wagoner Jr. "But it would be foolhardy to underestimate Nissan."

As turnarounds go, the Nissan saga is in a class by itself. In 1999 the company was straining under $19 billion in debt and shedding market share in both Japan and the United States Ghosn was also being undermined by Nissan insiders who wanted his reforms to fail. So when he was about to announce the closing of five factories, he didn't tell his own board of directors until the night before, recalls Jason Vines, who served as Nissan's North American public-relations chief early in Ghosn's tenure and now heads PR for Chrysler Group. And to ensure those in the know wouldn't spill the beans, Ghosn threatened: "'If this leaks out, I'll close seven plants, not five,'" Vines says. That boldness—and the factory shutdowns—led to menacing hate mail, and Ghosn began to travel with a bodyguard.

These days, though, Ghosn is more hero than target. Last year, Nissan reported profits of $4.6 billion on $68 billion in revenues, up 8%. It looks set to boost earnings by another 6% and sales by 9% this year, brokerage Morgan Stanley says. Nissan's $49.7 billion market capitalization is the second biggest in the industry, after Toyota's. It has overtaken Honda as No. 2 inside Japan. And Nissan leads the global pack in operating margins (11.1%).

Despite the problems with Canton, the brand is hot again. Nissan is turning out daring designs such as its sleek-but-muscular 350Z sports coupe, the curvaceous Altima sedan, and the round-backed Murano crossover. And in Japan, stylish numbers such as the March subcompact and the boxy Cube micro-van are driving sales. That's part of Ghosn's push to create what he calls "segment-defining" models. "Consumers either like a car or they don't, but that is OK," says Nissan design chief Shiro Nakamura. As long as a model isn't a bore and hits profit goals along the way, Ghosn gives his designers pretty free rein.

Yet the detail work needs to come up. The quality problems at Canton aren't the only difficulties the company has faced. Take the Quest minivan. First, Nissan underestimated demand for popular features such as snazzy skylights. What's more, the beige interior on the entry model turned off family buyers fearing spills from toddlers. Now, the Quest is getting big design changes, including darker interiors and sunroofs even in the cheapest versions. "You will see incredibly different results this fall," says Walt Niziolek, manager of Visteon's Mississippi plant, which makes many Quest cockpit parts.

Nissan still has some gaps in its lineup, too. It won't have a sub-$15,000 compact—a growing segment critical to brand loyalty that Toyota has exploited with its Gen Y Scion brand—until 2007. Ghosn continues to be skeptical of environment-friendly hybrid cars. So Nissan's first hybrid, a gasoline-electric Altima, won't hit showrooms until 2006. And even where it's filling gaps, Nissan needs to work out some kinks: The Titan, the first full-size pickup truck out of Japan, has been a disappointment. Consumers haven't been flocking to this monster as Detroit's Big Three kick in incentives on their models that are worth roughly twice the $1,500 Nissan offers on the Titan.

Ghosn, though, isn't postponing his return to the CEO's job in Paris. One factor in his favor is that Schweitzer—who will remain chairman of Renault—has done a good job spiffing up the French automaker. Renault is now the top-selling brand in Europe and, after tough restructuring, is light years away from its days as an industrial basket case. Quality still needs to come up. But thanks to rising profits and a deserved reputation for inspired design, Renault is on the offensive. It plans to hire 10,000 workers in 2005 to raise production in emerging markets such as Turkey, Slovenia, Russia, and Romania, where it has opened a plant to build a $6,000 sedan called the Dacia Logan. Renault has profited handsomely from Nissan, too: Its initial $5 billion stake has more than tripled in value.

More important for the company's global ambitions, Schweitzer and Ghosn have a stealth vehicle to drive integration. Early on, Schweitzer set up an Amsterdam-based company, Renault-Nissan BV, as a neutral forum where both sides could map out a common strategy for product engineering, model development, and computer systems, and leverage their combined size to squeeze suppliers for better deals. Once a month, Renault-Nissan's eight board members—four from each side—meet to make medium- and long-term decisions based on proposals by a dozen cross-company teams. Already, about 70% of the parts used by the two automakers are jointly purchased by the alliance.

The integration has been surprisingly smooth—in sharp contrast to the tumultuous marriage of Daimler and Chrysler. Renault today builds its Clio compact and Scenic minivan at Nissan plants in Mexico, while Nissan makes its Frontier pickup at a Renault factory in Brazil. The ultimate goal is to reduce the number of platforms, or chassis, the group uses to 10 in 2010 from the 34 it had in 2000. The goal is in sight: Nissan had 24 individual platforms in 1999, but uses only 15 today. That's important, because every shared platform can add $500 million-plus in annual savings for each carmaker, estimates Commerzbank. Renault will also share eight engine designs with Nissan.

When conflicts do arise, Schweitzer and Ghosn usually hash things out before alliance board meetings. After Renault acquired South Korea's Samsung Motors in 2001, the French company wanted Nissan to design the next large 4x4 sport utility for the Korean company. Ghosn resisted, but was finally swayed by Schweitzer's logic: Nissan had the best know-how in SUVs, so it should take the lead. It wasn't altruism on Ghosn's part, mind you: Nissan will get a royalty from Renault on each of the SUVs that is sold when it launches in 2007. "Every time there was a difficult decision," says Renault CFO Thierry Moulonguet, "Schweitzer and Ghosn worked out the right balance."

That's remarkable, given how different the two men are. Schweitzer, an intellectual who persuades with logic and nuance, prefers to lead from above. Ghosn, on the other hand, is in-your-face and reaches deep into an organization by constant–and often unannounced–visits to dealerships, test tracks, assembly plants, and parts suppliers. And he isn't shy about setting sky-high targets. Toshiyuki Shiga, a senior vice-president in charge of emerging markets for Nissan, recalls getting a call from Ghosn in early 2000. First the good news: Shiga had been promoted. Then the zinger: "He told me to make a clear strategy for Nissan in China, and he gave me two months to do it," laughs Shiga. Back then, Nissan sold just a few thousand vehicles in China annually, mostly imported from Japan. Shiga, though, jumped into motion and hatched a plan that led to a 50-50 joint venture with China's Dongfeng Motors. The duo just opened a plant in Guangzhou that will roll out six new models next year. Although Nissan is far behind market leaders Volkswagen and GM, the venture hopes to sell some 620,000 cars and trucks in China by 2007, double last year's level.

It's those surprise visits that really seem to energize Ghosn. On a recent swing through Nissan's Iwaki engine plant, 110 miles north of Tokyo, he was mobbed by eager factory hands. He doubtless enjoyed the attention, but at each stop it was evident he was looking for nuggets that would help him squeeze yet another ounce of productivity from the plant, which cranks out V-6 engines for such models as the 350Z and the upscale Infinity G35 luxury sedan. He worked the floor, chatting up assembly workers, drilling foremen, all to get that extra fact that would edge the company forward. Even if he got no cost-killing tips from line workers on this particular day, the visit clearly paid off for Ghosn, who knows he is nothing without an inspired workforce. "The only power that a CEO has is to motivate. The rest is nonsense," he says. As his next act begins, Ghosn's motivational powers must be stronger than ever.

Source: Brian Bremmer, Gail Edmondson, Chester Dawson, David Welch, and Kathleen Kerwin, "Nissan's Boss: Carlos Ghosn Saved Japan's No.2 Automaker. Now He's Taking on the World," *BusinessWeek Online*, October 4 2004.

QUESTIONS

1. What are the main elements of Ghosn's approach to leadership?

2. Why is he an effective leader?

3. What is his approach to managing conflict and influencing Nissan's managers and employees?

BusinessWeek CASE FOR DISCUSSION

The Six Ps of PepsiCo's Chief

As the head of a company best-known for soda and chips, PepsiCo's Steven Reinemund might be finding his job tough these days. But Reinemund doesn't worry about Americans' obsession over carbs and sugar. For him, it's just another opportunity to further expand PepsiCo's product family. Senior writer Diane Brady recently spoke with the PepsiCo chairman and CEO, who is one of *BusinessWeek*'s top managers of the year. Edited excerpts of their conversation follow:

Q: What do you think are some of your biggest accomplishments this year?

A: I think the operating performance of the business has certainly been gratifying this year–not without its challenges, but it has been strong and balanced in all of our businesses. That gives us confidence that we've got the right business formulas going forward.

The international business is really coming into its own now. A couple of years ago, we consolidated our international businesses into one organization. It has given us scale in lots of parts of the world.

Q: Do you find talent development more of a challenge overseas?

A: The principles transfer around the world. My role is to be the enabler of growth. That growth is business growth, but more importantly, it's people growth and helping to develop the leaders that we have around the world.

There are a couple of ways that I try to focus on it. One is to be accessible and be in the marketplace and get to know the leaders we have. I teach a class once a year for a subset of our middle managers.

Q: Why is it important for you to be involved in the teaching component?

A: It keeps me relevant on what's going on and what our people are thinking. It gives me a chance to influence and mentor our up-and-coming leaders. Out of those classes come the CEOs of the future.

But it also says to all of them that we all need to take a role in developing leaders. Leaders train leaders in this company. We believe in management development, and leaders do that. The most effective way to hire people, train them, and retain them is for the line leaders to get involved. We also want their feedback on what's important to them, and what will keep them motivated and involved in PepsiCo.

Q: What, to you, are the hallmarks of great leadership?

A: I think all of us as leaders should have a dynamic idea of what a leader is. I don't think you can copy it. You have to mold it yourself and change it over time. The value of listening to other leaders is to hone your model. Every leader has to have a foundation of who they are and what they value and look for in others. Mine involves the six Ps of leadership.

Q: What are the six Ps of leadership?

A: They're not meant to be the Holy Grail. They're just my view. The first P for me is Principles. You have to have a moral compass as a leader. It starts with basic beliefs and values. It's important to make clear to the people in the organization what those are, so you're transparent. They have to be consistent with the values of the organization, or there will be a problem.

If you look at all the issues that have happened in the corporate world of the last few years, it all boils down to a basic lack of a moral compass and checks and balances among leaders. We as leaders have to check each other. We're going to make mistakes. If we don't check each other on them, you get into trouble. Most of the companies that got into trouble had a set of stated principles, but the leaders didn't check each other on those principles.

The second is Perspective. That's an ability to dream, visioning that leads to strategies. It starts with a broader view of the world you live in. The example I use is Sam Walton. His vision lives today long after he's gone. It's about value to the consumer.

The third one is Passion. Passion is not style. There are a lot of different styles—charismatic, quiet, confident. But it all comes down to this motivating sense of commitment to what you do. I remember when I was a kid, Kennedy made the announcement that he wanted to put a man on the moon and bring him back safely to earth. That was so motivating and passionate. Nobody believed it could happen, but he inspired them with his passion.

The fourth one is Perseverance. That's sticking with it through the good times and the bad times—

mostly the bad. It means picking yourself up every day to go after it. The example I use is Roger Enrico, my predecessor, and the transformation that he did in the business in the mid 1990s. Very few people saw his vision. It didn't take right away, but he stuck with it. As a result, we have the possibility to be in a business today that's far better than it would have been had he not had that perseverance.

The fifth—and these are not necessarily grammatically correct, it's just how I remember them—is Performance. As I'm looking to select other leaders, it's important to remember that results count. If you can't get the results over the goal line, are you really a leader?

The last and probably most important one is People. If you can't build the people, if you can't leave an organization stronger than you found it, with more capable people than you inherited, then I question whether you're really adding value. I look at my predecessors— Don Kendall, Wayne Callaway, and Roger Enrico—and I think all three of them left the organization in a better place than they found it.

Q: How important have mentors been to you?

A: Absolutely critical. I can go back to being seven years old with my first mentor, and I can track through my whole life people who have had significant impact. My second-grade schoolteacher stepped in right after my father died. It was her first year of teaching, and I keep up with her all these years later. She stepped in and gave the extra care that made a difference.

I look at my seventh-grade social studies teacher who, when I didn't have a jacket to wear for a speech, gave me his so I could be up there with other kids who had sports coats on. And certainly in military and business, I've met many people who gave of themselves to share a bit about life and about their own experiences in encouraging me along the way.

Q: What are the challenges of your job?

A: You can never get complacent. The day that anyone says "Nothing keeps me awake," that's the day you're not trying to get better and looking over your shoulder. The shorter-term challenges going forward are to attract, develop, and retain great leaders.

Medium term, one of our greater focuses is diversity. To be a leader in consumer products, it's critical to have leaders who represent the population we serve. We're making progress in this area. But it's a marathon, and we're at mile 11. We've got a long way to go.

QUESTIONS

1. What are CEO Reinemund's six Ps of leadership, and why does he think they result in an effective leadership approach?

2. How do these six Ps relate to the concepts discussed in this chapter?

Source: Diane Brady, "The Six Ps of PepsiCo's Chief," *BusinessWeek Online,* January 10, 2005.

BUILDING YOUR MANAGEMENT SKILLS
Know Thyself

Do you enjoy taking charge in an emergency or leading a meeting? Over the past 20 years, professionals who study behavior in organizations have seen differences between good leaders and good managers. They have learned that their leaders need certain qualities to earn the right to lead others and deal effectively with change, as well as those needed to set direction, align employees, and motivate and inspire others to achieve goals. Would you like to know if you have these qualities? Assess your current skills and learn where you can improve by taking the self-assessment exercise on your Student DVD called "Do You Have What It Takes to Be a Leader?"

CHAPTER VIDEO
Breaking Through: Sylvia Rhone of Electra Records

The music industry has been traditionally characterized as a 14 billion dollar a year, white-male dominated business. That had been largely true until Sylvia Rhone was elevated to the position of Chair and CEO of Elektra Records. She is a single mother who can't sing or play music and started in the business as a $12,000 per year secretary.

While at Elektra, Rhone had the best years for hit records of any music company. In her first two years at the company, revenue tripled and in the third year, will go even higher. What makes her successful, according to experts in the industry, is that she has an instinct for what is marketable. Rhone herself characterizes herself as someone who has "guts" and is willing to take risks. Sometimes you win, and other times you lose, she says.

She has left her successful years at Elektra Records behind. She is now an executive with Motown Records. No doubt, her instincts and guts will serve her new company well.

1. How does Sylvia Rhone reduce uncertainty?

2. What type of leader do you think Sylvia Rhone is?

3. Of the four types of leadership approaches, which is most applicable to Rhone?

CHAPTER

7 Motivating and Managing People and Groups in Business Organizations

Learning Objectives

After studying this chapter, you should be able to:

1. Understand the nature and sources of work motivation and appreciate the way motivation is under the voluntary control of an employee.

2. Describe five different theories of work motivation and identify how they work together to determine work motivation.

3. Identify the characteristics of groups and teams and distinguish between important types of groups and teams.

4. Explain the factors that create high-performing groups and teams.

5. Identify the sources of organizational conflict and understand how bargaining and negotiation are used to resolve conflicts between people and groups.

WHY IS THIS IMPORTANT [?]

Why do you work harder in some classes than in others? Something motivates you to do a better job. Why do some of your classmates study more or less than you do? The same thing is true in organizations. Some people and groups are more motivated to achieve goals than others. Also, why is there more conflict within some groups than others? What causes conflict and how can it be managed to benefit the organization?

This chapter will help you understand how important it is for companies to motivate employees so they can achieve success for the company they work for and for themselves.

A Question of Business
How to Run a Restaurant

What is Dick's approach to motivating its employees?

Dick's Drive-In Restaurants is a five-store, family-owned hamburger chain based in Seattle, Washington. Founded in 1954, its owners have pursued an innovative approach to leadership and motivation in the fast-food industry, which is known for its high employee turnover and low-paying jobs. From the beginning, Dick's has always paid its employees well above the industry average and offers them many benefits, too. Dick's pays its 110 part-time employees $8.75 an hour, covers 100% of the cost of their health insurance, and provides employees who have worked at Dick's for six months up to $10,000 towards their college education. Dick's even pays its employees their regular wages if they perform four hours of volunteer work each month in the local community. Dick's competitors, on the other hand, national hamburger chains like Wendy's and McDonald's, pay their part-time employees the minimum wage ($5.85 an hour) and offer them no health insurance and few fringe benefits. When asked why Dick's adopts this approach Jim Spady, its vice president answered, "We've been around since 1954, and one thing we've always believed is that there is nothing more important than finding and training and keeping the best people you possibly can."

Dick's approach to leading and motivating its employees begins when it recruits new hires

straight out of high school. Its managers emphasize that they look for a long-term commitment from employees and that in return, Dick's will help and support employees by providing them with above-average pay, pension benefits, and tuition money while they work their way through school. With its supportive "family style" leadership, Dick's managers and employees help train new recruits and quickly bring them up to speed.

Dick's expects its employees to perform to the best of their ability to get its burgers, and its customers, out the door as fast as they can. Dick's employees don't wait to be asked to do something. They are proactive and do whatever it takes to provide customers the freshest burger Seattle has to offer.

Dick's does not expect its employees to remain with the company after they have graduated. However, it does want them to stay with the company until they graduate. And, here lies the reason why Dick's can afford to motivate its employees with generous pay and benefits. Employee turnover at the large burger chains is frequently more than 100% a year. In other words, a typical restaurant has to replace *all* of its employees at least once a year. As a result, these chains have to constantly hire and train new employees to get them up to speed. This is expensive and significantly increases their operating costs.

Dick's has discovered that if its employees stay with the company for at least six months, the resulting fall in operating costs more than offsets the extra pay and benefits employees receive. This makes for a "win-win" situation for the company and its employees. From the company's perspective, providing employees with greater rewards and a more satisfying work experience actually helps boost the chain's productivity and its profitability. From the employees' perspective, they enjoy the supportive "family" atmosphere that prevails in the restaurant, and they appreciate the good pay and benefits that make it easier for them to graduate from college. As Spady puts it, "Our philosophy is that if you want to be the best, you need the best people, and if you want the best people, you have to pay for them." If a person has to work his or her way through college, then Dick's seems like a good place to do it.[1]

Overview

Every company strives to make and sell the kind of goods and services customers want to buy. A crucial determinant of a company's ability to achieve this goal is its managers' ability to motivate its human resources. The opening case described how managers at Dick's Restaurants tried to create a work setting that encouraged employees to work hard, perform at a high level, and stay with the company. In this chapter, we examine how managers can motivate people and groups in order to do this.

First, we examine the nature of work motivation and describe five theories that together explain what motivates people. Second, we move up from the individual level to the group and team level. We identify several different types of groups and teams and discuss the factors that can increase or decrease their members' motivation.

We then turn to the issue of why conflict occurs between people and groups in the work setting and discuss how conflict can reduce efficiency and effectiveness. Finally, we examine how managers can use bargaining and negotiation to help resolve conflict and increase a company's performance. By the end of this chapter, you will understand the many issues managers face as they try to motivate employees, individually or in groups, to work hard and perform in ways that allow a company to pursue its business model successfully.

Motivation in Business Organizations

The principal determinant of an employee's willingness to work hard is his or her work motivation. **Work motivation** is the psychological force within people that *arouses* their interest, *directs* their attention, and causes them to *persist* and work *intensely* to find a way to achieve their work goals. Managers, of course, try to motivate employees to work hard, but employees ultimately control how much effort they will expend. This concept is illustrated in Figure 7.1.

Recall from Chapter 3 that employees can choose to do their jobs in a way that just allows them to meet minimum work performance requirements. Alternately, employees can choose to search for ways to do their jobs more efficiently and effectively. The

Figure 7.1
Voluntary
Employee
Behavior

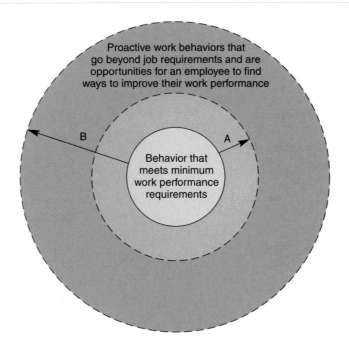

Proactive work behaviors that
go beyond job requirements and are
opportunities for an employee to find
ways to improve their work performance

B   A

Behavior that
meets minimum
work performance
requirements

work motivation The
psychological force within
people that arouses their
interest, directs their
attention, and causes
them to persist to achieve
their work goals.

inner circle in Figure 7.1 represents the minimum required work performance level. The two outer circles represent the level of performance employees could potentially achieve if they were motivated to perform at higher levels.

Employees know that if they do not perform at the minimum level, they risk being punished or sanctioned. This may motivate them to put in enough effort and work to reach this point. But what pushes employees to perform beyond this point? for example, to perform at the higher level represented by the length of Arrow A. And why would employees want to put in the enormous amount of effort and hard work needed to reach their peak performance level? represented by the length of Arrow B.

This is where work motivation comes into play. A company's owners and managers clearly want their employees to be motivated. But to achieve this, managers first need to understand the specific kinds of things that motivate them and then create a work setting in which this can happen. One principal factor that affects work motivation is a manager's approach to leadership, which we discussed in Chapter 6. Other factors relate to the psychological needs that affect the way the person thinks and feels about his or her job and company. To understand how these factors affect motivation, we need to discuss five important theories that together give us a good picture of the various sources of employee motivation.

Maslow's Needs Hierarchy Theory

**Maslow's needs
hierarchy theory**
A theory that specifies
why and how people try to
satisfy their needs through
their behaviors at work.

As we discuss in Chapter 1, people engage in business and other forms of human activity to increase their utility, or satisfaction. Maslow's needs hierarchy theory, illustrated in Figure 7.2, explains *what* specific needs people are trying to satisfy through their work behaviors. Abraham Maslow, a U.S. psychologist, first argued in the 1950s that *unsatisfied needs* motivate people to try to meet those needs in order to satisfy themselves.

At the base of Maslow's hierarchy are *physiological needs,* like the need for food, water, clothing, and sex. Only when their physiological needs are satisfied can people turn their attention to satisfying their *needs for security,* like the need for protection and safety to help them and their families prosper over time. For example, to satisfy their safety needs, people might form clans and tribes to protect themselves from harm and improve their welfare.

Once their physiological and security needs are satisfied, people then search for ways to satisfy the next higher-level need, the *needs for belongingness.* At this point,

**Figure 7.2
Maslow's Hierarchy
of Needs**

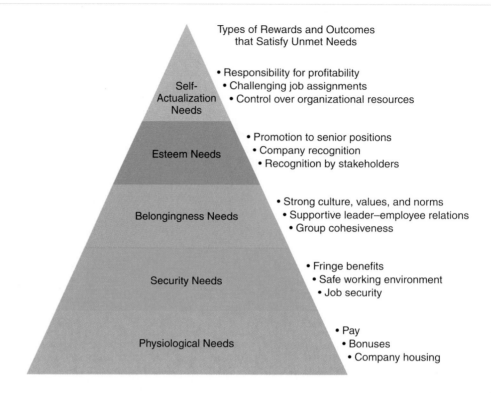

Types of Rewards and Outcomes
that Satisfy Unmet Needs

Self-Actualization Needs
• Responsibility for profitability
• Challenging job assignments
• Control over organizational resources

Esteem Needs
• Promotion to senior positions
• Company recognition
• Recognition by stakeholders

Belongingness Needs
• Strong culture, values, and norms
• Supportive leader–employee relations
• Group cohesiveness

Security Needs
• Fringe benefits
• Safe working environment
• Job security

Physiological Needs
• Pay
• Bonuses
• Company housing

Maslow argued, the desire for affection and love becomes increasingly important. Another kind of belongingness need is the desire to feel a part of something bigger than oneself, such as a clan, community, or nation. Patriotism and the love of one's country are behaviors driven by the need for belongingness.

Once people have satisfied their belongingness needs, they can then search for ways to satisfy their *esteem needs*–the need to be recognized for their skills, expertise, and contributions to society. This need can be satisfied when people achieve a level of prestige and a measure of recognition from others. Achieving such social approval becomes a visible sign of their personal success.

Once people have satisfied these kinds of "lower-level" needs, Maslow argued, they become free to search for ways to satisfy their "higher-level" *needs for self-actualization.* Self-actualization is the desire for personal self-fulfillment–a person's desire to be the best he or she can be. At this level, a person is driven to excel in an activity *for its own sake;* mastering an activity becomes an end in and of itself, in other words.

Self-actualization differs from person to person, however. Some people might achieve self-actualization by continually striving to improve their occupational or other skills. A stamp collector, for example, might be driven to obtain every single stamp issued by a particular country. A runner might become obsessed with building the personal fitness necessary to compete in a marathon. Other people might achieve self-actualization by immersing themselves in the arts or by helping other people. A scientist might achieve self-actualization by working intensely for years to find a cure for a particular disease.

self-actualization

The desire for personal self-fulfillment; that is, a person's desire to become the best he or she is capable of becoming.

MANAGERIAL IMPLICATIONS   Maslow's hierarchy is useful in a business context because it identifies the many different kinds of needs people try to satisfy at work and clues as to how to motivate them. Some of the many rewards or outcomes that motivate employees are listed in Figure 7.2. These rewards include things like salaries, bonuses, and greater job responsibility and autonomy. Outcomes include being recognized for one's successes, being in control of an organization's resources, and having the power to determine the rewards other people receive. The point here is that different employees desire different things, and a manager's job is to figure out what those things are. That said, employees will often be motivated to fulfill their basic needs before their higher-level needs. For example, if a firm lacks basic health-care insurance

Managers must motivate their employees if they want them to perform well. What are some of the types of motivators a manager can use?

expectancy theory A theory that argues that the motivation of employees depends upon whether or not they believe that performing at a high level will lead to the rewards they desire.

(a safety need), its employees are likely to be more motivated to find jobs that offer these benefits than they are motivated to meet the firm's goals.

The next four theories we discuss focus on *how* employees can be motivated to work hard in order to obtain the outcomes and rewards they personally desire. These theories also describe how specific factors in the work setting influence this motivation.

Expectancy Theory

Expectancy theory argues that work motivation is a function of an employee's belief (a) that working hard will allow the person to perform at a high level, and (b) that if the person does perform well, he or she will be rewarded for it (see Figure 7.3). According to this view, motivation is therefore a two-stage process. Several factors determine whether or not employees believe that working hard will lead to a superior job performance. Each of these factors is discussed next.

FACTORS AFFECTING THE EFFORT-TO-PERFORMANCE LINKAGE

Employees' *past experience* frequently provides them with information about how likely they are to succeed at a particular task. Employees who have repeatedly failed to achieve certain work goals in the past will tend to doubt their ability to achieve it in the future. As a result, their motivation to work hard will be diminished.

The implication for managers is that they need to do everything they can to strengthen the *effort-to-performance linkage.* The idea is to encourage employees to believe that if they do apply themselves and work hard, they will succeed. For example, managers should provide support and training to employees who are underperforming. Perhaps more experienced employees can teach the underperforming employees how to do their jobs more efficiently. Expressing confidence in an employee is also an important way managers can strengthen the effort-to-performance linkage. In this way, managers can help increase an employee's self-efficacy, the belief a person holds about his or her ability to succeed.

self-efficacy The belief a person holds about his or her ability to succeed at a certain task or in a particular situation.

Second, to strengthen the effort-to-performance linkage employees also need to believe that nothing in the work situation, *outside their control,* will prevent their hard work from resulting in superior performance. Suppose the level of one employee's job performance depends upon the job performance of other employees, such as when a carpenter assembles furniture parts made by two other carpenters. Suppose the carpenter has learned from past experience that the two other carpenters often make irregular table legs or table tops and that fitting together the pieces is a difficult, time-consuming process. The carpenter may come to believe that it will be impossible to assemble a high-quality table quickly, and, as a result, not be motivated to put forth more effort.

The implication for managers is that they need to identify the factors in the work situation that weaken the effort-to-performance linkage and reduce motivation. If managers can discover what's worrying employees, they can search for ways to help them succeed. For example, if the carpenter's manager discovers that the co-workers'

Figure 7.3
Linkages in Expectancy Theory

poor job performance is the source of his or her lack of motivation, the search for a solution can begin. Perhaps the two carpenters need further training, or perhaps the real source of the problem is a low-level of group cohesiveness. A manager can then try to solve these problems.

FACTORS AFFECTING PERFORMANCE-TO-OUTCOME LINKAGE   The second stage of motivation, according to expectancy theory, relates to how strongly employees believe that a superior performance will result in the outcomes they value. Managers therefore must reinforce the idea that there is a strong *job performance-to-outcome linkage.* One way to do this is to create an incentive structure that clearly links a certain performance level with certain rewards. This is the goal behind creating a *piece-rate* pay system. For example, in a piece-rate system, employees might be paid $2 for each of the first 50 units of a product they make each day, but then receive $4 for each additional unit they make over and above 50 units.

As we discussed earlier, different employees value different outcomes differently. For many people, pay is their principal incentive. These employees will therefore respond positively to attempts to strengthen the performance-outcome linkage by using money as the reward. By contrast, other people might be more motivated by jobs that are more interesting or flexible, offer further training, and greater responsibility over the firm's resources.

Managers need to consider how the various components of a company's incentive system work together to encourage employees to perform at a high level. Consider the issue of promotion. Some companies predominantly hire experienced managers from other companies to fill vacant job positions. If this is a common company practice, however, the company's employees who are motivated by the prospect of being promoted and earning a higher salary will come to believe that there is little chance of this occurring. The performance-to-promotion outcome linkage will be weak, and these employees will be more inclined to leave the company. This is why companies are often advised to "promote from within." By contrast, when employees are already being paid relatively well for what they do—like students working at Dick's Restaurants are—managers might need to reward them differently. For example, Dick's might offer students more flexible work hours or extra days off to study or take trips home.

Employees also must believe that nothing in the work setting outside their control will prevent them from obtaining the valued outcomes they seek. Suppose an employee has a manager who is well known for taking credit for the achievements of his or her subordinates. In this case, the manager's employees will have no motivation to come up with better ways to do their jobs because they do not expect to be recognized for their superior performance.

Employees who value time with their families will not be motivated to perform at a high level by the prospect of being promoted to jobs that require them to work late and on weekends.

Finally, it is important to understand that even if a company's employees have strong effort-to-performance and performance-to-outcome expectancies, this does not guarantee they will be motivated to behave the way the *company* desires. Employees are also motivated by the needs they can satisfy outside of the workplace, so managers must factor this into their decision making. If employees value time with their families, for example, then satisfying this need will have an impact on how much effort they exert and the performance level they aim for. These employees will *not* necessarily be motivated to perform at a high level if their jobs are so demanding they are required to work late or on weekends, for example. By contrast, an employee with a large family might be motivated by a job that offers good pay, health benefits, and job security. And, if this means working long hours, so be it.

Remember, employees *choose* how much effort they expend at work. Their motivation is under their control, although managers can attempt to influence it. The expectancy theory of motivation focuses on the thought processes that go on inside an employee's head as he or she calculates how hard to work to obtain the outcomes desired. Three other motivation theories that throw additional light on the way managers can strengthen the effort-to-performance and performance-to-outcome linkages are discussed next.

Goal-Setting Theory

People never know exactly what they are capable of achieving, until they actually try. You perhaps have heard the saying: "Nothing ventured, nothing gained." This is the idea behind goal-setting theory. To help managers evaluate how well their employees are performing, psychologists recommend that work goals be established for their jobs and that these goals be used to assess their performance. A **work goal** is something an employee is trying to accomplish when doing a job. A goal might be to make a particular piece of work, meet a work quota, demonstrate improved job skills, or to reduce the number of complaints from the company's customers.

Goal-setting theory suggests that the goals used to assess job performance should have five properties if they are going to encourage employees to try to achieve those goals. The five properties of goals are that they be *specific, challenging, measurable, results oriented,* and specify a *timeframe for completion.* These five properties are shown in Figure 7.4.

For example, a bank manager who tells employees to "do your best" is not providing any information that tells them how and what they should do to improve their performance. By contrast, a bank manager who tell employees "you have three months to develop a new IT program that shortens the time it takes to get an old bank statement to a customer who has requested one from seven days to two days" has set a *specific* goal. Now employees can focus on how to solve this specific problem. Based on their own knowledge of the bank's IT system, the manager needs to be reasonably sure that employees can achieve this goal, however. If employees believe the

work goal Something specific an employee is trying to accomplish when doing a job.

goal-setting theory A theory that suggests that if goals are to motivate employees, they should be specific, challenging, measurable, results oriented, and specify a timeframe for completion.

Figure 7.4
Five Characteristics of Motivating Goals

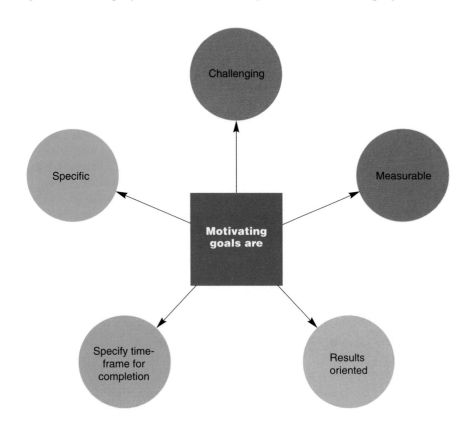

goal is much too ambitious, they will not be motivated to put forth the effort needed to achieve it. Goals should be challenging but not unattainable.

For similar reasons a goal should be stated in a way that allows both managers and employees to measure and evaluate the progress that has been achieved towards meeting the goal. It should be *results oriented,* in other words. If, after one month, employees are able to report they have reduced the request-fulfillment time to four days, everyone has a clear idea of what has been achieved and how far there is still to go. In general, goals should be set that relate to the four building blocks of gaining a global competitive advantage, discussed in Chapter 4—achieving superior productivity, quality, innovation, and responsiveness to customers. These goals provide ways to measure a company's performance and evaluate the success of its business model.

Finally, when managers set a timeframe for the completion of a goal, this also allows them and their employees to judge the progress made towards meeting it. In many cases, reaching a goal is usually the consequence of accomplishing a series of specific "subgoals." Although these subgoals are goals in their own right, they are part of what needs to be done to meet a principal goal—in this case, reducing the customer-response time to two days.

In turn, the bank's customer-response goal might be part of a larger, companywide goal set by the bank's president to "increase work productivity by 10% in order to save $200 million in operating costs." Remember, that the owners of the bank have set a goal for the bank manager, just as the lower-level manager in the bank set a goal for its IT employees. Goal setting occurs up and down the organizational hierarchy. The ultimate goal is that sought by the bank's stockholders: Increase the bank's profitability and its stock price. This hierarchy of goals is illustrated in Figure 7.5.

When these five principles are used to established work goals, they act as clear signals managers and employees can use to gauge performance: Employees understand why their efforts have, or have not, led to improved job performance (and better rewards). Managers can also give employees more accurate feedback about how they have performed, if they have met minimum performance requirements, and how they have performed relative to their co-workers. In the example of the carpenters above, a manager could tell the carpenter who assembles tables that other carpenters assemble five tables a day, whereas he only assembles four. The manager and carpenter could then discuss why this is happening.

When their work performance can be measured, employees can also calculate if the outcomes and rewards they receive are in line with how they have performed. Now, the reason for the carpenter's below-average pay raises becomes clear, and the carpenter can work with the manager to find ways to solve the problem.

WHY GOAL SETTING INCREASES MOTIVATION   In general, there are three reasons why goal setting helps to increase work motivation. First, a goal directs and focuses an employee's efforts toward achieving that goal. Second, the goal motivates the employee to be persistent. In other words, a goal is a constant reminder about what ultimately must be accomplished. Third, when people become used to achieving one goal after another, this helps them develop personal goal-attainment strategies that make them more effective over time.

Research has shown, in fact, that people who are successful tend to be goal oriented. They view the long run in terms of a series of specific, short-run subgoals that need to be achieved. Successful students, for example, might have a four- to five-year goal to obtain a degree. They have found that the best way to achieve this goal is to view each of the 40 different courses they must take as 40 specific, measurable, subgoals that must be met to achieve the main goal—a degree. Moreover, after a number of classes, they learn how to refine their goal-attainment

Did You Know?

In addition to the five universal needs in his hierarchy, Abraham Maslow believed two additional human needs are present in each individual: A need to understand the world around and a need for beauty.[2]

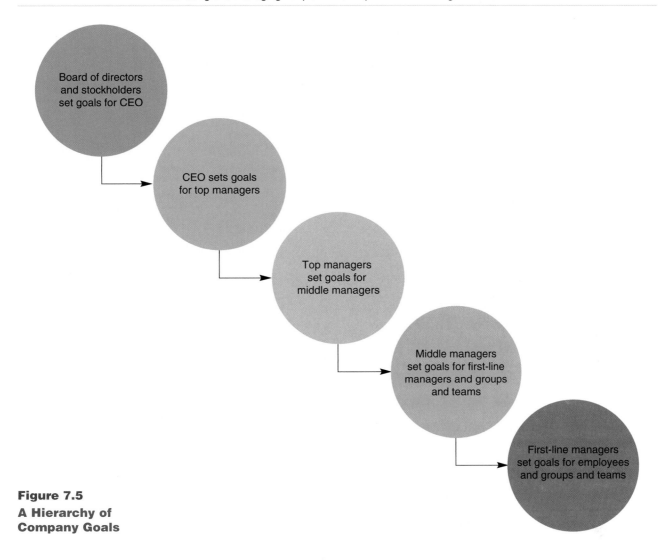

Figure 7.5
A Hierarchy of
Company Goals

strategies; they figure out better ways to study more productively and what they need to do to get an A, B, or C. Similarly, pursuing specific work goals will lead to a general increase in an employee's job performance.

MANAGEMENT BY OBJECTIVES Managers can use goal-setting theory to increase employee motivation by developing a management by objectives (MBO) work-performance review system. MBO systems are used to strengthen the effort-to performance and performance-to-outcome linkages discussed earlier. This involves setting specific, challenging goals and then reviewing employees' progress towards achieving them. The three stages in the MBO process are illustrated in Figure 7.6.

The MBO process begins when managers analyze employees' jobs to determine which specific, challenging goals need to be set to achieve a certain objective. When these goals have been selected, managers then develop work standards that establish clearly what constitutes a below-average, average, or above-average job performance. Employees should participate in the goal-setting process and provide input as to what a reasonable goal for them to achieve is. When employees are allowed to participate in the process, they tend to be more committed to the goals set. The employees' managers are also less likely to set unrealistic goals, which might actually hinder their performance or hurt their self-confidence. Also, both managers and employees tend to be more committed to finding ways to achieve jointly set goals because failing to do so reflects badly on both parties.

Let's return to the example of Tony Knowles, the snack food distributor, to illustrate each of the stages in the MBO process. Assume Knowles has been in business

management by objectives A work-performance review system that involves setting specific and challenging goals and then reviewing employees' progress towards achieving those goals.

Figure 7.6
Motivation through
Goal Setting and
Management by
Objectives

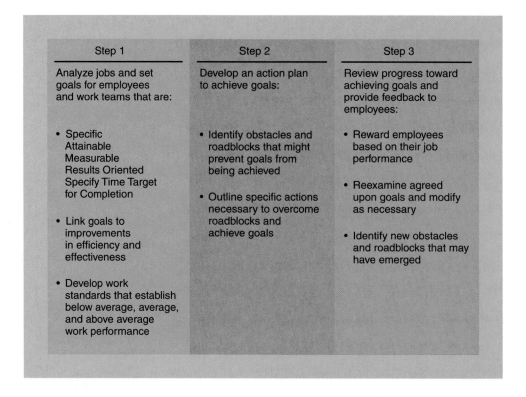

for two months, and his five drivers have learned their routes and are meeting their 25-visits-per-day quota. Moreover, Knowles's intuition has proven correct: Consumers like the new snack foods, and the number of outlets he needs to service is increasing quite rapidly.

Knowles tells his drivers that he plans to introduce an MBO performance review system. He plans to drive the routes again with his drivers and wants their input into how many extra visits per day would be a reasonable goal for them to achieve. His drivers are not particularly happy. They have just learned their jobs and already Knowles wants them to do more. However, he explains that meeting the higher visits-per-day goal will be linked to higher rewards. After covering their routes, Knowles and his drivers agree on the challenging goal of 30 visits per day.

At step 2 in the MBO process, the manager and employee "brainstorm" to develop an "action plan" that lays out specific behaviors needed to achieve the agreed-upon goals. Knowles and his drivers, for example, examine how the business's operations could be changed so that the drivers could increase the number of their daily sales visits to 30 a day. His drivers tell Knowles that they won't be able to reach the higher visits-per-day goal if the snack food supplies are not ready for pick up in the morning and in the afternoon when they need to restock their vans. The time it takes them to get the snack foods out of the warehouse and into their vans is time lost driving their routes. Given that snack food sales are increasing, Knowles decides to hire a new employee to take charge of getting the snack foods to the loading dock for quick pickup.

At step 3 in the MBO process, the manager meets with his or her employees to review their progress towards meeting the agreed-upon goals and gives them feedback on their job performance. Managers need to approach the review process in a positive way. The review should focus on providing support to employees and identifying ways they can improve their performance. Knowles's drivers are required to complete written reports of their daily outlet visits. Knowles then uses these reports to review their progress towards meeting their goals. The reports can also be used to pinpoint any emerging problems. He can then intervene selectively to correct these problems. In addition, to strengthen the commitment of his employees, Knowles plans to reward them as promised when they meet their goals.

The time period for reviewing progress and providing feedback varies depending on the nature of the job. For more complicated jobs, a longer time period of six months to a year might be appropriate. For less-complex jobs, a weekly or monthly review might be most suitable. In Knowles's case, a once-a-week review might be appropriate at the start. Then this period can be extended as he and his employees get up to speed.

STRETCH GOALS AND JOB LEARNING Most businesses today use some type of MBO system to motivate their employees. Often, MBO systems are used to maintain minimum performance standards and ensure employees put in a "fair day's work for a fair day's pay." But managers and employees can get into a rut—a routine of doing their jobs the same way over and over again. To prevent this from happening, some companies use modified MBO systems to encourage employees to "stretch" themselves. Stretch goals are highly ambitious goals put in place to energize employees to think "outside of the box" and perform at an even higher level. The idea behind stretch goals is to encourage employees to develop a *learning orientation* and to constantly question the way things are done. Stretch goals challenge them to experiment to find new and better ways of doing things. This facilitates creative, entrepreneurial work behavior. In a global environment, continuous experimentation and learning are needed for companies to survive and prosper.

stretch goals Highly ambitious goals put in place to motivate employees to perform at higher levels.

Stretch goals sometimes go unmet, but the important thing is to keep on trying. When the stretch goals *are* met, companies usually reward their employees more handsomely than they do for meeting their regular goals. This also helps motivate employees to continuously strive to act entrepreneurially. Jack Welch, the former CEO of General Electric, used stretch goals with great success at GE, and the practice later became widespread.

In Tony Knowles's case, once his drivers have met the higher, 30-visits-per-day goal, Knowles could then decide to challenge them with a stretch goal. A stretch goal might require each driver to provide sales leads that result in five new outlets being signed up each month. Knowles could then reward a driver who achieves this goal with a $200 bonus. Later, Knowles might consider adopting an even more ambitious approach: A team goal for his drivers. If together the drivers can devise a way to work their routes more efficiently and sign up even more accounts, he will pay each of them an even higher bonus.

Jack Welch, the former CEO of General Electric, once said, "We have found that by reaching for what appears to be impossible, we often actually do the impossible. And even when we don't quite make it, we inevitably wind up doing much better than we would have done."

Equity Theory

equity theory A theory that argues that employees will be motivated to achieve a goal only if they believe they will be rewarded equitably relative to their co-workers.

According to equity theory, employees will be motivated to achieve a goal only when they believe they will be rewarded *equitably* (fairly) for doing so. Basically, employees compare their own performance to that of their co-workers. They select co-workers like themselves—employees who do the same jobs, have similar education and experience levels, and so on—and compare their inputs and outcomes versus those of these people. Figure 7.7 illustrates three different possible results of the outcome-input comparison process.

In Figure 7.7a, two employees, A and B, have compared their inputs and outcomes against those of employees, X and Y. and have decided that they have been fairly treated. The perception that *all* employees have been evaluated and rewarded in a similar way increases A and B's beliefs that their performance determines the outcomes and rewards they will receive. This increases, or at least maintains, A and B's motivation to work hard and perform at a high level.

In Figure 7.7b, employees A and B feel they have received more favorable evaluations and rewards for what they have achieved versus X and Y. In fact, A and B feel

**Figure 7.7
Equity Theory
in Action**

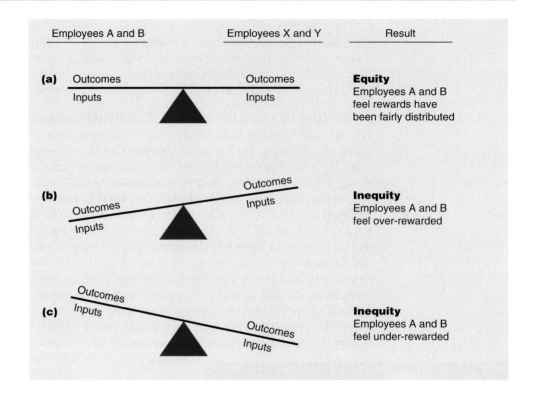

over-rewarded. In Figure 7.7c, A and B feel they have received less-favorable evaluations and rewards for what they have achieved versus X and Y. A and B perceive they have been *under-rewarded*. Both of the inequitable results in Figure 7.7 lead employees to question how accurately their managers are evaluating their performance and how fairly they are distributing rewards. They might even feel that they are being "picked on" or that their managers are playing favorites. In either case, the fact that they don't believe their efforts will be appropriately rewarded weakens their motivation.

According to equity theory employees A and B will withhold a significant amount of effort and perform only up to minimum standards. They are also likely to stop cooperating with their "over-rewarded" co-workers and feel less valued by the company. This will take a toll on their job satisfaction and possibly diminish their self-confidence. The result might be that they are absent from work more frequently and begin to search other jobs.

Tony Knowles has studied equity theory. He knows his five drivers are watching to see if he treats different drivers differently. They will also compare their job strengths and weaknesses against one another to try to determine if Knowles's evaluations match their own. In this way, drivers decide if he is distributing rewards in a fair and equitable way.

Knowles knows he should not act in a way that makes his employees think he is an unfair or arbitrary manager. He should take great care not to give the impression that he favors certain employees for non-job related reasons or that he gives the drivers he likes best better routes to work, more reliable trucks, or simply more supportive supervision. Using an MBO system and applying the same performance review standards across all of his employees can help Knowles (and all managers) behave in a fair and impartial manner. Suppose a driver starts to complain about unfair treatment and suggests Knowles is treating another diver who is a poorer performer in a more favorable way. If Knowles uses an MBO system and the same criteria to judge all of his drivers, he can show the driver that his or her poorer performance led to the poorer performance evaluation. Knowles now has a way to justify why the driver received a smaller bonus.

**Video
Small
Business
in Action**

Debbie and Leslie Busfield

Summary: The original video on your Student DVD introduces Debbie and Leslie Busfield, the wife and husband owners of Strongfield Trimco, Inc. The company provides framing for "high-end" homes in the Phoenix area. Prior to Debbie's involvement, the company provided the whole range of building services without a focus on a market niche. However, they could not sustain a high level of quality with such a diversified approach. The Busfields bought the business and focused its product/service so that it only does one thing but does it with the best quality—framing houses. Their sustainability for the business and business growth has been primarily through word of mouth.

Debbie notes that communication is at the heart of a successful business. To be successful, the entrepreneur must be unafraid to make mistakes. Success demands that you make a decision, even if it is not the "best" one. In that case, you adjust. You have to have the ability to be flexible and innovative by trying new ideas. Maintaining flexibility is critical.

Both Debbie and Les emphasize the importance of motivating their workforce by keeping them involved. They see their responsibility as owners and managers to create a place where people want to come to work. To that end, their management style is oriented toward encouraging and developing their employees. They take the perspective that problems are challenges. They recognize that people come to work for more than just a paycheck. They solicit ideas from employees and, more importantly, provide feedback to employees on the status of their ideas. They also recognize the need to be flexible in making changes in the work environment that are consistent with employees' needs. They are quite successful in this arena; they have a highly motivated workforce with very low turnover.

Discussion Questions

1. Using Maslow's Hierarchy of Needs theory, explain how the Busfield's "motivate" their employees.
2. Using equity theory, provide examples from the video that would illustrate the theories' principles.
3. How does Strongfield Trimco, Inc. "empower" its employees?

Job Enrichment Theory

job enrichment theory A theory that argues that employees will be more motivated if they have more control over the way they do their jobs.

job enlargement Motivating employees by expanding the range of tasks they do.

empowerment Expanding employees' tasks and responsibilities to allow them more freedom and autonomy over the way work is performed.

To encourage employees to perform at a higher level and be more satisfied with their work, several researchers have proposed that managers should design jobs in such a way that they offer employees greater rewards or desired outcomes. Job enrichment theory suggests that one way to motivate employees is to increase the degree of responsibility they have over the way they do their jobs. There are several ways of doing this.

First, a manager can increase the number of different tasks an employee has to perform in a particular job. This is called job enlargement. The manager might also encourage employees to develop new skills and abilities, perhaps by transferring them to other departments temporarily or by paying for them to get additional education and training. This helps remove the monotony of continually doing the same job, and many employees find it motivating. It also gives employees a better perspective on a company's overall operations and how they can work to improve them.

Second, a manager can empower employees. Empowerment involves continually expanding employees' tasks and responsibilities to give them more freedom and autonomy over the way work is performed. When employees have more control over their jobs, they can usually find a way to make them more interesting and satisfying. This can improve their efficiency and effectiveness and make them less likely to want to quit. Another way managers can make jobs more interesting is by setting specific, challenging goals for employees to achieve and then allowing them to decide how to organize tasks or pace the work to get the job done. Frequently, allowing employees to monitor and measure their own progress toward meeting their goals is a part of this process.

self-managed teams
Groups of employees who are given the responsibility to supervise their own activities and to monitor the quality of the goods and services they provide.

Last, but not least, managers can create **self-managed teams,** groups of employees who are given the responsibility to supervise their own activities and monitor the quality of the goods and services they provide. Members of self-managed teams assume many of the responsibilities and duties previously performed by first-line managers. When self-managed teams are used, the role of the first-line manager is to act as a coach or mentor; not to tell employees *what* to do but to provide them with advice and guidance in order to help them find better ways to perform their tasks. The story of John Deere, discussed in Business in Action, illustrates the way all these things can help improve employee motivation and improve a company's performance.

Business in Action

A New Approach at John Deere

In the 1990s, John Deere, the well-known agricultural equipment maker based in Moline, Illinois, experienced intense competition from Caterpillar and Komatsu, the other leading makers of agricultural equipment. Deere began to experience huge losses. In an effort to turn around its performance, the company laid off thousands of employees to reduce costs. But this was not enough to stem John Deere's losses. The man in charge of finding a solution, CEO Hans W. Becherer, was then forced to make some even more dramatic changes.

Becherer decided that John Deere should pursue a business model based both on improving product quality and lowering prices. To accomplish this, he knew that he and his managers would have to find new and better ways to utilize the company's employees and increase their motivation—despite the fact that many of their co-workers had been laid off. Becherer gave his managers the responsibility to empower John Deere's remaining employees and group them into self-managed teams.

Becherer also wanted his managers and employees to better understand what the company's customers wanted from its products. As part of the empowerment process Becherer decided that all factory employees periodically would be sent out to meet the company's customers. He empowered assembly-line employees to take limited leaves from their jobs so that they could interact with customers, just as the company's marketing and salespeople did. In this way they would learn about customers' likes and dislikes.

The result was that John Deere's factory employees brought a great deal of newfound knowledge back to the company and passed it along to the engineers responsible for creating improved products for John Deer. Their contact with customers also helped make employees more quality conscious. Becherer also took steps to increase the company's productivity. He made it clear to employees that if Deere were to survive and prosper, they had to find ways to "work smarter." Part of that effort included establishing an extensive training program to enhance the skills of John Deere's workforce. Every employee is expected to attend classes to learn better manufacturing techniques. Becherer also linked employees' pay directly to their skill development. As a

In an effort to improve its business model and products, John Deere CEO Hans Becherer sent the company's factory employees out to meet with its customers.

result, John Deere's workforce has become one of the most skilled and productive in the industry.

John Deere's self-managed work teams and employees now meet frequently as a group to find ways to continuously improve the company's work procedures to reduce its costs and increase its output. The overall result of the suggestions made by the self-managed teams has been a 10% cut in manufacturing costs and a significant reduction in customer complaints. John Deere is once again a profitable company and its managers and employees are enjoying greater job security and higher wages.[3]

As the story of John Deere suggests, managers who make job design choices that empower employees are likely to find that they behave proactively. Tony Knowles could learn some lessons from John Deere. Recall, that Knowles wants his drivers to be proactive, learn each other's routes, and search for new customers and ways to better satisfy their needs. One way for him to do this is to organize his drivers into a self-managed team, which would require a whole new leadership approach on his part. Because employees in self-managed teams are given the autonomy to make their own decisions and control their own activities, Knowles would need to shift from a directive leadership approach to a participative or achievement–oriented approach.

Once he is sure that his business is secure, the move to self-managed teams might be a good way for Knowles to keep his drivers motivated. Driving the same route every day becomes uninteresting for many people. His drivers therefore might like more variety and greater responsibility. They will also like the higher monetary rewards that accompany the higher performance that self-managed teams are often able to achieve. The question is, how does Knowles go about creating a self-managed team? We discuss how next.

Creating High-Performing Groups and Teams

The performance gains John Deere achieved by moving to self-managed teams suggests that many companies could benefit from such an approach. Today, most companies use teams in different functions and in different levels of their organizations. Below we discuss why groups, and particularly teams, can enhance employee motivation and a company's performance. We then look at some important types of groups and teams.

What Is a Group or Team?

People can work alone to create goods or services, but in many cases they can also work in a group or team. A **group** is a collection of people who follow similar work rules and norms and work towards a common, specific, and measurable goal. A **team** is a group of people jointly responsible for creating, managing, and changing the work rules and norms, if need be, to meet that goal. Once the goal is met, the team then establishes more challenging goals for itself to meet in the future.

Figure 7.8 illustrates how employees act when they work alone, in a group, or as a team. In Figure 7.8a, each employee receives inputs (chair legs and table tops) and then works alone to assemble a finished product (a table). In Figure 7.8b, the employees work as a group. Inputs are received by employee X, who performs the first task, and then hands off the work-in-progress to Y, who performs the second task and hands it off to Z, who performs the last task needed to create a highly polished table. Under this setup, how well one employee performs is likely to affect how well each of the other employees performs. If X fails to create a level tabletop, Y will not be able

group A collection of people who follow similar work rules and norms and work towards a common, specific, and measurable goal.

team A group of people who are jointly responsible for creating, managing, and changing work rules and norms to find better ways to achieve current and future goals.

Figure 7.8
Patterns of Interaction between Employees, Groups, and Teams

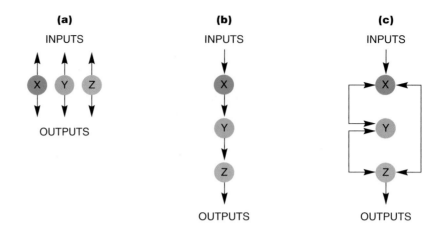

to thoroughly sand the tabletop, and Z will not be able to achieve a highly polished finish, so the performance of the group suffers.

Now look at Figure 7.8c, which illustrates how a team (versus a group) operates. As you can see, the employees do not merely hand off the work-in-progress sequentially. Instead, X, Y, and Z hand off the work to the member whose work contribution is most needed–that is, the member who has the skills currently needed to complete the task. This means that there is no fixed pattern of interaction between the members. If the work is to progress smoothly, they must coordinate their activities much more closely to anticipate one another's needs and respond quickly.

Types of Groups and Teams

functional team
People grouped together by virtue of their expertise, typically, by departments.

The most common type of team is a functional team. Functional teams are people grouped together by their area of expertise or by their department–marketing, manufacturing, accounting, sales, and so on. Frequently, subgroups composed of employees who work on the same project, or who share a particular specialization, are found inside each function or department. An example of a subgroup might be a group in a company's human resource department that focuses on employee training. A subgroup in the accounting department that specializes in accounts payable is another example.

A functional team must also coordinate its work with the organization's other functional teams. Take, for example, Verizon: When a cell-phone outage on Verizon's network occurs, the company's highly trained repair team swings into action. This team must work closely with the company's customer-service team to keep them informed about when service will be restored. Likewise, to develop systems less prone to future outages, Verizon's R&D team must work closely with the firm's repair and customer-service teams.

cross-functional team
A group of people from a company's various functions who pool their talents to increase the organization's efficiency and effectiveness.

As you might expect, teams are also created to bring together people with different skills and expertise. A cross-functional team is a group of people from a company's various functions who work together to increase the organization's efficiency and effectiveness. Reducing the cost of making a product and getting the product more quickly to customers are examples. In Verizon's case, a cross-functional team might consist of a member from repair, customer service, and R&D respectively.

When people are grouped into cross-functional teams, the artificial boundaries between functions disappear. Larger, companywide goals replace narrow, departmental goals. The result is often a dramatic improvement in performance: By using cross-functional teams, Chrysler is now able to introduce a new car model in two years versus five years. Likewise, Black & Decker is now able to create new products in months versus years. And Hallmark Cards can now get a new greeting card onto store shelves in weeks versus months. Cross-functional teams have also dramatically improved operations at Rubbermaid, as Business in Action suggests.

Business in Action

Using Teams at Rubbermaid

Managers at Rubbermaid, the well-known maker of over 5,000 different household products, were worried when the company's rate of product innovation fell dramatically in the 1990s. To fix the problem, Rubbermaid decided to create 20 cross-functional teams, each consisting of five-to-seven people from marketing, manufacturing, research and development, and so on. Each team focused its energies on developing new and improved products for a particular product line, such as Rubbermaid's garden, bathroom, or kitchen product lines.

The results were astonishing. Within the first year, the teams developed over 365 new products, and the rate of product innovation at Rubbermaid continues to increase annually. Today, the main challenge Rubbermaid faces is not creating new products but selecting from the hundreds of new product ideas its teams have come up with.[4]

In the first year following their implementation, Rubbermaid's cross-functional teams developed over 365 new products, and the rate of product innovation continues to increase year by year.

---

top management team A group consisting of the top managers of a company's major functions or business units.

virtual teams Teams whose members are connected by e-mail, the Internet, instant messaging, wireless laptops, and video teleconferencing.

A **top management team** consists of the top managers of a company's major functions or business units. Members of a top management team are responsible for increasing the profitability of the company and improving its overall business model. Finally, **virtual teams,** teams whose members are connected by e-mail, the Internet, instant messaging, wireless laptops, and video teleconferencing, are an emerging feature of multinational companies. Members of these teams might rarely, if ever, meet face to face. Multinational team members frequently move from client to client and country to country, communicating electronically with one another. The virtual team members of the consultant company Accenture are a good example. When Accenture's consultants encounter problems, using their laptops, they are able to access a problem–solution database. If they cannot find the solution to their clients' problems in the database, they contact their other team members via the Internet for help.

High-Performing Groups and Teams

Why is it that employees often perform at a higher level when they work in groups and teams than when they work separately?

First, when people work in teams, their shared identity and need for achievement can make them want to work harder. (No one wants to "let the team down," after all.) Recall from Chapter 6 that members of highly cohesive teams like each other and try to help one another perform better. The most-skilled members of the team can help those who are less skilled so that the performance of the team as a whole increases.

Second, groups and teams frequently monitor the performance of their members. In some instances (particularly in self-managed teams), the team can penalize members who do not seem to be pulling their weight. Groups and teams also develop norms that facilitate cooperation. Members might be encouraged to be courteous to one another, arrive on time for work, or work overtime to accomplish a task.

A third performance advantage of teams is that they often facilitate the division of labor and specialization. In a team, members can continually work out better ways to organize their tasks to get a job done more efficiently. Teams also generally allow

In large groups, people may feel that their individual work contributions are going unnoticed and they begin to slack off.

people to experiment with new ways to get the job done. Moreover, team members, not managers are responsible for controlling their own activities. As such, they are less costly to monitor and supervise.

Owens-Corning, the insulation maker, is another example of a company that used teams. One hundred employees work in teams in Owens-Corning's Tennessee plant. Each employee reports directly to the plant manager because all of the middle levels in the organization's hierarchy have been eliminated. Jointly, the members of the teams are responsible for making the plant's operational decisions. The plant manager intervenes only when requested to do so by a team member, and even then, only to act as a facilitator to help the team solve its own problems. The teams make employees most affected by a problem, fix it. Owens-Corning does not just use the teams to reduce costs, however. It does so to create an atmosphere of entrepreneurship and new opportunities for organizational learning. This has increased the motivation of the plant's employees tremendously.

In fact, the theories of work motivation we discussed earlier suggest several more reasons why groups and teams have an edge when it comes to performance. Employees' effort-to-performance and performance-to-outcome linkages can frequently be strengthened in a team because its members are frequently rewarded as a group. Moreover, many self-managed teams formally appraise the performance of their members. Not only does this strengthen the performance-to-reward linkage, it promotes the perception of equity and creates cooperation among the group. Groups and teams also make it easier for people to satisfy their belongingness and esteem needs. Employees each have a clearly defined position, so their contributions can clearly be recognized. Finally, because teams set their own goals, their members often feel more committed to meeting those goals.

The performance-enhancing advantages of a group or team disappears, however, if it becomes too large. Several problems can hamper the group's performance. First, team members begin to impede each others' ability to perform their tasks—they "get in each others' way," in other words. Second, in large groups, people are more likely to feel their contributions go unnoticed, which weakens the performance-to-outcome linkage. When this happens, team members will have a greater tendency to "free-ride," or "shirk." That is, they will expend less effort and let their team members shoulder the bulk of the work.

Thus, simply creating groups or teams is not enough to promote high work motivation and performance. The team members still have to figure out the best way to equitably allocate their tasks and coordinate their activities. They also have to create a system of rules and norms to facilitate the work process, set specific goals, and measure how well they are achieving them.

Conflict, Bargaining, and Negotiation

Organizational conflict is the discord that ensues when a firm's stakeholders attempt to thwart each other's efforts to achieve their goals and objectives. Conflict is an inevitable part of organizational life because the goals and interests of different stakeholders, such as managers and employees, are often incompatible. Organizational conflict also can exist between groups, teams, and functions that compete for resources, or between individual managers in competition with one another for promotion, for example.

The amount of conflict that occurs in a company reveals much about the level of its performance. When there is little or no conflict, this signals that the company's managers value conformity more than they do new ideas. It indicates that on the

organizational conflict
The discord that ensues when stakeholders thwart each other's attempts to achieve their goals and objectives.

whole, they will resist change and strive to maintain the status quo—even if it hampers the organization's performance.

Suppose, however, different managers and functions actively disagree about how a company should change its business model to improve its performance, and they have conflicting ideas they are trying to get adopted by their company. This conflict often signals that a company is open to new ideas and that its managers and employees are encouraged to look at problems from different points of view to increase efficiency and effectiveness. So, disagreements are often considered a necessary part of effective decision making.

Thus, not all conflict should be eliminated. Rather, it should be kept at a level that facilitates change and improvement. If the conflict becomes too great, however, the organization can become *dysfunctional*. This happens when the conflict between managers is such that they waste a company's resources to achieve their own goals versus those of the company. It can also occur when managers become more concerned about winning political battles than building the most competitive business model for their organization. If the conflict becomes so great that managers stop cooperating with one another, a company's performance will suffer.

Types of Conflict

Managers need to understand the types and sources of conflict and strategies to effectively deal with it. Three main types of conflict in companies are interpersonal, intragroup, and intergroup conflict. *Interpersonal conflict* is conflict between two or more people in a company. It often occurs because of differences in people's goals, interests, and values. For example, two top managers might experience interpersonal conflict because their values about the environment differ. One manager might argue that the organization should do only what is required by law to protect the environment. The other manager might counter that the organization should invest in pollution-abatement equipment even though the organization's current level of emissions is below the legal limit.

Intragroup conflict is conflict that arises within a group, team, or department. When members of the marketing department in a clothing company disagree sharply over how they should spend their limited advertising budget on, say, a new line of men's designer jeans, they are experiencing intragroup conflict. Perhaps some of the members want to spend the entire budget on magazine advertisements; others want to spend half of the budget on billboards and ads posted on city buses and in subways.

Intergroup conflict is conflict that occurs between groups, teams, or departments. A company's R&D department, for example, can sometimes experience intergroup conflict with its production department. The members of the R&D group might develop a new product they believe production can make inexpensively using the firm's existing manufacturing capabilities. The members of the production department, however, may disagree. They might believe that the existing facilities are insufficient and that the extra time and money it will take to make the product will hamper their productivity and increase their costs.

Sources of Conflict

Conflict in a company can spring from a variety of sources. The sources we examine here are incompatible goals, complex task interdependencies, incompatible reward systems, and scarce resources. Each of these sources is outlined in Figure 7.9.

INCOMPATIBLE GOALS   A major challenge for managers is to group people into functions and departments to achieve a *company's* goals. Unfortunately, once this is done, these functions and departments often naturally pursue incompatible goals. The result is conflict. Members of the production group, tend to focus on reducing costs and improving efficiency. In order to do this, they have to pay attention to what is presently coming off of the production line and how it affects current costs and product quality. This necessitates a short-term focus.

Figure 7.9
Sources of
Organizational
Conflict

In contrast, marketing and marketing managers focus on ways to increase sales and responsiveness to customers. Their time horizon is longer than that of production because they are trying to be responsive not only to customers' needs today, but also in the future. The actual cost to make the products customers want on a day-to-day basis is not an important priority for them. These differences in perspective are often a breeding ground for conflict.

Suppose production is making a customized product needed quickly by an important buyer, and the department is behind schedule. The marketing department believes that the delay will significantly reduce the potential sales of this product. So, the head of marketing insists that the product must be delivered on time—even if this means that production's costs will increase sharply (because of the need to pay production employees overtime, for example). The production manager says that she will do this if marketing will pay for the costs of overtime and so on. Both managers' positions are reasonable from the perspective of their own departments. Conflict is still likely, however, because the goals of the two groups differ so sharply. Managers further up in the hierarchy need to prevent these conflicts from escalating by prioritizing the firm's goals across its different departments.

COMPLEX TASK INTERDEPENDENCIES   Have you ever been assigned a group project for one of your classes and one group member consistently failed to get things done on time? This probably created some conflict within your group because the other members were dependent on the late member's contributions to complete the project. Whenever individuals, groups, teams, or departments are *interdependent,* the potential for conflict exists. Managers of marketing and production with differing goals and time horizons come into conflict precisely because their departments are interdependent. Marketing depends on production to make the products it sells as quickly as possible, and production depends on marketing to create customer demand for the products it makes.

INCOMPATIBLE REWARD SYSTEMS   The way in which interdependent groups and departments are evaluated and rewarded can be another source of conflict. Production managers are evaluated and rewarded on their ability to reduce production costs, maintain product quality, and stay within their operating budgets. Consequently, they are reluctant to make decisions that will increase costs, such as paying employees overtime to complete an order a customer needs right away. Marketing managers, in contrast, are evaluated and rewarded for attracting more customers and generating increased sales revenue. Consequently, they think that higher overtime pay is a small price to pay for increased responsiveness to customers that generates higher sales. Thus, conflict between production and marketing is to be expected. Business in Action illustrates how incompatible rewards caused a great deal of conflict at a prominent bank.

Business in Action

Dysfunctional Conflict in a Bank

The merger of two smaller banks, First Boston (based in New York), and Crédit Suisse (based in London), formed CS First Boston, a large investment bank. From the beginning, the U.S. and U.K. units of the new bank were at odds. Although the merger was formed to take advantage of the growing global investment banking business, the bankers in the two units wouldn't cooperate with one another. Bankers in both units openly criticized the banking practices of the other unit to anyone who would listen.

As long as the performance of one unit of the bank did not affect the other, the lack of cooperation between them was ignored. Analysts, however, pointed out that this lack of cooperation kept CS First Boston out of the top ranks of investment banks. In the 1990s, the performance of the European unit began to affect the American unit, and the conflict escalated.

First Boston was making record profits from issuing and trading fixed-income debt securities, so its managers were expecting hefty bonuses. However, those bonuses were not paid. Why? The London unit had made huge losses, and although the losses were not the fault of the Boston unit, the company's top managers decided not to pay bonuses to their U.S. employees because of the European unit's losses.

Punishing the bank's U.S. employees for an outcome that they could not control led to considerable conflict in the company. Relations between the U.S. and European units of the bank became even more strained and infighting between the firm's top managers ensued. Many of the employees affected by the conflict decided that the situation would not soon change, so they quit. Moreover, a large number of them were hired by competitors such as Merrill Lynch and Goldman Sachs. As a result, CS First Boston was left in disarray. Clearly, designing a reward system that does *not* promote conflict between groups, teams, and units should be a top priority for managers.[5]

What managers at CS First Boston lacked was a reward system that promoted cooperation, rather than conflict between the company's groups, teams, and units.

SCARCE RESOURCES Competition for scarce resources also produces conflict within companies. For example, functions and divisions often compete for more resources and a larger budget so that they can pursue a greater range of activities and hire more people. However, money is always limited, so conflict can occur as a CEO decides how best to allocate capital.

Resolving Conflict through Negotiation and Bargaining

If a company is to achieve its goals, its managers must be able to resolve conflicts between employees and groups of employees. It is always best when the parties in conflict can find the "middle ground" and resolve the conflict amicably. Compromise is possible when each party is willing to engage in a give-and-take exchange and to make concessions until a reasonable resolution is reached. When parties are willing to cooperate to find a solution each finds acceptable, a company is more likely to achieve its goals.

negotiation and bargaining A technique managers use to increase the chances that conflicting parties will reach a compromise.

Managers use negotiation and bargaining to increase the chances that parties in conflict will reach a compromise. Via negotiating and bargaining, the parties try to come up with mutually acceptable ways to reconcile their differences. But sometimes one or both parties view the negotiation and bargaining process as a "win or lose" situation in which one benefits only at the other's expense. This makes the bargaining process competitive and adversarial. As time goes on, each party draws an increasingly "hard line." They may begin to make unrealistic demands or become belligerent, and the conflict escalates.

The people involved in the bargaining process need to prevent this situation from developing. Instead, they need to work to create a situation that both parties can view as a win-win situation—as a situation in which they both get most of what they want. This is similar to the "make everyone a winner" political tactic discussed in the last chapter.

There are four specific tactics that managers can use to structure the negotiation and bargaining process to make compromise more likely: emphasize common goals; focus on the problem, not the people; create opportunities for joint gain; and focus on what is fair.

EMPHASIZE COMMON GOALS

Common goals are goals that all parties agree on regardless of the source of their conflict. Increasing organizational effectiveness, increasing responsiveness to customers, and gaining a competitive advantage are just a few of the many common goals that members of a company can emphasize during bargaining. Emphasizing common goals helps parties in conflict keep the "big picture" in mind—that they are cooperating to help a company succeed despite their disagreements.

FOCUS ON THE PROBLEM, NOT THE PEOPLE

Parties who are in conflict may be unable to resist the temptation to focus on the shortcomings and weaknesses of the other party. Instead of attacking the problem, they attack one another; they talk about the mistakes the other has made or criticize the personality or habits of the other party. This approach is inconsistent with reaching a compromise through bargaining. All parties to a conflict need to keep focused on the problem at hand and resist the temptation to discredit one another.

CREATE OPPORTUNITIES FOR JOINT GAIN

Once the parties to a conflict focus on resolving the source of the conflict, they can focus on finding creative solutions that will benefit them all. The parties try to come up with new alternatives that benefit each of them in ways they may not even have considered before.

FOCUS ON WHAT IS FAIR

In many bargaining situations, the parties naturally adopt the position that will benefit them the most. Each party will prefer the alternative that best achieves their objectives. To counter this tendency, one that will inevitably lead to conflict, it is useful to emphasize the need for fairness. This can help the parties come to a mutual agreement about the right way to proceed.

When managers pursue these four strategies and encourage other members of a company to do so, they are more likely to resolve their conflicts effectively through negotiation and bargaining. Again, a measure of conflict can increase a company's performance. Conflicts that go unresolved, however, can adversely affect a company, as CS First Boston discovered.

Summary of the Chapter

The principal determinant of an employee's desire to perform at a high level is his or her work motivation. Psychological forces within people affect how motivated they are. Managers can increase the motivation of their employees by understanding the six different theories of motivation discussed in this chapter and putting them into practice. They can also increase the motivation of their employees via job enrichment, enlargement, and empowerment techniques, as well as by implementing self-managed teams and controlling the amount of conflict in their organizations. This chapter made the following points:

1. Maslow's needs hierarchy theory explains the specific needs people are trying to satisfy through their behaviors at work.

2. Expectancy theory argues that people are motivated to pursue work behaviors they believe will result in the outcomes and rewards that satisfy their needs.

3. Goal-setting theory suggests that setting specific, challenging, measurable, results-oriented, and time-specific goals motivates employees to perform at a high level.

4. Management by objectives (MBO) is a popular performance review system that involves setting specific and challenging goals and then reviewing employees' progress towards achieving those goals.

5. Equity theory proposes that an employee's perception of the fairness of a company's review and reward process is an important determinant of his or work motivation. Employees compare their performance and rewards to those of other employees to evaluate whether or not they have been fairly treated.

6. Job enrichment theory suggests that the motivation of employees depends on the degree of control they have over the way they do their jobs.

7. A group is a collection of people who follow similar work rules and norms and work towards a common, specific, and measurable goal. A team is a collection of people who are jointly responsible for creating, managing, and changing work rules and norms to find better ways to achieve their current goals and establishing more challenging future goals.

8. Several types of teams are functional (departmental) teams, cross-functional teams, top management teams, and virtual teams.

9. There are several performance advantages associated with the use of groups and teams. However, these advantages can only be realized when managers design and manage the firm's teams correctly. When teams become too large, problems can ensue that hamper their performance.

10. Organizational conflict is the discord that ensues when an organization's stakeholders attempt to thwart each other's efforts to achieve their goals and objectives.

11. Four important sources of conflict are incompatible goals, complex task interdependencies, incompatible reward systems, and scarce resources.

12. Negotiation and bargaining is a conflict resolution technique used by managers to increase the chances that conflicting parties will reach a compromise.

13. Managers can use four specific negotiation and bargaining tactics to make a compromise more likely: emphasize common goals; focus on the problem, not the people; create opportunities for joint gain; and focus on what is fair.

Developing Business Skills

QUESTIONS FOR DISCUSSION AND ACTION

1. In what sense is employee motivation voluntary, or under a person's direct control?

2. What is self-actualization? Why is it a person's highest need, according to Maslow?

3. In what ways can managers use (a) expectancy, (b) goal-setting, and (c) equity theory to encourage employees to take a proactive approach and perform at a high level?

4. Think of a business setting in which you have worked. Use the six theories of motivation to describe how managers motivated employees in that setting? To what degree do you think they were successful?

5. When does a group become a team?

6. Why can groups and teams enhance an organization's performance? Under what conditions can groups result in lower performance?

7. *Action.* Find a manager who leads a group or team. What kind of team is it? What kinds of issues and problems arise when managing the team?

8. What is organizational conflict, and why can it be both an advantage and a disadvantage for a company?

9. What are the sources of organizational conflict? In what ways can negotiation and bargaining help people or groups in conflict resolve their problems?

ETHICS IN ACTION

A Lack of Teamwork: Free-Riding, or Shirking

As the chapter notes, sometimes when groups or teams become too large, their members are more likely to shirk, or free-ride—that is, let other members of the team bear the bulk of the work burden. If this happens, there is likely to be conflict.

Using the material on ethics from Chapter 5, think about the following issues:

- How do the four ethical principles explain the origin of free-riding in a group setting?

- How can managers design teams to eliminate this problem? What can the members of teams do to eliminate this problem?

- When and why does conflict in groups become unethical?

SMALL GROUP EXERCISE

How to Motivate New Teams

After reading the following scenario break up into groups of three or four people and discuss the issues involved. Be prepared to share your thinking with the rest of the class.

You are managers in a large building-products supply company. In the past, each of you was responsible for managing a different department consisting of 10 employees who stock shelves, answer customers' questions, and check out customers. You have decided that you can operate more efficiently if you organize these employees into work teams. You believe that the old system did not encourage employees to behave proactively. Indeed, you think

that the way the work situation was designed prevented them from finding ways to improve the business's operating procedures.

Teams will change how employees perform their tasks in many ways. You are meeting to decide how to change the way you lead and motivate your employees. Using the chapter material:

1. Discuss how the move to teams will affect your various leadership approaches.

2. Discuss how the firm's incentive system can be changed to encourage employees to work well together in their new teams.

3. Identify the new kinds of motivational issues that will arise and how you can use the motivation theories discussed in this chapter to deal with these issues.

DEVELOPING GOOD BUSINESS SENSE

What Motivates You?

Motivating employees is a complex task because employees essentially control their own performance levels. To help you understand how the different kinds of motivational techniques are likely to affect your *own* future work behaviors, use the chapter material to think about the following issues:

1. Using Maslow's hierarchy of needs, think about your past work and leisure behavior. Which kinds of needs have you been trying to satisfy the most? Which kinds of needs do you think you will be striving to satisfy in the future? What kinds of things might satisfy your needs for self-actualization?

2. In general, are you the kind of person who is most likely to want to perform at a minimum standard level or the kind of person who will behave proactively? Why? What could change this?

3. Using the six theories of motivation think carefully about which theory or theories would do most to strengthen your *own* personal beliefs that (1) more effort on your part will result in you performing at a higher level and that (2) if you do so, you will obtain the outcomes you desire.

4. Create your own "personal motivational model" that outlines the steps you could take to improve your performance at school or work.

EXPLORING THE WORLD WIDE WEB

Motivation

Go to any search engine on the Internet and type in "Anne Perlman CEO Moai Technologies." Then browse through the articles you find

(especially the *InformationWeek* article). **For more Web activities, log on to www.mhhe.com/jonesintro.**

1. What motivates Perlman to succeed in the e-commerce arena?

2. What approach does she take to motivate people and groups?

BusinessWeek CASE FOR DISCUSSION

Two Men and a Lot of Trucks

The Two Men and a Truck brand began simply enough. To help drum up business for her sons' part-time moving service in the early 1980s, Mary Ellen Sheets made a line drawing of two stick figures in a truck cab and placed an ad in the local paper.

It worked. In fact, too well. Sheets, a single mother and data analyst for the State of Michigan, kept receiving moving inquiries–even after her sons, Jon and Brigham Sorber, left for college. "One day, I came home from work and there were 12 messages on the answering machine," she says.

Sheets was understandably hesitant to just turn away business. So in 1985, she bought a used pickup truck for $350 and hired two men to do the heavy lifting. "That $350 was the only capital investment I ever made," Sheets says. And seeds for the nation's largest franchised moving company were planted.

SHORT HAULS. Today, Lansing, Michigan–based Two Men and a Truck operates in 27 states. The outfit made 250,000 moves last year, generating $150 million in revenue along the way.

Its success was born largely out of Sheets's early discovery that local, residential hauls–from Point A to Point B within the same city, as opposed to long-distance–were a greatly underserved market. She initially ran the part-time operation from her dining room. But as orders kept coming in and the business continued to grow, she found herself devoting more time and energy, and began drafting formal business plans and operating manuals.

In 1988, after putting her third and last child through college, Sheets finally felt comfortable with the risk of leaving her government job to run the company full-time. "Everybody said I was crazy," she recalls. "I had a good-paying job with health benefits and vacation." But she also says she had caught the entrepreneurial bug. "It was going pretty well. I was so scared, but I just wanted to do this so bad."

MAN'S WORLD. That same year, at the urging of a woman she met while speaking on a panel at Michigan State University, Sheets decided she could leverage and grow Two Men through franchising. A year later, she sold her first franchise to daughter Melanie, a pharmaceutical sales representative. Then her sons bought franchises, as did some of the moving men. "After we had sold 10 franchises, my attorney said, 'I think you are going to make it,'" she says. "But I always knew we were going to make it."

Today, there are 152 franchise locations. Franchisees pay an initial fee of $32,000, but capital costs (including trucks and office space) bring total startup costs to roughly $100,000. Royalties run 6% of gross revenue, with an additional 1% for advertising–considered standard in the franchising world.

Along the way, however, there have certainly been bumps in the road. For one thing, Sheets was never exactly embraced by the traditionally male-dominated trucking business. At one point early on, she says, competitors reported her for minor violations. She was eventually hauled into court when some of her truckers drove 10 miles outside the company's zone. Says Sheets: "We made a lot of mistakes and learned the hard way."

SATISFIED CUSTOMERS. Unlike the other moving companies she had seen, Sheets decided that Two Men would put a premium on customer service. "Moving had a cruddy reputation," she says. "I made sure everything was spotless. And we went out of our way for the customers." Sheets put her movers in uniforms and gave them business cards, charged by the hour instead of weight, and paid for any damage to be fixed. The company's mission statement remains: "Treat everyone the way you would want your Grandma treated."

From the start, Sheets handed out postage-paid reply cards, with just five questions, to her customers. Last year, the company received 66,000 responses. Sheets says that only 1% of the comments are negative—and she uses them as an opportunity. "We want to get it right with our customers," she says. "Sometimes we send them flowers or a gift if something went wrong." As a result, Two Men gets about 95% of its business from word-of-mouth referrals, eliminating the need for much advertising.

With no formal business background, Sheets says she has relied mostly on her own instincts and experience. She credits her time volunteering at a hospital crisis intervention center with helping her to handle customers over the phone. "It taught me empathy and how to listen," she says.

STICK MEN U. When it came to marketing, Sheets took a similar grassroots approach. She printed brochures and placed them in apartment buildings, handed out mugs with the Two Men logo filled with jelly beans, and turned the trucks into mobile billboards—displaying the original stick-figure logo. Her goal was, and remains, to bring a personal touch to an industry known for its uniformity and stressed-out customers.

Like most successful franchisers, Sheets realized the need for consistency. In 1998, she established Stick Men University, a comprehensive training facility at the company's Lansing headquarters. Here, franchisees and movers learn the basics—from answering a customer's first phone call to a handshake after the move is done. On site, there is also a two-story house set up to simulate many moving challenges, like transporting a piano down a narrow staircase and moving crates of fragile china.

At Two Men's computer lab, franchisees learn to pay their royalties electronically, check their colleagues' spending patterns, and communicate with each other about what's working and what's not. "I want them to be successful as fast as they can," Sheets says.

COMING HOME. Richard McBee, a former seventh-grade social studies teacher in Birmingham, Alabama, is the most successful among them. Eleven years ago, he decided to go into business for himself, and has since become Two Men's top franchisee—with $5 million in annual revenue, two locations, and a third in the works. "I'm still astonished at what we've done," he says.

The Two Men system and a well-respected brand convinced McBee to make his initial investment of $90,000. "I didn't feel comfortable getting into a business without a lot of support," he says. And once up and running, McBee made his own success by expanding his customer base slowly, and enlisting a payroll service and legal and tax advisers to help avoid mistakes along the way.

Two Men is once again a family affair. Sheets is CEO and daughter Melanie Bergeron is president and chief operating officer. After stints in the corporate world, Sheets's sons have returned—Jon is a franchise owner and board member, while Brigham works as director of licensing.

"I'm still shocked by our success," Sheets says. "I worked so hard, I never really knew how big it was." Indeed, the company that began almost by accident could easily be re-named One Family and a Thousand Trucks. Or more simply, a family success story.

Stacy Perman, "Two Men and a Lot of Trucks," *BusinessWeek Online*, April 14, 2005.

QUESTIONS

1. What motivates Mary Ellen Sheets? What personal qualities does she possess that makes her a successful entrepreneur and manager?

2. Why are high-performing teams vital to the company's success? What steps has Sheets taken to train her franchisees and their employees to build a competitive advantage?

3. What kinds of conflicts with customers typically occur in the moving business, and how does Sheets deal with them?

BusinessWeek CASE FOR DISCUSSION

Siemens's New Boss

Workers at a Siemens unit that makes X-ray machines and other diagnostic equipment were shocked when, in 1998, a cocky new boss asked them to work more flexible shifts to speed production. The new guy, a 40-year-old up-and-comer named Klaus Kleinfeld, even wanted some people to work weekends, then practically unheard of. Yet employee representatives knew the unit in the Bavarian town of Forchheim was getting beat up by rival General Electric Co. and that shareholders were nagging Siemens to dump its medical equipment unit. Everyone's job was on the line.

The negotiations were tough. But Kleinfeld won over workers, hanging around the factory asking detailed questions. He answered e-mails from employee reps almost immediately, even late at night, recalls Werner Mönius, chairman of the workers council in Erlangen, Germany, home base of Siemens Medical Solutions Division. "He was able to motivate people to pull together," says Mönius. The workers signed off on Kleinfeld's plan, which helped cut the time it took to build a $100,000-plus diagnostic scanner from six weeks to one. Siemens Medical is now Siemens's most profitable business.

And that cocky young boss? This month Kleinfeld, now 47, becomes chief executive of Munich-based Siemens, a $100 billion behemoth that operates in 190 countries and makes subways, light bulbs, power plants, auto parts, automatic mail-sorting equipment, and more. With 430,000 employees and 12 major divisions, Siemens is the rock of Germany Inc., which still needs to learn how to survive and thrive in a world where heavily taxed, slow-moving European companies operate at a disadvantage. If Siemens can reach new levels of profitability, maybe the rest of Corporate Germany has a chance, too.

Siemens Chief Executive Heinrich von Pierer and the company's supervisory board, which includes such corporate luminaries as Deutsche Bank CEO Josef Ackermann and former Allianz Group CEO Henning Schulte-Noelle, skipped over more seasoned top managers to choose the ferociously energetic Kleinfeld. He's a prime example of a new breed of German manager, fluent in English and comfortable in settings from Tokyo to Toledo. "This generation has grown up in a much stronger international environment than the earlier one," says Hermann Simon, chairman of Bonn consulting firm Simon-Kucher & Partners. "They understand the need to be global." With his big laugh and knack for storytelling, Kleinfeld knows how to network globally as well. He sits on several corporate and charitable boards abroad, including aluminum-products maker Alcoa and the Metropolitan Opera in New York. "I love him. He's a generous, funny man," says Beverly Sills, chairman of the Met, who gushes about Kleinfeld's ability to appraise opera performances.

If nothing else, Kleinfeld should help put to rest stereotypes about dour German execs. At a November dinner in Munich with business journalists, one Italian scribe waved his Nokia mobile phone in Kleinfeld's face and demanded to know how Siemens can compete with the handset industry's market leader. Kleinfeld replied by snatching the Nokia phone and dropping it in a glass of water. The message: We'll drown the competition. (Kleinfeld later gave the journalist a waterproof Siemens phone instead.) But the reporter's question was legitimate. Does Kleinfeld have what it takes to fix Siemens's money-losing mobile-handset business and other underperformers?

In its home market of Germany, where Siemens has 38% of its workforce—compared to 58% in 1994—employees are demonstrating a willingness to work longer and accept modest pay raises to keep jobs from moving overseas. Abroad, Siemens can draw on a lower-cost workforce and decades of experience to cash in on rapid growth in giant markets like China and India. In December, for example, Siemens won a $460 million order to supply locomotives to China's state railway. Profit in the fiscal year ended was up 40% over 2003.

But Siemens still suffers in comparison to archrival GE, whose shares have had a total return of 423% over the past 10 years, versus 273% for the German company. Von Pierer himself has admitted that he wasn't always able to push change as fast as he would have liked. It's not just a question of cutting costs. "In the innovation game, productivity and R&D matter more than cost structure," says William M. Castell, CEO of GE Healthcare. Siemens boasts that its engineers and scientists generate more than 8,000 inventions a year, but it needs to do more to turn those innovations into commercial products. Siemens was a leader in introducing mobile-phone handsets with color screens and built-in MP3 music players, for example, but wasn't able to translate its tech edge into market strength.

Can Kleinfeld succeed? He doubtless has the drive. Kleinfeld's father, a shipyard laborer who became an engineer by studying nights, died when the boy was 10. That was a "brutal" experience, Kleinfeld says, but the hardship that followed forged a determination to succeed. An only child, he stocked grocery shelves at age 12 and has held a job ever since. After studying business at Georg August University in Göttingen, Kleinfeld put in stints at a Nuremberg market research firm and at drugmaker Ciba-Geigy before joining Siemens's corporate sales and marketing department in 1987.

The new Siemens chief was a multitasker before anyone used the term. Many of his generation milk Germany's free university system for years. But Kleinfeld completed his doctorate at the University of Würzburg while working full-time at Siemens and raising a young family. (His wife, Birgit, is a teacher, and they have two school-age daughters.) "That was an extreme burden," recalls Ulli Arnold, now a business professor at the University of Stuttgart, who supervised Kleinfeld's thesis work on corporate identity and strategic management.

"ENDLESS ENERGY"

His stamina is already legend inside Siemens. "Working hard earns the right to play hard," Kleinfeld once told students at the University of Rhode Island, and he lives the creed. George C. Nolen, CEO of Siemens Corp., the company's U.S. unit, recalls returning from a European trip with Kleinfeld, who runs or lifts weights every day. "I was dead tired, and he runs the New York City marathon. The guy has endless energy," Nolen says.

Kleinfeld's résumé reflects ambition as well as talent. He has held 10 jobs within the company in 17 years, including building Siemens's in-house consulting arm into a power center. The unit had eight consultants when he took it over in 1995. Under Kleinfeld, it grew to 170 operating under direct control of the management board, and was involved in turnarounds of divisions such as power generation. It helped formulate and run the TopPlus program, a late-'90s drive to apply stricter standards to managers and fix or prune marginal businesses.

His job-hopping and role as an internal consultant have led to muttering that Kleinfeld is short on operational experience. "He's a bit full of himself," says one outsider who has worked with Kleinfeld. But his stint as a consultant has also allowed him to explore every corner of the far-flung Siemens empire. He enjoys regaling dinner partners with tales of his adventures, such as an all-night session with the glum managers of a troubled Japanese unit. By dawn, fatigue and sake loosened the managers' reserve: They worked out a new business plan.

NOT SO LONELY AT THE TOP

Winning friends and influencing people—and neutralizing the rest—is crucial at a vast company where local barons have built their fiefdoms over the years. Kleinfeld was one of the main inventors of One Siemens, a program designed to get company units to cooperate better to win business. He got a chance to put theory into practice when Siemens sent him to the United States in January 2001, first as chief operating officer, then, a year later, as CEO of New York-based Siemens Corp. Under Kleinfeld, units including Medical Solutions and Power Transmission & Distribution joined together to supply diagnostic equipment, software, telecommunications, and power to a new hospital being built in Temple, Texas, for Scott & White Healthcare System.

Kleinfeld won't enjoy unlimited power as he tries to crunch Siemens into a seamless unit. Formally, he is not CEO but chairman of the management board, a body that operates on the principle of consensus. He probably can't take such action without von Pierer's support. But he may get it. Siemens is scheduled to announce plans for the handset unit on Kleinfeld's first day as CEO, and von Pierer has said sale or closure are options. Even in labor relations, Kleinfeld has room to maneuver. Labor leaders know that they must give way on wages and hours to slow the outflow of jobs to Eastern Europe and China. "We can hinder it, but there's not much we can do to stop it," admits one top official of the IG Metall union, which represents Siemens workers.

A whole generation of young Siemens executives, keen to conquer the world and frustrated with the bureaucracy, is also rooting for Kleinfeld. Robert H. Schaffer, a Stamford, Connecticut, consultant who has helped design training programs for Siemens as well as GE, says that the mid-level managers at Siemens "are as bright and as aggressive as any I have met." Bright and aggressive—that describes Kleinfeld, too. The talent is there. But the task—transforming the prime symbol of Germany Inc.—is huge.

Jack Ewing and Diane Brady, "Siemens's New Boss," *BusinessWeek Online*, January 24, 2005.

QUESTIONS

1. What kinds of needs do you think Klaus Kleinfeld is trying to satisfy at work? Which motivation theory best explains his behavior?

2. What is Kleinfeld's approach to creating high-performing teams?

3. Why has bargaining and negotiation been important at Siemens?

BUILDING YOUR MANAGEMENT SKILLS
Know Thyself

How do you react when someone yells at you? Do you get angry and yell back or shut down and try to get away? Do you try to calm the person down and seek a solution? Conflict is inevitable between individuals and between groups, even when they share basic values and goals. Whether at work or in your personal life, understanding your own style of handling conflict and recognizing the responses of others can be very helpful. To learn more about it, do the exercise on your Student DVD called "What Is Your Primary Conflict Handling Style?"

CHAPTER VIDEO
The Container Store

The Container Store has no parallel in the retail industry. It pays its employees 50 to 100% above the industry average, has a turnover rate of 75% below industry average, and has the happiest, most empowered employees in the industry.

Garrett Boone, Co-Founder and CEO explains the company's philosophy throughout this video. He explains that the operating philosophy of The Container Store can be captured in the following maxim: "1 great person = 3 good people." Their hiring practices actually reflect these values. Their mission is not only to satisfy customers but to exceed their expectations. The video exemplifies this by citing examples of employee kindness to customers well beyond what is expected.

The video then traces the history of management theory beginning with Taylor and concluding with Vroom's expectancy theory model. The video provides examples from The Container Store that support theoretical tenets across several models. For example, Theory Y and Theory Z management principles apply to the belief in people to work effectively without close supervision and to work in a team environment. Herzberg's motivators and hygiene factors is exemplified by the 100% cross-training goal for all employees at the company. Development is also a key concern with Boone and his team: Drucker's MBO could apply here.

The video concludes by suggesting that one management theory of motivation does not and cannot fit all company models. The Container Store sees its business as "situational" requiring flexibility in terms of customer response. Empowerment is the only answer. Several of the values and practices of The Container Store clearly support a "situational" approach to management and motivation–they draw from Maslow, McGregor, Drucker, Herzberg and Vroom. Open communication is at the heart of the company's culture–it is a privately held firm but shares all information with employees including the financials. In a sense, the CEO sees "communication" as being the #1 core value of The Container Store and as such is equivalent with leadership.

1. What examples from the video on The Container Store support Maslow's motivational need for self-actualization?

2. How is empowerment used in the video case?

3. How does Herzberg's theory of motivators and hygiene factors relate to The Container Store?

8

The Structure and Culture of a Business Organization

Learning Objectives

After studying this chapter, you should be able to:

1. Discuss why organizational structure and culture are important determinants of a company's ability to pursue a profitable business model.

2. Identify the relationship between organizational design, structure, culture, and the environment.

3. Identify the main types of organizational structures companies can choose from to group their activities, employees, and resources.

4. Explain why the need to coordinate functions and divisions is an important element in organizational design, and list the main methods companies use to coordinate their activities.

5. Identify the nature and sources of organizational culture and understand the way it influences and shapes employee behavior and attitudes.

WHY IS THIS IMPORTANT ?

Have you ever returned a defective product and been met with a pleasant smile and prompt refund? Why is it easy and pleasant to do business with some companies and terrible to deal with others? The design of an organization, its formal structure, should make it easy for employees to satisfy customers. This chapter explains how companies organize work into jobs, departments, and divisions to create value as effectively and efficiently as possible.

There is more to it, however, than who reports to whom and whether the company is able to respond quickly to change. A company develops its own "personality" that shapes the way employees interact with customers and with one another. This chapter explains how corporate culture develops from an organization's shared values and norms.

A Question of Business
Sony's New "Networked" Organization

How and why has Sony changed its structure and culture?

In 1946, Akio Morita, a Japanese physicist, founded the company that was to later become Sony. Akio envisioned that his company would one day become the world's leading producer of state-of-the-art electronic products. For example, to achieve his vision, Morita created a corporate culture based on excellence and innovation and a corporate structure that would motivate his employees to work toward that goal. To give Sony's engineers the freedom to be creative and pursue new product ideas, he created separate product divisions. Each division specialized in making a particular kind of product, such as tape recorders, televisions, or radios. Moreover, each divisional manager was given complete control over the development of these products.

The result was that Sony's individual employees became intensely loyal and committed to the divisions in which they worked. They also competed vigorously with one another to develop the most innovative and profitable products on the market. Their efforts led to the creation of hundreds of new products each year, including the world's first tape recorder and pocket radio. By the 1980s, Sony was selling thousands of different products around the globe.

By 2000, however, Sony's new CEO, Nobuyuki Idei, realized Sony's business model was no longer working well in the new digital, Internet-

based environment. The kinds of electronic products customers wanted had changed. Idei saw that what Sony needed was "networked" electronic products—cameras, telephones, computers, stereos, and televisions—that worked seamlessly together. Sony would also need new advanced multimedia products that could store and play large digital files, including movies, music, video games, and electronic books.

The problem was that Sony's current organizational structure and culture had become a major liability. Its fiercely independent divisions were too used to protecting their own turf at the expense of the company's overall competitiveness. If Sony were to succeed in the new networked world, its culture would have to change. Idei needed to champion a new "knowledge based" culture based on cooperation and teamwork. Only by forcing the divisions to share their expertise could Sony quickly develop a wide range of networked products for the global marketplace.

Thus, in 2001, Idei redesigned Sony's structure and culture to change its employees' work attitudes and behaviors. He scrapped Sony's old organizational structure and replaced it with a new "networked" system that matched its newly networked business model. To accomplish this, he had Sony's engineers create a new knowledge-management IT system shared by the entire organization. The sophisticated electronic system linked up all of Sony's product divisions and pooled their collective knowledge. Then, to further integrate the divisions, Idei created cooperative, cross-functional teams made up of managers from Sony's different product divisions.

Finally, Idei began to focus on changing Sony's culture. He knew that establishing new cooperative values and norms would be difficult because Sony's engineers were used to behaving in an independent, competitive way. To counter this culture, Idei embarked upon an extensive companywide public relations campaign championing Sony's new networked culture. He clearly let Sony's employees know that to achieve the company's new goals, they needed to embrace teamwork and put aside their divisional goals.

Many divisional managers were not receptive to Sony's new structure and culture and resisted these changes, however. Nonetheless, Idei made them toe the line. Even Sony's "heroes," the people who had pioneered its major product breakthroughs, were forced to change. Ken Kutaragi, the innovator of the Sony Play Station, was known for his strongly independent attitude. To make Kutaragi conform to Sony's new culture, Idei gave him cross-divisional responsibilities, which naturally forced him to become a team player.

Although Idei continued to send a clear message to Sony's employees that they must change, his efforts met with only limited success. The company responsible for creating cutting-edge products like the Walkman failed to see that the future lay in new digital music players like Apple's popular iPod. To add insult to injury, agile competitors like Samsung and Panasonic were introducing networked products at a much faster rate than Sony was.

In an effort to regain its former momentum, Sony announced a sweeping managerial change in 2005. Idei stepped aside, and the former head of Sony Corporation of America, Howard Stringer, who is known for his digital expertise, was named its new CEO. What will Stringer's new business model for Sony be and how will he implement it?[1] •

Overview

The previous two chapters described many different ways companies and their managers can persuade employees to work hard, including the company's approach to leadership, its incentive structure, and the use of empowered teams. As Sony's experience suggests, however, an organization's structure and culture are also important factors that shape employees' behavior. In this chapter, we first examine how an organization's structure and culture affect its ability to pursue its business model successfully. Second, we examine the two main decisions involved in designing an organizational structure (1) how to divide up a company's activities, employees, and resources into functions and divisions; and (2) how to link and coordinate these functions and divisions. Lastly, we examine how a company's culture can make its organizational structure work to its advantage. By the end of this chapter, you will understand how and why a well-designed organizational structure and culture provide a good foundation for a profitable business model.

Structure, Culture, and the Organization's Business Model

organizational structure The framework of task-and-authority relationships in a company that coordinates and motivates employees to work together toward a common goal.

organizational culture The set of shared company values and norms that shape the way employees and groups interact with one another.

organizational design The process of creating an organizational structure and culture so that a company can pursue its business model profitably.

Sony has the most recognized brand name in the world. The Sony Walkman, Trinitron television, and Play Station 2 are just a few of the company's best-selling products. Given its track record, it might appear that Sony would be the last company to be concerned about the success of its business model. Yet, to stay competitive, Sony's top managers had to radically change that model. A total redesign of Sony's organizational structure and culture was needed.

As we noted in Chapter 1, organizational structure is the framework of task-and-authority relationships in a company that coordinates and motivates employees to work together toward a common goal. Its organizational culture consists of the values and norms employees share and how they affect their interaction with one other. Organizational design is the process by which managers create a specific type of organizational structure and culture so that a company can pursue its business model profitably.

Once a company decides what kind of work attitudes and behaviors it wants from its employees, its managers can then create specific task-and-authority relationships that promote those attitudes and behaviors—just as Akio Morita did for Sony. The challenge facing managers of all companies is to design a structure and culture that (1) *motivates* employees to work hard and to develop supportive work behaviors and attitudes, (2) *coordinates* the actions of employees and groups to ensure they work together efficiently and effectively, so that (3) a company can pursue its business model successfully.

The Business Model and Organizational Design

Figure 8.1 illustrates what it takes to implement a successful organizational design. A good organizational design will coordinate and motivate employees to create products customers want to buy. This leads to higher operating revenues for the company. Likewise, a well-designed structure and culture can help alleviate many organizational problems like conflict, slow or faulty decision making, and poor communication. This enhances a company's ability to operate more efficiently and leads to lower operating costs. As we describe in Chapter 1, a company's ability to increase operating revenues and reduce its operating costs result in *an increase in the profitability of its business model.*

How do managers decide what is the appropriate organizational structure or culture for a particular company? As Figure 8.1 illustrates, the design process starts with the business model. The business model outlines a company's goals and objectives and how it is going to compete for customers. Different kinds of business models often require different kinds of structures.

To encourage his engineers to produce high-quality electronic products, Akio Morita chose to use a product division structure. Akio also promoted values that stressed the importance of product innovation and excellence. Dell, by contrast, has a business model based on providing customers with low-cost products. To reduce the costs of assembling its products, Dell groups employees into empowered work teams.

The Contingency Approach to Organizational Design

The managers of a company not only need to create an organizational design, they must also be prepared to alter it. Like Sony, they must change the company's structure and culture to allow it to better respond to the changes taking place in the global environment.

Figure 8.1

Implementing a Profitable Business Model through Organizational Structure and Culture

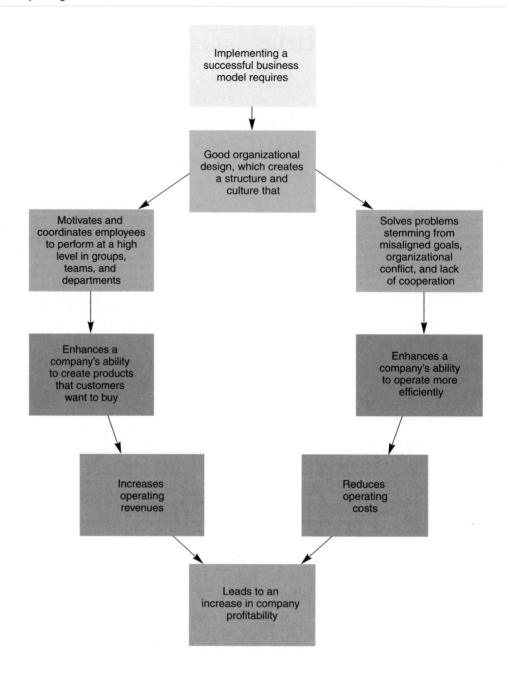

contingency approach to organizational design
A type of organizational design that depends on the changing forces in a firm's competitive environment.

Researchers call this the contingency approach to organizational design. The implication of contingency theory is that there is no "one best way" to design a company—design reflects each company's specific situation at a certain point in time. Moreover, as Sony's experience suggests, organizational design is a *dynamic* process. Just as a manager needs to match his or her leadership style to the characteristics of a particular work situation, so, too, must a company's structure and culture match the environmental contingencies affecting its business model. Companies are continually changing their structures to better match their business models. Managing this fit is a vital managerial task.

Next, we examine the different kinds of organizational structures companies can choose from. Each of these structures is based on a different way of grouping people and resources. First, we examine grouping employees by function and its advantages and disadvantages. We then look at grouping employees by divisions, either on a product, market, or geographic basis. Finally, we examine matrix structure, a special kind of structure used when a company needs to respond rapidly to change.

Functional Structures

functional structure
A structure that groups people together because of their expertise or the type of activity they do (typically into departments).

When managers group a company's activities, employees, and resources into functions they create a functional structure. Almost all companies create business functions or departments. Recall from Chapter 7 that a function is a group of people who work together and perform the same types of tasks or hold similar positions in a company. For example, the salespeople in a car dealership belong to the sales function. Together, car sales, car repair, car parts, and accounting are the set of functions that allow a car dealership to sell and service cars. Similarly, product design, manufacturing, sales, and customer service are the functions that allow Dell and Gateway to make and sell low-priced PCs. Figure 8.2 lists many of the most important functions typically found inside a business organization.

The managers of each function are responsible for predicting how changing competitive forces in the environment are likely to affect the performance of both their departments and the firm as a whole. For example, marketing managers need to be able to forecast the changing customer needs–something Sony has been doing poorly as of late. Similarly, manufacturing managers need to be able to identify new locations, such as countries abroad where the firm's products can be assembled at lower cost. Likewise, materials managers need to know where to find cheaper raw materials and components. Finance managers must be able to anticipate changing interest and currency exchange rates and assess their future impact on the company. (In Part 3, we examine in depth how managers and employees in *each* function of a company support its business model.)

Successful organizational design begins when a company develops a functional structure to better help it with these various tasks. Companies that fail to develop a broad range of functional skills risk failure For example, a company might have a great R&D department that develops a blockbuster product. But, if the company fails to develop effective marketing and sales functions to promote that product, it is unlikely to succeed in the marketplace.

To successfully control the activities of her employees as her company grew, Heida Thurlow created a functional structure for Chantal Cookware, based in Houston, Texas. It is shown in Figure 8.3.

Thurlow, a German-born mechanical engineer, patented a device that keeps the handles of saucepans and other kinds of cookware cool to the touch. To take advantage of her invention, Thurlow grouped all employees who perform tasks related to assembling the cookware into the manufacturing function, and all employees who handle sales to Chantal's 2,000 retail customers into the sales function. Engineers responsible for designing Chantal's expanding range of cookware are grouped into the product development function, and employees responsible for obtaining the inputs (steel, plastic, and heat-proof paint) needed to make the products are grouped

Figure 8.2
Grouping Activities by Function

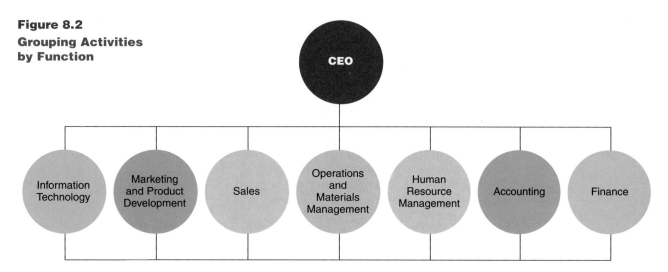

Figure 8.3
Chantal
Cookware's
Functional
Structure

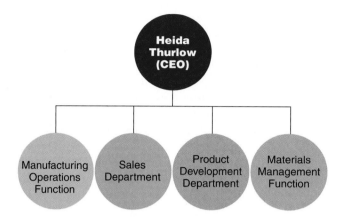

into the materials-management function. This structure suited the needs of Thurlow's growing company, especially as it battled against other upscale cookware makers like Le Creuset and Calphalon. Although Chantal started as a small company, it now earns more than $12 million in revenues annually.

Advantages of a Functional Structure

We just discussed how a functional structure helps a company pursue its business model successfully in a changing environment. Companies also group their activities by function to obtain the benefits from specialization and the division of labor discussed in earlier chapters. When each function specializes in one activity, its members become more skilled and productive. Functional structures also have several coordination and motivation advantages.

COORDINATION ADVANTAGES   Employees grouped together because they perform similar kinds of jobs can easily communicate and share information with each other. Because employees in the same function also approach problems from the same perspective, they can often make decisions quickly and effectively. A functional structure also makes it easier for people to learn from one another's experiences and improve their skills. This can result in an improvement in the company's overall performance.

MOTIVATIONAL ADVANTAGES   Grouping by function also improves a company's ability to motivate its employees. Because first-line managers are generally skilled in the function they supervise, they are in a good position to monitor and reward employees. Grouping by function also results in the development of function-specific values and norms that increase a department's performance. For example, it allows members to monitor another's performance, and it makes it possible for the company to use empowered teams. Finally, grouping by function creates a career ladder to motivate employees: Functional managers and supervisors are typically employees who have been promoted because of their superior skills.

Disadvantages of a Functional Structure

The founders of almost all companies begin by creating a functional structure to obtain the advantages just discussed. If a company's business model is successful it will grow, and as it does, its activities normally become more diverse and complex. At some point the functional structure that helped the company grow may no longer be sufficient. A functional structure can become a disadvantage under one or more of the following three circumstances:

1.   When the range of goods or services a company makes increases. Imagine the coordination problems that would arise, for example, if a company started to make cars, then decided to make computers as well, and then went on to add clothing to the mix. Could the *same* salesforce sell all three kinds of products? Most salespeople would not be able to learn enough about all three product lines to provide good customer service. Similarly, imagine the problems that would arise if one product development department tried to coordinate product development across all three product lines.

2. As companies attract customers with different needs. The needs of individual customers, for example, are often very different from the needs of large corporate customers. Each group requires its own customer service department that can provide advice tailored to its specific needs.

3. As companies expand nationally and globally. For example, servicing the needs of customers in different regions of a country, or different countries, by using a single set of manufacturing, sales, or purchasing functions becomes very difficult.

Divisional Structures: Product, Market, and Geographic

divisional structure
A structure that groups employees by function but allows them to focus their activities on a particular product line or type of customer.

To solve the aforementioned problems, companies often overlay their functional groupings with divisional groupings. A divisional structure allows a company's different functional groups to each focus on a particular product line or on a particular type of customer. When a company moves to any kind of divisional structure, its managers divide up into two groups: corporate managers and divisional managers. The job of divisional managers is to develop the most competitive business model for their particular divisions. The job of corporate managers is to supervise the performance of the company's divisional managers. Corporate managers are responsible for increasing the entire company's long-run profitability. Managers at both levels are responsible for monitoring changes in the competitive environment that can impact either the company's individual divisions or the corporation as a whole. We discussed earlier how former Sony CEO Nobuyuki Idei, together with his corporate and divisional managers, changed that company's business model to respond to the changing digital environment.

Companies can choose from three kinds of divisional structures: product, market, and geographic. Each is adopted to solve one of the three kinds of problems noted above.

Product Structure

product structure
A structure that groups functions into divisions that specialize in certain products.

When a company chooses to group functions so that it can make and sell a wider variety of products, it moves to a product structure. Managers and employees in each division can specialize in a particular kind of product. As a result, they are better able to manage their division's business model. Note that each product division has its *own* set of functions, such as accounting, marketing, and research and development.

The advantage of the product structure adopted by Gap Inc. was that managers of each store chain could develop a business model that was most effective for their particular chain.

**Figure 8.4
Product Structure**

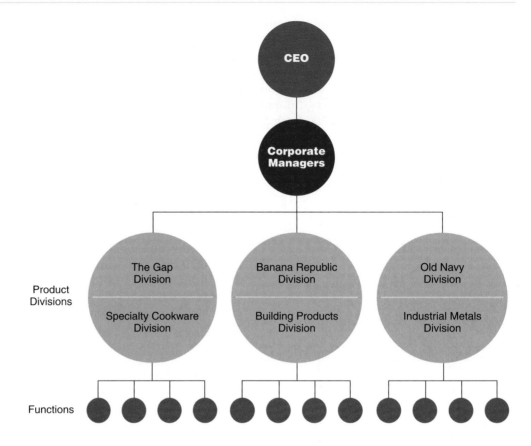

Figure 8.4 shows how a product structure can be used by (1) a company that chooses to expand the range of products it makes and sells within the *same* industry; and (2) by a company that decides to expand into new industries. Gap Inc. is an example of a company in the first category. Gap first operated The Gap store chain and then launched Banana Republic followed by Old Navy. These three chains are all in the retail clothing industry. The advantage of the product structure for Gap Inc. was that the managers of each chain were able to develop a business model most effective for their particular chain. This is similar to how each of Sony's divisions focused on a particular kind of electronic product.

Also shown in Figure 8.4 is a company that has established independent product divisions to make and sell a range of products in three different industries—specialty cookware, building products, and industrial metals. A company using a product structure might have any number of divisions. General Electric, for example, currently has over three hundred divisions producing products ranging from washing machines to light bulbs to electric turbines and television programs.

Market Structure

Sometimes the most pressing problem facing a company is that different types of customers buy its products, and these products must be customized to suit their individual needs. For example, a product's features, price, and even the level of after-sales service provided can vary a lot depending on the type of customer buying the product. To best service the needs of different types of customers, a company moves to a **market structure** and creates market divisions, each of which has a set of functions that specialize in the needs of a particular type of customer, as Business in Action illustrates.

market structure
A structure that groups functions into divisions, that serve different types of customers.

Business in Action

Dell's Market Structure

When Dell Computer began to grow rapidly during the 1990s, it quickly discovered that it could sell more PCs if it customized them to the needs of different types of customers. Home computer users, for example, typically have less of a need for high-powered PCs than business customers, who demand PCs loaded with business-specific software. By contrast, government and state agencies that buy large numbers of PCs usually require no-frills machines that can be bought at a discount price.

Dell's problem was how to make and sell a wide range of PCs and yet still keep its operating costs low. Operating costs often rise sharply when a company has to assemble many different models of a product, each of which is customized to the requirements of the buyer. Also, when a wide variety of products are made and sold, customer service becomes much more complex and expensive. Dell knew that providing high-quality customer service was absolutely vital. Its managers needed to find an organizational structure that would keep the company's operating costs low but still allow for excellent customer service. They decided that Dell should move from a functional structure to a market structure. Figure 8.5 shows the market structure that Dell created.

One way Dell saves money and passes the savings on to customers is by selling directly to them and avoiding the "middleman."

Dell created four market divisions as part of this structure. Each focused on the needs of a particular group of customers: corporate, small business, home computer users, and government and state agencies. The manager of each division and his or her employees focused on designing low-cost PCs to best met the needs of

Figure 8.5
Dell's Market Structure

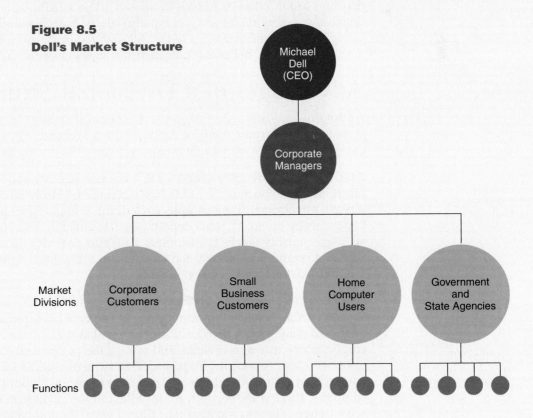

its customers. They also devised pricing strategies that would attract the greatest number of customers and yet allow Dell to maintain its high profit margins.

Dell's new market structure was successful. Its sales soared throughout the 1990s, and it has the best customer service rating of any PC maker in the industry as well as the lowest costs.[2]

Geographic Structure

geographic structure
A structure in which divisions are created to serve the needs of customers in a particular region, country, or world area.

Suppose a company expands rapidly both at home and abroad. This will make it difficult for the functional managers at the firm's home location to respond to problems that surface abroad. In this situation, a geographic structure, in which divisions are created to serve the needs of customers in a particular region, country, or world area, is often chosen. See Figure 8.6 for an example. Each of the divisions' functional managers, who are located in the geographical areas they serve, are in a better position to respond to the firm's customers in that area.

Consider Fed Ex: To provide guaranteed, next-day airmail package service, Fed Ex founder and CEO Fred Smith chose a *regional geographic structure* for his company. (See Figure 8.6a.) Large retail chains like Macy's, Neiman Marcus, and Brooks Brothers also use a geographic structure because the needs of their customers differ by region. For example, California customers need more swimsuits, whereas Midwestern customers need more down parkas. A geographic structure gives retail regional managers of these companies the flexibility to choose the range of products that best meets their customers' needs.

When managers adopt a *global geographic structure* (illustrated in Figure 8.6b), they locate different divisions in each of the world regions in which the company operates. Likewise, they adopt this structure to meet the needs of different customers. They also sometimes choose this structure when they need to find low-cost or high-quality suppliers abroad and facilitate the transfer of components and finished products between divisions around the world (see Chapter 4). The need to choose the right organizational structure to implement a company's global business model is a major challenge facing multinational managers today. All multinationals use some form of geographic divisional structure because it puts their managers closer to the scene of operations.

Advantages of a Divisional Structure

As the previous discussion suggests, divisional structures (product, market, or geographic) can overcome many of the problems associated with a functional structure as the size and complexity of a company increases. We discuss each of these next.

COORDINATION ADVANTAGES   Because each division contains its own set of functions, these functions are able to focus more precisely on a specific kind of good, service, or customer. For example, each division might have its own sales force, customer-service group, or R&D department. This narrow focus helps the company create higher-quality products customers want and provides them with better customer service. Communication between functions in a divisional structure is also easier and can improve the firm's decision making.

MOTIVATIONAL ADVANTAGES   As we have discussed, the move to a divisional structure results in the emergence of two types of top managers—corporate and divisional managers. A divisional structure makes it easier for a company's CEO and corporate executives to evaluate and reward the performance of the individual managers who lead its various divisions. This strengthens the linkage between performance and rewards. In addition, because there are two types of managers within the company, there is more room for middle and top managers to advance within the organization. These are major motivational issues for companies. Talented employees and managers who feel they are pigeon-holed will be quick to leave the company.

Figure 8.6
Geographic
Structure

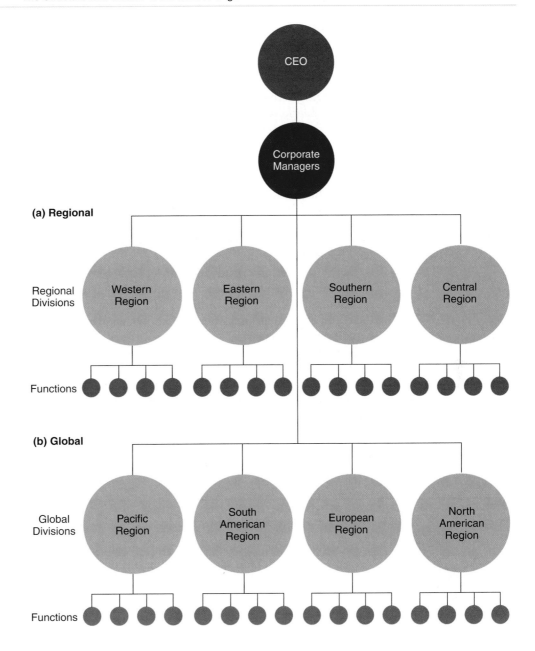

Furthermore, divisional managers enjoy a large measure of autonomy because they, not corporate managers, are responsible for divisional operations. This autonomy gives them a strong incentive to perform at a high level and encourage their employees to do so, too. Also, because divisional managers are close to their functional managers and employees, they are in a good position to monitor their performance. Finally, employees' close identification with their divisions can promote positive work attitudes and increase their commitment and loyalty to the company.

Disadvantages of a Divisional Structure

Although divisional structures offer large, complex companies a number of coordination and motivational advantages over functional structures, they have certain disadvantages as well. First, because each division has its own set of functions and managers, operating costs are much higher. Second, having more managers can result in communications problems, slower decision making, and lower performance. Third, divisions may begin competing with one another and pursue their own agendas, like they did at Sony.

Matrix Structures

matrix structure

A structure that groups people and resources in two ways *simultaneously*: by function and by product.

When forces in the global environment are changing rapidly, even a divisional structure may not give managers enough flexibility. For example, when customers' needs are changing rapidly or new technologies are emerging, managers often choose the most flexible kind of structure a company can adopt: a matrix structure. A matrix structure is chosen most commonly by high-tech companies that need to design, make, and sell new products continuously. In a matrix structure, managers group people and resources in two ways *simultaneously*: by function and by product. Employees are grouped into *functions* to allow them to learn from one another and become more skilled and productive. In addition, employees are grouped into *cross-functional product teams* in which members of different functions work together to develop a specific product. The result is a complex network of reporting relationships among product teams and functions that make a matrix structure, which is illustrated in Figure 8.7, very flexible.

Each member of a product team reports to two bosses: (1) a functional boss, who assigns employees to a team and evaluates their performance from a functional perspective, and (2) the boss of the product team, who evaluates their performance on the team. Thus, team members are known as *two-boss employees* because they report to two different managers.

Functional employees assigned to product teams change or rotate over time as the specific skills that a team needs change. At the beginning of the product development process, for example, engineers and R&D specialists lead product teams because their job is to develop new products. When a provisional design has been established, marketing experts are assigned to the team to discover how well the new product will meet customers' needs. Engineers might then rejoin the team to make any necessary modifications. Then, manufacturing employees join when it is time to find the most efficient way to produce the product. So, as their specific tasks are completed, team

Video Small Business in Action

One Smooth Stone

As shown in the original video on your Student DVD, "One Smooth Stone" specializes in developing and producing business theater for a wide array of corporate clients around the world. Its clients include companies such as Motorola and Nortel.

Employees at One Smooth Stone need expertise in both business- and corporate-event planning. One Smooth Stone only recruits highly trained, highly skilled, and self-reliant individuals who can work autonomously and as members of project teams. Given the customer-driven culture of One Smooth Stone, the teams must be empowered. When necessary, Stone will outsource work to companies with expertise it does not have. However, these vendors must embody the same core values as Stone.

The company has a flat, decentralized structure. Its values revolve around building a good relationship with its clients and employees and helping others. One Smooth Stone's entrepreneurial structure is exemplified in its strategic planning processes as well. For example, Stone's managers attempted to use a traditional approach to strategic planning but found that once they had articulated a strategy, it was obsolete. Stone now formulates its strategy via *strategic improvisation:* It provides a template to its project teams and then lets them generate strategic ideas for the company. The three values of success for One Smooth Stone are: (1) smart, (2) fast, and (3) kind.

Questions
1. Why would a functional structure be ineffective at One Smooth Stone?
2. Does a matrix structure adequately describe the organizational characteristics of One Smooth Stone?
3. A company's culture is a product of its values and norms. Describe the culture and its characteristics at One Smooth Stone.

**Figure 8.7
Matrix Structure**

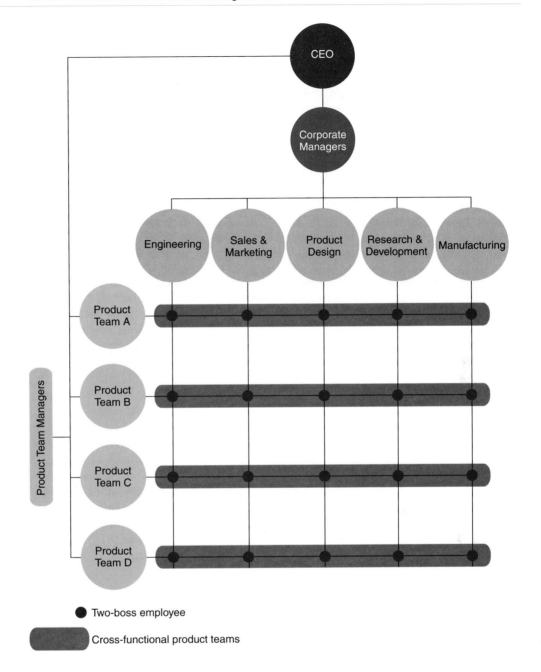

CEO

Corporate
Managers

Engineering   Sales & Marketing   Product Design   Research & Development   Manufacturing

Product Team Managers

Product Team A

Product Team B

Product Team C

Product Team D

● Two-boss employee

Cross-functional product teams

members leave and are reassigned to new teams. In this way, the matrix structure makes the most use of the company's human resources.

To keep the matrix structure flexible, product teams are empowered and team members make many of the important decisions about the product. The product team manager acts as a facilitator, trying to keep the project on time and within budget. The functional managers try to ensure that the product is the best that it can be in order to maximize its appeal to customers.

COORDINATION ADVANTAGES   Typically, a company uses a matrix structure for three reasons: (1) The company can develop new products more rapidly; (2) it can maximize communication and cooperation between team members; and (3) innovation and creativity are the key to the company's competitive advantage. Product teams permit face-to-face problem solving and communication and allow managers with different functional expertise to cooperate to develop competitive products.

MOTIVATIONAL ADVANTAGES   To understand how a matrix structure affects motivation, it is important to understand that the members of the product teams are generally highly qualified and skilled employees who are experts in their chosen fields. The matrix structure provides a work setting that gives these employees the freedom and autonomy to take responsibility for their work activities. Matrix structures make job assignments more interesting and challenging and encourage work behaviors that promote quality and innovation.

DISADVANTAGES OF A MATRIX STRUCTURE   As you might expect, matrix structures have some disadvantages, too. The dual reporting relationships that comprise a matrix structure have always been difficult for managers and employees to deal with. Often, the functional boss and the product boss make conflicting demands on team members who do not know which boss to satisfy first. In addition, functional and product team bosses sometimes come into conflict over precisely who is in charge of which team members and for how long. The jobs in a matrix are also very demanding, and because employees move from one team to another, they often feel the lack of a stable "home base." Both these factors can lead to feelings of stress and anxiety.

Because matrix structures are so difficult to manage many companies, such as Sony, choose to retain a product division structure but "network" their different product divisions by using cross-functional teams. This is discussed below when we examine the second main issue in organizational design: how best to coordinate functions and divisions.

Coordinating Functions and Divisions

The more complex the structure a company uses to group its activities, the greater are the problems of *linking and coordinating* its different functions and divisions. Coordination becomes a problem because each function or division develops a different orientation toward the other groups, which affects the way they interact with them. Each function or division comes to view the problems facing the company from their own particular perspective.

As we mentioned in Chapter 7, a company's manufacturing function typically has a very short-term view: It wants to keep costs under control and get the product out the factory door on time. By contrast, the research and development function has a long-term viewpoint because product development is a relatively slow process. R&D is often much less concerned about keeping costs low. These different viewpoints clearly make it harder for functions to cooperate and coordinate their activities. In a product structure, employees sometimes focus more on their division's products than the profitability of the whole company. (This is what the employees at Sony did.) They may refuse, or simply not see, the need to cooperate or share information and knowledge with the firm's other divisions. Essentially, each division can become so focused on its own customers it loses sight of the fact that its expertise, skills, and knowledge could benefit other divisions. In a geographic structure, the goal of customizing products to suit the needs of regional customers can conflict with the need to reduce global operating costs.

The problem of linking and coordinating the activities of different functions and divisions becomes more and more acute as the number of functions and divisions increases. For this reason, as companies grow and their business models become more complex, they must increase their coordination efforts. Three methods of promoting

Did You Know?

IBM and Endicott-Johnson—two widely-known firms located in Endicott, New York in the 1930s—had dramatically different cultures. Thomas Watson crafted a highly disciplined and standardized IBM sales force of dark suits and white shirts, whose motto was inscribed on signs reading "THINK." George Johnson, president of one of the nation's largest shoe manufacturers, believed in industrial democracy and eschewed hierarchy. Employees at Endicott-Johnson would taunt the IBM employees on their way to the pub after work, "While you're thinkin' we're drinkin'."[3]

coordination include (1) allocating authority; (2) specifying work rules; and (3) using formal integrating mechanisms to link functions and divisions.

Allocating Authority

To effectively coordinate the activities of their functions and divisions, managers must make a number of decisions about how and where to allocate authority in the organization. First, managers must develop a clear hierarchy of authority so managers at all levels, and in all parts of the company, know exactly whom they report to and what their responsibilities are. The *hierarchy of authority* is a company's chain of command—the relative authority that each manager has—from the CEO down through the company's middle managers and first-line managers.

The fewer managers a company has, the more employees each of them has to supervise. So, as a company grows, it is generally better able to coordinate its activities if its hierarchy of authority grows, or lengthens, as well. In addition, with two levels of top managers, like a divisional structure has, it also becomes easier to coordinate a company's activities.

As you read in this chapter, former Sony CEO Akio Morita implemented a product structure which eventually resulted in Sony lagging behind its competitors because its divisions refused to cooperate with one another.

TALL AND FLAT HIERARCHIES The number of levels in a hierarchy varies from organization to organization. In general, the larger the organization and the more divisions it has, the taller is its hierarchy. *Tall* organizations have many levels in the hierarchy relative to their size; *flat* organizations have few. See Figure 8.8 for an example. GM, for example, has about 10 levels in its hierarchy whereas Toyota only has 5. This helps to explain the huge difference in the profitability of the two companies for reasons discussed next.

To be sure, as a company grows, it needs more levels to function. However, when a company's hierarchy becomes *too* tall, coordination between the levels can become very difficult. Four types of problems arise in this case. Each is outlined in Figure 8.9. Hence, controlling the length of the hierarchy as an organization grows (or contracts) is a crucial managerial task.

**Figure 8.8
Tall and Flat
Structures**

Tall Structure
(10 levels)

Flat Structure
(5 levels)

Figure 8.9

**Problems in
Companies with
Too Many Levels
in the Hierarchy**

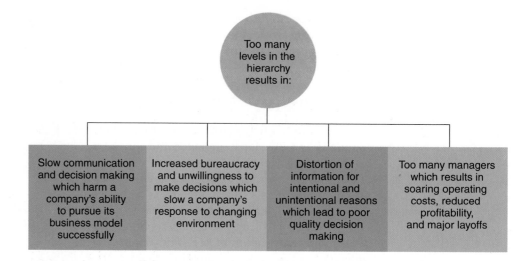

But why is this so? First, it can take an excessive amount of time for the decisions and orders of top managers to reach managers further down the hierarchy. Similarly, it can take too long for top managers to learn about problems occurring at lower levels. Feeling out of touch, top managers may want to verify that middle managers are following orders or require written confirmation of them. Middle managers, who know they will be held strictly accountable for their actions, start to spend their time writing reports to justify their decisions rather than trying to solve new problems. Over time, this can make a company highly bureaucratic as the amount of "red tape" increases. Middle managers might even try to avoid responsibility by making top managers make all of the company's day-to-day decisions. In other words, the firm's managers start to "pass the buck." This makes it much more difficult to change a company's business model quickly to take advantage of new opportunities or improve its efficiency as needed.

A second problem that arises when a company's hierarchy gets too tall is that information transmitted up and down the hierarchy starts to get distorted. This causes managers at different levels to interpret what is happening differently, and it creates a lot of communication problems. Finally, a hierarchy with too many levels indicates that a company is employing too many managers—and managers are very expensive. Large companies such as IBM and General Motors pay their managers billions of dollars a year; a tall hierarchy can therefore take a serious toll on a company's profitability. If the problem gets bad enough, they can be forced to lay off thousands of employees. Kodak is a case in point. In the last decade alone the company has had to lay off more than 60,000 employees.

THE MINIMUM CHAIN OF COMMAND   To prevent its hierarchy from becoming too tall, more companies are adhering to the principle of the minimum chain of command—the principle that a company should operate with the fewest managerial levels possible. This principle is being increasingly followed by companies in the United States and elsewhere as they try to reduce their costs to battle more effectively against their global competitors. Managers are scrutinizing their hierarchies to see how they can be made flatter, for example, by eliminating levels and giving the responsibilities associated with those levels to managers above and below.

CENTRALIZATION AND DECENTRALIZATION OF AUTHORITY   Another way managers can keep the levels in a company's hierarchy to a minimum is to *decentralize* authority to lower-level managers and empower employees. When managers and employees at lower levels are given the responsibility to make important decisions, the problems of slow and distorted communication are avoided. Moreover, fewer managers are needed because their role is not to make decisions but to act as coaches and facilitators so employees can.

**minimum chain-of-
command principle**
The principle that a company's structure should be designed with as few managerial levels as possible.

One manager who is constantly trying to empower employees is Colleen Barrett, the president of Southwest Airlines and the highest-ranking woman in the airline industry. At Southwest, Barrett is well known for continually reaffirming Southwest's message that employees should always behave proactively to provide better customer service. Her central message is that Southwest values its employees. Southwest employees are encouraged not to look to their superiors for guidance but rather to find ways to do their jobs better themselves. As a result, Southwest keeps the number of its top and middle managers to a minimum.

Decentralizing authority allows a company and its employees to behave in a flexible way even when it grows and its hierarchy lengthens. This is why managers are so interested in creating empowered teams and establishing cross-functional teams. These design innovations help keep a company flexible and responsive to the changing global environment.

Colleen Barrett, president of Southwest Airlines, is well known for continually reaffirming Southwest's message that employees should behave proactively to provide better customer service. What are the advantages and disadvantages of decentralizing authority?

Work Rules and Standard Operating Procedures

management by exception The use of rules and standard operating procedures to coordinate operations whereby managers only intervene to take corrective action.

Most companies also develop detailed systems of work rules and standard operating procedures (SOPs) to increase the coordination between their functions and divisions. Rules and SOPs guide employee behavior. They specify what employees should do when they confront a problem that needs a solution. When employees follow the rules that managers develop, their behaviors become *standardized*—they perform a specific action or task in the same way time and time again—and so their work is predictable.

With rules and SOPs in place, managers can manage by exception, that is, they intervene and take corrective action only when necessary. The rest of the time employees are coordinating their own activities. Because rules and SOPs also reduce the need for direct managerial supervision, they reduce operating costs. One dot.com company that successfully used rules and SOPs to keep its customers satisfied is discussed in Business in Action.

Business in Action

Never Underestimate the Power of Rules

The high-tech, dot.com image is not usually associated with the military image. However, managers of the thousands of dot.coms that went belly-up in the early 2000s might have benefited from some military-style discipline. Indeed, a few dot.coms that survived the shakeout did so because their managers used military-style procedures to coordinate their functions and ensure high performance. One of these companies is siteROCK based in Emeryville, California, whose COO, Dave Lilly, is an ex-nuclear submarine commander.

siteROCK's business is to host and manage other companies' Web sites to keep them up and running and error free. A customer's site that goes down or runs haywire

Most dot.coms fell apart in the early 2000s. Companies like siteROCK were able to stay afloat because their managers used procedures and rules to coordinate their functions and ensure high performance.

is enemy no. 1 at siteROCK. To increase coordination and improve the ability of siteRock's employees to respond to unexpected online events, Lilly decided the company needed a comprehensive set of rules and SOPs to cover all known major problems. Lilly insisted that every functional problem-solving procedure be written down. Then, he insisted that each function ensure their procedures were compatible with those of the other functions. siteROCK developed over 30 thick binders that list all the processes and checklists employees from all functions should follow when an unexpected event happens. Their job is to try to solve the problem quickly using these procedures.

The goal is 100 percent reliability. Detailed blueprints guide cross-functional planning and decision making—not seat-of-the-pants problem solving that might be brilliant 80 percent of the time but result in disaster the rest of time. At the end of a shift, employees spend 90 minutes doing paperwork logging what they have done. They write down any improved rules they have come up with so their co-workers can benefit from them, too.[4]

Integrating Mechanisms

A firm's hierarchy of authority and rules and SOPs are vital to its coordination. When a company like Sony has to change its business model quickly to respond to changes in the environment, however, they are often not enough. At this point, managers need to turn to another potent method of coordination: integrating mechanisms.

integrating mechanisms
Organizing tools that managers use to increase communication and coordination among a company's functions and divisions.

Integrating mechanisms are organizing tools managers use to increase communication and coordination among functions and divisions. The greater the need for coordination, the more complex tend to be the integrating mechanisms used by a company. UPS and FedEx, for example, both have geographic structures. To make this structure work efficiently, both companies have decentralized authority to their employees and drafted careful, timesaving rules and procedures. However, UPS and FedEx also employ integrating mechanisms such as empowered teams, customer-liaison personnel, and computer-controlled tracking equipment to allow their employees to manage transactions quickly and efficiently.

Four integrating mechanisms available to managers to increase communication and coordination are discussed below. These mechanisms—arranged from simplest to most complex—are listed in Figure 8.10 together with examples of the individuals and groups that might use them. In the remainder of this section we examine each one, moving from least to most complex.

DIRECT CONTACT   Encouraging more *direct contact* among different managers, functions, and divisions to solve a problem might seems like an easy thing to do. Often, however, it is not. We mentioned earlier that managers from different functions commonly have different views about what must be done to achieve a company's goals. But if the managers have *equal authority* (as functional managers typically do), the only manager who can tell them what to do is the CEO. If functional and divisional managers cannot reach agreement, no mechanism exists to resolve the conflict apart from the authority of the boss.

Resolving everyday conflicts, however, can chew up a top-manager's time and slow down the person's decision making. In fact, an increasing number of problems sent up

Figure 8.10
Four Kinds
of Integrating
Mechanisms

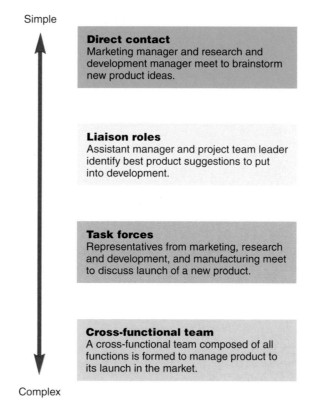

Simple

Direct contact
Marketing manager and research and development manager meet to brainstorm new product ideas.

Liaison roles
Assistant manager and project team leader identify best product suggestions to put into development.

Task forces
Representatives from marketing, research and development, and manufacturing meet to discuss launch of a new product.

Cross-functional team
A cross-functional team composed of all functions is formed to manage product to its launch in the market.

Complex

the hierarchy for managers to solve is a sign of a poorly performing organizational structure. To increase coordination among functions and divisions and to prevent these problems from emerging, top managers employ more complex integrating mechanisms.

LIAISON ROLES   Managers can increase the coordination among functions and divisions by establishing *liaison roles.* When the volume of contacts between two functions increases, one way to improve coordination is to give one manager in each function or division the responsibility for coordinating with the other. These managers may meet daily, weekly, monthly, or as needed. Liaison roles provide a way of improving communication across a company—something that is particularly important in a multinational company whose employees might meet no one outside of their immediate functions or divisions.

TASK FORCES   When more than two functions or divisions share many common problems, direct contact and liaison roles might not provide enough coordination. In these cases, a more complex integrating mechanism, a *task force,* may be more appropriate. One manager from each relevant function or division is assigned to a task force that meets to solve a specific, mutual problem. Task force members are responsible for communicating to their departments the issues addressed and the solutions recommended. When the problem or issue is solved, the task force is no longer needed, and members return to their normal roles in their departments or are assigned to other task forces.

CROSS-FUNCTIONAL TEAMS   In many cases, the issues addressed by a task force are recurring problems like the need to develop new products or find new kinds of customers. To address recurring problems effectively, managers are increasingly using permanent integrating mechanisms such as cross-functional teams (discussed in Chapter 7). An example of a cross-functional team might be a new product development committee responsible for the choice, design, manufacturing, and marketing of a new product. Such a project obviously requires a great deal of integration among functions if the new product is to be successfully introduced. The use of a complex integrating mechanism such as a cross-functional team can accomplish this. Intel, the

Figure 8.11
Sony's Cross-Functional Product Teams

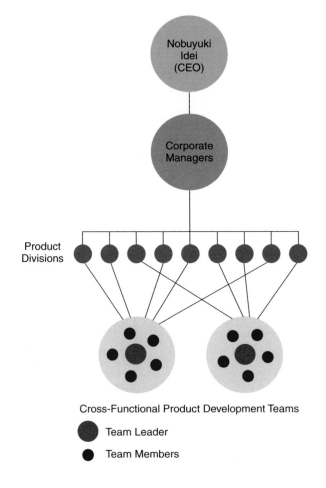

Cross-Functional Product Development Teams

● Team Leader

● Team Members

computer chipmaker emphasizes cross-functional teamwork, for example. Its structure consists of scores of cross-functional groups that meet regularly to determine which new kinds of chips Intel should focus its resources on.

The more complex a company, the more important cross-functional teams become. In fact, Sony's top managers used all four of these integrating mechanisms—but particularly, cross-functional teams—to design its new networked structure, shown in Figure 8.11.

Sony retained its product division structure. Then to speed up innovation, it created a whole series of liaison roles, task forces, and cross-functional teams comprised of many of its most experienced engineers and managers from the different product divisions. Their task was to speed up the flow of information and knowledge between Sony's many product divisions so the company could develop new products faster. Members of the cross-functional teams are held accountable for ensuring that divisions *do* cooperate and share their knowledge with one another. And, of course, Sony installed a companywide IT system to better coordinate its activities. We discuss the important subject of how to use information technology to integrate functions and divisions in Chapter 9.

Organizational Culture

Earlier, we defined *organizational culture* as the shared company values and norms that influence how people and groups behave and interact with one another. Just as a company's structure influences the behavior of its employees and groups, so do the values and norms embodied in its culture.

Values and Norms

company values
The shared standards a company's members use to evaluate whether or not they have helped the company achieve its goals.

company norms
Beliefs, attitudes, and behaviors that specify how a company's members should behave.

A company's culture is the result of its guiding values and norms. Company values are the shared standards an organization's members use to evaluate whether or not they have helped the company achieve its goals. The values a company might adopt include any or all of the following standards: excellence, stability, predictability, profitability, economy, creativeness, morality, and usefulness. Company norms specify or prescribe the kinds of shared beliefs, attitudes, and behaviors that a firm's members should hold and follow. Norms are informal but powerful rules about how employees should conduct themselves if they want to be accepted and successful. Norms can be equally as constraining as the formal written rules in a company's handbook, such as siteROCK's rules.

Companies might encourage workers to adopt norms such as working hard, respecting traditions and authority, and being courteous to others. Being conservative, cautious, and a "team player"; being creative, courageous and taking risks; being honest, frugal and maintaining high personal standards are other norms. Norms may also prescribe very specific rules to be followed, such as keeping one's desk tidy, cleaning up at the end of the day, taking one's turn to bring doughnuts to the office, and even wearing blue jeans and a T-shirt on a Friday.

Ideally, norms help the company shape its values. For example, a new computer company that has a culture based on values of excellence and innovation might encourage its workers to adopt norms about being creative, taking risks, and working hard persistently to obtain certain long-term rewards. Adopting these values and norms leads to an *entrepreneurial* culture. On the other hand, a bank or insurance company that values stability and predictability is more likely to emphasize norms of cautiousness and obedience to authority. Adopting these values and norms leads to a *conservative* culture.

Over time, members of a company learn how to interpret various work events and respond to them in ways that reflect the company's shared values and norms. Often these employees behave in accordance with the company's values and norms without even realizing they are doing so.

Sources of a Company's Culture

Where does a company's culture come from? What determines its values and norms? How do employees learn these values and norms and develop behaviors and attitudes that reinforce the company's culture? Four important sources of organizational culture are the values of a company's founder, organizational socialization, ceremonies and rights, and stories and language. These various sources are shown in Figure 8.12.

Figure 8.12
Sources of a Company's Culture

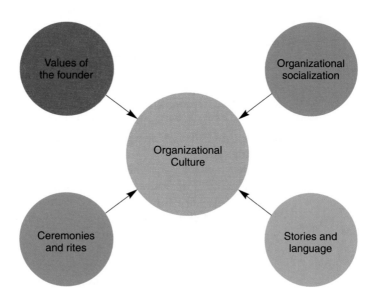

VALUES OF THE FOUNDER   One person who has a very important impact on the culture that emerges in a company is its founder. A founder, and his or her personal values and beliefs, greatly influence the values and norms that develop over time within a company. Founders tend to recruit managers who share their values and who, in turn, recruit employees who share theirs. Gradually the founder's values and norms permeate the entire company. For example, if a founder addresses his or her managers formally and insists upon formal modes of dress, this person's managers will expect the same from their subordinates.

Bill Gates, the founder of Microsoft, has created a corporate culture that reflects his personal values. Microsoft employees are expected to be creative, work long hours, and to "think outside of the box" (as Gates does). They are also encouraged to be themselves, dress informally, and personalize their offices. Gates also holds a host of company events such as cookouts, picnics, and sporting events to encourage cohesiveness, teamwork, and competition.

ORGANIZATIONAL SOCIALIZATION   As we discussed, employees quickly figure out and adopt the values and norms desired by their companies—often without realizing they are doing so. This is called organizational socialization. Most organizations have some kind of socialization program to help new employees "learn the ropes"—the values, norms, and culture of the organization. The military, for example, is well known for the rigorous socialization process it uses to turn raw recruits into trained soldiers. Similarly, through the design of its socialization program, the founder and top managers of a company transmit to employees the specific cultural values and norms they want employees to endorse.

Eventually employees behave in accordance with these norms and values not just because they *think* they have too, but because they *believe* they are the right way to behave. In other words, values and norms shape people's beliefs, behaviors, and attitudes. The way in which Michael Dell instilled his values in his company is instructive in this respect. Dell created a culture to mesh with the structure he designed for his company, as Business in Action illustrates.

organizational socialization

The process by which newcomers learn and absorb a company's values and norms and acquire the work behaviors and attitudes necessary to perform their jobs effectively.

Business in Action

How Michael Dell Created a Frugal Company Culture

Under the influence of its founder, Dell Computer developed a frugal organizational culture—one driven by Michael Dell's own values. These values reflect the origin of his company, which began when Dell and seven employees worked together around an old table to assemble the PCs they sold over the phone to customers. From the beginning, the only way the company could compete with giant competitors like IBM and Compaq was because Michael Dell was so focused on cutting costs. He sold PCs over the phone because he couldn't afford expensive advertising. Being frugal does not mean being cheap, however. Dell insisted from the beginning that his phone salespeople provide PC buyers with excellent customer service to ensure that the good word about his company's products spread.

How does Dell socialize new employees to be frugal? By sending them to Dell "boot camp," of course. New employees go to a Dell training center outside Austin, Texas, for four weeks. There they learn how to install the software needed to operate Dell computers, much of which is based on Microsoft's Windows platform. At the end of the boot camp they break into groups and are given a real business problem facing Dell to solve. They must arrive at a solution to the problem and then present their findings to a panel of instructors. During this training process new employees also learn the basic values and norms that guide Dell employees. They are also taught how to provide excellent customer service.

In order to acclimate new employees to Dell's frugal culture, Dell requires they attend a training camp in Austin, Texas, for four weeks and then "shadow" an experienced Dell employee for a week.

After boot camp, new hires engage in a week of "shadowing." They observe an experienced Dell employee performing the tasks they will need to do and are able to ask the employee questions, and quickly learn their jobs. This, of course, further inculcates new employees with Dell's frugal, cost-cutting values. And because Dell's employees are all trained in the same, focused way, they share these same values.

Dell's rapid growth has made the need to carefully socialize its employees increasingly important. Almost half of Dell's employees in 2005 were recruited during the previous three years. Apparently, this socialization has paid off. Despite its humble beginnings, Dell is now the world's largest and most profitable PC maker.[5]

CEREMONIES AND RITES Another way in which managers can create and shape organizational culture is by developing ceremonies and rites–formal events that recognize employees or groups who have acted in ways that benefit the company. The most common rites that organizations use to transmit cultural norms and values to their members are rites of passage, of integration, and of enhancement.

Rites of passage determine how individuals enter, advance within, or leave the organization. The socialization programs described above are rites of passage. Likewise, the way in which an organization prepares people for promotion or retirement are rites of passage.

Rites of integration, like office parties, company cookouts, and meetings held to announce the company's achievements, build and reinforce a common bond among a company's members. Southwest Airlines is well known for its efforts to develop ceremonies and rituals to bond employees to the organization by showing them they are valued members. Southwest holds cookouts in the parking lot of its Dallas headquarters, and its top executives often attend employee Christmas parties throughout the country.

Rites of enhancement, such as a company awards banquet, let organizations publicly recognize and reward employees' contributions. This strengthens their commitment to the organization.

Rites of enhancement, such as awards dinners, newspaper releases, and employee promotions, let organizations publicly recognize and reward employees' contributions. This serves to strengthen their commitment to the organization. By bonding members within the organization, rites of enhancement help promote group cohesiveness and employee commitment.

STORIES AND LANGUAGE Stories and language also communicate organizational culture. Stories about the managers and employees who helped the company in crucial ways provide important clues about its values and norms. They reveal the kinds of behaviors it values the most and the kinds of practices it frowns upon.

The strong customer-oriented values Sam Walton established for Wal-Mart are evident in the stories its employees tell. These employees tell stories about their co-worker Sheila, who risked her own safety when she jumped in front of a car to prevent a customer from being struck; about Phyllis, who administered CPR to a customer who had suffered a heart attack in her store; and about Annette, who gave up the Power Ranger she had on layaway for her own son so a customer's son could have his birthday wish.

Nokia, the Finnish company that is the world's largest wireless phone maker, attributes its success to its cultural values and norms. Nokia believes its values reflect those embedded in Finland's national culture: Finns are down-to-earth, rational, and straightforward people. They are also friendly and democratic and do not believe in a rigid hierarchy based either on a person's authority or social class. Innovation and decision making are pushed right down to teams of employees who take up the challenge of developing the smaller, more sophisticated phones for which the company is known. Although Nokia's culture, called the "Nokia Way" can't be written down, it is present in the values that cement its members together and in the language its employees use and the stories they tell about the company.

But the concept of organizational language encompasses not only spoken language but also how people dress, the offices they occupy, the cars they drive, and the degree to which they use formal or informal language to greet one another. Casual dress is associated with entrepreneurial cultures like those of Google and Microsoft. Formal business attire supports the conservative cultures of law firms and investment-banking companies such as Citibank and Goldman Sachs. The cultures of these companies emphasize conformity, respect for authority, and working within the bounds of one's job.

Characteristics of a Strong Culture

Researchers have identified several characteristics of *strong company cultures*, organizational cultures whose values and norms lead to highly motivated and committed employees who are prepared to work hard and help a company succeed. Companies with strong cultures have cohesive sets of values and norms that work together to motivate employees. Companies with strong cultures also develop *professional cultures*, meaning that they communicate to employees their desire to invest in them. These companies adopt employment practices that demonstrate their commitment to their employees, and they encourage members to reciprocate by doing a good job for the firm. Microsoft, Intel, and UTC, for example, emphasize the importance of maintaining long-term relationships with their employees. These companies try to avoid layoffs and develop employee career paths. They also invest heavily in employee training and development.

Furthermore, in companies with strong cultures rewards are directly linked to an employee's performance and to the performance of the company as a whole. Sometimes, employee stock ownership plans (ESOPs) are developed to allow employees to buy shares of their company at a discount. Southwest Airlines employees, for example, own over 20 percent of their company's stock. Dell also allows its employees to buy its stock at a discounted price. Employees who are also owners of a company have an additional incentive to help it perform well. Finally, companies with strong cultures encourage their employees to act like entrepreneurs. They design their structures and culture in such a way that employees know they have the freedom and autonomy to be proactive. Frequently this is done by decentralizing authority and empowering employees and teams to build a better business model.

Did You Know?

Nature may provide some wisdom for organizing companies. Long before businesses practiced job enlargement and cross-training, honey bees practiced it. Bees have two general roles within the hive but they minimize the time and energy spent moving about the hive looking for work by performing several subtasks within each area rather than specializing in one. So there's always a job within close reach.[6]

Summary of the Chapter

Organizational structure and culture shape the attitudes, behaviors, and performance of employees and groups in a company. A well-designed organizational structure can help facilitate a culture that makes managing employees and teams easier and gives the company a competitive advantage. This chapter has made the following major points:

1. The challenge facing managers of all companies is to design an organizational structure and culture that (1) *motivates* employees to work hard and to develop supportive work behaviors and attitudes and (2) *coordinates* the actions of employees and groups to ensure they work together so that (3) a company can pursue its business model successfully.

2. Organizational design is the process of creating an organizational structure and culture so that a company can pursue it business model profitably.

3. Organizational structure is the framework of task-and-authority relationships in a company that coordinates and motivates employees to work together toward a common goal.

4. Organizational culture is the set of shared company values and norms that shape the way employees interact with one another.

5. The two main decisions involved in designing organizational structure are (1) how to group a company's employees and resources into functions and divisions and (2) how to link and coordinate these functions and divisions. How well managers make these decisions determines how efficiently and effectively a company operates.

6. Most companies first choose to divide up their activities by function. This involves creating a functional structure that groups people together by virtue of their expertise or tasks, (generally by department).

7. A functional structure can become a disadvantage (a) when a company starts to produce a wide range of different kinds of products, (b) when it begins to serve many types of customers, each of which has a different set of needs, (c) when its operations expand geographically by region or by country.

8. To solve these problems, companies sometimes overlay their functional groups with divisional groups. Companies can choose from three kinds of divisional structures: product, market, and geographic.

9. When the competitive environment is changing rapidly, managers often choose a matrix structure. A matrix structure groups employees by function and by product and is very flexible.

10. Generally, the more complex a structure a company has relative to its size, the more problems it will experience coordinating its different functions and divisions. Many firms have therefore moved to flatter organizational structures.

11. Three methods of achieving coordination include (1) allocating and decentralizing authority by empowering employees and creating self-managed teams (2) specifying work rules and SOPs and (3) linking functions and divisions via direct contact, liaison roles, task forces, and cross-functional teams.

12. A company's culture is a product of its specific values and norms.

13. Four important sources of organizational culture are the values of the founder of a company, the process of socialization, ceremonies and rights, and stories and values.

14. Strong company cultures are those with values and norms that motivate employees to work hard and help a company succeed. These cultures link rewards directly to the employee's performance and to the performance of the company and emphasize entrepreneurship at all levels.

Developing Business Skills

QUESTIONS FOR DISCUSSION AND ACTION

1. Why is it important for managers to analyze the changing forces in the global environment when designing an organization's structure and culture?

2. What are the main functions of (1) organizational structure and (2) organizational culture.

3. When would a company move from a functional to a product structure? In what ways will its structure change as it makes this shift?

4. What kind of organizational structure would you expect to find in (a) a fast-food restaurant; (b) a company like General Electric or General Motors; (c) a biotechnology company?

5. What are the main issues when it comes to deciding how to allocate authority in a company? How would a company in which all authority is kept at the top function compared to a company that decentralizes authority and uses empowered self-managed teams?

6. *Action.* Interview the manager of a company to identify the kind of structure it uses. Why is the company using that structure?

7. What is the difference between a company value and a company norm? How would you try to create a culture that is best for (a) a hospital and (b) a car dealership?

8. How does the founder affect the development of a company's culture over time?

9. *Action.* Find the founder or manager of a company in your city. Interview the person to discover the kinds of company values and norms that guide the behavior of the company's employees. Where do these values and norms come from? How does the company socialize new employees? (Hint: During the interview, ask for examples of corporate ceremonies, rites, and stories.)

ETHICS IN ACTION

How to Lay Off Employees?

You are the top manager(s) charged with reducing high operating costs. You have been instructed by the CEO to eliminate 25 percent of the company's workforce, including both managers and employees. You must manage the layoff process and then reallocate authority within the company to increase its efficiency.

Some managers might decide to retain the employees easiest to work with and whom they like rather than the ones who are difficult or the best performers. Other managers might decide to lay off the most highly paid employees or redesign the firm's hierarchy to retain as much power and authority as they can themselves. Using the ethical principles in Chapter 5, think about the issues involved in the layoffs and the redesign of the organization as you answer the following questions:

- What ethical rules should managers follow when deciding which employees to terminate?
- What ethical rules can help managers best allocate authority and redesign their hierarchies?
- How can the use of ethical principles help managers make the layoff process less painful for employees?
- Do you think the way the layoff is carried out will have an effect on the employees who remain?

SMALL GROUP EXERCISE

Speeding Up a Company's Web Site Design

After reading the following scenario, break up into groups of three or four people and discuss the issues involved. Be prepared to share your thinking with the rest of the class.

You have been called in as consultants by the top functional managers of a Web site design, production, and hosting company whose new animated designs are attracting a lot of attention and a lot of customers. Currently, employees are organized into different functions like hardware, software design, graphic art, and hosting (as well as functions like marketing and human resources). Each function takes its turn working on a new project beginning with the customer's initial request to the final hosting of the Web site online.

The problem this company is experiencing is that it typically takes one year to get a site up and running. The company wants to cut this time in half to protect and expand its market share. The firm's managers believe its current functional structure is the source of the problem. They want you to suggest a better one.

1. Discuss ways to speed up the firm's current functional structure.

2. Discuss the pros and cons of moving to a matrix structure. Then, discuss the pros and cons of using cross-functional teams to coordinate between functions.

3. Which of these structures do you think is most appropriate and why?

DEVELOPING GOOD BUSINESS SENSE

Understanding Organizational Structure and Culture

Understanding how their company operates is an important task for new employees. It is often difficult for a person to do one's job successfully unless he or she understands the design of its structure and its values and norms in order to fit in. This exercise is intended to help you develop your understanding of organizational design and how it will affect you personally in the workplace.

If you currently have a job in a company, you can use this company to answer the following questions. Or, you can use a company you have worked for in the past. Alternately, locate a manager of a company and interview the person. Many managers are willing to give up 30 minutes of their time to help students learn about their businesses.

1. What kind of structure does the company use to group employees and resources? Draw a diagram showing the major functions or divisions. How can this structure promote the company's business model? What are some disadvantages? Would another structure be more appropriate?

2. Draw a diagram showing the company's levels and the job titles of the people at each level. Do you think this company has the right number of levels in its hierarchy? How centralized or decentralized is authority in the company?

3. How does the company coordinate its functions or divisions? For example, does it have extensive rules and procedures? Does it use cross-functional teams? Try to describe its approach.

4. What are the company's values and norms? How would you characterize the company's culture? In what way does its culture fit with its business model?

5. How does the company socialize its members? Does the company use ceremonies, stories, or other means to transmit its culture to its members?

EXPLORING THE WORLD WIDE WEB

3M's Structure and Culture

Go to 3M's Web site (www.3M.com), click on "Our Company," and then click on "3M Businesses." Read about 3M's different businesses. Then, click on the "History" link and read about 3M's innovations. Finally, answer the following questions. **For more Web activities, log on to www.mhhe.com/jonesintro.**

1. Which of the structures discussed in the chapter do you think is most appropriate for managing 3M's businesses? Why?

2. What kind of culture does 3M have, and how did it develop its norms and values?

3. What else does the story of 3M tell you about the way the company is designed and operated?

BusinessWeek CASE FOR DISCUSSION

Shaking Up Intel's Insides

Long before announcing a sweeping reorganization of Intel Corp.'s operating divisions in January 2005, CEO-designate Paul S. Otellini had been telling the world about a major shift in the chipmaker's strategy. Gone were the days, he said, when the company could get by with a single-minded focus on microprocessor design. Intel would instead focus more on bringing together chips and software into so-called platforms designed to perform specific tasks, such as showing movies on home PCs or keeping corporate computers virus-free. "For the first three decades of the company, we made mostly discrete chips. But they weren't designed to be used together . . . and they weren't marketed together," Otellini told *BusinessWeek*.

Now he's making it clear to employees that, under his leadership, Intel truly is entering a new era. Otellini was the first chief executive without an engineering degree at a company where gearheads have reigned supreme. He believes that to keep Intel growing, every idea and technical solution should be focused on meeting customers' needs from the outset. So rather than relying on its engineering prowess, Intel's reorganization will bring together engineers, software writers, and marketers into five market-focused units: corporate computing, the digital home, mobile computing, health care, and channel products–PCs for small manufacturers.

The reorganization is not without challenges, but if Otellini succeeds it will amount to a revolution. For years, Intel has built one-size-fits-all processors, then expected customers to adopt them in various markets. But tech companies increasingly are being asked to deliver solutions that respond to the end user's demands. Corporations, for instance, are looking to prevent their systems from crashing, but employees frequent sites that contain viruses or spyware. Intel has responded by developing chips and software that quarantine these PCs and limit the damage.

TANDEM APPROACH

Otellini's reorganization is supposed to ensure that such product tailoring becomes part of Intel's DNA. How will it work? The company's Centrino wireless notebook platform provides some clues. Intel first determined consumers wanted a powerful notebook with decent battery life that connected wirelessly to the Net. Armed with this knowledge, engineers and software writers designed a package of chips that would do that. Later, engineers and marketing people joined forces to create advertising that would persuade consumers to pay a premium for Centrino-powered notebooks. It worked: As of December 2004, Intel had 87% of the notebook PC market, says Mercury Research.

But imposing such a management structure across the company won't be easy. For one thing, Otellini has taken the unusual step of putting two execs apiece in charge of the two biggest groups, mobility and corporate computing. Intel has used this "two-men-in-a-box" approach before, but it will be particularly tricky under the new structure. Each unit will be responsible for several market segments; for example, the mobility unit will build platforms for notebooks, handhelds, and cell phones. So divvying up each co-chief's duties will be a challenge. Getting that right is crucial or the rank and file won't know whom to report to.

The new regime will cause a jolt to the culture. For decades, employees have been compensated for their own work. Now teams will be judged as a whole. Engineers, long the top dogs, may resist working with others. "It's like saying to a baseball player, 'Gee, we're deciding to play pro football,'" says Edward E. Lawler, a professor at USC's Marshall School of Business. "All of a sudden, the rules of the game are very different."

Otellini has begun to put the pieces in place. Now he'll need the teamwork of his people to pull it off.

Source: Cliff Edwards, "Shaking Up Intel's Insides," *BusinessWeek Online,* January 31, 2005.

QUESTIONS

1. What changes has Intel made to its organizational structure and why?

2. Which of the structures in the chapter is most like the one Intel currently uses?

3. What problems might Intel encounter with its new structure?

BusinessWeek   CASE FOR DISCUSSION

Fashion, with a Conscience

As founder and CEO of Men's Wearhouse, George Zimmer is known to the shopping public as the bearded company pitchman who declares "I guarantee it!" in his TV commercials hawking suits and sport coats.

Founded in 1973, the Men's Wearhouse chain has grown to more than 500 stores catering to the man who doesn't necessarily adore shopping. Stores are located in outdoor shopping centers, letting customers get in and out quickly. The $250 to $300 price tag for most Men's Wearhouse suits is budget-conscious. The merchandise isn't high-fashion, but it is practical and functional.

Behind the scenes, Zimmer has long worked to build a corporate culture that centers first and foremost on keeping his employees happy and loyal. That culture appears to benefit Men's Wearhouse: So

far this year, its shares have risen 25%, outperforming the 1% increase in the Standard & Poor's index of apparel retailers. Last year, earnings rose 23%, to $52.3 million, on sales of $1.4 billion, a gain of 7.5%.

To date this year, same-store sales [revenues for stores open at least one year] have risen 12%, including a same-store gain of 8.2% in the United States and Canada, and earnings have jumped 48%, to $33.3 million. Zimmer recently spoke with *Business-Week* correspondent Louise Lee about his background, his beliefs, and the company culture. Here are edited excerpts of their conversation:

Q: How did you get interested in the clothing business?

A: My father was a manufacturer and had been in suits. I'd been exposed to the apparel industry through osmosis my entire life. When I tried to think of starting my own business, the only thing I had any semblance of awareness of at the time was men's apparel. I never was a clotheshorse in a personal sense. It was a vehicle for a business. As the years unfolded, I was able to create an economic model.

Q: How does your job differ from that of other men's apparel companies?

A: Normally, the CEO of a men's apparel company is very involved in the merchandise side of the business, which is obviously mission-critical. We have both a direct manufacturing business as well as a merchandise team that buys from outside, and I have very little input into that process. The other execs who manage that are given great autonomy. It enables me to focus on other aspects of the business.

Q: So how do you spend most of your time?

A: The bulk of my time is focusing on our corporate culture, which is store operation—the intersection of employee, customer, brand, and merchandise. They all come together. I focus on the experience of our employees and customers, and how it can be improved year after year after year.

Q: How are your beliefs enforced throughout the company?

A: There's an enormous opportunity for us to unfold through our consciousness, through our ability to think. One of my real passions is the nonprofit Institute of Noetic Sciences. We study, scientifically, the phenomenon of consciousness. There's untapped power in our consciousness, which by the way, isn't just coming out of our brains. Consciousness is the intersection of the heart and the brain.

We've woven that thought into our [corporate] culture. What does that mean? You've got to have a company that starts with trust and fairness. I said in a speech a couple of years ago that compassion and forgiveness must sit at the board table side by side with accountability and responsibility. The voice I represent here is underrepresented in the business community.

Q: What kind of specific benefits does Men's Wearhouse have that directly reflect these values?

A: We have a fund, named after our first Hispanic district manager, that we set up six or seven years ago after he died. We ask employees to donate $1 per week through automatic payroll deduction. Executives put in thousands.

Employees apply for loans and grants, mostly grants, to cover unexpected expenses like a car repair. It's $250,000 a year, and it gets used.

We allow a sabbatical once every five years. We add three weeks of paid vacation to the three weeks of vacation you get, so every five years, you can take six weeks paid. This is for all full-time employees, including store-level and distribution-center employees. We encourage people to take six weeks all at once.

Q: How about fairness?

A: We have an ESOP [employee stock-ownership plan]. Ours is capped, meaning income above a certain number doesn't calculate into your distribution.

It's capped at $50,000, which is what the average store manager earns.

We originally had it capped at $200,000. After 5 or 10 years, I realized what that meant as to how money was being distributed. I said, Let's reduce the cap to $100,000. I remember resistance from certain execs and remember smiling at the resistance. Five years later, we lowered the cap to $50,000. We had less resistance from executives, but now we had resistance from district and regional managers.

I smiled because human behavior is human behavior. What we should condemn is selfish behavior, but not the instinct. That's an instinct embedded in us because it serves survival.

Q: Has anyone tried to take advantage of the culture of the company?

A: Ten years ago, we had a store manager who had a gambling problem. He stole bank deposits and asked for the opportunity to pay it back and stay with the company. We gave him a second chance. I said it wasn't an absolute necessity he be terminated if we thought this man could be rehabilitated.

This was a way of getting our money back, and sometimes people can change. But to be honest, most people don't change in this situation. Ultimately, he did it again and was terminated. You have to be prepared when using values like this to have situations not work out well.

Q: So your values are still worth the small cost?

A: For the number of people who take advantage of the values we operate with, the dollars you lose are not so great. The overall change in the corporate energy is still very positive. We do $1.5 billion in sales a year and make a lot of money.

We have millions of dollars of stealing in this company, just like at every company. But if an additional hundred thousand was stolen because we made decisions based on forgiveness and compassion and empathy, and the overall corporate culture was enabling us to earn $100 million pretax, our culture would be a good business decision.

This is not some New Age flighty business model with false nobility with no sustainable earnings. We're a company that's driving consistent and growing earnings over decades while using this business model.

QUESTIONS

1. Why does George Zimmer believe "you have to have a company that starts with trust and fairness"?

2. What are the core values and norms of Men's Wearhouse?

3. By what means did Zimmer create the values and norms of his company?

Source: "Fashion, with a Conscience," *BusinessWeek Online*, November 1, 2004.

BUILDING YOUR MANAGEMENT SKILLS
Know Thyself

Have you ever been "bawled out" by the boss for trying something new without asking? Are you encouraged to try new tasks, even if you make a few mistakes? It's useful to understand the way you prefer to work and decide whether you will fit into a company or department's culture before you accept a job. If you are creative and innovative, it is difficult to work in a very bureaucratic structure. It's helpful to know if you prefer clear rules, policies, and operating procedures. The exercise called "Identify You Preferred Organization Structure" on your Student DVD will help you assess your preferences.

CHAPTER VIDEO
Organizational Culture

NBB is a high-tech, environmentally conscious brewery that produces a world class beer. It employs state of the art cutting edge technology—even that which has yet to be fully proven. It combines the winning formula of high quality, low price, and maximum profit. Yet it accomplishes all of its goals with leading edge human resource practices.

The company uses lean manufacturing processes, through a relatively flat organizational structure that facilitates decision making, authority, and autonomy for individuals across the company. NBB emphasizes the number and quality of cases produced but equally emphasizes the satisfaction level of co-workers. New Belgium Brewery was the first company to introduce on-site child care. The CEO emphasizes that children are members of the broader NBB community and employees are encouraged to bring children with them to the workplace.

The corporate culture of NBB is strong and pervasive. The company has a set of core values and beliefs that it argues directly affect costs and profitability. Overall, NBB is characterized by decentralized authority and empowered employees. Open communication is the key to the company's success. Employee happiness and the establishing of real interpersonal relationships are at the core of New Belgium Brewery's corporate culture.

1. Why is corporate culture an important element in understanding businesses?

2. What is the key difference between a company's values and its norms?

3. What are the sources of a company's corporate culture? Is this true at NBB?

Part 3

A Functional Approach to Business

Part Three, *A Functional Approach to Business,* provides a detailed examination of the essential business functions and occupations necessary to create valuable goods and services that people will want to buy. Using the value chain approach, each of the principal functions involved in business commerce is examined. As you've probably seen so far, the book has used a "hands-on" approach to discussing these functions and their activities, so accounting, for example, becomes not about "crunching numbers" but about "measuring how efficiently and effectively resources are being used."

CHAPTER

9 Information Technology and E-Commerce:

Managing Information, Knowledge, and Business Relationships

Learning Objectives

After studying this chapter you should be able to:

1. Distinguish between data, information, and knowledge and identify the characteristics of useful information.

2. Explain the relationship between IT, competitive advantage, and profitability.

3. Discuss five major IT applications used by companies today to build competitive advantage.

4. Identify the major hardware and software components of IT and e-commerce and describe how they have evolved over time.

WHY IS THIS IMPORTANT ?

Think back to the last time you bought a new cell phone or computer. With all of the choices on the market, how did you decide which model was best for you? You probably did some consumer research to learn about the brands and features available, checked for the best price, and made a selection based on the information you had.

Managers do the same thing when making decisions. They need the best information available to support the value chain that creates a competitive advantage for their organizations. This chapter explains how companies can use information technology to increase their profitability.

A Question of Business

IBM's "E-Business on Demand" IT

In what ways can IBM's IT help improve a company's efficiency and effectiveness?

In the poor economic conditions of the early 2000s, the stock prices of most companies that make and sell information technology (IT) plunged as their main customers—other business companies—slashed their IT budgets. With their lower IT budgets, companies worked hard to find the types of computer hardware and software that would have the biggest impact on their profitability. Convincing a company to spend millions or billions of dollars to buy new kinds of software and hardware is a daunting task facing the salesforce of any IT company today.

One IT company that faces this challenge is IBM, which makes, sells, and services a vast array of computer hardware and software. To maintain its leading position in the competitive IT industry IBM's CEO, Sam Palmisano, announced a bold new business model for IBM based on new IT called "e-business on demand." Palmisano announced that companies that adopt IBM's new IT will obtain millions or billions of dollars in savings in operating costs—something very appealing to companies trying to make the most of their IT budgets.

To promote the new business model, IBM told its customers to think of information and computing power as a "fluid" like water that is contained in the hundreds or thousands of computers that

are the "reservoirs," or "lakes," of a large company's IT system. This water flows between PCs in a company's computer network via the fiber-optic cables that connect them. Thus, computing power, like water, can be moved between computers both inside and between companies—providing that computers are linked seamlessly together. Seamless means that the computer hardware and software do not create information "logjams" that disrupt the flow of information and computing power.

IBM's software engineers developed new e-business software to allow computers both inside and between companies to work seamlessly together. Among other things, this software allows computer operators to monitor hundreds of different computers at the same time and shift work from one machine to another to distribute a company's computing power to wherever it is most needed. This has several cost saving advantages. First, it allows companies to run their computers close to capacity, which greatly improves IT productivity and reduces operating costs. Second, to ensure that there was never any possibility its customers would experience a "drought," IBM proposed to use its own vast computer capacity as a kind of bank, or reservoir, that customers could tap into whenever their own systems might become overloaded. For example, IBM's e-business software allows companies to shift any excess workload from their network to IBM's computers, which means they do not have to invest tens-of-millions of dollars in extra computers—a huge cost saving. Third, when a company's computers are seamlessly networked, they can function as a "supercomputer," a computer with immense information processing power that can easily cost upwards of $50 million to purchase as a standalone computer, and tens-of-millions more dollars to maintain.

To show customers the cost-saving potential of its new e-business products, IBM decided it would be the first company to use it. Previously, IBM allowed its hundreds of different divisions to choose whatever software they liked to manage their own purchasing and supply chain activities. In 2003, Palmisano appointed star manager Linda Stanford to overhaul IBM's companywide supply chain—which purchases inputs worth $44 billion a year! Stanford was made responsible for developing software to seamlessly link all IBM's divisions into a single,

integrated computer network. When implemented, the new software resulted in a 5% gain in productivity, which IBM expects to repeat for the next 5 to 10 years. This will result in cost savings of over $2 billion annually. IBM was quick to tell its customers that they can expect to see similar savings if they purchase its e-business software.

IBM's new e-business system also has many other performance-enhancing benefits. Its thousands of IT consultants are experts in particular industries such as the car, financial services, or retail industries. They have a deep understanding of the particular problems facing companies in those industries and how to improve their business models. Palmisano told IBM's consultants to work closely with its software engineers to find ways to incorporate their knowledge into software that can be implanted into a customer's IT system to better manage its business model.

IBM is now developing 17 "expert systems," which are industry-specific, problem-solving software packages managers can use to make better business decisions as well as reduce operating costs. One of these expert systems is being developed for the pharmaceutical industry. Using IBM's new pharmaceutical expert system, a company's computer network will function as a supercomputer able to simulate and model the potential success of the many new drugs a company has under development. Currently, only 5 to 10% of new drugs make it to the market. IBM believes its new expert system could raise that rate to over 50%, which would result in billions of dollars in cost savings for drug companies.[1] •

Overview

We live in exciting times. Just decades ago, science-fiction writers like Robert Heinlein and Isaac Asimov imagined devices such as wrist-held videophones, virtual reality machines, and speech-programmed, hand-held computers. Today, companies like Palm, Hewlett-Packard, Nokia, Sony, and Microsoft are producing the computer hardware and software that makes these devices possible. Even science-fiction writers did not imagine the creation of the Internet or how that would dramatically change people's lives. We live in a different world than just a decade ago; advances in IT have changed the way people think and the very nature of business commerce, occupations, and organizations.

In this chapter, we examine how these dramatic advances in IT have affected business activity and the way companies compete in today's wired and wireless global world. First, we discuss the relationship between information, knowledge, competitive advantage, and profitability. Second, we discuss the five principal IT applications responsible for much of the increase in business efficiency and effectiveness today. Third, we describe the different hardware and software components of IT and e-commerce used to network computers both inside and between companies.

We then examine the battles currently raging in the IT industry between major companies. By the end of this chapter, you will understand the many ways in which IT allows companies to make better use of their resources to increase their efficiency, effectiveness, and profitability.

Information Technology and Profitability

In a historical sense, the IT revolution is the most recent cause of the global change in industrial business practices. To understand how IT has changed business and the way companies operate today, it is necessary to understand what information is and why it's become a crucial facilitator of business commerce.

Suppose you add up the value of the coins in your pocket and find you have $1.36 in change. You have been manipulating *data,* the numerical value of each individual coin, to obtain *information,* the total value of your change. You did so because you needed to know, for example, if you have enough money to buy a coke and a candy bar. Information is a set of data, facts, numbers, and words organized in such a way that it provides its users with knowledge. Knowledge is what a person perceives, recognizes, identifies, or discovers from analyzing data and information. Over time, the result of acquiring more and better information and knowledge is learning. Learning is an increase in the store of expertise or knowledge people have. Knowledge and learning give people the ability to better understand and respond to the economic environment in which they operate. As such, they are better able satisfy their wants and needs. Figure 9.1 illustrates the relationship between information, knowledge, and learning. In a business context, managers try to acquire more and better data and information that leads to increased knowledge. The more knowledge they possess, the better able they are to respond to the competitive business environment.

Information technology (IT) refers to the many different kinds of computer and communications hardware and software, and the skills of the designers, programmers, managers, and technicians who create and manage this technology. IT is used to acquire, define, input, arrange, organize, manipulate, store, and transmit facts,

information A set of data, facts, numbers, and words that has been organized in such a way that it provides its users with knowledge.

knowledge What a person perceives, recognizes, identifies, or discovers from analyzing data and information.

learning An increase in the store or stock of people's expertise or knowledge.

Figure 9.1
Information, Knowledge, and Learning

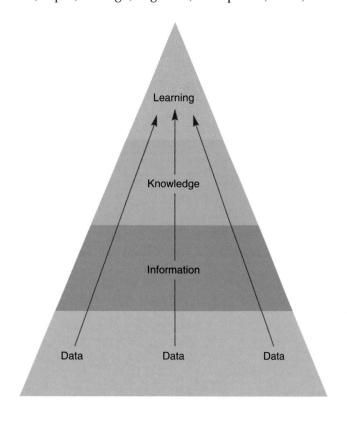

information technology The many different kinds of computer and communications hardware and software and the skills of their designers, programmers, managers, and technicians who create and manage it.

organizational learning Managing information and knowledge to achieve a better fit between a company's business model and the forces in its environment.

data, and information to create business knowledge and promote organizational learning. Organizational learning occurs when managers and employees are able to use information and knowledge to achieve a better fit between a company's business model and the forces in its environment. The result of organizational learning is increased profitability.

Useful Information and Knowledge

When managers and employees have information that gives them a greater understanding of the competitive threats and opportunities a company faces, they are in a better position. The usefulness of information depends, however, on whether it is complete, accurate and reliable, relevant, and timely. Figure 9.2 illustrates these characteristics, and each is discussed next.

COMPLETE   For information to be useful, it needs to provide a *complete picture* of a situation; salient facts or data that would alter a manager's assessment of a situation cannot be omitted. For example, a manager who fails to collect information about the cost of holding parts in inventory or the actual cost related to hiring, training, or paying employees lacks a complete picture of his or her company's true profitability. Similarly, a research team that fails to examine the research results of other scientists around the world is at a competitive disadvantage.

ACCURATE AND RELIABLE   The usefulness of information is a function of its accuracy and reliability. The greater its precision and freedom from error, the more likely the information is to be truly insightful, and the more confident managers can be basing their decisions on it. Basing important decisions on poor-quality information can obviously be disastrous. For example, if managers in different functions measure the cost of the same resources in different ways, the company's top managers will have a much harder time gauging the real profitability of the business.

RELEVANT   Before IT, information was very expensive to collect and process. Today, however, managers are awash with information. In fact, in many cases, they have *too* much information. What's relevant and what can be safely ignored is time consuming and costly for them to sort out. Moreover, information that is too detailed or complex can actually obscure rather than provide insight about a business situation.

Figure 9.2
Characteristics of Useful Information

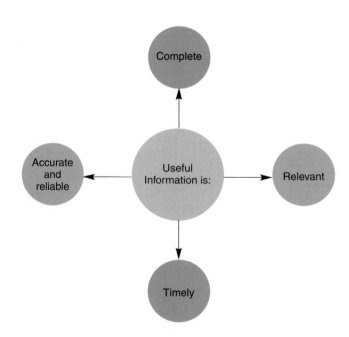

information overload
A situation in which managers have to process so much information it actually reduces their understanding of a situation.

Information overload is a term used to describe a situation in which managers have to process so much information that it actually *lessens* their understanding of a situation.

Suppose, for example, to find a way to increase profitability managers decide to collect information on every kind of product being made by their company's competitors. Then, they collect detailed information on all these products' features and their market share (to see which are the most popular). The managers now possess detailed information about which products were successful in the past. However, this does not provide them with much knowledge about what kind of products might be successful in the *future.* Moreover, while they are doing this research their competitors are developing newer products. The point here is that not all information is good information: To avoid collecting irrelevant information that can actually slow down a company's progress, managers need to think carefully about which information they truly need and what is relevant in a particular problem-solving situation.

real-time information
Information that is constantly updated.

TIMELY In today's rapidly changing business environment, it is essential that the information managers use to make decisions be as up-to-date as possible. Real-time information is information that is constantly updated. Most companies today purchase IT systems that give them real-time information. For example, when a company introduces a new product or reduces the price of an existing product, managers need real-time information about how well customers are responding to these moves and if the company's profitability is rising or falling as a result. If managers have to wait months to find this out, the company's market share might fall significantly in the meantime (because customers don't like the new product) or its profitability might drop precipitously (because the price cut isn't leading to more units sold).

Gaining a Competitive Advantage with IT

Recall from Chapter 4 that the four sources of a global competitive advantage are superior productivity, quality, innovation, and responsiveness to customers. The purpose of a company's IT is to provide managers at all levels and in all functions and divisions with the knowledge they need to achieve these goals. Figure 9.3 outlines these goals, which we discuss in depth next.

SUPERIOR PRODUCTIVITY IT gives middle managers the ability to collect and process more data and information about each individual task or operation involved in a functional activity. With the knowledge they gain, they can improve the

Figure 9.3
IT and Competitive Advantage

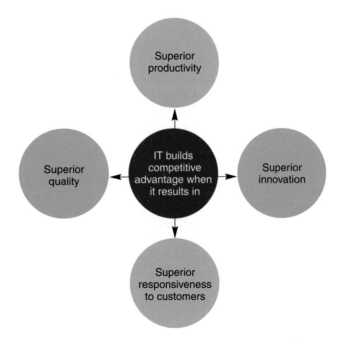

productivity of a particular function. Today, for example, manufacturing managers are able to collect data on hundreds and thousands of specific manufacturing operations. This gives them a much better understanding of how efficiently they are using the company's resources to make and sell goods and services. Even 10 years ago the costs of doing this would have been exorbitant. Now it is much cheaper. Moreover, as we learned earlier in the chapter, IBM now goes so far as to *promise* its customers that its systems will improve their productivity. In a sense, the productivity gains companies can achieve by acquiring good information makes the cost of getting that information even cheaper yet. In other words, good information pays off.

SUPERIOR QUALITY   IT gives managers the ability to accurately analyze the individual operations needed to make a product to understand where problems might lie. When they know where these errors lie, they can then work to eliminate them and improve product quality. Take a car engine, for example: A one-thousandth-of-an-inch difference between a piston in an engine and the combustion chamber it enters can have a dramatic impact on a car's performance. If the managers in charge of engine assembly can discover why such a gap is being created, they can redesign the components or manufacturing process to fix the problem and improve quality.

In service organizations, such as retail stores, IT makes it possible to collect information on many dimensions of quality. For example, managers in companies such as Amazon.com and LandsEnd.com use IT to track the percentage of customer orders that are correctly filled as a way of judging quality. Analyzing this information allows managers to pinpoint reasons why mistakes happen so corrective action can be taken.

SUPERIOR INNOVATION   IT can speed up product innovation in many ways. We learned, for example, how software created by IBM is helping pharmaceutical firms identify products most likely to succeed. By focusing on just those products, the firms are able to develop and market them more quickly. IT systems also allow a company's technical knowledge to be stored and constantly updated in the ongoing search for new products and ways to improve existing products. Similarly, electronic bulletin boards, chatrooms, and teleconferencing systems that allow scientists and engineers from all parts of a company to access constantly updated information speed up innovation.

SUPERIOR CUSTOMER RESPONSIVENESS   IT can facilitate a company's responsiveness to its customers in a number of different ways. Many companies use software systems to create a profile of each of their customers—a record of their likes and dislikes, buying habits over time, and so on. IT systems can also be used to track how customers are responding to a firm's advertising campaigns. For example, using sophisticated software, Amazon.com was able to discover that its advertising dollars were much more effectively spent when used to reach the company's present customers versus attract new customers. As a result, Amazon.com now advertises primarily on Web sites popular among its repeat customers.

Starbucks is another example. When Starbucks first began operating in the United States, finding places to put its stores was not a problem. Now, however, the company is already located in many of the prime real-estate spots. Instead of basing store location decisions on gut instinct (which is what Starbucks' managers used to do) the company now uses "location" software. The software analyzes consumers in a particular area (their demographics, income, and so forth) as well as the surrounding competition.

Did You Know?

In 1974, a pack of Wrigley chewing gum was scanned at a New Jersey grocery store. Today there are about five billion scans every day. The bar code traces its origins back to 1949 and a 27-year-old graduate student, Norman Joseph Woodland who drew dots and dashes in the sand to simulate Morse Code (he was on the beach, taking a break from school) and then extended them downward with his fingers. What appeared were thin lines resulting from the dots and thick lines from the dashes.[2]

Major Information Technology Applications

In this section, we focus on the five IT applications that have had the biggest impact on business: (1) transaction processing systems, (2) knowledge management systems, (3) expert systems and artificial intelligence, (4) enterprise resource planning, and (5) e-commerce. These applications are outlined in Figure 9.4. A company's **chief information officer** (CIO), the top manager of its IT function, is responsible for choosing and implementing a system in which these applications operate seamlessly and at the least cost.

Transaction Processing Systems

chief information officer The top manager of a company's IT function.

transaction processing system An IT system designed to collect, record, and manipulate the data related to a company's day-to-day business operations.

Transaction processing systems (TP systems) are designed to collect, record, and manipulate the data related to a company's routine, day-to-day operations. VF Jeans uses a TP system to connect with its sales outlets, such as department stores, where it collects data on the type and size of jeans selling the fastest. Its managers then take this information and, within hours, decide what to instruct the company's overseas manufacturers to make.

In the human resource management (HRM) function, a TP system is used to enter employee records like their personal data, employment history, and performance evaluations as well as process their pay and benefits. Accounting uses a TP system to enter and record data on each of the millions of transactions involved in making and selling goods and services. This basic information is then used to prepare a company's financial statements.

TP systems are the "backbone" of a company's IT. They perform all of the donkey work necessary to record the basic information a company needs to operate. Managers then manipulate and use this information to better understand how individual functions and the company as a whole are performing.

Knowledge Management Systems

knowledge management system An IT system that analyzes the information collected from the TP system but filters and analyzes it to make it more useful to managers.

Knowledge management systems (KM systems) take the information in a company's TP systems and filter and analyze it to make it more useful to managers. The problem facing IT managers when they design a KM system is to identify the most important information in the database *needed to solve a particular problem*. In other words, they need to be able to extract that information from the mass of data the company's TP system collects every day.

Figure 9.4
Five Major IT Applications

Transaction Processing

Knowledge Management

Expert Systems

Enterprise Resource Planning

E-Commerce

Managers in charge of VF Jeans, the company that produces Lee-brand clothing, use data from the company's TP system to alert them when the demand for a specific product is dropping or if a large number of people are returning a particular product.

best practices The set of skill-based competencies that allow a particular function to perform at its optimal level.

IT consultants Expert employees who use their knowledge and learning to solve their customers' IT problems.

To extract this information, a company first instructs its functional managers to develop a set of criteria about the information that needs to be collected. These managers then work with the company's IT personnel to develop a set of best practices, the set of skill-based competencies that allow a particular function to perform at a high level. A function's best practices are the optimal procedures by which it does its job, such as marketing finding new ways to attract new, online customers, product development using new software to innovate new products, and manufacturing developing novel ways to assemble a product.

Once these best practices are discovered, they are converted into computer code that works like a set of rules to scan the information in a company's transaction processing databases and recognize patterns that spell "trouble"–departures from the rules. When the KM system recognizes problems that are arising, it alerts the functional managers, who then must find the best way to respond to the problem. In VF Jeans, for example, hundreds of thousands of pieces of sales data are archived each day in its TP system. VF's sales managers then use this information to develop rules alerting them if the demand for a specific product drops or if a large number of customers are returning a particular product (which perhaps indicates there is a quality problem). These rules are then programmed into the KM system so managers can take quick corrective action as needed.

KM systems are especially important in service organizations that use IT consultants: employees charged with solving customers' IT problems. At IT consulting companies like Accenture, for example, each consultant is responsible for capturing the knowledge he or she gains while working with a client and giving it to Accenture's KM system managers. These people then sift through all of this input and determine the best practices consultants should use to provide state-of-the-art IT solutions for the company's clients. The information is then programmed into Accenture's companywide KM system so the firm's consultants anywhere in the world can access it at any time. Accenture spent over $2 billion developing its companywide KM system, and it employs 300 knowledge experts to manage it.

Expert Systems and Artificial Intelligence

expert system An advanced IT system that can reason through a company's information, diagnose problems, and suggest solutions.

IT has dramatically improved business decision making. Expert systems and artificial intelligence are now taking this decision making to a higher level. An expert system is an advanced IT system that can (1) reason through the information captured by a company's TP and KM systems; (2) recognize and diagnose patterns, problems, or issues related to that information; and (3) suggest solutions for those problems and issues. It is this third component of expert systems–the ability to suggest solutions to problems–that distinguishes them from ordinary KM systems. This ability is called "artificial intelligence."

artificial intelligence An IT system that reasons and learns like a human being.

Artificial intelligence allows computers to learn, and refine, their reasoning over time, much like a human being does. Let's look at VF Jeans again. An expert system might have the ability to use information about customers' current buying preferences to predict future changes in customer demand. By analyzing detailed information on operating costs, the expert system might be able to suggest ways to change the company's purchasing or manufacturing operations to reduce costs 12 or 18 months in the future.

Expert systems can be designed to perform similar kinds of high-level information processing for all of a company's functions. They can also provide top managers with a set of sophisticated analytic procedures that explain the fit, or misfit, between a company's business model and its environment. Recall that in addition to the pharmaceutical industry, IBM consultants are working to develop expert systems for 16 other industries. Hewlett-Packard, Oracle, and Honda are some of the other companies developing systems using artificial intelligence. Honda has even developed a child-sized robot called "Asimo." Asimo taught itself to climb stairs and jog using artificial intelligence software. Honda is hoping the robot will be running errands and delivering interoffice mail to Honda's employees perhaps by 2010.

Enterprise Resource Planning Systems

It is not sufficient just to give managers inside of a function better information and knowledge. They also need to be able to access information about the activities going on in the company's other functions. The greater the flow of information and knowledge among functions, the more organizational learning takes place, which allows managers to improve a company's business model. Enterprise resource planning (ERP) systems are multimodule applications software packages that coordinate all of a company's functional activities. ERP systems (1) help individual functions improve their operations and (2) improve the integration between functions.

enterprise resource planning (ERP) systems Multimodule applications software packages that coordinate all of a company's functional activities.

Choosing and designing an ERP system to improve the way a company operates is one of the biggest challenge's facing today's CIOs. To appreciate why almost every large global company installs an ERP system, it is necessary to understand the concept of the *value-chain*. We discuss this next.

ERP AND THE VALUE-CHAIN Recall from Chapter 1 that a company's value chain consists of the functional activities needed to make and sell goods and services profitably. Figure 9.5 lists these functions again (which are discussed in the remaining chapters in the book).

Recall from Chapter 1 that a value chain has two different types of functions: primary and support functions. *Primary functions* are those that are directly involved in making and selling goods and services: Marketing, product development, operations, materials management, and sales are successive steps in the value-creation process. These activities are primary because they produce the *value* customers find in a company's products. When the primary functions combined activities lower the costs of making a product, or create well-designed innovative products customers are willing to pay a premium price for, they add value to the firm and increase its profitability.

**Figure 9.5
Primary and
Secondary Value-
Chain Functions**

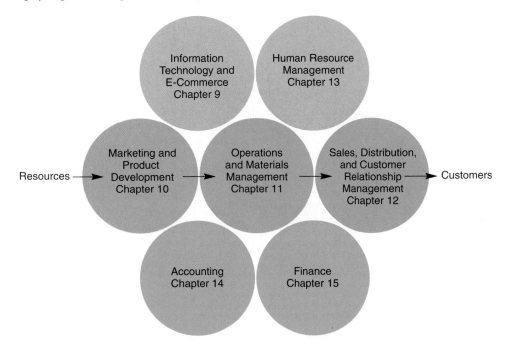

By contrast, a firm's *secondary functions* are those that measure, control, facilitate, and improve the way a company's primary functions perform. IT, human resource management (HRM), accounting, and finance are, in many cases, secondary functions.

In the value chain, each primary function, in sequence, contributes value to a product and then hands it off to the next function, which makes its contribution, and so on, down the line. The primary function of marketing, for example, is to uncover new or changing customer needs and to decide how to modify or create new products to respond to them. Marketing then shares this knowledge with the firm's product development groups, whose engineers and scientists work to develop and design these products. In turn, materials management and manufacturing work to find ways to obtain cheaper, better inputs and make the new products as efficiently as possible. Marketing and sales must then convince customers to buy these products.

The value chain provides a useful way to think about the sequence of functional activities necessary to create and sell products successfully. In an IT context, however, it also suggests that there is an enormous amount of information that must be coordinated. This is where the IT function can have the most impact on a company's profitability. Business in Action discusses an ERP system designed to do this, which is sold by SAP.

Business in Action

SAP's ERP Systems

SAP is the world's leading supplier of ERP software; it introduced the world's first ERP system in 1973. So great was the demand for its software that SAP had to train thousands of IT consultants from companies like IBM, Hewlett-Packard, Accenture, and Cap Gemini to install and customize its software to meet the needs of companies around the globe.

SAP's ERP system is popular because it manages a company's functional activities at all the stages in the value chain. Within the industry, the software has become known as *the* "expert system of expert systems." It contains the set of best practices SAP's engineers have found increase a business's efficiency, quality, innovation, and responsiveness. SAP claims that when a company reconfigures its IT platform and installs its software, it can achieve productivity gains of 30 to 50%—which can amount to billions of dollars in savings for a large multinational firm.

For each value-chain function, SAP installs a software module on its network. Each function then inputs its data into the module in a way specified by SAP. For example, the sales department inputs all of the information it gathers about customers; the materials-management department does likewise, as does marketing, accounting, and so on. The modules then reason through the information that has been input, and managers get real-time feedback about the firm's current state of operations and how to improve them. The managers also have access to the other function's systems and are alerted when their operations might be affected by those functions. All of this information is then relayed to the company's top managers, who consider the solutions offered by system and take action.[3]

SAP's ERP system is popular because it manages a firm's functional activities at all stages in the value chain.

Suppose, for example, marketing personnel discover some unmet customer need and suggest a type of product that can meet this need. They estimate that the company could sell 400,000 units of the product annually, if it were produced. Using

SAP's software, the company's engineers then develop a new, high-quality, low-cost product based on marketing's recommendations. While this is occurring, the firm's manufacturing managers monitor the development of the product via the system and make suggestions to the engineers about how to design the product in such a way that it will cost less to produce. Materials managers observe how the product is being developed and make suggestions to the engineers about the global suppliers that should be used or how the product should be altered so that certain suppliers or parts can be utilized. At the same time, the firm's human resource managers use the system to forecast the number of employees needed to make and sell the product and what this will cost.

SAP's software is multifunctional. For example, engineers in product development can use the system to design a new, high-quality, low-cost product, whereas manufacturing managers can use the system to keep operating costs to a minimum.

How does SAP's ERP software build competitive advantage and profitability? First, it speeds up product development so companies that can bring products to market more quickly generate higher sales revenue. Second, SAP's system focuses on how to drive down operating costs while maintaining high product quality. Third, SAP's system is focused on satisfying the final customer; its customer relationship management (CRM) module watches how customers respond to a new product and feeds back this information quickly to sales and the company's other functions.

To see what this means in practice let's jump ahead three months and suppose that the CRM component of SAP's ERP software reports that actual sales are 20% below target. It has further reasoned that the problem is due to the fact that the product lacks one crucial feature that customers want. The product is a smart phone, for example, and customers want a built-in, digital camera.

The sales function decides that this, indeed, must be done and alerts the managers of the firm's other functions. Now, they can also begin to make decisions about how to manage this development: The engineers in product development, for example, can figure out how much it will cost to develop the built-in camera and how long it will take. Managers in the other functions can monitor the engineers' progress and make suggestions for improvement. In the meantime, the firm's manufacturing managers are aware that sales of the older camera are slow and have already cut back on their production of that camera. Similarly, materials managers will have contacted digital camera makers to find out how much such a camera will cost and when it can be supplied. In the meantime, marketing will develop new sales forecasts to estimate demand for the modified product. It announces a revised sales forecast of 75,000 units of the modified product.

It takes the firm's engineers one month to modify the product, but because the managers in manufacturing and materials management already have information about it via SAP's software, the product hits the market only two months later. Within weeks, the company's sales department reports that actual sales are greatly exceeding marketing's new forecast. The company knows it has a winning product, and top managers give the go ahead for manufacturing to build a second production line to double production of the product. The firm's functions are expecting this decision because they have access to this information, too. In fact, they have already been experimenting with their SAP modules to try to determine how long it will take them to respond to such a move. In turn, they provide the other functions with this information so they can adjust their functional activities accordingly, much like a symphony orchestra works together.

Remember, all this quick and responsive action has been made possible because of the ERP system. Compare this to a paper-based system. In such a company, it would take much longer to find out about the slow sales and that the firm's projections were wrong. In the meantime manufacturing, producing according to plan, will have generated a huge stock of unsold products, which is a major source of operating costs. Also, because the product will be out of date, the company will have to sell it at a discount just to get rid of it. This will hurt the firm's profitability. In the meantime, managers from the different functions will have been making frantic phone calls and holding face-to-face meetings to decide what to do. It might take another six months for the modified product to be put into production. Perhaps as much as an entire year of huge potential profits will have been lost.

E-Commerce Systems

e-commerce Trade that takes place between companies, and between companies and individual customers via the Internet (or other IT systems).

E-commerce is trade that takes place between companies, and between companies and individual customers, using IT and the Internet. Business-to-business (B2B) commerce is trade that takes place *between* companies. (See Figure 9.6.) A main B2B software application is the **B2B marketplace,** an industry-specific trading platform set up to connect buyers and sellers using the Internet. To participate in a B2B marketplace, companies agree to use the same software standard. This allows them to search for and share information with each other. Together, they can work to find ways to reduce costs or improve quality. This is what the grocery industry is trying to do. Because profits are small in the industry, it is trying to adopt common software standards to make transactions between businesses less complicated and more cost effective. We discuss these B2B and B2C marketplaces in more detail in later chapters.

Business-to-customer (B2C) commerce is trade that takes place between a company and consumers. When a company uses IT to connect directly to consumers they do not need to use intermediaries like wholesalers and retailers. Like Dell computer, they make higher profits by selling directly to customers. The wine industry is an example. Many wineries now sell their wine straight to consumers via the Internet. Online storefronts are helping companies access customers directly and cheaply with a much wider range of products and information about them. Amazon has developed one of the most customer-friendly storefronts on the Web. Amazon's site offers a plethora of products from multiple stores, along with detailed information about the reliability of both the products and retailers that sell them—in many instances from current users of the products. Amazon.com is consistently rated top in online customer satisfaction.

Once again, here is Chip Wass' cartoon depiction of an electronic auction.

Figure 9.6
Types of
E-Commerce

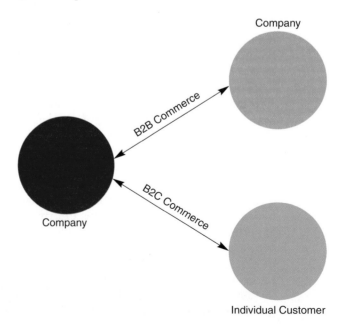

B2B marketplace An industry-specific trading platform set up to connect buyers and sellers using the Internet.

intranet A company's internal system of computers and Web sites accessible only by its employees.

Software developers like Microsoft, Oracle, SAP, and IBM are rushing to help Amazon and other companies put IT application to work on the Internet. Previously, the developers' software had been configured only to work on a particular company's system of interlinked internal computers or intranet. Now, they are developing software that links a company's network to its suppliers and customers around the world via the World Wide Web. SAP, for example, rushed to update its ERP modules to allow for transactions over the Internet. It calls its new B2B commerce software "mySAP." Today every one of SAP's modules is Internet compatible. Microsoft and IBM are doing likewise with their software. We discuss Internet applications and storefronts in greater depth in the chapters on marketing and sales, which appear later in the book.

Hardware Components of IT and E-Commerce

Total global spending on IT is over $1 trillion a year. The United States, with just 4.6% of the world's population, purchases about 50% of the world's computing and information processing power. In the view of many experts, the strength of the U.S. economy today is due to it being the world's leader in making and using IT. Some experts call the computer industry the "industry of industries" because its products have an immense effect on the performance and profitability of companies in most *other* industries.

Let's examine the way the IT industry has developed over the last 50 years and how it has affected businesses. In this section, we examine the hardware components of IT, and in the next section, software components. Throughout this discussion we also examine the way companies in the IT industry, such as IBM and Microsoft, are competing to be the leading IT suppliers.

Legacy Systems

legacy system The hardware and software components of a company's IT system at any one point in time.

The hardware and software components of a company's *existing* IT system are called its legacy system. A company makes a huge investment in its legacy system, one that can cost a multinational company billions of dollars to purchase and develop. Moreover, its IT managers, and managers and employees across the company, have spent an enormous amount of time to learn how to input data and use the system. Advances in IT frequently require a company to upgrade its systems, just as we as individual computer users have to upgrade our own systems from time to time.

To make the process of upgrading its legacy system smoother and easier, companies and their CIOs are increasingly choosing to buy most of their computer hardware, software, and services from one or a few leading IT companies like IBM or Hewlett-Packard. Large IT companies offer a complete suite of computer hardware and software from mainframes to laptops that work seamlessly together when installed. The IT consultants of these companies also know how to customize their systems to suit a company's particular needs and develop comprehensive training programs on the system for the company's staff. But what are the specific hardware components of a legacy system and how have they changed over time? We discuss this next.

Mainframe Computers

The first modern computer, the UNIVAC, was developed in 1951 using vacuum-tube technology. The result was a computer as big as a two-story house. Seven years later, Texas Instruments invented the integrated circuit. The integrated circuit allowed much smaller mainframes to be built. Instead of the size of a two-story house, each was about the size of a large living room. The computing power of the new mainframes was also many times greater. IBM ultimately became the leading developer of mainframe computers, and mainframes still serve as the center, or hub, of most

The first modern computer, the UNIVAC, which was developed in 1951, used vacuum-tube technology. The result was a computer as big as a two-story house.

companies' information processing and storage systems. IBM also became the leading developer of the software that runs mainframes.

Transaction processing systems for large companies were the principal kind of IT applications being developed at this time. Because it dominated mainframe computing, IBM became one, if not the, most profitable company in the world. The company then pumped those profits back into IT research and pioneered many of the advances in computer hardware that made computers thousands of times more powerful during the 1960s and 1970s.

In the age of mainframes, however, computers were in the "backroom." A firm's functional managers could only access them through the company's computer engineers. These people were responsible for maintaining the systems and inputting data. Upon request they would manipulate the data and provide the results to managers who requested it. Although a functional manager could request a spreadsheet to analyze sales figures, examine changes in production costs, or prepare the company's accounts, the way computers operated remained a mystery to most non-IT managers. Nonetheless, computers were used, among other things, for scientific research, to design cars, and to manage complex global financial accounts and transactions. Even though they were crude by today's standards, they helped companies to increase their efficiency and effectiveness in countless ways. By the 1970s, for example, General Motors possessed more computing power than any other company. The company's superior IT was one reason why it was then the largest, and most profitable, global carmaker.

Also during the 1960 and 1970s, other companies like Digital Equipment Corporation (DEC) and Hewlett-Packard began to offer smaller, less-powerful mainframe computers, called "minicomputers." Minicomputers were developed to provide IT applications for a particular function or product division. Thus, for example, each of GM's car divisions might possess several minicomputers dedicated to car design or accounting while the mainframe worked separately at corporate headquarters.

In the 1970s, software engineers were focusing their efforts on ways to improve a computer's "word-processing" abilities. Not only were computers just crunching numbers, they were increasingly being used by managers to work on word documents and then update, and store them. It was becoming clear that computers, rather than typewriters, could be used more efficiently to create all kinds documents. Companies began to look for ways for their mainframe computers to perform word-processing functions. One idea, then called the "office of the future," was to connect secretaries and clerks directly into mainframes through remote terminals located in a company's functions and departments. Note the focus on the mainframe computer. At this time it was unimaginable that there could be a computer on every employee's desk.

One significant departure from this approach was pioneered by DEC, which developed standalone minicomputers, or "workstations," dedicated to word processing. Often, each department in a company purchased one of these expensive machines, and managers gave their handwritten documents to workstation operators for inputting. DEC became a leader in this area and a very profitable company. It did not remain so for very long, however, because IT kept advancing and DEC had shown that word processing applications could be successfully performed by much simpler means than mainframe computers.

Microprocessors and Personal Computers

The dominance of the mainframe was challenged by Intel's 4004 microprocessor, or "computer on a chip," in 1970. The first chips were thousands of times less powerful than the "brains" of a mainframe and were not regarded as a substitute for mainframe

The buyers of the first Apple PCs were "early adopters" of computer products—people who enjoyed experimenting with new technology.

computing. However, they opened the door for "standalone" computing. Intel had the idea that an individual user could have a computer using its chip on his or her desk and then program it to do whatever he or she wanted it to do.

Apple Computer ran with this idea. In 1976 it introduced a kit form of the personal computer (PC) that it sold to computer enthusiasts worldwide. They could assemble a PC and then program it using some kind of computer language. This event turned the computing world upside down. The enthusiasts then began to experiment with ways to develop more powerful word-processing and spreadsheet applications for the PC. Many of them were so successful they went on to found companies such as WordPerfect, Novell, Word-Star, and so on.

Nonetheless, it took several years for the "hidden" significance of standalone PCs to register with leading computer makers. IBM and DEC, for example, were dominated by "mainframe thinking." Their company values and norms were based on the notion that computing would always be a centralized, technical activity. In a famous quote, Kenneth Olson, the founder and CEO of DEC (and a brilliant computer engineer in his own right), commented publicly that personal computers were merely "toys."

Olson's view, and the view of leading IT makers, soon changed. In the IT world, researchers are always striving to improve a particular technology, and so its capabilities improve over time—much as the power of a car's internal combustion engine has been increased dramatically over the last 100 years. Intel continued to plow back all its profits to develop ever more powerful generations of microprocessors, or chips. Its more powerful chips allowed software developers to continually write ever more powerful software applications improving the capabilities of PCs.

IBM didn't introduce its first PC until 1981. It was very late to respond to the emerging threat PCs posed to its mainframes.

Finally, in the late 1970s, an IBM manager named Bill Lowe, acting on his own initiative, convinced his company's top managers to put him in charge of developing a PC to compete with Apple. Lowe couldn't afford to wait for five years while IBM developed the hardware and software needed for the new PC, so, he decided to make the IBM PC by buying *all* of the components he needed from other companies. This was a major departure for IBM. Previously, all the technology needed to run IBM's products had been internally developed and then patented by the company.

The new IBM PC incorporated Intel's 8086 chip and had two floppy disk drives (the PC hard disk had not yet been invented). But to make all the PC's different components—its microprocessor, memory board, keypad, screen, printer, and so on—work together, the computer needed software. Developing the software in-house would have also taken IBM two or three years, so the company instead bought the right to use a software operating system owned by a small company in Redmond, Washington: This was Microsoft's MS-DOS system. Interestingly enough, Microsoft did not create MS-DOS. Bill Gates, Microsoft's founder, knew IBM was looking around for an operating system. He, too, lacked the time to develop one. However, he knew of a small company in Seattle that *did* have a viable operating system. Using $50,000 borrowed from his father, a wealthy Seattle lawyer, he purchased it, continued developing it with his colleagues, and renamed it MS-DOS. The rest is history.

Network Computers: Servers and Clients

The use of PCs spread rapidly during the 1980s. It also became clear during this time that linking an organization's PCs into a network could facilitate communication between PC users. IBM, DEC, Hewlett-Packard, and new companies like Sun Microsystems began to make powerful midrange computers known as network servers or "servers." These computers connect to individual PCs, or "clients," in the network. The relatively low cost and ease of programming and maintaining server–client networks (compared to the mainframe) soon made them very popular. Large, but particularly small companies that had limited IT budgets, increasingly began to use them as substitutes for mainframes.

The collection of client PCs linked to a central server became known as a "local area network" (LAN). Within any large company, there might be hundreds of LANs across its divisions, functions, or project groups. Each division or group could configure its own LAN, and load it with the software that best met its functional needs. This was a major turning point.

Companies like SAP realized that what companies needed was software that would allow each function or division to use its LAN most effectively, and software that could link all the different LANs to its mainframe computer so they could all work together to perform the sophisticated kinds of analyses needed to improve a company's business model, as we discussed earlier. The success of SAP's ERP software signaled to IT companies like Microsoft and Hewlett-Packard that they needed to develop software that would seamlessly connect PCs, LANs, and mainframes, as depicted in Figure 9.7, so that they could all share the same information and communicate with one another.

The World Wide Web and the Internet

Not surprisingly, software engineers realized that if computers could be networked at all levels *inside* of a company they could be networked *across* companies and countries. Scientists in universities and research centers around the world needed to find a way to rapidly transmit and share information. This led them to develop software connecting the databases of different institutions. A software scientist, Tim Berners-Lee, wrote the first HTML software code making it possible to post that information on Web pages. Hence, the Internet and World Wide Web were born. (Contrary to popular belief, the Internet was *not* created by former U.S. Vice President Al Gore.) Berners-Lee won a Nobel Prize in 2004 for his efforts.

The Internet is made up of all the computer hardware such as mainframes, servers, PCs, and the electronic network switches or routers, fiber-optic cable, telephone lines,

**Video
Small
Business
in Action**

Future Workforce

Summary: The future workforce is the topic of this *BusinessWeek* TV segment as shown in the video on your Student DVD. Innovation abounds if you know where to look for it. For example, the Canadian company, Taking It Global, has developed what it calls the "Technology Board of the Future." The organization is designed as a sounding board that provides insight into the views, perspectives, and needs of the future workforce. Fourteen students from around the globe are selected to participate as active members of the Technology Board. These students play a key role in identifying trends that will be invaluable to employers particularly in the area of technology needs of the future workforce. Specifically, the Board members are asked to provide input on how they will use technology in their jobs of the future. The film features short interviews with several of the Board members. Each of these students provides a variation on the same themes—the importance of empowerment, mobile technology, and education. They see these factors as essential for members of their generation and the workforce of the future.

Discussion Questions:
1. What are the major applications of information technology? Are the comments of the Board Members consistent with these applications?
2. Is innovation possible without a commitment to technology?
3. What is the effect of IT on occupations and careers?

Figure 9.7
Four Levels of IT and Computing

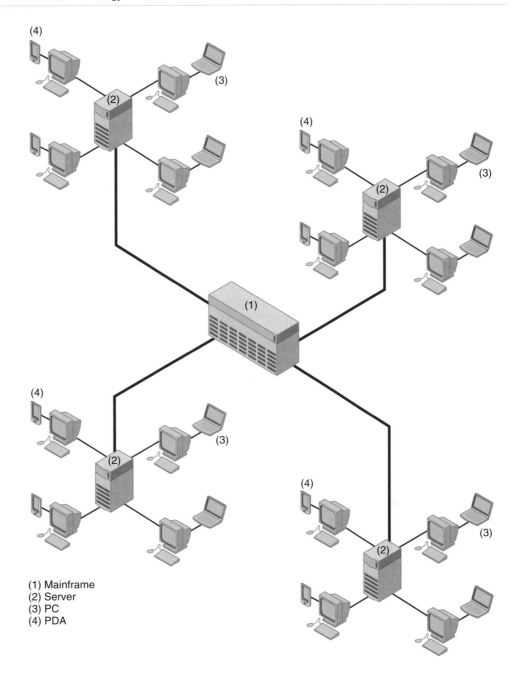

(1) Mainframe
(2) Server
(3) PC
(4) PDA

and wireless technology that connect them into a global network. Companies such as Cisco Systems, which was started by two scientists at Stanford University, pioneered the development of cost-effective network switches and routers that make it possible to link the computer networks of organizations together to form the Internet. A **router** transfers data between networks over the Internet and to its intended destination, such as a specific Web page or a computer anywhere in the world. In an effort to further improve communication between them, researchers later created the first e-mail systems. In 40 years' time IT has evolved from standalone mainframes confined to backrooms to the Internet, a worldwide network of computers with vast amounts of information accessible by anyone with a PC who wants to take the time or trouble to find it.

router Hardware and software that electronically transfers data between networks to its intended destination, such as a specific Web page or computer.

Ethernet A local area communication technology that transmits information between computers at speeds of between 10 and 100 million MBPs using coaxial or fiber optic cable.

Wired and Wireless Broadband Technology

Inside most organizations today, Ethernet cable connections are used to link clients to servers and servers to the mainframe. The Ethernet is a local area network (LAN) communication technology that transmits information between computers at speeds of between 10 and 100 million bits of information per second (MBPs) using coaxial or fiber-optic cables. Ethernet connections are found in networked offices, laboratories, residence hall rooms, and so on. Most people's first connection to the Internet was through a modem phone line connection. The problem with a phone line connection, however, is the limited capacity of ordinary phone lines to carry snippets of data, called "bytes." An Ethernet connection is much faster than a dial-up modem connection. The Ethernet can handle up to 10 million bits of information a second using a coaxial cable. By contrast, if you connect to the Internet through the modem in your PC, (which is mostly likely a 56K modem) you can transmit only 56,000 bytes per second. That's almost ten times slower.

broadband technology A type of communications hardware that allows for the rapid transmission of vast amounts of information.

To rapidly access information on the WWW, communications hardware has been developed that can handle many billions of bytes per second. Broadband technology is a type of communication hardware that allows for the rapid transmission of vast amounts of information like movies and music, for example. Without broadband technology, it might take many hours, or even days, to download a movie from a Web site. To picture broadband transmission, recall IBM's view of computing power as being like a fluid flowing through a pipe. Imagine how much fluid can flow through a pipe one inch in diameter; now imagine how much water can flow through a pipe ten feet in diameter. This is the difference between the information carrying capacity of an advanced broadband technology versus a 28K dial-up modem connection!

By 2000 another major IT breakthrough came in the form of *wireless* broadband technology service. *3G wireless* technology—the technology found in Web-enabled phones—is expected to become the dominant wireless technology; it offers a wireless phone connection to the Internet that is as fast as fiber-optic broadband technology. Other developments in wireless communication are described in the following Business in Action.

Business in Action

Wireless Broadband's Fast Takeoff

Since its introduction in 2001, a wireless broadband technology called Wi-Fi, short for "Wireless Fidelity," has been growing rapidly in popularity. Wi-Fi is a wireless Ethernet technology that operates in the 5Ghz band used for radio-based local area networks. Wi-Fi requires no wires or cables to connect a laptop to the Internet. Laptops from every room of a house or business, or in any location, such as a coffee shop or restaurant, can connect via an access point known as a "hotspot," assuming there's one within frequency range. A Wi-Fi user can also establish a wireless home network with say, six different PCs and laptops sharing access to files, a printer, the Internet, and even stereos, DVD players, and televisions within range. The drawback of the technology is that Wi-Fi hotspots broadcast no more than a few thousand square feet. Some companies like fast-food restaurants and hotel chains offer free Wi-Fi access as a selling point to computer users on the go. In 2003, Intel began selling Centrino, wireless-enabled laptop chips. With Intel's new chip installed, a separate Wi-Fi device no longer needed to be installed on a user's computer. It was already built into new machines.

Another wireless technology called Bluetooth has also become popular and is also being built into PC chips. Bluetooth is a wireless technology that can connect all the different pieces of a computer such as its hard drive, keyboard, screen, printer, and mouse. (It is not a broadband technology, however. It does

Hotels, restaurants, and airports are among the businesses trying to attract mobile computer users by offering Wi-Fi, or access points known as "hot spots."

Wi-Fi A type of Ethernet technology that allows computer users to access the Internet wirelessly.

not link the user to the Internet.) Bluetooth makes computer cables a thing of the past. It can also wirelessly link most devices such as PDAs, stereos, and televisions, into a home IT system.

In 2004, a major advance in wireless broadband arrived when a "super Wi-Fi" technology using a different radio wave frequency was announced. A hotspot equipped with the new technology will have a transmission range of up to 50 miles, similar to cellular phone towers. If and when this super Wi-Fi arrives, it will create serious competition for phone and cable companies.[4]

WIRELESS COMPUTERS AND PERSONAL DIGITAL ASSISTANTS It was this need for people to "compute on the go" that initially led to the development of laptop computers and personal digital assistants (PDAs) in the late 1990s. Using a laptop, with Wi-Fi, for example, a salesperson can perform on-the-spot number crunching, word-processing, and spreadsheet applications to give their customers an immediate response, such as a price quote. Hand-held PDAs were originally designed to perform specific business functions such as work and appointment scheduling, address-book keeping, note taking, and expense tracking. The first of these, introduced in 1996, was the Palm Pilot, an easy-to-use device that sold over 1 million units in just 18 months.

Most new smart phones connect wirelessly to the Web. Smart-phone users can also connect directly to their PCs or to their companies' LANs.

Also in the 1990s, IT companies like Intel and Texas Instruments began to develop more powerful microprocessors that allowed many functions of hand-held devices to be merged. Today, companies like Samsung, Nokia, Sony, and Motorola are making "smart phones." A smart phone is a combination wireless phone, PDA, and laptop. Many of these phones contain word-processing and spreadsheet applications, digital cameras and MP3 and video-game players. Smart phones can also connect to the Web. These amazing devices are continually growing in power and sophistication. They can increase business productivity in many ways. Employees dealing with customers or suppliers can input real-time information into the devices, which can then be transmitted wirelessly to a company's LAN. Because a company's databases are constantly updated, managers can make decisions using more accurate information. Employees negotiating with customers and suppliers in the field can request and obtain immediate assistance using their smart phones, PDAs, and laptops to draw on the information in their company's databases or information their colleagues or managers presently have. This is the ultimate IT goal of most companies: Linking wireless PDAs, smart phones, and laptops, together with the rest of their computer systems. The goal is to have all *four* levels of computing power (mainframe, LAN, PC or laptop, and PDA or smart phone) operate seamlessly together.

Software Components of Information Technology

The need to link the four different levels of computer hardware has helped drive the development of new and improved software. Whenever computers can be integrated, productivity can be increased. Of course, just as in the computer hardware industry, there are many software companies that are competing with one another to do this—SAP, Oracle, Siebel Systems, Microsoft, and IBM, are just a few of them. All the companies that compete in a particular segment of the software market, such as ERP, networking, or security software, try to attract the CIOs of corporations by claiming that their software is the best-of-breed solution, the highest-performing IT application currently available for a particular task. Next, we examine competition in different segments of the software market.

PC Software

best-of-breed solution
The highest-performing IT hardware or software application currently available for managing a particular information processing or multimedia task.

industry standard
A predominant type of technology used in an industry. Other technologies must be compatible with the industry standard in order to be widely adopted.

Microsoft, the world's largest software maker, is, of course, the maker of the Windows operating system, which is installed on more than 90% of the world's PCs. In the 1990s, Windows became the industry standard. Today, PC makers (with the exception of Apple) typically install the Windows operating system on new PCs. A software maker's ability to control an industry standard (like Microsoft has done with Windows) can alter the entire course of hardware and software development. Think of it as a sort of "snowball" effect: The value of any particular kind of software (like Windows), is a function of how many people use the software to communicate, share files, data, and so forth. The more people that can communicate with the software, the more important the software becomes for other people to have.

When a particular software program, such as Windows, becomes the industry standard, more and more software developers will write applications that work with it. In turn, this makes the software that has become the standard even more popular. This is precisely what has happened with Windows. Windows may or may not be the best operating system available; it is, however, the industry standard.

Networking Software

IBM, the originator of the mainframe is still the largest mainframe software maker. However, most of the software sold today is networking software—software that networks one company to another—including their mainframes, servers, PCs, laptops, and PDAs. Networking software allows companies to define, manipulate, analyze, update, store, and share data with one another. Oracle, the second largest software maker after Microsoft, achieved its position because it controls the industry standard for networked, database-management software. One reason for the success of Oracle's software is that it works with Microsoft's Windows software.

Another early leader in the networking software market was Sun Microsystems, which recognized that a gap existed in the market between mainframe computing (controlled by IBM), and PC computing (controlled by Microsoft). Sun focused its efforts on developing powerful servers capable of linking all of a company's servers and PCs together. Sun, in fact, hoped that its servers would one day *replace* most mainframes.

For several years Sun prospered, but it decided that to protect its competitive advantage, it would not make its networking software compatible with the Windows platform. This was a costly mistake because Microsoft later took aim at the server market. Because most PCs use Windows software, it was much easier for companies to use Microsoft's networking software than it was to use Sun's. Today, Microsoft controls over 70% of the server market, and SUN is not even a major player. In fact, Microsoft's biggest competitor in the server market is Linux, which controls a 20% share. Linux, and the threat it poses to Microsoft, is discussed in Business in Action.

Business in Action

Linux Takes on Windows

First developed for use at the mainframe level, Linux is a computer operating system that today works on servers and PCs. It is quickly becoming a very popular choice for CIOs in the server software market because it is relatively inexpensive compared to Microsoft's software. This is because Linux is *open source* software, that is, it is free to download and use. Any company can download the Linux operating software and then configure its computer hardware and software to use it. However, companies often need expert help to customize Linux to their legacy system. This is where the costs come in: Companies have to buy the application software and the expert service needed to install and maintain Linux.

Other companies like IBM, Red Hat, and Hewlett-Packard provide Linux-based software and services in addition to Linux. Indeed, one of IBM's prime e-business strategies is based on using Linux to keep a client company's costs low. In fact, in 2002, IBM announced it was spending $3 billion to make *all* of its software compatible with Linux. Hewlett-Packard has made a similar commitment, and Red Hat is also becoming a major Linux provider.

However, even after paying for these company's software and service, the potential cost savings of using Linux, rather than Microsoft are often enormous. It has been estimated, for example, that to license the Microsoft software necessary to connect just 100 of a client's PCS to a server would cost $40,000 per year. With Linux, that figure falls to several thousand dollars, and most of the money goes towards paying for Linux services, not for the software itself, which can quickly become obsolete.

Not surprisingly, by 2004, over 20% of companies had shifted to Linux. This has cut into Microsoft's revenues in a big way, and the company now views the Linux platform as a major threat. Indeed, one reason that companies like IBM, Hewlett-Packard, Sun, Oracle, and SAP are championing Linux and making their applications software compatible with it, is to reduce Microsoft's power in the software industry. If they can replace Microsoft Windows as the industry standard, they can sell more of their Linux-related software and services. Perhaps much of the profit that Microsoft currently receives from sales of its Windows software could then be captured.

Linux is also reaching down into the PC market. A Linux operating system for PCs, and its accompanying applications package, is currently available free. If users want support, they can buy it from a company like Red Hat at a price much lower than Microsoft charges for Windows XP. For example, in 2003, Wal-Mart sold a complete Linux-based PC for $485. By contrast, a PC loaded with Microsoft XP cost $150 more. If more and more software developers start to write user-friendly applications for Linux, then the gains Linux has made at the server level might trickle down to the PC level. Then, Microsoft will be in real trouble.[5]

Computer Security Software

firewall Software that gives a company's PCs safe access to the Internet but that blocks computers from outside the firm from gaining access to the company's intranet.

hackers People who seek to invade a company's databases and steal the information for malicious or illegal reasons.

The creation of the Internet led to a new software problem for companies—as well as opportunities for others: How to protect a company's systems and data from Internet intruders? Obviously, a company needs to protect the vital, proprietary knowledge contained in its databases from Internet users, some of which might even be competitors. At the same time, a company needs to open up its computers and network to enjoy the efficiency-enhancing benefits the Internet makes possible.

One way to achieve this protection is with a "firewall." A **firewall** is software that gives a company's PCs safe access to the Internet but that blocks computers from outside the firm from gaining access to the company's intranet.(See Figure 9.8.) A firewall is designed to keep out **hackers**, people who seek to invade a company's databases and steal the information in them, often for malicious or illegal reasons.

Figure 9.8
Protecting the Intranet from the Internet by a Firewall

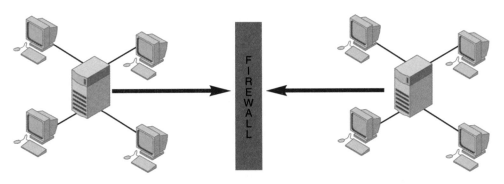

Internet   Intranet

computer virus
Software code deliberately written to harm hardware and software and corrupt files and databases.

The rapid growth of the Internet has also led to a rise in the number of computer viruses. A computer virus is software code deliberately written to harm a company's operating system and software applications software or corrupt its files and databases. Sometimes a virus can wipe out all the information on a computer's hard drive. Differentiating useful information that should be allowed through a company's firewall versus viruses is hard to do. This has led to opportunities for companies like Network Associates and Symantec. These companies work to identify new viruses and quickly write software code to kill them. People and firms are willing to pay for this service because they don't want their computer systems tampered with.

Wireless Hand-Held Software

Whether Linux will make inroads into Windows may depend on which company, or companies, gains control of the industry standard for wireless computing and PDA applications. Here, another competitive battle is currently raging between Palm, Microsoft, and Symbian, a division of Nokia. All have developed competing wireless hand-held operating systems for PDAs, smart phones, new tablet computers that can be networked to a company's computer system.

In the late 1990s, Microsoft realized that PDAs, such as tablet computers, and even, keyboard-equipped smart phones might become powerful enough to become *substitutes* for PCs and laptops. As sales of PDAs increased, sales of PCs would plunge—just as demand for mainframes plunged when powerful PCs became available—and this would threaten the dominant position of Microsoft's Windows software. To avoid this, Microsoft spent billions of dollars developing Windows PocketPC, a Windows operating system for wireless PDAs. Microsoft is striving to make PocketPC the industry standard to protect its competitive advantage. Again, the stakes are high; billions of dollars in future profits are up for grabs. Just as Microsoft hurt Sun when it moved into the server market, Microsoft's move into the PDA market has hurt Palm.

Nokia, the second largest IT company after Microsoft, is desperately trying to prevent Windows PocketPC from becoming the industry standard. Nokia is championing its own standard made by its Symbian division, which is also supported by Sony, Samsung, and Motorola. These companies know if they adopt PocketPC instead, it will inevitably become the industry standard.

IT and Business Occupations

Last, but not least, we should not forget the vital human component of IT. Today, over five million U.S. employees are involved in computer hardware or software development or IT management. More job growth in the last decade has occurred in the IT industry than in any other. Thousands of new occupational jobs such as those for LAN computer managers, expert systems analysts, database managers, and Internet design and hosting specialists have emerged.

Not only has IT created many new kinds of occupational specializations, it has also transformed many other kinds of business occupations. In many industrial settings, for example, computer-controlled technology now runs the production lines and employees at all levels in a company must have the skills necessary to

Did You Know?

According to Intel, computer processing capability is rapidly approaching the "Age of Tera"[6]:

Byte = 8 bits (one character)
Kilobyte = 1000 bytes (very short story)
Megabyte = 106 bytes (small novel)
Gigabyte = 109 bytes (pickup filled with paper)
Terabyte = 1012 bytes (a moderate university library)
Petabyte = 1015 bytes (half of all US college libraries)
Exabyte = 1018 bytes (all words ever spoken)
Zettabyte = 1021 bytes (180 million Libraries of Congress)
Yottabyte = 1024 bytes (180 billion Libraries of Congress)

manage the new computerized systems. In law offices and consulting companies, a major part of an employee's job is to contribute to its knowledge management systems and help improve its performance.

Finally, to understand how much IT impacts any kind of business occupation, consider how it has changed a truck driver's job. Only a few years ago it was common for a truck driver to receive a commission for delivering a load from one city to a second. Very often, the driver would then drive the truck back to the first city empty because it was difficult to get information about the kinds of loads that might need to be shipped from the second city back to the first. Today, most truck drivers have wireless laptops in their cabs linked to a national electronic delivery B2B marketplace. The database contains information about different loads that need to be trucked from city to city. So, a driver can discover what loads are available and then negotiate a price to haul it. Today, drivers rarely return with an empty truck and both drivers and the companies they serve benefit. Shipping costs can be spread over both outward and inward bound journeys. Goods get to consumers more quickly and can be priced more cheaply.

Clearly, never before has it become so important for people, no matter what their occupation is, to become computer literate and develop advanced computer skills. Computers are not toys; they are vital tools people can use to develop their human capital and make themselves more valuable in the marketplace.

Summary of the Chapter

All companies are feeling the effects of changing IT and e-commerce today. Creating and managing a modern IT system is a major challenge for managers at all levels and in all functions of a business organization. Increasingly, gaining competitive advantage and remaining profitable are coming to depend on the possession of a state-of-the-art IT system. This chapter has made the following main points:

1. Information is a set of data, facts, numbers, and words that is organized in such a way that it provides its users with knowledge. The more knowledge managers possess, the better able they are to respond effectively to the competitive business environment in which they operate.

2. Information technology (IT) refers to the many different kinds of computer and communications hardware and software and the skills of the designers, programmers, managers, and technicians who create and manage this technology. IT is used to acquire, define, input, arrange, organize, manipulate, store, and transmit data and information.

3. Four factors determine the usefulness of information: its completeness, quality, relevance, and timeliness. Real-time information is information that is constantly updated. Managers use real-time information to tell how well customers are responding to their products and if a company's profitability is rising or falling as a result.

4. By lowering the costs of information processing, computers make it cost-effective for managers to (1) acquire better data about their operations, and (2) manipulate data to increase their insight about how well a business is operating.

5. The five principal IT applications used in businesses are (a) transaction processing systems, (b) knowledge management systems, (c) expert systems and artificial intelligence, (d) enterprise resource planning systems, and (e) e-commerce systems.

6. The two main kinds of e-commerce are (1) business-to-business (B2B) commerce and (2) business-to-customer (B2C) commerce.

7. The main components of IT hardware are the legacy system, mainframe computers, microprocessors and personal computers; network computers, the Internet, wireless computers and personal digital assistants (PDAs); and wired, wireless, and broadband communication.

8. The main components of IT software are PC software, networking and mainframe software, computer security software, and PDA software.

9. More U.S. job growth in the last decade has occurred in the IT industry than any other. IT has created many new kinds of occupations and transformed other occupations.

Developing Business Skills

QUESTIONS FOR DISCUSSION AND ACTION

1. If you were the manager of a fast-food restaurant, what kinds of data would you collect to measure (a) productivity (b) quality, and (c) responsiveness to customers?

2. What is real-time information and why is it important in business today?

3. In what ways can IT be used to create a competitive advantage?

4. What are the main differences between a knowledge management system and an expert system?

5. *Action.* Find a manager of a company in your city. Interview the manager and identify the main kinds of software applications the manager uses to perform his or her job.

6. Why is the IT industry sometimes called the "industry of industries?"

7. What are the four main levels of computing? If you are the CIO of a large company, what are the biggest IT issues you face?

8. What is an industry software standard and in what ways does it affect the nature of competition between IT companies?

9. What is a tablet computer and how is it different from a laptop or a PDA?

ETHICS IN ACTION

Watching the Web Surfers

You are the IT managers of a company and have been asked by the CEO to install software that will allow you to track the Web sites employees are visiting using their work PCs. The CEO is concerned that some employees are spending too much time playing games, shopping online, or entering chatrooms to amuse themselves. The CEO wants to cut down on these activities. You will be responsible for monitoring the employees' Web-surfing activities.

Using the ethical principles in Chapter 5, think about the ethical issues related to installing Web-monitoring software. Then answer the following questions:

- Is it ethical for a company to monitor the Web sites an employee visits at work?

- Suppose an employee spends his or her lunch hour surfing the Web. Is it ethical to monitor the employee during that time?

- Suppose you find out that an employee who is one of your friends is spending a lot of time in chatrooms trying to find dates. How will you deal with this situation?

- Should employees be told that Web-monitoring software has been installed on the company's computers? Who will be allowed to see the records of the employees' activities?

SMALL GROUP EXERCISE

Laptops or PDAs for Salespeople?

After reading the following scenario, break up into groups of three or four people and discuss the issues involved. Be prepared to share your thinking with the rest of the class.

Your company is a major office supply chain with over 2,000 stores throughout the United States. It is known for excellent customer service, and its salespeople are continually visiting customers to demonstrate new products and help them with the ordering process. Currently, salespeople use laptops and plug into dial-up modems to connect back to corporate headquarters. Your CEO has asked you, a group of

IT managers, to debate the pros and cons of moving to a wireless computing system using PDAs and some kind of broadband technology.

Buying thousands of PDA devices for salespeople and paying for wireless broadband access will be expensive, and the new technology will probably cost a few million dollars or more a year to operate. Your job is to debate the pros and cons of moving to a wireless PDA system.

1. What are the pros and cons associated with salespeople using laptops or PDAs?

2. What are the main disadvantages or disadvantages associated with moving to the new IT system?

3. What features must the PDA have to make it a substitute for a laptop?

4. Which PDA operating system and type of broadband service will be best for your company? Why?

5. What might be some major problems associated with moving to the new IT system?

6. How would you measure if the use of PDAs has increased the productivity of the salesforce?

DEVELOPING GOOD BUSINESS SENSE

Buying Your Own IT

Personal and tablet computers, PDAs, and smart phones are expensive. So is the cost of the broadband service necessary to connect them to the Internet. Like CIOs, most individual consumers have budgets they have to stick to. The purpose of this exercise is for you to investigate the choices and costs of the new IT available on the market and which of it will do the most to increase your "business productivity."

Imagine you have $2,500 to spend on a new computing and communication system. You will be stuck with it throughout college, and you will be responsible for paying for all the hardware and software needed to run it—including broadband access. Search the Internet for relevant information, and then answer the following questions.

1. What are the pros and cons associated with buying a personal computer, a tablet computer, or a PDA equipped with an external keyboard?

2. Given your personal needs, which of these, or which combination of these, is best for you?

3. What would be the most economical, but functional, system given that technology is rapidly changing?

4. How will the nature of the operating systems these devices use affect your decision? For example, is Linux software an option for you? What must you be careful about to avoid buying hardware or software that is already outdated technologically?

5. Which broadband service should you choose? Why?

6. Calculate the cost of purchasing you ideal system. Did you meet or exceed your budget?

EXPLORING THE WORLD WIDE WEB

Using mySAP ERP

Go to the Web site of SAP, the ERP software company discussed in the chapter. Then click on "Solutions," "mySAP ERP," and read the business case about Phenix Optics at http://www. sap.com/solutions/business-suite/erp/pdf/CS_Phenix_

Optics.pdf (or any other case your instructor assigns). **For more Web activities, log on to www.mhhe.com/ jonesintro.**

1. Why did Phenix Optics choose ERP software to enhance its business performance?

2. What kinds of benefits did the company obtain by using mySAP ERP?

BusinessWeek   CASE FOR DISCUSSION

Nailing the Design before You Build

Saturn Electronics & Engineering Inc.'s growth strategy hinges on software. The privately held maker of electronic components in Auburn Hills, Michigan, wants to play in the global leagues to better serve its big manufacturing customers. For starters, Saturn has set up shop in the Philippines. There, some 40 engineers pick up work that is still pending when their U.S. counterparts head home at day's end. Adding a second day shift means Saturn can deliver products faster and more cheaply.

To make this transpacific collaboration go smoothly, engineering director Paul Fleck invested more than $1 million in two programs—one coordinates the on-line design process, the other watches over product-development costs. It was a gutsy move for a company with less than $400 million in revenues. But Fleck expects the new software from Agile Software Corp. to pay for itself within 18 months through a combination of cost savings and new business.

Saturn is just one of a growing crowd of midsize manufacturers spending big bucks on the industry's latest craze: product life-cycle management. PLM is unleashing a revolution in product development, with tools for improving everything from design and engineering to manufacturing and field service—even final disposal of discarded products. Market researcher CIMdata Inc. pegs PLM's sales this year at nearly $15 billion, heading to more than $20 billion in 2008.

In the 1990s, PLM was used mainly by automotive and aerospace giants. Early versions of the software were pricey integrated suites, but PLM vendors now offer separate modules, like the two that Saturn bought. Moreover, to small companies, PLM's promises sounded too much like the hype surrounding previous enterprise-software programs, which often didn't live up to their hoopla.

So what's different about PLM? That's simple, says Monica A. Schnitger, a senior vice president at market researcher Daratech Inc. PLM emphasizes new-revenue generation, or top-line growth, as opposed to cutting costs. "Most companies have done about as much cost-cutting as they can. The best way to increase revenue is to get better products to market more quickly."

That potential has universal appeal across all manufacturing sectors, not just in high tech. "Top-line growth is the key benefit," concurs Stephen A. Segal, chief information officer at Canada's Loewen Windows, which makes wood-framed windows and doors for luxury homes in a factory near Calgary. For its first PLM module, Loewen last year plunked down

$150,000 for a Catia computer-aided design and engineering (CAD/CAE) system from IBM. "Since everything we build is made to order, our lead times are typically four to six weeks," says Segal. "If we can knock off one week, the payback from faster revenues will be in the millions of dollars every year."

For large companies, PLM's product-portfolio management tools offer a different route to better top-line numbers. "At companies with complex portfolios, like Nike Inc. or Stanley Works, the key thing you want to understand is which products are worth investing in," says James E. Heppelman, executive vice president at Parametric Technology Corp., a PLM supplier in Needham, Mass. "PLM can tell you that," he says, by correlating the better-margin items with market intelligence on what's likely to sell.

TRICKLE-DOWN TECH

Some small and midsize companies that have been slow to see the light are getting pulled into PLM by the bigger manufacturers they serve. "Once they get a little experience, they see the benefits, too," says Robert M. Nierman, president of business strategy at UGS PLM Solutions, a unit of Electronic Data Systems Corp. "There's a trickle-down effect from the aerospace and auto industries, which bit off PLM first."

In the 1990s, Detroit had a huge anchor weighing down product development: incompatible CAD and product-data management (PDM) systems, where designs are stored with information on materials and CAE data. At General Motors Corp., each division had its own CAD and PDM system, and most couldn't talk to their counterparts in other departments, notes Michael Burkett, research director at market watcher AMR Research Inc. So when a CAD file got passed to a CAE system and then to a factory computer, the data had to be manually translated. Not only did manual reentry waste time, it led to countless errors. By the late '90s, the car industry's bill for fixing these goofs was running around $900 million a year, according to a study by the National Institute of Standards & Technology.

GM became a PLM champion when it started to clean shop in the mid-1990s. Product designs and related data were then stored on 1,500 different servers, says Burkett. Just consolidating that army of computers has saved millions in annual maintenance costs. In addition, GM launched a sweeping program to standardize its CAD and PDM tools so designs could flit instantly and flawlessly among computers. As GM brought in PLM software and insisted its suppliers follow suit, its product-cycle times steadily shrunk, from 44 months to the current 18 months.

PLM is also curbing the plague of engineering change orders. Such changes have been an eternal curse on factories everywhere. Detroit still handles some 300,000 orders of this sort each year, at an average cost of $50,000 each. And that can get multiplied tenfold if time and money must also be spent to revise the so-called jigs and fixtures that hold parts in machine tools or on assembly lines. "The PLM agenda," says Eric Sterling, a UGS vice president, "is to make sure it's right the first time, before you build anything."

Right-the-first-time designs: It's the mantra of both analysts and new PLM converts. "Getting the design right produces numerous benefits," says Oliver Masefield, vice president for engineering at Eclipse Aviation Corp. The Albuquerque startup is developing a small twin-jet plane—and leaning on a full-blown PLM suite to coordinate with suppliers in Japan, China, and Britain that will build the wings, nose section, and fuselage. Eclipse's supply chain will be guided by virtually perfect digital prototypes. "We model everything down to the minutest detail," Masefield says, "including each and every rivet."

Engineering-analysis tools that plug into CAD systems can now create digital prototypes so functionally realistic that Floyd Rose, head of Floyd Rose Guitar Co. in Redmond, Washington, didn't bother to build a physical prototype of an electric guitar he unveiled in 2001. He just used his Catia-created model to begin production—and moved up the launch date by several months.

In fact, when CAD equipment is linked to PLM's oversight capabilities, the system can become smart enough to suggest its own designs, which engineers then tweak. That's how Delta Marin, a marine-engineering company in Turku, Finland, developed a new bridge for big container ships. Designers fed into the computer the maritime regulations for visibility over and around the containers stacked on deck so captains can see a safe distance ahead of the ship, and the CAE system calculated what was permissible.

Such capabilities "are going to make a huge difference," says Paul G.P. Hoogenboom, CIO at RPM International Inc., a Medina (Ohio) chemicals company with subsidiaries in 17 countries. It markets Rust-Oleum paint and other products that also must meet many regulatory requirements. "With PLM, compliance is built into the workflow," he says. "The system won't allow you to create a formulation with a material" that isn't approved.

PLM towers over previous efforts to integrate product development, says AMR's Burkett. When other enterprise-software juggernauts came to market a decade or more ago, he notes, "the type of thought processes that now dominate manufacturing [in this online age] didn't even exist." The Internet changed mind sets—and PLM is fundamentally revamping the rules of product development to fit manufacturing's new global game.

Source: Otis Port, "Nailing the Design before You Build," *BusinessWeek Online,* May 31, 2004.

QUESTIONS

1. What is PLM software and why is it being used increasingly with CAD software?

2. How can this software be used to increase a company's global competitive advantage (for example, its superior efficiency, quality, innovation, and customer responsiveness)?

BusinessWeek CASE FOR DISCUSSION

Outsourcing Innovation

HTC? Flextronics? Cellon? There's a good reason these are hardly household names. The multimedia devices produced from their prototypes will end up on retail shelves under the brands of companies that don't want you to know who designs their products. Yet these and other little-known companies, with names such as Quanta Computer, Premier Imaging, Wipro Technologies, and Compal Electronics, are fast emerging as hidden powers of the technology industry.

They are the vanguard of the next step in outsourcing—of innovation itself. When Western corporations began selling their factories and farming out manufacturing in the '80s and '90s to boost effi-

ciency and focus their energies, most insisted all the important research and development would remain in-house.

But that pledge is now passé. Today, the likes of Dell, Motorola, and Philips are buying complete designs of some digital devices from Asian developers, tweaking them to their own specifications, and slapping on their own brand names. It's not just cell phones. Asian contract manufacturers and independent design houses have become forces in nearly every tech device, from laptops and high-definition TVs to MP3 music players and digital cameras. "Customers used to participate in design two or three years back," says Jack Hsieh, vice president for finance at Taiwan's Premier Imaging Technology

Corp., a major supplier of digital cameras to leading U.S. and Japanese brands. "But starting last year, many just take our product. Because of price competition, they have to."

While the electronics sector is furthest down this road, the search for offshore help with innovation is spreading to nearly every corner of the economy. Boeing said it is working with India's HCL Technologies to co-develop software for everything from the navigation systems and landing gear to the cockpit controls for its upcoming 7E7 Dreamliner jet. Pharmaceutical giants such as GlaxoSmithKline and Eli Lilly are teaming up with Asian biotech research companies in a bid to cut the average $500 million cost of bringing a new drug to market. And Procter & Gamble Co. says it wants half of its new product ideas to be generated from outside by 2010, compared with 20% now.

Competitive Dangers

Underlying this trend is a growing consensus that more innovation is vital—but that current R&D spending isn't yielding enough bang for the buck. After spending years squeezing costs out of the factory floor, back office, and warehouse, CEOs are asking tough questions about their once-cloistered R&D operations: Why are so few hit products making it out of the labs into the market? How many of those pricey engineers are really creating game-changing products or technology breakthroughs? "R&D is the biggest single remaining controllable expense to work on," says Allen J. Delattre, head of Accenture Ltd.'s high-tech consulting practice. "Companies either will have to cut costs or increase R&D productivity."

The result is a rethinking of the structure of the modern corporation. What, specifically, has to be done in-house anymore? At a minimum, most leading Western companies are turning toward a new model of innovation, one that employs global networks of partners. These can include U.S. chipmakers, Taiwanese engineers, Indian software developers, and Chinese factories. IBM is even offering the smarts of its famed research labs and a new global team of 1,200 engineers to help customers develop future products using next-generation technologies. When the whole chain works in sync, there can be a dramatic leap in the speed and efficiency of product development.

The downside of getting the balance wrong, however, can be steep. Start with the danger of fostering new competitors. Motorola hired Taiwan's BenQ Corp. to design and manufacture millions of mobile phones. But then BenQ began selling phones last year in the prized China market under its own brand. That prompted Motorola to pull its contract. Another risk is that brand-name companies will lose the incentive to keep investing in new technology. "It is a slippery slope," says Boston Consulting Group Senior

Vice President Jim Andrew. "If the innovation starts residing in the suppliers, you could incrementalize yourself to the point where there isn't much left."

Such perceptions are a big reason even companies that outsource heavily refuse to discuss what hardware designs they buy from whom and impose strict confidentiality on suppliers. "It is still taboo to talk openly about outsourced design," says Forrester Research Inc. consultant Navi Radjou, an expert on corporate innovation.

The concerns also explain why different companies are adopting widely varying approaches to this new paradigm. Dell, for example, does little of its own design for notebook PCs, digital TVs, or other products. Hewlett-Packard Co. says it contributes key technology and at least some design input to all its products but relies on outside partners to co-develop everything from servers to printers. Motorola buys complete designs for its cheapest phones but controls all of the development of high-end handsets like its hot-selling Razr. The key, execs say, is to guard some sustainable competitive advantage, whether it's control over the latest technologies, the look and feel of new products, or the customer relationship. "You have to draw a line," says Motorola CEO Edward J. Zander. At Motorola, "core intellectual property is above it, and commodity technology is below."

You can see this great divide already taking shape in global electronics. The process started in the 1990s when Taiwan emerged as the capital of PC design, largely because the critical technology was standardized, on Microsoft Corp.'s operating system software and Intel Corp.'s microprocessor. Today, Taiwanese "original-design manufacturers" (ODMs), so named because they both design and assemble products for others, supply some 65% of the world's notebook PCs. Quanta Computer Inc. alone expects to churn out 16 million notebook PCs this year in 50 different models for buyers that include Dell, Apple Computer, and Sony.

Now, Taiwanese ODMs and other outside designers are forces in nearly every digital device on the market. Of the 700 million mobile phones expected to be sold worldwide this year, up to 20% will be the work of ODMs, estimates senior analyst Adam Pick of the El Segundo (California) market research firm iSuppli Corp. About 30% of digital cameras are produced by ODMs, 65% of MP3 players, and roughly 70% of personal digital assistants (PDAs). Building on their experience with PCs, they're increasingly creating recipes for their own gizmos, blending the latest advances in custom chips, specialized software, and state-of-the-art digital components. "There is a lot of great capability that has grown in Asia to develop complete products," says Doug Rasor, worldwide strategic marketing manager at chipmaker Texas Instruments Inc. TI often supplies core chips, along with rudimentary designs, and the ODMs take it from there. "They can do the system integration, the plastics, the industrial design, and the low-cost manufacturing, and they are happy to put Dell's name on it. That is a megatrend in the industry," says Rasor.

Perhaps the most ambitious new entrant in design is Flextronics. The manufacturing behemoth already builds networking gear, printers, game consoles, and other hardware for the likes of Nortel Networks, Xerox, Hewlett-Packard, Motorola, and Casio Computer. But three years ago, it started losing big cell-phone and PDA orders to Taiwanese ODMs. Since then, CEO Michael E. Marks has shelled out more than $800 million on acquisitions to build a 7,000-engineer force of software, chip, telecom, and mechanical designers scattered from India and Singapore to France and Ukraine. Marks's splashiest move was to pay an estimated $30 million for frog design Inc., the pioneering Sunnyvale (California) firm that helped design such Information Age icons as Apple Computer Inc.'s original Mac in 1984. So far, Flextronics has developed its own basic platforms for cell phones, routers, digital cameras, and imaging devices. His goal is to make Flextronics a low-cost, soup-to-nuts developer of consumer-electronics and tech gear.

Marks has an especially radical take on where all this is headed: He believes Western tech conglomerates are on the cusp of a sweeping overhaul of R&D that will rival the offshore shift of manufacturing. In the 1990s, companies like Flextronics "completely restructured the world's electronics manufacturing," says Marks. "Now we will completely restructure design." When you get down to it, he argues, some 80% of engineers in product development do tasks that can easily be outsourced—like translating prototypes into workable designs, upgrading mature products, testing quality, writing user manuals, and qualifying parts vendors. What's more, most of the core technologies in today's digital gadgets are available to anyone. And circuit boards for everything from cameras to network switches are becoming simpler because more functions are embedded on semiconductors. The "really hard technology work" is migrating to chipmakers such as Texas Instruments, Qualcomm, Philips, Intel, and Broadcom, Marks says. "All electronics are on the same trajectory of becoming silicon surrounded by plastic."

Why then, Marks asks, should Nokia, Motorola, Sony-Ericsson, Alcatel, Siemens, Samsung, and other brand-name companies all largely duplicate one another's efforts? Why should each spend $30 million to develop a new smartphone or $200 million on a cellular base station when they can just buy the hardware designs? The ultimate result, he says: Some electronics giants will shrink their R&D

forces from several thousand to a few hundred, concentrating on proprietary architecture, setting key specifications, and managing global R&D teams. "There is no doubt the product companies are going to have fewer people design stuff," Marks predicts. "It's going to get ugly."

Close to the Heart

Still, most companies insist they will continue to do most of the critical design work—and have no plans to take a meat ax to R&D. A Motorola spokesman says it plans to keep R&D spending at around 10% for the long term. Lucent says its R&D staff should remain at about 9,000, after several years of deep cuts. And while many Western companies are downsizing at home, they are boosting hiring at their own labs in India, China, and Eastern Europe. "Companies realize if they want a sustainable competitive advantage, they will not get it from outsourcing," says President Frank M. Armbrecht of the Industrial Research Institute, which tracks corporate R&D spending.

Companies also worry about the message they send investors. Outsourcing manufacturing, tech support, and back-office work makes clear financial sense. But ownership of design strikes close to the heart of a corporation's intrinsic value. If a company depends on outsiders for design, investors might ask, how much intellectual property does it really own, and how much of the profit from a hit product flows back into its own coffers, rather than being paid out in licensing fees? That's one reason Apple Computer lets the world know it develops its hit products in-house, to the point of etching "Designed by Apple in California" on the back of each iPod.

Yet some outsourcing holdouts are changing their tune. Nokia long prided itself on developing almost everything itself—to the point of designing its own chips. No longer. Given the complexities of today's technologies and supply chains, "nobody can master it all," says Chief Technology Officer Pertti Korhonen. "You have to figure out what is core and what is context." Lucent says outsourcing some development makes sense so that its engineers can concentrate on next-generation technologies. "This frees up talent to work on new product lines," says Dave Ayers, vice president for platforms and engineering. "Outsourcing isn't about moving jobs. It's about the flexibility to put resources in the right places at the right time."

It's also about brutal economics and the relentless demands of consumers. To get shelf space at a Best Buy or Circuit City often means brand-name companies need a full range of models, from a $100 point-and-shoot digital camera with 2 megapixels, say, to a $700 8-megapixel model that doubles as a videocam and is equipped with a powerful zoom lens. On top of this, superheated competition can reduce hit products to cheap commodities within months. So they must get out the door fast to earn a decent margin. "Consumer electronics have become almost like produce," says Michael E. Fawkes, senior vice president of Hewlett-Packard's Imaging Products Div. "They always have to be fresh."

Source: Pete Engardio and Bruce Einhorn, "Outsourcing Innovation," *BusinessWeek Online*, March 21, 2005.

QUESTIONS

1. Why is the issue of whether a company should make its own hardware and software or buy it from another company so important today?

2. What factors affect the decision a company makes?

BUILDING YOUR MANAGEMENT SKILLS
Know Thyself

Do you like to have the latest cell phone or PDA available? Do you always sit in the same seat in class and resent having to move to another spot? Individuals deal with change differently. Some welcome it eagerly and others resist. What's more, people may react differently in some situations than others. In organizations, managers are often required to coordinate and implement change that meets some resistance. Try the exercise on your Student DVD called "Technological Change" to analyze the barriers to change in three scenarios.

CHAPTER VIDEO
Hillerich & Bradsby

Hillerich and Bradsby are best known for the first name in bats—the Louisville Slugger. Beginning in 1857 as a manufacturer of butter churners, the company became the leading supplier of baseball bats in the world. Baseball bats were the company's sole products until the 1960's when Golf and Hockey equipment were added to their product lines. Wooden bats were the only bats made by Hillerich & Bradsby until 1978 when they joined the aluminum bat market.

The culture is one of innovation based upon a strong family tradition of caring for one another, according to the CEO. Leaders are promoted from within the company and serve as coaches. These values were put to the test in the 1990s, however.

The computer system for the company, its Legacy system, would no longer be supported after the turn of the century (or Y 2K). Competition was getting fierce and the firm's internal systems were no longer efficient or effective. There were problems in all areas including order entry, production and inventory control. The company faced a crucial decision—to implement a system of connected stand-alone computers or to start over moving toward supply chain management that integrated all functions within a central database.

The decision was made to replace the Legacy system with an ERP system (Enterprise Resource Planning). The transition was long, difficult, and challenging. During the transition, management considered "pulling the plug on ERP." The investment in ERP was significant and no bottom line savings would be realized for a long period of time.

The transition took 18 months to configure the new ERP system; this resulted in high levels of stress throughout the organization, and mistakes on production and inventory abounded. It was five years before quantifiable savings were realized. However, with the new system 85% of orders are shipped on time and complete compared to only 40% using the Legacy system. Customer satisfaction ranges from 90-95% with the new system fully operational.

1. Which of the major applications of information technology did Hillerich and Bradsby turn to? Why?

2. Evaluate Hillerich and Bradsby's ERP system as it relates to two of the characteristics of useful information (complete and reliable).

3. What impact on "costs" do computers have in relation to IT?

10 Marketing and Product Development:

Creating and Positioning Goods and Services

Learning Objectives

After studying this chapter you should be able to:

1. Explain how marketing, product development, and sales must coordinate their activities to align a company's products with customer needs.

2. Describe how marketing research can identify customer needs.

3. Identify the four main elements of the marketing mix and discuss how the marketing mix is used to differentiate a company's products.

4. Describe how marketing research can identify the needs of different customer groups and market segments.

5. Differentiate between the three main approaches to market segmentation.

WHY IS THIS IMPORTANT ?

Does your car have a driver side airbag? Perhaps it is a later model that came equipped with driver and passenger side airbags and anti-lock brakes. Maybe it is an even newer model and has side airbags and a Global Positioning System (GPS). Manufacturers continually add new features and products to encourage consumers to upgrade to a better model, whether it is a car, a cell phone, or a PDA.

Developing and marketing products and services are primary functions in the value chain that are critical to creating the competitive advantage that are needed for a successful business model. This chapter explains the processes managers use to decide which innovations can be brought to market most profitably and how to appeal to markets that will be willing and able to buy.

A Question of Business
General Motors' Marketing Approach

How has GM's approach to marketing its cars changed over time?

In the 1920s, Ford was the leading car maker. Henry Ford based his business model on offering customers one kind of car—no matter what their different needs were. "You can have any color as long as it's black," Ford was known to say. By offering only one model, Ford kept its operating costs to a minimum and its car prices low to attract as many buyers as possible.

Ford's approach worked well until the U.S. car market started to change as the income of Americans rose. Alfred Sloan, GM's CEO, recognized that car buyers were willing to pay more for cars that offered them superior performance, features, or styling not available in an "average car" like the Model T. In essence Sloan had discovered that different groups or customers, who had different needs, had emerged in the car market. Sloan then created a business model to take advantage of this opportunity, a model based on marketing and selling different kinds of cars to better meet the needs of different kinds of car buyers.

To put his new business model into action Sloan took GM's twenty-two different car divisions and grouped them into five main divisions by brand: Chevrolet, Pontiac, Oldsmobile, Buick, and Cadillac. The models produced under these five brand names were organized into five price ranges, from least to most expensive. Chevrolet-brand cars were priced the lowest; Pontiacs were more expensive, and so on, up to the most expensive cars of all, Cadillacs.

Sloan spent millions of dollars to send a clear marketing message to customers that the cars in the next higher-priced division were different and superior in some way to the cars in the division below. He also made sure the style of cars offered by each division was different. So, for example, the cars in more expensive divisions had more chrome, bigger fins, bigger engines, and, of course, were larger than the others. He also gave each brand of car a kind of "personality," or "identity." Pickup trucks became closely associated with the Chevrolet division, a brand marketed to appeal to "hard working" Americans like farmers and tradespeople. Upwardly mobile Americans were encouraged to choose an Oldsmobile; successful professionals were encouraged to choose a Buick; and if people really hit the jackpot, then the ultimate choice was a Cadillac. Even more importantly, Sloan also made sure that a particular brand's *highest-priced* car always cost more than the *lowest-priced* car in the next brand up the line. This encouraged people who were thinking about buying a new car to continually think in terms of trading up to a more expensive brand.(In truth, persuading customers to buy a particular GM brand was less important to Sloan than making them GM customers for life.)

Sloan's marketing strategy was enormously successful. It resulted in a huge increase in sales of GM's cars. GM's marketing had convinced customers that—due to their own success—they should spend more money to get the GM car they deserved. The automaker's customers were very loyal, and, for decades, the company was the largest and most profitable in the world. In fact, until the 1970s, GM controlled a huge percent of the car market—over 40%.

This all changed, however, in the 1980s and 1990s when Japanese and European carmakers entered the U.S. car market with smaller, high-quality, more fuel-efficient cars aimed at economy-minded customers—a market segment that wasn't being served. Soon, these foreign automakers were introducing upscale cars and capturing customers in many different market segments. GM's cars were suddenly beginning to look old-fashioned, and the company's market share started to fall.

GM responded by changing the design of its cars. To cut costs, it shared the same product design and engineering across divisions. The problem was that Buicks and Cadillacs started to look the same, and the company's different brands lost their identity. Moreover, the design and quality of GM's entry-level cars were far below those of the Japanese.

In an effort to continue the fight, GM launched the Saturn brand name in the 1980s. It also told Cadillac's managers to find a unique new approach to styling these cars. Although these moves met with some success, customers still had no idea what GM Oldsmobiles, for example, were supposed to be offering them, and this division's entry-level cars attracted few buyers. In 2000, GM decided to close down the Oldsmobile division and introduce new Chevrolet, Pontiac, and Buick models at a rapid pace. However, the company's marketing message still failed to resonate with many consumers, and its market share continued to drop—to less than 30%.

When in early 2005 GM announced much poorer than expected sales, its stock price plunged to levels not seen since the early 1990s. The challenge facing its managers is to design, build, and then market the right model cars to better position itself against its Japanese and European rivals. GM believes it has the ability to do this and expects to recover by the end of the decade. Industry analysts are not so sure, however.[1]

Overview

As the story of GM's marketing efforts suggests, the goal of marketing and product development is to find ways to make customers want to buy a company's products. This is the first of two chapters that examine the many issues related to developing attractive new products and successfully marketing and selling them.

In this chapter we first describe the nature of marketing and the relationship between marketing, product development, and sales. Second, we focus on the three most important issues in marketing and market research, how to (1) identify and shape customer needs in a particular market, (2) identify different groups of customers or market segments, and create products to meet the needs of these groups, and (3) use the marketing mix to create distinctive or differentiated products that satisfy different customer needs and customer groups.

By the end of this chapter, you will understand how a company's profitability depends on the ability of its marketing function to send a strong and consistent message to customers about the value of the firm's products. Then, in Chapter 11 we take an in-depth look at some additional marketing mix issues–distribution, sales, and customer relationship management–that are becoming increasingly important today.

The Power of Marketing

We discussed in Chapter 1 how *profit,* from a customer's point of view, can be regarded as their judgments about whether or not they are better off by acquiring and consuming some good or service. I profit from trade when I believe that I have obtained something more valuable than the money I had to spend to get it. Money is a scarce resource, so a person always has to make choices about what products to buy.

If I have $100 to spend on clothing, for example, should I buy some casual shirts and pants or the business suit I know I will need for a future job interview? And, if I choose to buy the shirts, there is usually a range of competing products to choose from. Should I spend all $100 on that stylish Ralph Lauren designer shirt I have been wanting for some time? Or, should I spend my $100 on three good-quality shirts from Lands' End? People are always faced with this problem–they have to constantly decide which products will satisfy their needs the most.

Maslow's need hierarchy, discussed in Chapter 7, suggests some factors that affect this decision. For example, if satisfying my physiological and security needs is my most pressing goal, to save my $100 I might go to a local thrift store and search for the best donated shirts I can find. That way, I will have enough money to pay my rent. Or perhaps I will go to Wal-Mart or Target to take advantage of their low prices. If my budget is sufficient, then I might decide to use my $100 to satisfy my self-esteem or belongingness needs and go to a department store and buy a Ralph Lauren or Tommy Hilfiger shirt. My friends wear these brands, and the fact that I can afford to buy them sends a signal to others that I am "doing well." If I really want to make an impression and show the world how successful I am, I might go to Neiman Marcus or Nordstrom's and spend $500 on a silk Gucci or Versace shirt.

Some people actually do satisfy their self-actualization needs with the clothes they wear. Stunning designer clothes, made with the finest materials and workmanship are things of beauty to many people. People who perhaps have plenty money but are thrifty might self-actualize by managing to buy $500 worth of designer clothes on sale for $150. Often people do not realize that when expensive clothes have been marked down significantly, an exclusive designer shirt from Dillard's or Macy's can cost less than one of the designer lines sold at Wal-Mart or Target.

People who are good shoppers understand the *relative value* of different products and know how to make their money go the farthest. Indeed, research has shown that people who have the most money tend to be the thriftiest shoppers of all! Although rich people do not have to think twice about buying whatever shirt they want, when it comes to high-ticket items, they often want to spend their money wisely. On the other hand, people with the least money are frequently inclined to make spur-of-the-moment purchases. They are the people who see a beautiful shirt and "just have to have it," running up their credit card bills in the process.

As this discussion suggests, the factors that motivate people to buy different goods and services are complex because the needs of people are complex. Yet, the total amount of money consumers spend on goods and services drives the whole of a nation's economy. In fact, 65% of all sales in the United States are made by individual consumers. The U.S. economy is strong because its citizens have a considerable amount of buying power; they also feel confident about their ability to earn money in the future, which makes them less worried about going into debt.

Some people satisfy their self-actualization needs through the kinds of clothes they wear.

By contrast when people are uncertain about their future ability to earn money, they spend less and try to reduce their debt. If this happens an economy can falter and go into recession. When people purchase fewer goods and services, companies make less money and hire fewer employees. Some employees get laid off. Companies also cut back on their purchases of inputs and components. As a result, the suppliers of these inputs are also forced to lay off employees. Unemployed workers spend less, resulting in yet more layoffs. A vicious cycle develops. Over time, the total amount of spending power of people in an economy falls, and business goes from bad to worse. Marketing can help prevent this from happening, however, by boosting people's desire to spend their money.

What Is Marketing?

Let's now discuss marketing in terms of a company's activities versus the economy as a whole. The way in which marketing as a functional activity is viewed has been changing rapidly in the last decade. It used to be said that *marketing* was about getting the message about a product—its qualities, features, and ability to satisfy customer needs—to customers who would never be "seen." By contrast, *sales* was about getting the message to customers who *would* be seen, by salespeople, for example. Marketing relied on national advertising media like TV, radio, and newspapers to reach the "mass market"—the millions of anonymous customers a company could never reach using a regular salesforce.

marketing An organizational function and a set of processes for creating, communicating, and delivering value to customers and for managing customer relationships in ways that benefit the organization and its stakeholders.

Marketing is about persuading customers a product meets their needs and convincing them to buy it. Some people would argue that marketing is also about getting people to buy something they never even *knew* they needed. For example, Nike's marketers try to make people feel they *need* Nike sneakers. But what these people really need are foot coverings or shoes. A primary marketing task is to devise a marketing plan that will capture the attention of customers and create a place for the company's product—a *product image or identity*—in their minds, whether they need it or not.

Today, however, this has become a much more complicated task. First, the mass market has fragmented into many different groups of customers who have different needs, so reaching large numbers of customers who want any one particular product is much more difficult. Some marketers, such as Philip Kotler, an eminent scholar, argue that marketing has to focus on developing "one-on-one" relationship with the customer—that it must find a way for the company to build a personal rapport with customers because it is so much harder to get their attention these days: New communication media—the Internet satellite TV, cell phones and PDAs—mean that people are constantly being bombarded with information in multiple ways. Moreover, the growing number of products—cars, electronics, sneakers, shirts, food and drink, and music—in all kinds of categories have made it much more difficult for marketers to grab people's attention.

Table 10.1
The Changing Nature of Marketing

Definition of Marketing, 1985
"Marketing is the process of planning and executing the conception, pricing, promotion, and distribution of ideas, goods, and services to create exchanges that satisfy individual and organizational objectives."

Definition of Marketing, 2004
"Marketing is an organizational function and a set of processes for creating, communicating, and delivering value to customers and for managing customer relationships in ways that benefit the organization and its stakeholders."

Source: The American Marketing Association, *Marketing News*, September 15, 2004, p. 17.

Recognizing this, the American Marketing Association (AMA) decided to change its definition of marketing based on the need expressed by Kotler–the need to build relationships and deliver value to customers. The old and new definitions of marketing are presented in Table 10.1.

customer needs
Consumer needs that can be satisfied by the qualities or features of a good or service.

product development
The set of technical, scientific, and engineering processes involved in creating new or improved products to better satisfy customer needs.

sales The development and use of techniques to inform customers about the value of a company's products in order to persuade them to buy them.

customer relationship management The process of tracking the demand and satisfaction of customers in an effort to develop products they will want to buy on an ongoing basis.

Marketing, Product Development, and Sales

The new definition of marketing adopted by the AMA reflects the complexities just noted that make it harder for companies to get close to customers. When companies can get close to their customers, they are better able to understand their needs and deliver more value to them. Customer needs are needs that can be satisfied by what a good or service has to offer. In marketing today it is much more difficult to (1) discover unmet customer needs, (2) identify what kinds of products can meet those needs, and (3) develop new products that satisfy those needs better than competing products. Gaining access to this information is vital because marketers use it to decide what kinds of qualities or features a product should have and how it should be made. It also requires that marketing integrate its information-gathering activities with the firm's product development and sales functions. Product development relates to the technical, scientific, and engineering processes involved in creating new or improved products to better satisfy customer needs. Sales is the process of informing people about the value of a product and persuading them to buy it versus competing products. Customer relationship management (CRM) is the process of developing an ongoing relationship with customers to maximize the value the firm can deliver to them over time. (Sales and CRM, which are both vital aspects of the marketing task today, are discussed in more detail in Chapter 11.) Business in Action illustrates how, by listening to customers, 3M has created a plethora of best-selling products.

Business in Action

Creating New Products at 3M

3M is one of the most successful innovators of new products in the world. 3M uses many different technologies to create thousands of new and improved products for companies and individual consumers each year. To encourage successful new product development, 3M has set a challenging stretch goal. The stretch goal specifies that 30% of 3M's annual revenues be earned from the sale of products developed in the previous three years. This goal encourages the company's employees to behave like entrepreneurs and find new ways to create products customers will value and buy.

Sometimes, the process of developing new products at 3M begins with finding a technology to make a product that better meets an existing customer need. In 1904, for example, 3M's engineers discovered a new technology that allowed them to bond grit to paper. The result was a blockbuster product–the first sandpaper. 3M developed and marketed sandpaper because it firmly believed there was a large, unmet consumer need for such an inexpensive, easy-to-use abrasive.

In many cases, however, it is more difficult for a company to discern what the customer's needs are–or even to discover potential uses for a new product. The way two other 3M products, Scotch masking tape and Post-It Notes, were developed illustrates this. The story of Scotch tape begins when Dick Drew, a 3M scientist, visited an auto body shop in St. Paul, Minnesota, to test a new kind of sandpaper he was developing. Two-tone cars were popular then, and Drew watched as paint shop employees improvised a way to keep one color of paint from being over sprayed onto the other. The workers used a paint shield made up of a combination of heavy adhesive tape and butcher paper. Very often, as they pulled the shield off after the paint was dry, it took the other colored paint with it. Employees joked with Drew that it would be a good idea if 3M could develop a product that made the job easier.

Drew realized that what was needed was a tape with a *weaker* glue or adhesive that would not pull the paint off. He went back to his lab to develop such a glue and, after many attempts, used it to develop the first masking tape. Paint shop employees now had a way to detach butcher paper from a car and achieve a first-class paint job. Once the success of the new product was proven, Drew and 3M's marketing and salespeople began to think about other uses to which masking tape could be put. It soon became clear that the need for a reliable way to seal, wrap, or attach something meant that the uses for masking tape were endless. Drew continued his research. In 1930, he invented clear cellophane tape to better meet many of these other kinds of customer needs.

The next story starts the other way around—not with the customer but with the product. Spence Silver, a 3M scientist in its industrial glue division, discovered, by accident, a new type of glue with extremely low adhesive properties. Paper coated with this glue could be stuck in position, but then moved and repositioned. This meant that the glue and paper were too easy to remove for most uses.

A corporate culture that permits failure helps foster the creative thinking and risk taking required for innovation. If 3M hadn't kept Francis G. Okie on board after a couple of his inventions failed, he might never have come up with 3M's first successful product—waterproof sandpaper.

At first, it seemed like this innovation would go nowhere. But one scientist, Art Fry, found a personal use for the glue. Tired of the way pieces of scrap paper kept falling out of his church hymnal, Fry began to put this glue on the paper to keep it in place to bookmark songs. He also wrote notes on the paper, which could be easily lifted off. Other people watched him use these sticky pieces of removable paper and asked where they could get some. This encouraged Fry to think that he had possibly discovered a previously undiscovered customer need.

After Fry convinced 3M's top managers a sticky bookmark was a viable product, Post-It Notes were introduced in 1981 and proved an instant success. Today, they contribute over $300 million a year to 3M's revenues.[2]

As 3M's experience suggests, managing the linkage between the characteristics of a product and the customer needs it satisfies is a joint role played by marketing, product development, and sales. Figure 10.1 illustrates the ways these functions must coordinate their activities to create valuable new products. Let's assume the product creation process starts with marketing conducting consumer research to find a better way to design an existing product to satisfy customer needs. Marketing presents its suggestions to the company's product development group. The product development group then does its own research to discover how best to design and make the product. When the improved product has been developed, sales' responsibility is to inform and persuade people to buy it.

The product creation process does not stop there, however: Sales has uncovered new information about how customers are reacting to the product. Perhaps salespeople have discovered that the product is being used in ways that marketing had not expected—that is satisfying other kinds of customer needs. Sales discovers, for example, that masking tape is being used to hang light objects such as magazine pictures, photographs, and children's drawings on walls. To make the tape more convenient to use, people have been cutting the tape in half. Sales also notices the tape doesn't look very attractive on walls. Perhaps something could be done to make the tape not only smaller but also to make it look better?

Figure 10.1
How Marketing, Product Development, and Sales Cooperate to Get Products to Customers

Sales informs marketing that Scotch tape should be made in different widths, perhaps in five-, three-, and one-inch sizes. Marketing conducts further research to investigate potential opportunities and quickly confirms that an entire range of new product opportunities exist. If the tapes are developed to closely match the needs of different customers, many more customers will want to buy the product, and sales revenues could soar–the company might even have a blockbuster new product lineup on its hands.

Marketing has also discovered a need for a tape that is waterproof and asks product development to develop a waterproof glue. Finally, it appears that many customers find it frustrating when the end of the tape becomes "restuck" to the roll and is hard to find. Product development is asked to find a way to package the tape to alleviate this problem. (These events actually occurred at 3M.)

Product development engineers begin work to design and develop a whole series of different-width Scotch tapes. They even find ways to make the tape more attractive to users, including making it transparent so that it does not look unsightly when used to hang things on walls or paste photographs into albums. Sales, which has been observing these developments, now has to create a sales campaign to inform customers about the features of the new kinds of tape. Sales' goal is to persuade people to buy a roll of tape to discover how it can better satisfy their needs.

This process of aligning products with customer needs never stops. Sales continually informs marketing and product development about how customers are reacting to a new product, and marketing then conducts research to find yet more possible uses for a product, while product development continues to find ways to improve it. Enterprise resource planning systems, discussed in Chapter 9, are designed to link marketing, product development, and sales in just this way.

Marketing and the Business Vision, or Mission

Companies engage in marketing to promote their products and brands to customers. *Even the best designed product can fail if marketing hasn't devised a careful plan to persuade people to buy it and try it out.* To help attract customers, a company frequently shows its commitment to its customers and the value it intends to deliver to them in the way it frames its business vision, or mission. A company's business vision, or business mission, is a brief, concise statement of its business model that tells stakeholders *why* the firm is in business, *how* it intends to satisfy customer needs, and *why* it will satisfy their needs better than its competitors. From a marketing perspective, the purpose of a firm's business vision is to capture the attention of customers and spark the imagination and energy of its employees. Table 10.2 contains some examples of companies' vision statements.

As you can see from the vision statements in Table 10.2, companies focus on satisfying customers. Some companies go so far as to claim that their vision is to make products that will even "delight the customer." When you hear someone say, "That was the best money I ever spent" or "That was worth every penny," this is what has happened. Companies would like their customers to say such things about their products, but only some firms succeed–generally the ones that are most profitable in their industries. Nonetheless, both parties to an exchange must feel that they will profit, or be made better off, if the exchange is to occur. On the one hand, a company has to provide a product that the customer believes is more valuable than the price he or she had to pay to get it. On the other hand, the firm has to be able to charge a high enough price for the product to cover its costs and make a profit.

business vision (business mission)
A brief statement of a company's business model that tells stakeholders *why* the firm is in business, *how* it intends to satisfy customer needs, and *why* it will satisfy their needs better than its competitors.

Table 10.2
Business Mission, or Vision, Statements

Wal-Mart
"We work for you. We think of ourselves as buyers for our customers, and we apply our considerable strengths to get the best value for you. We've built Wal-Mart by acting upon behalf of our customers, and that concept continues to propel us."

Target
"Throughout Target Corporation, we are committed to offering our guests an exciting shopping experience that combines fashion newness, trend-right design, and superior quality with compelling value and exceptional convenience. Through innovative merchandising, marketing, and presentation, we provide our guests with more reasons to shop our stores, resulting in consistent top-line growth and market share gains."

Ford Motor Company
"We are a global family with a proud heritage, passionately committed to providing personal mobility for people around the world. We anticipate consumer needs and deliver outstanding products and services that improve people's lives."

The Product Life Cycle

product life cycle
The typical sequence of changes in demand for a product that occur over time.

One more important factor companies must consider when developing their business models is the product life cycle, which is the typical sequence of changes in demand for a product that occur over time. The demand for products that have been successful occurs in the four stages shown in Figure 10.2: the embryonic stage, growth, maturity, and decline. In the *embryonic stage,* a new product has yet to gain widespread acceptance, commonly because customers are unsure what the product has to offer. As a result, demand for the product is minimal. If a product does, indeed, become accepted by customers, demand for it takes off, and the product enters its growth stage. In the *growth stage,* many customers are entering the market and buying the product for the first time, so demand is increasing rapidly. Products such as cell phones and broadband Internet service are currently in this stage.

The growth stage ends and the *mature stage* begins when market demand peaks because most customers have already bought the product and relatively few first-time buyers remain. At this stage, demand is typically replacement demand. In the U.S. car market, for example, most cars are bought by people who already own a car and are either trading up or replacing an old model. The *decline stage* follows the mature stage if and when demand for a product falls. Falling demand often occurs when technological change makes a product obsolete and it is replaced by a newer, more advanced product. For example, demand for Kodak's film products is falling rapidly because the popularity of digital photography is soaring.

In fact, a main determinant of the length of a product's life cycle is the rate of technological change; a second is the pace at which consumer tastes are changing because of changing fads and fashions. In the car industry, for example, a five-year-old car design is likely to be outdated; its old styling will make it less attractive to customers. Similarly, in the restaurant business and fashion world, the demand for certain kinds of food and clothes changes rapidly.

Today, the length of the product life cycle is shortening because technology and customer tastes are changing more rapidly. The implications for marketing research are clear: The shorter the life cycle a

Did You Know?

Gatorade was developed by University of Florida researchers who were attempting to help the football team avoid becoming dehydrated in the Florida heat. The beverage created was tested on the Florida Gators football team and became known as "Gatorade." (The Gators had two winning seasons and won the Orange Bowl shortly thereafter.)[3]

**Figure 10.2
A Product
Life Cycle**

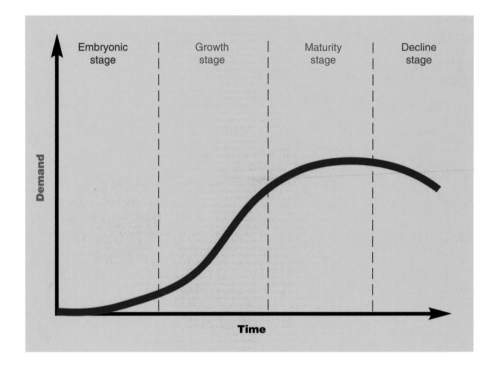

company's products have, the more important it will be for the company to constantly create and market new products quickly. In industries where product life cycles are short, companies must continually develop and market new products or risk going out of business. For example, a few years ago, Nokia was on top of the cell phone world. Just a short time later, the company watched its market share wane after it failed to develop new flip-style and camera phones. Similarly, the fashion house that fails to develop a new line of clothing for every season, or the small restaurant, club, or bar that is not alert to changing customer tastes will see a drop off in sales.

In the next sections of this chapter we outline the three main marketing activities involved in creating a successful business model: (1) identifying and responding to customer needs; (2) identifying customer groups and deciding which market segments to compete in; (3) using the marketing mix to differentiate products and to persuade customers to buy them.

marketing research
The systematic search for information that uncovers met and unmet customer needs, the different needs of different customer groups, and whether or not a product's marketing mix appeals to customers.

Marketing Research: Identifying and Responding to Customer Needs

Marketing research is the systematic search for information that uncovers customer needs, how these needs differ among customers, and whether or not a company's products appeal to customers. Marketing research begins by (1) identifying customers' existing needs for a particular product (2) uncovering unmet needs that the product does not satisfy, and (3) searching for ways to make a product that better suits those unmet needs. When marketing research correctly identifies customer met and unmet needs, the chance that product development will create a product customers want to buy increases. There are two important reasons for this:

First, when the needs of customers are known, product development can build into products those qualities, characteristics, and features that will most appeal to them. Second, both marketing and product development can work to make those products different and superior to those of their competitors. Five main methods are used by marketing and product development to obtain the information necessary to align a

Figure 10.3
**Identifying
Customer Needs
through Marketing
Research**

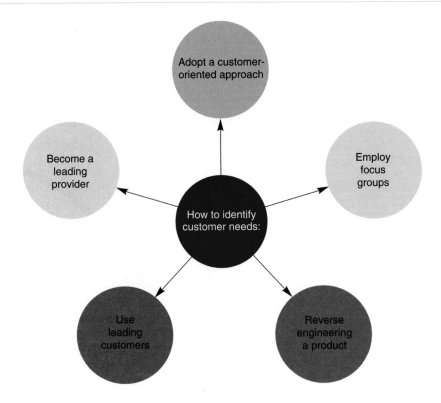

product with customer needs: (1) Using focus groups, (2) adopting a customer-oriented business definition, (3) involving leading customers, (4) becoming a leading provider, and (5) reverse engineering a product. These methods are shown Figure 10.3.

Suppose you are a marketing manager for a global carmaker. You have been put in charge of developing an entry-level car targeted at first-time buyers that will sell for less than $20,000. How will you begin to investigate what entry-level car buyers are looking for in a car in terms of performance, quality, reliability, and features that influences their purchasing decisions?

Use Focus Groups

A first approach to marketing research is to ask customers what they like and dislike about the characteristics of the firm's products as well as competing products. Marketers do this by creating focus groups. A focus group is a collection of people, such as entry-level car buyers, brought together to share their thoughts and feelings about a particular product and uncover how and why it satisfies or does not satisfy customer needs. Often, a company will hold several different focus groups to ensure it is collecting accurate information.

The biggest buyers of entry-level cars are people between 18 and 30 who are just beginning their careers. Marketing invites 10 to 15 of these people to inspect and then discuss a set of entry-level cars. During the meeting, the members of the focus group begin to talk about what they like or dislike about these cars. As they share their experiences, many points begin to emerge: Some members of the focus group, for example, express disappointment that most entry-level cars no longer have hatchbacks and fold-down rear seats to permit bulky objects or a great deal of cargo to be easily transported. This is important to younger people who frequently need to move their belongings from one apartment to another or to their family homes. They also comment that cars do not have convenient outlets in which to plug in MP3 players

focus group A group of people brought together to share their thoughts and feelings about a particular product and why it may or may not meet their needs.

Did You Know?

For every 7 new product ideas, about four enter development, 1.5 are launched, and 1 succeeds.[4]

or enough storage space for CDs. The focus-group participants also comment that the look and layout of the cars' control panels haven't changed in years.

Marketing personnel gather feedback of this kind from several focus groups. They begin to understand how and why the needs of entry-level buyers are changing. Armed with this new knowledge, they approach the firm's car designers and discuss these findings. Together, these groups rethink their approach to the design of the company's next generation of entry-level cars.

Adopt a Customer-Oriented Approach

The use of focus groups revealed vital new marketing knowledge. Simply overhauling and restyling the carmaker's existing entry-level cars would not be enough to "excite" and meet the needs of current entry-level car buyers who want a new kind of vehicle—a sporty-looking, cargo-carrying hatchback. If the firm's marketing personnel had merely focused on the characteristics of existing competing products without consulting the focus groups, they would have been taking a *product-oriented* approach. The problem with this approach is that it focuses on products—goods and services that have already been developed—rather than customers and their changing needs.

By contrast, a focus-group approach to marketing research is a *customer-oriented approach.* In other words, it starts with the customer. Not only does it focus on why existing products failed to meet customer needs, but also how future products could and should be designed. This might seem like an obvious approach to marketing research, but there are hundreds of stories about companies who began their research based on a product, not on customers. In addition to focus groups, companies can interview customers individually, ask them to fill out surveys, meet with them at trade fairs, and so forth. Kodak, profiled in Business in Action, could probably have changed its fortunes by doing more of these things.

Business in Action

Kodak's Flawed Focus

The history of Kodak illustrates the perils of adopting a product-oriented approach to marketing research. In the 1960s, the rate at which consumers were taking pictures was soaring. Kodak dominated the photo industry and was one of the most profitable companies in the world. But this is just the beginning of the story. About the same time that Kodak was profiting handsomely, a team of chemists working independently invented instant photography. The chemists offered to sell the technology to Kodak, but it rejected their offer.

Kodak's managers thought the company's customers would never accept the grainy, less-defined photographs that instant cameras produce. Its own silver-halide technology was so superior, why would anyone even think about buying such an inferior technology? Or so the managers thought. What Kodak had ignored, however, was the fact that many customers wanted to see their photographs instantly versus having to wait to have them developed. Polaroid later adopted the instant technology, which took a serious bite out of Kodak's profits.

Why did Kodak make this mistake? Because its managers had taken a product-, not a customer-oriented, approach. In other words, Kodak didn't put the needs of customers first. The company believed it was selling high-quality, glossy photographs. In reality, it was satisfying the need customers had to capture and record the images

Kodak's managers were too focused on the company's own products rather than their customers. As a result, Kodak missed out on a number of cutting-edge technologies that led to new, successful products like instant cameras and Xerox machines.

of their lives–their birthday parties, weddings, graduations, and so on. Moreover, people wanted those images *quickly* so they could share them right away with the people they had photographed. If Kodak had held just a couple of focus groups and shown participants the new instant cameras, it would probably not have made this mistake.

This was not Kodak's only gaffe, however. In the 1960s, the company was offered another new product: Xerography–photocopying, that is. Xerography was a major breakthrough. (If you have ever experimented with carbon paper, you surely agree.) Kodak's response? "What does Xerography, which produces poor-quality images, have to do with our products, which are based on high-quality silver-halide technology? This is not our business." Once again, Kodak missed out on being the leader in a new imaging technology that created an entire industry. Today, Kodak is in trouble. Digital photography is replacing silver-halide film at a rapid rate. The company's profitability is falling, and its future does not seem bright. If only it had consulted its customers more often.[5]

Involve Leading Customers

leading customers
Companies that improvise their own solutions to business problems because no products currently exist that can do so.

A third method of marketing research is to focus on leading customers. Leading customers are companies that are forced to improvise their own solutions to problems because no products currently exist to solve them. Recall, the paint shop employees in the 3M story. These employees had worked out their own quick fix to prevent over spray. They needed some kind of new product that would prevent this problem, but there was none available.

Staying close to your customers and observing what they are doing to "make things work" is a great way to identify needs that are going unmet. This has not been lost on companies like 3M. These companies routinely involve leading customers in their marketing and product development processes. They visit their facilities and watch what their employees do. They then develop products to solve the obstacles they encounter. Frequently, they ask their leading customers to test these new products. Over 60% of successful new products, in fact, are commercialized after companies uncover an unmet need their leading customers have.

In the 3M example, the paint shop employees knew they had a specific unmet need. But how does marketing go about discovering unmet needs when customers don't even know they have them? There are several possible ways. First, marketing experts watch and talk to people in focus groups, at their work, or in their own homes.

MTV is a good example. During the 1980s, MTV's new music video shows enjoyed phenomenal success. The network had a huge share of the 18- to 25-year-old viewing audience. But in the early 1990s, this changed. MTV's viewing audience plunged. MTV subsequently hired new hosts and made its video programming more upbeat and glitzy. Nothing worked. The network no longer seemed to connect with its viewing audience, and its product was not aligned with its customers' needs.

In desperation, MTV turned to a famous New York marketing company that researches the needs of customers by visiting their homes, following them around, and talking to them intensively for 24- or 48-hour periods. The company selected a number of typical MTV viewers, went with them to their homes and schools, and listened as they talked with their friends about their current issues and problems. It even went shopping with them and studied the products they bought. Focus groups were also held to find out what viewers thought about MTV's programming and what they wanted.

The company's findings astonished MTV executives. Viewers were no longer interested

Did You Know?

"Forrest Mars got the idea for M&M's® from seeing soldiers in the Spanish Civil War eat chocolate-covered lentils dipped in sugary candy."[6]

In order to win back viewers, MTV hired a marketing company to find out what they wanted. What the marketing company found was that viewers wanted to see people on MTV like themselves—people with whom they could identify.

in an endless string of music videos featuring famous rock bands. They wanted to see people like themselves onscreen—to see what they were wearing and what their interests and concerns were.

Armed with this new marketing knowledge, MTV understood why it was failing to meet the needs of its customers. It put into production a whole new series of shows, like reality-based TV programming based on strangers joining up for a road trip to an exotic location or partying on a beach. It developed chat, news, cooking, and other shows tied to its viewers' interests. Its new programming lineup proved appealing, and its viewing numbers soared.

Another way of discovering unmet needs is to allow leading customers "create" the ultimate product. Boeing has used this approach to its advantage. When Boeing was designing the interior layout of its newest passenger jet, the 777, it knew that its leading customers, major U.S. airlines, had different needs and uses for the plane. Boeing decided to use their expertise. It created a prototype of the interior of the new plane and asked each airline to send a team of specialists to configure the interior to match their particular airline's needs.

As each team worked to design a layout that best met their company's needs. They experimented with different seating arrangements, cabin layouts, and so on. Boeing's engineers closely watched each team's design decisions, asking them about why they were doing it in this way or that way. They then took all of the knowledge they had collected and used it to determine the best way to configure the aircraft as well as how to customize it to each airline's specific needs. This knowledge proved immensely valuable to Boeing, to the airlines, and to airline passengers. The 777 is regarded as the best designed aircraft ever; passengers often feel their journeys are much shorter because of the plane's efficient use of space, generous legroom, and amenities, like individual TV screens and game players.

Become a Leading Provider

Recall that the people who watched Art Fry bookmark pages with the first Post-It Notes wanted some for their own use. These people recognized they had a need only *after* the product had been created. As we discussed in Chapter 3, entrepreneurs are people who think they see an unmet customer need, or a "gap in the market." They envision a product that doesn't yet exist but that people will want to buy. Entrepreneurs are essentially leading providers—people or companies that believe their new products will better satisfy customers even though they have no sure proof of this.

leading providers
People or companies that believe their new products will better satisfy customer needs even though they have no sure proof of this.

The explosive growth of Starbucks is a good example of a leading provider. Howard Schultz, Starbucks' founder, noticed during a trip to Italy that a new "coffee bar culture" had become popular with Italians. Schultz believed there was an opportunity to duplicate this culture in Seattle. It worked. People learned to visit Starbucks, relax with their friends, and spend $4 dollars for a cup of coffee.

It's not just the coffee people enjoy at Starbucks, however. Over time Starbucks' has become a kind of coffee "club," where the price of admission is just a cup a coffee. It has become a kind of home-away-from-home, where busy people can meet their friends, do business, and socialize. Starbucks continues to alter the range of its products to anticipate its customers' needs. It has installed Wi-Fi service in its stores, for example, and music kiosks.

Another good example of how to be a leading provider is the way Izod changed the retail clothing market in the 1970s. Izod was the first company to "badge" its polo shirts. Sales of Izod's expensive crocodile-logo golf shirts subsequently soared. Within a few years the alligator logos became a symbol of their wearers' membership in the affluent, U.S. middle-class. U.S. clothing designers, particularly Ralph

Lauren, watched Izod's success and realized there was pent-up demand for high-priced, prestige designer clothing that would satisfy people's self-esteem needs. Ralph Lauren subsequently designed a line of Polo clothing and used innovative marketing to convince people it was worth spending $60 to buy a Polo shirt and join his exclusive "club" of well-dressed people. Previously, the average person had no idea he or she would want to spend a lot of money to wear a shirt with a special label. Izod, Ralph Lauren, Tommy Hilfiger, and others convinced them it was worth the price. As such, they became leading providers.

DEVELOPING AND SHAPING CONSUMERS' NEEDS: IS IT ETHICAL?

Marketing's ability to create or shape the customer's need for a particular product has ethical implications. As we discussed earlier, MTV is a very skillful marketer. Some people believe MTV actually uses its marketing expertise to create demand for products–like new rock bands. For example, by giving airtime to select rock bands, MTV persuades its audience that these bands are worth listening to. This then creates demand for the bands' CDs, concerts, and other products–and MTV shares in the profits. Some experts claim that, in fact, these bands are no more skilled or creative than any other talented rock bands waiting to be discovered. Rather than letting the buying choices of individual music lovers–the market–signal the rise or fall of a new talent, however, MTV does. This, these experts believe, is unethical.

If you were a member of an up-and-coming rock band, how would you feel about this practice? Is it ethical for MTV to create a successful rock group–one that would not have risen to fame based on its own talent? Is it ethical for MTV to make millions of dollars by promoting the group? How about other markets? Is it ethical for a company to use marketing to convince a teenager to spend $120 on a new pair of running shoes or $50 on a shirt, even though it means running up his or her cash-strapped parents' credit cards?

Some people would simply answer: Let the buyer beware–meaning that we are all responsible for our own personal actions. The other side of the coin is that the power of marketing, via constant advertising and promotion, can convince people to buy products that might harm them. Tobacco products and liquor are banned from appearing in certain media in the United States for this very reason. Breakfast-food companies are under fire for advertising sugar-laden cereals to children. But so are fast-food chains for advertising hamburgers on TV when America is facing an obesity problem. Unfortunately, these are complex issues with no clear-cut answers.

Reverse Engineer a Product

reverse engineering
The process of examining the products of one's competitors in depth in order to figure out what makes them successful.

Good marketing research involves taking a customer-oriented approach, as we have discussed. But it also necessitates carefully analyzing competing products. One way of doing this is through reverse engineering, which involves purchasing the products of competitors and carefully examining them to discover the qualities or features that make them successful or unsuccessful. Some companies are relentless in this pursuit. It is common, for example, for carmakers to first have marketing experts study competitors' cars and evaluate their features, styling, and specific characteristics such as acceleration, comfort, or internal noise level. Then, engineers break the car down into its component pieces to discover how the car works the way it does.

Did You Know?

Diverse American lifestyles have lead companies like Hallmark and American Greetings to create over 200 niche greeting cards for events like the adoption of an adolescent, birth of quadruplets, divorce announcements, and birthday cards to people from their pets.[7]

For example, when Ford was designing its first Mustang convertible, its engineers could not stop the car's body from shaking when it made a sharp turn. Desperate for a solution, Ford bought a Mercedes Benz convertible. Its engineers took it apart and discovered that it had a 100-pound block of steel behind the radiator. They copied this feature, solved the problem, and the Mustang became one of

When the marketing managers of the Hampton Inn were developing the concept for the new hotel chain, they stayed at and studied their competitors' hotels. With this knowledge, they were able to design a better business model for the Hampton Inn.

Ford's best-selling cars. Similarly, when the marketing managers of the Hampton Inn chain were developing the concept for the new hotel, they stayed in their competitors' hotels and studied the design of their guest rooms, furniture, service, the way room and bathroom noise was controlled, and so on. Armed with this knowledge, they were able to design a better product for travelers that has been very successful.

After reverse engineering their competitors' products, marketing managers then compare this information to information about their own products. Such a comparison helps them pinpoint key differences. An automaker's marketing personnel might discover, for example, that the firm's vehicle is underpowered compared to competitors' and that a new, more powerful engine in their car is necessary. They might also decide that a new design is needed to keep the look of the car up to date and that new color options should be added. Using the information it collects from this research, marketing starts to create a model of the product that will better meet customer needs. Of course, it is not enough just to identify these needs. The firm's product development and sales groups must be willing to respond to them, too.

Marketing Research: Identifying Customer Groups and Segments

As we just discussed, it's the job of marketing to research and identify customers' met and unmet needs so a superior product can be created. In many cases, however, companies do not produce just one type or model of a particular product; they produce *many* types or models because different groups of customers have very different needs. Let's discuss some of these types of customers.

Customer groups are groups of people who have a *similar need* for a particular product. Many customer groups can exist in a particular market because a product usually satisfies several different kinds of customer needs. In the car market, for example, some customers want basic transportation; others want top-of-the line luxury; still others want the thrill of driving fast sports cars. In the athletic shoe market, the two main customer groups are those people who use the shoes for sporting purposes and those who like to wear them because they are casual and comfortable.

Commonly, there are also *subgroups* within each customer group. These are people who have an even more specific need for a product. Inside the customer group of people who buy athletic shoes for sporting purposes, for example, are subgroups of people who buy shoes suited to a specific kind of activity, such as running, aerobics, walking, and tennis. (See Figure 10.4.) It's marketing's job to identify what kinds of needs buyers of a particular product have in order to identify different customer groups.

customer groups
Groups of people who have a *similar need* for a particular product because the product satisfies several different kinds of needs.

How Customer Groups and Market Segments Are Identified

To help GM, or any company, decide which products to develop to suit the needs of different kinds of customers, it is first necessary to *group* customers according to the similarities or differences in their needs. To identify the customer groups in a particular

**Figure 10.4
Identifying
Customer Groups**

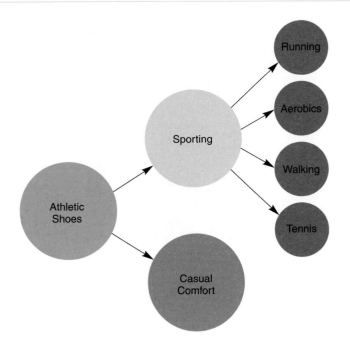

market, marketers perform research to discern the *primary need or use* a group of customers has for a product and their income or buying power (to determine the target price). Other important attributes of a customer group are then identified. Once a group of customers who share a similar or specific need for a product has been identified, this group is treated as a **market segment**. Companies then decide whether or not to make and sell a product designed to satisfy the specific needs of a customer segment.

market segment A
group of customers the
firm targets based on their
need for its products.

PRIMARY PRODUCT NEED   Companies first group customers according to their primary need or use for a product. In the car industry today, for example, six principal market segments have been identified, and most vehicles are made to satisfy the primary needs of customers in those segments:

- *Passenger sedans*, whose purpose is to get a person to work or transport a family around.

- *Minivans*, which combine the ability to carry six-plus people or large amounts of cargo.

- *Personal luxury vehicles*, top-of-the-line cars designed to pamper their occupants and satisfy their needs for personal esteem.

- *Sports cars*, whose purpose is to thrill their occupants and test their driving skills.

- *Sports utility vehicles* (SUVs), which were originally intended to be rugged, off-the-road vehicles but which today are increasingly being used for normal driving purposes.

- *Pickup trucks*, which primarily have a cargo-carrying role, although four-door passenger carrying versions are becoming increasingly popular.

Marketing researchers assign all the different kinds of vehicles produced by global carmakers to these six market segments according to which primary customer needs they satisfy. In this way they can identify which vehicles are competing products in each segment. Then marketers identify the features and characteristics of the most popular models inside of each segment to determine why they have the most appeal. This allows the company to better tailor future model cars so that they have these characteristics. This research also indicates where there might be a *gap* in the market–a segment where consumers' needs are going unmet. A famous example of a new vehicle developed to target a newly discovered market segment was Chrysler's introduction of the first minivan in 1983. Passenger sedans were by far the biggest selling vehicle before minivans, and later SUVs were introduced. Few vehicles on the market offered the ability to carry six-plus passengers or a large cargo after the rear seats had been folded down. Marketers at Chrysler, spotted a gap in the market for a new kind of vehicle that could satisfy both these needs simultaneously. The discovery of this new market segment, in fact, saved Chrysler from bankruptcy in the 1980s. The high profits Chrysler earned from its new minivan allowed it to create new kinds of vehicles to compete with those of low-cost Japanese carmakers.

PRICE RANGE The second customer attribute marketers need to identify in different market segments is differences related to how much customers are willing to pay for a particular product. Suppose, for example, that GM's marketers find that most passenger sedan buyers typically choose sedans in four prices ranges: $11-20,000, $21-30,000, $31-45,000, and $46-75,000. To attract the buyers, GM must make a sedan designed and priced for customers in each of these price ranges. This is exactly what it does: GM makes (1) entry-level, two- and four-door models such as the Chevrolet Aveo; (2) economy models such as the Cavalier; (3) upscale models such as the Buick Regal; and (4) luxury models such as the Cadillac Deville.

At present, Toyota is the carmaker that offers customers the most extensive range of vehicles, as illustrated in Figure 10.5. Toyota offers a vehicle targeted at almost all of the main segments and subsegments of the car market—something that explains why the company is so profitable.

OTHER DIFFERENTIATING CHARACTERISTICS After grouping customers into market segments by primary product need and price range, marketing researchers then work to identify other characteristics that demarcate their needs. Demographic variables such as buyers' ages, genders, education levels, occupations, and lifestyles are characteristics frequently used to differentiate between customer groups. GM, for example, might find that the buyers of one of its best-selling vehicles comprise a clearly defined group: well-off, retired professionals. To keep this important market segment's business, GM must be careful to develop new and improved car models that target their needs. In fact, the main buyers for GM's Cadillac Deville come from exactly this customer group. One of the main reasons GM developed its On Star vehicle-tracking system was to provide older people in this category with the assurance that if they break down or have a problem, they can obtain assistance anywhere and at any time.

**Figure 10.5
Toyota's Product
Lineup**

Price	Sports Utility Vehicles	Passenger/ Sports Sedans	Passenger Vans	Personal Luxury Vehicles	Sports Cars	Pickup Trucks
11-20K	RAV4 Scion xB	Echo, Matrix, Corolla, Prism Scion xA			Celica GT	Tacoma
21-30K	4-Runner, Highlander	Camry, Avalon	Sienna	Avalon	MR2, Spyder	Tundra
31-45K	Sequoia, RX330	GS 300, IS 300		ES 330	Camry Solara	Tundra Double Cab
46-75K	Land Cruiser, GX,LX	GS 430		LS 430	SC 430	

☐ No vehicle in category

Choosing Markets to Serve

Once market segments have been identified, a company has to decide whether to make products to serve *one, several,* or *all* of these segments. As shown in Figure 10.6, There are three main approaches toward market segmentation:

- First, a company might choose *not* to recognize that different market segments exist and make a product targeted at the *average, or typical, customer.* This results in *mass marketing,* the selling of a mass-produced product to all customers.

- Second, a company can choose to recognize the differences between customer groups and make a product targeted at most, or all, of the different market segments. This results in *multiple-segment marketing,* where different models of a product are made and sold to different customer groups.

- Third, a company might choose to target just one or two market segments and develop products for customers in just these segments. This results in *focused marketing.*

Operating costs increase when a company makes a different product for each market segment rather than just one product for the entire market. So why does a company do this? The answer is that although operating costs increase, the decision to produce a range of products aligned with the needs of customers in different market segments attracts many more customers, so sales revenues increase more than costs do. Recall from the opening case how GM's revenues increased when it offered customers many more car models and how customers were willing to pay premium prices to buy them. As long as a company's revenues increase faster than its operating costs, its profitability increases.

Does this mean *all* companies should decide to produce a wide range of products aimed at each market segment to increase their profitability? Not necessarily. It depends on how much the needs of customers in a particular market or industry vary. In some industries–like the automobile and computer industries–customers' needs differ widely by their income levels, lifestyles, ages, and so on. Consequently, a company that produces just one car model, compared to a company that produces 25, might find itself at a serious competitive disadvantage. To prevent this, all major global carmakers now produce a wide range of vehicles serving most market segments. Figure 10.7 shows the wide range of customer groups Dell serves in the computer market.

By contrast, in some markets, customers have similar needs. Often, the need to find low-priced products drives their buying choices. In this case, a company that chooses to use its resources to make and sell a single product as inexpensively as possible might gain a major competitive advantage. The average customer buys the product because it's "OK" and the "right" price.

Figure 10.6
Three Approaches to Market Segmentation

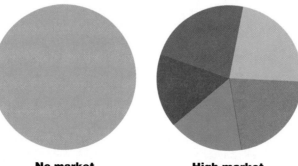

No market segmentation	High market segmentation	Focused market segmentation
A product is targeted at "average consumer"	A different product is offered to each market segment	A product is offered to one or a few market segments

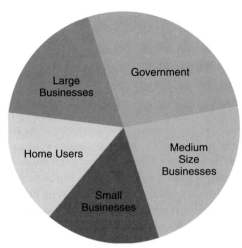

Figure 10.7
Dell's Main Customer Groups

This is the business model followed by companies such as BIC, which makes low-cost razors and ballpoint pens, and Arm & Hammer, which makes baking soda. These are products that most people have a similar use for.

This is also the business model followed by companies like Wal-Mart, with its mission to *buy* products from suppliers at as low a cost as possible, and then *sell* them to customers at as low a price as possible. BIC and Wal-Mart do not focus intensively on the different segments of a market. Instead, they decide to serve the needs of customers who want to buy products as inexpensively as possible. Wal-Mart promises everyday low prices and price rollbacks; BIC promises the lowest-priced razor blades that work.

The third approach to market segmentation is to target a product just at one or two market segments. To pursue this approach, a company must develop something very special or distinctive about its product to attract a large share of customers in a particular market segment. In the car market, for example, Porsche targets its products at specific market segments–sports-car buyers who can afford high-quality, high-priced vehicles. In 2003, however, Porsche departed somewhat from this strategy. It introduced the Cayenne SUV to compete against the SUVs produced by BMW and Lexus.

In a similar way, specialty retailers compete for customers in a particular market segment. Segments such as these might include consumers who are affluent and can afford to buy expensive handmade clothing, or consumers who enjoy wearing "trendy" shoes such as Nike's Converse brand. A retailer might also specialize in a particular style of clothing like Western Wear, beachwear, or accessories. Small companies are frequently better able to satisfy the needs of certain customer subsegments.

Video Small Business in Action

Father of the Bratz

This *BusinessWeek* TV segment on your Student DVD features Isaac Larian, an Iranian immigrant who founded the firm, MGA Entertainment, which manufactures fashion dolls for young girls. Larian has a tenacious drive and loves a challenge. His chief competitor is Mattel and its famous Barbie doll collection.

Larian's emphasis on autonomy and creativity has led many of Mattel's designers to leave the company to go work for MGA Entertainment. This has enhanced the company's ability to develop and produce the line of dolls called the "Bratz" collection.

The Bratz doll is the first doll ever to substantially cut into Barbie's market. Largely due to the success of the Bratz dolls, MGA Entertainment went from a small company to one grossing hundreds of millions of dollars. The dolls are considered the "anti-Barbie" and feature modern fashions that the target market, younger girls, find attractive. MGA prides itself on continuously reinventing the product and pushing brand extensions such as consumer electronics for young girls.

Currently, MGA and Mattel are locked in a legal battle concerning the designers who left Mattel for MGA. Moreover, it appears that the dominant market share commanded by Mattel is now under direct fire from MGA Entertainment.

Questions
1. Which type of market segmentation does MGA Entertainment use? Why?
2. If MGA Entertainment were to differentiate its product line by introducing new products directed at different market segments, what characteristics would be of interest as it developed its marketing plan?
3. What is one method Larian could use to differentiate his Bratz dolls from Mattel's Barbie dolls?

Often these companies are more attuned to their customers' specialized needs than their larger competitors are. Sometimes, however, a product marketed to a subsegment becomes so popular it takes off and becomes a major market segment in its own right. Dr. Marten boots, Volkswagen Beetles, and Mini Coopers are good examples.

Marketing Research: Differentiating Products via the Marketing Mix

product differentiation The process of setting a product apart from its competitors by designing and marketing it to better satisfy customers' needs.

marketing mix The combination of a product's qualities and features, its price, the way it is promoted and sold, and the places at which it is sold.

Once the marketing function has identified different needs of various customers and groups, its next task is to make recommendations about the characteristics a particular product should possess to satisfy them. Product differentiation is the process of setting the company's products apart from those of its competitors by designing goods and services that deliver more value to customers. Marketing accomplishes product differentiation via the marketing mix—the "4P's" of marketing. As Figure 10.8 shows, the marketing mix is a combination of the following: (1) the *product's* qualities and features; (2) its *price;* (3) the *promotion* used to inform and persuade people to buy the product; and (4) the *place* at which it is available for sale. Some marketers argue a fifth "P" be added to this list—*people.* They argue that companies are increasingly differentiating themselves by providing superior customer service excellence. *Customer-relationship management* (CRM), discussed in Chapter 11, is a technique for accomplishing this.

Developing the right marketing mix for a product requires a significant investment on the part of a company. The company has to spend a great deal of money on marketing research and the engineering activities necessary to develop the product. Then there are the costs associated with marketing and selling the product: It costs Ford $3 billion to design and sell a new car model, and it can cost a drug company $1 billion to create and advertise a new drug. Microsoft spent more than $1.5 billion to develop and sell Windows XP, for example. Moreover, when a company produces a range of different models of a product—each targeted at a different market segment—a separate marketing mix is needed for each. This further increases costs.

Given these high operating costs, all of a company's functions must work together to increase the firm's efficiency and effectiveness. If costs spiral out of control, the revenue the company hopes to earn by selling the product will not be sufficient, and the product will be unprofitable. The need to economize on the costs of product differentiation is a major determinant of the marketing mix.

Figure 10.8
Components of the Marketing Mix

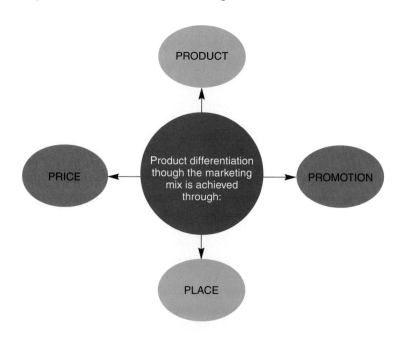

Product Branding and the Marketing Message

marketing message
A product-related message the firm's marketing department sends to customers about how and why a product will better satisfy their needs.

product branding
Using a unique name, design, symbol, or other element to differentiate a product from its competitors.

brand name The specific name, sign, or symbol a company uses to distinguish and legally protect the identity of its products.

brand loyalty The tendency of customers to consistently purchase a particular product over time because they believe it can best satisfy their needs.

product positioning
The process of customizing or tailoring a product to a specific market segment.

When a product's marketing mix is well-designed, it sends a strong marketing message to customers about how and why the product will better satisfy their needs. One way to do this is through product branding. Product branding is the process of using a unique name, design, symbol, or other elements of the marketing mix, to distinguish a product from its competitors. A brand name is the specific name, sign, or symbol a company uses to do this. In many cases, firms register their brand names to legally protect the identity of their products. The reward for marketing's ability to turn a product into a brand is brand loyalty, the tendency of customers to consistently purchase a particular product over time. Product positioning involves tailoring a product for a specific market segment relative to its competitors. The idea is to create a superior image or identity of the product in the "minds" of the customers in that market segment. Next, we examine *how* a marketing mix and these other elements are blended to send a strong marketing message to customers.

Products

The process of product differentiation starts when a company creates *real* or *perceived* differences between its products and those of its competitors. Marketing and product development work together to choose these qualities. Some of these differences are the result of superior engineering or product performance and are therefore tangible, or real. Other differences are perceived: They are the result of advertising and promotion that lead consumers to believe the product is superior to others.

CREATING REAL PRODUCT DIFFERENCES Normally, real differences between competing products stem from a company's ability to achieve superior *quality, innovation,* and *responsiveness to customers.* Companies that are able to differentiate their products in real, tangible ways will attract more customers. Moreover, these customers will often be willing to pay premium prices for their products.

Quality and reliability are crucial, real differentiating characteristics: Many people make their purchasing decisions based on product reviews, which generally focus on quality and reliability. These reviews are available online and also in magazines like *Consumer Reports. Consumer Reports,* for example, reviews a wide variety of products including appliances, food, mutual funds, and health-care products. The magazine's annual issue devoted to cars is widely used by car buyers to compare different autos.

Innovation that leads to the development of new and improved products is also a crucial, and very expensive, part of product differentiation. In many industries, companies introduce new or improved products every year as a way of maintaining their competitive advantage. Many people will pay a premium price to be the first to have a flat-screen TV, the latest PDA, or car model. Textbook publishers introduce new editions every few years featuring the latest and greatest information available in the marketplace and new learning technologies like online courses, Web site quizzing.

Finally, some companies are well known for their excellent after-sales service and responsiveness to customers. Wal-Mart, for example, rarely questions a customer who returns a product. Dell provides first-class support to customers who have trouble operating their new computers. The profits of competitors Home Depot and Lowe's rise and fall according to their ability to provide good customer support for home improvement projects.

CREATING PERCEIVED PRODUCT DIFFERENCES Marketing can also work to create *perceived differences* between a product and competitors' products. Often, this is achieved by appealing to one or more of the psychological needs of customers, including their needs for safety, prestige, status, or self-actualization. A company that can create the perception among customers that its products offer them

Ralph Lauren is one company that creates the perception among its customers that its products offer them more value than those of competitors. This leads to brand loyalty.

more value than those of competitors attracts more customers and creates brand loyalty.

We discussed earlier how Starbucks and Ralph Lauren created a "club-like" perception about their products, fulfilling the customer's need for belongingness. Similarly, BMW, Mercedes, and Rolex appeal to personal luxury, status, and self-esteem needs of their customers. Other companies like The Traveler's Insurance Company, Blue Cross/Blue Shield, and AAA appeal to customers' security needs.

Typically, companies try to create both real *and* perceived differences between their products and those of their competitors. Mercedes Benz products are an example: The vehicles are some of the best-engineered cars on the market and possess every advanced safety feature. They also confer prestige and status on their owners.

PACKAGING *Packaging* is a marketing mix choice that concerns the "look" or physical appearance of a product when it is presented and sold to customers. Factors such as the shape, color, look of the packaging, and the way a product is presented in a store display affect customers' perceptions. Upscale luxury products tend to be packaged in more elaborate ways than less-expensive products. This is why Ralph Lauren shirts are filled with tissue paper, pinned in elaborate ways, packed in green and gold boxes, and placed in Ralph Lauren shopping bags.

In contrast, at Sam's Club, which is owned by Wal-Mart, customers are not even provided with shopping bags. They are just provided with cardboard boxes to use if they wish. In the United Kingdom, supermarkets used to charge customers 10 cents for each plastic bag they used, so customers usually brought their own shopping bags. This situation changed when Wal-Mart bought a U.K. supermarket chain and began to supply bags free. Now most other U.K. chains do the same. These kinds of packaging decisions send a clear marketing message to customers about the quality of products: Wal-Mart emphasizes the low price of its products versus their quality; Ralph Lauren, by contrast, emphasizes that its products are high quality and worth paying a premium price for.

Price

Pricing is a complex issue in the marketing mix. For example, if a company chooses to differentiate its product based on innovation, quality, and responsiveness to customers, its product development and marketing costs increase. (Obviously, it costs more for a company to make a state-of-the-art product backed by good after-sales service than a basic, no-frills product.) The company will therefore need to charge a higher price for the product to offset these higher costs. But how much higher? As you can see, this is a critical decision: If the price is too high, customers won't buy the product; if it's too low, the firm might sell a large amount of the product but make little or no profit—or even worse, suffer a loss.

It's marketing's job to find out how much customers are willing to pay for a particular product. The **target price** is the price a typical group of customers are willing to pay for a product with a particular set of qualities—an entry-level car or a top-of-the-line luxury sedan, for example. Once the target price is known, a budget is then developed for each of the elements of the market mix—product development, marketing, sales, and so forth. If these budgets are exceeded, however, a company can find itself in trouble.

target price The price a typical customer will be willing to pay for a product with a particular set of qualities and features.

Did You Know?

Americans now spend more money annually on fast food than they do on higher education, personal computers, computer software, or new cars, or on movies, books magazines, newspapers, videos, and recorded music combined.[8]

DaimlerChrysler gave its engineers free reign to create a new, top-quality Mercedes Benz model in the 1990s. Unfortunately, the costs associated with development of the product skyrocketed, and so did the price of each new car.

DaimlerChrysler experienced exactly this problem in the early 1990s when it gave its engineers free reign to create a new, top-quality Mercedes Benz. Unfortunately, the development costs related to creating the car were astronomical. As a result, each automobile had to be priced at well over $100,000! Even well-heeled buyers were reluctant to buy a car at a price this high. DaimlerChrysler has since learned the importance of budgeting product development costs.

BMW, by contrast, offers a whole different story. In the 1990s, the German automaker set a target price for its new model 3 and 5 Series luxury sports sedans that was well within the price range of most U.S. sports-sedan buyers. BMW kept its prices "relatively" low (given the high cost of making a luxury sports sedan) so that it could increase its share of the U.S. luxury car market. Because sales revenues are a function of price multiplied by number of units sold, BMW hoped that by keeping its prices relatively low, it would attract many more buyers and increase its brand loyalty. BMW was correct. Its marketing mix turned out to be enormously effective. Sales nearly doubled as a result, and the company's profitability rose, too.

The important point to note here is that customers must find more value in a product than the price they pay for it, and companies must limit marketing and product development costs so that they can make the product, sell it, and still earn a good profit. A crucial marketing task is to discover the right target price—something BMW's marketers achieved, as have Toyota's. (See Figure 10.4.)

Promotion

promotion The way in which a company advertises, announces, publicizes, and pushes its products.

Even the best product sold at a great price will not succeed in the marketplace unless people can be convinced to try it out. Promotion relates to the way a company gets the attention of its customers—how it advertises, announces, publicizes, and pushes its products. Companies spend enormous amounts of money to differentiate their products via their promotional activities. Over 75% of the price of a box of washing powder goes to pay for the costs of promoting the product, for example; $300 to $6,000 of the price of a new car is used to tell customers how excellent it is. We are all familiar with the elaborate marketing campaigns companies use to introduce new products and inform us about how much their older products have improved.

Why do companies need to spend so much money on this? Because buyers are fickle, picky people who search for new products that can better satisfy their needs. Companies use promotion both to attract new customers and to build brand loyalty among existing customers. The fact is that that it costs much more to attract new customers than it does to keep one's existing customers. Promotion is one way of keeping customers committed to a product. Just as customers want reliable products, companies want reliable, loyal customers.

promotional mix The combination of advertising, sales promotions, public relations, and personal selling used to reach and persuade customers to buy a product.

In general, companies use promotions to inform customers about the physical attributes of their product and *persuade* them to buy them. Typically this involves using a promotional mix—a combination of advertising, sales promotions, public relations, and personal selling. These elements are discussed next.

advertising The paid, nonpersonal promotion of a company's goods and services using mass media to influence consumers.

ADVERTISING Advertising is the paid, nonpersonal promotion of goods and services by a company using mass media to persuade or influence consumers. Some advertising media include billboards, printed flyers, radio, cinema and television ads, Web banners, Web popups, skywriting, bus stop benches, magazines, newspapers, town criers, sides of buses, and taxicab doors. Three common techniques used in advertising are (1) repetition, (2) the bandwagon effect, and (3) testimonials. Most of us are familiar with repetition. We've all heard ads repeated over and over again on TV, radio, and elsewhere. The bandwagon effect implies that the product is widely used by others; those who don't use it, should "get on the bandwagon" and do so. Testimonials are used when an advertiser wants to promote the superior quality of its product. The testimony can come from ordinary users, experts, or others.

Using brand names and trademarks are part of the advertising process. Brand names help send a consistent marketing message to customers reinforced consistently over time. The Jaguar, Porsche, Jeep, Beetle, and Mini brands each conjure up something specific in most people's minds. Why? Because these brand names have been successfully promoted in consistent ways over time.

sales promotions
Nonpersonal, persuasive efforts designed to boost a company's sales immediately.

SALES PROMOTIONS   Sales promotions are nonpersonal, persuasive efforts designed to boost sales immediately. Some examples of sales promotions include coupons, discounts and sales contests, point-of-purchase displays, rebates, gifts, and incentive items. Each of these has many forms. Take coupons for example: They can be placed in free-standing booklets inserted into newspapers or magazines; put on shelves located next to products; printed on a customer's receipt; or posted on the Internet for downloading.

public relations The practice of conveying messages to the public through the media to influence people's opinions about the company and its products.

PUBLIC RELATIONS   Public relations (PR) is the practice of conveying messages to the public through the media to influence people's opinions about the company and its products. The media used to disseminate these messages include newspapers, magazines, radio, television, and the World Wide Web. PR experts usually target specific market segments to communicate to, such as the readers of a particular magazine or viewers of a particular television channel. Generally, however, firms don't pay directly for publicity. There are, nonetheless, costs related to getting the media's attention. PR personnel or firms must be hired to do this, which, of course, costs money.

personal selling
Direct, face-to-face communication by salespeople with existing and potential customers to promote a company's products.

PERSONAL SELLING   A crucial sales activity is personal selling, direct face-to-face communication by salespeople with existing and potential customers to promote a company's products. Personal selling is discussed in depth in Chapter 11, where we also describe how customer relationship management (CRM) works with sales and marketing to build customer relationships and increase the value delivered to customers. Suffice it to say that good, hardworking salespeople are critical to a company's success. Companies are keenly aware of this. That's why good salespeople are generally rewarded with large commissions and/or bonuses when they perform well.

Place

place The distribution and sales channels used to get both a product and its marketing message to the customer.

The fourth factor in the marketing mix is place, which refers to the channels, or pathways, used to get both the marketing message and product to customers. A company can choose a multitude of possible channels to reach its customers, as Figure 10.9 illustrates. Going to a "bricks-and-mortar" location like a department store, supermarket, or car dealership is still the main channel through which customers buy most products. The Internet is growing in importance as a channel to reach the customer, however. Sometimes customers will go to a store first to see a product and examine its features, packaging, and the way it is promoted. Then, they might buy it on the Internet to both get a lower price and avoid paying sales taxes (although they usually have to pay shipping charges). Bricks-and-mortar companies are aware that this occurs and are working to coordinate their virtual and real storefronts to keep their customers loyal.

Did You Know?

"Make it a habit to keep on the lookout for novel and interesting ideas that others have used successfully. Your idea needs to be original only in its adaptation to the problem you are working on."[9] ~ Thomas A. Edison

**Figure 10.9
Place: Different
Types of Marketing
Channels**

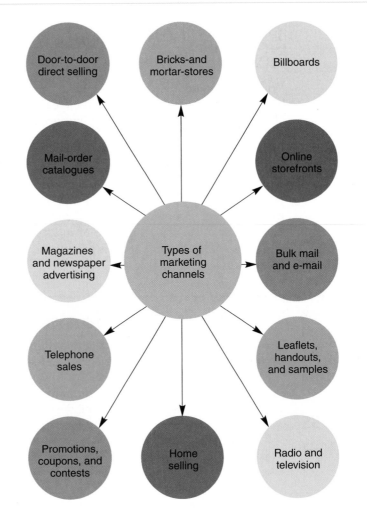

Other place channels include mail-order catalogues, newspaper advertising, bulk mail, telephone sales, e-mail, leaflets, and door-to-door selling. Selling in peoples' homes is also a widely-used channel to get a product directly to customers with a "personal touch." This channel is popular with companies such as Tupperware, Avon, and Mary Kay.

Deciding which of these channels is best suited to its business model is a part of a company's choice of marketing mix to differentiate its product. The aim is to use those channels to get closest to the customer and form the best relationships with them. Designer Ralph Lauren, for example, first started marketing his products to high-income customers in company-owned stores in trendy neighborhoods and resorts. To expand sales quickly in the 1980s, Ralph Lauren launched the concept of a "store within a store" and entered into alliances with department store chains like Macy's and Dillard's. These Ralph Lauren stores were highly differentiated from the department stores that surrounded them. They featured dark wood décor, expensive furnishings, and array of British cricketing trophies and pictures. All these place features were designed to conjure up the feel of an expensive private club.

The store-within-a-store concept was very successful, Ralph Lauren sales soared, and other designers such as Tommy Hilfiger and Nautica moved to imitate the concept. Today, large department stores are frequently composed of many stores. Often, the greater variety of clothing available attracts more customers so that all of the companies benefit.

Product Differentiation and Market Segmentation

When a company decides to make and sell many different types of a particular product, like cars, shoes, clothes, or digital cameras, differentiating the products to avoid customer confusion becomes very important. To accomplish this, a company chooses a different marketing mix (product qualities, price, promotion, place) for the product in each market segment in which it chooses to compete. As noted earlier, *product positioning* is the process of customizing a product to the characteristics of a specific market segment. Product positioning also, however, requires marketers to clearly distinguish between the products to avoid customer confusion. Customers need to understand why some of a company's different products are better suited to their needs than others. This requires a high degree of marketing precision. The following Business in Action describes Ralph Lauren's product positioning choices.

Business in Action

Product Positioning at Ralph Lauren

Ralph Lauren (RL) Company competes in only two market segments of the retail clothing market: the exclusive designer segment and the high-priced–high-quality segment. RL then divides each of these two market segments into subsegments (shown in Figure 10.10). The company's brand managers must position the different product lines to appeal to the specific clothing needs of customers in each subsegment.

On the *product* dimension, RL's positioning is based on the quality of the materials and workmanship required to make its clothes. Its top-of-the-line designer clothes are handmade and use luxury materials such as silk and cashmere, which can cost thousands of dollars. The quality of materials then drops to fine cottons, wools, and linens in the high-end segment. Design is a particularly important differentiator of the women's brands: RL's Black Label brand competes with Dior and Versace in the evening wear segment of the market, whereas its Blue Label Brand is oriented towards more casual, yet exclusive clothing that can be worn at home or in the office. The Ralph brand focuses on floral designs; Pink Pony on the country-club sports segment; and as with the men's brand, Polo Jeans Co. concentrates on upper-end casual clothing.

As you might expect, the *price* of RL's clothing is also positioned to differentiate its products. Although *all* of the company's products command premium prices, a men's cashmere shirt can cost $300 in RL's Purple Label brand, whereas a similarly styled cotton shirt in Polo Golf might sell for $50. Marketing makes sure that the prices of the different clothing brands signal their value to different customers.

In terms of *promotion*, RL advertises its various brands in the media most likely to be read by customers in each market segment. Polo Golf is widely advertised in sporting magazines; its Polo Jeans lines in upscale magazines like *Vanity Fair*, and its exclusive lines in fashion magazines like *Vogue*, *GQ*, and *Food & Wine*.

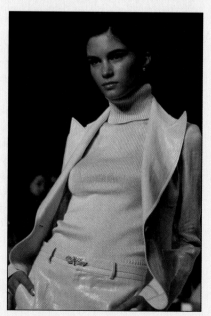

Ralph Lauren's marketing managers make sure that the prices of the company's different clothing brands clearly signal their value to the company's customers.

Figure 10.10
Product Positioning at Ralph Lauren

	Men Sub-segments	**Women** Sub-segments
Exclusive Designer	Purple Label (Designer)	Black Label (Designer
	Polo Ralph Lauren (Work/casual)	Blue Label (Work/casual)
Upper End Segment	Polo Jeans Co. (Upper Casual)	Polo Jeans Co. (Casual)
	Polo Sport (Lower casual)	Pink Pony (Sporting)
	Polo Golf (Sporting)	Ralph (Floral designs)

Finally, with regard to *place*, RL's casual and sporting brands are widely available in department store chains. Its exclusive designer brands are sold through boutiques in top-of–the-line department stores like Neiman Marcus and Saks Fifth Avenue and in its own 130 company-owned stores. Finally, RL owns a chain of stores in outlet malls to sell its overstocked clothing at discounted prices, such as its staple Polo shirts and shorts.[10]

RL ran into problems with its product positioning in the late 1990s when customers perceived that the "distance" between its different brands and the brands of its competitors had fallen. After it went public in 1997, its drive to increase revenues and profits led RL to make more clothing than it could sell at the premium prices it wanted. Faced with a large amount of unsold inventory, it began to sell its clothes in places such as Sam's Club and other discount stores. This seriously weakened RL's exclusive image, and it had to lower the price of its clothes in the upper-end clothing segment or customers wouldn't buy them. At the same time, the popularity of Tommy Hilfiger and other brands increased thereby eroding RL's unique image in people's minds.

RL's experiences illustrate the problems related to product positioning. It is a complex, demanding task. Being able to develop the right marketing mix to position a range of different products strengthens a company's business model. How well marketing managers are able to do this, however, determines a company's profitability and often its very survival.

Summary of the Chapter

Marketing is a powerful tool that can help a company develop and differentiate its products to meet the changing needs of its customers. Because marketing motivates people to purchase goods and services, it is a major driver of a company's profitability and the health of a nation's economy. The chapter made the following major points:

1. *Marketing* is the organizational function responsible for uncovering the needs of customers and creating customer relationship programs to deliver value to them over time. *Product development* relates to the technical, scientific, and engineering processes involved in creating new or improved products that better satisfy customer needs. *Sales* relates to the development and use of techniques to inform and persuade people about the value of a company's products.

2. Customer needs are needs that can be satisfied by the qualities or features a good or service has to offer. Marketing research is conducted to collect information about customer needs and the way these needs differ from customer to customer.

3. The three main challenges marketing managers face to understand their customers are to (1) identify their existing needs (2) find ways to better satisfy existing needs (3) discover unmet needs.

4. Customer groups consist of people who have a similar need for a product. Many customer groups normally exist in a market.

5. Once a significant group of customers who share a similar need for a product has been identified, this group is treated as a market segment. A market segment is a set of customers companies target by making and selling a product designed to satisfy their specific needs.

6. Market segmentation is the process of grouping customers based on differences in their needs or preferences for products. Companies then need to decide which products to make and sell to which market segments.

7. A company can choose between one of three approaches towards market segmentation: ignore differences between groups and make a product aimed at the "average" customer; make a different product aimed at most or all market segments; or focus on producing a different product for just one or two market segments.

8. Product differentiation is the process of setting goods and services apart from their competitors by designing them to better satisfy the needs of customers. In practice, product differentiation is the result of the design of the marketing mix—the combination of (1) the product's qualities and features; (2) the product's price; (3) the promotion mix used to inform and persuade people to buy the product; and (4) the places at which the product is made available for sale.

9. When a company decides to make and sell many different types or models of a product, designing the marketing mix to differentiate between the products becomes much more complex.

Developing Business Skills

QUESTIONS FOR DISCUSSION AND ACTION

1. What different roles do marketing, sales, and product development play in the process of creating products that better satisfy customers' needs?

2. Why is it so important for a company to adopt a customer-oriented marketing approach?

3. How should (1) an appliance manufacturer and (2) a fast-food company go about the process of finding better ways to satisfy customers existing needs?

4. What are the four main elements of the marketing mix? How does the design of the marketing mix create product differentiation?

5. Why is product branding an important marketing activity?

6. How does a company go about identifying different customer groups and needs?

7. What are three main approaches to market segmentation? Why would a company want to make many products for many market segments if this increases costs?

8. Why does product positioning and the design of the marketing mix become an important determinant of a company's success of when it decides to segment the market and offer customers many different products?

9. *Action.* Contact the marketing manager of a department, office, or home-supply store and find out what approach to product differentiation and marketing segmentation the store uses.

ETHICS IN ACTION

The Limits to Marketing

As the chapter discussed, it is possible for companies to generate demand for products by clever marketing and promotional activities. Because most people only have a limited amount of money to spend, the question becomes, can marketing actually reduce the utility of customers if it convinces them to buy products that they later learn do not really satisfy their needs? Cigarettes and liquor, which can harm people's health, are examples of such products. Using the ethical principles discussed in Chapter 5, think about and answer the following marketing-related questions:

- What ethical guidelines should companies follow when marketing their products to avoid doing their customers harm?

- When a company advertises and promotes its products, what ethical considerations should determine what is acceptable or unacceptable advertising and promotion?

- What clear examples of unethical marketing can you think of?

SMALL GROUP EXERCISE

Supermarket Competition

After reading the following scenario break up into groups of three or four people and discuss the issues involved. Be prepared to share your thinking with the rest of the class.

You are marketing managers in charge of designing the marketing mix for a new supermarket in your city. You need to find the best approach to differentiate the supermarket from others and target the market segments that seem to offer the best chance of developing a competitive advantage.

1. List the supermarkets in your city and identify their approach to product differentiation and market segmentation. In other words, what are the main elements of their marketing mix and what kind of customer groups are they attempting to attract?

2. On the basis of this analysis, what type of marketing approach do you think will best succeed in the local market? What will the specific elements of your marketing mix be? Which market segments will you choose as your primary targets? What will you do to attract them?

DEVELOPING GOOD BUSINESS SENSE

Marketing a Restaurant

Marketing is big business. One way to think about its importance as a value chain activity is to compare the marketing advantages of large, nationwide companies with millions of dollars to spend on marketing against those of smaller, local companies who are closer to their customers. Using the restaurant business as your focus, complete the following assignment:

1. How can a nationwide restaurant chain use its marketing resources to give it a competitive advantage in any local market?

2. Given its scarce resources, how should a local restaurant try to market its product to compete against national chains?

3. Which national and local restaurants are most popular in your local market? What elements of their marketing mix helps to explain this?

EXPLORING THE WORLD WIDE WEB

P&G's New Marketing Approach

Go to Procter & Gamble's Web site (www.proctergamble.com), click on "News," and then click on "Management Speeches and Perspectives" and read

"The Future of Marketing" by Jim Stengel. **For more Web activities, log on to www.mhhe.com/jonesintro.**

1. What new issues and changes are confronting marketers today?

2. How is P&G altering its marketing activities to respond to the changes taking place?

BusinessWeek   CASE FOR DISCUSSION

Branding: Five New Lessons

The last time detergent and toothpaste giant Procter & Gamble Co. made a bid for razormaker Gillette Co., it was out of desperation. Back in 2000, when the Cincinnati giant made an unsolicited bid, Gillette was a bargain: Despite its hit Mach3 razor, a series of earnings disappointments had hammered the stock. P&G was struggling, too, and so were a lot of other once-invincible brands. With fracturing TV audiences moving to the Web and cable, the classic 30-second spot that had made household names of the likes of Mr. Clean and Tide was losing traction. Consumers were starting to identify more with niche markets than with the one-size-fits-all brands that had long been the backbone of the consumer-products industry. Retail shelves were stocked with private-label rivals. Most frightening of all: The information-packed Internet threatened to expose those brands as nothing special. The age of the giant, mass-market brand seemed to be dead–and so was a P&G-Gillette deal.

Oh, what a different story it was on January 2004, when it was announced that the wedding was on. Sales growth at both companies is on a tear, earnings and margins are up, and hit products are rolling out of their labs. P&G's sales growth is running at 8% a year, excluding acquisitions–-double the rate of the late 1990s. And the once-struggling razormaker fetched a price of $57 billion, 19 times earnings before interest, taxes, and depreciation. Why did Gillette do the deal? "I have a simple formula," says CEO James Kilts. "Strength plus strength equals success."

Are brands back? Well, yes and no. It's not that the doomsayers were all wrong. Media are becoming infinitely more complex. Big retailers–especially Wal-Mart Stores Inc.–are more powerful than ever, pressuring the profits that big brands need to fuel marketing and innovation. And every year surveys show consumers becoming more cynical about advertising. No wonder so many brands have faltered: Coca-Cola, Levi Strauss, Kodak, Ford–the list goes on.

But the savviest brand managers have adapted, creating a new paradigm in which innovation is king, marketing is diffuse and personal, and size can be an advantage. Nothing shows this more than perennial No. 1 detergent Tide, where P&G's stepped-up consumer research, brand extensions, and ads have reawakened it within a moribund category.

Here are five lessons from classic companies and upstarts alike. All are thriving by managing brands differently than companies did in the heyday of the mass market.

1 Innovate. Innovate. Innovate.

Why would P&G tinker with Tide? Long the detergent leader, Tide would seem best left alone, a profitable annuity on years of mass-market flogging in the 60s, 70s, and 80s. But P&G has tinkered nonetheless, combining strong technology and consumer research to push sales up 2.6% over the last year in a category that is growing less than 1%. The secret: a widening family of detergents and cleaners that now includes everything from Tide Coldwater, for cold-water washing, to Tide Kick, a combination measuring cup and stain penetrator.

Innovation isn't always built from scratch. P&G is a master at transferring technologies from one brand to another. Tide StainBrush, a new electric brush for removing stains, uses the same basic mechanism as the Crest Spinbrush Pro toothbrush–also a P&G brand. Gillette, too, is adept at cross-pollination. Its latest winner is the battery-operated M3Power, the result of a collaboration between the company's razor, Duracell battery, and Braun small-appliance units. Despite a 50% price premium over what Gillette charged for its previous top-of-the-line razor, the M3Power has captured a 35% share of the U.S. razor market in seven months.

2 Move Fast–Or Lose Out

Not only are customers hooked on innovation, they're demanding it faster. Handbag designer Coach Inc. once introduced new products quarterly; now they come out monthly. On Coach's Web site, the new line currently features a bevy of options, from a $498 suede tote bag covered in an oversized pink and purple logo pattern to the "Coach Soho Nappa Small Tortilla," a white leather number with a tassel and a $328 price tag. "For brands to stay relevant, they have to stay on their toes. Complacency has no place in this market," says CEO Lew Frankfort. In any given month, Frankfort says, new products account for 30% of U.S. retail store sales.

3 Minimize Exposure to Wal-Mart

Wal-Mart is the key customer for any consumer product brand today. But balancing those sales with plenty of others is vital to a brand's health: For most suppliers, the more you sell to the world's biggest retailer, the less you make. In a recent study by consultant Bain & Co. of 38 companies doing 10% or more of their volume through Wal-Mart, only 24% sustained above-average profitability and shareholder returns. P&G, which sells 18% of its goods through Wal-Mart, was one. It has done so by shifting business away from basic products such as paper towels, which can easily be knocked off by a private label, to higher-margin products such as health and beauty care, including its line of Olay skin products.

It's not as if Wal-Mart is the only game in town—though sometimes it might seem that way. Besides low prices, Americans crave convenience. Increasingly, consumers are shunning supermarkets and buying food at convenience stores, fast-food outlets, club stores, and elsewhere. Recognizing that, Kellogg Co. began thinking outside the supermarket aisle in 2001 when it bought Keebler Co. and its links to vending machines. Now, Nutri-Grain bars, Pop-Tarts, and even single-serving cereal bowls are available at many more places, and the Battle Creek (Michigan) company has gone from providing breakfast cereals to round-the-clock snacks.

4 The New Media Message

The splintering media, it turns out, hasn't been all bad. P&G is a longtime master of what a former exec calls "surround-sound marketing"—everything from in-store demos to pitches on Wal-Mart TV, engulfing shoppers in the brand message. But it has also become a pioneer of new techniques, such as integrating its Crest Whitening Expressions Refreshing Vanilla Mint into a recent episode of the TV show *The Apprentice*. The goal is to both target specific customers and to fit the medium to the message. When research showed that girls wanted to know more about Tampax, P&G shifted a chunk of advertising from TV to print and created a Web site called Beinggirl.com. "It's hard to convey a lot of information and stuff that's kind of personal in a 30-second TV ad," says Ted Woehrle, vice president for North American marketing. "Print and online were terrific."

5 Think Broadly

Rather than define itself by its products, P&G has expanded its mandate to become a solver of every problem in the home. While toothpaste rival Colgate-Palmolive Co. was focusing on the tube, P&G grabbed greater "share of the mouth" with innovations such as the inexpensive spin toothbrush and premium-priced Whitestrips teeth-whitening kits.

Apple Computer Inc., which was late to market with its digital music player, the iPod, took the lead nevertheless with a combination of great product design and marketing brains. But why were consumers willing to accept a computer maker as a consumer-electronics company? Because Apple made its brand stand not for desktop computing but for imagination and fun. "The iPod is about creative people doing creative things," says David Placek, president of Lexicon Branding in Sausalito, California.

Such thinking can fuel a rise to megabrand status in a fraction of the time it once took. The proof: Starbucks Corp. The Seattle-based coffee chain does plenty of core innovation. Credit for part of its holiday profit surge of 31.2% belongs to its new pumpkin spice latte. But that's just the start. Anne Saunders, senior vice president for marketing, sees the cafes not just as a place to slurp java but as somewhere "to connect with other people or as a getaway." That broader vision has led to offerings such as music and wireless Web connections.

Today, 30 million people visit a Starbucks each week. The average customer stops in 18 times a month. With no tagline and sparse traditional advertising, Starbucks has gone from an idea to being one of the most popular and valuable brands on the planet in under 20 years. "Starbucks, based on the old model, shouldn't be able to happen," says Kelly O'Keefe, CEO at brand strategy firm Emergence. But it has—and it's a whole new world.

Source: Nannette Byrnes, Robert Berner, Wendy Zellner, and William C. Symonds, "Branding: Five New Lessons," *BusinessWeek Online*, January 14, 2005.

QUESTIONS

1. Why are the five new lessons in product branding each important in today's market?

2. What changes in the market have made these new lessons necessary today?

BusinessWeek   CASE FOR DISCUSSION

Reps and Marketers: Across the Great Divide

"I love our marketing department. They're great," Bart repeated. He then went on to itemize all the ways marketing provides support to the CollabNet sales team, including participation in sales calls and sales meetings, and collaborating on campaign plans and objectives. In fact, he listed every item that every other sales team said was lacking, as if he was from a parallel universe where the normal polarity was reversed.

I was so impressed by what I heard from Bart, that I asked him to introduce me to his vice president of marketing. I wanted to hear first-hand how Collab-Net built a functioning relationship between its sales and marketing teams, I wanted to understand what kept that relationship working, and I wanted to know whether or not it was paying dividends.

Bart introduced me to Bernie Mills, CollabNet's marketing vice president, and we shared a long discussion about their sales and marketing approach. Though Mills is clearly in command of his marketing program, he didn't lead off by taking credit for CollabNet's marketing and sales success. In fact, he recounted events during his rise to the vice president's position that have framed his marketing philosophy.

"Early on, the vice president of sales requested marketing's participation in the sales process," Mills recalled. "Not because he needed help closing sales, but because he wanted me to see opportunities in the channel." During one series of sales calls, the sales vice president invited Mills on a side trip to visit a prospect in a new market segment he was targeting. "We had talked about the opportunity on a theoretical level," Mills said, "but he wanted to give me a first-hand experience as to what the opportunity actually was. I was thrilled to participate, but it also helped me to understand the points he was trying to make as we continued to have a healthy debate over the level of emphasis we should put on that area of our business."

The experience doesn't sound all that remarkable, and Mills frames it by recalling that the sales vice president was actively trying to sell him on the new opportunity. But the elements of effective integration aren't remarkable: collaboration, client-interaction, consideration, and debate. What is remarkable is that such a simple recipe is lacking in so many companies.

MEETING OF MINDS. CollabNet certainly appreciates the importance of collaboration. Its successful software tools are designed for enabling and enhancing collaboration among far-flung software developers over the Web. Whether or not Collab-Net's market success can be attributed to its deep understanding of collaboration, there is plenty of evidence that the outfit practices what it preaches. It is a culture that encourages collaboration.

Mills reports that both CollabNet's sales and marketing teams continually reach across the traditional divide, and that his marketing department treats the sales team as its first customer base. "The channel is the customer—our sales team. They're the ones who will be in front of the client. And treating sales as a customer means understanding their requirements." As an example, Mills recalled a typical encounter with the sales team.

CollabNet's Worldwide vice president of field operations, Ken Comee, wanted marketing to develop a sales kit for a product launch. Some marketing departments would go their own way, while others might just follow the sales director's instructions. Mills approach was like a consultative sale. "We had a number of meetings with sales, first to build a collaborative list of requirements, and then to negotiate over the issues we didn't see the same way. When we finally built to that list, we showed up at launch with a kit already vetted by sales."

THE OTHER GUY'S SHOES. "Sales is selling one-to-one. Marketing is selling one-to-many," he began. "For sales, that means selling deal-to-deal, quarter-to-quarter, while marketing needs to focus on the longer-term picture. We need to understand and respect that difference."

Understanding and respecting the difference between sales and marketing only comes by making the effort to listen and consider other points of view, which is certainly an aspect of leadership. As Mills put it: "Marketing needs to lead with a listening ear. Marketing doesn't need to have all the good ideas; they just need to be able to recognize them."

TALK IS CHEAP. Bill Portelli, CEO of Collab-Net, set out at the beginning to create at CollabNet a culture of collaboration and communication, a culture supportive of cross-functional integration, a culture where people challenge each other to perform.

Yeah, sure, we've heard it all before. But that's precisely the point. We've heard all of these things before because it's common sense. And yet, like so many other things, like not dieting or continuing to smoke or not getting enough exercise, we all know what needs to be done—yet persistently fail to do it.

SHARED GOALS, COMMON LANGUAGE. Portelli's recipe for a collaborative culture is simple: Establish clear goals that everybody understands, focus communication on solving business problems, give your team ownership over its product, hold them accountable for successes and failures, and specifically hire people who buy into that approach. Of course, the devil is always in the details, so I asked Portelli how this plays out day-to-day in the roles of sales and marketing at CollabNet.

In order to understand CollabNet's approach, you first need to understand one thing about the company: it values marketing. At CollabNet, marketing is not just about creating PowerPoint presentations and sales collateral, but about playing a pivotal role in understanding market demand and translating that into products that can be sold profitably. As Portelli puts it, "Marketing is very much a lynch pin in our organization. Both engineering and sales look to marketing to arbitrate what we're going to build next, and why."

So, turning back to the creation of a collaborative culture, the sales, marketing, and engineering efforts need to continually understand what each is trying to achieve, and that means clear goals and metrics against which performance can be measured. At CollabNet, sales and marketing work together toward revenue and booking targets, and engineering and marketing work together toward product road maps and dates. There is a clear value chain in which every team understands the critical role that every other team plays.

"It's important to have complete transparency of what the sales force is trying to accomplish," Portelli says, "as well as what engineering is trying to accomplish. So it starts at the executive level by having everyone understand these tradeoffs and metrics, and how we're trying to drive ourselves."

Getting marketing involved directly in the sales channel is a critical part of CollabNet's process, not only for getting marketing and sales on the same page, but getting on the same page with the client and engineering, or, as Portelli puts it, "the whole value chain that connects the client with the product that ultimately has to get out the door."

For Portelli, what starts at the foundation as a cultural imperative to collaborate and communicate openly, naturally builds into the business tactics that help CollabNet thrive in a challenging market. Communication isn't just about playing well with others, it's about getting the right information to the right people at the right time to be able to beat the competition and make a profit, and every team has specific responsibilities around communication.

BEDROCK VALUES. Portelli again frames things around his internal value chain. "Getting in front of your clients, understanding their pain points, and then making the client a part of the process, along with sales and marketing, and then actually delivering something that the market wants, and then supporting it—that goes a long way to client satisfaction, and of course making money with everyone feeling good about it."

Marketing's role in all of this is to "take input from the broadest possible group of stakeholders that matter, and synthesize it into some direction for engineering." Those inputs include market dynamics, direct client feedback, and feedback from the teams that service and support clients day-to-day.

The sales function is also built on communication. "Sales' role is to go out there and really listen to what particular clients want . . . and to work closely with marketing so that marketing understands it as well, and that the right kinds of information can be fed back into the product development process."

None of these ideas will be new to anyone in business. These are the ideals we read about in every business text book. The difference at CollabNet is that these ideals have been turned into bedrock values that Portelli and his team have pursued from the start, and continue to pursue from the start with every new employee.

Source: Christopher Kenton, "Reps and Marketers: Across the Great Divide," *BusinessWeek Online,* May 26, 2004 (Part 1); June 14, 2004 (Part 2).

QUESTIONS

1. How can communication between marketing, sales, and product development increase a company's performance?

2. How has CollabNet's CEO, Bill Portelli, created a culture in which these three functions work together effectively?

BUILDING YOUR MANAGEMENT SKILLS
Know Thyself

Do you enjoy playing an instrument? Some people prefer to express themselves by painting, making jewelry or pottery, or writing. Maybe you like to solve problems and find new ways to do things. We each need to express our creativity in different ways. Businesses need people who are creative to help develop new products, improve systems, and create marketing messages. Try the assessment exercise called "Assessing Your Creativity Quotient" on your Student DVD to help you understand your creativity and give you some good ideas of how to enhance it.

CHAPTER VIDEO
3M Greptile Grip Golf Glove

3M Corporation is a highly diversified multi-million dollar company known for technology and innovation, but not necessarily as a strong "brand" in the sports industry. Its entrance into the sports industry represents an interesting process in product development and successful marketing.

The new product development process at 3M occurs in stages beginning with strategic product development, the successful cycle concludes with the commercialization of the product. 3M used this approach in the successful introduction of the Greptile Grip Golf Glove.

Critical points in the development cycle include market segmentation where specific target markets are identified and research conducted. Questions are raised such as "what can we do to prolong an individual's relationship with the sport?" Or "How can we introduce individuals to the sport?" In this case, the sport is golf. After targeting their market segments, 3M looks to screen the product for effectiveness. For example, they found that the Greptile glove had 610% more grip than traditional golf gloves and 340% more than special grip gloves currently on the market.

The business analysis stage follows where the problem of overcoming the perception that 3M is not a sports brand is addressed. In 3M's case, innovation and technology are clearly related to the sports industry and they use the power of the innovation brand to overcome obstacles to entry.

Development and test marketing of the glove are the next steps in the process. Development is concerned with how to make a stylistic, functional and affordable product; test marketing is concerned with how the consumer and retailer respond. During this phase is where packaging of the product became an apparent issue, not the product itself.

The final process is commercialization of the product where the benefits of the ownership and superiority of performance are communicated to the consumers.

1. How does 3M differentiate its sports brand from its other product lines?

2. What is the "marketing message" of 3M?

3. Would you consider Greptile Grip Golf Glove to be a product "brand"?

11 Sales, Distribution, and Customer Relationship Management:

Reaching and Satisfying Customers

Learning Objectives

After studying this chapter you should be able to:

1. Understand the relationship between marketing, distribution, sales, and personal selling.

2. Discuss the main distribution channels a company can use to reach customers and the factors that determine distribution channel choices.

3. Differentiate between different approaches to personal selling and explain why the nature of a company's products determines the selling approach.

4. Outline the major issues and problems that arise during each stage of the personal selling process.

5. Explain how customer relationship management can improve the profitability of the sales and distribution process.

> **WHY IS THIS IMPORTANT ?**
>
> Have you ever wondered why Avon relies primarily on direct sales, and Dell on telephone and Internet sales, for their competitive advantage? Also, why Lands' End systems for handling customer returns are a benchmark for many other companies?
>
> After reading Chapter 11, you will understand why choosing the right approach to sales and distribution, the one that best fits a company's business model, creates the most value for customers and profit for a company. This chapter also explains how effectively developing and managing relationships with customers can create an advantage that makes a company a market leader.

A Question of Business
Avon Is Calling in Every Way It Can

Why is Avon so successful at marketing and selling its products?

Avon reported record profits in 2005 on booming global sales of its well-known makeup, soaps, hair care, jewelry, and other products. Since its founding over 100 years ago, Avon has used personal home selling by sales reps, its "Avon ladies," to distribute and sell its products. Today it has 4.9 million sales reps located around the world who generate the majority of its $76 billion in revenues.

Avon is hardly an old fashioned marketer, however. Under its hard-driving CEO, Andrea Jung, it is pioneering ways to promote its products using new sales and distribution channels. Jung, for example, has been pushing the Avon ladies to make use of the Internet to increase sales. In the late 1990s, she recognized the importance of the Internet as a method of direct distribution to customers—one that fits perfectly with its personal selling approach. Avon created a sophisticated online storefront to display its products and inform customers about their high quality and value for the money.

At first, this Internet, direct-distribution approach caused considerable anxiety among Avon reps. They were worried that the sales made on the Internet would bypass them, thereby reducing their commissions. Jung worked hard to show reps that once Internet customers had bought and tried Avon's prod-

ucts, they would likely become good prospects for the reps. To convince them of this, she set up a program whereby the reps would also earn a commission when their customers purchased directly from Avon's online store.

Reassured, reps soon found that that the Internet sales actually complemented their personal selling efforts. After a customer went online to make a purchase, the Avon rep in the customer's area could follow up and offer the person additional help. The reps quickly discovered that Avon's Web site was, in fact, a great tool for getting new sales leads. Today almost 60% of Avon reps use the Web to generate sales leads.

Under Jung's leadership, Avon has begun to distribute and sell its products in a number of other ways, too. First, Avon is reaching beyond the typical customer it has served in the past, the 30- to 55-year-old woman. Jung decided to target the critical 16- to 24-year-old woman to attract and build brand loyalty among younger customers. The sales potential of this market segment is enormous; the 17 million women in this segment spend a full 20% of their income on personal care products.

In 2003, a new Avon division called *Mark* debuted to distribute a new line of hip cosmetics designed specifically to meet the needs of younger women. To attract younger customers, Avon decided to recruit a new generation of Avon reps from the same demographic group. Jung hopes that by training the new sales reps about how to respond to the needs of younger customers, the company can better customize the personal selling process for people in this market segment. Avon also recognizes that many of these reps will eventually replace its older reps. So hiring them now will help the company build an "army" of highly trained reps it can count on in the future. In addition, Avon began distributing its products through retailers such as J.C. Penny to increase its presence in department stores—where younger women typically do their cosmetic buying.

Avon is also expanding globally. A number of its cosmetics and jewelry lines are designed to appeal to customers in many different national markets. In fact, more than 3 million of its sales reps are located in countries abroad. Avon does not just distribute its U.S.-made products globally, however. Rather, it designs and makes products in the countries in which they are sold. This has also paid off handsomely because many products developed to appeal to customers in a particular overseas market, such as colors of lipstick and jewelry, have then been marketed successfully to U.S. customers.

Small wonder then that the innovative sales and distribution methods it is using to promote and sell its products resulted in record revenues and profits for the company. Its biggest challenge to increase profitability in the future is to reach and attract younger women who hitherto have had a "neutral" image of the company. If it can successfully sell its new line of Mark cosmetics to younger women, and attract new customers, Avon's future looks pretty indeed.[1]

Overview

How Avon is changing the way it reaches and sells to customers illustrates the challenges companies face today as they try to better manage their sales and distribution activities. As we discussed in Chapter 10, customers are fickle buyers. They constantly search for products that better meets their needs and need to be persuaded to buy and try new products. As a result, companies need to use marketing to find the best ways to promote and place their product to attract the most customers to buy them and increase sales and revenues. In this chapter, we focus on specific aspects of the promotion and place components of the marketing mix discussed in Chapter 10. Specifically, we examine the distribution and sales methods a company uses to place, promote, and dispose of its products. The ways Avon is changing the methods it uses to reach and attract customers illustrates the many challenges involved in managing a company's sales and distribution activities today. Avon is using new distribution channels, such as the Internet, to attract new and existing customers. It is also changing its sales approach by targeting a new customer group, younger women, and recruiting younger sales reps to distribute and sell to these customers.

First, we discuss the kinds of distribution channels a company uses to sell and distribute its products. Second, we examine the different kinds of personal selling approaches a company uses to manage these distribution channels. The stages involved in the face-to-face personal selling process and the ingredients that lead to successful personal selling are then described. We pay a great deal of attention to the issue of personal selling because in today's world, each of us has to be able to "sell ourselves." We need to be able to sell ourselves to prospective employers, for example, or make a bargain on a vehicle at a car dealership, or negotiate a real estate deal. Even finding a spouse requires a bit of "salesmanship." This is why we discuss the sales process in detail in this chapter. Finally, we examine the ways new information technology, such as CRM software, can improve the profitability of a company's sales, distribution, and marketing activities. By the end of this chapter, you will understand how a company's sales and distribution methods affect its ability to reach customers and deliver more value to them.

Distribution and the Sale of Products to Customers

distribution The selection of the distribution channels to reach and deliver products to customers most efficiently and effectively.

distribution channel The specific method a company uses to sell and deliver its products to customers.

Distribution involves the selection of the distribution channels to reach and deliver products to customers most efficiently and effectively. A **distribution channel** is the specific method a company uses to do this—to place, present, and deliver its products to customers. Sales are the activities involved in locating customers and then informing and persuading them to buy a company's products. A crucial sales activity is **personal selling**, direct face-to-face communication by salespeople with existing and potential customers to promote a company's products. The terms *sales* and *distribution* are used together because each activity is necessary for a company to reach and satisfy customers.

Types of Distribution Channels

In Chapter 10 we discussed several types of marketing distribution channels companies use to reach customers and inform them about their products. Here, we focus on four main kinds of distribution channels (1) company-owned or licensed distributors, (2) independent wholesalers, (3) retailers, and (4) direct distribution to the customer. The different channels are outlined in Figure 11.1.

COMPANY-OWNED OR LICENSED DISTRIBUTORS Many companies choose to sell their own products through a company-owned sales and distribution network. A company such as this establishes a chain of sales and service centers and

Figure 11.1
The Four Main Product Distribution Channels

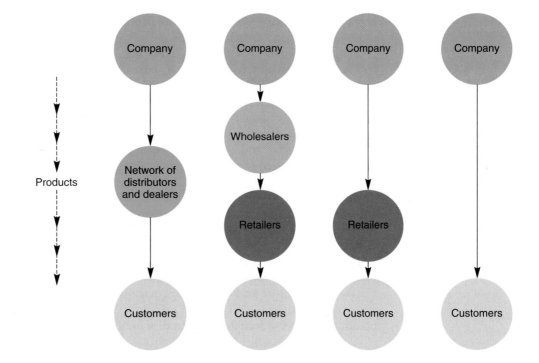

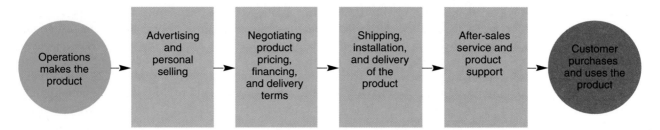

**Figure 11.2
Sales and
Distribution
Activities Involved
in Managing the
Upstream Value
Chain**

personal selling Direct
face-to-face communication
by salespeople with
existing and potential
customers to promote a
company's products.

**downstream value
chain** All of the activities
related to managing a
product from the time it is
made to the time it is
delivered and used by
customers.

**licensed distributors
or dealers** Independent
companies that buy the
rights to distribute, sell,
and service a company's
products within a specific
geographical area.

exclusive dealerships
Distributors that are
licensed to stock and sell
only one brand of a
product.

warehouses in the geographical areas in which it will operate. Xerox, for example, has hundreds of sales and service centers in all 50 U.S. states. In each of these areas, the company's salespeople call on customers, some of whom order the company's copying machines and other products. The machines that have been ordered are then shipped to the area sales office, and Xerox's after-sales service and support technicians install them in customers' businesses.

When a company owns its distribution network, it has total control over the way its products are delivered and sold to customers. In other words, it controls the down-stream value chain—all of the activities related to managing the product from the time it is made to the time it is delivered and used by customers. Activities in the downstream value chain directed at the customer include advertising and promotion, the personal selling process, product pricing, financing, delivery, installation, and after-sales service. These activities are shown in Figure 11.2. When a company controls all these activities directly, it can be highly responsive to the needs of its customers and provide them with a high level of service.

The downside of owning and operating a nationwide distribution system to control the downstream value chain is that it is very complex and expensive—it requires a major capital investment. To reduce these costs but still allow them to reach as many customers as possible, some companies develop a network of licensed distributors or dealers—independent companies that buy the rights to distribute, sell, and service its products within a specific geographical area. Frequently, licensed dealers are not allowed to carry competing products. For example, carmakers like Ford and Nissan typically distribute and sell their products through a nationwide system of exclusive dealerships. Exclusive dealerships are licensed to stock and sell only *one* brand of product, such as a car. (Sometimes, however, particularly in small towns, a dealer might be allowed to sell two or more brands.) When only licensed distributors and dealers are allowed to sell a company's products, the company is able to maintain considerable control over the way the products are distributed and sold—even though it does not own the distributorships.

Most companies provide intensive training to their licensed distributors. The distributors are instructed how to sell, customize, install, and service the company's products. Companies also establish a set of rules, best practices, and performance goals that distributors are expected to follow and achieve—such as sales and customer satisfaction goals. If a distributor fails to meet these sales goals, it can be penalized, and, in some cases, even stripped of its license.

A company's control over the *supply* of products to its dealers also gives it the ability to motivate them to meet their sales goals. One of Toyota's sales goals, for example, is to minimize the number of customer complaints it receives about a particular dealership. Should the number of complaints about a dealership become unacceptable, Toyota can punish it by reducing the total cars it is allocated each month. With fewer cars to sell, the dealership's profit falls. This will motivate its managers to solve customers' problems rather quickly.

Franchising is also a form of licensed distribution. For a fee, franchisees are allowed to use a company's business model. However, the company granting the franchises is allowed to monitor and control the activities of its franchisees to protect its brand name and reputation. McDonald's, Gold's Gym, and Midas Muffler are among the companies that use franchising as a distribution channel.

wholesaler An intermediary or broker that buys products from manufacturers and then resells them to other companies, such as retailers, which in turn distribute them to the final customer.

final customer The person who actually uses or consumes a product.

WHOLESALERS   Many companies use independent wholesalers to manage the distribution of their products. A wholesaler is an intermediary, or broker. It buys products from manufacturers and then resells them to other companies, such as retailers, who distribute them to the final customer. (The final customer is the person who actually uses and consumes a product.) Many manufacturers use wholesalers to reduce the enormous distribution and sales costs necessary to reach and attract customers. Unlike licensed distributors, however, wholesalers can carry competing products. Indeed, they stock the range of products that they believe will most appeal to their customers.

When a company uses wholesalers to distribute its products, it loses some control over the way they are delivered and sold. Because of this, a manufacturer has to negotiate with its wholesalers to ensure its products will be effectively promoted and advertised. It often has to pay wholesalers a fee to perform this service, in fact. The manufacturer also hires salespeople to regularly visit wholesalers to ensure its products are being given a sufficient amount of shelf space and promotion.

retailers Intermediaries who sell other companies' products to the final customer.

RETAILERS   Retailers are intermediaries who sell other companies' products to the final customer. In the past, it was common for manufacturers to distribute its products through hundreds of wholesalers, which then supplied thousands of retailers that sold them to millions of final customers. In the grocery business, for example, food companies like Dole and Kraft would ship their products to large, regional, food-product wholesalers, which would then sell and distribute them to countless small supermarkets.

Today, retailers like national supermarket chains and discount stores are electronically linked to their suppliers. Using an IT-based distribution system, retailers, not wholesalers, are now the intermediary between manufacturers and the final customer. As a result, large retail chains like Kroger's and Wal-Mart now have considerable power to drive a hard bargain and demand steep price discounts from manufacturers.

Another common form of retailing that has emerged involves establishing an online storefront to reach customers via the Internet. Virtual retailers can design their Web sites to provide customers with large amounts of information about an enormous range of products. They can also offer recommendations and rankings of competing products to help the customer make a decision. Increasingly, online retailers are trying to personalize the distribution system by creating long-term relationships with customers. Amazon.com, with its "One-Click" checkout system, is a good example of an online retailer that early on realized it would be an advantage to have customers establish online accounts containing their shipping addresses, credit card information, past transactions, and products that have interested them. The ability of online customers to avoid paying state sales taxes has also increased the popularity of online retailing.

direct distribution Distribution channels used to deliver and sell products directly to the final customer.

DIRECT DISTRIBUTION   Direct distribution occurs when a company delivers and sells products straight to the final customer. A company can select from many different methods to directly reach the final customer. One method is direct advertising in newspapers, magazines, and television. The customer fills out an order form in a magazine and mails it to the company or places an order over the phone. The company then ships the product directly to the customer. Many companies also create a company-owned, online storefront and use the Internet as a direct distribution channel. An online storefront can be a relatively low-cost method of sales and distribution, especially because it can cut out wholesalers as well as bricks-and-mortar and virtual retailers. In the textbook industry, for example, books used to be distributed and sold only through book wholesalers and bookstores. Now, students can visit a textbook publishers' Web site and buy a

Did You Know?

The average American receives 330 pieces of direct mail each year.[2]

Companies like Pampered Chef hold shopping parties in people's homes. Sales reps demonstrate their products, take individual customers' orders, and transmit the orders to the company, which then ships the products to the rep, who distributes them to customers.

copy directly online, often at a reduced price. Of course, textbook publishers still distribute and sell their books to bricks-and-mortar stores and other online retailers like Barnes & Noble and Amazon.com to maximize their ability to reach customers. Similarly, thousands of insurance companies, mortgage brokers, and specialty retailers have gone online to interact directly with customers.

The way Michael Dell used the direct distribution channel to make Dell the global leading provider of PCs illustrates the importance of this channel. In the 1980s, Dell's original strategy to compete with Compaq and IBM was to sell his PC directly to final customers using newspaper advertising and over-the-phone selling. This low-cost way of attracting customers allowed him to charge lower prices for PCs than his competitors. IBM and Compaq, by contrast, sold their higher-priced PCs through licensed dealers. As the use of the Internet started to explode, Dell took his business online and created a storefront that worked side-by-side with the telephone to sell to customers. This direct distribution channel not only made intermediaries unnecessary but also allowed Dell Inc. to be highly responsive to its customers.

By contrast, other companies employ national salesforces. Such a company divides a country into sales regions or "territories" and assigns salespeople to each to manage the sales and distribution activities there. Companies such as Avon and Tupperware are examples. These companies hold shopping parties in people's homes. Sales representatives demonstrate their products, take individual customer orders, and transmit the orders to their companies, which then ship the products to their reps, who distribute them to customers.

The Distribution Mix and How It's Chosen

distribution mix The combination of channels a company selects to place, promote, sell, and deliver its products to customers.

A company's distribution mix is the combination of channels it selects to place, promote, deliver, and sell its products to customers. For any company, the crucial issue is to select the channels that align the products it sells with the needs of its customers most efficiently and effectively. If it makes the right choices, a company reaches and attracts the most customers. Andrea Jung, for example, started a new distribution channel to sell Avon's new Mark line of cosmetics to younger women. By changing Avon's distribution mix, she better aligned Avon's cosmetics with the needs of younger women. She also pioneered the selling of Avon's products through the Internet to reach and attract more customers. As we mentioned, textbook publishers use wholesalers and retailers and also are finding that the Internet is a viable distribution-mix channel.

Factors Affecting the Choice of Distribution Mix

When a company selects the channels to distribute and sell its products it needs to consider three main factors (1) the characteristics of its products; (2) the need to customize its products; and (3) the importance and expense of the purchase to the customer. These three factors are illustrated in Figure 11.3.

complex products Products with qualities and characteristics that make them difficult for customers to evaluate.

PRODUCT CHARACTERISTICS   Distributing and selling a product becomes more difficult and expensive as a product becomes more complex. Complex products are products whose qualities and characteristics make them difficult for customers to evaluate. If I go to the supermarket, for example, I can see and touch the fruit and vegetables to determine which are freshest; judging these products is a relatively easy and straightforward process. If I go to a computer store or car dealership, however, I can see and touch the computers and cars, but this still tells me little about their reliability and how they will stand up to constant use. Complex

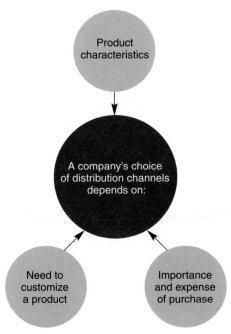

Figure 11.3
Factors Affecting the
Distribution Mix

products can only be evaluated thoroughly *after* they are purchased and used over long periods of time. The reliability of a new car or appliance, for example, might take years to evaluate. (By contrast, I know if an apple is rotten the moment I bite into it.)

Companies that make and sell complex products must do more promotion and sales to inform and persuade customers to buy them. Aligning a complex product with customer needs therefore requires greater communication between the buyer and seller. Companies selling apples or table salt do not need to provide customers with as much information about their products. By contrast, a carmaker has to provide glossy brochures, a 100-page operating manual, and employ salespeople to educate customers. This necessitates that companies "get close to customers." Companies that make complex products get close to their customers by choosing a distribution mix that uses distributors, dealers, or a national salesforce, as illustrated in Figure 11.4. Each of these channels involves the use of a highly trained team of sales and service specialists who can provide customers with information and promote a product's qualities and features. A company with an established dealer network is also in a position to assure customers that it can provide excellent after-sales support if problems do occur.

On the other hand, when a company sells less-complex products that customers can easily evaluate for themselves, it usually distributes the products through wholesalers and retailers or distributes them directly to the final customer. Advertising becomes the most important way to promote products distributed via these channels.

THE IMPORTANCE OF THE PURCHASE TO THE FINAL CUSTOMER

Some companies make products that customers have to give considerable thought to before purchasing. Expensive products such as luxury cars, ERP software, and heavy earth-moving equipment are examples. Because these purchases require spending large amounts of money, buyers actively seek out information about their quality versus the quality of competing products. The more significant a purchase of a product is to customers, the more likely a company is to use distributors, dealers, or a national salesforce to sell that product. Like with complex products, well-trained salespeople

Figure 11.4
The Choice of
Distribution Mix

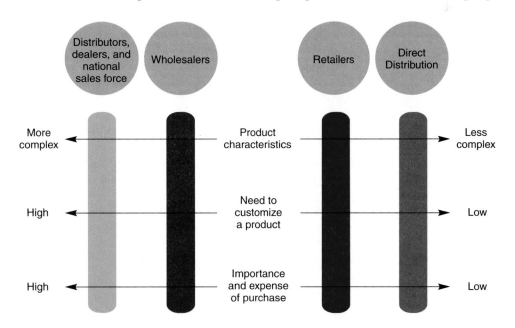

Companies that use these three factors to determine the distribution mix obtain a competitive advantage.

must be on hand to provide customers with information and "coach" them through the buying process. However, this also gives the company more control over how the product is marketed and sold.

By contrast, some companies make relatively inexpensive products that are bought by millions of buyers every day. Products such as soap and detergent and food products made by companies such as Procter & Gamble and Kraft are examples. Consumers don't spend much time making these kinds of buying decisions. Even if a customer decides he or she made a mistake after buying a product, all is not lost. The customer has only spent a small amount of money on the product, after all. Like less-complex products, when a product is relatively inexpensive and a less-significant purchase, the company uses intermediaries to get it to the customer. Once again, promotion through advertising is much more cost effective than using a salesforce to reach customers. Companies that make less-expensive products nonetheless work hard with their distributors and retailers to find the best ways to display and sell them. The goal of companies selling standardized products is to make the products "stand out" in stores so that they are easily visible to customers.

THE NEED TO CUSTOMIZE A PRODUCT   The second factor that affects the type of distribution and sales mix a company uses is the degree to which specific knowledge about the customer must be collected to customize the product to meet their needs. If a company makes or provides a customized product, salespeople will need to collect a great deal of information about what exactly the customer wants. Health insurance policies, mortgages, and custom homes are examples of products that fall into this category. A lot more face-to-face or phone contact is required in this case. By contrast, if a company makes a standardized product that it offers to everyone, such as a can of beans or a ream of paper, little or *no* customer contact is required in the selling process. Customers simply evaluate the qualities and features of competing products and then decide which one to buy.

Video Small Business in Action

Outsourcing

A polarizing debate concerning the outsourcing of U.S. jobs overseas is featured in this *BusinessWeek* TV video on your Student DVD. On the one hand, companies see outsourcing as a strategic approach to realize cost savings and improved efficiencies that will actually increase jobs over the longer term. For example, projections show an increase of 317,367 new jobs by 2008. For example, in order to achieve the longer-term increase in jobs, there will be a 21 billion dollar savings by exporting computer jobs overseas. These new jobs will be higher skilled and better paying. Furthermore, the low technology, low skill jobs that are being outsourced are no longer aligned with the skill level and needs of the modern U.S. workforce.

The other side of the debate suggests that companies who use outsourcing as an employment strategy are engaged in unethical business practices. Proponents of this view see the exportation of jobs "offshore" as a direct cause of the loss of U.S. jobs. The issue of outsourcing can be seen across industries with two notable exceptions: health care and education.

The debate does not show any sign of abating. Regardless, the data show clearly that the best jobs go to those with the best skills. That means that there is a need to focus on increasing the skill level of the U.S. labor force.

Discussion Questions
1. What are many businesses doing in today's economy to reach and attract more customers? Would these methods potentially lead to outsourcing?
2. Health care and education seem to be immune to outsourcing. Using the material from the chapter, cite reasons for this phenomenon?
3. Is the process of Customer Relationship Management (CRM) appropriate for outsourcing?

Collecting information about specific customers is a demanding and time-consuming sales activity. It greatly increases the costs of managing the distribution and selling process. This explains why companies that sell complex, expensive, or customized products also choose a distribution mix based on the use of distributors, dealers, or employ a national salesforce to get the word out and promote their products. By contrast, the more standardized or inexpensive the product a company makes, the more likely the company is to use advertising, intermediaries, and direct distribution to sell to the final customer.

Gaining a Competitive Advantage with the Right Distribution Mix

Companies that choose the right distribution mix are able to achieve a competitive advantage by reaching a large number of buyers through most cost-efficient channels. Avon is one of these companies. Cosmetics are complex products. Users often have a hard time figuring out what kinds of cosmetics and colors work best for them. Trained facial and makeup artists are needed to help customers decide which type of cosmetics best suit their personal skin tones and how best to apply them. Obviously, cosmetics affect the way people look and their appearance is an important concern to most people. Because many brands of cosmetics are expensive, buyers often welcome the advice of trained salespeople like Avon has. Avon also recruited younger salespeople and began selling its products in departments stores. This distribution mix is working well for Avon.

Rather than using a national salesforce to demonstrate their luxury cosmetics lines like Avon does, Estee Lauder and Lancome use makeup specialists located in department stores. Avon is now also using this distribution channel, as well as the Internet to sell its products.

Interestingly, cosmetic companies like Revlon, which primarily distribute and sell their low-priced cosmetics through drug and discount stores, have run into major financial problems recently. Customers are less attracted to their products even though they charge much lower prices for them. In many cases, the lower prices that consumers have to pay for these cosmetics still doesn't compensate them because the failure rate of the products is so high (because the customer has chosen the wrong color and so forth, because of lack of advice). This puts Revlon and other companies using this channel at a competitive disadvantage. Some of these firms and their retailers are now attempting to overcome this problem by offering unconditional money-back guarantees to buyers who end up with cosmetics they don't like. As you can see, a company must select the most cost-effective distribution channels it can. But it also has to balance this priority against its need to attract as many customers as possible.

THE IMPACT OF IT As we note earlier, advances in IT are dramatically changing distribution methods. These days, customers can even customize products themselves online. For example, using Expedia.com, we can all customize our own vacation packages or our stock portfolios on E*Trade. BMW allows would-be car buyers to create their "ideal" cars on its Web site. Retail clothing stores like Sears and The Gap allow their customers to input their physical dimensions online so they can see how different types of clothing will fit them.

This "self-entered" data is making it much easier for companies to collect information about their customers, which is actually making it less complex and easier to distribute and sell products to them. More companies have become motivated to directly distribute their products online as a result. Take the banking industry, for example. There are now a number of banks that exist only "virtually." So far, no major U.S. bank has completely done away with its bricks-and-mortar branches. Instead, banks have added online banking to their distribution mix. This channel allows them to reach more customers—customers located anywhere in the world.

Approaches to Sales and Selling

As we discuss in Chapter 10, sales and personal selling are a vital part of the promotional activities involved in reaching and delivering products to customers efficiently and effectively. (Recall that *personal selling* occurs when a salesperson sells to customers directly, either face-to-face or via an electronic medium, like a telephone or computer.) In some industries personal selling is paramount: Which products wholesalers and retailers choose to stock, for example, or which drugs doctors decide to prescribe, often depends on a salesperson's ability to inform and persuade customers that *their* company's product is superior and thus the best choice. As you would expect, the selling approach adopted by companies depends on the type of product being sold and how well the approach satisfies the needs of customers. (An interesting case about Pfizer's salesforce is at the end of the chapter.)

technical selling
Selling that requires a company's sales representatives to impart detailed technical information to their customers.

missionary selling
Selling that occurs when a salesperson educates customers, builds goodwill, and performs promotional activities to encourage them to purchase a product at a later date.

agent A, person, or intermediary, acting on behalf of final customers.

Selling Complex Products

When products are complex, customized, and expensive, they lend themselves to three personal selling approaches: *technical, missionary,* and *creative selling.* These approaches, which are outlined in Figure 11.5, demand the most use of a salesperson's skills and effort, and so are relatively high-cost methods of selling. However, they are often required when a company uses distributors, dealers, or a national salesforce to sell its products.

TECHNICAL SELLING Technical selling becomes especially important when a company's products are technologically oriented or when they must be customized to suit the needs of specific customers. In this situation, it is essential that salespeople be able to communicate the technical aspects of the product to would-be customers. The ability to close a sale often depends on the salesperson's ability to convince customers that the product *does* meet their needs—and does so better than competitors' products. Often this makes it necessary for salespeople to reassure customers that the company stands by its products and will give them the after-sales support they need to learn how to operate and maintain the product. Selling million dollar X-ray machines and advanced scanners to hospitals, for example, requires a high level of technical selling. In this type of a selling situation, the salesperson's ability to "get close to" or form a personal relationship with the customer is vital. Frequently, the same salesperson will service the needs of the same set of customers over a long period of time in order to "bond" with them.

MISSIONARY SELLING Missionary selling also requires salespeople to have detailed product knowledge and be able to impart that knowledge to customers. However, missionary selling differs from technical selling because the goal is not to close the sale immediately. Rather, missionary selling involves a salesperson educating customers, building goodwill, and performing promotional activities such as supplying them with product samples and literature so they will purchase at a later date.

Missionary selling is used most often when the potential customer is an **agent,** a person acting on behalf of final customers. The way in which pharmaceutical companies go about selling prescription drugs is a good example of missionary selling. These companies do not sell

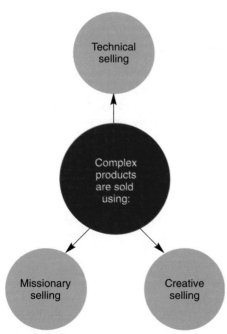

Figure 11.5
Approaches to Selling Complex Products

directly to the final customer. They cannot, because only doctors (who act as agents) can write prescriptions. Instead, large drug companies like Merck and Pfizer employ thousands of sales reps to visit doctors on a regular basis. Their task is to inform doctors about the superior qualities of the company's drugs and to handout free samples doctors can give to their patients.

Although this is an expensive way to sell a product, research shows, in fact, that doctors are most likely to prescribe the drug promoted by the salesperson who visited them last. In 2002, drugmaker Warner Lambert announced it intended to hire 2,000 additional salespeople to promote its drugs for just this reason! Missionary selling, and the advertising that accompanies it, is a major factor contributing to the high price of prescription drugs today.

creative selling
Selling that requires salespeople to combine their technical knowledge and personal selling experience to craft creative and unique ways to better meet the needs of their customers.

CREATIVE SELLING   Creative selling occurs when salespeople combine their technical knowledge with all their personal selling skills searching for creative and unique ways to better meet their customers' needs. This might involve finding new ways to use a product or combine products, if need be. In other words, the salesperson uses every means available to close the "gap" between a product and customers and convince them that it *does* meet their needs. Often this means that the salesperson has to work closely with customers and continually probe them to determine what it is they are looking for.

Suppose an IBM software sales rep is trying to sell a multimillion-dollar ERP system to a large company. The sales rep needs considerable technical expertise; the rep also needs the ability and experience to appreciate what the company's specific needs are and then show the company's decision makers how the software will solve these problems. For example, if the company really likes some of its existing software applications, the rep might have to find out a way to make these older applications work well with IBM's new ERP system. Similarly, a real estate broker who sells million-dollar homes needs the ability to appreciate what a particular client is really looking for in a house. By asking the right questions and listening carefully, a creative broker can narrow down 500 homes a prospective buyer could potentially view to a final list of 25 and close the sale more quickly. When products are complex, there is usually a lot of scope for salespeople to engage in creative selling. If the salesperson can uncover a crucial piece of information about a problem a customer is experiencing and find a special solution to it, he or she can often win the business.

Many of the types of issues involved in selling complex products come up in the auctioneering business, discussed in Business in Action. Although selling works of art worth millions of dollars might seem far removed from ordinary selling, it is not. Note how crucial it is for the salesperson, the auctioneer in this case, to have a great deal of expertise. Note also the great lengths the auctioneer goes to develop personal relationships with customers. Likewise, a salesperson at Best Buy or Macy's who listens carefully to the problem a customer is having and finds a creative solution to solve it will also be able to close more sales. Moreover, when the customer returns, he or she will often seek out that salesperson, resulting in repeat business for that person and a steady stream of commissions.

Business in Action

Going, Going, Gone . . . at Sotheby's

How do you get wealthy people to spend millions of dollars to buy a modern work of art? Creative selling by the art auctioneer is often vital to selling such a product. One of the world's leading art auctioneers is Tobias Meyer, the head of contemporary art at Sotheby's, the world's leading auction house. Meyer's first selling task is to get wealthy people who own important works of art to put them up for auction. The only way for him to get owners to sell is to convince them that they will receive a premium price for their art. Meyer's second task is to find other wealthy people who are willing to pay a premium price to own the work of

Sotheby's Tobias Meyer, the world's leading art auctioneer, has to persuade buyers and sellers they will both be better off trading artwork worth millions of dollars.

connoisseur A person with immense knowledge about a particular type of product and who can identify the qualities that make it valuable.

art—and to convince them that they have made a good purchase. In other words, Meyer has to persuade both buyers and sellers that they will both be better off trading a work of art worth millions of dollars.

To perform well in such a complex sales situation, a fine art auctioneer must be an art expert in his or her own right. A connoisseur is a person with immense knowledge of a particular type of product, such as paintings or antique furniture or cars. A connoisseur can identify what makes a particular product unique and valuable. Meyer has such credentials. When he was only seven he advised his mother to buy a painting by Cy Twombly, a modern American artist that cost several thousands dollars. Today the painting is worth several millions.

To learn his business, Meyer studied fine art, visited most of the world's fine arts museums, and apprenticed himself to an antiques dealer who was a connoisseur in early furniture and silverware. He achieved his present position in his 30s because he was recognized as a connoisseur in his own right. Armed with such a reputation, a broker of expensive works of art can convince buyers and sellers about the true market value of a painting. An auctioneer acts as an intermediary who links buyers and sellers and receives a commission in return. At Sotheby's that commission is at least 10 percent of the work's selling price, so the sale of a $5 million painting nets Sotheby's $500,000 in commission.

Using his connections in the art world, Meyer identifies wealthy collectors willing to part with a work of art. He also searches for owners of paintings who have little idea of their real value in today's art market because prices have soared. Once he has found a hot property, Meyer informs as many interested buyers as possible about the painting's forthcoming sale to increase demand for the work. In the art market, as in all markets, a product's price depends upon how many buyers compete to own it.

One example of the way Meyer goes about his business was evident when he was viewing an art exhibition in Germany. He noticed that one of Andy Warhol's most famous paintings, *Orange Marilyn*, a painting of Marilyn Monroe, was still owned by a private collector. Sensing that the owner did not know its real value today, he engaged in some creative selling. He informed the owner he thought it would fetch a record price at auction, possibly $4 million or more. A few weeks later the owner agreed to let Meyer and Sotheby's manage its sale.

To sell the painting at such a high price, Meyer had to engage in more creative selling. He invited 30 major art collectors to a lavish dinner in New York, promising them "they would meet a woman who had left America decades before and had just come back." When his guests had dined, and their curiosity was at a peak, Meyer dramatically uncovered the painting and used his knowledge to explain its uniqueness and place in modern U.S. art. He also expressed his belief that it would command a record price, far higher than a Warhol painting had ever sold for before. In this way, he created excitement and competition among collectors to possess it. He continued to communicate with collectors and promote the painting further until the sale day arrived. Bidding for the painting was vigorous, and it sold for $17.3 million! As Meyer's actions suggest, creative selling is a major part of the sales process in the art world—and in selling all kinds of complex products.[3]

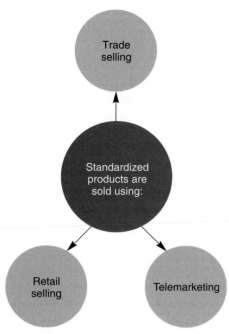

Figure 11.6
Approach to Selling Standardized Products

trade selling Selling done through intermediaries, such as wholesalers and retailers, which manage the sale of a company's products to other companies.

retail selling Selling to the final customer—the person who buys a product for his or her own use.

telemarketing A sales method used to contact prospective customers exclusively by phone.

Selling Standardized Products

Fewer problems confront a salesperson selling more standardized products. Although the salesperson must still be able to clearly communicate the product's qualities, because customers have fewer problems evaluating them, this is easier to do. So, when selling standardized products a salesperson's main task centers on being helpful, courteous, and responsive to customers, especially to earn a customer's repeat business. Three approaches to selling standardized products are *trade selling, retail selling,* and *telemarketing.* These approaches, which are outlined in Figure 11.6, are most commonly used when selling products to intermediaries and directly to the final customer.

TRADE SELLING Trade selling involves managing the sale of one company's products to other companies. Trade sellers can be intermediaries, such as wholesalers and retailers. They can also be companies that purchase products to use as inputs for making their own products. A food company like Kraft, for example, uses trade selling to distribute its food products to wholesalers and retailers like supermarkets, and to other food makers and restaurant chains that use its cheese and sauces as ingredients in making their own products—like pizza, for example.

In the trade selling business, customers understand what they are looking for in a product. As a result, they can easily evaluate the products of a company like Kraft. Thus, the principal task in trade selling is negotiation—negotiating issues such as pricing, financing, and delivery. Trade selling typically takes place between companies in related industries, like food-product companies and restaurant companies, for example.

RETAIL SELLING Retail selling involves selling to the final customer, a person who buys a product for his or her own use (or family's use). The main goal of retail selling is to provide customers with the product information they need, keep the product in stock on store shelves, process customers' orders quickly and correctly, and handle the packaging and delivery of the product.

Sales associates in a retail setting can be passive or proactive in the way they handle customers, however, which has a direct effect on a company's profitability. Recall that the sales and profitability of both Home Depot and Lowe's are tied to the quality of the customer service provided by their sales associates. How well these associates are able to advise customers often determines whether or not the customers proceed with their home-improvement projects—and buy Lowe's and Home Depot's products.

TELEMARKETING Telemarketing involves persuading customers over the phone. It is a common method used to get customers to try or switch products, particularly standardized products. Some companies have their own telemarketing departments. Many others, however, use the services of telemarketing companies that employ hundreds of people in call centers to represent various companies. Indeed telemarketing can reduce, and even eliminate, the need for a company to employ its own salesforce.

Today, however, many companies are finding telemarketing to be an increasingly ineffective channel. Most people feel that telemarketing is an obtrusive, annoying method of personal selling. Of course, it's relatively easy to hang up on telemarketers or otherwise screen their calls. Even people who unwittingly answer their phones and don't hang up are frequently unreceptive to the products being sold. To overcome this problem, some companies have reverted back to door-to-door sales, a trend discussed in Business in Action.

Business in Action

When the Sales Call Gets Very Personal

In the 1990s, the use of telemarketing by companies such as phone service and credit card providers increased dramatically. Improvements in IT made it possible for computers to automatically dial the phone numbers of consumers repeatedly until they picked up. At this point, a sales rep would come on the phone line and begin his or her "pitch." To prevent such unwelcome calls, customers began to use services such as Caller ID and gadgets like the TeleZapper. Finally, in 2003 national legislation was passed that allows customers to register their names on a "do not call" list with the Federal Trade Commission. Over 60 million phone numbers were on this list by 2004.

In an effort to continue to reach potential customers, some companies have resorted to an old-fashioned method of door-to-door sales. Companies like AT&T, SBC, Comcast, and countless utility companies began sending out thousands of door-to-door sales reps to "connect" with people at home. Of course, when they hear a knock at the door, many people believe it's their friends or neighbors paying them a visit, only to discover it's a sales rep. For most people, it's harder to slam a door in someone's face than it is to hang up the phone.

Just as complaints about phone selling soared in the 1990s, so, too, are complaints about door-to-door salespeople on the rise today. Clearly companies want to attract customers rather than repel them. Even though communications have improved, many companies still have a hard time finding good distribution channels that allow them to continue to grow their sales. For these reasons and those discussed in Chapter 10, marketing and sales have become much more complex today.[4]

Telemarketing is under fire. Because of Caller ID, the TeleZapper, and 2003 legislation allowing customers to be put on a "do not call" list, companies are reverting back to door-to-door sales.

Stages in the Selling Process

Now that we have described the main types of distribution channels and approaches to personal selling, we can turn to the many important issues involved in the actual selling process. Imagine that you have an engineering degree and have been recruited as a salesperson by John Deere & Company to sell farm equipment. What kinds of skills and knowledge do you need to be successful in your new sales position?

First, technical selling requires an in-depth knowledge of a company's products. So, you can expect to attend intensive training programs designed to teach you about the company's various products and those of its competitors. This training will help you align John Deere's products with the needs of your customers and demonstrate why they are the best choice. Second, you will need training to help you manage the typical issues that arise during the six stages involved in selling complex, expensive products. These issues are outlined in Figure 11.7, and each is discussed next.

Prospecting for Customers

prospects Potential customers for the goods and services a salesperson is offering.

The first stage in the selling process is to search out and find **prospects,** potential buyers of the goods and services you are offering. You will need to identify as many prospects as possible. The more contacts you make, the more John Deere products you are likely to sell. This involves identifying people and companies in your sales territory that need the kind of products you are selling but have yet to buy them from your company. Why, for example, does a major construction company in your region always buy its equipment from Caterpillar or Kubota?

An essential part of a salesperson's job is to do research and investigate prospective customers to find the answers to such questions. This research might involve:

- Examining the prospect's promotional materials and Web site and the kind of projects it has been engaged in.
- Making indirect inquiries about the prospect by questioning existing customers or the prospect's customers.
- Discovering how the type of equipment the prospect buys differs from the equipment you sell
- Finding out which person or persons in the prospect's company makes the purchasing decision and how best to approach them.
- Determining the company's financial status to ensure it has the money to buy the equipment (a *qualified prospect* is one that can afford to purchase your products and is therefore a sales lead worth pursuing).
- Using this information prepare to make a case as to why your product better meets the prospect's needs.

Based on this information, you will then forecast the chances of your getting the prospect's business. Because your time and resources are limited, this will help you identify the "hot prospects" and focus your sales effort on them. Meanwhile, there are likely to be prospective customers in your sales territory currently looking at equipment and trying to decide what to buy. It is vital that they know how to reach you, especially because you are new to your position and sales territory. So people get to know you, you will want to do some self-promotion by, for example, creating a Web page, sending out brochures and flyers with a personal note and business card to people in your territory, and so forth.

Obtaining referrals from existing, satisfied customers is a very good way to obtain new prospects. When prospects contact you, it is clear a satisfied customer has recommended you. This creates a favorable selling situation. So, along with prospecting for new customers, a new sales rep needs to keep his current customers happy–not only to increase their business but to get referrals.

To keep your customers happy it's important to keep good records on them as well as on customers you hope to do business with in the future. For example, salespeople can use their records to create mailing lists targeted at a specific type of prospect and feed them information whenever there is a chance a certain product might interest them. Recall the importance of missionary selling in building goodwill. A few hours spent listening to customers and taking time to inform them about new products can pay off with new sales later.

Making the Initial Contact

Because salespeople only have so much time, it is crucial for them to target their most *likely* prospects first. This is what people mean when they tell you to "grab the low-hanging fruit first." In other words, grab it before someone else does. Customers who have done business with you before, who have been referred to you by other customers, or who are actively looking for products are "low hanging" fruit, so to speak.

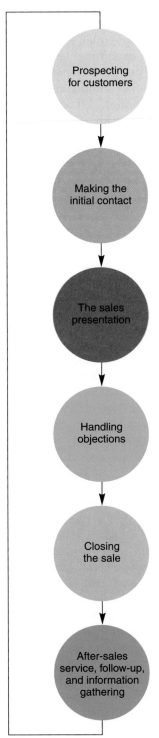

Figure 11.7
Six Stages in the Selling Process

(Prospecting for customers → Making the initial contact → The sales presentation → Handling objections → Closing the sale → After-sales service, follow-up, and information gathering)

cold call The first contact a salesperson has with a customer, either by e-mail, phone, or in person.

When you first initiate the contact with the customer, or make a cold call, either by e-mail, phone, or in person, any information that can personalize the conversation and show you are knowledgeable about and interested in the customer will create a favorable selling situation. Cold calls made in person are usually the most successful way to reach a prospect and get their time and attention. Again, it is more difficult to slam the door in someone's face than it is to slam the phone down.

But there are costs associated with personal vists–the time and money it costs to drive to the prospective customer's place of business and then to wait until the customer has the time or inclination to talk. For this reason, salespeople often e-mail or call customers first to determine the likelihood of a successful encounter. Getting a prospect's door open and seizing an opportunity to make a sales pitch, is not as easy as it sounds. Salespeople who look for ways to make themselves known to prospects in advance, have a much better chance of getting their "foot in the door." Of course, if the prospect initiates contact with you, it is important to respond quickly. The longer it takes to respond to the customer, the "colder" the call becomes.

Making the Sales Presentation

A salesperson may or may not be invited to make a detailed sales presentation upon his or her first visit with a prospect. If and when a prospect does indicate a desire to listen to such a presentation, the sales moment has arrived. Now, many of the communication issues we discussed in Chapter 6, such as active listening, become important. A salesperson's goal is to rapidly align the company's product with the needs of customers. To do this, she has to listen carefully to what the customer is looking for. What needs are driving the purchasing decision? Is it quality, price, the product's features, or delivery time? Some experts advise that the best sales approach is to get the prospect to do most of the talking. Then, using their technical expertise salespeople can show the prospect how a product matches their requirements. If the salesperson launches into a detailed product description prior to uncovering this information, however, he or she is quite likely to say exactly the wrong thing. This gives the prospect the opportunity to end the sales call.

When the presentation of the product ultimately does begin, it's important to be enthusiastic and excited about it. If the salesperson isn't excited about the product, the customer isn't likely to be either. The prospect is always on the lookout for cues from salespeople that might help them to evaluate the quality of the product they are being offered. Is the machine going to be reliable and will the salesperson provide prompt customer service? A salesperson who arrives late and lacks the necessary sales tools (brochures, facts, figure, prices, and so on) does not send the prospect a favorable message about the kind of service customers can expect in the future. By contrast, a salesperson who arrives with testimonials from satisfied clients, has everything on hand to make an effective presentation, is relaxed, courteous, and willing to listen has a much greater chance of success.

Don't make prospects feel uncomfortable by pressing them for an immediate decision. It may take 5 to 10 sales contacts to get a potential customer to commit to buy a product–personal selling is a time consuming activity. Instead, invite potential customers to try out your product and make it clear that you have

A salesperson needs to carefully listen to what a customer is saying before launching into a "spiel" about the company's products. Why is this important? Have you ever encountered a salesperson who talked about everything else but what you were interested in?

time to spend with them and can provide any information they might need to evaluate the product.

Salespeople must expect delays and failure. That said, a salesperson should never be shy about actually "asking for the customer's business." His or her job is to persuade the prospect to buy the company's product, after all. If a customer doesn't make a purchase, the salesperson shouldn't be afraid to ask why not. The problems with a product might be ones that can be easily solved by a different product later. They can also help the rep when it comes to dealing with the next potential customer. If, however, a prospect mentions having an unbreakable, 20-year relationship with a competitor's sales rep, this tell the rep not to waste any more time with the potential customer. At this point, his or her time would be better spent locating promising new sales leads.

Handling Objections

A typical sales encounter is rarely all smooth sailing. The very nature of sales and the selling process is to convey information that persuades prospects a particular product *does* match their needs. Savvy buyers are aware of this, however, and also know how to question a salesperson to uncover things that are *not* being said. A salesperson might emphasize product quality and after-sales service, for example, and sidestep the fact the product costs 20% more than its main competitor. When the issue of the higher price is eventually raised, the information a salesperson provided about the product and how well he or she presents it might convince the prospect it is well worth paying extra for.

During a typical sales encounter, it is common for prospects to make many objections or say why they *don't* plan to buy the product. Some objections will concern the product's features or its price. Alternately, a prospect might make a statement like, "I already buy the product from your competitor." From the prospect's point of view, making objections is a way of getting more information out of the salesperson. It is also a way to assess how anxious a salesperson is to sell the product. In this way, the prospect can gauge how much of a price discount the salesperson might be willing to buy. So, savvy buyers make real objections. Often, however, they do so just to see how a salesperson reacts. This is actually a useful part of the selling process because more information gets exchanged between the buyer and seller. However, salespeople need to learn to anticipate the kinds of objections that buyers typically come up with so they can respond quickly and easily to them.

Some companies actually provide their salespeople with a response sheet listing answers to typical objections they will face. Another way to counter opposition is for the salesperson to "agree" with a prospect's objection, but then to counter with the "yes, but" statement, which involves offering the prospect more information that overcomes the objection. This once again opens the selling door. At every point in a sales visit it is important to uncover the real reasons why a customer is hesitating to make a purchase, so a salesperson can try to resolve them and close the sale.

Did You Know?

How $100 is spent in an American grocery store[5]:

$50.00 - Perishables
$11.20 - Beverages
$ 5.42 - Staples, condiments, other
$ 8.37 - Non-food grocery
$ 6.33 - Snack foods
$ 8.13 - Main meal items
$ 3.83 - Health and beauty care
$ 3.81 - General merchandise
$ 2.89 - Pharmacy

Closing the Sale

At some point during the sales visit it becomes clear a prospect is reaching a decision about whether or not to buy a product. Often, the prospect alerts the salesperson to this by asking specific questions about a product's availability, features, price, financing, warranties, or delivery time. Prospects might also mention problems they had with their previous suppliers to signal a salesperson to convince them they won't have a similar bad experiences with the new product. Finally, they may start to ask a salesperson personal

Free financing or discounted prices if the customer "buys today" are tactics salespeople commonly use to close deals.

questions, or questions about the company they work for and the other products it sells.

It is important for a salesperson to know when to end a sales presentation and not shower a prospect with too much information. Salespeople need to stop talking long enough to give the customer enough time to say, "OK, I'll buy it" and make the deal. For many products, particularly complex ones, the "point" of sale is like a teeter-totter where a prospective buyer needs, or sometimes wants, to be pushed over the "edge" to make an important buying decision. Salespeople have to listen closely to their customers (recall active listening from Chapter 6) to sense when they are approaching this edge. When the customer has reached this point, it is a good time for the salesperson to offer "extras," such as an extended warranty to induce the person to buy. Other extras commonly offered are free delivery or financing, or a discounted price if the customer "buys today."

Savvy prospects, however, also know when a deal is closing. They will often try to prolong the sale to get the salesperson to throw in more and more extras. They might for example, keep bringing up the fact that a competitor's prices are lower. Or they will ask for a day or two to think about the purchase to give the impression the sale is not going to close. Each time it seems to a salesperson the deal is about to close, the prospect asks for something extra–and often they get it!

Salespeople need to understand the selling game taking place. Part of the game is knowing when to offer customers something extra and when to hold back–perhaps by saying something like, "I can't go lower than that; it's the lowest price I've offered all month." However, because they need to close the sale to meet their sales targets, it is often easy for them to give too much away. The problem in sales is that closing a sale by offering a steep price discount, free delivery, and so on, will generate higher sales and sales revenues. But everything extra given to a customer reduces the profitability of each sale (and in most cases, the salesperson's bonus). On the other hand, failing to close a sale and meet one's sales target can result in zero bonus pay. Moreover, many salespeople (those who sell cars are a good example), work strictly on commission. If they don't sell anything, they don't get paid. (Now do you understand why these people seem overeager to make a deal?)

Many times, however, it is best for the salesperson to slow down and try to discern where the prospect is really coming from. What's exactly driving his or her purchasing decision? This can help the salesperson determine how much extra will have to be given away to make the sale and whether this makes the sales worth it. This is frequently when the rep's sales manager gets involved–his or her job is to prevent the salesperson from giving too much away!

Doing After-Sales Service, Follow-Up, and Information Gathering

To gain the customer's loyalty, get referrals from them, and grow one's customer base, it is essential for salespeople to follow up immediately after the sale to begin building a long-term relationship with the customer. Did the product perform as expected? Were there delivery problems? What else could be done to help the customer? Even if the customer *has* experienced a problem, he or she is more likely to be more forgiving if you take the trouble to find out about it and work to fix it. For many customers, simply having someone listen to their complaints can alleviate much of their aggravation. Recognize, too, that if you promise to help your customers resolve a problem, you need to follow through on your promise. If you don't do these things,

buyer's remorse A phenomenon that occurs when a customer believes he or she made a poor purchasing choice.

buyer's remorse can result. Buyer's remorse occurs when a customer believes he or she has made a poor purchasing choice.

Follow-up also gives salespeople additional access to their customers and the opportunity to discover if any of the company's other products might fit the customer's needs. In addition, a salesperson is often able to generate additional service business. Long-term contracts to service complex products, such as machinery, equipment, and computer systems, are a major source of revenue for many companies. General Electric, for example, sells its turbines and jet engines at near giveaway prices. GE make money on these products by providing customers with after-sales service.

In general, good after-sales service makes customers very loyal to the company, in part, because so few companies do a good job of it. This builds goodwill, promotes a company's reputation, and generates repeat and referral business. Satisfied—and dissatisfied—customers talk about a company's products. Salespeople can actually use this information to their advantage. For example, if a salesperson can gather information from a prospective customer about how the competition is failing to satisfy the customer, he or she has an excellent opportunity to "steal" the business. The information is also an important source of "market intelligence" for the firm. Good market intelligence helps the company's marketing and product development groups created new and improved products. The role salespeople play in entering this information into a company's customer relationship management system is discussed next.

Customer Relationship Management

customer relationship management system An IT-based knowledge management system designed to track a company's customers— what they are buying, how satisfied they are, and how their demands are changing.

A **customer relationship management** (CRM) **system** is an IT-based knowledge management system designed to track a company's customers—what they are buying, how satisfied they are, and how their demands are changing. Among other things CRM monitors are the selling efforts of the firm's salespeople, the delivery of products via the firm's distribution channels, and after-sales service. CRM systems link all of these different activities together. The result is that marketing and sales managers have a better understanding of how each of these activities are affecting customer satisfaction and the firm's sales revenues and costs. CRM systems can help increase a firm's profitability, which explains why they are one of the fastest growing software applications today.

CRM systems have three interconnected components, which are shown in Figure 11.8: sales and selling, after-sales service and support, and marketing. Using the CRM system, every member of the firm's sales and marketing functions, from the salesperson in the field right up to the director of corporate marketing, have real-time access to information about these functions. Next, we discuss the ways in which the three components of CRM systems can improve a company's sales and marketing efforts.

CRM and Sales

Suppose that the only data a sales manager has access to are the total sales revenues generated by each of the firm's salespeople in the last 30 days. The information is not broken down in terms of the revenues generated from existing customers versus new customers. Also, suppose salespeople are not required to provide their sales managers with written input about the needs and preferences of their existing customers or prospective customers. How do you think this will affect the firm?

If the information the sales manager receives shows only that the revenue generated by a particular salesperson has increased, this tells the manager little about the actual profits being earned from those sales. The salesperson may have met or beaten his or her sales target and earned a bonus, for example, but if most of those sales were made at deeply discounted prices, this could be a problem. It's entirely possible that the sale of these products actually reduced the company's profits.

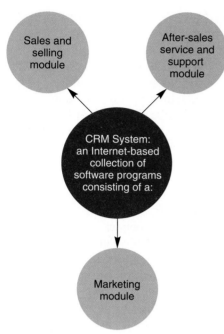

Figure 11.8
Components or Modules of a CRM System

Additionally, if salespeople don't share information about their current and prospective customers, sales managers cannot get a feel for who these customers are or why sales to them are or are not closing. If sales managers lack this information, they will often be at a loss when it comes to helping their reps maximize sales in their territories. It might be that customers would order more of the company's products if they could be delivered more quickly, or if the customers were offered a bigger discount than their salesperson could authorize. The sales manager will not know, however, and will be unable to intervene and close the deal. Similarly, a salesperson might have a hot prospect but be unable to close a deal without the help of a team of other salespeople with more experience or expertise. If no system is in place to flag managers with this information, sales will be lost. Another problem that could occur is that the rep who cries the loudest for help, will get it. Meanwhile, quieter reps with better prospects and bigger sales deals on the line might not get it.

Other important dimensions in the sales process are pricing, financing, and order processing. In many companies, to close a deal, a salesperson has to send the paperwork to a central sales office to check the customer's credit, approve special financing, offer a price discount, and determine shipping costs and delivery dates. In some companies, different departments handle these activities, so it can take a long time to get a response from them. This keeps customers waiting—something which often leads to lost sales. Until CRM systems were introduced, these kinds of problems were widespread.

Implementing a CRM system starts at the salesperson level. Companies like SAP provide CRM systems that specify, in detail, what kinds of information salespeople need to collect and input. Generally this includes information about their existing customers, such as the nature and size of their purchases, their changing needs, and their specific demands for price discounts or fast delivery. Salespeople are also required to input information about their prospective customers, including information about why or why not the prospect seems willing to purchase the firm's products. In addition to information about customers, they are also required to input data on (1) the amount of sales to new and existing customers; (2) the dollar value of the price discounts or "extras" they have given customers to close the sale; and (3) the amount of time and money spent selling to each customer.

As each salesperson inputs the required information into the CRM system, it is analyzed using the best practices software, and managers get a much clearer picture about what's going on. Each salesperson's individual sales performance can be assessed, and the profitability of each sale closed can be calculated. Sales managers can also tell if "star" salespeople—those who generate high sales revenues—are doing so only by offering their customers steeply discounted prices. Sales managers can also assess how much business is being generated by new customers and which salespeople have the most success in this area. Because the system contains information about how these sales were closed, sales managers can use it to educate the entire salesforce.

Each member of the salesforce also knows which prospects other members of the salesforce are working on and the kinds of problems they are encountering as well as their successes. Salespeople can share this information and brainstorm solutions to common customer problems. This fosters a kind of mentoring environment. Over time, salespeople begin to realize they are part of a "team" and that they will all benefit if they cooperate and use the CRM system collectively. Some companies using CRM

Did You Know?

Although it is common to find things sold in large packages in the United States, consumers in the Philippines more often buy items in small units or *tingi:* A single cigarette, a single disposable diaper, one painkiller pill, or small units of cell phone credit.[6]

A CRM system allows salespeople to share information with one another, including the customer objections they encounter and how they deal with them successfully. This helps everyone close more sales.

systems, in fact, base their sales bonuses not just on each salesperson's performance but also on the performance of the salesforce as a whole for this very reason. This encourages salespeople to input the necessary information into the system, which, of course, requires extra effort on their part.

Finally, by using a CRM system, a company can close more sales because it has more accurate information about its customers' needs. The sales module builds up a detailed case history about each customer, which helps salespeople plan their future visits to customers and better anticipate their needs. It also alerts salespeople to opportunities to sell additional kinds of products or services to customers.

CRM and After-Sales Service and Support

When a company implements the after-sales service and support CRM module, salespeople are then required to input detailed information about their follow-up visits to customers. Because the system documents every customer's case history, salespeople can instantly access a record of what occurred during a previous phone call or visit. They are now in a much better position to be responsive to their needs. This can be especially helpful when there is turnover, and a new sales representative takes over a territory.

CRM also allows a company to improve the company's after-sales service delivered by its customer service representatives. Telephone providers like Sprint and MCI, for example, require their reps to collect information about all of their customers' inquiries, complaints, and requests. This information is then recorded electronically in a customer log. The CRM module can analyze this information to evaluate if the customer service reps are meeting or exceeding the company's service standards.

Moreover, the CRM system identifies why customer complaints are occurring in the first place. The company's sales managers can then work to eliminate the sources of these problems and improve the after-sales support customers get. Finally, the CRM system can identify the "top ten" best service and support practices. These best practices can then be taught to all sales reps. Business in Action describes how one health-care insurance company improved its sales and after-sales procedures dramatically with a CRM system.

Business in Action

How Choosing a CRM System Helped Empire HealthChoice

Empire HealthChoice Inc., the largest health insurance provider in New York, sells its policies through 1,800 independent sales agents. For years, these agents were responsible for collecting all of the customer-specific information needed to determine the price of each policy. Once they had collected the necessary information, the agents called Empire to get their price quotes. After waiting days to get these quotes, the agents relayed them back to customers, who often then modified their requests to get the cost of their policies lower. When this occurred, the agent had to telephone Empire again to get a revised price quote. Because this frequently happened several times with each transaction, it often took more than 20 days to close a sale, and another 10 days for customers to get their insurance cards.

Recognizing these delays were resulting in lost sales, Empire decided to examine how a CRM system could help improve the sales process. Its managers chose a Web-based system so agents could calculate the insurance quote for themselves online. Once an agent has entered a customer's data, a quote can be generated in just a few seconds. The agent can continually modify the policy while sitting face-to-face with the customer until a policy and price are agreed upon. As a result, the sales process can now be completed in just a few hours, and customers receive their insurance cards in two to three days.[7]

After Empire HealthChoice Inc. adopted a CRM system, it found that it could sell and finalize an insurance policy in just a few hours—a process that used to take the company 20 days.

CRM and Marketing

As we discussed, the "market intelligence" salespeople put into a CRM system creates a knowledge database that can improve the effectiveness of the firm's marketing research activities. Marketing managers have access to detailed customer profiles, their purchases, and reasons why they were or were not attracted to the company's products. Armed with this knowledge, the marketing department can help improve the marketing and sales process in many ways.

First, it becomes possible to track the effectiveness of a company's advertising and marketing campaigns in real-time. For example, if the company's salespeople report that many prospective buyers were attracted by ads placed in a certain magazine, on a certain Web site, or aired over a certain radio station, the marketing department can quickly divert more of its budget to promoting its products through these channels. Similarly, when a salesperson reports a "hot" prospect, marketing can intervene and send in a marketing expert to help the rep close the deal, if need be.

Second, the information provided by the CRM system can help marketing improve its product differentiation and market segmentation. It may become clear, for example, that a customer group targeted by marketing has a specific need that is not currently being met by the company's product. With real-time CRM information, marketing can work with product development to redesign the product to better meet customer needs. Similarly, CRM information can reveal that the potential of a particular market segment is much larger than marketing had originally thought. Marketing can then move quickly to focus its advertising and promotion campaign squarely on this segment. Via the CRM system, the company's sales and support groups are also alerted to these changes taking place. This will allow them to modify their activities and frame their presentations to better target the promising new market segment. Managers can use the CRM system to analyze each of the many crucial activities that go into the sales, distribution, and marketing process to pinpoint ways to increase revenues and reduce the company's operating costs.

Summary of the Chapter

Companies today have more distribution options available to them than ever before. Deciding how to better reach, sell, and distribute products to customers has therefore become a more complex task. For any company, however, the crucial issue is to select the channels that align the kind of products it sells with the needs of its customers most efficiently and effectively. This chapter has made the following major points:

1. Distribution relates to the way companies sell to customers and deliver products to them. A distribution channel is the specific method a company uses to accomplish this.

2. Sales are the activities a company needs to engage in to locate customers, provide them with information about its products, and persuade them to buy them.

3. The four main distribution channels companies use are (1) wholly owned or licensed distributors, (2) independent wholesalers, (3) retailers, and (4) direct distribution to the customer.

4. A company's distribution mix is the combination of channels it selects to sell and distribute its products. For any company, the crucial issue is to tailor its distribution mix so that the nature of its products is aligned with the needs of its customers.

5. Three factors that affect a company's choice of distribution mix are (1) the complexity of a product; (2) the importance of the purchase to the buyer, (3) and the degree to which a product must be customized to meet the needs of customers.

6. Companies selling complex, expensive, or customized products use either wholly owned or licensed distributors or employ a national salesforce.

Companies selling standardized, inexpensive products use intermediaries, like wholesalers and retailers, or sell directly to their customers. Advertising is usually the most effective way of promoting these kinds of products.

7. Today, the emergence of new distribution channels, large national retail chains with buying power, and the Internet are changing the way companies distribute and sell their products.

8. Personal selling is vital for companies that sell complex, customized, or expensive products.

9. Three approaches to personal selling are technical, missionary, and creative selling. These sales approaches are time intensive and result in higher sales and distribution costs.

10. Three approaches to selling standardized products are trade selling, retail selling, and telemarketing.

11. The personal selling process is made up of a series of six stages:(1) prospecting for customers, (2) making the initial contact, (3) presenting the product, (4) handling customers' objections, (5) closing the sale, (6) and providing after-sales service.

12. A customer relationship management system (CRM) is an IT-based knowledge management system designed to track a company's customers— what they are buying, how satisfied they are, and how their demands are changing. CRM monitors the selling efforts of the firm's salespeople, the delivery of products via the firm's distribution channels, and its after-sales service.

13. CRM systems have three main components, sales and selling, after-sales service and support, and marketing. These components are linked together so that all of the company's sales and marketing employees have real-time access to information about the company's downstream activities.

Developing Business Skills

QUESTIONS FOR DISCUSSION AND ACTION

1. What are the four main distribution channels a company can use to reach its customers?

2. What factors determine a company's choice of distribution channels?

3. Why does selling to an agent differ from selling to the final customer?

4. In what ways can direct distribution through the Internet improve a company's distribution mix?

5. Why is personal selling an important aspect of the distribution process, and what kinds of personal selling are associated with each channel?

6. Imagine you are a salesperson selling expensive, custom-made bicycles. What kind of approach to selling would you use to sell to specialized bicycle retailers?

7. *Action.* What are the stages of the selling process? Using a visit to a car dealership as an example, list the kinds of car buying issues that come up at each stage for (1) a car buyer and (2) the salesperson responsible for selling cars.

8. *Action.* Find a salesperson in your city and interview the person to determine the kind of personal selling they do and the main challenges they face.

9. What is CRM? In what ways can CRM systems help marketing managers better target and respond to customer needs?

ETHICS IN ACTION

Information and Persuasion in Selling

Salespeople need to make a living. They know if they don't close the sale, it hurts their chances of meeting their targets and earning bonuses. If they fall far short of meeting their targets, they can even lose their jobs. Using the ethical principles discussed in Chapter 5 address the following issues.

- How far should a salesperson go to convince a customer to buy a product—even if the salesperson knows the product doesn't meet the customer's needs?

- Is a salesperson obligated to reveal information about a product that might result in the loss of a sale?

- To what extent is it the customer's responsibility to make the inquiries necessary to determine if a product matches his or her needs?

- What kinds of events in the sales process might lead customers to believe they have been unfairly or unethically treated?

SMALL GROUP EXERCISE

How Best to Distribute a New Soft Drink

After reading the following scenario break up into groups of three or four people and discuss the issues involved. Be prepared to share your thinking with the rest of the class.

You are a group of food-science students who have discovered a combination of herbs and spices that make a great, new, revolutionary soft-drink syrup. You've convinced a local restaurant to try this syrup out in their soda machine, and the response from its customers has been overwhelming. Customers love the soda's flavor. Better yet, the drink only has a few calories. All of you are eager to start a new business venture to market the syrup. Together, you have managed to borrow $50,000 from your families to fund the project. Now you have to decide how to distribute and sell your new product.

1. What kind of distribution mix should you initially use to distribute and sell your product?

2. What kind of personal selling will be necessary to get (1) local restaurants and stores, and (2) a regional soft drink bottling company to try your product?

3. Assuming your venture goes well, how will you change your distribution mix to reach more customers over time?

4. What kinds of sales and promotional activities will be necessary for you to grow the sales of your syrup?

DEVELOPING GOOD BUSINESS SENSE

Which Company's Web Site Is Best?

The Internet is a distribution channel that offers many opportunities for small businesses to reach a wide number of potential customers. However, some Web sites attract many more customers than others. Think about why some Web sites are better at reaching customers than others. With this in mind, go to the following Web sites: Amazon.com, Wal-Mart.com, and Landsend.com. Shop around on each site and then answer the following questions:

1. In your opinion, which of these sites best attracts shoppers and creates customer loyalty. Which of the sites does the poorest job, in your opinion?

2. What factors (convenience, speed, appearance, and so forth) made you decide one company's Web site was a better direct distribution channel than the others?

3. In what ways does Wal-Mart's nationwide system of bricks-and-mortar stores give it a distribution advantage over a purely online store?

4. What kinds of distribution advantages do purely online stores have over those that use a bricks-and-mortar channel?

EXPLORING THE WORLD WIDE WEB

Siebel and CRM

Go to Siebel (www.siebel.com), a major supplier of CRM software. Click on "About Siebel" followed by "Customers and Case Studies." Choose a product or industry from the pull-down list that interests you and read a case study about a company. Then answer the following questions. **For more Web activities, log on to www.mhhe.com/jonesintro.**

1. What are the problems the company was trying to solve by using Siebel's CRM software

2. In what ways did the CRM software help solve these problems?

BusinessWeek CASE IN THE NEWS

Netflix 1, Wal-Mart 0

Is the tide finally turning for Netflix? For the past two years, wave after wave of competitors had threatened to capsize the DVD rental-by-mail pioneer. Retail giant Wal-Mart Stores entered the market with prices that undercut Netflix. So did Blockbuster Entertainment, which has quickly amassed nearly 1 million subscribers. And e-tailer Amazon.com, which opened a rental service in Britain last year, hinted that it might create its own U.S. service, too.

Now it looks like the competitive storm is dying down—on the surface, at least. Wal-Mart abandoned ship, turning over its DVD rental service to Netflix and promising to promote its service in return for links advertising DVD sales on Walmart.com. "It's great to have the world's largest retailer as a partner," says Netflix Chief Executive Reed Hastings. He got the deal rolling during a dinner last January with Wal-Mart Chief Marketing Officer John Fleming, who handles the company's online operations.

That's not all. Just the day before, Blockbuster announced it's testing higher prices for its online rental service, which currently undercuts Netflix's $17.99 monthly fee (for three DVDs at a time) by about $3 a month. And its aggressive move into DVD rentals by mail could get short-circuited by top shareholder Carl Icahn, who has recently said he wants Blockbuster to cut costs and focus on the basics.

MINIMAL IMPACT? Still, it's not smooth sailing yet for the six-year-old Netflix—and investors know it. After lifting the stock as much as 17% in early trading May 19, Netflix ended up just 4%, to $16.13 a share—still far below its high of $39.77 early last year. The reason: For the short term, anyway, the company's situation hasn't changed that much. "Neither of these announcements does much for Netflix," says Dennis McAlpine, managing director of McAlpine Associates, a market researcher in Scarsdale, N.Y. "The impact will be minimal."

Why? For one thing, the benefit from the Wal-Mart deal won't extend much beyond the elimination of what has proved to be a minor competitor. McAlpine estimates that the world's largest retailer had less than 100,000 DVD rental subscribers. That's a pittance next to Netflix's 3 million-plus, which is why Netflix says it doesn't expect any material impact from the deal.

What's more, it still faces some pretty potent competitors, both real and potential. Chief among them: Blockbuster. The chain has said it will invest $170 million this year in its online-rental operation. And while Icahn has indicated little willingness to spend on such new initiatives, for now Blockbuster's aggressive pricing remains in force. "I don't think BBI is less dangerous—maybe more, as they feel like they have to be more aggressive with their customer acquisition and pricing strategy," writes First Albany

Corp. analyst Jason Avilio in an e-mail to *Business-Week Online.*

SMALLER RIVALS. And Amazon is still looming. It's not saying when, if ever, it will offer a DVD-rental service in the United States, and the exit of Wal-Mart is a powerful statement that it's tough to start from scratch in the face of Netflix's momentum. Even so, that may well spur Amazon to forge a partnership instead, perhaps with Blockbuster. That might present an even more powerful enemy for Netflix.

Netflix also faces challenges from below. A startup called Peerflix, for instance, lets individuals swap DVDs for 99 cents a trade, avoiding the need to build costly distribution centers and a huge library of DVDs, as Netflix has. "For us, every household in America is a distribution center," says Peerflix CEO Billy McNair, whose company has 25,000 DVDs in circulation compared with Netflix's 40,000 different titles. "The capital efficiency of a peer-to-peer model is real obvious."

STILL SEEKING PROFITS. But no doubt about it, Netflix is sitting prettier today. Wal-Mart's exit reveals how much of a headstart Netflix has, and how its hold on the market is stronger than skeptics thought. And its first-quarter results indicate that it's managing to keep pace with Blockbuster. As a result, even though Netflix had a first-quarter net loss of $8.8 million, its sales rose 54%, to $154.1 million, and subscribers jumped by 56%. "We're continuing to invest heavily," says Hastings. "But we've seen our business grow steadily for the past 20 quarters."

The big question is when Netflix's progress will pay off with consistent profits. Avilio estimates that if the new competitive environment could allow Netflix to raise its monthly fees by $2; that would improve profits quickly, by $96 million a year. But he thinks it will be next year before Blockbuster would raise prices broadly. So as far as Netflix has come, it has a long way to go before Reed Hastings can catch his breath.

Source: Robert D. Hof, "Netflix 1, Wal-Mart 0," *BusinessWeek Online,* May 20, 2005.

QUESTIONS

1. How are distribution channels in the movie-rental business changing?

2. What are the advantages and disadvantages of the channel Netflix uses?

3. How is the competition between movie-rental companies changing, and why did Wal-Mart make a deal with Netflix to handle its DVD rental service?

BusinessWeek CASE IN THE NEWS

Pfizer's Funk

Every weekday, some 38,000 Pfizer Inc. sales reps fan out around the globe. Armed with briefcases full of free drug samples, reams of clinical data, and lavish expense accounts for wining and dining their quarry, the reps infiltrate doctors' offices and hospitals. Their goal: to persuade medical professionals the world over to make Pfizer drugs the treatment of choice for their patients' aches and pains.

This massive sales force—roughly the size of three army divisions—is just the advance guard in Pfizer's quest for world drug domination. Equally important is the drugmaker's $3 billion annual ad budget. A pricey array of prime-time commercials and glossy magazine ads show vibrant people freed from the threats of heart disease, hay fever, and a dismal sex life. Sure, consumers can't just go out and buy this stuff:It has to be prescribed by a doctor. But Pfizer and the industry have learned that stoking demand among consumers puts irresistible pressure on doctors. That's why Pfizer is now the fourth-largest advertiser in the land.

Efforts such as these impose huge fixed costs. Pfizer, for example, now spends twice as much on sales and administrative expenses—$16.9 billion last year—as it does on research and development. And it employs 15,000 scientists and support staff in seven major labs around world. As long as those labs are churning out a steady stream of blockbuster drugs for Pfizer's gargantuan sales force to promote, this mass-market approach is extremely profitable. Pfizer, which has more than its share of megasellers, including such familiar names as Lipitor, Viagra, and Zoloft, earned $16 billion last year, not counting discontinued operations and onetime items, on sales of $52 billion.

There's only one problem:The blockbuster model doesn't really work anymore. Pharmaceutical companies, Pfizer being the leader, have sent so many sales reps into the field that they're tripping over one another. The company's once-vaunted labs, along with those of most of the industry, have hit a dry patch, with introductions of promising new treatments slowing alarmingly. Some of Pfizer's recent launches have been duds. (Ever heard of Caduet or Inspra?) The diseases Pfizer and others now chase are harder to defeat with a one-pill, mass-market solution. HMOs and the like are putting the brakes on skyrocketing drug spending.

That's why Pfizer has quietly circulated a memo telling its employees to brace for a restructuring that analysts expect will slash billions from the company's cost base. That's not to say Chairman and CEO Henry McKinnell, 62, has accepted the end of the blockbuster era. While he acknowledges that Pfizer is heading into rough times, he also argues that the company is primed for a resurgence. And he has become the public face of an industry that these days seems only one step above the tobacco business in public opinion. That's him on C-SPAN for an hour, trying to soothe callers irate over the high price of drugs. That's him calmly looking into the camera in TV ads as he explains how Pfizer's scientists are pushing for cures for the greatest of human scourges. He simply won't cotton to the notion that his company's go-go years are gone-gone.

Quite the opposite. McKinnell argues that there are a host of untreated diseases that represent huge potential markets. He says Pfizer's internal research is presenting more great opportunities than ever before—indeed, the company is on track to file 20 new drug applications in the five-year period ending in 2006. And he boasts that a number of those are potential blockbusters.

The thing about the blockbuster model is that it gives you great leverage. But it cuts both ways. Each of Pfizer's sales reps costs close to $170,000 per year including car, computer, and benefits, estimates Credit Suisse First Boston analyst Catherine J. Arnold. That figure doesn't change a lot if the company's sales are soaring or falling. So a big-selling drug can generate fantastic margins as sales ramp up. Pfizer generated an astonishing $45 billion in gross profits last year. That works out to $1.2 million per sales rep. Celebrex, with rich 90% gross margins, according to analysts, contributed some $3 billion of that.

But watch what happens if those blockbusters fizzle. If Celebrex gets yanked from the market, profits per sales rep immediately drop to $1.1 million—a 7% decline in productivity. If several drugs fall dramatically, which will inevitably happen as patents run out, and if others fail to take off quickly, that massive sales force could quickly become a massive millstone. Even without the unexpected loss of one of the blockbusters, Pfizer's net income is expected to fall nearly 9% this year, to $14.7 billion, as generics begin to launch and big franchises such as the Cox-2 drugs take hits.

Clearly, McKinnell needs to do something. The Stanford University PhD in business, who blows off steam shooting his Sig Sauer handgun as a guest at the FBI firing range in Quantico, Virginia, will soon take aim at a major restructuring. According to the late-January memo obtained by *BusinessWeek*, McKinnell has ordered a top-to-bottom review intended to make the drug giant more flexible and less bureaucratic. But don't expect him to make big cuts in his sales machine. Sources say Pfizer's overhaul will entail having salespeople call on fewer doctors and talk about fewer products—with the goals of cutting down on the repetitive pitches doctors get and making it easier to determine who's most productive. And the sales force will shrink, though largely through attrition and selective cuts. Employees have been told that decisions on cost reductions and the like will be announced to Wall Street around the April analyst meeting. Friedman, Billings, Ramsey & Co. analyst David Moskowitz figures McKinnell may slash as much as $3 billion in expenses over the next several years.

Amy Barrett, "Pfizer's Funk," *BusinessWeek Online,* February 28, 2005.

QUESTIONS

1. Why has Pfizer increased the size of its sales-force so much in recent years?

2. What advantages and disadvantages have resulted from having such a large salesforce?

BUILDING YOUR MANAGEMENT SKILLS
Know Thyself

Have you had a friend or co-worker tell you that you are a good listener? Although we often think of someone in sales having to be articulate, that's only part of the story. Good listening skills are valuable to sales people and others who manage relationships with customers, co-workers, and even in your personal life. It's important to listen well so you understand what others need from you or from your company. Your Student DVD has an exercise called "Active Listening Skills Inventory" that will give you insights into your current skills and give you ideas for improving.

CHAPTER VIDEO
New Belgium Brewery

Production and operations management is the focus of this video featuring the New Belgium Brewery (NBB) a very successful and award winning microbrewery in Colorado.

The modest beginning of NBB contained the formula for its future success. A full bottling shift produced only 60 cases; yet the customer feedback on the quality of the beer was tremendous. The question was how to ensure the highest quality of a small batching process and convert it to a much larger production run. The answer can be found in effective production and operations management principles.

NBB is a high-tech, environmentally conscious brewery that produces a world-class beer. It employs state-of-the-art cutting edge technology—even that which has yet to be fully proven. It combines the winning formula of high quality, low price, and maximum profit.

The reasons for its operations management success is NBB's focus on high quality through its transformation process where it converts its various inputs (yeast, malt, water, etc) to outputs (beer, waste water, etc.). The company achieves efficiencies through its supply chain management processes where it fully utilizes its facilities by employing machines and technology and reducing the need for direct labor. Within the supply chain management process, it focuses on purchasing, inventory control, servicing operations, quality assurance, and finished goods. It accomplishes its goals through a relatively flat organizational structure and has equal emphasis on the number of cases it produces and the satisfaction level of co-workers. New Belgium Brewer is truly a self-managed production operation.

1. What methods are employed by NBB to ensure high quality?

2. What are the key components involved in comparing manufacturing to service organizations?

3. What are the five main sources of operating costs affected by Operations Materials Management?

12 Operations and Materials Management:

Managing the Production and Flow of Goods and Services

Learning Objectives

After studying this chapter, you should be able to:

1. Describe the nature of the operations and materials management process and explain how it can create a competitive advantage for a company.

2. Identify the five main components of operations and materials management costs and the methods companies use to reduce them.

3. Differentiate between the three major kinds of operating systems companies use to produce goods and services.

4. Understand the way total quality management can significantly improve both quality and productivity.

5. Describe three materials management methods companies use to improve the flow of resources into and out of production and increase operations efficiency.

WHY IS THIS IMPORTANT ?

Flour, eggs, sugar, baking powder, chocolate, and shortening don't create much excitement when they are in the kitchen cupboard. They create a lot more excitement when someone transforms them into a cake. Whether it's a cake, a computer, or a legal document, operations and materials management processes create value in a household or a company.

A company's operations require inputs such as raw materials or parts and the skilled people and equipment to transform them into useful products. After you read this chapter, you will understand why the management of a company's supply chain and transformation processes determine how much value it can create for customers.

A Question of Business
UTC Is on Top of Its Game

Why does UTC have such an efficient and effective operating system?

United Technologies Corp. (UTC), based in Hartford, Connecticut, is a *conglomerate*, a term used to describe a company that owns a wide variety of other companies that operate in different businesses and industries. Some of the companies in UTC's portfolio are better known than UTC itself, such as Sikorsky Aircraft Corporation, Pratt & Whitney, the aircraft engine and component maker, Otis Elevator Company, Carrier Transport Air Conditioning Inc., and Chubb Corporation, the security and lock maker.

In the 2000s, UTC has been one of the most profitable companies in the world. The reason, so its CEO George David claims, is that he has created a sophisticated business model for his company based on improving the operating and materials management systems in all its diverse businesses. To understand how David continually improves UTC's operating system, it is necessary to go look at how his career as a manager in many of UTC's different divisions has shaped his thinking.

David joined Otis Elevator as an assistant to its CEO in 1975, but within one year Otis was acquired by UTC during a decade when "bigger is better" ruled corporate America and mergers and acquisitions, of whatever kind, were seen as the best way to grow a company's profits. UTC sent David to manage its South American operations,

and later gave him responsibility for the company's Japanese operations. Otis had formed an alliance with Matsushita to develop an elevator for the Japanese market, but after being installed widely in Japanese buildings, the "Elevonic 401" proved to be a disaster. It broke down much more often than elevators made by other Japanese companies, and customers were concerned not only about the reliability of the elevators but also about their personal safety.

Matsushita was extremely embarrassed by the elevator's failure and assigned one of its leading total quality management experts, Yuzuru Ito, to head a team of Otis engineers to find out why it performed so poorly. Under Itos's direction they created a set of "process" techniques, which involved all of the employees responsible for producing the elevator—managers, designers, and production workers—to analyze why the elevators were malfunctioning. This intensive study led to a total redesign of the elevator. When the new and improved version was launched worldwide, it met with great success, and Otis's share of the global elevator market increased dramatically.

David was subsequently named president of UTC in 1992. He was given the responsibility to cut costs across the entire company including its important Pratt & Whitney division. After he successfully reduced UTC's cost structure, the company's board of directors appointed him as CEO in 1994. Now responsible for all of UTC, David decided the best way he could work to increase UTC's profitability was to find ways to improve efficiency and quality of all its diverse businesses. He convinced Ito to move to Hartford to take responsibility for championing the kinds of improvements that had transformed the Otis division. Ito then began developing UTC's TQM system, which is known as *Achieving Competitive Excellence* or ACE.

ACE is a set of tasks and procedures used by all of a company's employees to analyze every aspect of the way a product is made. The goal is to find ways to improve quality and reliability, to lower the costs of making the products, and, in particular, to find ways to make future products better. David makes every employee in every one of the company's functions at every level take responsibility for achieving the incremental, step-by-step gains that can result in innovative products.

David calls these techniques "process disciplines." He has used them to improve the operating and materials management systems in all of UTC's companies. His success can be seen in the rising performance of UTC. In the decade since he took control, he has quadrupled UTC's earnings per share, and its stock price has boomed in the 2000s.

David and his managers believe that the gains that can be achieved from its process disciplines are never-ending because its own research and development groups continue to produce innovative products at a rapid rate, and the company has continued to improve its companywide operating systems. The company also continuously acquires other manufacturing companies that can benefit from its expertise. Once UTC's systems are put into place in its new companies they then perform much better. This, in turn, increases UTC's profitability and its future looks bright indeed.[1] •

Overview

UTC's ongoing efforts to increase quality, boost efficiency, and create new, innovative products suggest how important it is for companies to continually search for ways to improve the way they make and sell goods and services. In this chapter, we examine why operations and materials management are vital functions in a company's value chain. First, we define operations and materials management (OMM) and explain how it can be such an important source of a company's competitive advantage. Second, we look at the sources of OMM costs and their relationship to profitability. Third, we describe three important forms of operating systems a company can adopt to increase productivity and quality. Finally, we look at three important materials management techniques that a company can use to improve its performance and gain a competitive advantage. By the end of this chapter you will understand the crucial role operations and materials management play in terms of making better use of a company's resources and speeding goods and services to customers.

The Nature of Operations and Materials Management

The last two chapters discuss the vital role that marketing, product development, and sales play in discovering customer needs, developing products to meet those needs, and then getting them to customers. Once a company has chosen which products to make and sell to customers, the actual process of creating goods or providing services begins. Operations, or an operating system, are the value-creation activities that convert a company's inputs into finished goods and services. The interaction between members of a surgical team performing open-heart surgery, the cooperative efforts of assembly-line employees standing along a moving conveyor belt to make a car, and the coordinated behaviors of lawyers, a judge, detectives, and courtroom personnel involved in a criminal trial are all examples of different kinds of operations and operating systems. In each case, value is being created by the specific activities used to bring about change and create value, for example, to cure a patient, assemble a car, try a legal case, or make a high-quality doughnut.

Materials management is the set of activities that control the flow of resources *into* and *out of* the operating system. For a manufacturing company, materials management activities on the *input* side include the activities necessary to find and purchase high-quality raw materials or low-cost components and get them to the firm's operational units as efficiently as possible. For a service organization, input activities include controlling the flow of patients into a hospital or diners into a restaurant, for example. Materials manage-

Manufacturing companies such as General Motors, Boeing, and Dell create value by using their operating systems to turn inputs into outputs—products such as cars, aircraft, and PCs.

operations A company's system of value-creation activities used to transform inputs into finished goods and services.

materials management The set of activities that control the flow of resources into and out of a firm's operating system.

ment activities at the *output* side include (1) controlling the inventory of finished goods, (2) ensuring enough employees are available to provide high-quality customer service in banks or stores at busy times, and (3) distributing goods and services to customers.

The Operations and Materials Management Process

The functional activities involved in operations and materials management are usually viewed as a three-stage process illustrated in Figure 12.1. Value creation takes place at all three stages: input, operations, and output.

At the input stage, a company's materials management expertise determines how much value the company creates for customers. For example, Amazon uses its materials management expertise to keep the books, CDs, and electronics in inventory that most appeal to customers. Similarly, McDonald's works with hamburger bun manufacturers and beef and egg producers to make sure the fast food it produces is as fresh as possible. If Amazon's customers were unable to find the popular new books they want on the company's Web site, or McDonald's customers found the company's hamburger buns were always stale, these companies would be doing a poor job at the input stage.

It's not just the quality of inputs that are important at this stage, however. It's also their flow—how well they move into and out of the company. Amazon's success, for example, depends critically on how quickly it can ship its books and other products to customers. To further speed up delivery, Amazon has formed alliances with companies such as Circuit City. Customers who order products stocked by Circuit City on Amazon's site can now pick up the products in their local Circuit City stores instead of having to wait for the products to be mailed to their homes. Likewise, a fast-food company's ability to deliver customers tasty fast food quickly is critical to its success.

Figure 12.1
The Operations and Materials Management Process

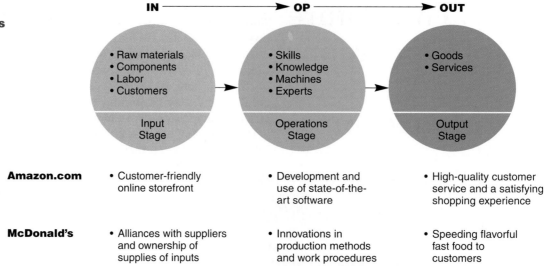

	Input Stage	Operations Stage	Output Stage
Amazon.com	• Customer-friendly online storefront	• Development and use of state-of-the-art software	• High-quality customer service and a satisfying shopping experience
McDonald's	• Alliances with suppliers and ownership of supplies of inputs	• Innovations in production methods and work procedures	• Speeding flavorful fast food to customers

The way a company combines the skills and knowledge of its employees with its machinery and computer systems to change inputs into outputs also determines how much value the company creates at the operations stage. A good operations process ultimately creates products that satisfy customers. A few years ago, McDonald's managed to create a fast-cooking burger machine and installed it in its stores. Unfortunately, the burgers didn't taste as good. In 2003, McDonald's announced it was changing its cooking operations to restore the charbroiled flavor its customers wanted. Likewise, although Amazon's online storefront is considered the best in the business, the company's success still depends heavily on the ability of its employees to develop even better software to track the changing needs of customers.

A company uses the revenue it earns from the sale of goods and services to customers to purchase more inputs and resources, such as new raw materials, new computer software, or additional highly skilled employees. Then, the value-creation cycle begins again. A company that continues to satisfy people will find that its sales revenues increase steadily over time. This, in turn, allows the company to buy additional and better resources to create even more value for customers—and profit for itself.

Video Small Business in Action

Mom-preneurship: Stroller Strides

This NBC segment, as shown on your Student DVD, introduces Lisa Druxer, the founder of the company "Stroller Strides." Druxer is a new mother who left a full-time career in fitness services to become a full-time mom. With her experience in the fitness industry, a new child, and plenty of time and energy, she found herself exercising while taking her daughter for a walk in the stroller. Druxer is creative and talented with considerable drive and energy. This gave rise to an innovation that combined full-time motherhood with her former career in fitness. The new business start-up integrates mothers spending time with their children with a physical fitness work-out. While new-business start-ups are a high-risk venture, Druxer had the full support of her husband even though she had never run a business before.

Today, Stroller Strides is a successful venture with over 100 sites nationwide. Her advice to individuals contemplating a new business startup includes: remaining flexible, having a sense of humor and to cut revenue projections by 50% while increasing by a factor of 2, projected expenses.

Discussion Questions
1. Using Stroller Strides as a model, explain how its operations add value that change inputs into outputs of goods and/or services.
2. What are the main sources of operating costs for Stroller Strides?
3. Would total quality management be relevant for Stroller Strides?

Amazon is a good example. The company has found that the number of its repeat customers continues to grow—as have its revenues. Likewise, McDonald's enjoyed enormous success throughout the 1990s. The company's combination of low prices and fast service created customer loyalty. In the 2000s, the growing perception that McDonald's food was not only less flavorful but also fattening lowered its appeal to health-conscious customers, who switched to fast-food chains like Subway sandwiches. In response, in 2003 McDonald's announced that it intended to change its operations. Not only would its new cooking methods result in better tasting food, it was also introducing new lines of healthy foods to its menu, such as a line of premium salads using grilled chicken. Many analysts are expecting McDonald's to introduce a new line of sandwiches as soon as it has developed the operational proficiency needed to do this efficiently. However, it will require extensive changes be made to McDonald's operating system. The company's thousands of restaurant managers, for example, will have to be retrained, and they will then have to retrain all of McDonald's crews.

Using Operations and Materials Management to Gain a Competitive Advantage

How well a company controls its operations and materials management activities will have a big impact on the overall profitability of its business model and its ability to create a competitive advantage for itself. Recall from Chapter 4 that the four building blocks necessary to gain a competitive advantage are superior productivity, quality, innovation, and responsiveness to customers. Figure 12.2 shows how this relates to operations and materials management.

Figure 12.2

Operations, Materials Management, and Competitive Advantage

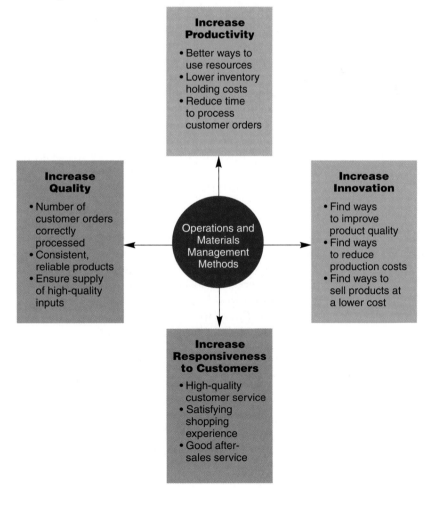

Productivity

To continue with our example of Amazon and McDonald's, to achieve superior *productivity* both companies must continually search for better ways to use their resources to create value for customers. Amazon can increase its productivity by reducing the time it takes to process customers' orders. McDonald's has installed clocks in some of its restaurants that show customers and employees the time it takes to complete an order—and to encourage speedy service, of course.

Amazon's early business model assumed that the Internet would give it a competitive advantage because the costs of operating an online storefront are a fraction of the costs needed to operate a national chain of bricks-and-mortar bookstores such as Border's. Once Amazon's business started to grow, however, the company found that it needed to invest over $10 billion to build the five huge warehouses necessary to serve its U.S. operations. These high costs resulted in huge operating losses in the early 2000s, but the major gains in productivity it derived from the new warehouses subsequently allowed Amazon to return to profitability by 2004.

QUALITY   For both Amazon and McDonald's the number of customer orders that are accurately processed is a major indicator of product quality. When customers return books or fast food because it is not what they ordered, operating costs rise and reduce the company's profitability. In fact, studies show that companies that can reduce the number of incorrectly processed orders from 3% to less than 1% can significantly increase their profitability. Of course, the quality of a product can only be as good as the quality of the inputs that go into making it. Cars and computers, for example, are only as reliable as the components used to make them. Ensuring that the firm has a reliable supply of high-quality, low-cost inputs is therefore crucial. (We discuss more about the quality of components later in the chapter.)

INNOVATION   Innovation not only involves creating new and improved products, but also finding new and better methods to make them—methods that will increase product quality or reduce operating costs. McDonald's has long been a leader in making innovative kitchen equipment to speed up the production of fast food. Indeed, Ray Kroc, the entrepreneur who built the McDonald's chain, got his start by selling state-of-the-art machines that could make six milkshakes at a time. A major operating challenge facing McDonald's is to create a burger-cooking method that simultaneously improves flavor and keeps costs low. As we discussed earlier in the chapter, the company found a way to speed up the cooking process, but flavor suffered. Introducing innovative new lines of salads and sandwiches also means McDonald's will have to purchase and ship a wider range of products to its thousands of restaurants—and salad is one of the most perishable of all foods.

Amazon faces several OMM innovation challenges, too. The company has already spent hundreds of millions of dollars to install and develop innovative new IT systems, such as SAP's ERP system, to meet its materials management needs. That said, it needs to continually upgrade its storefront IT to create an increasingly better shopping experience for its customers. Amazon also needs to adopt new methods to allow it to control the way it acquires, stocks, and ships the thousands of products it currently sells. Radio frequency tags could be the answer. Radio frequency tags allow a firm to "earmark," or track, each product that goes into and out of its warehouses.

Did You Know?

Henry Ford popularized the assembly line but did not invent it. Mechanized assembly lines were used in milling and baking and in packing houses over 200 years before Ford.[2]

RESPONSIVENESS TO CUSTOMERS
Finally, OMM plays a major role in creating competitive advantage by increasing responsiveness to customers. Customers, for example, prefer quick service to slow service, and good not poor after-sales support. Good OMM facilitates this. In Amazon's case, good OMM practices help ensure that books are always in

stock when customers request them and that "hot" new books are added to Amazon's title list when customers begin demanding them.

Similarly, it is vital that McDonald's rapidly change the kinds of fast food it offers when customer tastes change. The physical setting in which the company serves food is also important to customers. McDonald's has invested billions of dollars to upgrade and refurbish its older restaurants to improve their appeal to today's more sophisticated customers. It is also installing WiFi in many of its restaurants.

BALANCING COSTS VERSUS REVENUES It is important to note that a company must pay attention to all four competitive-advantage sources. A company that puts all its efforts into reducing costs to increase efficiency, for example, can easily lose sight of the fact that this might lead to lower quality, lower innovation or lower responsiveness to customers—which will reduce the demand for its products, revenues, and profitability. For example, operating costs often rise as the range of products a company designs, makes, and sells increases. McDonald's provides us with yet another example here: Some analysts believe the chain was slow to offer a wider variety of food because it was too focused on reducing its operating costs. McDonald's wanted to keep its costs low so it could keep prices low, of course. But, when the company's sales plummeted along with its profitability, McDonald's managers realized they had to find low-cost ways to offer customers new kinds of meals.

Gateway provides another example. Gateway became concerned about the high costs associated with providing after-sales service to its PC customers. To reduce costs, it ordered its customer service representatives *not* to help customers when they installed software on their new PCs that conflicted with Gateway's installed software. Customers became infuriated. Within months, news of Gateway's poor customer service spread, and sales of its computers plummeted. Not surprisingly, the PC maker's top managers have since reversed this order.

In both these cases, the attempt to reduce costs led to reduced revenues because Gateway and McDonald's were not providing customers with what they wanted—innovative, quality products, and/or good customer service. As we discuss in other chapters, investing capital to improve a product or customer service can increase operating costs. This is not a problem, however, as long as the investment maintains or increases the company's revenues. Moreover, if revenues do increase more than costs—something that normally happens if managers have made the right choices—a company's profitability will also increase. The success of a company's business model is based on increasing revenues through skillful marketing and product development, for example, and on reducing operating costs through well-designed operations and materials management methods.

Some analysts believe that McDonald's was slow to change its food offerings because it was too focused on reducing its operating costs.

Operations and Materials Management Costs

Let's now review the sources of operating costs involved in OMM activities to understand their impact on a company's profitability. The five main sources of operating costs affected by OMM activities are the costs of (1) raw materials and components, (2) plant, (3) labor, (4) inventory, and (5) distribution. These costs are outlined in Figure 12.3.

Raw Materials and Component Costs

Inputs such as raw materials and component parts comprise a significant percentage of companies' total operating costs, particularly companies that makes physical products

Figure 12.3
Five Major
Components
of OMM Costs

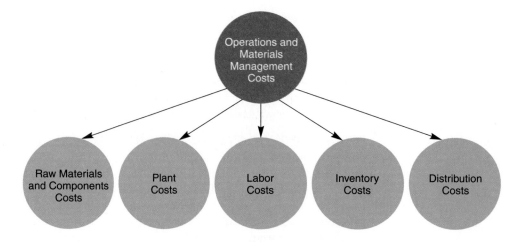

such as cars, aircraft, aluminum cans, computers, furniture, or hamburgers. A firm's materials management function is responsible for finding companies that supply high-quality, low-cost raw materials and components. As we discussed in Chapter 4, companies are now searching around the world for these inputs, so global outsourcing has become commonplace. To remain competitive, most multinationals now buy their component parts in countries where they can be acquired inexpensively.

Other companies go so far as to purchase the companies that supply them with their raw materials and components. This gives them greater control over the supply of inputs they receive, which can be especially important for critical inputs. Purchasing its suppliers can also help a company lower the cost of its inputs and increase their quality. McDonald's, for example, purchased vast cattle ranches in South America to allow it to obtain low-cost, high-quality beef. Similarly, Dole owns huge banana and pineapple plantations in the Caribbean and Hawaii. For Dole, the need to maintain control over the quality of the bananas it sends to U.S. supermarkets—to ensure they are neither too green nor too ripe when sold—was a major consideration.

Plant Costs

Plant costs, the cost of the machinery, computers, tools, buildings, and equipment needed to transform inputs into finished products is the second component of OMM costs. When Intel decides to make a new kind of microprocessor, it knows it will cost $1 to 2 *billion* to build and equip a factory with the technology necessary to make the chip. One of the goals of OMM is to find ways to reduce plant costs. Companies also have the option to outsource their operations and contract with manufacturers abroad to make their products. Nike and The Gap, for example, do not make their shoes and clothes. Manufacturers abroad that can make these products at a lower cost do. Still other companies prefer to lease, rather than own, their plants, and even their head-quarters and retail stores. This way they don't have to invest scarce capital in buildings and equipment or pay to maintain them.

Another way to avoid the high plant and capital costs associated with making and selling products is by franchising. Today, for example, it would cost a new company tens of billions of dollars to establish a nationwide chain of retail outlets. Few new companies can raise the capital needed to do this. By franchising, a young company can quickly increase its national presence and invest its capital in vital marketing and product development activities to grow its sales. Companies such as McDonald's, Subway, Midas Muffler, and Gold's Gym reduce their operating costs by making their franchisees invest the capital needed to open stores. This allows these companies to use their capital in other ways. The choice of how to use a company's capital to get the best return on its investment in buildings, machinery, and equipment is a complex materials management issue. Later in the chapter we discuss how companies design their operating systems to do this.

Many U.S. companies establish maquiladoras near the U.S.-Mexico border in order to take advantage of the low-wage rates there.

Labor Costs

The labor costs involved in making or providing goods and services are a third component of operating costs. For many companies, particularly service companies, labor is their biggest cost. The cost of labor is a function of (1) the number of employees needed to produce a given quantity of outputs and (2) the amount each employee must be paid—something which is often a function of the employee's skills, knowledge, and experience, (3) the health and social insurance benefits each employee is given. For many companies, benefits make up one-quarter to one-third of their total labor costs. The kind of technology a company uses also determines its labor costs, as we discuss later.

maquiladoras U.S. companies' manufacturing plants in cities along the Mexican border.

Today, to take advantage of the low cost of labor in countries overseas, companies often ship the machinery and computers they need to make their products to these countries and establish factories there. Many U.S. companies took this route to enter Mexico and establish **maquiladoras,** the name given to U.S. companies' manufacturing plants in cities along the Mexican border. In the last decade, China's low labor costs have made it the location of choice for most multinational companies.

The decision to set up manufacturing operations in a country abroad, rather than just contract with manufacturing companies in that country to make a product, often depends on the complexity and sophistication of the machinery and equipment needed to make the product. The machinery needed to make clothes and shoes, for example, such as cutting and sewing machines, is relatively simple. Hence, using a company overseas to make these products is often the lowest cost method. If GM decides to make cars in China, however, no Chinese carmaker possesses the knowledge and equipment needed to assemble cars to its specifications. GM must make the multibillion dollar investment needed to build and operate a factory there. This is, in fact, what GM has done. Because such a large investment is needed, multinationals try to locate countries that have a stable political and economic system to minimize their risks. (Companies obviously do not want their factories ravaged by war, a poor economy, or risk their being seized by corrupt national governments or lawless citizens.)

Frequently, labor costs increase when a company requires employees with more skills, knowledge, and experience to provide customers with services. A hospital is a good example. Hospitals need highly skilled nurses, doctors, radiographers, and other kinds of medical specialists to provide high-quality patient care. Since these people also work around the clock to deal with patient emergencies, high labor costs are associated with running a hospital—something that helps explain high health-care costs.

To reduce their labor costs, many service companies search for ways to redesign their production systems. Companies such as supermarkets, department stores, and fast-food restaurants have found many ways to have customers perform some of their own services. Today, we take for granted that we gas our own cars, scan our own groceries, and bus our own tables. But this wasn't so in decades past. If customers want better quality customer service today, they often have to pay extra for it—luxury food stores, department stores, and expensive restaurants pass their higher labor costs on to customers in the form of higher priced products.

The Internet has become an important labor-cost reducing tool for many companies. Checking and bill paying, buying and selling stocks, and planning and booking vacations online are now tasks many customers do for themselves—work previously handled by customer service reps. Customers also benefit, however, because they have the ability to easily access their banking or credit card records, brokerage records, and visually choose the seats they want on a flight, for example. Plus, they don't get put on hold waiting for a customer service rep to come on the telephone.

Inventory Costs

inventory The resources—materials, supplies, and goods—a company holds in stock.

work-in-process goods The semifinished goods and services that move through a company's production process.

Inventory is the quantity of resources—materials, supplies, and goods—a company has in stock. Inventory is held at three stages in the OMM process, which are shown in Figure 12.4. At the input stage, inventory consists of raw materials, component parts, repeat customers, and so on. At the operations stage inventory consists of **work-in-process goods,** semi-finished products moving through the production process, such as partially assembled computers and cars or patients being treated in hospitals. At the output side, inventory consists of the stock of finished products ready to distribute to customers.

Holding inventory at each of these stages is expensive for companies. A company's capital is tied up in these items and no return is received on them until revenues are generated from their sale. One way to reduce these costs is with IT. IT can help managers better forecast the inputs required to makes the inputs and finished products it needs to have on hand to meet demand in a certain period of time, a day or week, for example. Another way to reduce inventory costs is to shorten the time it takes to assemble or manufacture a product. The faster that inputs can be assembled into finished products and shipped out the door to customers, the lower the costs of holding these inputs in inventory is. Suppose, for example, a luxury carmaker currently spends two weeks to make a $60,000 car. The cost of the inputs needed to make the car increases every day until the car is gradually assembled—and then shipped and sold. If the firm's operations can be redesigned so the car can be made and sold in one week versus two, the cost of the company's inventory will be reduced by half.

**Figure 12.4
Three Types
of Inventory**

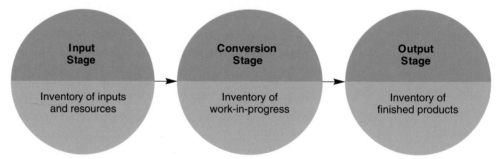

Finally, at the output side a major inventory cost is the stock of finished products a company holds in inventory, such as an appliance maker that stores thousands of refrigerators in its warehouses, or a carmaker that has thousands of cars sitting in the parking lots surrounding its assembly plant. Ideally, a company would like to ship products to customers as soon as they are made—then it will receive the sales revenues from them as quickly as possible. Every day a car spends on the lot of a carmaker, and then on the lot of a car dealer, operating costs increase. A typical car dealership that carriers an inventory of 500 cars may have $10 million tied up in its stock of cars (assuming the average cost of each car is $20,000). This is why car dealers are so anxious to get them off the lot!

On the other hand, suppose a company is cautious and decides to make only a small amount of a product to avoid having high inventory-holding costs. But if the product becomes extremely popular, the company won't have enough of it on hand. Most customers don't like to wait for products; frequently they will buy a rival's product instead. If this happens, the firm will lose a large amount of sales revenues—surely more than it saves on inventory-holding costs.

When a company makes just enough of a product to satisfy customer demand, it is maximizing sales revenues while minimizing its inventory costs. But this is a difficult thing to accomplish. Companies frequently make too much or too little of a particular product. Companies that make too much of a product often have to sharply discount their price to sell them. This reduces their profitability and can result in major losses. Due to overproduction, Dial, the soap company, was once forced to sell soap at such a deep discount that it lost an astonishing $300 million.

By contrast, good forecasting and inventory management practices are hallmarks of Dell. Dell has become the market leader by driving down operating costs–including its inventory-holding costs. Dell involves its suppliers in the component design process; informs them months in advance of its future requirements; and makes its suppliers establish warehouses close to its assembly operations so they, rather than Dell, bear the costs of holding inventory. Because Dell has the lowest operating costs of any PC maker it can offer its customers lower prices while still earning a 20% profit on each PC sale. None of its competitors can match its prices and make this same level of profit because their OMM costs are higher.

Distribution Costs

distribution costs The cost of getting products to customers.

The fifth major component of operating costs is distribution costs, the costs of getting products to customers. Transporting a car to a dealership costs hundreds of dollars. BMW, in fact, directly bills its customers about $650 per automobile to have their cars shipped. Similarly, when it is not offering free shipping, Dell charges $65 to ship a PC to a customer's home. Dell and BMW's delivery charges are visible to customers, but often delivery costs are built into the price of products, so consumers can't tell readily what they are. In 2003, Amazon reported a record increase in its revenues after it began to offer customers free shipping on orders over $50. Internet customers are sensitive to paying the extra cost of shipping. By building the shipping cost into the price of its products so it wouldn't be apparent, Amazon boosted its sales significantly.

Because high delivery and shipping costs increase the price customers have to pay for a product, companies, of course, try to find ways to reduce these costs. Cases of soft drinks are heavy and expensive to transport, for example, so to reduce shipping costs, Coca-Cola and PepsiCo just ship their syrups to regional and local bottlers and fast-food restaurants. The companies Coke and Pepsi ship to then mix the syrups with water and locally distribute the soft drinks produced. This keeps distribution costs to a minimum.

To reduce the high costs associated with shipping and distributing products abroad, multinationals often establish manufacturing operations abroad or contract with companies in countries overseas to make their products for them. Dell, for example, opened a large manufacturing plant in Ireland to supply countries within the European Union with its PCs, and a plant in Malaysia to serve the Asian region. Chemical and plastics makers such as DuPont, Shell, and Monsanto license the rights to manufacture many of their heavy, bulky products to companies around the world. This is more profitable than making these products in the United States and then shipping them elsewhere.

A major distribution decision companies have to make is whether to distribute their products themselves or outsource the task to other companies. Some companies, such as Anheuser-Busch, Dillard's, and Wal-Mart own their own trucking fleets and perform their own distribution activities. But many smaller companies contract with specialized trucking companies such as Hunt, Knight, and Yellow Freight to handle the shipping of their products because this reduces their costs. To grow their profits, both UPS and FedEx are becoming increasingly involved in not only the distribution of different companies' products but *all* of their materials management activities, including their inputs. Because UPS and FedEx are so efficient at what they do, they can perform materials management activities at a lower cost than these companies can. This lowers the multinationals' operating costs and frees up capital to invest in value-chain activities that generate more profit–by increasing global marketing, for example.

To grow their profits, FedEx and UPS are contracting with multinationals to take control of their materials management activities. This involves managing both the flow of inputs into their operation systems as well as distributing their finished products.

Of course, the Internet has changed the way companies transport their products to customers, too. Hundreds of millions of transactions take place each year between customers and company that have virtual storefronts. Now companies no longer have to ship their products to wholesalers or bricks-and-mortar stores, which boosts their profitability. The growth of the Internet has been a major source of revenue for companies like UPS and FedEx, which have seen the volume of packages they handle soar. In turn, this has allowed them to find ways to reduce their own operating costs and pass the savings on to their customers.

Types of Operating Systems

Now that we have discussed how OMM activities affect a company's operating costs and competitive advantage, we can take a close look at the different ways in which goods and services are produced. In other words, we are going to examine the different types of operating systems that are used to make goods and services. The three types of operating system we discuss below are small-batch production, mass production, and flexible production. (See Figure 12.5.) Then, we discuss how techniques like Total Quality Management (TQM) are used to improve operational efficiency and effectiveness.

Small-Batch Production

small-batch production An operating system designed to make one-of-a-kind or small quantities of customized products.

customized products Products designed to match the needs of individual customers.

Companies like Krispy Kreme that use small-batch production make one-of-a-kind or small quantities of customized products. Customized products are products that are designed and made to more closely match the needs of individual users—like a doughnut lover's desire for freshly made, Bavarian-cream filled doughnuts topped with fresh raspberries and Belgium chocolate. Other examples of companies that use small-batch production include a specialty furniture maker that makes chairs designed according to customers' specifications; a team of surgeons and nurses who are experts in heart transplant surgery; and software consultants who can modify ERP software to suit the needs of companies in the pharmaceutical industry.

In small-batch production, the operating methods used depend heavily on the judgment of employees about how and when to use machines and equipment. A custom furniture maker, for example, uses an array of tools—including lathes, hammers, planes, and saws—to transform boards into a chair. However, which tools are used, and the order in which they are used, depends on how the furniture maker chooses to build the chair. Likewise, as Business in Action suggests, Krispy Kreme employees have to decide how to utilize the machines needed to make doughnuts. The employees have to decide how and when to reconfigure the machines to make exactly the type and quantity of doughnuts that are in most demand, for example.

Figure 12.5

Three Types of Operating Systems

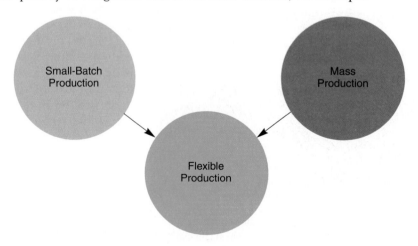

Business in Action

How Krispy Kreme Makes Doughnuts

Founded in 1937 in Winston-Salem, North Carolina, Krispy Kreme has grown to become a leading U.S. specialty retailer of premium quality, yeast-raised doughnuts. Krispy Kreme's doughnuts have a broad customer following and command a premium price because of their unique taste and quality. Although it only had 100 stores in 1999, by 2004 it had over 300. As it has expanded rapidly, Krispy Kreme has gone to great lengths to develop and use advanced operating and materials management methods to maintain the high quality of its doughnuts and increase its responsiveness to customers. Krispy Kreme calls its store operations "doughnut theatre" because the physical layout of its stores is designed so that customers can see and smell the doughnuts coming out of its impressive, company-built, doughnut-making machines.

What are the OMM elements of Krispy Kreme's business model? The story starts with the 65-year-old company's secret doughnut recipe that is kept locked up in a vault. None of its franchisees know the recipe for making its dough. The company sells the ready-made dough and other ingredients to its stores where they are changed or converted into the finished product–doughnuts. Even the machines used to make the doughnuts are company-designed and produced so no doughnut maker can imitate its unique cooking methods and thus create a similar, competing product.

The doughnut-making machines are designed to produce a wide variety of different kinds of doughnuts in small quantities. Each store makes between 4,000 and 10,000 dozen doughnuts per day that are sold in the store and it outlets such as supermarkets and convenience stores. Krispy Kreme is constantly refining its operating system to improve efficiency. For example, in 2003 it redesigned its doughnut machine to include a high-tech extruder that uses air pressure to force doughnut dough into row after row of rings or shells. Employees used to have to manually adjust the air pressure as the dough load lightened. Now, however, this is all done automatically. A new doughnut icer tips finished pastries into a puddle of chocolate frosting. Before the machine was invented and installed, employees had to dunk the doughnuts two at a time by hand. Although these innovations may seem "small," across hundreds of stores and millions of doughnuts they add up to significant gains in productivity.

To operate its small-batch production system efficiently, Krispy Kreme must have the different ingredients on hand just when they are needed so the doughnuts are fresh. Krispy Kreme therefore developed a state-of-the-art materials management method to control the supply and quality of its inputs. The company uses SAP software, for example, and developed an online portal called mykrispykreme.com. Franchisees can log on to mykrispykreme.com and order exactly what supplies of ingredients they need, when they need them. Second, the OMM information franchisees need to operate their stores, such as how to make a new kind of doughnut or repair a broken machine, is also available at mykrispykreme.com via streamed video. Franchisees even have access to predictive modeling software that helps them forecast how many doughnuts they should make each day due to changes in the weather and other factors. (More doughnuts are sold on cold, rainy days, for instance.)

Krispy Kreme's sweet rise to success was followed by an equally dramatic sour fall in 2004, however. Its company-wide inventory and operating costs had become bloated; lower profitability resulted, and the company's stock price plummeted. In the future, Krispy Kreme will have to tighten up its belt to remain competitive.[3]

Krispy Kreme calls its operations "doughnut theatre." The physical layout of its stores is designed so that customers can see and smell the doughnuts coming out of its doughnut-making machines.

The advantage of small-batch production is that the operating system is flexible–employees can change their work procedures and adapt their techniques to suit the orders of individual customers. This gives a company the ability to produce a wide range of products that can be customized. Small-batch technology allows a custom furniture maker, for example, to satisfy the customer's request for a certain style of table made from a certain kind of wood. For similar reasons, high-fashion designers and makers of products like fine perfumes, custom-built cars, and specialized furniture use small-batch production.

OPERATING COSTS   As Krispy Creme's story suggests, small-batch production is an expensive operating system and results in higher operating costs. Costs are higher when only small quantities of a particular product are made. In addition, a lot of time and effort is spent in fine-tuning a product and then finding the best kinds of inputs to make it–so raw materials and labor costs tend to be higher, too. As a result, the goods and services that small-batch production creates command higher prices. Specialized health care, custom software installations, Krispy Kreme doughnuts, or a Rolls-Royce car are examples of products you will have to pay more for because small-batch production processes were used to produce them. However, the price *has* to be very high if the company making the product is to profit.

Mass Production

mass production An operating system based on the use of automated machines and standard operating procedures to make work routine and create a large number of standardized products.

standardized products Products that are identical.

Mass production is an operating system based on the use of automated machines and standard operating procedures (SOPs). SOPs have been worked out in advance, which makes the work easy, or routine, so much less employee judgment is needed on a day-to-day basis. Companies that operate mass production systems manufacture large quantities of standardized products, that is, products that are identical, such as a razor blade, aluminum can, or hamburger. Instead of a group of skilled employees using hand tools to make a piece of custom furniture, for example, employees positioned along a production line use high high-speed saws and lathes to cut and shape boards into uniform components that are then assembled into thousands of identical tables or chairs. Each employee follows a standard operating procedure to perform one of the specific tasks needed to complete the final product.

Effective materials management is a crucial requirement for mass production systems to operate efficiently. The raw materials and component parts used to assemble a product must be made to a consistent quality and specifications to prevent problems from arising during the assembly process. To make a standardized product you must have standardized components–so the task facing materials management is to find reliable suppliers or to ensure a company can make its own high-quality inputs.

To increase their efficiency, service organizations like fast-food restaurants, airlines, and discount stores have imitated the mass production methods used by manufacturers. McDonald's, for example, devoted its energies to creating machines and SOPs that would allow its employees to make its food as quickly and inexpensively as possible. Similarly, Southwest Airlines decided to use only one kind of plane, the Boeing 737, to standardize its operations. This maximizes the ability of its employees to efficiently operate and service its fleet.

Instead of a group of skilled employees using hand tools to make a piece of custom furniture, employees on a mass production line use high-speed saws and lathes to cut and shape boards into uniform components that are then assembled into thousands of identical tables or chairs.

OPERATING COSTS   Mass production is a highly efficient operating system that results in low operating costs. Costs are lower because when large, often millions, of units of the same product are made, companies *learn* how to reduce costs, and they design machines and technology to make the process more efficient. The costs of making a product such as a table, PC, or car fall dramatically when mass production processes are used.

Because its operating costs are lower, a mass producer can reduce the price of its products. This will substantially increase customer demand. Recall that Henry Ford changed manufacturing history when he pioneered the assembly of the Model-T car using mass production methods (replacing the old small-batch method). His use of a moving conveyor belt, uniform car components, and employees who each did a specific task in sequence increased productivity and manufacturing efficiency a thousand times over. By shrinking operating costs, Ford was able to lower the cost of a Model-T and create a mass market for his cars. Similarly, McDonald's, Southwest, and Wal-Mart have all created mass markets for their products.

As you can see, mass production is essentially the opposite of small-batch production. It allows a company to achieve a competitive advantage via high productivity, low operating costs, and low product prices. The downside of mass production is that it is hard to be responsive to customers and provide them with products that better fit their needs. A customer has to select from what is on McDonald's menu, for example, or from what shirts Wal-Mart chooses to carry, or what colors Ford chooses to offer on its car models.

Flexible Production

Suppose an entrepreneur creates a new form of operating system and founds a new company that can achieve the advantages of both small-batch *and* mass production. Now, it can make small batches of a wide range of customized products at little or no extra cost than a company that uses mass production methods. This will attract more customers because the company can rapidly introduce new products that incorporate innovative features and the latest design trends. This gives the company a competitive advantage.

flexible production
An advanced operating system that combines the benefits of mass production with the benefits of small-batch production.

Many companies today are attempting to do just this. They are searching for new ways to design their operating systems to make them flexible enough to respond to changing customer needs but also to keep costs to a minimum. These new developments in OMM have resulted in what is known as flexible production, an advanced, computer-based operating system that allows mass production to achieve the benefits of small-batch production but at a lower cost. Computer-integrated manufacturing and flexible employees and work teams are integral elements of flexible production.

computer-integrated manufacturing A manufacturing technique that controls the changeover of machines from one operation to another via computer software.

COMPUTER-INTEGRATED MANUFACTURING In flexible production, a more complicated sequence of operations is needed to make a wide variety of customized products. The key to preventing costs from increasing in such a system is to use computer-integrated manufacturing (CIM). CIM is a manufacturing technique that controls the changeover from one operation to another by means of the commands given to machines through computer software. A CIM system eliminates the need to physically retool machines to produce different or customized products. The operating system is composed of a series of computer-controlled machines or robots, each capable of performing a range of different production operations. A master computer schedules the movement of products by a series of robots. Unlike a dedicated machine, a robot can be reprogrammed instantly to perform a number of different tasks. The robots can "behave" flexibly, in other words, unlike a dedicated machine. As a result, they can be used to create many different kinds of products. Besides being so flexible, this type of an operating system also results in lower costs: The cost of reprogramming a robot instantly to act differently is much less than the cost of retooling or changing

Did You Know?

Willis Carrier designed his first air conditioning system in 1902 for a New York printer who struggled with temperature and humidity affecting his paper and ink. Carrier solved a variety of production problems by applying chilled air to the manufacturing of razor blades, tobacco, soap, and bread, before taking it to stores and theaters and airplane repair in hot climates. Sixty years later, air conditioning was popularized for home use.[4]

over a dedicated machine, or buying and installing an entirely new one. Motorola's cellular phone and pager factory illustrates many of the operational advantages of robots and flexible production.

Business in Action

Motorola's Factory of the Future

Motorola is one of America's oldest consumer electronics organizations. The company developed the world's first car radio in 1930 and quickly entered the home audio and television market. Today, Motorola is a global leader in digital and wireless communications technology and a leading producer of cell phones. Nonetheless, it faces intense competition from companies such as Samsung and Nokia.

To compete effectively, Motorola created a "factory of the future" that is able to customize products, such as cell phones, to the individual needs of customers within hours. At its futuristic factory at Boynton Beach, Florida, Motorola can make a customized phone in just two hours.

This is how the customization process works: A salesperson in the field takes the customer's order for a cell phone designed to operate on a specific frequency range and have one of a number of customized features, such as a particular type of digital camera. The salesperson electronically relays this information as a bar code to the factory. There the CIM system scans the specifications and creates the circuit board design for the pager.

The production process is then handled by a series of computer-controlled robots. As the cell phone passes down the production line, each robot reads the bar code and performs the necessary operations. Each cell phone in the line can be made to order because the CIM system automatically selects the sequence of operations needed to assemble it to a customer's specifications. The finished products are then electronically scanned, tested, and shipped to the customer. Not surprisingly, customers like Motorola's ability to provide them with customized products, and demand has soared.[5]

FLEXIBLE EMPLOYEES AND WORK GROUPS Flexible production is not only achieved through computers and machines, however. It is also achieved by the way employees are organized and controlled. In mass production, employees learn only the specific work procedures necessary to complete a single operating task. Moreover, because employees perform their tasks in sequence, any alteration in the task of one employee directly impacts the performance of all the others. This makes it difficult or impossible to change the design of the product coming off the assembly line.

With flexible production, employees' tasks are more complex because SOPs continually change depending on which customized product is next up for assembly. Employees must develop the different skills needed to assemble different products. Generally, an employee first develops the skills needed to accomplish one operating task and then over time is trained to perform all the other tasks that need to be done to make a product. Employees can then be moved when and where they are most needed.

flexible work team A team of self-managed employees who assume responsibility for performing the operating tasks necessary to make a part, or all, of a product.

Flexible work teams are a hallmark of flexible production. A flexible work team is a group of employees who assume responsibility for performing the operating tasks necessary to make a part, or all, of a product. A flexible work team is self-managed: The team members jointly assign tasks and decide which employees should perform which tasks as necessary. So, production line employees who were used to being assigned to perform one specific task along the assembly line are now placed in work groups that are given the responsibility for managing all of the operations needed to make a part, or all, of a product.

Figure 12.6
The Use of Flexible Work Teams to Assemble Cars

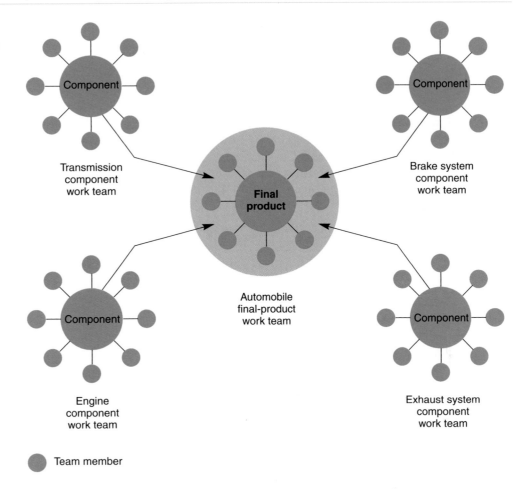

Transmission component work team

Brake system component work team

Final product

Automobile final-product work team

Engine component work team

Exhaust system component work team

● Team member

At a Ford plant, for example, one work team might be responsible for all the operations involved in the assembly of the car's transmission. This team then sends the work-in-process to the body assembly area, where another team takes over and fits the transmission into the car body. Figure 12.6 illustrates the way in which flexible work teams perform their activities. Separate teams assemble different components and turn those components over to the final-product work team that completes the finished product.

Globe Metallurgical, which makes specialty steel products is a leader in the use of flexible production, something that has allowed it to surpass its competitors in product quality, sales, and profit growth. Globe began experimenting with flexible, self-managed work teams when ten managers and thirty-five salaried employees were charged with the task of increasing the productivity of two of Globe's furnaces. They began to experiment with ways to reorganize operations to increase the efficiency of work operations. All the old work SOPs were abandoned, and different ways to sequence tasks were tested. It soon became clear that productivity could be increased if welders, crane operators, furnace operators, forklift operators, stokers, furnace tappers, and tapper assistants worked cooperatively in teams.

By trial and error, managers discovered that a flexible work team of seven employees, who could each perform all the others' jobs, could efficiently operate one furnace. Each team was put under the supervision of a team leader who took the responsibility of coordinating the team's work schedule with those of the

Did You Know?

One study showed that the value stream for a can of soft drink—creating the can, the cardboard box, and the drink itself—required 319 days, but all but 3 hours of that time, the product was waiting for the next stage of processing. The Japanese call this *muda* or "waste" in the production process.[6]

other teams. Every day brought new suggestions, and after several months Globe found that by using flexible work teams it could operate its furnaces with only one-third of the employees that were previously necessary.

Another way in which flexible work teams can be organized to increase productivity is by experimenting with new production layouts, that is, the way employees are physically grouped into work cells or pods to assemble a product. For example, Bayside Controls, a small gearhead manufacturer in Queens, New York, converted its thirty-five person assembly line into a four-cell design where seven to nine employees form a cell. The members of each cell perform all the measuring, cutting, and assembly operations involved in making the gearheads. Bayside's managers say that the average production time it takes to make a gear has dropped to two days from six weeks, and it now makes 75 gearheads a day—up from 50 before the change.

production layout The way teams of employees are physically grouped into work cells or pods to assemble a product.

Improving Operations Quality: Total Quality Management

Flexible production and the use of flexible teams and CIM are not only directed at improving productivity but also at increasing product quality. The members of flexible work teams, for example, are also responsible for controlling the quality of their performance, and the finished products that result. Increasingly, companies are adhering to the principles of total quality management. Total quality management (TQM) is an operations technique aimed at continuous improvement—improvement in product quality and the reduction of production time and waste. The idea behind TQM is to *empower* employees to find ways to improve the work process as UTC (discussed in the opening case) has done.

total quality management An operations technique used to continuously improve the production process, increase the quality of products, and help companies lower their operating costs.

One important TQM step is to solicit suggestions from lower-level employees about how to improve the quality of the organization's products.

A company that introduces TQM often begins by *benchmarking* some other company that does a particular functional activity extraordinarily well. The company then seeks to match that company's performance. Achieving this objective becomes similar to achieving a stretch goal, discussed in Chapter 6—it is a challenging objective that managers and employees work hard to do. Let's look at a couple of examples. To improve quality, Daimler-Chrysler benchmarked Lexus's low defect rate as the standard it sought to achieve. Similarly, UPS used FedEx's guarantee of overnight delivery as a benchmark when designing its own overnight delivery service. In fact, UPS searched so relentlessly for ways to achieve this benchmark that some analysts today think its overnight operations are now even more efficient than FedEx's.

In addition to establishing benchmarks, other important steps in TQM include:

- Identify defects. Trace them back to their sources, and fix quality problems.
- Design products that are easy to assemble.
- Identify customer needs. Translate those needs into quality requirements, and see that these quality requirements shape the production system of the organization.
- Work to break down the barriers between functional departments to get the cooperation needed among them to improve operating methods.
- Solicit suggestions from lower-level employees about how to improve the quality of the organization's products.

Employees in a TQM system are expected to make suggestions that improve all aspects of the work process. They then share their ideas with their managers so that it

quality control circles
Team meetings in which production employees discuss ways to improve operating quality and productivity

can be communicated throughout a company. New ideas often originate in quality control circles, meetings in which production employees discuss ways to improve operating quality and productivity. Research shows that the many small, incremental changes to work operations that a company's employees and managers make over time add up and pay off.

Advanced Materials Management Methods

Managing the flow of resources in to and out of the operating system is a complex functional activity. Earlier, we discussed how materials management methods such as outsourcing, licensing, and ownership of manufacturing operations abroad can reduce operating costs. Next, we discuss three other materials management methods that are often used to build competitive advantage: computer-aided materials management, global supply chain management, and just-in-time inventory systems.

Computer-Aided Materials Management

computer-aided materials management A technique that relies on computers to manage the flow of raw materials and component parts into and out of a company's operating system.

Computer-aided materials management (CAMM) is used to manage the flow of raw materials and component parts into and out of the operating system. The ways CAMM can increase efficiency is illustrated by the difference between the *push and pull* approaches to materials management.

Traditional mass production uses the "push" approach. Raw materials and components are pushed into the operating system according to a previously determined plan—a plan based on some forecast of how many units of product need to be made and which therefore might be accurate or not. Computer-aided materials management, by contrast, uses the "pull" approach. The flow of inputs is not governed by a mere forecast, but by real-time customer orders for a particular product. The inputs needed to make the product are pulled into the operating system in response to the output stage (the demand of customers) not a push from the input stage (sales forecasts).

VF Inc., the manufacturer of Wrangler and Lee jeans, meets customer demand using the pull approach. As VF's jeans sell out in stores, the stores issue requests by computer for VF to make jeans with the appropriate styles or sizes. VF's OMM functions then pulls in raw materials, such as cloth, zippers, and thread, from suppliers as they are needed. If VF used the push approach, its master plan might say, "Make 30,000 pairs of style XYZ in May"; and at the end of the summer 25,000 pairs might remain unsold in the warehouse because of lack of demand. The pull system means that specific products are produced when they are needed.

Computer-Based Global Supply Chain Management

global supply chain management The coordination of the flow of raw materials, semifinished goods, and finished products around the world.

Earlier in the chapter we talked about how companies are searching globally for supplies as well as searching for new ways to deliver their products around the world. Global supply chain management is the coordination of all of these activities. Coordinating the flow of resources, components, and final products becomes more complex as multinationals expand their operations abroad to take advantage of national differences in operations and materials management costs. To deal with global coordination problems, companies have increasingly adopted CAMM systems to manage their global supply chains. The system used by Bose Corporation, profiled in the following Business in Action illustrates how a CAMM works.

Business in Action

Bose's Global Supply Chain

Bose Corporation, based near Boston, Massachusetts, manufactures some of the world's best-known high-fidelity speakers. Bose purchases most of the components that go into its speakers from independent suppliers. About 50% of its purchases are from foreign suppliers, the majority of which are in the Far East.

The challenge for Bose is to coordinate this globally dispersed supply chain to minimize its inventory and transportation costs. Minimizing these costs requires that component parts arrive at Bose's assembly plants just in time to enter the production process and not before. Bose also has to remain responsive to customer demands. This means that the company has to respond quickly to increases in demand for certain kinds of speakers, such as outdoor speakers in the summer. Failure to respond quickly can cause the loss of a big order to competitors. Since Bose does not want to hold extensive inventories at its Massachusetts plant, the need to remain responsive to customer demands requires that Bose's suppliers be able to respond rapidly to its changing demand for components.

The responsibility for coordinating its global supply chain to simultaneously minimize inventory and transportation costs *and* respond quickly to customer demands belongs to Bose's logistics managers. These managers have contracted with W.N. Procter, a Boston-based freight forwarder and customs broker. W.N. Procter uses a CAMM called "ProcterLink" to provide Bose with real-time information on the flow of components and its finished products, as they move through the global supply chain.

When a shipment leaves a supplier, it is logged into ProcterLink. From that point on, ProcterLink can track the flow of components as they move across the globe toward Massachusetts, where Bose has its operations. This system allows Bose to fine-tune its production scheduling so that supplies enter the assembly process exactly when they are needed.

How well this system works was shown when one of Bose's Japanese customers suddenly doubled its order for the company's speakers. Bose had to gear up its manufacturing in a hurry, but many of its components were stretched out across long distances. Using ProcterLink, Bose was able to locate the needed parts in its supply chain. It then broke them out of the normal delivery chain and moved them by airfreight to get them to the assembly line in time for the accelerated schedule needed to meet the customer's request.[7]

The challenge for Bose is to coordinate its globally dispersed, supply-chain activities to minimize its inventory and transportation costs. What are some ways Bose can do this?

As the Bose example suggests, the use of computer-based global supply chain management allows a company to improve its responsiveness to customers, minimize its costs, and build competitive advantage. UPS and FedEx have expanded their outsourcing operations to serve the needs of global companies by establishing huge warehouses in countries around the world. They now manage a company's global inventory and coordinate the transfer of inputs and outputs to wherever they are needed around the world. This service is particularly important for companies that manufacture high-value, high-price products such as computer components and software, cell phones, and digital and electronic devices which generate higher sales revenues the faster they are delivered to customers.

Just-in-Time Inventory Systems

just-in-time inventory system An inventory management system whereby inputs are delivered to the firm just when they are needed rather than being purchased and warehoused prior to their use.

Another advanced materials management technique is the just-in-time inventory system. Developed from the Japanese kanban system (a *kanban* is a card), a just-in-time inventory (JIT) system requires that the inputs and components needed to assemble a product be delivered to the operating system *just* as they are needed—neither earlier nor later—so that inventory can be kept to a minimum. In other words, when a JIT inventory system is used, components enter the production system immediately; they are not warehoused for days or weeks before being used.

Components are kept in bins, and as they are used up, the empty bins are sent back to suppliers with a request on the bin's card (kanban) for more components. CAMM is necessary for a JIT system to work because computerized linkages make possible the rapid transfer of information between a company and its suppliers. Just-in-time systems were originally developed in Japan during the 1950s and 1960s, as Business in Action illustrates.

Business in Action

The Kanban System in Japan

The Japanese *kanban* system of just-in-time inventory was originally developed at Toyota during the 1950s by a mechanical engineer, Taiichi Ohno. Ohno was a middle manager in charge of one of Toyota's component factories. Ohno was trying to achieve two goals: First, he wanted to reduce the costs associated with stockpiling inventory before it was used in the assembly process. Second, he wanted to improve the quality or car components to improve the quality of Toyota's cars.

At the time, vast amounts of component parts were produced at once and then stored in a warehouse until they were needed. Ohno saw a major problem with this approach. He reasoned that if there was a defect in a part, it would not be discovered for weeks or months, when the part was needed in the assembly process. Ohno decided to experiment with a new component operating and delivery system. He began to produce and send component parts in small quantities from his factory to the assembly line in a small, wheeled container known as a *kanban* just as they were needed. Assembly-line employees emptied the *kanban,* and the return of the *kanban* container was treated as the signal to produce another small-batch of component parts. So, the process repeated itself.

The system worked well, Ohno was able to get rid of most of the warehouse space needed to store inventory. Moreover, short production runs meant that defects in parts showed up at the assembly line almost immediately, which helped enormously to identify and eliminate the source of a defect. As a result, Ohno's machine shop quickly gained a reputation for quality within Toyota. Over the years, Ohno was repeatedly promoted for his efforts and was given the authority to spread his *kanban* innovation, first within Toyota and then to Toyota's suppliers.

During the 1970s, other Japanese companies copied Toyota's revolutionary *kanban* system. Much of the subsequent success of Japanese companies globally during the 1980s can be attributed to the improvements in product quality that were brought about by the wide-scale adoption of the *kanban* system in Japan, a full decade before managers in Western companies imitated the idea.[8]

A JIT system can extend beyond components to raw materials. A company may supply Toyota or Ford with taillight assemblies, for example. The taillight supplier, however, assembles taillights from components (screws, plastic lenses, bulbs) provided by yet other manufacturers. So, to reduce costs and increase quality, the taillight supplier also operates a JIT system with *its suppliers,* which in turn operate JIT

Figure 12.7
Just-in-Time Inventory Systems

systems with their suppliers, and so on. Figure 12.7 illustrates a just-in-time inventory system that goes from the customer, to the store, and then back through the manufacturer and original suppliers.

JIT systems are crucial for efficient flexible production operations. The ability to order components as they are needed allows a company to rapidly change the design of the products it makes to respond to changing customer needs. The company is not forced to carry on making an unpopular product simply because it has a large inventory of parts that need to be used up.

Summary of the Chapter

Operations and materials management are some of the most important and interesting functional activities that take place within a company. Today, changes in global competition and advances in IT are making OMM one of the most challenging tasks facing companies, managers, and employees. This chapter made the following major points:

1. Operations are the value-creation activities that transform inputs into outputs, or goods and services.

2. Materials management is the control of the flow of resources into and out of a company's operating system.

3. The functional activities involved in operations and materials management take place at three stages: the input, operations, and output stages.

4. How well a company controls its OMM activities is an important determinant of the profitability of a company's business model.

5. The five main sources of operating costs are the costs of raw materials and components, plant, labor, inventory, and distribution.

6. Three main types of operating system are small-batch production, mass production, and flexible production.

7. Small-batch production is an operating system designed to make one-of-a-kind or small quantities of customized products that closely match the needs of individual users.

8. Mass production is an operating system based on the use of machines and standard operating procedures to control the work process. Companies that use mass production systems are able to reduce their operating costs and lower their product prices.

9. Flexible production is an advanced, computer-based operating system that combines the benefits of mass production and small-batch production. This is achieved by the use of computer-integrated manufacturing and flexible employees and work teams.

10. Total quality management is an operations technique whose goal is the continuous improvement of a company's operating system to increase quality and reduce costs.

11. Three other materials management methods often used to create a competitive advantage are computer-aided materials management, global supply chain management, and just-in-time inventory systems.

Developing Business Skills

QUESTIONS FOR DISCUSSION AND ACTION

1. How do OMM activities create value and a competitive advantage at the input, operations, and output stages?

2. What are the three types of inventory costs, and why is it important for a company to reduce its inventory-holding costs?

3. How does small-batch production differ from mass production?

4. How would a fast-food restaurant operate differently if it used small-batch production compared to mass production?

5. In what ways can flexible production and the use of flexible work teams help create competitive advantage?

6. *Action.* Find a manager responsible for some aspect of a company's operations. Talk to the manager about the way the company handles its input, operations, and output processes.

7. What is TQM, and why is it important for a company to improve the quality of its products?

8. What are the alternative ways in which a company can manage its global supply chain activities?

9. *Action.* How does a just-in-time inventory system operate? Go to Dell's Web site and analyze the way it manages its JIT system.

ETHICS IN ACTION

Changing Operating Systems

Advanced operations and materials management techniques often lead to new work arrangements that dramatically reduce the number of employees needed to operate the production process. Consider the following quote from Jerry Miller, a former employee of US West, whose team of billing clerks lost their jobs after the company began to use flexible work teams. "When we first formed our teams, the company came in talking teams and empowerment and promised that we wouldn't lose any jobs. It turns out all this was a big cover. . . . We showed them how to streamline the work, and now 9,000 people are gone. It was cut-your-own-throat."

Using the ethical principles discussed in Chapter 5, think of the issues involved in changing the nature of a company's operating system and answer the following questions:

- When a company needs to change its work procedures to increase productivity, what ethical guidelines should it follow? For example, what kinds of information should it provide employees, and what kinds of guarantees should they be given?

- If employees begin to do different kinds of tasks and work in self-managed teams, what kinds of work and pay procedures should be introduced to ensure they are fairly treated?

SMALL GROUP EXERCISE

How to Operate a Computer Store?

Read the following and then break up into groups of three or four people and discuss the issues involved. Be prepared to share your discussion with the rest of your class.

You are the operations managers of a company planning to open a chain of large computer stores in major cities. You plan to offer small businesses a range of hardware, including servers, PCs, and cell phones, and software applications that work on both the Windows and Linux platforms. Your business model is to offer small businesses "one stop shopping." Your designers, salespeople, installers, and service and maintenance employees will be expected to provide a solution that matches each customer's specific needs.

You are meeting to decide how to design your operations and materials management processes to provide the best quality solutions at the lowest possible cost.

1. Analyze the problems, issues, and tasks employees will have to solve to best provide such a service to customers.

2. Based on this analysis, what kind of work methods and procedures will be needed to achieve your goals? In particular, what kind of operating system–small-batch, mass, or flexible production–will you use?

3. How will you organize employees and coordinate their activities?

4. What kinds of materials management techniques will you need to develop to control OMM costs and yet provide excellent customer service?

DEVELOPING GOOD BUSINESS SENSE

Why Do Operating Systems Differ?

Many people take the way goods and services are provided to them for granted. They do not think about the nature of the operating system that produces the goods and services they receive. To improve your understanding of how OMM processes work, complete the following assignment.

1. Choose three companies and observe how employees do their tasks. These can be three different fast-food restaurants or three entirely different types of companies, such as a fast-food restaurant, a department store, or the emergency room of a hospital.

2. Think about the differences in the operations involved in the input, operations, and output stages of these companies. Try to identify the nature of their operating systems. Are employees organized in different ways? If so, why? If possible, talk to the managers and employees in these operations to further your analysis.

3. What are the main kinds of OMM costs companies have? How does this affect their OMM operations?

4. How do companies design their operating systems to give them a competitive advantage?

EXPLORING THE WORLD WIDE WEB

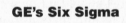

GE's Six Sigma

Go to GE's Web site (www.ge.com), click on "Our Company," and then "Company Information." Then click on "Six Sigma" and read about how GE is using Six Sigma to improve its OMM process. **For more Web activities, log on to www.mhhe.com/jonesintro.**

1. What is Six Sigma, and it what ways can it be used to reduce the costs of a company's OMM process?

2. In terms of a company's input, operations, and output stages, how can Six Sigma be used to create a competitive advantage?

CASE FOR DISCUSSION

A China Price for Toyota

Five years ago, Toyota Motor Corp. stunned the auto world by embarking on a plan to slash costs 30% across the board for the car parts it buys–from air-conditioning ducts and door-assist grips to windshield wipers. The bold plan to squeeze its own network of traditional suppliers, known as a *keiretsu*, was designed to make sure the Toyota group would retain its competitive edge against a spate of global auto alliances such as DaimlerChrysler, which promised gigantic synergies from their bigger size.

DaimlerChrysler is still struggling to make its merger pay off. But Toyota's cost-cutting program–

dubbed CCC21, or Construction of Cost Competitiveness for the 21st Century—has been a remarkable success. With just one year to go, the plan is on track to save the auto maker some $10 billion over its five-year time frame. Not only is CCC21 sourcing components more cheaply but Toyota has also improved the parts' quality. The program has even bested archrival Nissan Motor Co., whose chief executive, Carlos Ghosn, kicked off the savings scramble in 1999 by pledging 20% cuts in procurement costs.

But where does Toyota go from here? Even after putting its supply network through the wringer, Japan's No. 1 carmaker can ill afford to rest easy. Toyota may be under more pressure now to cut costs than when it began CCC21. So the drive is on to replace expensive materials, benchmark Toyota's auto parts against Chinese-level pricing, and squeeze its Japanese suppliers further by relying more on non-*keiretsu* parts makers. "We need to adjust our cost-cutting drive to meet a whole new set of challenges," says Katsuaki Watanabe, 62, the executive vice president who helped devise and supervise CCC21. In a sign that streamlining is still a top priority, the company announced that Watanabe will take over as president of Toyota from Fujio Cho.

STEEL SHORTAGE

Watanabe is a demon at spotting costs that no one even knew existed and eliminating redundancies that few had noticed. Under his prodding, one Toyota CCC21 team disassembled the horns made by a Japanese supplier and found ways to eliminate six of 28 components, resulting in a 40% cost reduction. No part has been too mundane to escape the Watanabe squad's notice. His favorite example: interior assist grips above each door. There once were 35 different grips. Now, Toyota's entire 90-model lineup uses just three basic styles. Toyota gearheads call this process *kawaita zokin wo shiboru*, or "wringing drops from a dry towel." It's an unending, excruciating process, but essential to Toyota's bottom line.

But even Watanabe needs a new game plan to counter what's coming. Among the most pernicious threats: the surge in prices of crucial items such as sheet steel due to higher costs for raw materials like iron ore and coal. Blame China's voracious demand for steel and a shortage of Asian blast furnace capacity—factors that are unlikely to go away anytime soon. What's more, the strong yen means Toyota's reported profits from outside Japan come in lower, increasing the pressure to cut expenses.

These burdens come just as the automotive giant's latest cost-cutting push has started to run out of steam. The company acknowledged its cost cuts will likely total just $1.7 billion for the fiscal year ending in March, 15% short of its annual target, in large part because of the surge in sheet steel prices. Nikko Citi-group Ltd. notes that the pace of cost cuts has slowed to $388 million in the most recent quarter, down from $582 million a year earlier.

To cope, Watanabe is pushing Toyota to winnow down the number of steel parts it uses in an average vehicle from 610 to about 500, although it won't say by when or how much savings that will net. Toyota will probably turn to more steel substitutes such as aluminum and heavy-duty advanced plastics and resins. Moving away from steel goes hand-in-hand with the company's longer-term goal of cutting the weight of its vehicles to increase fuel efficiency and rust-proof durability.

That said, there's a limit to how many steel parts Toyota can replace. There's also no guarantee that prices of aluminum and petrochemicals won't sky-rocket to the point where those materials are no longer cost-effective substitutes.

Something more is needed—and that's the China benchmark. Under CCC21, Watanabe's lieutenants identified about 180 key parts, then figured out who the world's most competitive suppliers of those parts were—companies like Robert Bosch of Germany, Delphi Corp., and the Toyota Group's own Denso Corp. The Toyota cost-cutters used this information as the "benchmark" against which Toyota's *keiretsu* suppliers had to compete. The *keiretsu* outfits must learn how to meet the benchmark—or risk losing the business. Toyota worked with affiliate Denso, for example, to consolidate production of air-conditioning vents to just four key styles, down from 27 previously. That resulted in a 28% cost reduction. Watanabe still wasn't happy: He had wanted just three.

Now the exercise goes to a whole new level. The boom in auto production in China is nurturing a car-parts industry—with both multinational suppliers and local companies—providing new data on how low prices can go. For now, that's mostly limited to commodity-type components such as assist grips, not high-end modules and core parts like brakes. Toyota officials say the rise of China has raised the bar for its *keiretsu* suppliers. They increasingly must push their prices toward the Chinese level to keep Toyota's business. "China has become an important new benchmark for us," says Watanabe.

This doesn't mean Toyota will soon start importing all its parts from China for use in its Japanese and U.S. factories. Analysts say it may be a decade before the parts makers in China can go toe-to-toe with components made in Japan, South Korea, and the United States The ultralow defect rates for parts made in Japan, for example, can be as important to cutting prices as cheap fixed costs. Even so, benchmarking against the Chinese price forces suppliers to come as close as possible to matching it without sacrificing quality. That involves rethinking everything, from the number of designers assigned to making any one part, to the supply chain involved in sourcing components, to the utilization rates of equipment at a parts factory.

The China benchmark will increase the pressure on Toyota's traditional suppliers. But so will the company's efforts to court more non-Japanese suppliers to find the best price. And parts makers like Bosch and Delphi, which turn out everything from air bags to transmissions, are now more willing to meet demanding specifications. Bosch, for example, supplies the complete brake system for the Toyota Avensis sedan and the diesel-injection system for the Toyota Yaris subcompact, both made in Europe. Toyota won't say how much of its parts purchasing comes from its *keiretsu* versus outsiders, but non-Japanese suppliers are eager to win a bigger share. No wonder: The auto maker expects its global sales to hit 8.5 million vehicles by next year, about 1 million more than in 2004. That will put it on a par with General Motors Corp., the world's largest carmaker. "Toyota is an important customer for Bosch," says Bernd Bohr, chairman of the company's automotive group. "We maintain a close cooperative relationship with Toyota and in development projects."

Non-*keiretsu* suppliers see their best chance in markets where Toyota is expanding fastest, especially China, where the Japanese automaker is eager to catch up with established rivals like GM and Volkswagen. "This is a great opportunity for outside suppliers to increase their business with us," says Watanabe. Those suppliers would love ultimately to win orders on a global basis—including in Japan, where local suppliers account for all but a fraction of the auto giant's parts purchases.

PART OF THE FAMILY

To show the depth of its commitment, Delphi now sends technicians to Toyota headquarters in Toyota City to collaborate on the blueprints for new parts, and invites Toyota execs to tour its plants and offer suggestions for improving productivity and increasing quality. Although Delphi won't disclose how much business it does with Toyota, less than 10% of its roughly $1 billion in Asian revenue comes from the Japanese. The company, however, says it has high hopes for supplying more to Toyota from its 13 plants in China. "We are becoming part of Toyota's extended *keiretsu* family," says Choon T. Chon, president of Delphi's Asia Pacific unit. And part of Watanabe's ruthless drive to cut costs to the bone.

Source: Chester Dawson and Karen Nickel Anhalt, "A China Price for Toyota," *BusinessWeek Online*, February 21, 2005.

QUESTIONS

1. In what ways did Toyota's CCC21 plan improve the efficiency of its OMM process?

2. How is Toyota continuing to find ways to increase efficiency?

3. How is low-cost Chinese competition helping Toyota reduce its OMM costs?

BUILDING YOUR MANAGEMENT SKILLS
Know Thyself

Have you ever been to a Krispy Kreme Doughnut store or watched food being prepared at McDonald's or a large cafeteria? At Krispy Kreme stores you can observe the entire production process. The arrangement of equipment and people determines the speed of production, customer response time, and overall efficiency of the operation. The goal of process selection is to determine the most economical processes and sequences needed to transform inputs into the company's product or service. Do you think you could design an effective layout of people and equipment? The exercise on your Student DVD named "Facilities Layout" will explain more about it and let you apply your knowledge of facilities design.

CHAPTER VIDEO
Jet Blue

Jet Blue defines itself as a "customer service company." From its innovative mission statement to the teamwork displayed by its employees, Jet Blue is focused on its customers.

Rather than a traditional mission statement to guide it, Jet Blue has defined five (5) core values that serve to direct all activity: safety, caring, fun, passion, and integrity. There is a constant focus on ensuring that all details are correct; that courtesy is practiced at all levels. Their rapid success is attributed to their exclusive focus and emphasis on their customers.

Through 2002, Jet Blue achieved its efficiencies from Point to Point routes and flying only one type of aircraft. As of 2003, however, the company acquired 100 Brazilian made Embry Air jets which resulted in 800 new markets. Despite the new aircraft, the operating philosophy remains intact—focus on customers. Strong internal relations and training constantly reinforce these key principles. Whether the Jet Blue experience is a sustainable competitive advantage can only be judged by watching it perform into the future.

1. How does Jet Blue differentiate its service from that of its competitors?

2. What is the "marketing message" of Jet Blue?

3. Would you consider Jet Blue to be a product "brand"?

13 Human Resource Management:

Acquiring and Building Employees' Skills and Capabilities

Learning Objectives

After studying this chapter, you should be able to:

1. Describe the five components of a human resource management system and the way they work together to help a company obtain a competitive advantage.

2. Appreciate the issues involved in the process of recruiting qualified people to join a company and the steps involved in the selection process.

3. Explain how training and development activities help to build the abilities, skills, and knowledge of a company's employees.

4. Understand why the process of appraising employees' performance is a major factor influencing the way they wish to contribute to achieving a company's goals and objectives.

5. Explain why linking pay to performance in a fair and equitable manner is an important source of employee motivation and commitment to a company.

6. Appreciate the importance of good labor relations and the importance of collective bargaining in aligning the goals of employees and companies.

> **WHY IS THIS IMPORTANT** ?
>
> Have you ever had an employment interview, received a job offer, but decided not to take the job? Do you agree that people are a company's most important resource? Human Resource Management is the function responsible for working to recruit, train, evaluate, and compensate employees.
>
> This chapter explains that HRM is actually several interrelated processes that work to support the entire organization by finding and retaining a work force capable of achieving organizational goals.

A Question of Business
GE's Human Resource Management System

How does GE use its HRM system to build competitive advantage?

General Electric (GE) is composed of over 300 separate operating divisions that make products as diverse as light bulbs, jet engines, television programs, and appliances. What ties this diverse company together is the way it has created a human resource management system used in all 300 divisions to encourage and motivate managers and employees to work hard to achieve GE's goals.

The process starts when GE sends its recruiters to schools and colleges to find and attract well-qualified applicants to meet its specific occupational needs—its need for skilled production employees and service personnel, sales representatives, engineers, management trainees, and so on. GE uses a sophisticated recruitment process to select people for these jobs, and it has developed job-specific tests to determine if applicants have the skills they need to perform at a high level. Using these tests, it narrows down the hundreds of thousands of job applicants who apply to GE each year, to a final list of several thousand people who are then invited to attend a job interview. GE's functional managers, human resource managers, and the employees these applicants will be working with, meet personally with the applicants to assess their fit with a specific job and the company.

After selecting which applicants will be offered jobs, GE then puts its well-organized training programs into action. The company

spends over a billion dollars each year on employee training and development activities, in fact. Each of its divisions has is its own advanced training programs designed to teach employees the specific skills needed to do their jobs and do them well. To train its future managers, GE has created its own university in Crotonville, New York. Here, middle managers who are rising in GE's hierarchy attend intensive training programs to develop advanced management skills. GE's CEO and top managers spend many days a year teaching these training programs. The company also uses these programs to identify "star" managers who have the talent needed to fill its top management positions in the future.

GE uses a companywide performance appraisal system to decide which of its employees are most likely to benefit from these advanced training programs as well as other types of training. The performance appraisal system requires all managers to use the same kinds of procedures to evaluate the performance of every one of their subordinates. GE also uses these appraisals to weed out and terminate employees who do not perform up to its minimum requirements. Its managers are told to rank employees into categories, including the top and bottom 10% of performers. The company then terminates the bottom 10% of performers each year.

GE is particularly quick to terminate managers who put their personal interests before the company's interests. It also gets rid of managers who diminish the motivation of their subordinates. GE describes these managers as the kind who "smile up and kick down," meaning they try to make themselves look good for higher-ups but do little to train and motivate their subordinates. GE believes that its managers must continually train and mentor their subordinates if they are to become high performers. It also wants its managers to cooperate and share their knowledge to continually increase the company's performance.

To motivate all its managers and employees to perform at a high level, GE is careful to link their personal performance to rewards such as pay increases, stock options, and promotions. Its employees know exactly what they need to achieve to increase their chances of being rewarded and promoted. GE is convinced that providing incentives for high performance, and accurately identifying those who perform at a high level, is the key to its continuing success.

Finally, GE has excellent relationships with the hundreds of unions that represent the interests of its thousands of employees. It works hard to build good union-company relationships because it knows that obtaining the goodwill of its employees and unions is the key to achieving high profitability and long-term success.[1] •

Overview

GE has invested billions of dollars to create a human resource management (HRM) system that allows it to acquire and build a high-performing workforce that labors to achieve its ambitious goals. For example, GE expects all its operating divisions to be the leading companies in their respective industries. Its employees are always in high demand by other companies because they have received excellent training and have developed extensive job knowledge. Indeed, its top managers are often recruited to become the CEOs of other leading companies. GE's goal, however, is that its best performers will never want to leave the company, which is one more reason why it has created a fair and equitable HRM system to provide the training, interesting jobs, rewards, and chances for success that keep its employees motivated to work hard.

In this chapter, we examine how a company's HRM system is used to acquire and build employees' skills and capabilities. Remember, their skills and abilities create much of the value in the products a company makes and sells. First, we provide an overview of the five main components of human resource management: recruitment and selection, training and development, performance appraisal and feedback, pay and benefits, and labor relations. Second, we examine each of these components in turn, focusing on how a company that creates a fair and equitable HRM system can use it to increase efficiency, quality, innovation, and responsiveness to customers. By the end of this chapter, you will understand why a company's human resources are often the ultimate source of its competitive advantage and profitability.

The Components of a Human Resource Management System

In Chapter 1, we note that business is goal-directed behavior aimed at using the four productive resources—land, labor, capital and enterprise—to make and sell goods and services. In the previous chapters, we discuss all of the value-chain functions and activities involved in making and selling goods and services. Now, we can turn our attention to the people who perform these functional jobs and tasks—a company's human resources, or labor. **Human resources** include all the people a company employs—its CEO and top managers, the middle managers throughout its functions, and the nonmanagerial employees who perform the thousands of specific tasks that need to be done to create goods and services.

human resources
The people a company employs, from its CEO and top managers, the middle managers throughout its functions, to its nonmanagerial employees.

human resource management The set of activities designed to recruit high-quality employees and then improve their skills and capabilities.

Human resource management (HRM) is the set of activities designed to acquire high-quality human resources, and then build employees' skills and capabilities so they can perform their jobs more efficiently and effectively. The primary responsibility of the HRM function is to develop a company's HRM system, which has five main components: recruitment and selection, training and development, performance appraisal and feedback, pay and benefits, and labor relations. These components are shown in Figure 13.1. The task of HRM managers is to build a HRM system that allows a company's functions, and the people within them, to work in ways that lead to superior efficiency, quality, innovation, and responsiveness to customers—the four building blocks of a competitive advantage. Like IT, HRM is a secondary function. It is not directly involved in the value chain that gets a company's products to customers, but its activities improve the performance of all of the firm's other functions.

When a company's HRM system gives it a competitive advantage, then, like GE, the company creates more value and profit, and all of its stakeholders benefit. Customers benefit by receiving higher-quality products. Shareholders receive increased dividends. Employees benefit because a profitable company has more money to spend to train its employees, improve their skills, and reward them for their hard work. A company can also offer its employees more opportunities for promotion to more interesting and better-paid jobs. Last, but not least, the more profitable a company, the less likely it is to lay off employees, so workers enjoy more job security.

Figure 13.1
The Five Components of the HRM System

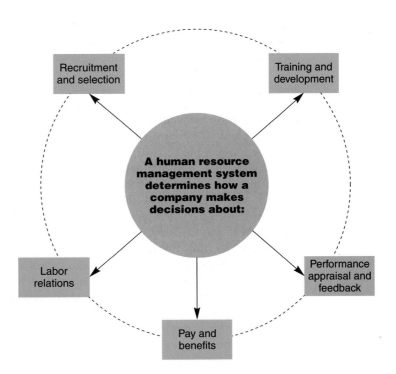

Video Small Business in Action

More People Leaving Corporate America

A new trend has emerged among high power professionals as shown in the NBC video on the Student DVD. Many younger professionals are leaving corporate America and are going it alone. From Sparky's Hotdogs to massage therapy and ethnic wallpaper, former corporate level managers are seeking new business opportunities.

The aftermath of 9/11, the corporate ethics scandals, and the loss of trust have given rise to a significant increase in new business startups. In fact, it is the largest boom in this area in over six years. Even more troubling is that the brain drain is occurring among the more valuable corporate human resources—that is the departure of younger employees. Over one-third of new businesses are formed by individuals under the age of 40; women are a larger share of this percentage than ever before.

Discussion Questions

1. What potential impact does the "brain drain" (as shown in the video) have on the management of human resources?
2. What is the most severe implication of the number of people leaving corporate America?
3. What impact does the brain drain have on the function of human resource planning?

To understand the way the five components of the HRM system work together to build competitive advantage, suppose you are an entrepreneur whose mission is to start a company to make a state-of-the-art home video game. You worked on the game during your last three years of college and developed a prototype that you recently demonstrated to a firm of venture capitalists. They were so impressed with the sales potential of your game that they provided $6 million to fund the development of your game. Now you can develop and finish your game's software and work to make it compatible with Sony's PlayStation and Microsoft's X-Box. To finish the game, you need to hire 10 video game developers to help you design and write the final game software.

Your first task is to *recruit and select* 10 new employees who can write great video-game software code. Where will you find these people, and how will you determine if they do have the skills and experience you need? Suppose you advertise in video game magazines or on popular Internet gaming Web sites for game software writers, and you receive 150 replies. What criteria will you use to identify, say, the best 30 prospective job applicants? Then how will you narrow this list down and select the best-qualified 10 job applicants? These are some of the many issues that entrepreneurs (and of course HRM managers) grapple with as they search for the people who have the skills needed to create blockbuster products.

During your search for these 10 employees, you identify two job applicants who are obviously creative and highly talented software writers. However, they have no experience writing video-game software code. If you hire these two people, you will then need to put the next HRM component, *training and development,* to work. Your task will be to train these people so that they quickly develop the skills needed to write highly complex game software. Since your software is also unique, you also have to teach all 10 employees how to write *new* code so that it works seamlessly with yours. Each of these employees will also have his or her own unique and valuable skills. To take advantage of these skills, you need to ensure the employees will share their knowledge with one another in training sessions and on-the-job. If the training is a success, the result will be higher quality code written in a shorter time—and increased efficiency and effectiveness.

Suppose your 10 programmers have been working with you for a month. You have closely observed their work and are pleased because you recruited a talented group of people. However, there is some variation in the pace and quality of their work. Two or three programmers are contributing much more than the others. One in particular has exceptional skills and has written code that significantly improves the speed at which your game operates. On the other hand, there is one person who is frequently late or absent from work, and one who is working at a very unacceptable level.

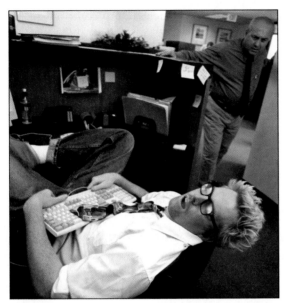

Average or poorly performing employees who do not receive extra awards might be motivated to work harder to obtain them—or they might decide to quit.

performance appraisal The task of accurately identifying differences in the level and quality of the work employees do and providing them with feedback that increases their performance levels.

labor relations The process of working with employees, or the unions that represent them, to create work rules and a negotiation process to resolve disputes between them.

At this point, you need to put the third component of the HRM system to work, *performance appraisal.* **Performance appraisal** is the process of evaluating the quality of the work employees do and providing them with feedback to increase their performance levels. When you hired your employees, you told them you would review their performance in a month's time, so now your task is to provide them with feedback. For example, you are responsible for informing your high-performing employees that you appreciate their contributions and that they will be rewarded. You also have to share with under-performing employees that you are concerned about their low performance level. You need to explain what they need to do to improve their performance and inquire about any problems that might be causing it.

Now each employee's performance has been appraised, it is time to use the fourth component of HRM, *pay and benefits.* To encourage your best game designers to continue to perform at a high level, you need to reward them with pay raises, bonuses, or even stock options so they will share in the profits you hope your new video game will generate. When high-performing employees are rewarded, they are more likely to stay with a company. Average or poor performers who do not receive extra rewards might be motivated to perform better to obtain these rewards. Or, they might decide to quit if they don't believe greater rewards will come their way in the future.

The last component of HRM, **labor relations,** is the process of working with employees—or the unions that represent them—and then creating work rules that define the responsibilities of the two parties. The negotiation process used to resolve disputes between the two must also be agreed upon. Negotiations between a company and its employees or unions typically take place over pay and benefits, work practices, and health insurance. Since your employees are not members of a union of software code writers, you do not have to negotiate with a union. Nevertheless, you do have to maintain good working relationships with your employees—just as you would have if a union did represent them. This is important because if one or more of your 10 employees decide to go on strike or quit, you would be in a very difficult situation. Most companies, particularly larger ones, set up committees to establish procedures that govern pay and benefits, work practices, and so on.

As you can see, each of the five HRM components affects the others. Together they determine if employees will cooperate in ways that result in innovative, high-quality products. If, for example, you were successful and hired motivated, talented people, these employees would probably help "train each other" to improve their game-code writing skills. In turn, your performance appraisal task would become easier—you would then be able to give your employees mostly positive performance feedback. In this case, your main problem might be to find enough money to pay for the substantial pay raises you want to give your employees for their hard work!

On the other hand, suppose you had made a few mistakes and hired employees whose performance was slowing down the development of your game. You could start an intensive training program to improve their performance, but then you would have to spend your time to train them, which would slow down game development.

So, to encourage employees to find ways to improve their performance, you start to appraise their performance on a weekly or monthly basis. This might motivate some programmers to try harder; but it might demotivate others and make them quit. If any of your employees quit, you will have to spend your valuable time recruiting and training new employees. This will leave you less time to focus on perfecting your game, again, slowing down its development.

All these problems, which frequently arise when new or improved products are developed, suggest how difficult it is to manage human resources—and how crucial the HRM function is. The way a company and its managers design and control the five aspects of its HRM system affects the performance of its employees and the way its functional groups cooperate to achieve its business model. For example, employees who believe they have been unfairly appraised or treated poorly by their managers might become demotivated and deliberately slow down the pace of work. Similarly, a manager who plays favorites and does not appraise the performance of his or her subordinates equitably is likely to poison the working relationships among the members of a function. Some companies have a history of poor labor relations because they fail to develop an effective HRM system. The result is a constant series of strikes and lost pay and profit that benefits no one.

Well-designed HRM systems, such as GE's, can prevent these "people problems" from occurring. Good HRM systems also align the goals of managers and employees with those of their companies. Companies must also ensure that their HRM systems comply with the complex set of national and state labor laws and regulations. Some of the most important national laws are presented in Table 13.1. In the rest of this chapter we examine the way the five components of the HRM system should be designed to work together to increase a company's efficiency and effectiveness.

Table 13.1
Some Important Laws Affecting HRM Practices (Organized by date)

National Labor Relations Act, 1935	Passed to control the collective bargaining process between companies and labor unions and prevent unfair labor practices, such as employers threatening employees with loss of jobs or closing down plants if they join or vote for a union.
Fair Labor Standards Act, 1938	Established national minimum hourly wage for jobs
Taft-Hartley Act, 1947	Established restrictions on union practices deemed unfair to employers or union members, such as preventing non-striking employees entering the workplace or threatening to harm them.
Equal Pay Act, 1963	Requires organizations to pay same wage or salary to men and women performing equal work.
Title VII of the Civil Rights Act, 1964	Makes it illegal for an employee to fail or refuse to hire or discharge a person, or discriminate against him in any other way on the basis of that person's race, color, religions belief, gender, or national origin.
Age Discrimination and Employment Act, 1967	Prohibits discrimination against employees over 40 years old.
Occupational Safety and Health Act (OSHA), 1970	Gives the federal government the power to establish and enforce occupational safety and health standards at work.
Americans with Disabilities Act, 1990	Prohibits job discrimination based on disability and requires employers to make accommodations for disabled workers.
Civil Rights Acts, 1991	Provides legal avenues for employees who believe they have been discriminated against to take action against employers and allows for award of compensatory and punitive damages under Title VII.
Family and Medical Leave Act, 1993	Requires employers with over 50 employees to provide up to 12 weeks of unpaid leave for serious personal or family reasons.
Drug-Free Workplace Act, 1998	Goal is to reduce use of illegal drugs at work and allows regular testing for certain jobs, such as truck drivers

Recruitment and Selection

recruitment The process of identifying and attracting a pool of qualified job applicants.

selection Creating the set of job- and company-specific criteria that determines which job applicants are the best match for a particular job and company.

Recruitment and selection are all the activities involved in acquiring human resources. Recruitment involves developing and using a company-specific set of rules and SOPs to identify and attract the best pool of qualified job applicants. Selection involves creating the set of job- and company-specific criteria that allow a company's managers and employees to choose the applicant best suited for a particular job and the company.

Human Resource Planning

Human resource planning is the process of forecasting the type and number of employees a company will require in the future to meet the objectives of its business model. To begin this process, HRM managers first analyze what skills and capabilities a company's current workforce has. Then they must work with the managers of the firm's other functions to decide what kinds of human resource requirements the company will need in one or two years' time. By comparing the makeup of the firm's present workforce with the one it will require in the future, HRM managers can identify how many, and what kind of employees, they will need to recruit, or alternatively, lay off because of changing business conditions. A carmaker looking two years into the future, for example, might decide it needs to recruit 300 design engineers to develop innovative new car models. It might also decide to layoff 200 IT employees because it has signed an outsourcing contract with IBM to manage its information systems. Two important tools that help HRM managers determine future needs are workflow and job analysis.

KORN/FERRY INTERNATIONAL

To hire top managers, sometimes companies use the services of executive search firms like Korn/Ferry International to do their recruiting.

human resource planning The process of forecasting the type and number of employees a company will require in the future to meet the objectives of its business model.

WORKFLOW ANALYSIS   Workflow analysis is conducted to identify what kinds of jobs will be required to allow each value-chain function to perform efficiently and effectively in the future. Sales and distribution managers, for example, analyze the tasks their functions currently perform, and consider how factors such as customers' increasing use of the Internet, or the widening range of products their company is making, will affect the kinds of skills their employees will need in the future.

Workflow analysis also involves pulling apart the many tasks involved in moving a product along the downstream value chain toward the customer to determine ways to perform them better. The goal is to find ways to link and coordinate sales and distribution jobs to increase efficiency and customer responsiveness. Workflow analysis tells managers how jobs *should* be changed to find better ways to manage its functional activities in the future.

job analysis The process of obtaining detailed information about the tasks and responsibilities involved in each job in a company.

position analysis questionnaire A written method of job analysis that asks jobholders and their managers to answer detailed questions about the skills and abilities employees need to do a particular job.

JOB ANALYSIS   By doing a workflow analysis, a company can identify how existing jobs need to change to allow a company to operate more efficiently and effectively in the future. The next step in HRM is job analysis, the process of obtaining detailed information about the tasks and responsibilities related to each job in the company. When managers know what each job involves, they can work to redesign jobs, that is, change the tasks and responsibilities of each job to increase efficiency. Jobs can also be redesigned to make them easier or more motivating.

There are several ways to do a job analysis. First, people who hold a specific job in a company are asked to describe the various tasks and duties they perform. Second, managers can also use a position analysis questionnaire (PAQ) to analyze jobs. The PAQ is a written method of job analysis that asks jobholders and their managers to answer detailed questions about (1) the skills and abilities employees use on the job, 2) the range of employees' job activities, and (3) the technology such as machines and computers employees use.

Based on this workflow and job analysis, managers better understand the different tasks people in each job must do and how best to do them. Now they have two vital

Figure 13.2
Technical Sales
Representative

> ## JOB DESCRIPTION
>
> Sales Mission. The sales mission is to meet the sales revenue
> and distribution channel profit targets each quarter
> through the effective management of the sales territory.
>
> Job Responsibilities.
> - Develop and manage sales territories and distribution channels
> - Develop and increase market share per dealer
> - Develop, train, and collaborate with dealers
> - Co-develop sales strategies, targets, and budgets
> - Continuous development of personal sales skills
>
> Performance Evaluation Goals.
> - Sales revenue
> - Profit per dealer
> - Dealer satisfaction
> - Sales specific errors
> - Expenditures relative to budget
> - Personal skills development
>
> ## JOB SPECIFICATIONS
>
> Personal Skills and Abilities.
> - High level of personal integrity, honesty, and responsibility
> - Motivated to close deals, and energized by competitive
>   sales situations
> - High stamina and endurance
> - Team player and customer-service oriented
> - Well-organized and skilled in prioritizing tasks and bringing
>   them to closure
>
> Required Professional Skills and Experience.
> - College degree
> - Four-years experience selling high-end products or services

job description A list of
the specific tasks, duties,
and responsibilities that
make up a particular job.

job specifications A
written list of the required
skills, abilities, and
knowledge needed to do
a particular job.

kinds of information to use in the recruitment process. First, they can write a job description, a list of the specific tasks, duties, and responsibilities that make up a particular job. Second, managers can now write job specifications, a list of the required skills, abilities, and knowledge needed to perform that particular job. These are essential tools in the recruitment process. For example, companies use these job descriptions and specifications to decide how to advertise for new recruits. Figure 13.2 contains a typical job advertisement for a salesperson.

External and Internal Recruitment

HRM planning tells managers what kinds of job positions need to be filled, and what qualifications the employees who will fill them need to possess. With this information, companies can begin to search and advertise for job applicants. The two methods of finding qualified applicants are internal and external recruitment.

internal recruitment
A policy of promoting
employees who already
work for a company.

Internal recruitment involves a policy of promotion from within; employees who already work for a company are recruited first. If the job is a promotion for the employee, it often requires the person to take a more complex or demanding job within the same function. A retail salesperson being promoted within a company to do trade or technical selling is one example. A promotion that involves an internal candidate moving to a managerial position to supervise his or her former co-workers is another.

To identify employees who have the skills and motivation to move to a more responsible position, a company asks their managers or supervisors for recommendations. Companies also internally advertise open job positions using their intranets, by posting vacancies on bulletin boards, and by sending e-mails to employees. Employees who believe they are ready to move to more responsible positions are then allowed to apply for these jobs.

Promotion from within is a policy that helps a company retain its highest performing employees. It encourages them to believe that if they work hard and develop better skills, they will move to positions with more responsibility. Recall that one's career, which often is the result of a series of promotions, is a major motivating factor for many people.

external recruitment
A policy of filling advanced job positions with applicants from outside of a company.

On the other hand, if a company has a policy of external recruitment—that is, if it fills its more advanced positions with qualified applicants from outside of the organization, this is likely to demotivate its employees. Employees who see no prospect of promotion from within are likely to begin looking for new job opportunities elsewhere. In other words, they become the qualified applicants who apply at *other* companies!

In practice, a company might have a 50/50 internal/external recruitment policy, meaning it seeks to fill half of its more advanced positions with employees from within the company and half from outside; or it may have a 70/30 or 80/20 policy. Which policy it chooses depends on factors like the number of qualified applicants there are within its own ranks, and how many positions it needs to fill.

External recruiting is obviously the method used most to fill entry-level positions, that is, jobs on the lowest step of the career ladder. To fill these positions a company selects the communication channels that allow it to identify and reach a large number of qualified applicants. This can involve sending company brochures to entry-level candidates, holding job "open houses," making recruiting visits to career centers and colleges, and advertising in local or student newspapers. To attract higher-level applicants, a company might advertise in major newspapers, trade journals, magazines, and employment Web sites that target people in specific occupations, such as marketers, software developers, or engineers.

There are some disadvantages associated with external recruitment. First, it is expensive and time consuming because managers from HRM and all of the company's other functions must go on recruiting visits to identify attractive applicants. Electronic recruiting is less expensive. It also makes it easy for job applicants to submit their résumés to companies—so much easier in fact, that many people apply for jobs they are not suited for. Then, HRM managers must spend more time sifting through the job applications to find the most qualified applicants. But most companies will still take the opportunity to make use of the Internet to search for well-qualified candidates at low salaries—even if they have to look globally—as Business in Action illustrates.

Business in Action

IT Recruiters Rush To Bangalore

What company would not want a large supply of qualified programmers who will work for a fraction of the going wage rate in the United States? Few U.S. firms can resist such a deal. Companies like IBM, HP, Oracle, and Accenture are rushing to Bangalore—India's equivalent of Silicon Valley. There, skilled programmers with two years' experience earn about $533 a month, one-fifth of their U.S. counterparts.

These U.S. companies are rapidly expanding the size of their Indian operations to take advantage of its low-cost, skilled labor. IBM, which has thousands of Indian employees, wants to add several thousand more, and both Oracle and Accenture plan to double their staff in India in the next few years. Indian employees, linked to their U.S. companies through the Intranet, can also maintain their companies' computer networks and provide computer hardware and software support for their customers around the globe. U.S. companies continually advertise on the Web in the *Times of India,* attracting thousands of applicants, who then visit the futuristic offices built by these companies in Bangalore. By simply going across town to work for a U.S. company, these employees can earn 30% more.

Ironically, many high-tech Indian companies were founded to take advantage of the low-cost labor services they could provide in the $68 billion global outsourcing market. Demand is high for low-cost computer services, such as customer help

Today the top 1,000 Indian high-tech companies operating in Bangalore are under intense pressure to retain their best employees. U.S. companies are luring them away with a 30% pay increase to join their India-based operations.

desks, software development, and "backroom" IT support to maintain a company's databases. Dell, for example, currently outsources over half of its customer support activities to Indian companies such as Infosys and Wipro, two global leaders in the outsourcing industry.

Now, however, there are new predators on the competitive landscape. The massive recruitment being done by U.S. companies in Bangalore is putting pressure on Indian high-tech companies. Although the Indian companies once focused their efforts on providing low-cost labor services, they are now under intense pressure to increase their salaries. If they don't, they will have a hard time retaining their best employees and remaining competitive.[2]

The Selection Process

A typical selection process involves four main "screening" steps. These steps can be viewed as a "funnel." The wide end of the funnel represents the initial pool of applicants, and the narrow end, the choice of a final candidate, as shown in Figure 13.3. At each step, the goal is to gain relevant information to narrow down the number of applicants qualified to move down the funnel. At each step, the task of HRM is to collect the information that determines whether or not an applicant should proceed through the "selection gate" or be disqualified. At each step, care must be taken not to disqualify job applicants who might be suited for the job for non-job related reasons. It should be noted, too, that the four steps do not always occur in the order shown in Figure 13.3 but can differ from company to company. For example, testing might occur before interviewing candidates or vice versa.

STEP 1: SCREENING APPLICATIONS AND RÉSUMÉS   Once a pool of applicants for a particular position has been amassed, the selection process begins. Note that a company might receive hundreds of applications for a particular position. Now begins the process of winnowing down the potential list of applicants to find the person who best matches the particular job that needs to be filled and is the best fit for the company.

At every stage in the selection process, ethical and legal concerns make it vital that applicants are not disqualified for non-job related reasons. Many laws, such as Equal Employment Opportunity (EEO) laws, the Civil Rights Act (1991), and the Americans with Disabilities Act (1991), govern the way U.S. companies make their selection decisions. (See Table 13.1.) These laws are designed to prevent discrimination against

Figure 13.3
The Four Steps in the Selection Process

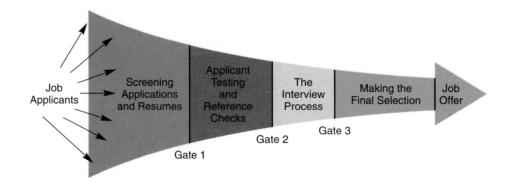

people and groups because of their age, gender, race, religion, and so on. Companies who break these laws can be fined tens of millions of dollars. HRM professionals are responsible for understanding these laws and ensuring an applicant is not disqualified for inappropriate reasons. They are also responsible for educating the firm's managers and other employees involved in the selection process about these laws.

The background information solicited on job application forms and résumés is first used to screen applicants. Recruiters use this information to select the applicants that appear to have the skills and experience best matching a particular job description. Depending upon the job, the highest level of education obtained, number of years and type of work experience, or special skills, such as the ability to speak a foreign language or overseas-assignment experience, are examples of the types of screening criteria used. Because the volume of résumés received for a particular position can be huge, some companies use software to scan them and sort out applicants. Career-Builder.com offers a software-screening service called IntelligentHire for companies. Companies pay a fee to have IntelligentHire screen out the 10 most qualified and interested applicants posting for a job on CareerBuilder's site.

In addition to asking for résumés, most companies ask applicants to fill out standard job application forms. The questions companies ask on their job application forms should not attempt to elicit information that would disqualify an applicant for *non-job related reasons*, however. Questions concerning age, race, marital status, and religion cannot be put on the forms. By the same token, it is unethical for job candidates to exaggerate or lie about their qualifications. This is harder to do on a standardized application form than it is on a résumé, which is why companies use them. Job application forms also usually require applicants to sign them, verifying the information they have listed is true and verifiable.

STEP 2: APPLICANT TESTING AND REFERENCE CHECKS   After the screening process is over, a company might still have a large pool of applicants who meet the basic job requirements. To further narrow the applicant pool and determine which people go down the funnel, HRM needs to obtain additional job-specific candidate information. Typically, to economize on selection costs, HRM managers use standardized tests that show an applicant's ability to do a certain job. Some of the standardized tests companies use are listed in Figure 13.4. *Standardized* means the identical test is used to screen all applicants for a particular position.

Skills tests gauging an applicant's typing ability or hand-eye coordination are common tests. Some companies require applicants to take personality tests to determine if they have personal qualities needed to do a certain type of job. A job in sales, for example, might require applicants be tested for their people skills. Physical tests are often conducted as well. Eye and hearing tests are routinely given to airline pilots and locomotive engineers, for example. Drug tests are also common, particularly when a person's on-the-job performance could put people's lives at risk. Job applicant testing must be done for valid job-related reasons, however. If companies that use these tests cannot justify their use for job-related reasons, they risk being sued by applicants who believe the tests discriminated against them for reasons such as gender, race, and so on.

Background investigations have also become standard procedure for many companies to protect against a variety of threats ranging from embezzlement and theft of merchandise to workplace violence. Some state courts have ruled

Did You Know?

The best and worst jobs in the United States according to the *Jobs Rated Almanac*:

Worst Jobs	Best Jobs
1. Lumberjack	1. Biologist
2. Fisherman	2. Actuary
3. Cowboy	3. Financial planner
4. Ironworker	4. Computer-systems analyst
5. Seaman	5. Accountant
6. Taxi driver	6. Software engineer
7. Construction worker	7. Meteorologist
8. Farmer	8. Paralegal assistant
9. Roofer	9. Statistician
10. Stevedore	10. Astronomer

Figure 13.4
Types of Standardized Tests

Physical Ability Tests	• Hand-eye coordination • Muscular power and endurance • Flexibility, balance, and coordination
Cognitive Ability (Intelligence) Tests	• Verbal skills such as skills in using written and spoken language • Numerical skills such as skills in working with numbers • Reasoning ability such as skills in working through problems and scenarios
Job-Related Performance Tests	• Typing skills • Driving skills • "In-basket" exercises that involve tests of specific activities that will be performed on job (e.g., office worker, receptionist, sales associate)
Personality Tests	Measure personality traits such as: • Extroversion • Agreeableness • Conscientiousness • Honesty
Personal Health Tests	• Drug Testing • Medical Examinations

that companies can be held liable for negligent hiring if they fail to do adequate background checks. Federal law requires a comprehensive background checks for all childcare providers, for example. It also prohibits convicted felons from engaging in financial and security-oriented transactions. Among the checks are social security verification, past employment and education verification, and a criminal records check. A number of other checks can be conducted if they pertain to the job being hired for. They include a motor vehicle record check (for jobs involving driving), a credit check (for money-handling jobs), and military records.

Like the application process, many checks that were once done manually are now being done online using existing computer databases. To comply with different state laws regarding privacy and to treat all applicants fairly and consistently, most large companies now outsource at least part of the background screening process to third-party background screening companies. This can cost between $4 and $80, depending on the types of checks requested, the number of references contacted, and the number of counties searched for criminal activity. They can generally be e-mailed to the company within a few hours or a few days. In addition a number of job boards like Yahoo! and Hot Jobs now have online screening allowing an applicant to conduct his or her own self-background check and post it online prior to any sort of interview. The idea is to demonstrate to propsective employers that the applicant has a clean criminal record, a good job history, and would make a good employee. Because drug testing, reference and background checking are expensive, they are usually reserved for final candidates.

STEP 3: THE INTERVIEW PROCESS   After the number of applicants has been narrowed down via testing, companies generally interview applicants. Human resource managers, together with the managers of the functions that have job openings, look over the remaining pool of applicants and decide which ones to invite for an interview. They may, for example, decide to invite three of the twenty applicants in for an interview. Interviewing is expensive because it's a very time-consuming process. HRM's goal is to select the best applicants to interview at the lowest possible cost (least managerial time and effort).

Many companies regard interviews as the most critical part of the selection process. The more important the position, the more face-to-face interviews a candidate is likely to have to go through. The most common interviewing methods are (1) *structured,* and (2) *nondirective* interviewing. In structured interviews, the job description for the open position is used to create a series of standard questions that all applicants are asked. Because each applicant is asked the same questions, interviewers can make direct comparisons between candidates in order to choose the best one.

To give applicants more scope to show their abilities one technique in structured interviewing is to create a scenario: a made-up incident about a job-specific event that might occur in the course of that job. Each applicant is then asked how he or she would respond to the event. Applicants for a bank teller's job, for example, might be asked how they would respond to (1) a customer who becomes rude after being informed his or her account is overdrawn, (2) a customer who asks to withdraw all of the funds in his or her account, and (3) a customer who turns out to be a bank robber.

Structured interviews are most commonly used to select applicants for lower-level jobs. When a company needs to determine if candidates have the skills and qualities necessary to perform complex or demanding jobs, such as those in research or management, nondirective interviews are used. Nondirective interviews do not ask applicants to respond to the same set of predetermined questions. Rather, questions are open ended to give applicants ample opportunity to reveal their skills, abilities, and strengths and weaknesses. In a nondirective interview, the interviewer might ask applicants to describe what they like most about their current job or what problems they seem to encounter most on a day-to-day basis. An interviewer might probe into how different applicants prefer to work with other people. For example, does a particular applicant express a preference for a team-oriented or a "go it alone" work approach? The most appropriate answer depends on the kind of skills needed to do a particular job and the kinds of values and norms a company wishes its employees to possess.

Some companies involve several people in the interviewing process to identify the best applicant for the job. A group of potential future co-workers might take applicants out to lunch and use this time to evaluate which person they would most prefer to have on the team. For senior positions, job applicants are interviewed by a series of managers at all levels, so each manager can form his or her own opinion about each applicant. The managers then meet to share their views and debate each candidate's job-related strengths and weaknesses.

Today, most interviewers like to use open-ended, behavioral interview questions to probe candidates and extract useful information. Many of these questions involve scenarios to find out how applicants would respond to particular situations, although each person might be asked different questions. Some examples of the kind of general, but hard-to-answer questions often asked of job candidates are listed in Table 13.2.

All questions used should be job-related, however. For reasons discussed earlier, companies must be careful that errors or biases do not creep into the interview process. Indeed, the interview process needs to be carefully planned so interviewers clearly understand that their questions should focus on the fit between the applicant and the job and company. They also need to know what kinds of questions are inappropriate or illegal, like ones about personal characteristics, such as a person's age religion, or if they are single, married, or have children. Finally, interviewers must be counseled how to prevent their personal biases from

Did You Know?

High labor demand in the early 1900s nudged firms to experiment with early human resource practices. Companies like NCR, Heinz, and Procter & Gamble employed "welfare work," providing their employees with clubs, cafeterias, insurance and savings plans, classes on child rearing and dancing, kindergartens, libraries, and retirement homes.[3]

Table 13.2
Some Examples of Open-Ended Interview Questions

Give me an example of a situation in which you used good judgment to solve a school- or work-related problem.

How do you motivate yourself to finish an assignment or task that you do not want to do?

Tell me about a person you knew or a boss you had that did things very differently from you. How did things work out?

What are your three greatest personal achievements or accomplishments to date?

Give me an example of a time when you set a goal and were able to achieve it.

What leadership positions have you held? How would you describe your leadership style?

Give me an example of a situation in which you motivated others to do what you wanted them to do.

Tell me about the people you like to interact with best at school and work, and people you prefer to avoid.

Give me an example of when you showed initiative and took the lead.

Tell me about a time when you were under stress and had too many things to do. How did you prioritize your tasks?

affecting their evaluations of job applicants. Some examples of questions that are appropriate or inappropriate or illegal to ask in a job interview are presented in Table 13.3, which also shows how even general interview questions can be inappropriately and illegally used.

STEP 4: MAKING THE FINAL SELECTION   After all of this information gathering and analysis is completed, the final decision about which applicant to choose must be made. This is a crucial decision because of the high costs associated with recruitment and selection. It has been estimated that the cost of filling each position at the entry level averages between $1,000 and $5,000. For more advanced positions, the cost averages between $10,000 and $20,000. If the wrong decision is made and the candidate doesn't work out, the company has to start all over again. This essentially *doubles* the cost of filling the position. Thus, it is imperative that companies do everything in their power to makes the right recruitment decisions in the first place. A company should commit its scarce resources to purchase the skills and knowledge of a person who is likely to remain with the firm for a number of years.

The final decision made is also important to job applicants as well, of course. Most applicants hope that they will be the one selected to fill the open position. To behave ethically, and, of course, legally, a company has an obligation to make the selection process as fair and equitable as possible. Those who are not chosen should be informed of the decision promptly and thanked for the time and effort they have put into the process. If they were on the final applicant list, they might be encouraged to apply for a similar job at a later date. The way a company handles the process of giving bad news to applicants is a sign of the way it does business—and even of its commitment to its own employees.

Training and Development

Once a company obtains the human resources it needs to pursue its business model, it faces the next HRM challenge—to improve the skills of its workforce to build a competitive advantage. The ability of people to continually learn new and improved skills and increase their job knowledge explains why a company's human capital is often its greatest asset. Microsoft sells almost $30 billion worth of its products every year that are created by only 50,000 employees. This amounts to $600,000 generated per employee annually. The amount of yearly sales generated per employee is one measure of the quality of a company's human resources and how well employees have been trained and developed.

Table 13.3
Appropriate and Inappropriate Interviewing Questions

Personal Characteristics Questions	Appropriate and Allowable	Inappropriate and Illegal
Age	Are you over 18?	How old are you? What is your date of birth?
Race	(No acceptable questions)	What is your race or ethnicity? What country were you born in?
Height\Weight	(No acceptable question unless it is directly related to job requirements)	How tall are you? What is your weight?
Religion	(No acceptable question)	What is your religious affiliation? Do you go to church?
Disabilities	(No acceptable question unless it is directly related to job requirements e.g., Can you lift 100 lbs?)	When was your last physical? Were any health problems discovered?
Marital/Family Status	(No acceptable questions)	Are you married or divorced? How many children do you have? How old are they? Are any other family members living with you?
Citizenship	Do you have a legal right to work in the United States?	Are you a U.S. citizen or permanent resident?
Educational Experience	How many years of education do you have? What is your highest qualification? What kinds of work experience do you have?	When did you graduate high school? Has any of your education or work experience been associated with any religious affiliation?
General Interview Questions	What are your strengths and weaknesses? What is most important to you in a job?	Do you have any personality or mental problems? How important is spending time with your family?
	Describe a work-related problem you faced and solved? What about one you didn't solve?	Do you have any personal issues or problem that affect the way you behave at work?
	What kinds of work activities excite and motivate you?	In what way does your age or family status affect the things you enjoy at work?
	What kinds of people do you like to work with?	Do you prefer to work with people who have the same gender, ethnicity, or age as you?
	How would you describe the way you interact with others? How do co-workers view you?	How does your age, personal and religious values, and your physical appearance affect the way you work with others?
	What are your career objectives in the short and long term?	How does your age and family status affect your short- and long-term career objectives?

training and development The process through which companies increase their employees' work skills and knowledge to improve their job performance.

Training and development is the process through which companies increase their employees' skills and knowledge to help them do their jobs in ways that lead to superior efficiency, quality, innovation, and customer responsiveness. For example, customer service reps can be trained to use CRM systems and ask customers questions about their changing product needs. Engineers and scientists can be reimbursed for attending professional programs and courses in which they learn about the latest technical developments. Production-line employees can be trained to operate new, more efficient, computerized equipment. Managers at all levels can be taught how to implement total quality management (TQM) techniques throughout a company. Recall how production personnel working for John Deere & Company venture into the field to talk to farmers to improve the design of the company's products. Most large companies provide their employees with a good number of training and development opportunities.

Training and development is an expensive component of a company's HRM system, however. Every hour employees spend in training is time they do not spend on the job. In addition, sending employees to skills-training courses taught at night schools and colleges is a major expense. To reduce their training costs, many companies use independent training consultants and "outsource" their employee training. Other companies provide training in-house, meaning they use their own training experts and facilities. GE has its own college, for example, and McDonald's has its own "Hamburger University," in Oak Brook, Illinois, which has graduated over 65,000 of its managers.

Training-Needs Analysis

To make training cost effective, a company must invest its scarce training dollars in activities that lead to measurable improvements in the way its individual employees, groups, and the company as a whole perform. Performance-enhancing training often involves teaching employees how to use new, function-specific techniques such as customer relationship management. For example, Merck invests millions of dollars to train its sales force in the latest CRM techniques to increase sales of its prescription drugs. An example of organizationwide, performance-enhancing training is the decision of a company to implement an ERP system that extends across all of its functions and divisions. IBM gets paid tens of millions of dollars to train employees to use these new systems once they are installed in companies.

training-needs analysis A method of identifying the kinds of employee training that will result in the greatest performance gains.

To make cost-effective, training investment decisions, a company's HRM managers conduct a **training-needs analysis**—a method of identifying the kinds of employee training that will result in the greatest performance gains. (See Figure 13.5.) Training-needs analysis starts when managers identify the many company-specific ways training programs can be developed to increase efficiency, quality, innovation,

Figure 13.5 Training Needs Analysis

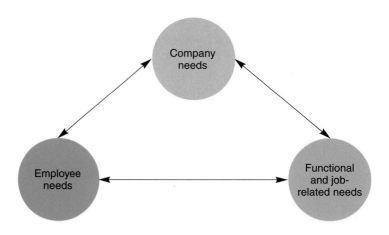

and/or responsiveness to customers. When Citibank identified that inefficient, poor quality customer service was causing the company to lose accounts, it invested $1 billion in a companywide, TQM training program to improve service. Citibank claims the investment resulted in a 15% increase in the number of customer accounts it has and $2 billion in cost savings.

Once a company decides which building blocks of a competitive advantage to work on, each function is instructed to perform workflow and job analysis to identify "training gaps." A **training gap** is a specific type of training needed by employees to improve the company's operating efficiency, products, and so forth. Managers in each function then decide which employees will need training, how much they will require, and who will provide it.

training gap A specific type training an employee needs to acquire.

Unfortunately, many companies fail to do a training-needs analysis on a regular basis. They end up spending their training dollars on the wrong programs or wrong employees. Other companies wait until problems such as lost sales, increasing customer complaints, rising costs, and high employee turnover signal that major problems exist before doing additional training. High-performing companies always anticipate their training needs in advance, and like GE, they work proactively to continually improve their employees' performance over time.

Types and Methods of Training and Development

Companies need to provide employees with several different types of training and development. The goal is to choose the type that will have the biggest impact on their work performance. New employees are given job skills and orientation training, for example; junior managers may be given advanced management training in persuasive communication and managing cross-functional teams. When all employees need a specific form of training, such as diversity training, the training often begins at the top of the organization and cascades downward as each manager takes responsibility for training their subordinates, and so on, down the line. This approach is also typically adopted when a company decides to introduce TQM and/or a new ERP system.

There are many different employee training methods companies can choose from. The primary consideration is to choose the training method that results in employees not only *learning*, but also *retaining* the skills and knowledge they have acquired. A secondary consideration is to choose the training method that is most cost effective.

on-the-job training Training employees receive in the course of doing their jobs.

A popular method of training that satisfies both these concerns is **on-the-job training.** Basically, employees learn how to do their jobs while actually doing them. Working side by side with their supervisors and co-workers helps new employees learn quickly. And because they put their new skills to work immediately, the training is more likely to be retained. When more complex or specialized kinds of training are required, however, different training methods are required. Figure 13.6 lists many of these methods.

The use of Internet-based methods of training is increasing rapidly. It is highly cost-effective for a company to record its training practices on video and then stream them over the Internet. All employees can access the video from their computers at work or at home, whenever the wish. Recall that Krispy Kreme's franchisees can easily access the company's online library of training programs via the Internet. Because the training information is presented visually, skills-based learning is easier and retained longer. Many companies also create instruction booklets with helpful animated charts, figures and diagrams to accompany their online training. Another advantage of online training is that when changes in a company's work procedures occur, they can quickly be put on the firm's training Web site. Employees are then able to review the new procedures immediately without having to wait for training sessions to be scheduled. Wal-Mart is one company that updates its store managers and employees this way.

Figure 13.6
Methods of
Training and
Development

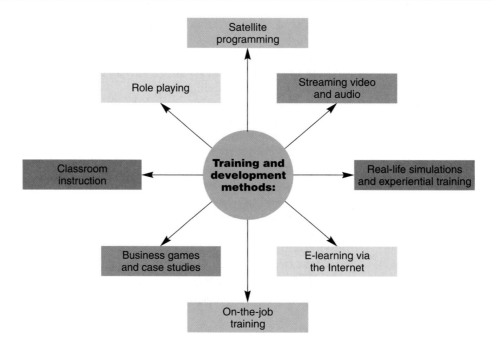

Performance Appraisal and Feedback

performance appraisal The process of evaluating the contributions an employee has made toward a company's functional and corporate-wide goals.

performance feedback The communication of performance appraisal information to employees to influence their future performance levels.

One way to measure how well employees retain what they learn from training is to regularly appraise their performance. **Performance appraisal** is the process through which managers review and evaluate the contributions an employee has made towards achieving a company's functional and corporate-wide company goals. **Performance feedback** is the process through which managers communicate the results of this evaluation process to employees to persuade them to maintain or improve their level of performance.

Performance appraisal and feedback help motivate employees to work hard and perform at a high level in three main ways. First, the performance appraisal is used to decide how to distribute rewards, such as salaries, bonuses, and promotions to employees. It is also used to make decisions about which employees to terminate or lay off. Second, performance appraisal and feedback gives employees information about their strengths and weaknesses, and provides managers with information they can use to make decisions about which employees could benefit from additional training. Many CEOs have risen up the corporate hierarchy because they received consistently positive performance evaluations and received advanced management training.

Third, because managers appraise the performance of their employees in terms of how their activities have furthered the company's goals, it helps to align their performance with the company's overall business model. For example, suppose the business model of your video game company centers around two competitive criteria: (1) Creating innovative games, and (2) getting them to market quickly. The performance of the video-game code writers should then be evaluated based on these two criteria, and the writers rewarded accordingly. This will "align" their goals with the goals of your video game company. In other words, it will motivate them to quickly create innovative games—which is just what you want them to do. In addition, if the company is to achieve a competitive advantage, the performance measures used to appraise its employees must be explicitly tied to measures of efficiency, quality, innovation, and responsiveness to customers. As you can see choosing the right set of performance measures can mean the difference between gaining a competitive advantage or not.

As in the case of recruitment and selection, the performance appraisal process must be conducted in a fair, equitable, and legal way. A manager typically reviews the performance of many people, just as an interviewer talks to many job applicants. To ensure equity, the set of performance measures a manager uses must result in an accurate evaluation of the contributions of all the different employees performing a similar job. Moreover, employees must *know* which set of measures managers will use to evaluate their performance. If they don't know, they are likely to be caught by surprise during their performance appraisals. This can leave them with the impression they have been treated unfairly by their managers, which, of course, will have a negative impact on their motivation.

Performance Appraisal Methods

When managers are observing and assessing the performance of their employees, there are two kinds of things they can evaluate: (1) the *results,* or *outcomes,* of an employee's activities, (2) the specific employee *actions* or *behaviors* that produced those outcomes. The most cost-effective way to appraise performance is to evaluate results or outcomes, which explains why results-based performance appraisals are often used. When an appraisal is performance based, managers measure the outcomes that directly result from the way each employee has done his or her job. For example, managers might measure high, acceptable, or unacceptable performances in terms of how many units of a product each employee makes each day or week; or how many customer problems each employee solves per hour, or how much revenue each salesperson generates each month.

For many jobs, particularly more complex and responsible jobs, the outcomes of each employee's performance can only be assessed over a long time period such as a month or year. For example, the performance of a new vice president of marketing or a team of research scientists can only be assessed over a one- or two-year time frame. For this reason, managers evaluate the performance of these employees by observing whether or not employees are engaging in the specific behaviors needed to achieve successful job-related outcomes.

When a performance appraisal is behavior based, a manager identifies a series of important job-related behaviors and then rates each employee's performance (high, acceptable or unacceptable) in terms of these behaviors. For example, each video game developer might be appraised using measures of behavior such as the ability to (1) take the code written by other developers and improve it, (2) create new game characters and improve the game's story line, and (3) work cooperatively with co-workers in a team situation. The founder of the video game company would then assess how effectively or ineffectively each game developer engaged in these three behaviors and give the developer appropriate performance feedback.

Management by objectives, the goal setting and evaluation process we discuss in Chapter 7, is a method of performance appraisal. The objectives that managers and subordinates agree upon can be results oriented or behavior oriented. These objectives then become the performance measurers used to appraise an employee's behavior. Research has shown that MBO systems can be highly effective when properly implemented. Employees given difficult, specific, objectives are generally motivated to work hard to achieve them.

Some companies use a *forced-ranking* method of performance appraisal. Forced rankings require managers to rank their subordinates from the best to the poorest performers. Like GE, a company might instruct managers to identify the top and bottom 10% of performers. The top 10% might receive extra rewards and training opportunities. The bottom 10% might receive counseling to improve their performance (or be terminated). The forced-ranking method causes managers to think carefully about the accuracy and fairness of their performance evaluations.

With a behavior-based performance appraisal, a manager identifies a series of important job-related behaviors and then rates each employee's performance in terms of these behaviors.

Who Appraises Performance?

Most managers have done their subordinates' jobs at some point in their careers, so they are generally well qualified to evaluate how their employees are performing. Sometimes, however, it is difficult or impossible for managers to assess how well employees are performing their jobs. A manager, for example, might have dozens of employees to supervise, so there is no time to evaluate how well each one is performing. Or, employees might work in a large team, which makes it difficult for a manager to identify each employee's individual performance. Some employees, such as buyers and salespeople who work in the field, can be difficult to observe. Likewise, an expatriate manager who heads a company's foreign subsidiaries abroad can also be difficult to observe. In these kinds of situations the information managers use to appraise the employee is often supplemented by information provided by other people, as Figure 13.7 illustrates.

Sometimes peers or co-workers are asked to provide information about each other's job-related behaviors. In a team situation, for example, each member might be given the same set of measures to evaluate the performance of every other team member. A manager can then use all team members' performance ratings to help assess the relative performance of each member and provide the employee with feedback.

Managers are also evaluated by *their* managers. Generally, the higher managers are in the firm's hierarchy, the less time they have to study the specific activities of the managers working below them. It may be difficult to identify a manager's unique job-related skills or abilities, for example, or to evaluate the way they motivate their subordinates. To address this problem, some companies also evaluate a manager's performance using information provided by their subordinates. Subordinates are in a good position to evaluate their managers' skills and to comment usefully on their management style and how it can be improved. We discussed in the opening case how GE uses subordinate ratings to weed out managers who "smile up and kick down." Accurate subordinate appraisals can be difficult to obtain, however. Subordinates will be reluctant to give negative feedback on their managers if they believe their bosses are being told "who said what" or will be able to figure it out. We discuss in the opening case how GE uses subordinate ratings of their managers to weed out those managers who "smile up and kick down."

Sometimes employees are asked to appraise themselves. They might be required to write an account of their activities and achievements over the last year, assess how well they accomplished their objectives, and describe how they can improve their performance in the future. Of course, most people have the tendency to paint an overly "rosy" picture of their performance—to take credit for outcomes due to luck or chance and to blame their failures on factors beyond their control. Nonetheless, the use of self-ratings can be useful because it helps employees focus intensely on their own activities.

Figure 13.7
Who Appraises Performance?

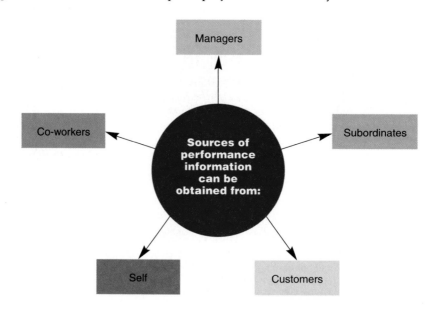

It also makes them feel like they have some say in the appraisal process and that it is therefore more equitable.

Customer reviews and surveys are also becoming popular as a means of obtaining information about the activities of employees in sales and service positions. When employees know that customers will be surveyed and that their evaluations will be used in the performance appraisal process, they are more likely to be motivated to respond to customers' needs. Customer appraisals can also be a source of objective information used to pinpoint employees' personal strengths and weaknesses.

360-degree performance appraisal The process of using multiple sources of information to appraise an employee's performance.

A company that uses multiple sources of performance information to appraise its employees uses a 360-degree performance appraisal. By collecting information from multiple sources, a company can more objectively evaluate their employees to prevent personal biases from creeping into the appraisal process. No matter what appraisal method a company uses, however, it must be careful the method does not cause employees to behave in unethical or illegal ways, as Business in Action illustrates.

Business in Action

How Not to Do Performance Appraisal

In 2003, 12 major U.S. banks and stockbrokers such as Citigroup, Merrill Lynch, and Morgan Stanley agreed to pay $1.4 billion in fines to settle a U.S. government lawsuit that claimed they provided faulty financial advice to their clients. Their bad advice resulted in their clients losing tens of billions of dollars when the stock market crashed. At the center of the lawsuit was the charge that top managers of these companies failed to adequately appraise and control the behavior of their stockbrokers, who advised a large number of clients to buy stock in certain companies simply to earn high sales commissions. Merrill Lynch's brokers even joked by e-mail with each other about how ridiculously poor the the stock recommendations they were making to their clients were.

The Securities and Exchange Commission (SEC), the government agency that supervises the business activities of U.S. companies, believed that the managers of these brokers deliberately ignored the fact the brokers were misleading clients. Why? Because the brokers were earning a higher commission by selling these particular stocks, which motivated them to sell more shares, thereby increasing the companies' profits. In performance appraisal meetings, the managers did not question the soundness of their brokers' investment advice, preferring to focus on the volume of stock sales each of them generated. The SEC is continuing its efforts to punish these people for their unethical and illegal behavior. For example, in 2004, the agency subpoenaed the companies' HRM records to see how the firms were rewarding the performance of their brokers. The SEC wants to prove that the managers in these companies used their performance appraisal systems not to ensure their brokers acted legally and in accordance with company policies, but to increase company profits at the expense of their customers.[4]

Merrill Lynch's stockbrokers joked by e-mail with one another about the poorly performing companies they recommended their clients buy. Part of the problem related to how the brokers were rewarded.

formal appraisals Appraisals conducted on a regular basis to provide employees with ongoing performance feedback.

Giving Performance Feedback

There are two main ways to give employees performance feedback. Formal appraisals are conducted on a regular basis to provide employees with performance feedback that will become part of their company employment record. They are also used to make

Table 13.4
Guidelines for Effective Performance Feedback

Avoid criticizing an employee's general approach to work; focus on specific work outcomes or behaviors that are causing problems.

Identify the source of problems the employee is experiencing and identify specific ways of solving the problem.

Focus on specific work outcomes and work behaviors that an employee can improve upon; do not focus on "personality" or "personal style" issues.

Provide positive feedback whenever possible and praise specific outcomes or behaviors at which the employee is doing well in the course of providing ongoing negative feedback.

Take advantage of informal appraisal opportunities to provide constructive feedback to motivate employees to improve their performance.

---

informal appraisals
Appraisals that take place as managers and subordinates meet from time to time to discuss important work issues.

important reward, and training and development decisions. **Informal appraisals** take place as managers and subordinates meet from time to time to discuss important ongoing work issues, such as current work projects or sudden problems. Informal appraisals give managers the opportunity to offer employees help, advice, and performance feedback.

Most employees enjoy receiving positive feedback, but few like to hear bad things about themselves. So, when managers give negative feedback, it is important they clearly explain to the employee what kinds of outcomes or behaviors resulted in the poor appraisal. The need to supply accurate feedback to employees is one more reason why it is vital to identify the specific outcomes and behaviors associated with high and low job performance. Then, a manager and employee discuss why the employee failed to meet specific performance objectives. Managers are not stating their "opinions." They can justify their evaluations using employee-specific performance information. This way, employees also understand what they need to do to improve their performance ratings. Of course, it is easier to give positive than negative performance feedback. Even when the feedback is positive, however, managers still need to explain clearly to the employee which specific work outcomes and behaviors led to the positive review. Some guidelines for giving effective performance feedback are presented in Table 13.4.

Pay and Benefits

pay The monetary rewards, such as wages, bonuses, and salaries, associated with a particular job.

benefits The monetary rewards, such as paid health care, life insurance, sick and vacation pay, and pensions, employees receive because they are a member of a company.

Pay is the monetary reward associated with a particular job or position in a company. Different types of pay include base pay, overtime pay, and pay bonuses for high performance. **Benefits** are the monetary rewards employees receive by virtue of the fact that they are a member of a company. These benefits include things like paid health care and life insurance, sick pay, paid vacations, pension plans, and so on. In addition, companies are required by law to pay employee taxes such as social security, workers compensation, and unemployment insurance. These government-funded programs provide benefits to employees when they retire, if they become disabled or injured on the job or laid off.

Pay Structures

Recall from Chapter 7 that equity theory suggests employees compare the *outputs,* or rewards, they receive and the *inputs,* or effort, they need to obtain them, against those of their co-workers. An employee's perception of the fairness of the reward process will have a big impact on his or her work motivation. It is therefore critical for managers to design the HRM system, and particularly the performance appraisal process, to make the distribution of rewards among employees as equitable as possible.

Managers must consider many issues when designing an equitable pay structure. A **pay structure** determines the relative pay and benefits received by employees performing different types of jobs or jobs at different levels in a company's hierarchy—from the CEO down to entry-level employees. A pay structure is based on differences in the skills, abilities, and knowledge required to do specific kinds of jobs. The pay and benefits associated with a particular job typically depend on how much that job affects important company goals such as its profitability. The level of rewards received by an engineer in product development who creates a profitable product, the director of marketing who manages a successful sales campaign, or the CEO who creates a successful business model are tied to the impact their activities have on the company's revenues and profits.

One important decision a company must make when designing its pay structure is to choose its **pay level,** which refers to the average salary a company chooses to pay its employees *compared* to other companies in its industry. A company, for example, might choose to pay its employees above, below, or at the industry-average pay level. Some companies, such as Microsoft, Merck, and IBM choose to pay their employees above the industry-average pay level. These companies are trying to recruit and retain the best employees in the business in order to gain a competitive advantage. Of course, this increases the operating costs of these companies. These higher costs are acceptable, however, if the companies can charge a premium price for their products because their employees create better quality products or provide better customer service.

On the other hand, some companies pay below-average wages to keep their costs as low as possible. Fast-food chains like McDonald's and Taco Bell, for example, pay at or just above the minimum wage. The result is often an employee turnover rate of over 200% per year. Recall from Chapter 7 that Dick's restaurant chain pays its employees 25% above the average pay level, but it has very low employee turnover.

Most companies survey and benchmark the pay levels of other companies in their industry to decide how high to set their own pay level. Very often conditions in an industry, like intense competition between companies to hire certain kinds of skilled employees, determine how high a company sets its pay level. In 2003, for example, the declining fortunes of the airline industry led many labor unions representing pilots, flight attendants, and mechanics to accept large pay reductions to try to keep their companies profitable. In 2004, all of Delta Air Lines' employees took a 33% pay cut, shaving a billion dollars off of the company's labor costs. Obviously, these employees hope that if conditions improve, Delta's pay level will increase.

Types of Incentive Pay

Companies design their pay levels and pay structures to motivate employees and groups to perform at a high level. Incentive pay links the size of the rewards employees and groups receive directly to their success in achieving specific work outcomes and behaviors. Incentive pay systems are found at the individual, group, and company level. Each system is discussed next.

INDIVIDUAL INCENTIVE PLANS Piecework plans, in which the pay employees receive depends on how many units of a product each employee makes, is a popular pay system. Piecework plans are used only when each employee's individual performance can be measured accurately, such as when employees work separately to assemble a product or provide a service.

Commission systems resemble piecework systems except that they reward not how much employees produce but how much they sell. They are commonly used to motivate salespeople to generate new business to increase a company's revenues. Often, the pay level of salespeople depends primarily on how much commission they earn. Some "star" salespeople who can generate an enormous volume of sales might earn a million dollars a year or more in industries such as finance or consulting.

Merit pay is a pay system that links superior performance directly to higher rewards, normally in the form of a certain percentage increase in salary. An employee

pay structure The relative pay and benefits received by employees doing different types of jobs or jobs at different levels in a company's hierarchy.

pay level The average salary a company chooses to pay its employees compared to other companies in its industry.

incentive pay The extra rewards employees receive when they achieve specific work goals.

piecework plans Pay plans that link the pay employees receive to the number of units of a product an employee makes.

commission systems Pay plans that link the pay employees receive to the amount of revenue they earn by selling a company's products.

merit pay A pay system that links superior performance directly to higher permanent rewards, such as a certain percentage increase in salary.

who makes $35,000 a year and receives a 10% merit pay increase will make $38,500 the next year as his or her "base" salary. If the employee continues to perform at a high level, a 10% merit pay raise the next year will increase his or her base salary to $42,350. So, the higher each merit raise, the more an employee's salary grows each successive year.

Unlike merit pay raises, which increase an employee's salary more and more each year, **bonus pay** is a one-time reward that an employee receives for accomplishing some specific work task. For example, to speed sales of a new product, a company might offer a salesperson a $10,000 bonus if he or she sells 5,000 units of the product in the first six months following its introduction into the marketplace. However, unlike merit pay, this $10,000 is not added to the salesperson's base salary. Each year the salesperson has to work hard to earn a new bonus. An example of a company that achieved great success by using a new merit pay system is profiled in Business in Action.

bonus pay A one-time reward employees receive for accomplishing a specific goal.

Business in Action

Fujitsu's Merit Pay System

In Japan, when an employee joins a company, he or she normally remains there until retirement. In other words, the Japanese have traditionally been loyal to their companies for life. Employees slowly progress up the corporate hierarchy to more senior positions over the years. In many, if not most of these companies, an employee's pay is tied much more to one's seniority than one's performance. In fact, formal performance appraisals are rarely used to make pay decisions.

But the poor performance of many Japanese companies in the 2000s has prompted the nation's managers to reevaluate their reward systems. One such company is Fujitsu, a leading IT company that was concerned about its declining performance. To improve its performance, Fujitsu radically overhauled its HRM system. It scrapped its traditional pay system, which linked pay to seniority, and introduced a new merit pay system for its 5,500 managers. Now, Fujitsu uses a twice-a-year performance appraisal process to make merit pay decisions and decide which managers to promote.

Fujitsu was so pleased with this change it later decided to extend the merit pay system to all of its 47,000 employees. The unions who represent its employees agreed to use the new HRM system so long as Fujitsu used clear and valid job-related measures to evaluate employee performance. The merit pay system is also helping quell the departure of Fujitsu's most talented employees. Because being promoted to higher positions took so long, many of these super-talented employees were taking jobs with foreign companies—companies that allowed them to climb the corporate ladder faster.[5]

To improve its performance, Fujitsu scrapped its traditional pay system (based on seniority) in favor of a twice-a-year performance appraisal process used to make merit pay decisions and decide which managers to promote.

As Fujitsu's experiences suggest, the promotion to a new, higher-level position that offers a significant increase in pay and benefits is an important reward for employees who compete to rise up a company's hierarchy. The highest-performing supervisors become the next generation of middle managers, for example, and the highest-performing middle managers become the next generation of top managers. Promotion is a crucial reward because the size of salaries and bonuses rises sharply as managers rise in the hierarchy. A CEO earns a salary that is twice, and often many times, higher than the manager directly below him or her in the hierarchy. In 2003, for example, the average CEO in the top Fortune 200 companies earned $5.4 million, almost double the $2.4 million earned by the next highest-ranking executive.

GROUP AND COMPANYWIDE REWARD SYSTEMS   The growing importance of teams, particularly cross-functional teams, as a way of increasing profitability has led many companies to implement group-based reward systems to encourage high team performance. However, a company consists of many groups that must cooperate with one another if it is to achieve its goals. To encourage these groups, teams, and individual employees to cooperate, a company often implements a reward system that pays a bonus to *all* employees if the firm achieves its revenue and profit goals. Popular reward systems at the group and company levels include profit-sharing plans, employee stock ownership plans, and organizationwide bonuses.

profit sharing plans
Pay plans that reward employees on the basis of the profit a company earns in a particular period, usually a year.

Profit sharing plans reward employees on the basis of the profit a company earns in a particular period, usually a year. These plans encourage employees to take a broad view of their jobs and find ways to help a company increase its performance. Rather than reward employees on the basis of short-term profits, however, a company might also establish an employee stock ownership plan (ESOP) and allow employees to buy its shares at below-market prices. Once they buy shares in their company, employees now own a small part of it. This, in turns, motivates them to find ways to improve its performance. Over time, employees may come to own a substantial number of a company's shares. Southwest Airlines employees own 18% of its stock, for example. Wal-Mart, has always given its employees stock options. In fact, a Wal-Mart employee who participated in the company's ESOP program from the time of its inception until today would now have stock options worth over $1 million!

employee stock ownership plan   A plan that allows employees to buy a company's shares at below-market prices.

organization bonus systems   The one-time rewards employees receive if a company achieves cost savings, quality increases, and so on, in a specified time period.

Finally, organization bonus systems reward employees if a company achieves cost savings, quality increases, and so on in a specified time period. These bonuses are generally based on how well each employee has performed. Consequently, organization bonus systems are most common in assembly-line settings or service companies where companies can calculate exactly how much each employee's contributions resulted in lower costs or higher revenues. Lincoln Electric is one company well known for the success of its organizationwide, cost-savings plan. Each year Lincoln Electric sets a cost-savings target and rewards all of its employees with a bonus if they meet that target.

Labor Relations

Labor relations is the process of establishing rules and practices between a company and its employees that specify how its human resources should be employed and rewarded. Many important national laws have been passed governing labor relations practices. (See Table 13.1.) When managers and employees develop labor relations practices that allow them to resolve human resource issues and establish good working relationships, both employees and the company they work for benefit. In many cases, however, companies and their employees cannot reach agreement over human resource issues such as working conditions, pay levels, and benefits.

A company with a great deal of capital—or a large share of the market in which it operates—wields considerable power in the labor market when it comes to pay structures and levels. In a situation such as this, individual employees have little power to influence a company's HRM practices. The way individual workers counteract this power is by banding together, or forming unions. This gives them greater leverage, or bargaining power, to negotiate with companies. Trade unions are organizations that represent the interests of employees who hold similar types of jobs in a particular industry. Steelworkers' and car workers' unions are examples. Trade unions bargain and negotiate over pay, benefits, and working conditions with the companies that employ these workers.

The International Brotherhood of Teamsters is the world's most powerful labor union. What do you think are the benefits of being in a union? What are the pitfalls?

labor relations The process of establishing rules and practices between a company and its employees that specify how human resources should be employed and rewarded.

trade unions Organizations that represent the interests of employees who hold similar types of jobs in a particular industry.

Historically, trade unions emerged because workers needed to negotiate fairer employment deals with growing industrial companies. When employees form a trade union, they can use their increased bargaining power to obtain a greater share of the profit a company creates. Recall from Chapter 2 how both Carnegie and Rockefeller chose the lowest pay levels possible and paid no attention to issues such as on-the-job health and safety. Workers saw the high profits these companies were earning and believed they deserved a greater share of those profits.

As we discussed in Chapter 5, a company consists of different groups of stakeholders. Each group makes a contribution to the firm with the expectation of getting something in return. Stakeholders must cooperate with one another to help the company produce goods and services people want to buy. However, these groups of stakeholders also compete with one another to increase their share of the company's profits. Top managers expect to receive a high return for the expertise they lend the company's business model, for example. Similarly, stockholders who lend their capital to a company expect to receive dividends and want the value of their stock to appreciate. Employees expect safe working conditions, a fair day's pay for a fair day's work, and health and pension benefits.

As Figure 13.8 suggests, each group of stakeholders has its own goals and interests. These goals and interests overlap somewhat with one another because all of the stakeholders have an interest in seeing the company succeed. But the stakeholders' interests are not identical. Managers, for example, are likely to want to find new, more efficient ways to operate the company even if it means many workers will lose their jobs. Obviously, workers don't believe this is in their best interests.

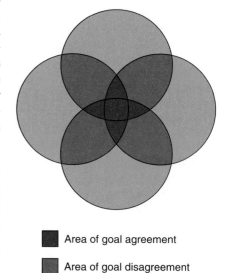

■ Area of goal agreement

■ Area of goal disagreement

Figure 13.8
Competition and Cooperation among Stakeholders

Union-Management Relations

industrial conflict The clash that occurs when workers and unions attempt to obtain a greater share of a company's profits at the expense of other stakeholders.

When workers believe a company's owners and managers are not sharing the company's profits with them fairly, the groups come into conflict with one another. Industrial conflict is the clash that occurs when workers, and the union that represents them, attempt to gain a greater share of a company's profits but are thwarted by managers who want to use the profits to benefit other stakeholders. When workers perceive that a company's owners and managers are not sharing the profit the company produces fairly, they come into conflict with them. Trade unions work to resolve conflict such as these by giving workers the power to resist the demands that managers make of them.

working-to-rule When workers perform their jobs exactly as specified in their employment contracts but do no more.

Some of the signs that a conflict is brewing are events that slow down the work process or bring it to a standstill. For example, if employees begin working-to-rule, they do their jobs *exactly* the way their employment contracts specify, but they do no more. In practice, this significantly slows down the pace of work because there are always "unwritten" tasks workers must do if work is to go smoothly. For example, there may be no rule specifying that a worker should shut a machine down if it is obvious it is malfunctioning, or help another worker who is in trouble, yet workers routinely do this to protect the workplace. When they are working-to-rule, however, they do not. So if a machine breaks down or the other workers cannot handle a problem, production may be slowed or halted. This is what happened during a bitter labor dispute in California in 2002. Members of the Longshoreman's Union, which represents dockyard workers and dockyard owners, behaved in exactly this way. The result was that the pace of work slowed down to 65% of normal.

lockout When managers decide to shut down a company's operations until workers are willing to accept the employment conditions being offered to them.

strike A situation that arises when workers refuse to do their jobs in an attempt to bring the work process to a halt.

Sometimes a company engages in a **lockout**, meaning that managers decide to shut down the company's operations until workers are willing to accept the employment conditions it is offering and return to work. Unions can also call a **strike**, a situation that arises when workers refuse to do their jobs in an attempt to bring all work to a halt. To cope with the strike, a company might try to hire new workers or have its managers operate the firm's machinery and equipment to keep at least some production going on. Workers on strike will sometimes try to prevent this from happening, and conflict breaks out.

Whenever these events occur, all stakeholders suffer. Essentially, the company's profits and workers' pay are disappearing. The purpose of labor relations is to prevent such disruptions, or at least reduce their severity. All stakeholders benefit from this because bitter conflicts poison good working relationships between managers, workers, and the unions that represent them.

Collective Bargaining: Resolving the Conflict

collective bargaining The process through which union representatives and managers negotiate a binding labor agreement over work-related issues, such as pay, benefits, and grievance procedures.

integrative bargaining solution A "win-win" solution that allows both parties to benefit from the labor contract agreed upon.

attitudinal structuring The attempt by negotiators on each side to influence each other's attitudes during the bargaining process.

Collective bargaining is the process through which union representatives and managers negotiate a binding labor agreement, or contract, over work-related issues such as pay, benefits, work rules, safety conditions, job security, and the way workers' grievances will be handled. Thus a labor contract acts as a vehicle that allows a company and unions to communicate and share information and ideas to solve common issues and problems.

Collective bargaining is a complex process. Negotiators on each side try to influence the bargaining process in ways that favor their own interests and objectives. Negotiators on each side understand, however, that it is in both their interests to reach what is called an **integrative bargaining solution**. This is a "win-win" solution that allows both parties to benefit from the labor contract agreed upon. An important component of the bargaining process is **attitudinal structuring**, in which negotiators on each side try to influence each other's attitudes. For example, negotiators might strive to keep the bargaining process amicable so it will be quicker and easier to reach and agreement. Otherwise, negotiations might drag on for months. If negotiators can create a positive bargaining situation, this reduces the potential for bitter conflicts like damaging strikes.

The opposite occurred in the collective bargaining process between the dockyard workers and owners discussed earlier. In their negotiations, both sides arrived at the bargaining table with hostile attitudes. Dockyard owners were determined to get new rules that would allow them to computerize the dockyards, which would have resulted in 25% of dockworkers being laid off. Obviously, the dockworker's union was determined to prevent this happening. Angry clashes ensued, and at one stage the owners hired bodyguards to accompany them to the negotiating table—hardly a tactic that would suggest to union negotiators that the owners had a win-win solution in mind.

Like any other contract, the terms of a labor contract, once agreed upon, bind both parties. However, employment contracts can, indeed, be altered if circumstances change and both parties agree to the changes. For example, the need to change a company's business model to improve its profitability might motivate managers to change the company's work procedures. This is not a problem if both parties agree to the changes. Often, however, they do not.

To manage the disputes that arise when a labor contract is already in force, the parties often rely on

Because industrial conflicts are costly to all stakeholders, managers and unions often resort to methods like mediation and arbitration to facilitate the negotiation process.

grievance procedures
Labor-contract rules used to resolve disputes between companies and their employees.

grievance procedures agreed to during the course of their original negotiations. Grievance procedures establish the rules both parties will observe to resolve disputes should they arise. When formal grievance procedures exist and managers and unions meet regularly to discuss ongoing issues, it becomes easier for the two groups to negotiate and resolve these issues—before they lead to conflict.

Sometimes, however, the grievance procedures outlined in a labor agreement are still not enough. One method to resolve continuing disputes is mediation and arbitration. Mediation is a conflict resolution method that involves the use of a neutral third party (a mediator) who listens to the facts of the case and both parties' views. The mediator then tries to "open up" the negotiation process and get each set of negotiators to understand what is reasonable so that both parties can come to a "meeting of the minds." A mediator has no formal authority to impose a solution on the parties in conflict, however. By contrast, an arbitrator does. In arbitration, an arbitrator—also a neutral third party—studies the situation dividing the two parties and imposes a binding solution on both. A *binding solution* is one that both parties must accept—even if they disagree with the terms of the contract they initially agreed to. Professional sports disputes are frequently settled by arbitration when players and owners cannot agree on the terms of their contracts. Many of these disputes occur simply because the dynamics of the sports-entertainment industry are changing so rapidly.

mediation A conflict resolution method that involves the use of a neutral third party, or mediator, to help labor and management resolve their differences and reach an agreement.

arbitration A conflict resolution method that involves the use of a neutral third party to negotiate and impose a binding agreement on labor and management.

As with all other HRM issues, creating and maintaining a fair and equitable relationship between employees and the companies they work for is an underlying theme of labor relations and collective bargaining. Creating a win-win situation for all stakeholders is the ultimate goal of the HRM function. Ensuring that all aspects of a company's HRM system are managed in a fair and just manner is one of the best ways for HRM managers to achieve this.

Summary of the Chapter

Managing human resources to obtain a competitive advantage and superior profitability is a difficult and demanding task for the HRM function and for all of a company's managers and employees. Each of the components of the HRM system must be carefully designed and managed, which is a complex matter today because intense global competition is taking place and work practices are constantly being changed to help companies adapt to this competition. This chapter made the following major points:

1. Human resource management (HRM) is the set of activities that must to be done to acquire good employees and build their skills and capabilities so they can do their jobs better.

2. A company's HRM system has five components: recruitment and selection, training and development, performance appraisal and feedback, pay and benefits, and labor relations.

3. Recruitment involves all of the activities a company engages in to identify and attract a pool of qualified applicants to fulfill its human resource needs. Selection is the process of deciding which applicant is the best suited for a job and the best fit for the company.

4. Human resource planning is the process of forecasting the type and number of employees a company needs to meet the objectives of its business model. Two important tools of human resource planning are workflow and job analysis.

5. The two methods of finding qualified applicants are internal and external recruitment. Internal recruitment involves a policy of promotion from within the company; external recruitment involves filling open positions with qualified applicants from outside of the organization.

6. A typical selection process has four main steps, screening applications and résumés, applicant testing and reference checks, interviewing, and making the final selection. Companies have a legal and ethical obligation to make the selection process as fair as possible.

7. Training and development is the process through which companies improve the skills, abilities, and knowledge of their employees. Training-needs analysis is a way of determining which employees need which kind of training.

8. Performance appraisal is the process of evaluating the degree to which individual employees have

contributed to a company's functional and corporate-wide goals. Performance feedback involves communicating this evaluation to employees to persuade them to maintain or improve their performance levels.

9. Managers need to select the right set of performance measures—the ones that will do the most to improve a company's competitive advantage—and communicate them clearly to employees.

10. Different types of pay include base pay, overtime pay, and bonus pay. Benefits are the monetary rewards employees receive, such as paid health care and life insurance, because they are members of a company.

11. A pay structure determines the relative pay and benefits received by employees doing different types of jobs or jobs at different levels in a company's hierarchy. A company's pay level determines the amount a company chooses to pay its employees relative to other companies in its industry.

12. Incentive pay links the size of the rewards employees receive directly to their success in achieving specific goals. Incentive pay systems are found at the individual, group, and company levels.

13. Trade unions are organizations that represent the interests of workers who perform a similar type of job in a particular company or industry.

14. Collective bargaining is the process through which union representatives and managers negotiate a binding labor agreement, or contract, over work-related issues such as pay, benefits, work rules, safety conditions, and job security.

Developing Business Skills

QUESTIONS FOR DISCUSSION AND ACTION

1. How do the five components of a HRM system work together to help a company recruit and develop the human resources it needs to achieve a competitive advantage?

2. *Action.* Go to a store and observe and interview the sales associates as they do their jobs. Using the information you collect, analyze the various tasks involved in their jobs, and write a job description for a sales associate.

3. Why is it important for a company to use both internal and external recruitment?

4. As a new employee, what kinds of training and development experiences would help you most to understand your new job?

5. Why is performance appraisal an important HRM activity? What kind of measures should managers use to evaluate performance?

6. As an employee, how would you react to negative performance feedback?

7. What combination of incentive pay systems do you think best motivates employees? What would motivate you the most?

8. What role do trade unions play in the HRM process? Why is it important that companies and unions work together to build good working relationships?

ETHICS IN ACTION

Interviewing and Appraising Employees

There are many ethical issues related to human resource management. Using the ethical principles discussed in Chapter 5, think about the following issues and how you would deal with them if you were a manager.

- When interviewing job applicants, how would you be influenced by their personal characteristics, such as their appearance and manner?

- How should you act to prevent your own personal biases and likes and dislikes from influencing the selection of the final candidate?

- As the manager conducting a formal performance appraisal, how might the ethical principles discussed in Chapter 5 help you to (a) decide on how you should measure and evaluate your subordinates and (b) influence the way you give performance feedback?

- As a subordinate being appraised, how would you respond to (a) positive and (b) negative feedback if you believe that you manager is acting in a fair and honest manner?

SMALL GROUP EXERCISE

Choosing a Team Leader

Read the following and then break up into groups of three or four people and discuss the issues involved. Be prepared to share your discussion with the rest of your class.

You are the employees of a company that is changing its work methods and is going to use self-managed teams to assemble the range of ergonomic office chairs it makes. The chairs have been selling fast because they ease the back pain many workers experience when they sit in front of computers all day. Your company has asked you to form your own teams and conduct a series of interviews with your co-workers to determine who will lead each team.

1. Select five of the nondirective interview questions in Table 13.2 (or create your own), and then use the questions to interview each of the members of your group.

2. Each person should interview all of the other members of the group while the other group members listen in.

3. Each person should write down the person they think should be the team leader and give three reasons for his or her choice. (You cannot choose yourself.)

4. Based on these written assessments, did your group reach a consensus on which person should be the team leader? If you did, what information did you obtain from the interview process that led you to make such a decision? If you did not agree, what information do you think you need to collect to help you make a decision?

DEVELOPING GOOD BUSINESS SENSE

Selecting a Company to Work For

Most people want to find a job that offers them opportunities to develop their skills and increase their well-being over time. When interviewing with companies, however, it is often difficult to decide which company offers the best opportunity. All companies want to hire the best people they can, so sometimes a company will paint an overly rosy picture of what new employees can expect. With this in mind, answer the following questions:

1. What kinds of information do you need to know about a company to decide if it is the right one for you?

2. What kinds of sources will you use to get the information you need to make a good job choice?

3. When you are asked to interview with a prospective employer, what kinds of questions do you need to be sure to ask about the company? Create a list of the 10 questions you will ask of *all* of the companies with whom you interview to gather the most information.

4. In many cases, you can pick up cues about what the company is like from the people who interview you. Think of some unstructured interview questions that you can use to discover (a) how the company treats its employees, (b) how much it wants to invest in them, and (c) what the value and norms of the company are and how well you will fit into it if you were to be hired.

EXPLORING THE WORLD WIDE WEB

Writing a Monster Résumé

Go to the Web site Monster.com. The Web site contains a lot of useful information about jobs and careers and resources about how to apply for jobs. Go to Monster's résumé resource center (http://resume.monster.com/) and read the advice Monster offers about how to write a good résumé. Then, pick a job and company you are interested in working for. Practice writing a résumé that you believe will lead the company to select you, out of hundreds of job applicants, for an interview. **For more Web activities, log on to www.mhhe.com/jonesintro.**

BusinessWeek CASE IN THE NEWS

10 Employer Secrets Worth Cracking

Thank goodness the labor market is finally loosening up, and more good jobs are becoming available. Still, finding a new position is tough enough that you don't want to make a wrong move.

So here's a critical point to consider: All employers have secrets that you'll want to uncover–things like a drastically underfunded pension plan, a *laissez-faire* attitude toward new regulations, or using high tech to snoop on employees. Then there's the more intangible, but often the most serious, problem you need to watch out for: Getting stuck in a corporate culture where you don't fit in and have little chance of getting ahead.

Even if you're not considering a new job but just evaluating your prospects at a current employer, here are 10 questions that you should have answered. In many cases, it would be impolitic to ask outright and, you won't find the answers in the employee manual, but you can find ways to ferret out the information you need.

1. Will this company be able to take care of me in retirement?

BusinessWeek's July 19 cover story, "The Benefits Trap," revealed that many large companies don't have enough assets to cover their pension obligations. At the same time, many of those companies are reducing retiree medical benefits in hopes of boosting the bottom line.

A classic mistake most people make when contemplating a career move is to base their decision too much on annual compensation and forget to consider the value of benefits, says executive coach Paul Bernard, principal of Paul Bernard & Associates in New York. "For baby boomers this is a big issue," he says.

How to find out: Pension plan details are in a footnote to the company's annual report, so you can check to see if your plan is funded adequately. Find out if the health-insurance program for retirees has been scaled back recently. If it hasn't, the next few years might bring cuts.

2. Is the 401(k) program loaded with lousy funds?

Securities regulators are now looking into whether poorly performing funds end up in employee retirement plans because of alleged revenue-sharing arrangements between the mutual-fund company and the plan provider. Big changes in these deals are coming, says Pete Swisher, of Unified Trust Co., which creates 401(k) plans for small- and midsize companies. "In general, your plan shouldn't include any funds that have been inferior choices for a while," he says.

How to find out: Get a list of all the funds in the plan and see how many have returns below the 50th percentile in their category for a year or longer, suggests Swisher. Another method: See how the funds are rated on *BusinessWeek*'s Mutual Fund Scorecard. Most of the funds in the plan should rank better than a "C."

3. Will I keep getting stock options?

Just because option grants have been lucrative in the past doesn't mean they'll continue to be. Due to accounting changes (new rules are likely to require options to become an expense on the balance sheet), companies are scaling back on allocations to employees. Some are replacing them with grants of restricted stock, but usually in smaller amounts.

What you can do: Companies can't tell you ahead of time how their plans will change, says Deborah Sawyer, an executive recruiter at Morgan Howard Worldwide. But be ready: If the plan changes, your total compensation should stay roughly the same even if options make up a smaller percentage.

4. Does the company snoop on its employees?

It probably does more than you think. Software is increasingly being used to monitor workers. A June survey from software firm Proofpoint and Forrester Research found that 43% of companies employ staff to watch outbound e-mail, mainly looking for leaks of confidential memos and intellectual property. "A little frightening, isn't it?" says Gary Steele, CEO of Proofpoint, which sells e-mail-monitoring software.

Internet Security Systems unveiled a service in May that first analyzes how much nonbusiness related surfing employees are doing and then provides filtering software to block offending Web content. Hyperion offers sales managers "dashboards" that show daily progress on all deals in the pipeline. Hyperion Chief Executive Jeff Rodek says companies should share information they gather with employees or risk coming off as "Big Brother."

What you can do: It's legal for companies to read employee e-mail, so use a private e-mail account for all personal communication, advises Steele. You can try asking about employee monitoring, but you may not get a straight answer. It's best to assume you're being watched.

5. Is the company able to cope with all the new regulatory scrutiny?

It may seem like old news, but the deadline for complying with major provisions of the sweeping corporate governance legislation known as Sarbanes-Oxley, is just coming up in November. A July 14 survey from PricewaterhouseCoopers found that 79% of respondents said their company still has work to do to comply. Senior management needs to be paying attention to compliance issues or risk being ensnared in a regulatory net that can affect the company stock and, indirectly, employees' job security.

How to find out: One way is to assess the role of internal auditors. "If internal audit is held in high esteem, that's a strong indication that the company has a solid compliance strategy and is running a tight ship," says Harald Will, chief executive of ACL Services, which provides internal-audit software. Keep up on company news to see if it has already run afoul of regulators.

6. Is turmoil at the top likely?

Employees at Credit Suisse First Boston were caught by surprise recently when Chief Executive John Mack agreed to step down. Perhaps they shouldn't have been. He was sharing the CEO role with his European counterpart at parent company Credit Suisse Group. That's often a sign that one of them is dispensable.

"There are lots of cases where most people are shocked, but the astute employee saw the signs all along and already had it figured out," says Sawyer. Is your boss due to retire soon? Does a wave of consolidation in your industry mean your company is available to be swallowed up? If major change is coming, consider how potentially disruptive that could be, advises Bernard.

How to find out: Don't focus too narrowly on dynamics within your own division. Follow company and industry news. Pay attention to management shifts at the top.

7. What is the company's hidden culture?

Any long-term employee knows the hidden culture at their company. Is it hard charging and aggressive? Or is it a more sensitive, consensus-driven place? "That's extremely important to know if you're the new kid on the block," says Bernard.

If you don't fit in, you might have trouble succeeding. You may be able to find a similar position at a company with a culture that suits you better. "If someone is very outgoing and likes a work environment with open communication and without a lot of structure, they might get frustrated at a place with a very traditional, rigid, structure where executives are shut off," says Tim Carrington, senior vice president for strategic support services at staffing firm Aerotek. "The better the cultural fit, the more fulfilled we find the person is," he says.

How to find out: Before you start, go out to lunch or have drinks informally with a few people who work there, advises Bernard. Also, check out the job boards on Web sites like TheVault.com for company scuttlebutt—just be sure to take this kind of griping with a grain of salt.

8. Is the company as family-friendly as it claims?

Morgan Stanley is now reeling from a $54 million settlement over sex-discrimination charges. No doubt the employee manual promised a work environment hospitable to women and minorities. Maternity and paternity leave and flextime arrangements are other areas where official corporate policies may differ markedly from reality.

What happens to the careers of women who go part-time after having children? Do men ever really take paternity leave? Anyone with young children or planning on having them should check out the unofficial policies.

How to find out: Talk to employees with kids at the company. For women, see if women are in positions you aspire to and find out about their career paths.

9. What's the (real) travel and expense policy?

This might sound like small potatoes, but for executives in sales or consulting, it's something to watch for, says Bernard. Just as cultures vary at different companies, so may one applaud you for taking clients out to a fancy lunch while another would wonder why coffee and a doughnut wouldn't suffice.

Bernard says clients have recently complained to him that it can take 60 to 90 days to get reimbursed for expenses or that they're now required to fly coach. If you're going to be taking lots of trips to Europe and are accustomed to flying first class, this is something to check out.

How to find out: Again, your best source is informal chats with current employees.

10. Is the company in good financial shape?

Finding this out is No. 1 for employees at startups, as many people learned during the dot.com bust. Is there strong venture-capital funding? Are there lots of deals in the pipeline? What's the burn rate? Says Sawyer: "If you're going to go to work for a company that's venture-capital backed, you have to be able to ask smart questions." Even employees at large companies (think Enron or WorldCom) are wise to plumb company finances these days.

How to find out: At a private company, you may be able to see the books if you sign a nondisclosure agreement, says Sawyer. If you work at a public company, check out its balance sheet, debt rating, or average stock rating. *BusinessWeek Online* has such information in its corporate snapshot on public companies (see "estimates and opinions" and "company financials").

It's impossible to find all the secrets of a company without spending a long time working there. But if you ask the right questions and look for answers from the right sources, you'll learn plenty.

Source: Amey Stone, "10 Employer Secrets Worth Cracking," *BusinessWeek Online*, July 15, 2004.

QUESTIONS

1. What are the 10 secrets worth knowing about a company when you apply for a job?

2. Where can you find the information you need to make a judgment about whether or not a company is a good employer?

BusinessWeek — CASE IN THE NEWS

Gap's MBA Hiring: A Clothes Call

Denise Mooney has been an MBA recruiter for Gap Inc. since August 2004. Before that, she served as the program manager at the Center for Responsible Business at the Haas School of Business at the University of California, Berkeley. She has also worked for Bain & Co., a strategy and management consulting firm.

Gap's well-known brands include Old Navy and Banana Republic. The key to getting hired by the company lies in demonstrating retail industry knowledge, says Mooney, who recently spoke with *BusinessWeek Online* Reporter Jeffrey Gangemi. Here are edited excerpts of their conversation:

Q: How do you decide where to recruit?

A: We have chosen a few schools where we are building close recruiting relationships. We go to each of them in the fall and give a presentation describing the types of opportunities for which we're recruiting. We do most of our recruiting for full-time positions in the fall and for internships in the spring. We're fortunate to be based in the San Francisco Bay Area, where there are a lot of California-based schools with great MBA programs. We also consider great candidates from other programs, but our focus is on a few core schools.

Q: When do you offer internships?

A: My recruiting efforts are for MBA programs, so I would be doing recruiting for students between the first and second year, for 10 weeks. We have a summer internship for both undergraduate and MBA students. The number of internships varies by the year. Some of the primary job roles are finance and company planning, strategy, inventory optimization, store operations, marketing, merchandising, and human resources. Within those functions, there are different brands recruiting for interns. For example, we may have a finance internship for Old Navy, Banana Republic, and Gap.

Q: What do you look for in a potential employee?

A: A candidate needs to have passion, appreciation, and knowledge of Gap and the retail industry. Proven leadership experiences, proven analytic strengths, and the ability to work well in a cross-functional team is also a critical success factor. Additionally, Gap has a strong commitment to corporate social responsibility, and we look for that same commitment in the people we hire.

Q: What's it like to work at Gap?

A: I've had an incredibly positive experience working for the organization. I can tell you that it's a great place to work for women—70% of our employees are women, and we were just named to the National Association of Female Executives top 30 list. We're getting high ranks from nongovernmental organizations and the public for our social responsibility efforts.

Source: "Gap's MBA Hiring: A Clothes Call," *BusinessWeek Online*, February 14, 2005.

QUESTIONS

1. Make a list of the qualities and skills that The Gap uses to recruit new employees.

2. Even though these employees are MBAs, think ahead. What kinds of academic and nonacademic learning experiences could you engage in now to develop the qualities and skills to succeed in the job market of the future?

BUILDING YOUR MANAGEMENT SKILLS
Know Thyself

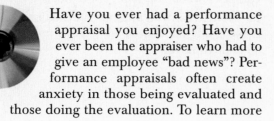

Have you ever had a performance appraisal you enjoyed? Have you ever been the appraiser who had to give an employee "bad news"? Performance appraisals often create anxiety in those being evaluated and those doing the evaluation. To learn more about performance appraisal, try the "Appraisal Methods" exercise on your Student DVD. In many organizations, a poor performance will result in additional training. The exercise about "Training Methods" on your Student DVD will help you understand how different training methods are selected for specific situations.

CHAPTER VIDEO
Patagonia

Patagonia is a very progressive global company. With stores in North America, South America, Japan, and Europe, Patagonia has a set of values that sets it apart from all other firms.

Michael Crooke, CEO, explains that employees at Patagonia are treated in a very different fashion than traditional firms. *Fortune* magazine has rated the company as one of the best places to work year after year. Its core values are based on an emphasis on environmental and social issues. This approach influences their human resource practices as well.

It begins with their hiring practices. They only hire individuals who are "great" with a high degree of passion for "something." The company attracts individuals with similar values to that of the corporation. It appears that the approach has staying power given that there is only a 4% turnover rate each year. Crooke describes the global workforce as highly committed not only to Patagonia but to environmental and social causes worldwide.

There is a flex time policy that allows people freedom to do other things while getting their jobs done on their own schedules. Further, people must have an intimate connection with the product that they are developing. So if an employee is developing surf board technology, he/she is expected to be surfing.

The company has a very innovative "internship" program that provides opportunities for employees to work in a grass roots social group with full pay for 60 days after one year of employment. Other progressive practices include the integration of child centers throughout their "campus" (pioneered in 1987) and a 1% "earth tax" that provides after tax dollars to offset the effects of pollution by the company.

1. How do Patagonia's HR practices affect innovation at the company?

2. Is there evidence of training and development at Patagonia?

3. How are employees "evaluated" at Patagonia?

Accounting:

Measuring How Efficiently and Effectively Resources Are Creating Value and Profit

Learning Objectives

After studying this chapter, you should be able to:

1. Explain how the success of a company's business model can be measured by financial accounts, and describe the various kinds of activities that accountants perform.

2. Analyze a company's balance sheet and describe how it balances the assets a company owns against the capital owed to its creditors and stockholders.

3. Explain how the income statement is used to measure a company's bottom-line profit and the various costs and expenses that must be deducted to arrive at this total.

4. Understand why the need for cash, as well as profit, affects a company's business model and how the cash flow statement measures the cash that flows into and out of a company.

5. Appreciate how financial ratios can be used to analyze the information in a company's financial statements and how they help both managers and investors evaluate a company's current and future profitability.

WHY IS THIS IMPORTANT ?

When you take a course such as this one in college, you have a goal. How will you know if you have reached it? You will probably take some tests, work on papers, or participate in projects that result in grades required to complete the course. They are a measure of your success. Managers who develop business models also want to measure whether they have succeeded in achieving company goals.

After reading this chapter, you will know how managers and other stakeholders measure how well their company is performing. They need to know if their company's business model is succeeding. This chapter is about accounting, the means managers use to track costs, revenues, and profit margins and measure company performance.

A Question of Business

How to Measure Performance in the Sporting Goods Business

Why is Dick's the most profitable sporting goods store?

In the early 2000s, the five biggest U.S. sporting goods retailers were the Sports Authority, Gart Sports, Big Five, Galyan's, and Dick's Sporting Goods. Of these five, Dick's has the highest profitability as measured by the accounting information contained in its financial statements. Dick's business model increases its revenues and reduces its costs in ways that lead to the best return on the capital that is invested in its business. This capital allows it to buy the productive assets and resources it needs to operate in the sporting goods business. What are the elements of Dick's successful business model?

First, Dick's is a full-line sporting goods retailer, and it offers a wide range of brand-name sports and athletic clothing and equipment. Currently, Dick's operates over 140 stores in the Eastern United States and has plans to enter many new cities. Over the past five years, Dick's has focused on growing its store chain so it can sell an increasing amount of high-priced, brand-name products. Brand-name products command a premium price, and this premium price means that Dick's can earn more profit for every dollar it invests in its sporting goods inventory to sell to customers.

Dick's gross margins have increased over the last five years from 21 to 26.5%, and this has

greatly increased its profitability. As we discuss later in the chapter, gross margin is the profit left over after the costs of purchasing the raw materials or components that go into making a product have been paid for. In retailing, the cost of paying for the products a company sells, like the sporting goods in Dick's stores, subtracted from the revenue it receives from their sale, determines its gross profit margin.

Rising gross margins are enormously important for a company because even a small increase in gross margin translates into a large increase in profits. Dick's gross margins are much higher than its competitors because it has been able to attract more people to its stores to buy the expensive brand-name products it sells.

But why do customers shop at Dick's rather than, say, the Sports Authority? Dick's is known for its excellent quality of customer service. In each of its five "stores within a store"—Golf Pro Shop, Footwear Center, Cycle Shop, Sportsman's Lodge, and Total Sports—its well-trained sales associates provide customers with expert advice on which products will suit them best. Excellent customer service results in increased sales revenues because (1) good advice encourages customers to buy more products, (2) good advice encourages them to purchase more expensive products. If sales associates can clearly explain to customers why more expensive products offer them better value for their money, for example, because of their superior quality and features, customers are more likely to buy them.

On the cost side of the equation, the main advantage Dick's has over its competitors is that, like Wal-Mart, it has a first-class inventory management system. Dick's "turns over its inventory," meaning the speed at which it sells the sporting goods in stock in its stores, at a much higher rate than its competitors. The faster a retail company can sell its inventory, the lower its costs will be relative to the amount of its sales revenue. This is because the capital it has used to purchase the inventory (sporting goods, in Dick's case) is being used more efficiently. For example, Dick's turns its inventory over at a rate of 3.83 times a year compared to its rivals, who average around 2.5 times. This is 65% ($2.5/3.83 \times 100 = 65.2\%$) faster than they are, which means Dick's can buy and sell 65% more inventory using the same amount of capital than its competitors. Once again, this translates into huge cost savings and increased profitability.

The combined effects of Dick's higher gross profit margin and inventory turnover rate can be seen in its return on invested capital (ROIC), the most accurate measure of a company's profitability. Dick's ROIC in 2003 was 11.8%. The chain's competitors, by contrast, earn between 9% and 10%. The ROIC figure means that for every dollar of capital Dick's invests in its business, it earns a profit of 11.8 cents (compared to competitors' 9 or 10 cents). This is a good profit return in any industry. It also puts Dick's in the same league as leading retailers in other segments of the retail market, such as Lowe's, Best Buy, and Bed, Bath, & Beyond.

Dick's reward for its superior efficiency and profitability translates into higher earnings per share for its investors than its competitors. More investors therefore want to buy Dick's stock, so its price goes up. In recent years, the price has soared because its business model allows it to use its capital so efficiently to create value and profit.[1]

Overview

In the previous chapters, we analyze how the activities of all of a company's functions contribute to the value customers believe its goods and services have. Dick's growing sales and profitability suggest that it has created more value for customers than its competitors. Dick's has a competitive advantage because its managers invested its capital to create a business model that attracts more high-spending customers to its stores.

Accounting is the function in a company that records and analyzes the thousands of transactions related to making and selling products that customers want to buy. The information provided by accounting allows managers to measure how well a company's business model is working to create profit—and thus how profitable a company is (Chapter 1 explained why profitability is such an important measure of performance).

In this chapter, we first examine the various kinds of activities involved in accounting and the different types of accountants involved in the accounting process. Second, we describe the terminology, or "language," of accounting, discuss the way in which accountants record and measure a company's value-creation activities, and how they present this information in financial statements. Third, we analyze the financial measures and ratios a company's stakeholders use to evaluate its past, current, and future performance and profitability. By the end of this chapter, you will understand the crucial role the accounting function plays in helping a company generate more value, cash, and profit from its operations—something that benefits all of its stakeholders.

The Nature of Accounting

As we mention in Chapter 1, the *value* a company creates can be measured by the amount that customers are willing to pay for its products. To make products that customers want to buy, a company has to invest its capital in resources such as raw materials, components, machinery, computers, and the employees who have the functional skills necessary to make and sell its products. Thus, on the one hand, a company receives revenue from the products its sells. On the other hand, it has to bear all of the costs and expenses involved in making them. The primary goal of a company is to make a *profit*, and it can only do this if the revenues it earns from the sales of its products exceed the costs and expenses of making them.

Accounting makes its functional contribution by providing the tools and methods a company needs to accurately measure its revenues, costs, expenses, money, assets, and capital so managers can evaluate how much profit their business activities are generating. As the story of Dick's suggests, accounting methods provide managers with the information they need to evaluate if their company's business model is earning a profitable return on the capital invested in it.

Accounting is the process of (1) collecting, measuring, and recording raw financial data; (2) organizing this data using agreed-upon accounting rules and methods to create useful information about a company's financial performance; and (3) analyzing this information and reporting and communicating the results of this analysis in financial reports and statements. A company's accounting system is the financial information system it uses to measure, record, analyze, and report all of the transactions involved in its value-creation process.

accounting The process of collecting financial data, organizing and analyzing it using agreed-upon accounting rules, and reporting the results in financial statements.

accounting system The financial information system a company uses to measure, record, analyze, and report all the transactions involved in its value-creation process.

Accounting and the Company's Stakeholders

All of a company's stakeholders are interested in the financial reports and statements that result from the work of the accounting function. Managers at all levels use these financial statements to analyze the past performance of a company, or one of its functions, over a specific reporting period—normally 3-,6-,9-, and 12-month periods. The information in these financial statements allows managers to break down the sources of a company's revenues, costs, and expenses. For example, managers can learn which products have generated the most sales revenue for the firm and then make changes to its product lineup. The managers might, for example, decide to drop a marginally profitable product to increase the firm's overall profitability. Similarly, by examining which products cost the most to make or sell, they can identify areas where they can try to increase operating efficiencies to reduce these costs—like finding new ways to increase inventory turnover, for example.

Managers at all levels in the company can also use these financial reports and statements to help improve a company's performance. Many of the reports that accounting generates are specific to a function—that is, they provide a detailed breakdown of how the function has spent the money in its budget to fund its activities. By using enterprise resource planning software in conjunction with accounting information, managers can often identify new best practices. Using customer relationship management software in conjunction with accounting information, for example, marketing and sales managers can evaluate how changes in sales and service activities have affected operating revenues and costs.

But it's not just managers who are interested in a company's financial statements. Regular employees are interested, too. These statements provide employees with information about the ongoing financial health of their companies. If their companies are healthy, workers know they have greater job security and more opportunities

Did You Know?

Best-selling author John Grisham received an undergraduate degree in accounting.[2]

Most employees would prefer to work for a company whose sales and profitability increase over time, such as Wal-Mart, because they know they have job security and there are more opportunities for promotion.

for promotion. Another reason employees are interested in a company's financial statements is that they often own stock or stock options in their companies, and so, like outside stockholders, they are interested in its performance. In fact, companies like Microsoft, Wal-Mart, and Dell that give their employees stock options often make it a point to show each employee how his or her activities directly affect the firm's financial performance. For example, a sales manager can use accounting information to show customer service reps how the length of time it takes them to solve customers' problems affects expenses over a certain time period. Similarly, a manufacturing manager can use accounting information to show employees how a new time-saving method of assembling a car will reduce production costs.

A company's stock price rises and falls as the information contained in its financial statements reveal how its operating performance has changed over time. Companies whose financial statements show continually rising sales, cash, and profit attract investors seeking to earn a good return on the money they have to invest. When a company suddenly reports lower-than-expected earnings for the previous accounting period, say three months or a year, its stock price often plunges because investors worry its downward performance may continue. As investors sell the firm's stock, this signals that the firm needs to improve its business model to solve its problems. The price of a company's stock is affected by the figures in its financial statements, so it is vitally important that accountants follow agreed-upon accounting rules to analyze and report financial information—something we discuss in detail below. For example, in 2003, McDonald's stock price fell by 70% to a record low after it reported falling revenues at its restaurants. Scrutinizing the accounting information in its financial statements, McDonald's board of directors decided it needed to replace the company's CEO, rapidly cut costs, and offer new menu choices to increase sales. Amazingly, within three months, McDonald's stock recovered 50% of its value!

Other stakeholders, too, examine a company's financial statements for information about its activities. The government, through agencies like the Securities and Exchange Commission (SEC) and the Internal Revenue Service (IRS), has a major interest in ensuring companies follow legally-accepted accounting practices in reporting their financial performance. And, also that companies pay the taxes that are due on their profits—just as people pay the taxes due upon their personal incomes. A company's suppliers are also concerned about its performance, especially because most suppliers offer buyers 30- or 60-days' credit. Suppliers want to be sure the companies that are their customers are in a good financial condition to pay for their inputs.

Finally, the general public has a strong interest in the performance of companies; a nation with financially healthy companies enjoys a constantly rising standard of living. Also, a company's stance on ethics and social responsibility is important to the public because it affects the well-being of everyone in a society. Recall that we mentioned in other chapters how the scandals at Enron, WorldCom, and other large companies devastated the investments and pensions of millions of Americans and cost millions of employees their jobs.

In sum, the information and knowledge that the accounting function provides is enormously important to all of a company's stakeholders. A company's yearly financial statement is a kind of "snapshot" of its health. Because most companies publish financial statements that show the results of their past five or ten years of performance, stakeholders can get a "moving picture" of the company's health over time. This gives them insight into the source of a particular company's competitive advantage (or lack of it), such as Dick's in the opening case.

The American Institute of Certified Public accountants (AICPA) is the premier national professional association for CPAs in the United States.

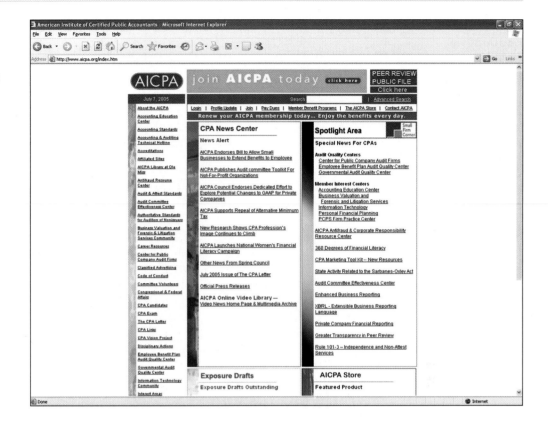

Over time, as managers compare the changes they make to a company's business model with changes in the performance information contained in its financial statements, they obtain valuable knowledge about the key "drivers" of the company's success. They then use this knowledge to find new ways to increase a company's profitability. Remember, however, that financial statements provide a picture of a company's performance in the *past*—they cannot be used to accurately predict its performance far into the future because conditions both inside of a company and outside within its industry can change rapidly.

Types of Accounting Activities

Several specific kinds of accounting activities must be done to measure the flow of resources into a company and flow of goods and services out the door. Figure 14.1 illustrates five principal accounting activities, which range from those needed to collect the thousands and millions of pieces of raw data about all of the company's transactions, to preparing the annual financial statements that summarize its overall financial performance.

bookkeeping The record-keeping activities needed to monitor and track all of the financial transactions related to making and selling goods and services.

The accounting process begins with bookkeeping, the record-keeping activities needed to monitor and track all of the financial transactions involved in making and selling goods and services. Some of the most important data that accounting tracks and records are the payments a company receives for its products and the payments it has to make for the resources it uses to make them:

First, accounting has to record all the details involved in each sales transaction such as how much of a product was shipped to each of its customers, how much each customer was charged for the product, and so on. As payments come in, accounting has to make sure they are deposited into the correct accounts. It balances the company's checkbook, and controls who has access to incoming funds.

Second, accounting is responsible for keeping track of all of the purchase orders submitted by a company's functions for raw materials, component parts, computers,

**Figure 14.1
Accounting
Activities**

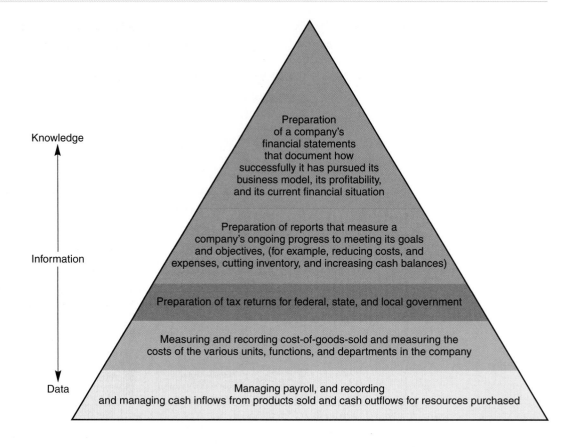

Knowledge

Preparation
of a company's
financial statements
that document how
successfully it has pursued its
business model, its profitability,
and its current financial situation

Information

Preparation of reports that measure a
company's ongoing progress to meeting its goals
and objectives, (for example, reducing costs, and
expenses, cutting inventory, and increasing cash balances)

Preparation of tax returns for federal, state, and local government

Measuring and recording cost-of-goods-sold and measuring the
costs of the various units, functions, and departments in the company

Data

Managing payroll, and recording
and managing cash inflows from products sold and cash outflows for resources purchased

equipment, and so on that add value to the company's products. All the machinery and equipment needed by manufacturing, the advertising time bought from radio and television stations, and the computer hardware and software IT orders for all a company's functions, is paid for by the accounting function out of each function's budget. Because many of these resources are bought on credit, accounting employees need to keep track of when these payments are due, pay them on time, and record them as expenditures of each individual function. For example, advertising would be paid for out of marketing's expense budget and computers out of IT's budget.

Accounting is also responsible for making sure the firm's employees get their weekly or monthly payroll checks. By recording all these payments, accounting can provide each function with a detailed breakdown of the cost of the human resources each function uses. This is important when making HRM decisions. The total of all the wages and salaries paid to employees are called *gross wages,* or *gross earnings,* and they also have to be calculated and reported in a company's financial statements. Gross wages also determine the amount of employee-related government and state taxes a company must pay. Accounting is responsible for making these payments, too, as well as seeing to it and that the property taxes the company owes on its land and buildings are paid. It is also responsible for sending dividend checks to the company's stockholders.

Finally, the purchase price and dates of all of the company's fixed, or long-term assets, must be recorded. For example, the costs of a new computer-controlled assembly line, additional office furniture, and a company's fleet of cars or trucks must all be recorded. By doing so a company can accurately depreciate its assets, that is, calculate the cost or reduced value of the assets as they wear out. The amount of this depreciation is then reported as an expense in the firm's financial statements.

Once all of the transactions related to making and selling a company's products have been recorded, accounting can perform more complex kinds of activities. These activities center around calculating the total sales revenues a company receives and the total costs and expenses involved in making its products. Accounting provides this information in regular financial reports that managers use to assess how efficiently and

depreciate The act of calculating the reduced value of the assets a company uses to make and sell its products.

effectively the company's resources or assets are being used. Finally, accounting prepares the company's official financial statements that provide an overview of a company's performance. This information can then be presented in a way that allows stakeholders to calculate the company's profitability and financial health.

The Rules of Accounting: GAAP

generally accepted accounting principles A set of accounting rules and procedures U.S. companies must follow to ensure their financial standing is being reported accurately and honestly.

All U.S. companies must prepare their financial statements according to generally accepted accounting principles (GAAP), a set of rules and procedures developed over time by accounting experts to ensure stakeholders obtain a clear and accurate picture of the financial standing of companies. These rules are legally enforceable. Companies and accountants who break them can be punished with fines and/or imprisonment. When *all* companies use the *same* set of accounting rules, it becomes much easier for stakeholders to evaluate one company's performance relative to others. This is particularly important to investors who are trying to identify the companies likely to provide the most return on their capital.

Unscrupulous managers sometimes try to manipulate and falsify accounting data to paint a more positive picture of a company's performance. Managers do this to protect the value of the company's stock and increase the value of the salary, bonuses, and stock options they receive when stakeholders believe a company is performing well. A well-established set of accounting rules greatly reduces such fraudulent behavior, although, as with any system of rules, there are always loopholes and ambiguities unethical managers can exploit.

In addition, in the United States, independent accountants with no financial ties to a particular company must legally review a company's financial statements and the data used to create them. These accountants are then required to make a declaration that a company's financial statements have been prepared in line with GAAP guidelines and that they present a true and fair account of a company's financial position and operating results.

Types of Accountants

certified public accountants People who have taken 150 semester hours of accounting courses and have passed the CPA exam administered by the American Institute of Certified Public Accountants.

audit The formal evaluation of the fairness and reliability of a company's financial statements.

To perform the accounting activities necessary for a company to meet these strict professional and legal requirements, companies employ two types of accountants: inside and outside (independent) accountants. Both kinds of accountants are required to pass stringent professional examinations ensuring they have the skills necessary to accurately prepare a company's accounts. Most of these people are certified public accountants (CPAs). CPAs must have taken 150 semester hours of accounting courses and passed the CPA exam administered by the *American Institute of Certified Public Accountants*. Only accountants who have passed this exam are allowed to audit, or formally evaluate the soundness of a company's financial statements and sign off on them.

EXTERNAL ACCOUNTANTS There are two main types of external accountants. First, there are the thousands of CPAs who work for one of the Big Four accounting firms of Ernst & Young, KPMG, PricewaterhouseCoopers, and Deloitte Touche Tohmatsu. Second, are the thousands of other CPAs who often work together in small public companies or in partnerships to provide their services to medium- or small-sized companies and to individual people. The key services external accountants provide center around auditing, tax preparation, and financial planning.

Did You Know?

Question: Where would you find the Office of the Chief Accountant?
Answer: The U.S. Securities and Exchange Commission.

The office is responsible for insuring that auditing policy and practice deliver trustworthy financial reporting for investors.[3]

The Big Four generally audit the books of large, public companies. The Big Four employ thousands of experienced professional accountants and financial analysts who have the broad range of skills needed to audit a large company's accounts. Typically, a large company selects one of the Big Four as its auditor, and then the two companies develop an ongoing auditing relationship that can last for many years. The cost of an audit for a large company can run into millions of dollars a year.

One initiative that Congress was looking into after the collapse of the accounting firm Arthur Andersen was to limit the auditing contracts between large companies and their auditors to a five-year period. (We discussed this earlier in the book, if you recall.) This would prevent the development of close relations between a company's top managers and its auditors that might lead them to "cook the company's books," that is, deliberately hide or distort a company's financial information. If a company's top managers know its financial accounts will be scrutinized by a different team of auditors from a different Big Four firm, in a few years' time, they are less likely to behave illegally because there will be a much greater risk of being caught. To date, such a bill has not yet been passed by Congress.

One measure that *has* been passed by Congress is the Sarbanes-Oxley Act, which requires a company's CEO, CFO, and external auditors to "sign off" on its financial statements. By doing so, these people are made personally and legally liable for any accounting irregularities discovered in the statements. Although, some companies use inappropriate accounting methods to inflate their revenues, others do the opposite: They actually underreport their revenues and profits, as Business in Action describes. (An interesting article about the recent changes to accounting rules and the way some companies "fudge" their numbers appears at the end of the chapter.)

Business in Action

Cooking versus Smoothing the Books

Many of the accounting scandals that occurred at companies like WorldCom, Tyco, and Qwest involved top managers deliberately "cooking the books" to inflate profits. There are different ways to do this. One way is by recording phony sales revenues. Another way is by deliberately underreporting or failing to record the firm's expenses.

Managers have always known that cooking the books to inflate profits is a serious crime they can go to jail for. By contrast, "smoothing the books"—a technique used to *underreport* profits—used to be regarded as a much-less-serious violation of the rules. Smoothing the books occurs when managers push revenues and expenses into other reporting periods than the ones in which they should be reported. For example, if a company's future prospects seem poor, pushing profits earned in one period to the next period will make it look like the company is earning stable or slightly increasing profits over time.

Executives at the telecommunications giant WorldCom committed accounting fraud that led to the largest U.S. bankruptcy in history.

Why would managers risk smoothing the books? The fact is that top managers are under intense pressure from Wall Street to show steadily rising sales and profits. If a company fails to meet its profit target or falls short of the profit stock analysts are forecasting, the price of its shares will plummet—sometimes by as much as 10 to 20%. So, if a company is making a lot of profit one year but suspects it will not make as much in the future, its managers might be tempted to smooth the books—push the extra profit forward to future years. By holding the profits in a so-called "cookie-jar reserve," they can protect their bonuses and stock options in subsequent years.

In 2003, however, it became apparent that the U.S. government wasn't going to tolerate smoothing anymore. Ripples ran through the financial community when Freddie Mac, the huge government-sponsored mortgage broker, fired its CFO and CEO for reportedly smoothing out its profits—underreporting them by over a billion dollars, in this case. Apparently, both managers felt that when interest rates started to rise, Freddie Mac's profits would slip badly. Their goal was therefore to smooth out Freddie Mac's profit stream over the course of several years. However, when a new team of auditors from Ernst & Young uncovered the practice, the ruse was up. Freddie Mac's stock price plunged by 19% following the announcement, and the SEC also began to investigate the two executives personally. Not only had the CEO and CFO signed off on the accuracy of the company's books, they sold their Freddie Mac stock before its price collapsed.[4]

managerial accountants
Accountants who specialize in preparing and analyzing the financial data used by managers.

financial accountants
Accountants who specialize in preparing financial data, following GAAP rules, for use by outside stakeholders.

INTERNAL ACCOUNTANTS A company also employs internal accountants as auditors to scrutinize the financial data used to prepare its statements. The role of these people is to ensure that revenue and expense figures are accurately recorded and that the appropriate accounting rules have been properly used to report the data. There are many complex GAAP rules surrounding the way a company is allowed to depreciate and write off the assets it uses to make and sell its products, for example. If these rules are wrongly applied, a large company could find that it has misstated its profits by hundreds of millions of dollars.

Internal auditors must also be on the lookout for deliberate fraud by employees responsible for recording and reporting financial information, by those who are responsible for handling its cash and other valuable assets, and those who create its internal financial accounts. Internal auditors ensure employees have not embezzled a company's operating funds, for example.

Beyond auditing, a company employs different kinds of accountants. Usually these people are divided into two areas of expertise: managerial accountants, who prepare and analyze financial data for use by managers, and financial accountants, who prepare financial data following GAAP rules for use by people outside of the firm (stakeholders, the government, and so forth).

Managerial accountants need to have a good grasp of business principles to interpret the data they are analyzing. They are often highly talented managers in their own right who rise to become the CEOs of their companies. Managerial accountants analyze a company's revenue and cost structure and report it to managers in a way that helps them improve the performance of the business. Some of this information must be kept secret, however. If a company reveals too much financial information, its competitors will have a better idea of where its competitive advantages lie. No company wants to share information such as this! Most companies, for example, do not break down the source of their revenues by product line or by operating division. They also do not provide a detailed breakdown of their expenses because this would help competitors understand why a particular company has lower costs, for example.

In a 2003 financial statement, Microsoft provided a breakdown of the profits earned by its individual products for the first time ever. The statement revealed most of the company's profits were earned from the sale of Microsoft's Windows software and that many of the firm's other products, such as MSN, Xbox, and Windows hardware, were actually losing money.

There are several specializations inside of managerial accounting. *Financial analysis* involves analyzing the financial implications of different kinds of business model decisions such as changing one of the 4Ps of marketing, adding a new product line, or acquiring a company. Financial analysts also use their expertise to decide how a company should manage the sale of its stock to investors, or how to invest its own cash in securities, like the stocks and bonds of other companies. At this level, the distinction between accounting and finance becomes blurry. We examine these important issues in depth in the next chapter.

Tax accountants specialize in preparing a company's tax returns and ensuring the company abides by all the laws and regulations that govern its operations in a particular country. These people are also responsible for finding ways to structure a company's operations to reduce its total tax bill, say, by locating its operations abroad or registering the firm's headquarters in a country that levies little or no taxes on corporations. Many large companies, including Seagate, Tyco, and Ingersoll-Rand avoid paying U.S. taxes in just this way. Even though they operate largely within the United States, these companies are registered in Bermuda. Finally, *cost accountants* are responsible for calculating the many different costs related to companies' production and distribution processes. These costs include inventory costs, work-in-progress costs, and the costs of different kinds of physical work arrangements. Cost accountants analyze these costs and look for ways to improve the firm's processes in order to lower them.

Accounting and ERP Systems

The use of ERP software platforms has changed the way financial information is recorded and analyzed. In the past, collecting and recording basic financial data was a time-consuming and expensive activity. Now, advanced financial software can collect and process this information more quickly and inexpensively than ever before. Many bookkeeping activities are being automated, for example, and today financial data flow freely throughout a company so employees have a better understanding of how well its business model is working.

The functional modules of ERP systems, such as the CRM component we discussed in Chapter 12, also allow a company to collect more detailed and valuable information about how and where revenues and costs are being generated. The result is that functional and top managers have much more useful, timely, and accurate information to help them analyze all aspects of a company's operations. This often leads to the development of new and improved best practices across a company. Advanced IT systems provide managers with financial information that gives them more insight into how the various elements of their business model work together to affect profitability.

Accounting Concepts and Financial Statements

Managers at all levels of the company, from the CEO down to its first-line managers, need to understand financial statements and the accounting methods used to prepare them. The strengths and weaknesses of a company's business model—and of its different functions—can be identified from the information in its financial statements. Similarly, individual investors should not invest their capital to buy the stocks of individual companies unless they can (1) read a company's financial statements, and (2) analyze them using the tools discussed later in the chapter to assess the potential future risks and returns associated with their investments. When a person invests in a high-performing mutual fund that contains the stocks of hundreds of companies, fund managers have already performed this financial analysis on behalf of investors.

To read and analyze financial statements, you first need to understand the meaning of the basic terms of accounting. The best way to do this is to look at the types of information provided by the three main kinds of financial statements companies use: a company's balance sheet (or statement of financial condition), its income statement, and its cash flow statement.

The Balance Sheet

balance sheet A summary of the financial condition of a business at the end of a day of a specific reporting period.

assets The productive resources a company owns as well as all of its financial investments.

liabilities The financial obligations a company incurs by borrowing money or buying productive resources on credit.

The balance sheet is a summary of the financial condition of a business at the end of the day of a specific reporting period, such as December 31, 2003. The balance sheet reports the main types of assets *owned* by a company, its liabilities or what it *owes*, and its stockholders' equity or what it is *worth* (see Figure 14.2). Assets are the productive resources that a company owns, such as the cash it has on hand in its checking accounts, its land, buildings, equipment, and computers, its inventory of products ready for sale to customers, and all of its other investments.

Liabilities are the financial obligations that a company incurs by borrowing money from banks or buying productive resources from suppliers on credit. When a company borrows money, it is said to "take on debt." Of course, the company has to pay the interest that accumulates on the debt as well as the debt itself when it is due. Thus, liabilities are the sums of money a company owes its creditors. Note that these creditors have the first claim on the company's assets if problems arise and the firm cannot pay them what they are owed.

Figure 14.2

Balance Sheet for Starbucks
In thousands, except share data

Fiscal year ended	Oct 3, 2004	Sept 28, 2003
ASSETS		
Current assets:		
Cash and cash equivalents	$ 299,128	$ 200,907
Short-term investments – available-for-sale securities	329,082	128,905
Short-term investments – trading securities	24,799	20,199
Accounts receivable, net of allowances of $2,231 and $4,809, respectively	131,015	114,448
Inventories	422,663	342,944
Prepaid expenses and other current assets	71,347	55,173
Deferred income taxes, net	81,240	61,453
Total current assets	1,359,274	924,029
Long-term investments – available-for-sale securities	135,179	136,159
Equity and other investments	171,747	144,257
Property, plant and equipment, net	1,471,446	1,384,902
Other assets	85,561	52,113
Other intangible assets	26,800	24,942
Goodwill	68,950	63,344
TOTAL ASSETS	$ 3,318,957	$ 2,729,746
LIABILITIES AND SHAREHOLDERS' EQUITY		
Current liabilities:		
Accounts payable	$ 191,574	$ 168,984
Accrued compensation and related costs	208,927	152,608
Accrued occupancy costs	65,873	56,179
Accrued taxes	63,038	54,934
Other accrued expenses	122,245	101,800
Deferred revenue	121,377	73,476
Current portion of long-term debt	735	722
Total current liabilities	773,769	608,703
Deferred income taxes, net	46,683	33,217
Long-term debt	3,618	4,354
Other long-term liabilities	8,132	1,045
Shareholders' equity:		
Common stock and additional paid-in capital – authorized, 600,000,000 shares; issued and outstanding, 397,405,844 and 393,692,536 shares, respectively, (includes 1,697,100 common stock units in both periods)	956,685	959,103
Other additional paid-in capital	39,393	39,393
Retained earnings	1,461,458	1,069,683
Accumulated other comprehensive income	29,219	14,248
Total shareholders' equity	2,486,755	2,082,427
TOTAL LIABILITIES AND SHAREHOLDERS' EQUITY	$ 3,318,957	$ 2,729,746

stockholders' equity
The total capital invested
in a company over time as
well as the past profits it
has retained in its
business.

Companies use the money they borrow to invest in their businesses. Thus, although the term liability has a negative tone to it, in reality the money a company borrows is a major source of the capital it needs to build its business model! Some liabilities or debt is good because "it takes money to make money." The key thing for a company, like an individual, is not to take on so much debt that it is impossible to pay it back. Companies pay back their debts and the interest due on them from the profits they make.

The other main source of a company's capital is its stockholders' equity or equity, the total capital that has been invested in the business by its founders and stockholders over time, as well as all of the profits a company has made and *retained* in its business. If a company uses the profit it makes to pay interest on its debts, or dividends to stockholders, then its stockholders' equity goes down. If a company can keep the profits it makes in its business, its stockholders' equity goes up. Together liabilities and equity make up the total amount of capital that a company has invested in its business. In practice, this capital is used to buy the assets and resources it needs to fund its business model.

As discussed in detail next, when a company makes a profit, this is recorded on the right-hand, or capital, side of the balance sheet as an increase in equity. However, profits are also used to buy productive assets. Asset purchases are represented by the increase in the value of the company's assets on the left-hand, or asset, side of its balance sheet.

Everything the company has—money, machines, land, equipment, and so forth, which are recorded on the left-hand side of the balance sheet—must come from *somewhere*—either from stockholders' investments, the company's earnings, or money the firm has borrowed, which are recorded on the right-hand side of the balance sheet. This is why it is called a *balance sheet*. The statement is designed so that the two sides always balance. This way, managers, investors, and other stakeholders can track how well their capital is being used to produce profit and surplus cash—the two main indicators of a company's profitability.

THE BASIC ACCOUNTING EQUATION   The basic equation of accounting is that what a company owns, minus what it owes, is what it is *worth*. It is as follows:

$$\text{Assets} - \text{Liabilities} = \text{Owners' Equity}$$

Increases in the size of owners' equity over time indicate how well a company is performing. These increases (or lack of them) tell stakeholders how much profit a company is earning and how much profit it is plowing back into its business (rather than paying dividends to stockholders, which takes profit out of a company) to increase its future performance. Recall from Chapter 1 that profitability measures how well a company is using and investing its capital to create products that can be sold at a price that generates profits. A sharply rising owners' equity shows that a company has achieved this. It is a signal of a strong financial position.

In accounting, the information on the balance sheet is presented in a rearranged form because the central task of accounting, as just noted, is to keep track of how well a company is using its capital to purchase assets that generate profit. This is best achieved by balancing assets against liabilities and equity, the total capital invested in a company. In balance sheet format the accounting equation is rewritten as:

$$\text{Assets} = \text{Liabilities and Owners' Equity}$$

**double entry
bookkeeping** A method
of recording the dual
effects of a business's
financial transaction so
that the company's assets,
liabilities, and owners'
equity are always in
balance.

As just noted, the accounting equation must always be in balance. This means that the firm's total assets must always be the same dollar amount as the firm's total liabilities *and* owners' equity. Accountants achieve this and balance financial accounts using double entry bookkeeping. Double entry bookkeeping involves recording the dual effects of a financial transaction on a company's assets and liabilities. Thus, if a company purchases $1 million of component parts on credit, this is recorded as a $1 million increase in its assets, but also as a $1 million increase in its liabilities—this is how the equation is kept in balance. If a company simply purchases $1 million in components outright, the balance sheet would simply show $1 million less in cash and $1 million more in inventory on the asset side of the equation. Because both cash and inventory are assets, the total amount on the asset side (left-hand side) remains the same and still balances with the amount on the liabilities and owners' equity side (right-hand side) of the balance sheet.

When stockholders look at a firm's balance sheet, they can see the financial risks they face by investing in the company. Should a company go bankrupt, its assets must first be used to settle its liabilities to its creditors, such as the companies that supplied its inputs and the banks and institutions that loaned it money. Its assets will be sold, and these debts will be paid first. The balance sheet shows how much money is owed to creditors, and thus how much, if any, money would be left to pay the company's stockholders once creditors' claims have been settled. So, if a company has few real assets and large sums of money owing in liabilities, potential investors see that the chances of getting their capital back are very poor. This helps investors get a sense of the *risks* involved in investing capital in a company. For example, a new company with few assets, or a large company with a high level of debt, are both risky investments.

Table 14.1 presents an abbreviated version of Dick's balance sheet. A balance sheet reports the main types of a company's assets, liabilities, and stockholders' equity. The various "lines" on the balance sheet report the specific information potential investors need to know to evaluate the soundness of its financial situation—which is why the balance sheet is also sometimes referred to as a *statement of financial condition*.

ASSETS As noted earlier, assets are the productive resources a company owns or has the right to collect, such as the right to collect cash from customers who have bought on credit and owe the company money. On a balance sheet, assets are listed in the balance sheet in order of **liquidity**, which means how fast they can be converted into cash. Thus, the most liquid asset—cash—appears at the top of the asset column. The next most liquid asset is *accounts receivable*, the monetary value of the cash owed to a company by customers who have bought its goods and services on credit. *Inventory* is the stock of finished products a company has on hand to ship to customers, *and* the stock of raw materials, components, and semi-finished products that will be made into finished products. *Prepaid expenses* are things like insurance premiums, rent, salary advances, and equipment maintenance agreements that a company has already paid for.

liquidity Assets listed in the firm's balance sheet in order of how fast they can be converted into cash.

Table 14.1
Dick's Balance Sheet (in millions of dollars)

Assets		Liabilities and Equity	
Cash	$ 11.1	Accounts Payable	$125.2
Accounts Receivable	16.4	Accrued Expenses	59.2
Inventory	233.5	Current Portion of Long-Term Debt	0.2
Prepaid Expenses	5.6	Income Tax Payable	35.5
Other Current Assets	8.7		
Total Current Assets	$275.3	**Total Current Liabilities**	$220.2
		Long-Term Debt	$ 3.4
Property, Plant, and Equipment	$143.9		
Accumulated Depreciation	(63.8)	Other Liabilities	12.2
Net Property, Plant, and Equipment	$ 80.1	**Total Liabilities**	$235.7
		Capital Stock Invested	$130.3
		Retained Earnings	10.2
Other Long-Term Assets	$ 20.8	**Total Stockholders' Equity**	$140.5
Total Assets	$376.2	**Total Liabilities and Stockholders' Equity**	$376.2

current assets The total value of a company's cash, accounts receivable, inventory, and prepaid expenses.

On a balance sheet, accountants work out the monetary value of a company's cash, accounts receivable, inventory, and prepaid expenses. These are then totaled and reported as a company's **current assets**. Current assets are often called *working assets* because they are being constantly used to make products that are then sold to generate revenue, profit, and still more cash.

Next on a balance sheet are reported noncurrent assets or long-term assets, meaning those that will not be converted into cash within a 12-month period. These assets include things like the firm's plant, its equipment, land, furniture, and computers. They are often lumped into a category called *property, plant, and equipment (PP&E)*. Because the constant use of assets such as these causes them to wear out and become less valuable over time, they are depreciated. The net figure for depreciated PP&E is then reported. Finally, *other assets*, a catchall category that includes intangible assets, such as the estimated value of a company's brand name and its patents is reported.

The total assets reported at the bottom of the balance sheet are the sum of current assets, fixed assets minus depreciation, and other assets. The information on current assets is particularly important to investors because it tells them how much ready cash a company has to pay its debts, and how quickly a company can convert its assets to cash if it needs to. We discuss this later.

current liabilities Debts that are payable within one year's time, including accounts payable and accrued expenses.

LIABILITIES   Liabilities are the amounts of money a company owes its suppliers, creditors, and so on. **Current liabilities** are debts that are payable within one year and include accounts payable and accrued expenses. *Accounts payable* are the money a company owes its regular suppliers for inputs, merchandise, or services it has received but not paid for. *Accrued expenses* are unpaid expenses that gradually build up over time. These expenses include things like the value of pension benefits and vacation pay owed to employees, profit-based bonuses, or employee stock options.

Notes payable is the account where the firm records the interest due on its bank loans that must be paid within one year. *Long-term debt* is money borrowed for a period longer than one year. A $250 million loan at a 5% interest rate payable over a 10-year period is an example of a long-term debt. Large companies like Disney and Viacom might have $6 billion or more in long-term liabilities. The *current portion of long-term debt* consists of the interest that is due on that debt within the next 12 months. *Income taxes payable* are whatever sum of money a company owes the government that will be paid when due. The sum of all these different liabilities is recorded as a company's *total liabilities* on the right-hand side of the balance sheet.

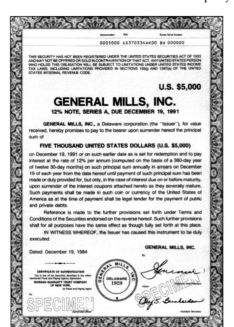

A General Mills stock certificate.

STOCKHOLDERS' EQUITY   Companies issue different types of stock. All companies issue *common stock*, the most common kind of stock; some also issue *preferred stock*, which gives its owners certain legal rights common stockholders do not have, such as the right to a regular dividend or the right to a company's assets after its creditors.

Capital stock invested includes the original money used to start the company and all the additional money raised by issuing and selling additional company stock. *Retained earnings* is the total of all the profits a company has earned over time that have not been returned to stockholders in the form of dividends. **Total equity** is the sum of the firm's capital stock invested and its retained earnings. The monetary value of total equity increases when a company makes a profit, and hence increases its retained earnings, or when its sells stock, which increases its capital stock. Once again, this information provides important information for potential investors. When a company's total equity is increasing, this suggests it is in good financial condition, and it usually leads investors to bid up the stock price.

When a company retains its earnings, its shareholders' equity increases. However, as we discussed earlier, each side of the equation must balance. Therefore, the other side of the equation—the company's asset side—must increase, too. This balancing act is achieved by

total equity The sum of the capital stock invested in a business in addition to its retained earnings.

increasing the firm's cash account (or current and fixed assets if the firm uses the cash to buy these types of assets). As we noted earlier, this balancing act allows stakeholders to evaluate how well a company is using its capital to purchase assets that result in increased sales revenues and profits. The balance sheet does not tell stakeholders *how or why* a company's revenues or profits are rising, however. This is the role played by the income statement, the second financial statement.

The Income Statement

income statement The financial report that summarizes the results of a company's profit-making activities in a specific time period.

bottom-line profit The amount of net income, profit, or earnings a company reports on the bottom line of its income statement.

In the balance sheet, the profit (or loss) a company makes is reported in terms of changes in its assets, liabilities, and owners' equity. The balance sheet does not show how a company used its assets to make its profits; in other words, it provides few clues about why a company's business model is successful. Many more clues are provided by the information in the income statement, which summarizes and reports the results of a company's profit-making activities in a specific time period (hence, it is sometimes called the *profit and loss statement*).

The basic equation used to compute a company's bottom-line profit, the amount of *net income, profit, or earnings* (these terms all mean the same thing) a company reports on the "bottom line" of its income statement, is presented below. As we discuss later, the figures for sales and net income provided in the income statement, in conjunction with the figures for assets, liabilities, and equity provided on the balance sheet, allow accountants to create important financial ratios that provide insight into a company's financial performance—especially its profitability.

Sales Revenues – Expenses = Profit (or Loss)

Sales revenues are reported on the first line of the income statement. Sometimes, the terms *sales* or *net sales* are used instead of *sales revenue*. Figure 14.3 shows graphically what the equation means.

To calculate their net income, companies first deduct from their sales revenues (or sales) the cost of goods sold. Table 14.2 presents an abbreviated form of Dick's income statement. The *cost-of-goods-sold* (COGS) is the cost of all the assets (raw materials components, and so forth) used to make the products that generated the sales revenue. Companies that resell products they buy from manufacturers to the final customer, such as Dick's, count the cost of purchasing these goods as their cost of goods sold. (Dick's calls this "cost of revenue.")

matching principle An accounting rule that requires that the expenses incurred to make and sell products be deducted from the revenues generated by their sale during the same accounting period.

Note that *inventory expense*, the cost of the products that have been made, but not sold, in a particular reporting period, are not included in calculating the cost of goods sold. These costs are not charged as an expense on the income statement until the products are actually sold. They are reported as a current asset on the balance sheet. There is a very important reason for this. A central GAAP accounting principle is the matching principle, which requires that that the expenses (costs) incurred in making

Figure 14.3
Sales, Expenses, and Profit

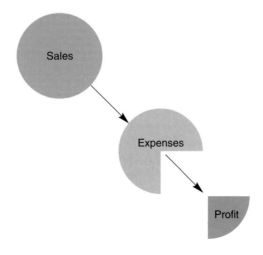

Table 14.2

Dick's Income Statement (in millions of dollars)

Sales Revenue	$1,272.6
Cost of Revenue	935.2
Gross Profit	**$337.4**
Selling, General, and Administrative Expenses	$262.8
Research and Development	–
Depreciation	–
Other Operating Expenses	5.6
Total Operating Expenses	**$1,203.5**
Operating Income	$69.1
Interest Expense	(5.3)
Net Income before Taxes	63.8
Provision for Income Taxes	25.5
Net Income after Taxes	**$38.3**

accrual basis of accounting The principle that a company's income statement should reflect the revenue received when the company makes a sale, not when payment is actually received.

and selling goods and services be deducted from the revenues generated by the sale of the company's products *during the same accounting period.*

Similar to expenses, when it comes to reporting their revenues, companies must follow what's called the accrual basis of accounting. It is based on the principle that the income statement should reflect the revenues the company earns when it makes a sale or provides a service, *not* when it actually gets paid. Likewise, the cost of the resources used to make and sell products should be recorded when they are sold, *not* when the firm pays for them. As we mentioned earlier, some unethical managers are tempted to report revenues and expenses in periods in which they aren't generated. This can distort a company's financial performance by making it appear that a company is far more profitable (and in some cases, unprofitable), than it really is.

gross profit The amount of money left over after a firm deducts the cost of the goods it has sold from the revenues earned from them.

The amount left over after a firm deducts the cost of goods it sells from the revenue earned from the sale of these goods is called gross profit (or *gross margin*). Bottom-line profit is then determined by deducting all the firm's other expenses from gross profit. Table 14.3 lists some major sources of these costs.

Sales and marketing expenses are sometimes broken out separately from the other expenses because they can significantly affect a company's profitability. When investors know how much it costs a company to sell its products compared to its competitors, they get important information about its marketing skills and its ability to attract and retain customers. Dick's has chosen to lump all these costs together to "hide" its cost structure. Note that Dick's has no research and development expenses because it is in the retail business rather than in the pharmaceuticals or high-tech business where R&D costs are a major expense. It also has a category called "other operating expenses" which lumps together some of the kinds of expenses noted in Table 14.3.

Table 14.3

Types of Expenses

- Sales and marketing expenses
- Depreciation of operating assets that last more than one year (buildings, cars, trucks, computers, office furniture, machinery, equipment, and so forth)
- Property taxes on land and buildings
- Payroll costs (wages, salaries, and benefits paid to employees)
- Utilities, telephone, and insurance
- Office supplies
- Cost of services such as IT, legal, and auditing costs
- Interest paid on loans

All these expenses are then totaled to form *total operating expense*. Now, a company's *operating income* is reported; this is what income is left over after costs *and* expenses are subtracted from sales revenue. Finally, interest expenses (interest charged on a company's debt), and income taxes payable, are deducted from operating income and the result is net income, or bottom-line profit.

net income A company's total profit after deducting the cost of the goods it has sold as well as all of its other expenses.

Net income is the company's total profit or earnings that reflect adjustments for cost of goods sold, all other expenses, interest, and taxes. It is referred to as the "bottom-line profit" because it is what the firm has really earned from its value-creation activities. Note once again that the terms "profit," "earnings," and "income" all have the same meaning—the amount left over when costs and expenses are deducted from sales.

Before we look at the many financial ratios managers and investors use to determine how successfully a company's business model is working, we first have to examine the third financial statement, the statement of cash flows.

The Statement of Cash Flows

Keep in mind that income or profit is not the same as cash-in-hand. A highly profitable company might show lots of income on its income statement but have very little cash left over to pay its bills. This is because some companies, especially young ones, have to spend all of their money to pay for the productive assets they need to set up their operations and make and sell their products. Sometimes, however, the cash a company receives from these sales is not being generated fast enough to pay a company's ongoing expenses even though in the future the firm might be able to generate lots of cash. With too little immediate cash on hand to pay its bills and cover its current liabilities, a company might go bankrupt. To ensure the firm's survival, managers therefore have to make sure that both the business's long-term profit and short-term cash flow objectives are met. Even the best business model won't be successful if the firm lacks adequate cash flow. As such, cash flow has to be closely monitored.

cash flow statement A financial report showing how much cash a company generated during a specific time period, including where the cash came from and how it was used.

cash The value of a company's assets that can be converted into cash immediately.

This is what the cash flow statement does. The cash flow statement shows how much cash a company generates during a specific financial period, where it came from, and how the company used it. In accounting, cash refers to the value of a company's assets that can be converted into cash immediately. Cash includes not only the money in a company's checking accounts but the value of the securities it owns, such as stocks and bonds that can be quickly liquidated and sold.

Stakeholders are not just interested in the amount of profit a company makes. They are also interested in how a company's cash flow is increasing or decreasing during a specific period, and the reasons for this change. To show stakeholders where the cash is coming from, accountants divide a company's cash flow into three basic categories when they report them in its cash flow statement:

- *Cash flows from operating activities*, that is, the cash flows that result from a company's profit-making, value-creation activities.
- *Cash flows from investing.* The cash flows that result from a company's use of its cash to invest in buying and selling stock, bonds, property, buildings, or money market funds and the cash payments it receives from these activities.
- *Cash flows from financing.* The cash flows that result from a company's financing activities like selling its shares to investors, paying dividends to stockholders, and repaying debt.

Did You Know?

The New York County District Attorney's office—on which the television show "Law and Order" is based—employs forensic accountants to prosecute securities and banking fraud, money laundering, tax crimes, and racketeering.

The net increase or decrease in a company's cash during the financial period is calculated by adding the three types of cash flow together. This is represented in the *net change in cash line* shown at the bottom of the cash flow statement. Dick's cash flow statement shows a small increase in cash of $2.2 million (see Table 14.4).

Table 14.4
Dick's Statement of Cash Flows (in millions of dollars)

Net Income	$38.3
Depreciation	14.4
Deferred Taxes	(5.0)
Noncash Items	3.1
Changes in Working Capital	10.4
Cash from Operating Activities	**$61.1**
Capital Expenditures	($29.0)
Other Investing Cash Flow Items	6.4
Cash from Investing Activities	**($22.6)**
Financing Cash Flow Items	$9.1
Cash Dividends Paid	–
Issuance (Retirement) of Stock	31.7
Issuance (Retirement) of Debt	(77.3)
Cash from Financing Activities	**($36.4)**
Net Change in Cash	**$2.1**

The most important kind of cash flow is the cash flow from a company's operating activities because this tells stakeholders how much cash-in-hand a company's business model is generating. Successful businesses must generate cash to maintain and increase their operating or profit-making activities. Dick's cash flow from operating activities is $61.1 million; this cash came from the net income, or profit, generated by sales to customers, from the extra cash Dick's received from an allowance for depreciation, and by an increase in its working capital.

working capital The amount of cash left over after a company subtracts its current liabilities from its current assets.

A company's **working capital** is the amount of cash left over after its current liabilities are subtracted from its current assets (figures obtained from the balance sheet). Working capital is the amount of money a company has to "work with" and invest in more assets to generate increased sales in the future. When stakeholders see that a company's working capital is increasing over time, this is a good sign that its business model is working well. As you can see, both Dick's working capital and cash from its operating activities have increased substantially because the company's business model has proven very successful.

The reason the net change in cash flow is so small ($2.1 million) is that Dick's has been reinvesting most of its cash to grow its business (capital expenditures of $29 million), which has resulted in a negative cash flow from its investment activities of $22.6 million. Dick's has also been paying off its long-term debts to creditors (Issuance/retirement of debt $77.3 million), which has resulted in negative cash flow from financing activities of $36.4 million. Investing capital in its business and using capital to pay off its debts are very positive signs that a company is generating a lot of cash.

As you can see from this example, looking just at the net change in cash can be misleading. A cash flow statement, like the other statements, has to be analyzed line-by-line to understand how a company is using its capital to generate profit and cash. Even so, Dick's has a *positive cash flow* meaning that it had more cash at the end of the period ($2.3 million) than at the beginning. As we pointed earlier in the chapter, startup companies often have a *negative* cash flow, meaning that more cash is flowing out of the business than coming in, so they have less cash on hand at the end of the period. This often means they cannot cover their short-term obligations or future investment needs. They may go bankrupt unless they can convince investors to provide them with more capital and cash—capital and cash they cannot yet generate from their business model—to buy the assets they need to pursue it.

Using Financial Ratios to Analyze a Company's Performance

financial ratios Ratios that measure different aspects of a company's performance.

Together, the balance sheet, the income statement, and the statement of cash flows provide a lot of information about a company's profitability and financial situation. To really use this information to evaluate how well a company is doing, however, managers and investors take the figures in its financial statements and compute **financial ratios**. Financial ratios measure different aspects of a company's performance and profitability.

Financial ratios are formed by dividing one piece of financial information by another. Managers and investors use them as benchmarks to (1) study a company's changing performance over time and (2) compare a company's performance to other companies in its industry. Financial ratios permit this because they cancel out the effects of differences between companies, such as the size of their operations and revenues. So, for example, Wal-Mart's profitability can be analyzed year-by-year, or it can be directly compared to a small chain of discount stores that operates only in the middle of Montana. This allows investors to determine how well a company is using its capital to generate profit and cash.

Managers use financial ratios to help them understand how changes in their business model will affect the figures in their company's financial statements in the future. In other words, managers use financial ratios to understand how decisions about product pricing and promotion, product development, HRM policies, and so on, will affect their company's bottom-line profit and future profitability. Will reducing the price of their products lead to increased profitability, for example, or reduce it? By using financial ratios to *analyze* the performance of their own company, and their competitors, managers can pinpoint where they should make changes to improve the performance of the firm.

Similarly, by using financial ratios to compare the performance of a company against other companies, investors increase their chances of picking the best company to invest in. Investing in stock is like betting on a horse race. Investors want to pick the best horse. To help them do so, they must use financial ratios. To get a more accurate picture of a company's future prospects, investors must also read a company's announcements and press releases, stories about the company in the media, and the reports of industry analysts. Investing one's personal capital in a company's stock is a very risky business; it is not a decision to be taken lightly.

The three main types of financial ratios used to calculate a company's performance are *liquidity ratios, asset management ratios,* and *profitability ratios.* Each type is discussed next.

Investing in stock is like betting on a horse race. Investors want to pick the best stock. To do so, they use financial ratios to compare the performances of companies.

Liquidity Ratios

As we discussed earlier, a company must have the cash necessary to pay its bills when they are due. A company can pay its bills if it has enough cash on hand, of course, or it can generate cash quickly by selling its products in inventory or collecting on its accounts receivable. Liquidity ratios measure a company's ability to pay its bills when they are due. They are an important short-term measure of company performance. Two important liquidity ratios are the current ratio and quick ratio.

CURRENT RATIO   The current ratio is a test of a company's solvency—its ability to pay off liabilities that will come due within one year. The ratio is a rough measure of whether the company's cash on hand, plus the cash generated from its accounts receivable, plus the cash it will receive from the sale of its product inventory to customers in the coming year are sufficient to pay for the liabilities that must be paid that year. The current ratio is calculated as follows:

$$\text{Current Assets / Current Liabilities = Current Ratio}$$
$$(\text{Dick's } 275.3 / 220.2 = 1.25)$$

A company with a 2/1 current ratio has twice the current assets (for example, cash, accounts receivable, and inventory) it needs to pay its current liabilities (accounts payable, accrued expenses payable, and so forth). This company is in a very safe, comfortable position. A company with a 1/2 ratio might be close to going bankrupt. Dick's with 1.25 can cover its current liabilities but seems to have less of a safety cushion. As the opening case describes, however, Dick's also has excellent inventory turnover, which means cash is coming in fast but also being used quickly to purchase more inventory. Nonetheless, the cash is being put to good use and not just sitting in a bank. This is why Dick's current ratio is not very high. However, this is not a problem.

QUICK RATIO   The quick ratio is a more stringent test than the current ratio of a company's solvency. This test excludes a company's inventory from consideration because it might be impossible to sell that inventory. For example, a company might make too much of a product and then have to sell it to customers at a steep loss. The quick ratio is calculated as:

$$\text{Cash + Receivables / Current Liabilities = Quick Ratio}$$
$$(\text{Dick's } 11.1 + 16.4 / 220.2 = .125)$$

A ratio above 1.0 means a company can pay off its current liabilities. When this ratio falls below 0.5, this might sound an alarm, but once again, it is necessary to look at a company's entire financial picture. Dick's has a very low quick ratio, but this is because it is continually converting its cash into store inventory, which is then sold to generate more cash to buy more inventory, and so on. Dick's is constantly putting its *working capital* (which includes its cash and inventory) to good use.

Asset Management Ratios

Assets are the engine of a company's value-creation activities. The question that interests stockholders is how efficiently and effectively managers are putting them to use to generate revenue and profit. Asset management ratios, however, do not measure how much profit is generated. Rather, they measure whether or not managers have constructed the elements of a company's business model to give it a "bigger engine" than its competitors to create profits. In other words, these ratios measure if a company has the ability to *efficiently* generate increasing profits over time. Indeed, asset management ratios are commonly viewed as measures of operating efficiency.

INVENTORY TURNOVER RATIO   We discussed how Dick's quick inventory turnover was a source of the company's competitive strength. Inventory, of course, is the stock of products a company has on hand in anticipation of future sales. The longer the inventory goes unsold, the higher is its "carrying" cost—the expense of owning it. Also, the longer it goes unsold, the more likely products in inventory are to become obsolete as other companies introduce better products. The inventory turnover ratio measures how quickly inventory is being shipped and sold. It is calculated as follows:

inventory turnover ratio A measure of how quickly a firm's inventory is being sold.

$$\text{Cost of Goods Sold / Inventory = Inventory Turnover}$$
$$(\text{Dick's } 935.2 / 233.5 = 4.0)$$

A company like Dick's with an inventory ratio of 4.0 turns over its inventory four times each year, that is, around every 91 days (365 days/4 = 91 days). A high inventory turnover ratio indicates that the company's products are very attractive. Higher sales revenues are being generated, and the firm's carrying costs of holding the inventory are lower. Lower expenses also imply higher profitability. As an investor, to see how this gives Dick's a competitive advantage, you could compare this figure to those of Dick's competitors. As we discussed in the opening case, Dick's much faster inventory turnover means it is operating more effectively and efficiently than its competitors.

asset turnover ratio
A measure of how well a company's assets are turned over or being put to use to generate sales.

ASSET TURNOVER RATIO   The asset turnover ratio is a measure of how well a company's assets are turned over or being put to use to generate sales. The higher the sales the better, because this means a company's assets are being better utilized. Imagine you have a bread truck that can deliver 1,000 loaves of bread a day, but then you find a way to use it to deliver 5,000 loaves of bread a day. In this case, you have made a much better (more efficient) use of the money you have invested in the truck. Asset turnover is calculated as:

$$\text{Sales / Total Assets = Asset Turnover}$$
$$\text{(Dick's 1,272.6 / 276.2 = 4.6)}$$

An asset turnover ratio of 4.6 is very high; it shows that Dick's is using its capital very efficiently to purchase the assets (mainly its inventory of sporting goods but also its information technology, and so on) to generate cash. Companies like Dick's that are growing their sales rapidly are those that achieve a high asset turnover ratio–one more sign of their high performance.

Profitability Ratios

Many different profitability ratios can be used to measure a company's financial performance. Each ratio relates a company's profits to some other piece of financial information such as sales, equity, or total capital to measure how effectively a company's business model is generating profit and cash. We discuss four profitability ratios below: gross margin ratio, return on sales, return of equity, and return on

Video Small Business in Action

Franchising

Franchising is a more expedient way of self-ownership according to the *Business Week* TV video on your Student DVD. Purchasing a franchise as a way to go into business for oneself has fewer barriers than attempting a new start-up small business. A franchise is a proven system with considerable support for the franchisee. Front-end expenses vary. Some franchises can require substantial fees where others have significantly lower annual costs.

Just Dogs Gourmet is the featured franchise for the segment. The franchise fee is approximately $65,000 per year; however, the owner indicates that their gross sales will exceed $200,000 this year. The second part of the segment features an interview with Rieva Lesonsky, the editor of *Entrepreneur Magazine*. She reinforces the observation that financing a franchise through a small business loan is relatively easier than other business start-ups. They are "known" systems and with SBA Loans, the federal government guarantees the loan. The franchise fee is only one part of the franchise agreement. Royalty payments to the franchisor range between 8 and 15% of gross sales.

As in any small business venture, the individual must have a passion and love for the business. The top 5 Franchises are (1) Subway, (2) Curves, (3) Quiznos, (4) Jackson Hewitt Tax Service and (5) UPS Store.

Discussion Questions

1. What type of expense would the franchise fee be considered? What about the royalty payment?
2. What type of financial statements would be needed for the small business owner who runs a franchise? Would these financial statements be shared?
3. Why would a manager (owner) of a franchise small business have to manage his/her business model?

invested capital (ROIC). Unlike the other financial ratios discussed above, profitability ratios are multiplied by 100 and expressed as a percentage, for example, a 24% return on sales.

GROSS MARGIN   Starting at the top of a company's income statement an important ratio is gross margin, which is calculated as:

$$\textbf{Gross Profit (or Sales − COGS)/ Sales} \times \textbf{100} = \textbf{Gross Margin}$$
$$\textbf{(Dick's 337.4 / 1272.6} \times \textbf{100} = \textbf{26.51)}$$

gross margin A measure of how much of each sales dollar is left over after a firm pays for the cost of goods sold.

When gross profit is divided by sales, gross margin indicates how much of each sales dollar is left over after paying for the cost of goods sold. Another way of putting this is that gross margin measures how much profit can be potentially earned after a company has paid for the costs of goods sold. Thus, the higher the gross margin, the more likely a company is to earn higher profits–after it has paid all of its expenses. In some industries like the supermarket industry, the gross margin can be 5% or less. In the home video game industry, it might be 90%. This means, that, in general, companies in the video game industry have a greater potential to earn profits than those in the supermarket industry. Figure 14.4 illustrates how much potential profit is left once the cost of goods has been paid for.

Managers and investors like to see a high gross margin because it indicates better cash flow and profit. In Dick's case, investors can see that its managers have worked successfully to improve its gross margin over time. Relatively small improvements in gross margin, in fact, can lead to a big increase in a company's gross profit. Suppose a business has a gross margin of 5% in one period and 7% in another on sales of $20 million. In the first period, the company made $1 million in gross profit. In the second, it made $1.4 million. In other words, a 2% difference in gross margin resulted in $400,000 in additional gross profit! Figure 14.5 illustrates how Dick's gross margins have increased over time.

profit margin A measure of how much profit a company generates from its sales.

PROFIT MARGIN   Profit margin, also called *return on sales* (ROS), measures how much profit a company generates from its sales. It differs from gross margin because *all costs and expenses* are deducted from sales to determine net income (profit), and then the net income is divided by sales. The result is the "profit margin." Sometimes it is tempting to assume that because a company has high sales, it has high profits, but look at Figure 14.6. As you can see, Sport's Authority has the highest sales but lowest profits of the four biggest sports retailers.

The profit margin is useful when investors are trying to compare the relative performance of companies of different sizes (like Wal-Mart and the small retail store in

**Figure 14.4
A Look at Gross
Margin**

Figure 14.5
Dick's Gross
Margin

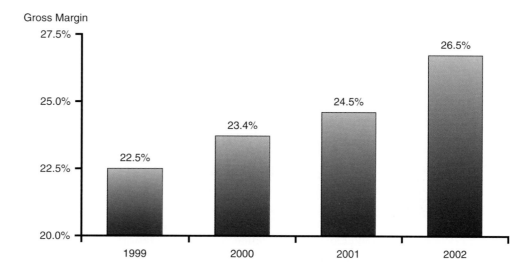

Figure 14.6

Sales and Net Income of Four Major Sports Retailers, 2002 ($ in millions)

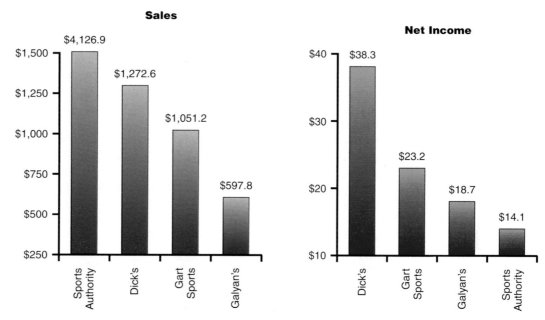

Montana we mentioned earlier in the chapter). The profit margin controls for this by showing how much profit (net income) a company earns on each $100 of sales. Profit margin is calculated as follows:

Net Income / Sales × 100 = Return on Sales (ROS)
(Dick's 38.3 / 1272.6 × 100 = 3%)

The profit margin indicates how much profit was earned on each $100 of sales after *all* expenses and costs are subtracted from sales. Dick's 3% profit margin tells managers they are making $3 in profit on each $100 of sales–much higher than its competitors.

Like the gross margin, a small change in a firm's profit margin can have a big impact. Suppose a business has a 2% profit margin in one period and 3% in the next period on sales of $500 million. In the first period, the company will therefore have made $10 million in profit; in the second, it will have made $15 million. In other words, a 1% increase in ROS resulted in a $5 million (50%) increase in profit! A 5–10% profit margin is common in many industries, although some like the supermarket industry have very low ones, around 1–3%. However, they make up for it by selling billions of dollars of products every year. For example, in 2004, Kroger's profit margin was less than 2%, but its net income was $1.2 billion on sales of $52 billion.

For the first half of 2003, Dick's reported an increase in return on sales, or profit margin, from 3 to 3.6%. If Dick's were to have sustained the 3.6% ratio for the entire year, the result would have been a 20% growth in profit. In fact, Dick's did achieve this! Business in Action, by contrast, describes how profit margins have been shrinking in the funeral business and how one company is dealing with the problem.

Business in Action

Shrinking Margins in the Funeral Industry

Service Corp. International, based in Houston, Texas, is the world's largest funeral-services company. But in recent years, Service Corp. has run into trouble. Between 1998 and 2003, for example, its stock price plummeted, falling from $47 to just $4! (The price has since recovered to about $9 per share.) One reason for the company's troubles was due to $4 billion it borrowed to fund an ambitious expansion plan to take over funeral home chains in countries around the world. Today, however, a large part of its problem is due to shrinking profit margins in the funeral business.

Consider this, however: By 2025, the annual number of deaths in the United States is expected to hit 3 million—up 25% from 2003 because of the aging of the baby boom generation. This might seem like a positive development for Service Corp. because it suggests that its revenues could potentially soar by 25%. But things are changing in the funeral business. More and more baby boomers wish to be cremated rather than buried, and the average cremation costs 55% less than the average burial costs. In addition, whereas the number of people choosing to be cremated was only 30% in the 1990s, that figure is expected to rise to almost 50% by 2025. As a result, the profit margins involved in the funeral business are shrinking rapidly, too, from well above 60 to 70% a decade ago, to less than 50% today, and perhaps only to 30 to 40% in the future.

One strategy Service Corp. is using to increase its profit margins is increasing the range of products and services it offers to customers.

This spells big trouble for Service Corp. unless it can find a way to increase its sales revenues. One strategy the company is pursuing involves increasing the range of products and services it offers customers to get its profit margins back up. Today, all of Service Corp.'s funeral homes offer far more than caskets and flowers. In a sense, they are getting into the "entertainment business." Every funeral is now videotaped, and tapes are available for sale as mourners leave the chapels. The company also arranges funeral receptions at the homes of bereaved families, and increasingly in places like local art museums and zoos. It also provides all the food and beverages for these funeral receptions. Finally, its in-house travel agency arranges discounted flights for relatives and friends attending the funeral.

By providing all these extra services, Service Corp. can double the revenues it obtains from a cremation and, of course, increase the revenues it can earn from burials as well. As long as it can keep its cost of goods sold and other expenses under control, it hopes that the result will be increasing profit margins in the funeral business in the years ahead.[5]

return on equity A measure of how much profit a company has earned on each $100 of stockholders' equity invested in the business.

RETURN ON EQUITY AND EARNINGS PER SHARE   Return on equity (ROE), sometimes called return on investment (ROI), tells managers and investors how much profit a company has earned on each $100 invested by stockholders in the business. The higher the return on equity, the more a company's managers are adding to the value of its owners' investment, which is why it is sometimes called *return on investment.* ROI is calculated as:

$$\text{Net Income / Owners' Equity} \times 100 = \text{Return on Equity (ROE)}$$
$$(\text{Dick's } 38.3 / 140.5 \times 100 = 27.25)$$

Dick's has a very high ROE, which is not surprising in view of the efficient way it is using capital to generate cash and profit. Its ROE is well ahead of its major competitors and one reason why its stock is so attractive to investors.

Another measure that stockholders use to determine how well their company is building the value of their capital is earnings per share calculated as:

$$\text{Net Income / Total Number of Shares} = \text{Earnings Per Share}$$
$$(\text{Dick's } 38.3 / 20.25 = \$1.89)$$

earnings per share A measure of how much profit a company has earned for each share of its stock issued.

Instead of dividing by the value of the owners' equity in the balance sheet, this ratio divides by the number of shares the company has issued. The earnings per share tells stockholders now know how much profit a company has earned for each share of its stock. Dick's, for example, earned $1.89 per share, a very large amount given that its stock was trading in the $20 range. Once again, these measures are useful in making a comparison across time, and across companies, to evaluate how well a company's managers are making use of its capital to generate profit.

return on invested capital A measure of how much profit a company generates for each dollar invested in its business.

RETURN ON INVESTED CAPITAL   Today, most financial analysts believe return on invested capital (ROIC) is the best measure of a company's profitability. ROIC allows managers and investors to measure how much extra cash, or profit, a company generates for each dollar that is invested in its business. The more cash generated per dollar of investment, the greater is a company's profitability. ROIC tells an investor how efficiently *and* effectively a company is being run; indeed ROIC is often viewed as a measure of management's effectiveness.

A company's ROIC is calculated by dividing its net income, or profit, by the *total capital* invested in the business. Total capital includes both a company's liabilities (minus noninterest bearing current liabilities) *and* its owners' equity. Note ROE just measures how well a company uses equity capital to generate profit; it ignores the capital a company borrows from creditors. Thus, it is a less-accurate performance measure. The formula used to calculate ROIC is:

**Figure 14.7
Return on Capital
Income, 2002**

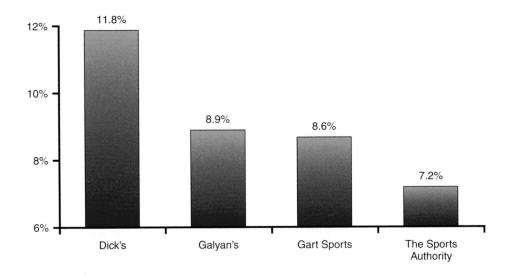

**Net Income / Total Capital = Return on Invested Capital
(Dick's 38.3 / 376.2 × 100 = 11.8% (adjusted)**

Dick's ROIC is 11.8% (which has been adjusted for specific business factors), which, as Figure 14.7 illustrates, is the highest of its competitors and the strongest indicator of its ability to generate profit and cash.

Another way to use ROIC to evaluate Dick's performance is to compare it to leading companies who operate in different segments of the retail industry, like the office supply, retail-book industry, and so on. Figure 14.8 shows how Dick's compared against other "best-in-class" retailers, that is, those who are the top performers in other segments of the U.S. retail market. As you can see, Dick's ranks in the middle of this group, indicating that the company is performing well relative to the best U.S. retailers. This is another reason why Dick's stock is viewed by many as being a very good investment. In general, the higher the ROIC, the more valuable is a company, and the higher will be its stock price. This is why the price of Dick's stock has soared.

What has been happening in the sporting goods industry since the early 2000s, is one reason why it's extremely important to look at and analyze a company's numbers using financial ratios. What changes would you expect the strongest and weakest companies in the industry to make to their business models to improve their future financial performance?

**Figure 14.8
ROIC Best-in-Class
Retailers, 2002**

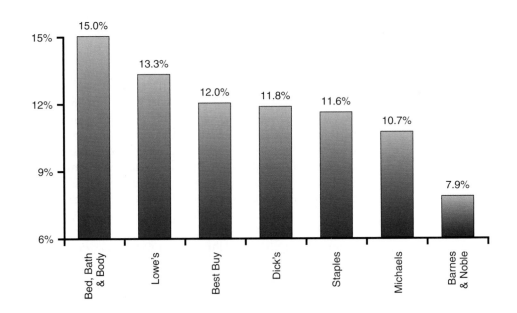

In 2003, Galyan's ran into cash flow problems because it expanded too rapidly. As a result, its stock price fell. Dick's saw an opportunity to acquire a company with a strong business model at a favorable price and made a successful takeover offer for Galyan's. Galyan's stores have now been integrated into Dick's store chain, and Dick's now has a stronger U.S. presence because it has more sporting goods stores in more cities. The result for Dick's has been increasing profitability.

Also in 2003, the two weakest chains, the Sports Authority and Garts, decided to merge in an effort to reduce their operating costs and improve their performance. So far the merged company, which kept the Sports Authority name, has not seen much improvement in its performance as measured by financial ratios. Combining the two less-efficient companies into one did not allow them to match Dick's performance. The merged company still does not have the strong business model that Dick's has. In the future, comparing the financial ratios of the leading sporting goods companies will tell the story about whether their business models are resulting in a competitive advantage and increasing profitability.

Summary of the Chapter

As this chapter suggests, the figures in a company's financial statements may look cut-and-dried, but they can tell an interesting story about why some companies are more profitable than others. The accounting function plays a major role when it comes to providing managers with the information they need to build and sustain a successful business model. All the different financial ratios used to measure performance highlight different aspects of a company's performance. They all point to better ways that value can be created and a company's performance improved. This chapter made the following major points:

1. Accounting is the process of (1) collecting, measuring, and recording raw financial data; (2) organizing this data using agreed-upon accounting rules and methods to create useful information about a company's financial performance; and (3) analyzing this information and communicating the results of this analysis in financial reports and statements.

2. All of a company's stakeholders are vitally interested in the financial statements that result from the work of the accounting function—and the manner in which accountants follow agreed-upon accounting rules and standards to prepare those statements. The information provided in these statements allows both inside and outside stakeholders to evaluate its performance.

3. To ensure that a company reports financial information in an accurate and honest way, all U.S. companies must prepare their financial statements according to generally accepted accounting principles (GAAP), a set of rules and procedures developed over time by accounting experts.

4. Companies employ two kinds of accountants—inside and outside accountants. Internal accountants called auditors scrutinize the financial data used to prepare the company's accounts to ensure revenue and expense figures are accurately reported in accordance with GAAP. External auditors then evaluate the accuracy of the work performed by the company's internal auditors to ensure they reported the firm's financial statements in a way that provides a true picture of its operating performance.

5. The three main kinds of financial statement are a company's balance sheet (or statement of financial condition), its income statement, and its statement of cash flows.

6. The balance sheet is a summary of the financial position of a business at the end of the day of a specific reporting period, such as December 31, 2003. The balance sheet reports the main types of assets owned by a company, its liabilities or what it owes, and its stockholders' equity or what it is worth. This is why the balance sheet is sometimes referred to as a statement of financial condition. The basic equation of accounting is that what a company owns, minus what it owes, is what it is worth or Assets – Liabilities = Owners' Equity.

7. The purpose of the income statement is to summarize and report the results of a company's profit-making activities in a specific time period (hence, it is sometimes called the profit and loss statement). The basic equation used to compute a company's bottom-line profit, the amount of net income or profit a company reports on the bottom line of its income statement, is Revenues – Expenses = Profit(or Loss).

8. A company's cash flow must be managed to ensure the firm's short-term and long-term survival. The statement of cash flows shows how much cash a

company generates during a specific financial period, where it came from, and how the company used it. In accounting, cash refers to the value of a company's assets that can be converted into cash immediately.

9. Together, the balance sheet, the income statement, and the statement of cash flows provide stakeholders with the information they need to analyze a company's financial situation and the way in which its assets, liabilities, equity, profit, and cash are increasing or decreasing.

10. Financial ratios are useful because they benchmark the company's performance (1) over time and (2) against the performance of other companies.

11. The three main types of financial ratios used to calculate a company's performance are liquidity ratios, asset management ratios, and profitability ratios.

12. Liquidity ratios measure a company's ability to pay its bills when they are due; they are a vital short-term measure of a company performance. Two important liquidity ratios are the current ratio and quick ratio.

13. Asset management ratios do not measure how much profit or cash is generated; they measure whether or not managers have created a business model that will give it the ability to efficiently generate increasing profits over time.

14. Several different profitability ratios can be used to measure a company's financial performance. Each ratio relates a company's profits to some other piece of financial information such as sales or equity to measure how effectively managers are using a company's capital to create profit and cash.

15. Return on invested capital (ROIC) is the ratio most financial analysts use to get a good picture of a company's present and future profitability. A company's ROIC is calculated by dividing its net income or profit by the total capital invested in the business.

Developing Business Skills

QUESTIONS FOR DISCUSSION AND ACTION

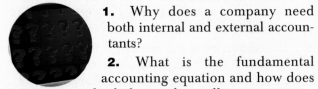

1. Why does a company need both internal and external accountants?

2. What is the fundamental accounting equation and how does the balance sheet allow a company and its stakeholders to keep track of its financial transactions?

3. What are the main types of a company's assets, and what are its liabilities and stockholders' equity?

4. What is the main purpose of the income statement? What is the difference between gross profit and bottom-line profit?

5. Why is it vital that a company pay attention to both its profits (income) and cash flows? Why is profit not the same as cash?

6. Why are financial ratios used to analyze the information contained in a company's financial statements?

7. What different kinds of knowledge do (a) liquidity (b) asset management and (c) profitability ratios tell stakeholders about a company's performance?

8. What is the difference between a gross margin and a profit margin?

9. Why is return on invested capital the best measure of a company's operating efficiency and effectiveness?

ETHICS IN ACTION

Cooking the Books

As the chapter discusses, top managers and their external auditors sometimes act unethically and illegally to manipulate the figures in a company's financial statements. Their goal is to convince stakeholders that the company's business model is generating more profit and cash than it really is to protect the company's stock price. The SEC proposed limiting the length of the auditing relationship between a company and a Big Four accounting firm to five years to try to prevent such unethical and illegal behavior from occurring. Using the ethical principles discussed in Chapter 5, consider the following issues:

- What do managers stand to gain by "cooking" a company's books?

- How does cooking the books harm other stakeholder groups? What effect does it have on (a) stockholders, (b) employees, and (c) society?

- Do you think a five-year time limit on an auditing relationship is a good way of preventing accounting abuses?

- What other kinds of methods could be used to prevent managers from engaging in unethical kinds of accounting practices?

SMALL GROUP EXERCISE

Rising Sales but Falling Profits

Read the following and then break up into groups of three or four people and discuss the issues involved. Be prepared to share your discussion with the rest of your class.

You are the top managers of a company that used to enjoy growing profit margins and increasing profitability. However, in the last two years, it has become clear that your company's business model is not working. Although your sales are still increasing, your profitability is declining. You are meeting to try to discover the source of the problem.

1. What kinds of information in the company's financial statements will be most helpful to you as you search for a solution?

2. Which of the financial ratios discussed in the chapter will help you the most in understanding the source of the problem?

3. Based on your analysis, what steps should you take to turn around your company's performance?

DEVELOPING GOOD BUSINESS SENSE

Comparing Dick's to the Sports Authority

One way of learning the language and methods of accounting is to go through the calculations involved in creating the financials used to analyze a company's financial statements. Since we have used Dick's as our running example throughout the chapter, a useful exercise is to compare its current performance against its main competitor, the Sports Authority, which had higher sales but lower profitability.

1. Go to the Sports Authority's Web site and Dick's Web site and print out each company's three current financial statements. Also, examine their annual reports on their Web sites to get a feel for how these companies' business models work.

2. Calculate each of the ratios that were discussed in the last part of the chapter for the Sports Authority.

3. Compare these ratios to those of Dick's and describe what the differences mean.

4. On the basis of this analysis, try to identify the major differences between the business models of the two companies that led to these financial results. Also, if time permits, try to collect more information about the companies that will help you get at the principal reasons for their different levels of performance.

5. On the basis of this analysis, which company would you invest your own money in?

EXPLORING THE WORLD WIDE WEB

A Career at PwC?

Go to the Web site of PricewaterhouseCoopers (www.pwc.com), the accounting giant. This site offers not only a wealth of information on accounting issues but also on career issues. Click on "Careers," select "USA" from the pull-down list, and then click on "Campus Candidates." Take the quiz to identify whether or not you might be suited to a job in accounting and look at the other career information the Web site offers. **For more Web activities, log on to www.mhhe.com/jonesintro.**

1. Do you think a job in accounting would suit you? Why or why not?

BusinessWeek   CASE FOR DISCUSSION

Fuzzy Numbers

Construction giant and military contractor Halliburton Co. did something mind-boggling last year: It reported earnings of $339 million, even though it spent $775 million more than it took in from customers. The company did nothing illegal. Halliburton made big outlays in 2003 on contracts with the U.S. Army for work in Iraq–contracts for which it expected to be paid later. Still, it counted some of these expected revenues immediately because they related to work done last year. Investors didn't get the full picture until six weeks later, when the company filed its complete annual report with the Securities & Exchange Commission. Halliburton says it followed generally accepted accounting principles (GAAP).

Maybe so, but after three years of reforms in the wake of corporate scandals, the Halliburton case illustrates that earnings remain as susceptible to manipulation as ever. Why? Because accounting rules give companies wide discretion in using estimates to calculate their earnings. These adjustments are supposed to give shareholders a more accurate picture of what's happening in a business at a given time, and often they do. Bean counters call this accrual accounting, and they have practiced it for decades. By accruing, or allotting, revenues to specific periods, they aim to allocate income to the quarter or year in which it was effectively earned, though not necessarily received. Likewise, expenses are allocated to the period when sales were made, not necessarily when the money was spent.

The problem with today's fuzzy earnings numbers is not accrual accounting itself. It's that investors, analysts, and money managers are having an increasingly hard time figuring out what judgments companies make to come up with those accruals, or estimates. The scandals at Enron, WorldCom, Adelphia Communications, and other companies are forceful reminders that investors could lose billions by not paying attention to how companies arrive at their earnings. The hazards were underscored again when mortgage-finance giant Fannie Mae said its primary regulator had found that it had made accounting adjustments to dress-up its earnings and, in at least one case, achieve bonus compensation targets. The company said it is cooperating with government investigators. The broader concern is that corporate financial statements are often incomplete, inconsistent, or just plain unclear, making it a nightmare to sort out fact from fantasy. Says Trevor S. Harris, chief accounting analyst at Morgan Stanley: "The financial reporting system is completely broken."

Indeed, today's financial reports are more difficult to understand than ever. They're riddled with jargon that's hard to fathom and numbers that don't track. They're muddled, with inconsistent categories, vague entries, and hidden adjustments that disguise how much various estimates change a company's earnings from quarter to quarter, says Donn Vickrey, a former accounting professor and co-founder of Camelback Research Alliance Inc., a Scottsdale, Arizona, firm hired by institutional investors to detect inflated earnings.

The upshot: The three major financial statements–income, balance sheet, and cash flow–that investors and analysts need to detect aggressive accounting and get a full picture of a company's value are out of sync with one another. Often, the income and cash-flow statements don't even cover the same time periods. "A genius has trouble trying to get them to tie together because different items are aggregated differently," says Patricia Doran Walters, director of research at CFA Institute, the professional association that tests and certifies financial analysts. "You have to do an enormous amount of guessing to even come close."

Many of the reforms adopted by Congress and the SEC will not remedy the situation. Most are aimed at policing the people who make the estimates rather than the estimates themselves. And some changes have yet to go into effect. No doubt, chief executives and auditing committees are paying closer attention to the numbers, and accounting experts believe there are fewer instances these days of outright fraud. But that's to be expected in a stronger economy. The big question is whether increased scrutiny is yielding more realistic estimates or just more estimates documented by reams of assumptions and rationalizations. We'll only know the answer when the economy begins to falter and corporate earnings come under pressure.

Already, recent academic research suggests that the abuse of accrual accounting is pervasive across a broad swath of companies. And it's enough to goad Wall Street into action. Aware that executives have tremendous opportunity to manipulate the numbers through their estimates, the market is on alert, delving more vigorously than ever into the estimates that go into compiling earnings. Over the past two years, investment banks have beefed up their already complex computer programs to screen thousands of companies to find the cheerleaders who make very aggressive estimates.

As analysts and investors drill deeper into these financials, they're finding some nasty surprises. Accounting games are spreading beyond earnings reports as some companies start to play fast and loose with the way they account for cash flows. That's a shocker because investors always believed cash was sacrosanct and hard to trump up. Now they're discovering that cash is just as vulnerable to legal manipulation as earnings. Companies from Lucent Technologies Inc. to Jabil Circuit Inc. have boosted their cash flow by selling their receivables–what customers owe them–to third parties. Says Charles W. Mulford, accounting professor at Georgia Tech's DuPree College of Management and author of an upcoming book on faulty cash reporting: "Corporate managers, knowing what analysts are looking at, say: 'Let's make the cash flow look better.' So the game goes on." A Lucent spokesman says it sells receivables to raise cash more cheaply than it could by borrowing the money. Jabil did not respond to questions.

Even with Wall Street's heightened scrutiny, many pros think the situation won't improve anytime soon–and it may well get worse. That's because accounting standard-setters at the Financial Accounting Standards Board (FASB) are deep into a drive to require companies to make even more estimates–increasing the potential for further manipulation of their bottom lines. One example: It's requiring companies to estimate changes in the value of a growing list of assets and liabilities, including trade names and one-of-a-kind derivative contracts. Eventually, companies will have to make corresponding adjustments, up or down, to their earnings.

There's some logic in FASB's position. It wants to improve the way changes in the value of corporate assets are reflected in financial statements because they can have a significant impact on a company's value. FASB argues the new estimates should be reliable since many will be based on known market prices. Unfortunately, others will rest on little more than educated guesses that in turn depend on a lot of other assumptions. "When you do that, you reduce the reliability of the numbers, and you open up the doors to fraud," says Ross L. Watts, accounting professor at the William E. Simon Graduate School of Business Administration at the University of Rochester.

FASB is understandably gun-shy about imposing even more rules on businesses. It has spent the last three years, and lots of political capital, trying to put in place requirements to expense the cost of stock options and to limit off-balance-sheet arrangements. But it has come up short by not insisting on financial statements that show in a simple way what judgments have gone into the estimates. FASB Chairman Robert H. Herz doesn't feel any urgency to do so.

He argues that investors and analysts aren't yet using all the information they now have. Besides, he adds, he doesn't want to pile too many new requirements on companies. After the recent reforms, Herz says: "Right now, [they] are very tired."

Tired, maybe, but not tired enough to renounce numbers games. Even among execs who wouldn't dream of committing fraud, there are plenty who are ready to tweak their numbers in an effort to please investors. In a Duke University survey of 401 corporate financial executives in November, 2003, two out of five said they would use legal ways to book revenues early if that would help them meet earnings targets. More than one in five would adjust certain estimates or sell investments to book higher income. Faulty accounting estimates by execs caused at least half of the 323 restatements of financial reports last year, according to Huron Consulting Group.

The cost of this obfuscation is high. According to studies of 40 years of data by Richard G. Sloan of the University of Michigan Business School and Scott Richardson of the University of Pennsylvania's Wharton School, the companies making the largest estimates–and thus reporting the most overstated earnings– initially attract investors like moths to a flame. Later, when the estimates prove overblown, their stocks flounder. They lag, on average, stocks of similar-sized companies by 10 percentage points a year, costing investors more than $100 billion in market returns. These companies also have higher incidences of earnings restatements, SEC enforcement actions, and accounting-related lawsuits, notes Neil Baron, chairman of Criterion Research Group, a New York researcher where Richardson consults. "Given the pressure on executives to reach expected earnings, it is not surprising," says Baron.

That's why more portfolio managers are using sophisticated screening to identify companies that make aggressive estimates and those that don't. Sloan and Richardson discovered that if you had sold short the companies with the biggest estimates and bought those with the smallest, you would have beaten the market 37 out of 40 years and by a huge margin–18 percentage points a year before trading costs. Now, Goldman Sachs Asset Management, Barclays Global Investors, and Susquehanna Financial Group, among others, are employing versions of the Sloan-Richardson models to guide their investments. Strategists at brokerages, including Sanford C. Bernstein Research, Credit Suisse First Boston, and UBS have built model portfolios using similar techniques.

Others on Wall Street seek an edge by going even further: They're deconstructing and rebuilding companies' financial reports. Morgan Stanley's Harris recently led an 18-month project aimed at filtering out the effects of accounting rules that can distort results from operations. His team gathered some 2.5 million data points and held countless discussions with analysts of individual companies. In an early test, the exercise determined that Verizon Communications Inc.'s pretax operating profit in 2003 was $13.7 billion rather than the $16.2 billion Morgan Stanley's star telecom analyst had first calculated using GAAP. That's mainly because GAAP allows companies to include estimates for what their pension plans will earn as current profits. A Verizon spokesman said the company has been careful to disclose its assumptions and tell investors how much its pension accounting boosts earnings.

Here are some of the ways companies can legally use accounting rules to inflate—or deflate—the earnings and cash flow they report:

ESTIMATE SALES With the stroke of a pen, companies can use estimates that make it appear as though sales and earnings are growing faster than they really are. Or, if they fear lean times ahead, they can create a cookie jar of revenues they can report later. Hospital companies, such as Health Management Associates Inc., report revenues after estimating discounts they will give to insurers and for charity cases. These discounts are typically two-thirds of list price, so a slight change in what HMA figures they will cost could have a large impact on its income. Vice President for Financial Relations John C. Merriwether says the company uses conservative estimates.

Getting the revenue right isn't easy. Computer software vendor IMPAC Medical Systems Inc. says three different auditors gave differing opinions on when it could count revenue from certain contracts that included yet-to-be-delivered products. Its latest auditor, Deloitte & Touche, resigned just 10 weeks into the job after declaring that the company had counted revenue from 40 contracts too soon. IMPAC Chairman and CEO Joseph K. Jachinowski says he's asking the SEC how to book the contracts.

PREDICT BAD DEBTS How companies account for customers' bad debts can have a huge impact on earnings. Each quarter they set aside reserves for loan losses—essentially guesses of how much money owed by deadbeats is unlikely to be paid. The lower the estimate, the higher the earnings. On July 21, credit-card issuer Capital One Financial Corp. reported quarterly results that would have been 3 cents a share below Wall Street estimates had it not reduced its reserves, says David A. Hendler, an analyst at researcher CreditSights. Capital One CFO Gary L. Perlin says the company made the change because it is lending to more credit-worthy customers now.

Sometimes companies on opposite sides of the same deal use different estimates. An example: Reinsurance companies have reserves of about $104 bil-

lion to pay claims they expect from property-and-casualty insurers. But the P&C insurers have booked $128 billion in payments they expect to receive from the reinsurers, according to Bijan Moazami, an insurance-industry analyst at Friedman, Billings, Ramsey Group Inc. He says the property-and-casualty companies will cut earnings as it becomes clear they won't collect all the money. Hartford Financial Services Group Inc. and St. Paul Travelers Cos. took such charges this spring, of $118 million and at least $164 million after taxes, respectively. The Hartford said it acted after reviewing its reinsurance arrangements. A St. Paul Travelers spokesman says: "We are comfortable with our estimates."

ADJUST INVENTORY By changing the costs they estimate for inventory that will be obsolete before it can be sold, companies can give their earnings a substantial boost. Vitesse Semiconductor Corp. took inventory expenses of $30.5 million in 2002 and $46.5 million in 2001. In 2003, it took no expenses but wrote off $7.4 million against a previously established reserve for obsolete inventory. Had it not tapped its reserves, the $7.4 million would have come out of current earnings, notes Terry Baldwin, an accounting analyst at researcher Glass Lewis & Co. Instead, Vitesse was able to report earnings of about 2 cents a share more than it could have otherwise. Vitesse's vice president for finance, Yatin Mody, says the company properly counted the costs in 2002 when it foresaw that the goods were likely to become obsolete because of the telecom bust.

Inventory accounting can produce even more bizarre outcomes. Last year, General Motors Co. reported an extra $200 million in pretax income after using up more inventory than it replaced. In standard last-in, first-out inventory accounting, when the older and less costly goods are sold at today's prices, profits look better. But GM's future earnings could be hit if it needs to replace inventory at higher prices. GM says it properly applied accounting rules to its inventory management.

FORECAST UNUSUAL GAINS OR LOSSES The ability to time big and unusual gains or expenses can give companies plenty of control over their numbers. For 2003, Nortel Networks Corp. reported an earnings rebound when it reversed a portion of the $18.4 billion in charges it had logged for restructuring costs, bad customer debts, and obsolete inventory in the preceding three years. But last April, the company said it "terminated for cause" its chief executive, its chief financial officer, and its controller amid an ongoing review and restatement of financial reports. In August, Nortel said it had fired seven more finance officers. Now the company says it had paid out $10 million in executive bonuses based on the trumped-up rebound. Nortel's new managers say they're trying to get the money back and that an independent panel "is examining the circumstances leading to the requirement for the restatements."

MASSAGE CASH Because analysts and investors are focusing on cash flow from operations as an indicator of financial health, those numbers are now a prime target for massaging. Companies have had to report cash flows since 1988, classifying them into one of three categories: operating, investing, and financing. By exploiting loopholes in GAAP rules, they can make their operating cash look a heap better. For example, in their consolidated financial statements, Boeing, Ford, and Harley-Davidson count as cash from operations the proceeds of sales of planes, cars, and bikes that customers bought with money they borrowed from the companies' wholly owned finance subsidiaries. As a result, cash from operations is higher, even though the companies didn't rake in any more of it. In its quarter through March, Boeing Co. reported $268 million in cash from operations that actually reflected what the company classified as investments by Boeing Capital Corp. in loans to customers to buy aircraft. Without the transactions, Boeing would have reported a $363 million drain of operating cash. For all of 2003, such transactions contributed $1.7 billion of Boeing's $3.9 billion in operating cash. The company says it has been preparing its accounts this way for years, and the method conforms to GAAP rules. Boeing began disclosing the amounts in a footnote in mid-2002. Harley-Davidson Inc. Treasurer James M. Brostowitz says its loans are properly disclosed, and analysts can make adjustments as they see fit. A Ford spokesman says the company's accounting complies with GAAP and accurately reflects its business.

The simplest way for companies to pump up their cash is to sell what customers owe them to a third party. Increasingly, companies carve out these receivables from their most creditworthy customers, sell them at a discount, and then present the move as smart capital management that boosts liquidity. Such deals give analysts fits because they are really financing actions. Jabil Circuit sold some receivables in an arrangement with a bank in the two quarters ended in May. That added $120 million, or nearly half of the $275 million of operating cash flow it reported in the period. But Jabil had to sell its receivables at a discount and recognize a $400,000 loss. The company did not provide comments after repeated requests.

Some transactions just keep operating cash flows looking pretty: Companies can use excess cash to buy securities when business is booming and then harvest it by selling them when the business runs cold. In 2003, Ohio Art Co., the tiny maker of Etch-A-Sketch drawing toys, used cash from operations to buy $1.5 million worth of money market funds. It sold them

this year, boosting cash flow. CFO Jerry D. Kneipp says the company relied on its auditors in reporting the transactions. Cable company Comcast Corp. reported $85 million in additional operating cash flow in 2003 from sales of securities. Though this move was by the book, it distorted cash flow from operations. Comcast says that before 2002 it counted such proceeds as cash from investments. It changed the way it reports such deals to meet a 2002 FASB standard.

Mergers, too, can cloud the numbers. Consider again the HMA hospital chain. It regularly has a higher ratio of receivables to sales than do its peers—a red flag to analysts because it might be a sign that a company is booking more revenues than it will ever collect. But HMA's Merriwether says the high receivables are explained largely by its steady acquisitions of hospitals, about four a year. With each deal, it has to submit new paperwork to the government and private insurers and wait weeks before they will pay new patients' bills, he says. With a continuous flow of deals, says Sheryl R. Skolnick, an analyst at Fulcrum Global Partners who has recommended selling HMA's stock, "you have no idea what is going on."

One of the quickest, but most fleeting, ways companies can increase cash flow is to shrink their working capital. That can include selling off inventory, pressuring customers to pay quickly, and stalling payments to suppliers. While executives often claim that these moves make the company increasingly powerful and profitable, the opposite may actually be the case. General Dynamics Corp. , for example, boasts in its 2003 annual report that it "has proven itself an industry leader in generating strong cash flows, which have enabled it to enhance returns through strategic and tactical acquisitions and share repurchases." Cash generation was "particularly strong" in 2003, it said. But while cash flow from operations rose to $1.7 billion from $1.1 billion the year before, half of the improvement came from slashing inventories in 2003 after adding to them in 2002. While cutting inventory may make sense given the weakened market for planes, it was a one-time cash boost from downsizing a business, not a sign of strong future cash flows. A company spokesman notes that Chairman and CEO Nicholas D. Chabraja told analysts in January that while General Dynamics' cash flow may fluctuate from year to year, it has tracked earnings over the past five years, even as the company was investing for growth in other areas.

The way companies are spinning their cash flows looks to some analysts as worrisome as the press releases announcing "pro-forma" earnings that companies cultivated during the 1990's tech-stock bubble. General Motors, for example, boasted in a January press release that it had "generated" $32 billion in cash in 2003. "That's outrageous," says Marc Siegel, a senior analyst at the Center for Financial Research & Analysis. GM had actually borrowed about half of that money by issuing bonds and convertible securities. The automaker says it had explained publicly the steps it was taking to get that cash number.

Concentrating too much attention on short-term cash flows can have significant effects. It could discourage companies from making investments that could add to economic growth and boost returns on capital. "They are routinely saying 'no' to valuable projects," laments Campbell R. Harvey of Duke University's Fuqua School of Business. Some stocks, such as Computer Sciences Corp., now tend to move up when they report higher "free cash flow," a measure that looks better when companies scrimp on capital investments. CSC declined to comment. The danger, warns Morgan Stanley's Harris, is that "we can end up inducing people to make wrong economic decisions for appearance purposes. Then the investor will lose." Indeed, CFOs' desire to show high free-cash flow may be one reason corporate investment is now far below average.

THE SOLUTIONS For now, investors are left largely to their own devices to make sense of companies' numbers. Auditors—the first line of defense against financial shenanigans—are under scrutiny by a new oversight board, which is rewriting audit standards. And while the SEC's Corporation Finance Div. has started prodding companies to disclose more of their critical accounting estimates in public filings, the results so far are spotty, and many disclosures are buried in dense text. FASB is talking about revamping the income and cash flow statements, but not for at least a couple of years.

There's plenty that regulators could do now to improve the quality of financial information. FASB should put aside some of its less pressing projects and turn its full attention to making it easier for investors to get behind companies' earnings numbers. If the form and presentation of financial statements were cleaner and more consistent, investors would be better able to spot accounting tricks. For example, earnings statements could be recast to distinguish between profits that come from selling products from those that come from ever-changing estimates. "You want to understand the subjectivity involved in these different numbers," says the CFA Institute's Walters.

The statement of cash flow needs a lift, too. Regulators must change the mirror-image presentation in which increases in cash show up as negative numbers and decreases as positive. They also have to define more clearly what constitutes an operating, investing, or financing item.

And FASB should make it easier for investors to make reliable comparisons. An obvious and simple step would be for companies to present their statements of cash flows for the same periods as their earnings statements. Even better would be to show the cumulative earnings and cash flows for the previous four quarters as well. Now most companies simply compare the latest quarter's earnings with those for the same quarter a year before, but present a year-to-date statement of cash flows without a comparison. Many financial analysts rearrange company data to highlight meaningful comparisons, but they have to build special spreadsheets for the task, and they need a library of past reports to feed into them. Companies should also clearly display in tables—not just in text—the changes they make in reserves.

With better and more consistent information in financial statements, investors would be able to reward and punish companies based on the quality of their accounting. "Then [investors] would start providing some discipline by discounting stocks when they aren't sure what the numbers are going to be," says Lynn E. Turner, a former SEC chief accountant and now research director at Glass Lewis. What's more, auditors would be on increased alert knowing that investors are looking over their shoulders.

Because companies will be using even more estimates in the future, they'll have even more opportunities to hype their results. To avoid future blowups, investors need a clear picture of a corporation's finances. Investors shouldn't have to wait for another Enron for regulators to tackle these issues.

Source: David Henry, "Fuzzy Numbers," *BusinessWeek Online,* October 4, 2004.

QUESTIONS

1. What is the accrual accounting method and why is it important?

2. In what ways can companies manipulate the information in the three major financial statements to artificially inflate their company's performance?

BUILDING YOUR MANAGEMENT SKILLS
Know Thyself

Do you think you might like to be an accountant? All managers have to understand financial statements to gauge whether the plans they have implemented are succeeding. You can practice building the financial statements needed to analyze an organization's financial well-being by trying the exercises on your Student DVD titled "Income Statements" and "Balance Sheets". They are the basis of the financial ratios that provide feedback to managers.

CHAPTER VIDEO
AON

Aon Company is a financial services company that provides accounting and other financial services for a broad range of clients including insurance agencies and other large corporations. They have over 100 offices around the globe with about 9 billion dollars in annual revenue. The role of accountants in Aon is central to its business.

The video discusses managerial, financial and tax accounting and the roles that each play at Aon. The central role that accounting plays in any organization is that of organizing, categorizing and interpreting financial data. Accounting is probably the oldest business function; in fact, earliest languages were based on the recording of transactions.

The video details the six-step accounting cycle from the analysis and recording of transactions through the preparation and analysis of financial statements. The basic accounting equations such as Assets = Liabilities + equity and Revenue – COGS = Gross Margin are discussed within the context of Aon.

In addition to the traditional accounting roles offered by Aon, they provide catastrophe modeling for insurers and re-insurers in assessing the potential financial impacts of hurricanes. They also have pioneered the terrorism financial model after they lost 175 colleagues in the 9/11 disaster.

1. What is the definition of Gross Margin?

2. What is the difference between an income statement and a balance sheet?

3. Identify the steps in the accounting cycle.

15 Finance:

Balancing Risk and Return to Increase Profitability

Learning Objectives

After studying this chapter, you should be able to:

1. Appreciate the crucial relationship between risk and return and the way it affects all business finance decisions.

2. Understand short-term capital management and the tools managers use to increase the rate of return on capital.

3. Understand long-term capital management and the tools used to manage it, like net present value and breakeven analysis.

4. Describe four different methods companies can use to finance capital investments.

5. Differentiate between the roles debt and equity securities play in financial decision making.

WHY IS THIS IMPORTANT ❓

Did you have to make decisions about how to finance your college education? Have you or your parents saved enough to pay for it or do you plan to use a combination of loans, scholarships, grants, or work to pay your bills? Your education is an investment that carries some risk that you try to reduce by choosing a college, a major course of study, and working hard to get good grades. You are investing time and money to gain knowledge that will prepare you to get a better job than you could without it, but the labor market could change.

Businesses also have to take risks when they decide how to finance the business model they hope will be successful. To learn more about how managers and entrepreneurs decide how to finance their businesses and the way they balance risk with potential for earnings, read Chapter 15.

A Question of Business
First Up, Then Down at Disney

Why did Disney's financial performance first rise and then fall?

When Michael Eisner became the CEO of Walt Disney in 1984, the company was in big trouble. Despite its world famous brand name and valuable assets such as its amusement parks, movie studios, and library of famous Disney movies, the company wasn't making a profit. Indeed, Disney was losing money. Its investors wondered how this could possibly have happened to a company that had once been so successful. What had gone wrong?

Michael Eisner knew what had gone wrong. He knew from analyzing the company's financial statements that Disney wasn't making the best use of its assets to generate cash flow and profits. A company may have superior assets, but unless it has a management team that understands how to make the most use of them, their ability to create value and profit will not be realized. Eisner looked for ways to use Disney's assets more productively.

In the 1980s, the number of visitors to Walt Disney theme parks was increasing each year. Eisner realized that customers were receiving substantially more value from their visits to its theme parks than the entry price they paid, so he reasoned that the entry price could be greatly increased without losing customers. He was right. Within five years, Eisner raised park-entry prices by over 50%, with no loss of cus-

tomers, and Disney's profit margin rose sharply. Eisner also recognized that the company's movie-making assets—its film studios, creative writers, and animators—were not being sufficiently utilized. He instructed studio executives to find ways to increase the number of films Disney made each year. He also started another studio called Touchstone Pictures to make low-cost movies using Disney's existing movie-making assets.

In addition, Eisner decided that the value of Disney's famous film library wasn't being utilized to maximize the company's profits. Eisner believed that the best way to realize the value of Disney's movie assets was to put movies like *Snow White* and *Pinocchio* on videocassettes and sell them directly to final customers. This also brought in billion of dollars in new revenues. Because the costs to make and sell the videos were low, profits from them were very high.

The changes Eisner made to Disney's business model sharply increased Disney's return on its invested capital, turning the company into a cash-making machine. The turnaround was so dramatic that the price of Disney's stock soared from $5 to $50, buoyed by constantly increasing cash flows and profits.

Eisner's new business model worked well until the mid 1990s, but then the company seemed to run out of steam—its money machine started to produce fewer and fewer new dollars. Some analysts believe Disney's problems began in 1995 when Eisner decided to acquire Capital Cities/ABC for $19 billion. Capital Cities/ABC owned the ABC television network and major TV channels like ESPN, television-program making studios, and a chain of radio stations. Eisner claimed the merger would result in huge cost savings and more creative programming because it would allow both companies to make better use of their assets. However, the assets of the merged company did not work well together to improve profit margins and profitability.

Under Eisner, Disney also started to invest large amounts of capital in other major projects. Disney bought sports teams, started Walt Disney cruises, and increased the number of television programs it made. Disney also opened up new theme parks in Europe and Asia. However, most of these investments did not generate enough cash flow and profit to justify the investment made in them. By the late 1990s, the figures in Disney's balance sheet and income statement showed as much. In fact, the figures actually showed a falling return on the company's invested capital (ROIC). Despite the huge number of assets Disney owned, they were generating less cash and reducing the company's profitability!

Disney's profit margins fell as its operating costs and expenses soared. Its new movies, particularly its new animated movies, were not well-received by moviegoers. The ABC network fell to third place in the TV rankings, which reduced television advertising revenues. The merger between Disney and Capital Cities/ABC, it seemed, had merely turned the firm into a monster-sized entertainment company.

When Disney announced lower earnings in 1999, its stock price plunged. In fact, its stock price dropped from a high of about $50 in 1998 to $15 in 2002, and it was trading in the low $20s in 2004. Most of the shareholder value Eisner created in the 1990s was wiped out, and he was criticized for accepting tens of millions of dollars in salary and stock options even as Disney's stock price plunged.

Eisner nonetheless continued to try to find new ways to use Disney's assets to once again create value. He revamped its film division in an effort to make hit movies at lower costs, changed ABC's programming, and sold off its loss-making chain of Disney stores. However, in 2004, Eisner announced he would step down as Disney's CEO by 2006. In 2005, Robert Iger, Eisner's hand-picked successor became Disney's new CEO and investors hope he will be able to find better ways to use the company's assets to generate cash and profit.[1] •

Overview

A company is a collection of assets, but the way those assets work to create value for customers and profit for a company depends on how well they are put to work. A company's business model is its plan of action for using its assets to create cash flow and profit. However, it takes considerable entrepreneurial and managerial skills to decide how to put assets to their most highly valued use—to maximize company profitability. Michael Eisner's initial decisions about how to employ Disney's assets were successful, but his subsequent failures show how complex and uncertain financial decision making is.

In this chapter, we examine how the activities of the finance function can help a company make better use of its assets and help secure the capital necessary to purchase those assets. First, we examine the nature of finance, different kinds of financial activities, and the way financial analysis is used to maintain and increase the return on a company's capital. Second, we examine issues involved in short-term and long-term capital investment and budgeting, such as how to best manage working capital and how to decide which new projects a company should invest its capital in. Third, we examine the issues involved when companies borrow capital and how they finance their activities through issuing debt and equity securities can also affect profitability. By the end of this chapter, you will understand the crucial ways in which finance helps managers increase a company's value-creation capabilities and its long-run profitability.

What Is Finance?

Finance is the set of activities people and companies engage in to decide how best to invest their capital so it generates additional cash, profit, and capital in the future—which increases *profitability*. As we note in Chapter 2, the use of money makes it possible to price and value assets more accurately and to exchange them so they move towards their *most highly valued use*—to the specific business activities that create the most value and profit. When assets are put to their most highly valued use, the value of those assets increases, and they generate a higher rate of return (profitability) for their owners. The goal of finance is to use capital to purchase assets that can be invested in ways that lead to the highest rate of return possible—to maximize profitability.

finance The set of activities people and companies engage in to decide how to invest their capital so that it generates more cash, profit, and wealth.

The principles of finance apply to all kinds of assets. People who go to college invest money to increase the value of their human capital. They can then use their new assets— superior skills and knowledge—to move to higher paying (more profitable) jobs. A person's motivation leads him or her to develop new skills and discover where those skills are most valuable and will generate the highest long-run returns. Similarly, landowners who work to improve their land and make it more productive increase the value of their assets. Their reward is better crops or higher rents and increased profitability. Finally, entrepreneurs who notice opportunities to use assets to make new products that better satisfy customer needs can earn enormous profits.

Entrepreneurs, managers, and investors who understand how to invest capital in the most profitable ways—that is, people who can put capital to its most highly valued use—can dramatically increase the returns they receive on that capital. Stockholders, for example, receive higher returns in the form of increased dividends and higher stock prices, and managers receive higher salaries and more stock options.

A person can attend a conference to develop new skills and discover where those skills are most valued to generate the highest long-run returns possible.

The Relationship between Risk and Return

Before we go on to discuss the main activities involved in finance, it is necessary to understand what the concept of "rate of return" on capital means and to appreciate the relationship between risk and the rate of return (or risk and return). The rate of return on an asset or investment is a financial ratio similar to those discussed in Chapter 14. It tells companies and individual investors how much they have gained or lost by investing their capital in a specific way during a certain time period, such as a year. The rate of return is calculated as:

$$\frac{\text{Value of the Asset Now} - \text{Value at Time of Purchase}}{\text{Value of the Asset at Time of Purchase}} \times 100$$

So, on the one hand, if I invest $500 in 2006, and in one year my investment has grown to $600, my annual rate of return is $600 – $500/$500 × 100 = 12%, meaning I have increased the value of my investment by 12%. On the other hand, if my investment falls in value to $400, my rate of return is $400 – $500/$500 × 100 = –20%. I have lost 20% of the value of my investment. An investor obviously wants the highest rate of return possible. Everyone would be happy if the value of their capital doubled or tripled each year. But what determines the rate of return on a specific capital investment?

When people or companies possess assets or capital, they have two main financial goals. On the one hand, they want to *preserve or protect* the value of their capital, meaning they don't want its value or purchasing power to fall over time. On the other hand, they would like to see the value and purchasing power of their capital increase or appreciate as rapidly as possible. In finance, the way people balance or "trade off" these two goals affects the rate of return they receive.

When investors make capital appreciation their main goal, they have to find ways to invest their capital that will result in high rates of return. In general, to obtain a higher rate of return, people have to "lock up" their capital in specific ways, and for longer periods of time. This increases the uncertainty surrounding their investment. Essentially, by locking up their capital to obtain higher returns, investors are forced to put their capital at greater risk–the risk of obtaining a return that might be far smaller than they expected and the risk of losing their capital altogether.

For example, if an investor decides to buy the stock of a new company that has yet to bring its new product to market, there is enormous uncertainty about whether the product will succeed or fail. To encourage investors to lock up their capital in such a risky project, the company will have to reward them with very high rates of return. As we discuss later, the potential rates of return that can be earned on stocks such as these are enormous, but so are the potential losses.

Similarly, the longer the period of time people are required to lock up their capital in an asset, the greater is the uncertainty surrounding their future rate of return. Suppose an investor identifies a profitable investment that will result in a good rate of return but will require locking up the capital for five years. The next day the investor discovers an investment opportunity that offers double the rate of return. However, the investor cannot make the new investment because the money is now tied up in the previous investment. So, for investors to take the risk of locking up their capital for long periods of time, they have to be compensated with higher rates of return.

The least risky strategy for investors to preserve the value or their capital, and hopefully increase it, is to find an investment that allows them to lock up their money for the shortest period of time (hours or days) and isn't very risky. A person can achieve both these goals by investing in the "overnight money market"–money market funds, that is. However, the rate of return received on money market funds, which is determined by current interest rates, is relatively low precisely because it is a low-risk investment.

By contrast, suppose an investor decides that that he or she wants to maximize his or her rate of return. In other words, capital appreciation is much more important to the investor than just preserving its value. To obtain a high rate of return, the investor will search for opportunities to invest in assets that have the potential to generate the most profit. However, such investments generate the highest rates of return precisely because investing in them is a highly risky business. Buying stock in new company in the process of developing a new product or investing in assets such as warehouses, duplexes, or strip malls are examples of risky investments. The uncertainty

Did You Know?

Of all the notes printed by the Bureau of Engraving and Printing, $1 notes make up about 45% of currency production. The life span of a $1 Federal Reserve Note is 22 months. In 1934, the Bureau of Engraving and Printing issued a $100,000 note but the $100 note has been the largest denomination of currency in circulation since 1969. It costs about 6 cents to produce a $1 note.[2]

Examples of investments with highly uncertain rates of return include assets like duplexes, strip malls, and stock in startup companies.

related to predicting the future success of such a company's business model, or the price of duplexes and warehouses 10 years into the future makes these investments very risky. People who invest in money market funds can withdraw their funds and virtually always get back their original capital invested as well as earn a small amount of interest. But, this is not always true for investors who buy stocks, bonds, and physical assets, such as land and buildings. Investors in a new company, for example, might find that the value of their investment rapidly rising or falling depending on whether the company's business model is succeeding or failing. Similarly, changing economic conditions affect the value of investments like shopping malls and duplexes. In good times the value of these investments goes up, but in bad times their value goes down. This makes the investments very *volatile*: The price of each will rise and fall sharply as people's opinions change about the rates of return likely to be earned from them.

risk premium The extra reward investors demand for bearing the additional risks associated with a speculative investment.

A basic principle of finance is that the *higher the risk involved in investing in a particular asset, the higher the rate of return people will require to compensate them for bearing those risks*. In other words, investors will demand to be paid a risk premium—an extra reward for bearing the additional risk associated with such an investment. Investors will not bear the risks of investing capital in assets such as stocks, bonds, land, and buildings unless they feel confident they will be able to earn a much higher return (risk premium) on these investments compared to less-risky investments such as investing in money market funds.

In finance, all kinds of capital investments must be compared in terms of their relative risks and returns. For example, if an investor buys stock in a new biotechnology company, the uncertainty associated with predicting its future success requires this investment to carry a high risk premium. An investor receives this premium in the form of a rapid rise in the value of the stock *if* the company succeeds. By contrast, if an investor buys stock in a company like Kroger, which already has a profitable business operation, there is much lower uncertainty surrounding its future success, so this investment carries a much lower risk premium. In this case, the investor will receive lower dividends and see a more gradual increase in Kroger's stock price.

One way investors try to reduce their risk is by relying on large, institutional investment companies to protect their interests—something increasingly important given the rash of recent corporate scandals. Business in Action discusses institutional investing.

Business in Action

The Increasing Power of Institutional Investors

The collapse of the stock market in the early 2000s made large mutual fund companies like Fidelity and TIAA/CREF realize they needed to try to prevent investors from losing billions of dollars caused the collapse of companies like Enron, WorldCom, Tyco, and Arthur Andersen. Mutual funds pool and invest the funds of many investors. This gives the funds a great deal of buying power in the stock market. That said, they don't control the companies they invest in. So how can these companies prevent abuses from occurring?

Take the California Public Employees' Retirement System (CalPERS), the largest public-sector pension fund in the United States. CalPERS manages over $190 billion for over 1.4 million of its members. Because the fund is so large, it is a major shareholder in many U.S. companies and therefore has a vital interest in their performance. During the 1990s, CalPERS realized that it had an increasing duty to protect the interests of its investors by paying more attention to what the top managers and boards of directors of these companies were doing.

In order to protect its investors, the California Public Employees' Retirement System monitors and influences the behavior of companies it invests in. The goal is to make sure that the top managers of these companies don't pursue their own interests at the expense of shareholders.

Out of concern for their shareholders, CalPERS and other mutual funds have taken a number of specific actions. One action relates to the "antitakeover" provisions managers sometimes create for their corporations. These provisions protect managers from corporate raiders who might like to take over a company, a process that would earn a lot of money for shareholders but might cost managers their jobs. Mutual funds are also attempting to intervene in long-run management decisions, like the acquisition of companies that might hurt the value of an acquiring company's stock. The funds have also been showing an interest in controlling the salaries and bonuses that top managers give themselves, many of which have reached record levels in recent years. Mutual funds have also demanded that companies clarify their accounting procedures and lobbied for new rules making it much more difficult for companies to hide illegal transactions–transactions that benefit managers but hurt other stakeholders. As the power of mutual funds and other institutional investors increases, so does the power of shareholders and other organizational stakeholders.[3]

Business Finance

Capital is the heart of business finance and financial analysis. Because it provides the funds used to purchase assets (productive resources), capital is a firm's lifeblood. Business finance is about increasing the rate of return on a company's invested capital (ROIC) because this is the best way to maximize the market value of stockholders' equity. Investors bid up the stock price of companies that have a high ROIC because it a sign that these companies have the potential to generate high cash flow and profits in the future. Let's look at Figure 15.1, which shows how a company manages capital to create profit–that is, how managers "use money to make money."

Stockholders' equity, including retained earnings, is the main source of the capital a company uses to buy the assets it needs to pursue its business model. The other source of capital is the money a company borrows to buy assets and finance its operations–company debt. If a company's business model works, and it puts these assets to good use, this generates a net cash flow and profit. In other words, more dollars flow into the company than flow out. The more dollars that flow in versus flow out,

Figure 15.1
The Cycle of Profit

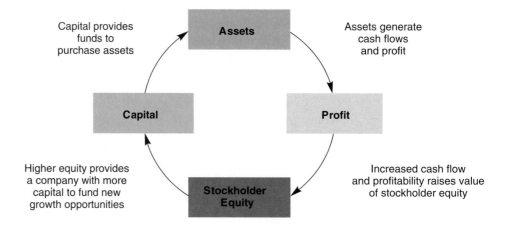

the higher a company's return on its invested capital will be, and the greater will be the value of its stockholders' equity. In turn, the greater the value of its stockholders' equity, the higher the company's stock price will rise as investors compete to own a share of the business.

The role of business finance is to ensure that the methods a company uses to borrow, invest, spend, and even lend its capital lead to a rate of return that maximizes the present market value of its stock (See Figure 15.2.)

Figure 15.2
Four Ways to Use Capital

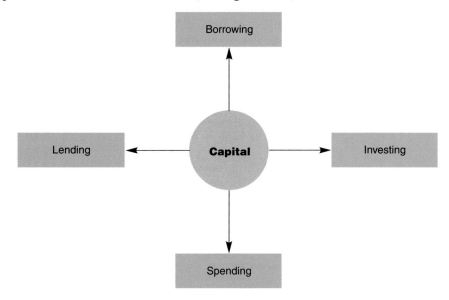

The two main kinds of financial activities used to manage these four uses of capital to achieve this are (1) capital investment and budgeting, which involves choosing how to invest in and manage assets to increase ROIC, and (2) capital financing, which involves choosing how to raise money to pay for these assets in the most cost-effective way. These are the issues addressed in the rest of this chapter.

Capital Investment and Budgeting

capital investment and budgeting The development of a financial plan and budget to manage and invest capital so that it leads to the highest return on invested capital that can be obtained.

short-term capital management The financial decisions involved when a company purchases resources to make products that will be sold within a one-year period.

Companies engage in capital investment and budgeting to manage and invest their capital in ways that lead to the highest ROIC they can obtain. Financial decisions about how to spend and invest a company's capital are some of the toughest and most critical decisions managers make. Because they are committing, or "locking up," stockholders' capital in specific business projects for long periods of time, financial managers must do all they can to evaluate which of these projects will result in the best returns. The effect of these investment decisions will be seen in the way a company's bottom line profits changes over time.

Recall that firms list their assets on their balance sheets in terms of decreasing liquidity (the length of time it takes to convert them to cash). Because the length of time a company's capital is locked up in an asset affects risk and return, capital investment decisions differ depending on whether the asset being purchased is short term (current), or fixed (long term). We examine some of the basic financial issues related to managing short- and long-term assets next and focus on a few key financial tools managers use to maximize the return on their company's capital.

Short-Term Capital Management Decisions

When a company orders raw materials and components and makes products that will be sold within a one-year period, short-term capital management decisions are involved. As we discuss in Chapter 14, accountants work out the monetary value of a company's cash, accounts receivable, inventory, and prepaid expenses, and then report this on a company's balance sheet as current assets. Companies try to manage their current, or short-term, assets in a way that speeds up the conversion of cash into products and products back into cash as a result of sales. A company's working capital is the amount of "free cash" or "funds" available to feed a business's operating activities. It is calculated as:

Current Assets − Current Liabilities = Working Capital

Working capital increases if the company's business model succeeds and its current assets, such as cash-on-hand or accounts receivable, increase, or its current liabilities, like current debt and accounts payable, decrease. By contrast, working capital decreases if current assets fall or current liabilities increase.

The reason it is so important to use working capital efficiently to speed the flow of cash out of and into a company is that this working capital has a time value attached to it. The longer working capital is tied up in inventory, the longer a company has to wait to get paid for its products. This slows the flow of cash into a company, and so the company receives a lower return on its working capital.

Financial managers can help reduce the amount of money a company has tied up in current liabilities so it can be put to use to make and sell more products. To better understand how this can be done, let's look at the stages involved in making and selling goods and services and the decisions involved at each stage. Figure 15.3 illustrates the relationship between a company's operating cycle and the cash flows associated with it.

The operating cycle begins when a company purchases an inventory of raw materials and components and ends when a company receives the actual payment of cash for them after they are converted into products and sold. The longer the operating cycle, the longer a company's working capital is tied up in its business. As Figure 15.3 suggests, timing related to paying for inputs (cash outflows) and timing related to collecting for products sold (cash inflows) are not directly connected. The two activities move on their own cycles.

For example, after a company purchases its inventory, it normally has to pay for it before the inventory is made into finished products and sold. The longer the inventory period, the higher the carrying costs a company must fund. Then, as products are sold, the length of the accounts receivable period once again determines how long it will be before a company receives payment. In the meantime, a company has to bear the costs of buying more inventory. So, for both these reasons, more cash is initially flowing out of the company than is flowing in. This "cash flow gap" is greater the longer a company's operating cycle is. To keep the company operating, or *solvent,* its managers will have to either borrow cash or hold enough cash-on-hand to purchase the resources it needs until it gets paid by its customers. This is why cash flow is so important: If a company does not have the funds to purchase these resources or cannot borrow enough money to buy them until it gets paid by customers, it will go out of business.

Figure 15.3

Managing the Short-Term Operating Cycle

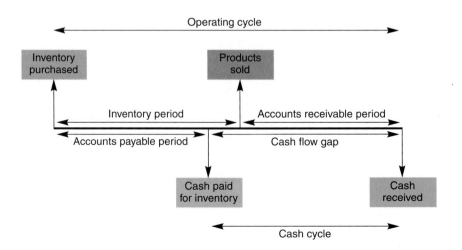

Managers in the firm's financing function try to find ways to shorten the operating cycle to reduce the amount of working capital tied up in the business's operations. One way of doing both of these things is to shorten the time money is tied up in inventory. This is why managers use techniques such as just-in-time inventory systems and sophisticated ERP systems to speed up the flow of inputs into a company and distribute products to customers more quickly. Dell Computer does this by having its suppliers locate their warehouses next to its operations, for example.

Another way to reduce inventory-holding costs is to try to obtain the best credit terms possible from suppliers. In other words, to get suppliers to lengthen a company's accounts payable period so it can wait much longer before it has to pay them. The bigger the customer, the more power it has to demand more favorable credit terms from its suppliers and make suppliers bear the carrying costs of holding the "inventory." As you learned, Dell does this. Dell is a master at managing its inventory to reduce the amount of working capital tied up in it. The computer maker's reward is rising gross profit margins. Recall from Chapter 14 how even small increases in gross margins can greatly increase a company's cash flow and profits.

Financial managers can also look for ways to reduce the size of the cash flow gap by, for example, changing the company's lending or credit policies. Remember, credit also has a carrying cost because a company's working capital is locked up in the finished products that customers have purchased but not yet paid for. If the company has a 60-day credit policy, perhaps managers can change it to 30 days. Alternately 60-days' credit might be given to new customers to get their business, but existing customers given only 30 days to pay.

Companies can also use their ERP systems to speed up the flow of their cash receivables. The faster the collection of accounts receivable, the faster money flows in, and the better use a company makes of its working capital. Developing a cash budget that estimates future cash receipts (cash in) and cash going out to pay bills is a vital, short-term financial planning activity. It tells managers if they will have a cash surplus or deficit so they can address any cash flow problems before a financial crisis occurs.

Long-Term Capital Budgeting Decisions

long-term capital budgeting The financial decisions involved when a company chooses how to invest capital for extended periods of time.

Long-term capital budgeting decisions involve choices about how to invest capital for extended periods of time. There are many different ways in which managers can invest their company's capital, for example, to improve existing products, to make new kinds of products, or even to acquire the assets, such as the products of another company. The role of finance in long-term capital spending and investment decisions is to help top managers maximize the return on a company's capital. To help the firm make these decisions, financial managers forecast the different rates of return a company would earn by investing its capital in a variety of different ways. For example, financial managers could forecast the return a company would receive if it invested its capital to make and sell either or all of three different products. A company's top managers can then use this information to decide which product will do the most to help increase the company's return on its capital.

Long-term capital investment decisions are always made in the context of uncertainty and risk. Managers never know for sure how successful their new projects and business model will be, but they can try to forecast the future stream of revenues and costs that will result from an investment decision.

net present value analysis The financial analysis needed to determine the true rate of return of a proposed capital investment. It tells managers how much a long-term project would earn in today's dollars if it were undertaken.

NET PRESENT VALUE ANALYSIS One of the most important forecasting tools involves estimating the true rate of return of a proposed investment. Net present value (NPV) analysis is the financial analysis needed to determine the true rate of return of a proposed capital investment. It tells managers how much a long-term project would earn in today's dollars if it were undertaken.

To perform an NPV analysis, managers first use all their skills and experience to forecast the value of the future stream of revenues or cash flows that will result from an investment in a project, for example, the launch of a new kind of soft drink. However, since that stream of revenues will be obtained over a 15-year period in this case, the managers have to "discount," or reduce, the value of these revenues to their current or "present" value in order to compare them to the current, or present, cost of capital the company needs to invest to get the new soft drink to the market.

To discount the future stream of revenues to their present value, a company has to consider what the total cost of capital locked up in the project for the next 15 years will be. To work out this cost, a company calculates how much it will have to pay in interest to borrow the money to launch the soft drink project. For each of the 15 years of the project, they subtract the cost of the capital to fund the project from the future stream of earnings the company expects to receive from it.

Keep in mind that this is capital that could be generating revenue if the company chose to invest it in another way. Consequently, financial managers also calculate how much money the company could expect to make if the funds were invested in, say, the stocks of other companies rather than investing it in the project. Based on all of this analysis, financial managers then calculate a company's cost of capital. The cost of capital is essentially the average rate of return a company could expect to earn from investing its capital in any number of ways.

After discounting the value of future cash flows in this way, if the future stream of revenues is higher than the current cost of the assets used to bring the new soft drink to the market, a project is said to have a *positive* NPV. If the project has a *positive* NPV, investing in it will increase the company's rate of return on its capital and its ROIC. Thus, managers should make the investment because this is the most profitable way to invest the company's money. If NPV is *negative,* however, then the investment should not be made because it will result in a rate of return lower than the company would receive if it invested its money in some *alternative way.* A complementary tool that helps managers decide which projects to invest in is called a breakeven analysis. It is discussed next.

BREAKEVEN ANALYSIS   To perform a breakeven analysis, managers estimate the potential sales and costs associated with a project and then discount the stream of future cash flows from it back to the present to determine if its NPV is positive. The **breakeven point** is the point where the sales level of the project *just* covers all its costs and expenses but no profit is earned. Figure 15.4 illustrates the breakeven point. The shaded area prior to the breakeven point shows the loss involved at each level of sales. The shaded area following the breakeven point shows how profit increases once this critical point is reached. This has some interesting financial implications.

First, the figure reveals how all new projects start out deeply in "debt." The company's money is tied up in these ventures, and it has to bear all of the risks associated with the capital investment. So, at the beginning of a project, potential losses are enormous. However, they quickly fall as sales revenues start to increase. Put another way, the figure illustrates how a company only starts to approach the breakeven point—where it will get back the cost of its capital and begin to report a profit in an accounting sense—on the last units of the product it sells. This is why it is so vital a company's sales forecast be accurate. If the sales forecast is overoptimistic and the sales target is not reached, disaster will result. Not only will the firm not earn a profit, it might even experience major losses. If it isn't able to make it at least to the breakeven point, managers will have to seriously consider shutting the project down.

When sales *do* reach the breakeven point, however, this shows that managers have a good grasp of the business. Now suppose managers decide to be cautious and choose a conservative sales figure. Looks what happens as sales go past the breakeven point in this case. As Figure 15.4 illustrates, the gap between revenues and costs widens rapidly as sales go beyond this point. At the breakeven point, all of the firm's fixed, or long-term, costs of the project have been covered. For example, interest and debt payments on the firm's equipment and facilities can be very steep. So, once these costs are covered, it is a major "weight" off of the

breakeven point The sales level that just covers all of a project's costs but where no profit is earned.

Did You Know?

The amount you'll earn if you save $1 a day for 60 years at 10% annual interest: $1,107,708.[4]

**Figure 15.4
Breakeven
Analysis**

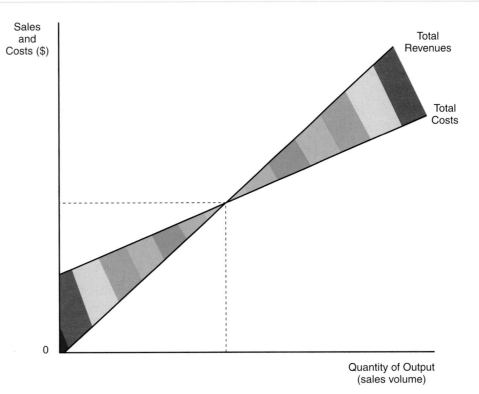

Sales
and
Costs ($)

Total
Revenues

Total
Costs

0

Quantity of Output
(sales volume)

variable costs Costs
that are only incurred
when the firm makes
and sells products.

firm's shoulders. Fixed costs must be paid whether or not the firm is able to sell a single unit of its product. However, once these costs are covered, the only other costs the firm has to pay for are variable costs–costs that are only incurred when the firm makes and sells products, like the cost of goods sold and so forth. In other words, all sales above the breakeven point result in a rapidly increasing rate of return, as shown by the difference between the revenue and cost curves. This reveals an important financial lesson. A company might have to wait a long time to cover its fixed costs, but once it does and passes its breakeven point, cash flows and profits are ever increasing.

Once a project is up and running, efficiently using the firm's working capital can help it reach its breakeven point more quickly. Recall from Chapter 14 how financial analysis shows that when managers can increase inventory turnover or asset turnover by only a few percentage points, profitability rises sharply. Figure 15.5 illustrates why. By increasing these ratios, managers speed up cash flows into and out of the firm's operations, thereby lowering operating costs.

In Figure 15.5, lower operating costs are illustrated by the shift of the firm's cost curve downwards from C_0 to C_1. Now in addition to the profits that result from increasing sales (represented by the top shaded area), profits are increased by good cash management (represented by the bottom shaded area). You can see how much the two work together to increase the rate of return on invested capital and profitability.

CAPITAL BUDGETS   For a company to accurately calculate its breakeven point, it must do a good job of making long-term investment decisions. A breakeven analysis embodies the revenue and cost assumptions managers make about a project's rate of return. If costs were to rise above those forecasted, the project's breakeven point would move to the right, and the project might not make a profit. So, once cost projections have been agreed upon, a budget must be developed so the company stays within these forecasts.

capital budget A set of
rules for allocating funds to
the different functions of a
firm to achieve a
predetermined rate of
return on its investment.

This is what a capital budget does. A capital budget is a set of rules for allocating funds to a firm's different functions. The goal of the capital budget is to achieve a predetermined rate of return on an investment. It is essentially a "straightjacket" that forces managers to limit their spending and find ways to keep costs down. When the total expenses of a project are broken down by function, every manager knows what they have to spend to make the project a success and yet stay within the budget. This

**Figure 15.5
Breakeven
Analysis and
Inventory Turnover**

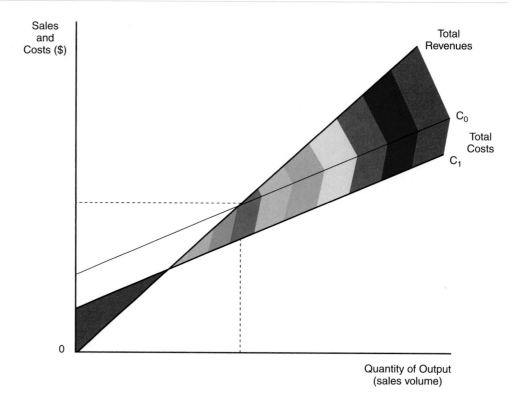

is why a capital budget is regarded as a set of rules. Of course, given the level of uncertainty and risk associated with any new venture costs often do increase in unexpected ways. When cost overruns occur, budgets force managers to go to their superiors to approve additional funding. However, most managers think twice about going to their bosses and asking for more money.

A Company as a Portfolio of Investments

A company can be looked at as a "portfolio," or collection of different investments or projects. Some of these projects might have a positive NPV, and some might not. Only projects with a positive NPV will generate positive cash flows and profits, however. In addition, each of a company's different products can be looked at as an individual project. It is the job of brand managers to decide how to invest in a product to increase its return. In a large company like Procter & Gamble or Kraft Foods, a **brand manager** is responsible for a particular type of branded product, such as Tide detergent or Pace picante sauce, to maximize its profitability over time. Brand managers make the kinds of short- and long-term financial decisions we just discussed.

brand manager A manager responsible for managing a brand-name product.

In terms of long-term decisions, brand managers need to figure out how to increase revenues or reduce costs related to the products they manage. This might involve finding a different way to package Tide, such as in a tablet form, investing in research and development to make Tide clean clothes better, or even moving the production of Tide to low-cost locations like Mexico. In terms of short-term decisions, the Tide brand manager might need to think about developing a new advertising campaign or adding a new fragrance to the product to attract more customers. He or she might also focus on finding ways to better manage inventory and distribution to increase the cash flow from Tide and reduce the costs of producing it. The goal of all these financial decisions is to increase ROIC and stockholders' equity.

Many large companies are not just collections of different products, they are also collections of different companies. General Electric is a collection of 300 different companies, and GE's CEO, Jeffrey Immelt, treats each of these companies as a separate investment project. Every year the performance of each division is evaluated by criteria such as ROIC. If a division fails to meet the company's profitability targets, Immelt and his managers have to figure out how its performance can be improved or whether it should be divested and sold. GE can then use the capital from the sales of underperforming divisions to invest in other projects likely to earn higher rates of return.

To make such decisions, the CEO and top corporate executives of a company like GE perform what amounts to a NPV analysis of each division to determine its potential future contribution to the company. This financial analysis helps identify those divisions that offer the greatest potential for increasing GE's ROIC as well as those divisions whose performance is reducing ROIC. A company like GE would then invest its capital in the divisions that will contribute the most to its long-term return on capital.

Financial managers also use NPV analysis to determine if it would be profitable to use a company's capital to acquire or merge with another company. These are difficult and complex financial decisions. Managers have to forecast the future income streams and costs that will result from combining the operations of *both* companies. The opening case discusses how Disney's managers did a poor job of forecasting the future rate of return that resulted from its merger with ABC. This acquisition is regarded by many as a failure. Another example of a failed merger, this time between Hewlett-Packard (HP) and Compaq, is discussed in Business in Action.

Business in Action

Analyzing the Assets of HP and Compaq

Many analysts thought that the acquisition of Compaq by HP in 2002 would be a failure and that it would not result in the huge cost savings HP had forecast. Before the buyout, however, Carly Fiorina, the CEO of HP, and Michael Capellas, the CEO of Compaq, and their top management teams engaged in some very detailed NPV analyses. Their goal was to forecast what would happen to expenses and costs if the operations of their many different divisions, and their marketing and distribution channels and sales forces, were combined.

Their financial analysis forecast that the combined company would achieve over $3 billion in cost savings over a three-year period. Thus, combining their operations would result in a positive NPV and increased profitability. By September 2004, HP claimed it had already realized $2.3 billion in savings and that the buyout was proving to be a success.

Despite research that shows mergers and acquisitions often reduce rather than increase returns, Carly Fiorina, the former CEO of HP, and Michael Capellas, the former CEO of Compaq, convinced shareholders that combining the two companies would lead to greater cost savings and a competitive advantage. But things didn't turn out that way.

In January 2005, however, the financial results showed HP was still unable to match Dell's low operating costs—operating costs created by Dell's efficient short- and long-term financial management practices. Unlike HP, Dell has never acquired companies to increase the return on its capital; in fact, most research suggests mergers and acquisitions actually reduce returns not increase them. Nevertheless, they are still favorite tactics companies use to try to increase their long-run profitability. That said, who knows what rate of return HP and Compaq would have earned individually had the buyout not taken place? By 2005, both companies might have been generating low or even negative returns because of Dell's increasing performance. Nevertheless, in the spring of 2005, HP's board of directors, disappointed at Carly Fiorina's continuing inability to reduce operating costs since the merger, removed her as its CEO and began the search for a new CEO who might have better luck.[5]

As this discussion suggests, long-term financial investing and budgeting revolves around increasing the potential future returns of a company's present investing activities. This is the stuff of "big business" or "high finance." Financiers and investment experts like Warren Buffet gamble billions to buy companies with assets they believe are undervalued and could be put to a better use under a new management team. If these experts are correct, they can make short-term financial decisions that improve the way these companies' assets are used to greatly increase their cash flows and profits. The stock prices of these companies then generally soar, and their shareholders earn high returns.

Capital Financing

capital financing The development of a financial plan to allow a company to obtain the money it needs to fund its activities at the lowest possible cost.

Just as a company makes short-and long-term investment decisions, so it must make short- and long-term choices about how to pay for both its current and fixed assets. Capital financing is the process a company engages in to get the capital it needs to fund its investments at the lowest possible cost. In this section, we first consider the sources of short-term financing, and then move on to look at the sources of long-term financing, in particular debt and equity financing.

Remember throughout this discussion that we, as individuals, confront the same basic financial issues as companies. Just as a company builds up a portfolio of assets over time, so does each of us in the form of assets such as personal skills, possessions, a house, family, money and capital in stocks, land, and so on. Just as a company's goal is to maximize the value of its stockholders' equity, so people desire to maximize their personal value. The principles of finance remain the same no matter if a company or person is doing the investing; so does the goal—to maximize the return on capital invested.

Short-Term Financing Methods

When managers engage in short-term financing, they try to minimize the cost of getting the funds a company needs to finance its operating cycle. The method they choose is determined by the makeup of their company's working capital, that is, by the percentage of working capital the firm has tied up in inventory, accounts receivable, final products, and cash-on-hand (cash reserves). Let's now look at each of these short-term financing methods.

CASH RESERVES   Companies that have large sums of cash-on-hand are likely to fund their own operations. However, growing companies like Dick's Sporting Goods, discussed in Chapter 14, which are expanding rapidly do not have large sums of cash lying around. These companies are constantly pumping cash back into their operations to buy more inventory, hire more employees, and so forth to keep up with the rising demand for the products the firms sell. They often use up cash as fast, or faster, than they can generate it. In fact, efficient companies often need more cash because they are putting it to the best use—not because they are in trouble! Potential lenders have to take this in consideration. They do this by looking at a company's income statement and balance sheet to determine if it is requesting a loan that will be put efficiently to use or if it needs a loan because it is operating inefficiently and merely burning through cash.

unsecured loan A loan not backed by valuable assets pledged to guarantee the loan will be paid back.

line of credit A short-term, unsecured loan a company can draw against as its accounts payable become due.

UNSECURED AND SECURED LOANS   The most common way to fund a temporary cash deficit brought about by the different lengths of the accounts payable and accounts receivable periods is to arrange a short-term unsecured bank loan. An unsecured loan is one that is *not* backed by *collateral*, that is, by valuable assets, like land, buildings, and inventory, pledged to guarantee the loan will be paid back. A company that obtains an unsecured loan for a short period of time typically obtains a line of credit—a budgeted amount of funds, such as a $500,000 loan, that it can "draw" against when its accounts payable become due. A *revolving* line of credit is

Firms can take out short-term, unsecured loans from banks like Wells Fargo & Company to pay for their short-term debts, such as accounts payable.

simply a line of credit that extends over two or more years. Of course, the company must pay interest on the unsecured loan or line of credit it has been given. It can also pay back the amount of money it originally borrowed early to reduce the loan balance, if it believes this is the best use of its cash.

Secured loans, by contrast, are backed by assets. Companies (or people) that are perceived as being a "high risk" typically are required to take out secured, short-term loans and sometimes pay a risk premium, such as a higher rate of interest. High risk means that there is some doubt about whether or not the borrower has the ability to pay back a loan. Moneylenders, like other investors, also seek to obtain the highest return on their capital. They therefore demand a risk premium to invest in projects such as these.

secured loan A loan backed by valuable fixed or current assets.

ACCOUNTS RECEIVABLE FINANCING Sometimes companies finance their short-term cash needs by selling their accounts receivable. Accounts receivable financing involves *factoring*. Basically, the company sells the rights to its future accounts receivable at a discounted (factored) price to a broker in order to generate immediate cash. For example, a company might factor $1 million of its accounts receivable by selling them for 97 cents on the dollar. It obtains $970,000 and the remaining $30,000 is the commission earned by the broker. This is a relatively expensive method of obtaining a loan. It is nonetheless common in certain industries like the clothing industry. In the clothing industry, for example, the accounts receivable period is long because clothing makers frequently give department stores 90 or 120 days to pay for the goods they buy. However, clothing makers must pay their suppliers in just 30 to 60 days. So, to cover the cash flow gap, they sell the rights to their accounts receivable to brokers, who then take over the collection of the accounts.

commercial paper Short-term, unsecured debts or notes issued at a certain rate of interest for up to nine months.

COMMERCIAL PAPER To reduce short-term financing costs, companies perceived as being low risk, such as well-established, profitable companies, borrow money at low interest rates by issuing commercial paper. Commercial paper consists of short-term, unsecured debts or notes issued at a certain rate of interest for up to nine months. Because of their excellent reputations, blue chip companies can sell these notes to investors at a much lower interest rate than the rate a bank would charge for the same loan. For example, a company might issue a note paying 4% interest, whereas a regular bank loan might be at 8%. So, by issuing the notes, the firm saves 4% in interest costs. Large, established companies seldom need short-term financing, however, because they have large cash flows—cash flows that are usually in excess of the money they need to fund their current operations. More likely, these companies face a different problem: How to invest or spend the extra cash they have on hand to increase the rate of return earned by their stockholders.

Long-Term Financing Methods

Many of a company's most important investment decisions involve the purchase of fixed assets such as land, buildings, machinery, and information technology that will be used for several years to produce a particular kind of product. When Intel, for example, decides to build a new factory to produce its next generation of microprocessor, it has to decide how to finance the $3 billion it will cost to build and equip the factory.

The three ways most companies fund their long-term capital investment projects are by (1) spending their retained earnings, (2) issuing debt securities, and (3) selling equity securities. A fourth method involves outsourcing production so the firm doesn't have to invest its capital in machinery and plants. These methods are illustrated in Figure 15.6.

Figure 15.6
Methods
of Obtaining
New Capital

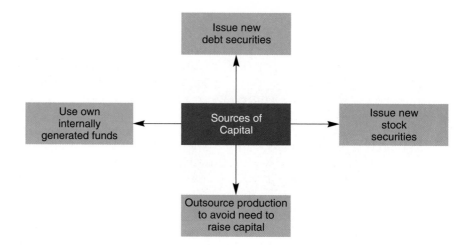

Intel is a successful company with billions of dollars of cash-on-hand. It could pay cash for the factory it wants to build, or it might choose to keep its cash to invest in another project, perhaps the acquisition of another company. If it decides to fund its investment by borrowing $3 billion, it could do so by issuing debt securities, such as bonds. (We will explain more about debt securities in a moment.) Intel might also decide to issue new capital stock and sell it to investors to raise the $3 billion. Lastly, Intel could decide to *avoid* the $3 billion capital cost of the factory by outsourcing the chip's production to another chipmaker. Some small chip-designing companies take this approach. Several factors determine which method of financing a company decides to use.

First, the choice of how to raise capital to fund operations depends on the *relative cost* of financing via these different methods. Obviously, a company wants to borrow money on the most favorable terms possible to keep costs to a minimum. The rate of interest a company will have to pay to borrow capital depends upon how potential lenders evaluate the risks of loaning a company the funds it needs. Companies perceived as risky prospects will have to pay higher rates of interest to obtain a loan.

How high a rate of interest potential lenders will charge for a loan depends on the story told in the company's financial statements. If the company's financial ratios show its managers are using the company's existing capital efficiently, the firm can borrow funds at a lower interest rate. A company like Dick's that has an excellent ROIC will pay a much lower rate of interest than a company with a low ROIC, especially if the latter already has a lot of debt.

leverage The ability to use borrowed capital in ways that have the potential to lead to high rates of return.

A second important factor that determines the method a company uses to raise capital is financial leverage. Leverage is a financial term that refers to the ability to use borrowed capital—someone else's money—in ways that have the potential to lead to high rates of return. A simple example of leverage is the act of taking out a mortgage to buy a house. Suppose a person decides to borrow $500,000 at 5% interest rate for 15 years to purchase a house. The homeowner is betting that the total amount of interest he or she will have to pay over the life of the mortgage will end up being less than the amount that the house will appreciate by in value over the 15-year period. The difference between the price received when the house is sold and the total interest that has been paid on it is a measure of how much the homeowner has *leveraged* the borrowed capital to create a profit. In a way, the leveraged, or extra, return the homeowner receives is the reward for bearing the risk of tying up his or her capital in the house for 15 years when it could have been invested in a different way. Home ownership is an investment that has paid a high rate of return in the past, so homeowners have typically profited by taking on debt to buy houses because of the leverage it offers.

Just as a person takes on debt to buy a house, a company takes on debt when it uses borrowed capital to fund a new project. If managers have performed an accurate NPV analysis, however, the profits the project eventually generates will be sufficient to pay the interest on the debt; and if the project passes the breakeven point, the company has used (leveraged) someone else's money to make more money. Leverage is an important source of profit. In fact, if a profitable opportunity to put borrowed capital to good use arises, it is "good" to be in debt. But because of uncertainty, this strategy can also result in disaster. However, to get higher returns, investors must bear higher risks.

hedge funds Mutual funds that use highly leveraged investments to try to rapidly increase investors' capital returns.

Only the shrewdest investors can manage the high or speculative risks associated with borrowing capital to profit from leverage. Hedge funds are mutual funds run by shrewd analysts (fund managers) who invest in highly leveraged investments to try to aggressively increase investors' returns. These analysts invest in speculative ventures with rates of return so high that investors can double or triple their money in just a few months. If the fund managers make the wrong bets, though, they can lose investors' capital just as quickly. This is why only wealthy investors with a net worth of at least $1 million can legally invest in hedge funds—rich people can afford to lose a large amount of their capital; poor people cannot!

The increasing risks associated with using debt financing to borrow more and more money explains why, at some point, a company starts to issue stock. Each investor, as an owner, participates in the benefits and risks associated with investing his or her capital in the company when buying stock. The investor will receive his or her share of the profits the company generates in the future no matter how large (or small) those profits are. Thus, the potential upside and downside risks and returns from such an investment are unlimited. By contrast, debtholders only receive a specified interest payment for lending their money to a company no matter how much profit a company makes. However, debtholders or creditors have first claim on the company's assets if it cannot pay the interest on the debt, or the principal, which consist of the money originally borrowed. So, although debtholders returns are limited, so are their risks.

principal The amount of money originally borrowed.

capital structure The balance between the amount of capital a company raises through debt and the amount it raises through equity.

To manage the costs associated with raising capital, companies have to decide how to balance the amount of capital they raise through debt and the amount they raise by issuing stock. This balance is known as the company's capital structure. Now that we have discussed the main factors influencing a company's choice of financing methods, we can take an in-depth look at debt and equity securities.

Video
Small
Business
in Action

Starting a Business: Rieva Lesonsky Discusses How to Start a Business

Starting your own business is risky, according to the video from NBC on your Student DVD. Risk is part of the process of a new business venture. However, mitigating the risk is an important part of the process according to Rieva Lesonsky, editor of *Entrepreneur Magazine*.

In order to manage risk, the new business owner should have a solid business plan that h/she follows step by step. Software abounds to provide assistance to the entrepreneur. Go to Bplan.com for examples. Lesonsky suggests having a "risk quotient" for oneself in terms of how much risk you are willing to tolerate. She cautions that a new business consumes your life; you need to invest your time, money, and energy in order to be successful.

According to the Small Business Administration, more than 50% of new businesses fail within the first year and more than 95% fail within the first 5 years. Given these factors, Lesonsky suggests that one incorporate to create a wall between your personal "self" and your business "self." Finally, if you do fail, she suggests that you learn from your mistakes.

Discussion Questions

1. What are the methods of obtaining new capital? What is the most frequently used method for new business start-ups?
2. What does the term "finance" mean and how does it relate to the new business start-up?
3. What does breakeven analysis provide for the new business start-up?

Debt Securities: Bonds

debt securities
Investment documents that provide evidence of a company's legal obligation to repay within a certain period of time the money it borrows and make regular interest payments on that money in the meantime.

bonds Common types of debt securities issued by a company for a period of more than one year.

Debt securities are investment documents that provide evidence of a company's legal obligation to repay within a period of time the money it borrows and make regular interest payments on that money in the meantime. **Bonds** are debt securities issued by a company for a period of more than one year. They are one of the most common types of debt securities. To create a bond, a company's lawyers prepare a *deed of trust* or *bond indenture,* and a trustee, often a large commercial bank, is appointed to represent the interest of the bondholders (the people who buy and invest their capital in the bonds). The bond indenture describes the terms under which the bonds are issued, such as their value, a description of the assets used as security for them, if any, and details about interest rates and repayment terms of the principal.

Bonds issued by companies usually have a *face value,* or *par value,* of $1,000, which is the amount paid to a bondholder at the maturity date—the date the bond is due to be repaid. Companies have to find buyers for their bonds, so they pay to have their bonds *rated,* meaning ranked in terms of the riskiness or creditworthiness of the company that issued them. The two main companies that rate bonds are Moody's and Standard & Poor's. These firms rate the bonds of different companies based on the careful assessment of a company's financial statements, its business history, its current standing against its competitors, and the size of the debt it already owes. These ratings assess the likelihood that a company will default on its debts, meaning that a company will not be able to repay the interest and principal due in the future. Moody's and Standard & Poor's also estimate the revenue that would be received from the sale of the company's assets if they need to be sold to pay bondholders. The ratings range from AAA or Aaa, which are given to the bonds issued by companies assessed to have the lowest level of risk, to the lowest rating, D, which is reserved for bonds that are already in default.

The rating of a particular bond can change over time as the financial condition of the company that issued it changes. A company that becomes weaker because of increased competition in its industry might have its bonds downgraded, which means they are now rated as a riskier investment. The riskier a company, the higher the rate of interest it will have to pay investors to purchase its bonds. Also, owners of existing bonds will suffer when the risks of investing in a particular company's bonds increase because other investors will only agree to buy these bonds at a *discounted* or reduced rate. So, if current bondholders need to sell their bonds, they will take a loss. That is, they will receive less than the $1,000 face value they paid for the bond. As with all investments, the level of risk determines the level of potential future returns.

A key point about bonds, and debt financing, is that the value of a bond that has been issued changes over time as the general interest rate changes *even though the interest rate paid on the bond has not changed.* In other words, the interest rate was "locked in," so to speak, when the bond was issued. In general, as interest rates in the economy rise, the price, or par value, of bonds already issued falls because their rates of return relative to other investments have fallen. By contrast, as interest rates in the economy fall, the value of bonds already issued increases because their rates of return relative to other investments have increased. Investors, and bond mutual funds, make (or lose) money buying and selling bonds by betting on how changing risks and interest rates will affect the future prices of bonds.

The company that issued the bond will also be affected by changing interest rates. If interest rates in the economy go up, the company will be happy because it only has to pay the

Bonds, like the IBM bond shown here, usually have a face value (par value) of $1,000, which is the amount the company must pay the bondholder at the bond's maturity date—the date the bond is due to be repaid.

lower interest rate that will endure for the life of the bond, normally at least 10 years. Suppose, however, interest rates fall, as they did in 2003, down to 1 or 2%. Now the company that issued a bond that carries a relatively high rate of interest, say, 6%, is worse off. The high interest rates it agreed to pay on the bonds when it issued them reduces its return on investment, which can lead to financial trouble ahead.

To avoid such problems, many bonds contain a feature in the original bond indenture called a call provision. This gives a company the legal right to "call in its bonds," which means it can exercise the right to buy its bonds back from bondholders and repay its debt early to avoid high interest-rate payments. This provision is similar to the one in mortgage contracts that allow homeowners to refinance their mortgages to obtain lower rates when interest rates are falling.

Companies are not the only kinds of organizations that issue bonds, however. The U.S. Government is, in fact, the biggest bond issuer of all. When the government wishes to borrow money for more than one year to fund new government expenditures and its existing debts, it sells U.S. Treasury bonds to the public. For the investor, Treasury bonds are attractive because there is little or no risk of default—the government can issue new bonds to cover interest payments and repay the principal due on old bonds. Indeed, one of the major reasons why the government issues new bonds, and one reason the national debt increases over time (currently U.S. government debt is over $6 trillion) is to pay the principal and interest due on bonds it has issued in the past.

SELLING AND BUYING BONDS   Every day the amount of money that changes hands through the trading of bonds is many times larger than the money generated by the trading of stocks. Financial Web sites and publications such as *The Wall Street Journal* publish a list of the daily prices at which government and corporate bonds issued are trading. Figure 15.7 shows a typical bond entry, which reports a bond's current financial information to buyers and sellers.

The first column, *Bonds*, describes the issuer of the bond, in this case the Zylon Corp; 7 3/4 means Zylon is paying a 7 3/4 percent interest rate on the bond meaning its owner will receive $75 per year in interest (on the par value of a $1,000 bond); 07 means that the bond will mature in 2007, the year in which the principal must be repaid. On this day, the closing price of the bond was 106 1/4 meaning that the $1,000 bond is selling for $1,061.25, a 6% increase in its par value. It is selling for a higher price because it is paying a much higher interest rate than the one currently prevailing in the bond market—so the bond's *relative* rate of return has increased. When 30 of these bonds were traded the previous day, the price of the bond increased by 25 cents compared to the day before, which suggests that bond investors are betting that further falls in interest rates may be likely (which increases an existing bond's relative rate of return). The current yield tells an investor what the current rate of return on a bond is, which is 7.3% in Zylon's case, a figure obtained by dividing a bond's original interest rate by its current closing price (7.75%/$1,061.25 = 7.3%).

As noted earlier, bondholders have the first claim on a company's assets, before its owners, should it get into financial trouble. For this reason, bonds are perceived as being a less risky investment than stocks and therefore earn a lower rate of return than stocks. This is why bonds are regarded as a comparatively "conservative" investment and why people who are concerned about preserving their capital, as well as increasing it, should have both bonds and stocks in their personal portfolio. The more cautious or risk averse investor are, the greater the proportion of bonds they should hold in their portfolios. But even the most cautious investors understand the time value of money. Rather than investing in, say, low-earning money market funds, most people will buy bonds. What investors absolutely should not do is leave their cash

---

call provision A company's legal right to buy its bonds back early from bondholders to avoid high interest-rate payments.

current yield A financial measure of a bond's current rate of return. It is obtained by dividing the bond's original interest rate by its current closing price.

**Figure 15.7
How to Read
a Corporate
Bond Table**

BOND	CURRENT YIELD	VOLUME	CLOSE	NET CHANGE
ZYLON 7 ³⁄₄ 07	7.3%	30	106 ¹⁄₄	1/4

under a mattress where it earns no interest. If the economy is experiencing inflation, which is the case with most countries, the value of their money—that is, what they are able to buy with it—will drop.

Equity Securities: Stocks

equity securities The capital stock certificates a company issues giving shareholders the legal right to its assets and dividends from its profits.

initial public offering The first time the owners of a company's stock offer it for sale to the general public.

Equity securities are the capital stock certificates a company issues giving their owners legal rights to a company's assets (after creditors and bondholders) and the right to receive dividends from any profits the company makes. The initial public offering (IPO) is the first time the owners of a company, who currently own all of the units or shares of stock in the company, offer their stock for sale to the general public. As in the case of bonds, following legal procedures, a company announces a formal intention to sell a certain percentage of its stock to raise capital. An IPO is normally handled by an investment bank that advertises the sale and generates interest in the stock to increase its initial offering price. Obviously, the higher the initial price of the stock, the greater will be the amount of capital the IPO generates for the company. Once the stock is sold, the increase or decrease in its value depending on the demand for the stock determines the return the company's former stockholders receive.

Companies can issue more stock over time if they need it to fund their further growth. When a company does issue more stock this is said to *dilute* or weaken the value of its existing stockholders' equity because there are now a greater number of shareholders with a claim on the company's assets and income stream. For example, if a company issued 100 million shares initially, and then issued 100 million more a year later, when the 200 million shares are divided by net income, earnings per share fall by half. Obviously, existing stockholders do not like this dilution of their equity—it makes their stock less valuable. Indeed, when a company issues additional stock, the market value of the stock usually falls sharply in the short term because there is simply more supply of the stock than demand for it. However, providing the company uses the funds it raises to continue to grow profitably, demand for its stock will pick up over time, and its stock price will continue to rise.

TYPES OF STOCK   To assess the risks involved in investing in a company's stock and to assess what rate of return an investor should expect to achieve by bearing the risks of buying a particular company's stock, financial analysts classify them by their risk-return profile. Four main types of stock are blue-chip stocks, growth stocks, income stocks, and speculative stocks.

Blue-chip stocks are the stocks of the most prestigious companies such as DuPont, General Electric, IBM, and Procter & Gamble. These companies have a record of high cash flows and profits and for paying dividends to stockholders. They are a low to moderate risk and have provided a good return historically.

Growth stocks are those perceived to have the potential to generate high future cash flows and profits because their business model is based on making or selling new products that could earn millions or billions of future sales. A company whose stock is regarded as a growth stock, like Dick's Sporting Goods, does not pay dividends because it reinvests its profits back into its operations to increase sales. Companies such as these normally range from medium to high risk. The goal of both a growth stock company and its investors is capital appreciation: a rise in the price the stock sells for. If the firm's business model succeeds, investors who have risked their capital to buy and hold the stock receive high returns. Successful growth stock companies like Microsoft and Wal-Mart, eventually become the blue-chip companies of the future.

Income stocks are those primarily bought because their company's business model is perceived as being low risk and because historically the firm has regularly paid its investors high dividends. Investors do not view income stocks as being a good chance for long-run capital appreciation. Indeed, sometimes their dividend yields may be lower than the interest-rate payments they could have earned had they purchased bonds. Still, with stocks, unlike bonds, there is some chance for capital appreciation.

Yahoo! stock is considered speculative stock because the company is perceived as being a risky investment. The company's potential is great, but no one knows if or when the stock price will rise.

Often, these are the stocks of companies who are perceived to be safe bets in bad economic times because they provide goods and services, such as food products or insurance, which people always have to buy.

Speculative stocks are those of companies that are thought to have enormous upside potential but that currently have low sales. As measured by their financial ratios, they are perceived as being extremely risky investments. Nevertheless, they are highly valued by investors because of their enormous potential for future sales growth. Investors will pay *relatively* much more to own the stock of these companies than blue chip companies because of this potential. Investors lucky enough to buy and hold the stock of a company that does succeed are the ones who can "retire tomorrow." During the dot.com boom, for example, the shares of companies like eBay, Yahoo, Amazon.com, and AOL were valued at hundreds or thousands of times more than companies like Wal-Mart and GM. This has all changed now, and Wal-Mart is once again valued more highly than most dot.coms. By 2004, however, the share prices of the strongest dot.coms, like Yahoo, eBay, and Amazon.com, had once again soared. Investors apparently decided these dot.com stocks had the most potential to succeed in the long term.

SELLING AND BUYING STOCKS   Once company stock has been issued, it is traded on various types of stock markets. The purpose of the market is to increase the number of buyers and sellers interested in a particular stock. This helps ensure all of a company's stock is more accurately valued and priced. The two biggest stock markets are the New York Stock Exchange (NYSE) and the NASDAQ. Traditionally, the NYSE is home to large, profitable, blue-chip companies, and the NASDAQ is home to young, high-tech, or information-technology companies. In general, companies listed on the NASDAQ are perceived as being riskier investments than the typical company listed on the NYSE. Historically, a new company might first trade its stock on the NASDAQ, but if it prospers and its sales and profits increase, it would move to the NYSE.

Information about stocks is listed in most daily newspapers. Financial Web sites such as Morningstar.com, Yahoo, and MSNBC also contain vast amounts of financial information about every company traded on any stock market in the world—including their past financial statements and ratios. Entering a company's stock symbol, say GE, for General Electric, in the search bar on Yahoo! Finance will call up many different kinds of information about a company. If you click on profile in the box below the company's current stock price, you will find even information about the company. And, at the bottom of the left column, if you click on performance or financial ratios, the company Multex provides a complete financial analysis of the company.

The typical way of reporting in a daily newspaper how a company's stock has performed on a given day is shown in Figure 15.8. Each column of the table provides specific financial information about the stock. The first column or term *YTD % Change* tells an investor how much the value of a stock has changed on a year-to-date percentage basis. In this example, Liz Claiborne, the apparel company's stock, has risen in value by 7.1%. Next comes the *52-week high and low values* that a particular stock has traded at. Liz Claiborne's stock has ranged in price from a high of $32.46 to a low of $21.38 in the previous 12 months. The next column, STOCK(SYM), shows the abbreviated name of the stock, LIZ CLAIB, and its stock exchange symbol, LIZ. Then comes the term *DIV*, which refers to how much, if any, dividend a company pays to its stockholders. LIZ pays a 23-cent yearly dividend. That is, an investor receives 23 cents for each share of LIZ stock owned. The *YLD%* column tells the investor the dividend yield of the stock in percentage terms. It is the dividend divided by the closing price of the stock, in this case, .9%.

Figure 15.8
How to Read a
Stock Table

YTD % CHG	52-WEEK HI	52-WEEK LO	STOCK(SYM)	DIV	YLD %	PE	VOL 100s	CLOSE	NET CHG
7.1%	32.46	21.38	Liz Claib (LIZ)	.23	.9	10	5481	23.65	-0.13

price-to-earning ratio
A way of valuing a stock by dividing its closing price by its annual earnings per share.

The next column provides information about the stock's price-to-earning ratio, PE, which we discussed in the last chapter. The price-to-earnings ratio is a way of valuing a stock by dividing the closing price by annual earnings per share (EPS). Stocks normally are valued at some PE multiple such as 7, 15, or 26, meaning that a company is valued at 7, 15 or 26 times its current earnings. LIZ has a 10PE, so it is valued at a respectable 10 times its current earnings. Next, the volume column, *VOL 100s*, tells an investor how many shares of a stock were traded in quantities of 100 on that day. On this particular day, 548,100 shares of LIZ were traded. The *CLOSE* column shows the price at which the stock closed on that day. Finally, *NET CHG*, the last column, shows how much the stock price increased or decreased compared to its closing price on the previous day. LIZ decreased in value by 13 cents, an insignificant amount given the closing price of the stock.

Non-Operations Investing and Financing

An important aspect of both capital investing and financing is how a company chooses to spend the capital it has generated to achieve the best rate of return. Recall from the balance sheet that the most important kind of cash flow is cash flow from current operations that increase a company's working capital. Much of this cash is used to fund the future operating cycle.

Another category of cash flows, however, are those that result from a company's financing activities. These are the cash flows a company receives from investing its capital not in its operations but from buying stock and bonds and money market funds, and any other non-operations uses of its money. Companies must invest all of their capital in a way that will generate the highest rate of return for stockholders.

Sometimes, to increase the rate of return, a company will buy the stock of other companies. For example, a company might buy stock in its suppliers to signal them that they should cooperate harder with the company to find ways to increase operating efficiencies. This might involve implementing a JIT inventory system or finding ways to increase inventory turnover. Sometimes a company buys government and corporate bonds to increases the rate of return on its capital. Microsoft, for example has over $30 billion in current assets from retained earnings. To get the best return for stockholders, Microsoft's financial managers invest this money in the combination of securities they calculate will lead to the highest return, but they also keep enough of the money in securities that can be liquidated (turned into cash) easily should Microsoft decide to make a major acquisition in the coming months.

treasury stock Stock a company buys back from the public and becomes part of stockholders' equity on the firm's balance sheet.

Another financing option open to a company is to buy back its *own* stock on the open market. A company buys back its own stock when it believes its stock price is currently too low and is undervalued by the market. As a company buys back its own stock, it reduces the number of shares outstanding, and so the value of the remaining shares usually increases because the supply of them has been reduced. This is the opposite of dilution, discussed earlier. When a company buys back its own stock, this rewards investors because the higher stock price results in capital appreciation. The stock that a company buys back is known as treasury stock; it becomes part of stockholders' equity on the balance sheet. An interesting example of how a company could potentially reward its stockholders is provided in Business in Action.

Business in Action

Should Doctors Own Stock in Hospitals?

Throughout the last decade, there has been an increasing trend for medical doctors to become stockholders in the hospitals and clinics in which they work. Sometimes teams of doctors in a particular area join together to open their own clinic. Other times, large hospital chains give doctors stock in the hospital. Such a trend has the potential to cause a major conflict of interest between doctors and their patients.

Take the case of the Columbia/HCA hospital chain, for example. In the 1990s, Columbia began offering doctors a financial stake in the chain, a move designed to encourage doctors to send their patients to Columbia hospitals for treatment. The problem is that when they become owners, doctors then have an incentive to give their patients minimum standards of care in order to cut costs and increase the hospital's bottom line, or more likely to overcharge patients for their services and reap extra profits that way. In addition, the financial link between doctors and hospitals means that other hospitals, which might do a better job minimizing postoperative infections or managing general patient care, will not be used by these doctors.

In the 1990s, Columbia/HCA Retreat Hospitals began offering doctors a financial stake in the company so they would encourage patients to be treated at the chain's hospitals.

There has been some support for banning doctors from holding a financial stake in their own clinics and hospitals. In 2002, a major HMO owned by doctors settled charges that it used its power to demand lower prices from its suppliers and high fees from its patients. However, doctors claim that they are in the same situation as lawyers or accountants and there is no more reason to suppose that they will take advantage of their patients than these professionals might.[6]

Finally, a company might decide that it can get the best return on its capital if it buys the total amount of stock issued by another company and takes it over. In November 2004, for example, Oracle, which had been in a long, complicated battle to acquire software maker, PeopleSoft, offered to pay PeopleSoft's stockholders $24 a share, which put the value of the company at $8.8 billion. Oracle made the offer because it believed the acquisition would significantly increase the future value of its cash flows and profits and increase the return on its capital.

Summary of the Chapter

Corporate finance and investment is a fascinating subject. In a world full of uncertainty and risk, managers attempt to make the investment decisions that maximize the present value of their company's stock price. Finance provides a set of tools for quantifying that uncertainty and risk. It helps managers make better decisions. This chapter made the following major points:

1. Finance is the set of activities a company engages in to decide how to raise, use, and invest money so it generates more cash, profit, and capital in the future.

2. All investments must be compared in terms of their relative risks and returns. The higher the risks associated with an investment, the higher the rate of return people will demand from that investment.

3. Business finance is about increasing the rate of return on a company's capital to maximize the market value of stockholders' equity.

4. Capital investment and budgeting involves developing a financial plan and budget to manage capital so that it leads to the highest return on invested capital (ROIC).

5. Short-term capital management decisions are involved when a company buys resources to make products that will be sold within a one-year period. A major goal of short-term capital management is to increase the efficiency of the company's working capital by speeding up the firm's operating cycle.

6. Long-term capital budgeting decisions involve choices about how to invest capital for extended periods of time. Managers make these decisions in part by estimating the net present value (NPV) of a proposed investment—forecasting the value of the future stream of revenues that will result from it, reducing those revenues to their current *(present)* value, and comparing them to the firm's current cost of capital. If the NPV of a project is positive, then a company should invest in it.

7. A breakeven analysis forecasts the revenues and costs associated with a project to locate the point at which the project's sales just cover all of its costs without a profit being earned. When a project reaches its breakeven point, the revenues and profits earned from it increase rapidly.

8. The goal of capital financing is to obtain the money a company needs to fund its activities at the lowest possible cost.

9. The goal of short-term financing is to minimize the costs associated with financing a company's operating cycle. The method of financing managers choose is determined by the makeup of their company's working capital, that is, by the percentage of working capital it has tied up in inventory, accounts receivable, final products, or cash-on-hand.

10. The three ways most companies fund their long-term capital investment projects are by (1) spending their retained earnings, (2) issuing debt securities, and (3) selling equity securities. A fourth method involves outsourcing production to another company so it does not have to invest its capital to buy machinery and plants.

11. Securities are investment documents that give investors a legal claim against the assets of a company.

12. Debt securities are investment documents that provide evidence of a company's legal obligation to repay within a certain period of time the money it borrows and make regular interest payments on that money in the meantime.

13. Equity securities are the capital stock certificates a company issues giving the owners of the certificates the legal right to a company's assets and the right to receive dividends from any profits the company makes.

14. An initial public offering (IPO) is the first time the owners of a company offer their stock for sale to the general public.

15. Four main types of stock are blue-chip stocks, growth stocks, income stocks, and speculative stocks.

Developing Business Skills

QUESTIONS FOR DISCUSSION AND ACTION

1. What is the relationship between risk and return? What increases the risks involved in a particular investment?

2. What are the goals of business finance?

3. What is the goal of short-term capital management, and why is it important to make good use of a company's working capital?

4. What is the goal of long-term financial management, and how does NPV analysis help managers make better investment decisions?

5. What is the breakeven point and why is it important?

6. What are the four methods of long-term financing?

7. What are the differences between debt and equity securities?

8. What are the advantages and disadvantages associated with each type?

9. What is an IPO?

10. What are the four main types of stock and why are they different?

ETHICS IN ACTION

Patients and Capital

You are a group of doctors who own stock in your hospital. You have been asked to draw up a list of guidelines that all hospital doctors should follow to behave in an ethical way and put patients' interests first. Using the ethical principles from Chapter 5, consider the following issues:

- How can doctors change the way they treat their patients to speed up a hospital's operating cycle and make better use of the hospital's working capital?

- Although such changes might increase the return on their capital invested in their hospital, will these changes increase or reduce the quality of patient care?

- Draw up a list of the most important guidelines that doctors should follow to ensure they are treating their patients ethically while making efficient use of their capital.

- How much, if any, stock should doctors be allowed to own in the hospitals in which they work?

SMALL GROUP EXERCISE

Disney's Store Troubles

Read the following and then break up into groups of three or four people and discuss the issues involved. Be prepared to share your discussion with the rest of your class.

Often managers fail to correctly forecast the potential return on an investment because they lack knowledge about the business. Disney, for example, had never operated a chain of retail stores in the fiercely competitive retail and cruise ship industries. In particular, its managers failed to understand the

problems related to maintaining high profit margins in the company's retail stores.

1. How could Disney have shortened the operating cycle of its stores to make better use of its working capital?

2. Because its retail stores failed, Disney must have overestimated potential future sales, future costs, or both. How does this affect the accuracy of its breakeven analysis?

3. What different kinds of choices could Disney have made to protect the capital invested in its stores?

DEVELOPING GOOD BUSINESS SENSE

Financing at Dick's and the Sports Authority

In Chapter 14, you analyzed the financial statements of Dick's Sporting Goods and the Sports Authority. Now, taking a finance rather than an accounting perspective, go back to the Web sites of the two companies, examine their annual reports

and other relevant documents, and consider the following issues:

1. What are the main differences between the short-term capital management decisions made by the two companies? How are these decisions reflected in their financial ratios, like their inventory and asset turnover ratios?

2. How have these two companies chosen to finance their long-term investments? Are there differences in the mix of debt and equity they use to fund their operations?

3. What difference does this make in terms of their long-term financing? Which company finances its activities in the most cost-effective way?

4. What other differences exist between the way these companies finance their activities?

5. Dick's is growing rapidly. How might this change its long-term financial decisions in the future?

6. What steps has the Sports Authority taken to improve either its capital management or capital financing decisions?

EXPLORING THE WORLD WIDE WEB

The Functions of the FTC

Go the Web site of the Federal Trade Commission (www.ftc.gov), which contains a wealth of financial information and advice for consumers as well as businesses. Click on "Consumers" and you will see a list of useful FTC reports about careers, vocational training, and so on. Now click on the "Guide to the Federal Trade Commis-sion" link and read the introduction and sections on its three main bureaus. **For more Web activities, log on to www.mhhe.com/jonesintro.**

1. What are the main functions of the Bureau of Consumer Protection?

2. What are the main functions of the Bureau of Competition?

3. What are the main functions of the Bureau of Economics?

BusinessWeek   CASE IN THE NEWS

E*Trade Rises from the Ashes

Mitchell H. Caplan insists he never doubted that E*Trade Financial Corp. would survive. Not when shares of the online broker and bank plunged from more than $60 at the peak of the Internet frenzy to below $3 in 2002. Not even when the outfit lost a total of $428 million in 2001 and 2002. "I felt great about the business model," says the 47-year-old lawyer-turned-entrepreneur who rose to chief executive two years ago and was charged with getting the company on track. "I knew that if we stuck with it, we would get our story out."

Caplan's optimism has paid off. While E*Trade was given up for dead after the dot.com bust, its prospects now look bright. The nation's third-largest online broker just wrapped up its second profitable year in a row, earning an estimated $376 million on $1.52 billion of revenue. The company also told Wall Street that earnings could come in above $400 million this year on as much as $1.8 billion in revenues. Investors have bid E*Trade's stock up to $14 a share. "They survived the bubble, and they've come out the other end much stronger," says Friedman, Billings, Ramsey Group Inc. analyst Matthew J. Snowling.

Sure, the stock market rebound has helped, but much of the credit goes to the buttoned-down Caplan. Confronted with a culture that ignored red ink as long as the stock price climbed, he quickly went to work cutting costs and focusing the business. E*Trade no longer splurges on $2 million Super Bowl commercials. Instead of the $500 million a year it once spent on marketing—more than the entire U.S. liquor industry spends on ads—it will lay out a modest $140 million this year. Caplan also dispensed with distracting sidelines: a national ATM network, kiosks in Target stores, a palatial New York retail branch that sold E*Trade souvenirs, and a TV business-news service. New ventures, such as a string of small store-front offices in major cities, are rigorously vetted for profitability. "I am adamant—and as a team we are all adamant—about financial returns," he says.

RUBBER CHICKENS

Symbolic measures may have been as important in instilling discipline in the ranks. Breaking with E*Trade's wild past, Caplan moved the headquarters from Menlo Park, Calif., to New York City. Left behind were the propeller beanies and rubber chickens, geeky props that kept the atmosphere loose. Now jackets and ties are *de rigueur.* There are fewer employees, too: about 4,000, down from 5,000 at the peak.

Caplan joined E*Trade just as the Net frenzy was ebbing in 2000. A native of Virginia, he earned a law degree and an MBA from Emory University in Atlanta and practiced law in New York for five years. In 1989 the entrepreneurial bug bit, and he launched a branchless savings and loan, TeleBank. He figured customers would bank by phone, mail, and ATMs to get cheaper rates on loans and higher yields on deposits.

Eventually phone access became Net access. That drew E*Trade's attention: It soon plunked down $1 billion in stock to buy TeleBank. As Caplan integrated his bank into E*Trade's fast-growing brokerage operation, he focused on "boring stuff," he says, such as growth in revenue and earnings and return on equity. Impressed with Caplan, E*Trade's board elevated him from chief banking officer to North American head and then to president and chief operating officer.

By the time Caplan became CEO in January 2003, the company was in free fall. The former CEO, the exuberant Christos M. Cotsakos—who once had employees stand on chairs and shout corporate principles to each other—had run into criticism over an $80 million pay package he took while E*Trade was losing millions. Cotsakos was forced to return some $21 million. E*Trade's stock, worth about $26 a share when Caplan sold his bank, had shrunk to just a few dollars, hitting Caplan and fellow TeleBank investors in the wallet. "I felt like a passenger on the Hindenburg," recalls Thomas C. Danziger, a New York lawyer and longtime friend of Caplan's who says his investment had swelled to eight figures only to plunge to six figures.

Once in charge, Caplan and his colleagues focused on exploiting E*Trade's bank, where the company had a clear edge over rivals Charles Schwab Corp. and Ameritrade Inc. By offering banking products such as checking accounts and loans at bargain rates to trading customers, E*Trade has built the nation's eighth-largest thrift. It has become a big profit center, too, accounting for nearly 40% of revenues and 48% of profits. Overall, the company boasts some 632,000 bank accounts and 2.9 million active brokerage accounts, up from 170,000 bank accounts and 2.4 million brokerage accounts in early 2000.

BUYING A RIVAL?

After stripping E*Trade down to its basics, Caplan is now searching for growth. He has reorganized his management team around retail and institutional customers, hoping to appeal to hedge funds and institutional traders as well as individual investors. He's also interested in acquisitions. Last year, Caplan explored buying rival TD Waterhouse Investor Services Inc.—until he realized that a stock deal would give the firm's parent, Toronto-Dominion Bank, too big a stake in E*Trade. He is currently sizing up Ameritrade, whose $5.3 billion market capitalization slightly tops E*Trade's. "We've got the infrastructure," says Caplan. "We've got our costs down. Now let's complete the creation of the franchise." For its part, the relentlessly acquisitive Ameritrade is open to deals of all sorts, its executives say. Looking at the changes Caplan has made, Ameritrade CEO Joseph H. Moglia says: "Mitch has done an excellent job."

Much as Caplan's fixes have helped, he's facing tougher competition than ever. On Jan. 3, Scottrade Inc., the No. 6 online broker—and the cheapest of the major players—cut its fees. Charles R. Schwab, back in charge of his old company, is also dropping prices, although Caplan argues that Schwab is only playing catch-up. Schwab, which recently crept ahead of Ameritrade to become the online-trading leader, is ramping up its own bank, and Ameritrade is planning to launch one, too. Schwab is "a killer company," admits Caplan, but he's confident that E*Trade's customers will stay loyal.

If it would help shareholders, Caplan says he would sell E*Trade. Still, there's little doubt he would rather come out on top. "Mitch always wants to win," says Arlen W. Gelbard, Caplan's former college roommate, now president of E*Trade's bank. Indeed, the longtime tennis buddies rarely keep score on the court anymore to keep the games from getting too competitive. But investors are keeping score—and so far, Caplan is winning.

Source: Joseph Weber, "E*Trade Rises from the Ashes," *BusinessWeek Online,* January 17, 2005.

QUESTIONS

1. What steps did E*Trade CEO Mitchell Caplan take to turn around the company's performance and increase its profitability?

2. What steps might he take in the future to realize more value from the company?

BusinessWeek CASE IN THE NEWS

Media: Breaking Up Is Easy to Do

On March 16, Viacom confirmed that it was considering splitting the $22.5-billion-a-year company. One piece might comprise CBS, Infinity Broadcasting, and outdoor advertising, say sources, while the other would consist of red-hot MTV, its other cable networks, and the Paramount studio. Its theme park and book-publishing businesses may be put on the block. Wall Street applauded the news, with the stock rising $2.70, to $37.

Viacom is among a growing number of media outfits that feel frustrated by how the markets perceive their businesses. Of late, investors have been less than enthusiastic about the industry. In the past year, the Bloomberg Media Index, made up of 37 companies, posted a 3% return, versus a 10% gain for the benchmark Standard & Poor's 500 Index.

REDSTONE'S EXAMPLE? "These companies feel misunderstood and undervalued," says Gigi Johnson, executive director of the Entertainment and Media Management Institute at the UCLA Anderson School of Management. "There was a time when size mattered more than consistency, but it turns out it's hard for investors to decipher these companies and assess their business risks on their own. If you are buying Viacom today, you're buying an overly diversified media company, one in almost every sector of the industry's future."

The moguls are conceding that it's time to try a new strategy. "For whatever reason, [media stocks] have fallen out of favor with Wall Street, and I can't explain that," says Viacom Chairman Sumner Redstone who, over the course of 50 years, built his family owned drive-in operation into the huge corporation it is today. "As Shakespeare said, 'A rose by any other name is just as sweet.' Now I'll have two roses."

Does Redstone think other outfits will follow Viacom's lead? "Every media company is facing the same thing right now," he says. "I don't know if any of them will do what we have done, but I know that every one of them will be considering it."

They have already started. Just a day before Viacom's announcement, John Malone's Liberty Media, a holding company of sorts with a jumble of investments in various media companies, announced plans to spin off its 50% stake in cable networks Discovery Communications, along with a Hollywood post-production outfit, Ascent Media.

GARAGE SALES. On February 25, Walt Disney sold off its Mighty Ducks hockey team for $60 million, a paltry gain on the $50 million the company spent to launch the team in 1992. This follows last November's sale by Disney of its U.S. chain of 400 stores to The Children's Place. The Mouse House is also considering exploring the sale of its European chain of retail stores, which it valued at $36 million as of last September.

And consider the poster child of media merger mania: Time Warner, which agreed to sell itself to America Online in 2000 at the height of the Internet boom for $130 billion, a record deal. It created a $40-billion-a-year company that was widely viewed as having too many disparate pieces.

After the stock of what was then called AOL Time Warner took a beating in the market, newly appointed CEO Richard Parsons began in 2002 to sell off what would eventually total more than $5 billion in assets, including the Warner Music Group, a CD manufacturing business, a 50% stake in Comedy Central, and two Atlanta sports teams. Now the company, whose stock has risen 80%–to about $18–in two years, is mulling a public offering of its cable business.

"SYNERGY" DISCREDITED? There's a huge catalyst for splitting these companies: the current abundance of private equity money looking for investment opportunities. It makes for an enticement to executives seeking to jettison declining but steady cash flow businesses. Private equity firms have been gobbling up media companies from Warner Music to PanAmSat to Hollywood Entertainment, as well as taking a major position in a Sony/MGM venture.

After years of bombardment with unrelenting sales pitches from media companies about the importance of scale and "synergies," should investors now feel duped as they witness the companies pull themselves apart? "In the end, it's probably a good thing for shareholders that this is happening," says UCLA's Johnson.

It was Wall Street that dictated to the media companies what they wanted to see, not vice versa, says Robert Kindler, global chief of mergers and acquisitions at JPMorgan Securities, which is advising Barry Diller's Interactive Corp. on its spin-off of online travel business Expedia. "The best companies are the ones responding to what investors want. And investors today want more focused businesses. They have less faith in conglomerates."

Yet it's far too early to know whether media deconsolidation will benefit investors in the long run. The only guaranteed winners will surely be investment bankers like Kindler, who get the fat fees whether they're putting companies together or taking them apart.

Source: Tom Lowry and Ron Grover, "Media: Breaking Up Is Easy to Do," *BusinessWeek Online,* March 17, 2005.

QUESTIONS

1. What problems arise when investors try to evaluate the performance of companies that own many different kinds of businesses?

2. Why would breaking up a company into pieces allow these media companies to realize more value from their business assets and increase their financial returns?

BUILDING YOUR MANAGEMENT SKILLS
Know Thyself

How do you make up your mind when you have to make a big decision such as choosing a college or buying a car? Perhaps you gather as much information as you can through Internet research, ask parents or friends what they think, or just decide based on what you like. This chapter on Finance is about the decisions managers make to balance risk and potential gain, debt or equity financing, and how to invest profits to use a company's resources to create the maximum value for stakeholders. To learn more about the way you make decisions, try the exercise on your Student DVD "Your Preferred Decision-Making Style".

CHAPTER VIDEO
Winning Advice—Jack Welch

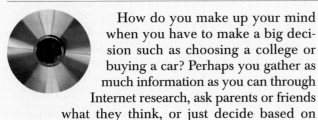

At the time of this interview from *BusinessWeek TV,* Jack Welch had recently authored his book, *Winning.* Several questions are asked of Welch: (1) How do you lead, hire, and get ahead? The answer, according to Welch, is to look for individuals who are smarter than you are, who have high levels of energy, who are action oriented, and get the job done. (2) How are managers distributed in the company? According to Welch, there are three tiers—the top 20 percent, the middle 70 percent, and the bottom 10 percent. The job is to grow individuals—try to move the middle 70 percent up and to try to encourage the bottom 10 percent to move on. He says that all employees should know where they stand in the company. It is the manager's responsibility to ensure that all employees know this. Welch says that when you become a manager it becomes all about your employees, not about you.

1. How might you relate the finance concept of risk to that of hiring a talented executive?

2. What is the most difficult thing about being in management, according to Welch?

3. What is the best thing about being a manager, according to Welch?

Appendix to Chapter 15

Managing Your Personal Finances

There is a very close connection between people's personal finances and careers. Excluding those with private or inherited wealth, the amount of a person's lifetime earnings directly relates to the number of years of his or her education and training. Educational qualifications are the main determinant of what kinds of jobs, occupations, and careers people will pursue over the course of their working lives. Nevertheless, while the number of years of a person's education is the main determinant of a person's lifetime *earnings*, this does *not* necessarily mean that a person will become *wealthier* over time. The ability to accumulate capital and wealth, as opposed to earning income, is the result of a person's ability to understand how scarce and valuable a commodity money is and how to use, manage, and invest it wisely. This appendix provides some guidelines to help people think about how to manage their personal finances so that over time their increased earnings *do* translate into increased capital and wealth.

Perhaps the best place to start to understand the financial management process is to look at how a business organization makes financial decisions about spending, saving, and borrowing money.

In Chapter 15, we discussed how companies borrow money and take on debt to fund ventures they hope will earn them a large stream of *future* income and profit. Note, however, that most companies only take on debt to fund future *wealth-creating* ventures. In other words, they borrow money only when they believe they can use that money to generate more money and profit. If they are successful, the profits earned are retained in the company, and the firm's assets and shareholders' equity increase in value.

Established companies normally only take on debt to fund *current expenditures* as a last resort—when their capital and assets are becoming exhausted and they need to borrow money to keep them solvent, or "above water." For example, a company might be unable to pay for its current expenditures because of an unexpected, short-term cash flow problem it believes is only temporary. By contrast, a company's cash flow problems might be due to the fact that its business model is failing and its owners or managers are desperately searching for a source of funds to keep the business solvent in order to avoid bankruptcy.

When a company has no retained earnings or stockpile of cash, it has to search for financial institutions or private investors that will lend it money. However, most potential lenders will not loan a company money unless they believe it will be possible to get their money back by selling the company's assets if it goes bankrupt. Bondholders and debtors have first claim on a bankrupt company's assets, not its stockholders or owners. Even if banks or private investors are willing to assume the risk of lending a troubled company money to solve its short-term cash flow problems, they will do so only at high rates of interest. This makes it very expensive for a company to pay off these loans. Similarly, private investors will usually demand a large chunk of the company's equity or stock in return for loaning a company in trouble money. If the company fails, they will then take control of it and its assets.

What does this mean for an ordinary person—someone who has to decide how to spend, save, and borrow money to fund his or her current and future expenditures—someone who has to maintain his or her current lifestyle, pay for ongoing education and training, and save money for retirement? Just as companies only succeed if they have a viable business model, to succeed people must increase the value of their current and future human capital. Successful financial planning also necessitates that people, like businesses, consider the amount of money they need now as well as in the future, say, in a year's time. Only by looking into the future can people (and businesses) make ongoing financial spending and saving decisions that maximize their utility.

Spending Decisions

The fact is that most people, no matter how wealthy they are, *never* have enough money to completely satisfy their needs and desires. Money and capital are scarce, but the amount of goods and services that can be bought to satisfy one's current and future needs is not. This is why people have trouble managing their personal finances. There are always many more goods and services that people would like to buy than they can afford. Given the sheer range of enticing products available for purchase–food, clothing, electronics, jewelry, cars, and homes–it is not surprising that many people throw caution to the wind, spend more money than they own, and go into debt. Even people who know they need to economize and choose less-expensive options such as lower-priced clothing and cars frequently spend more money than they should because they overestimate their future income and underestimate the problems of paying off debt.

As we noted in Chapter 1, strangely enough, research shows that the people who *do* make the best spending and saving decisions–people who spend their money wisely in ways that provide them with the most current *and* future utility–are those who have the most money to spend. These are the richest people in a society–the so-called "millionaires" (although today a person needs to have a net worth of over $20 million to match the spending power of the millionaires of decades past). In large part, the richest people are able to make the best financial decisions because with a secure financial "safety blanket," they have the luxury of being able to look ahead–to decide how best to spend *and* save their money on an ongoing basis so that they maximize their present and future utility. These people do not have to worry about how to put food on the table, or how to pay this month's rent or credit card bills.

Nevertheless, even people who lack a financial safety blanket and have inadequate or limited funds, must also make financial decisions in the way the richest people do if they are to avoid financial disaster and make their limited funds stretch as far as possible. No matter what their income level, this process always begins with the need for people to carefully consider the future consequences of their present spending decisions–even though this often involves hard decisions, such as forgoing purchasing new clothing, DVDs, or going out on a Saturday night. By looking at the future consequences of their spending, however, people can more effectively decide how to allocate their money to pay for ongoing necessities like food, rent, and utilities. Second, it helps them not to spend money they do not yet own. In other words, it helps ensure people do not get into debt and borrow money they cannot pay back–the worst possible financial situation a person can be in, as we discuss below.

Personal financial management begins with a careful, meticulous, and painstaking assessment of how to spend whatever money is available to get the most utility or benefit from it. Understanding how to spend money wisely is something that has to be learned, and it is often learned the hard way. Unfortunately,

financial learning often begins when a lack of money forces people to think carefully through the present and future consequences of their spending decisions. These decisions are of equal and often more importance than the decisions they make about what classes to take, where to live, and whom to select as their friends, lovers, or eventual marriage partners.

Developing and Keeping a Personal Budget

Financial management begins with developing and keeping a personal budget, just as a company's accountants monitor a company's income and expenditures so managers know the consequences of their spending and investment decisions. Research suggests that a higher proportion of millionaires than people in other income brackets develop and stick to a budget. There are good reasons for doing so.

Developing a budget is the best way for people to get a grip on their spending so that they can evaluate if they are using their money in the best possible ways. It begins first with identifying how much money you spend on an ongoing basis; and second, with analyzing how and where you are spending that money. Table 1 provides a checklist that covers many of the goods and services that most people buy on an ongoing basis. Completing the checklist is a worthwhile exercise. Take some time looking at your past bills, receipts, and bank statements over the course of the last six months. Then estimate the amount of your average monthly personal expenses and compare it to your monthly income to determine when and why you had money left over or if you have overspent.

Obviously, the worksheet needs to be tailored to your personal situation. People still living at home, for example, may or may not pay rent whereas people living in an apartment obviously do. Those who have saved the money necessary for a down payment on a home may be paying a mortgage. Indeed, one reason people live at home is that it gives them the opportunity to save on living expenses and pay their higher-education costs.

Completing this worksheet is especially useful for people contemplating life changes that will significantly affect their expenses, such as the decision to leave home and move into an apartment, to assume the monthly costs of a new car payment, or to budget

Table 1
Worksheet

Expenses		Entertainment	
Shelter		Dining Out	
Mortgage or Rent	_____	Cable/Videos/Movies	_____
Utilities		Magazines/Newspapers	_____
Heat		Vacations	
Electric	_____	Other	_____
Garbage/Sewer/Water	_____	**Education**	
Telephone	_____	Tuition and Fees	_____
Property Taxes	_____	School Supplies	_____
Insurance	_____	Books	_____
Furnishings	_____	**Savings**	
Maintenance	_____	Financial Institution	_____
Homeowner's Association Dues	_____	Company Savings Plan	_____
Transportation		IRA	_____
Car Payment/Lease	_____	Other	_____
Insurance	_____	**Family Needs**	
License/Registration	_____	Life Insurance	_____
Maintenance	_____	Child Care	_____
Gasoline	_____	Child Support	_____
Parking/Tolls/Taxi/Bus	_____	Pets	_____
Food		Allowances/Gifts	_____
Groceries	_____	**Additional Items**	
Lunches/Snacks	_____	Donations	_____
Health Costs		Membership Dues	_____
Insurance	_____	Taxes (Not Already Withheld)	_____
Doctor(s) Bills	_____	Other	_____
Dentist Bills	_____	**Credit Payments**	
Prescription Drugs	_____	Credit Card	_____
Clothes		Credit Card	_____
Purchases	_____	Credit Card	_____
Cleaning/Laundry	_____	Department Store	_____
Personnel		Gasoline Card	_____
Haircuts/Cosmetics	_____	Student Loan	_____
Alcohol/Tobacco	_____	Other	_____
Other	_____	**Total Expenses**	_____

Income	
Paycheck	
Paycheck	_____
Gratuities	_____
Dividends/Interest	
Pension/Social Security	_____
Child Support	
Gifts	_____
Total Income	_____

(continued)

Table 1 (continued)
Your Net Worth

What You Have

Take-Home (After-Tax) Pay	$_____
Checking/Savings Accounts	$_____
Certificates of Deposit (CDs)	$_____
Security Deposit	$_____
Investments	$_____
Loans Owed to You	$_____
Cash in Your Pocket	$_____
Other (Birthday Checks, Allowances, Etc.)	$_____
Total of What You Have	$_____

What You Owe

Rent	$_____
Car Loan	$_____
Student Loans	$_____
Credit Card(s)	$_____
Store Charge Cards	$_____
Money You Owe (Friends, Etc.)	$_____
Other Outstanding Debt	$_____
Total of What You Owe	$_____

What You Have	**$_____**
What You Owe	$(_____)
Your Net Worth	$_____

ahead for future education costs. The extra expenses associated with a move to an apartment, for example, are surprisingly high and often amount to several hundred dollars a month. After people have a grasp of their budgets and the way their income is earned and spent, they can more accurately answer questions such as, "Do I have sufficient income to pay for the monthly expense of living in an apartment?" "Is spending this amount of money on rent a good decision given the fact that I am currently trying to save money for my education or make a down payment on a new car or house?" "Suppose I share an apartment with other people? How much will this reduce my expenses so I can still save money each month?"

Keeping a budget and performing these kinds of financial calculations allow people to evaluate their spending-habit patterns and change them to meet their financial objectives, such as buying a car or establishing a long-term savings plan. Of course, once a person has worked out a budget and decided how his or her income should be spent or saved, the person must then watch his or her ongoing spending to ensure it stays within those guidelines. Just as managers want real-time information about how a company's income and expenditures are changing, so people need to be continuously aware of how much money they are taking in and giving out (spending) on an ongoing basis.

Financial Guidelines for Staying within a Budget

Given that people usually want to spend more money than they possess, sticking to a financial budget that keeps them "in the black," meaning that their income exceeds their expenditures, is not an easy task. What financial guidelines or rules should people use to budget their money to help them stay in the black as opposed to going "in the red," meaning their expenditures exceed their incomes so they go into debt? Moreover, beyond the short-term goal of keeping one's head financially above water, how can people increase their long-term capital and wealth?

RULE 1: Do *Not* Take on Debt Unless You Currently Own the Money Necessary to Pay Off the Debt!

The personal decision about how and when to borrow money on credit and "take on" or "get into debt" is one of the most complex, difficult, and significant decisions a person can make. But many people who get into debt do so without thinking, often because they do not understand the immense future consequences of this decision. In other cases, people get into debt by accident rather than design because they don't stick to a budget and own too many credit cards. It's sad but true: Many people don't begin to manage their personal finances to create a financial safety blanket and wealth for themselves until they are perilously in debt.

Charles Dickens summed up the need for financial budgeting in his classic book *David Copperfield.* As the character Mr. Micawber puts it:

Income twenty pounds, expense twenty pounds and sixpence: Result—unhappiness. (spending one dollar too many)
Income twenty pounds, expense nineteen pounds, nineteen shillings and sixpence: Result—happiness. (having one dollar left over)

In Dickens's day a person who could not pay back that sixpence (dollar) at the end of the month could be put into debtor's prison and left there to rot; debtors even had to beg for food to survive. Society provided people with a clear message—do not borrow money you cannot pay back.

The same platitude remains true today except under one circumstance: In general, it is acceptable to go into debt when the debt is incurred to fund the costs of the education and training a person needs to build his or her human capital. A person investing in his or her education is the equivalent of a company investing in a new commercial venture that it hopes will earn high future profit. Assuming this investment in education pays off, and as noted earlier, research suggests that it does, it becomes acceptable and financially prudent to borrow money to obtain educational qualifications. The same is true for investing in assets such as the car and clothing necessary to succeed in business. Of course, borrowing money to buy a dwelling to avoid the costs of paying rent, finance a new business, or buy rental property might also be financially sound decisions. However, these kinds of borrowing decisions are obviously far in the future for a person worrying about paying back the sixpence currently owed.

Today, however, many people borrow money just to fund their current or ongoing expenses and have little or no money available to pay it back. The most common way people spend more than they can pay back is by using credit cards to finance their purchases. In the last decade, credit card companies began issuing their cards to people with little income and no credit history. In fact, most of the growth in the use of credit cards today is by people under the age of 25–those most likely to have limited incomes. The reason credit card companies make cards so accessible is simple–the profit they earn from the high rates of interest they charge to borrow money is enormous, many billions of dollars a year.

In 2005, for example, a person with a good credit history could probably have borrowed $5,000 from his or her bank or credit union for around 9 to 11% interest, assuming the person also agreed to pay the balance and interest off in two years. By contrast, borrowing $5,000 using a credit card would have involved paying an interest rate of 15 to 20% or more. Moreover, there is *no* requirement that a person using a credit card pay back a sufficient amount of money each month to pay off the interest and principal borrowed. As a result, many credit card borrowers, lacking the money to pay off any part of their credit card balance, only make the "minimum payment" they are required to each month. *But this does nothing to reduce the total amount of money they owe on the card!* Add to this the fact that many people continuously take on more debt because they keep on using the card to pay for ongoing expenses. As a result, their credit card balances balloon over time. In turn, this means that the amount of money they have to pay each month just to pay interest on their balances increases–and remember credit card users are already paying a very high rate of interest.

This credit-card-balance, interest-payment trap puts people in a frightening situation: They end up being permanently saddled with an ever-increasing amount of credit card debt they can't pay off. Accumulating a credit card balance (or any form of debt) that cannot be paid off will put a person on the road to financial ruin and personal bankruptcy. However, unlike in the past, the passage of the Bankruptcy Protection Act in 2005 now largely prevents people from declaring personal bankruptcy and wiping out their credit card debts. Under the new act, credit card debt never goes away. Even if people declare bankruptcy, they still have to work out payment schedules with their credit card companies. At the same time, these people suffer because their inability to pay off their credit cards saddles them with a poor credit history that adversely affects many aspects of their lives, such as their ability to obtain utility or phone service, a student or car loan, or an apartment or home.

Thus, to avoid the credit-card-debt trap, you absolutely must follow **Rule No. 1:** *For every dollar you spend using a credit card, make sure you have enough in your personal savings account so that you can pay off your balance in full each month.* The reality of successful financial management is that just as a company with zero cash flow will soon go into bankruptcy, so a person who consistently borrows more than he or she earns will go the same route. A new business has to have a stock of capital to survive until it can generate revenues from customers; people have to have a stock of savings before they can take on debt to fund necessary future expenditures. This is the reality noted by Mr. Micawber, who was always relying on an "unexpected fortunate event," such as a gift or an inheritance to help him avoid the debt trap.

A second important rule when borrowing money using credit cards is to use only *one* credit card. When people use only one credit card, it easy for them to go online and review the pattern of their credit card purchases to find out how much debt they have accumulated so they can be sure they pay it off monthly. However, when people use several different cards, it becomes much more difficult to keep track of how much debt they are accumulating, and therefore easier to ignore the total debt. When only one card is used, however, reality bites: It is then easy to compare one's debts to one's savings. This makes it less likely a person will run up a high credit card balance. People also need to be aware of the so-called "interest free" charge cards they constantly receive in the mail. The fact is that many of these cards carry a zero interest rate only if the holder can pay off his or her balance in full each month! The bottom line is that people with no savings should not use credit cards.

RULE 2: Do Everything Possible to Build Short-Term and Long-Term Savings

Ideally, experts recommend that people accumulate a sufficient amount of savings to pay for at least three months of ongoing expenses should they lose their jobs. For most people the principal way they earn money is by working at a job. But if the job does not pay enough to allow a person to save money, then a second or third job becomes necessary. Nonetheless, working several jobs to earn and save money in order to be able to borrow money in the future is financially worthwhile.

Take credit cards, for example: Assuming people *do* pay off their balances (or at least part of their bal-

ances) on time each month, they develop a good credit history. This is vital to their ability to build long-term financial wealth. It is something of a paradox that a person cannot build up a good credit record without having a history of paying off their debts on time. So, to show they are reliable debtors, people need to borrow and pay back modest sums of money in order to be able to borrow increasing amounts of money in the future. For example, a person with a good credit card payment record can often obtain a sizeable loan at a low interest rate. This also allows the person to use leveraged (borrowed) money, say to buy a home. Home ownership has many advantages. Houses offer all kinds of income tax benefits and usually appreciate. In addition, by taking out a mortgage, you can eventually own your own home, which you cannot do as renter. Property owners, by contrast, use the rent you pay them to pay off the mortgage they assumed to purchase the rental property you live in. Instead of you, your landlord enjoys the advantages of leveraged money, that is, using other people's money to make money. But if you lack savings or have failed to develop a good credit history, you may have no choice but to continue to pay monthly rent versus buy a home. Moreover, if you are in a low-income bracket, your rent can often amount to one-half or more of your monthly income.

So how do low-income earners manage to pay off their credit card bills or even save money? The hard answer is that it is often very difficult or impossible for them to because they are caught in a "poverty trap." Millions of people are in this unfortunate financial situation. They are burdened with such high rent and credit card payments they cannot get out of the trap. Once again, this is why investing in education is so important. The ability to develop personal human capital and get a higher paying job helps people escape the trap—but only if they live within their means—that is, if they spend less than they make.

To help people do this, experts recommend that parents teach their children from the earliest age possible to save 10% or more every month, even if their income amounts to just a small allowance. One important reason for this is to teach kids to exercise self-discipline when it comes to spending. Another reason is that the longer the time period money is invested for, the more it appreciates in value because of the magic of compound interest. This is an advantage that the young more so than the old can especially benefit from. Money invested wisely today and left to accumulate is worth much more than money invested at a later point in a person's life. As an example, suppose I invest $1,000 at 10% for a period of 10, 30, 50, or 70 years. Ignoring income taxes on interest earned, the value of that $1,000 at the end of each time period would be $2,594, $17,449, $117,391, and a whopping $789,747. The value of the original sum invested increases exponentially over time because the interest earned each year on the principal then begins earning interest too. The result is a type of "snowball" effect. This "compounding" interest effect on the value of money is truly amazing and one more reason why people should start to save at a young age. However, this advice is hardly useful to people who are struggling just to keep their heads above water financially and pay off their credit card balances.

RULE 3: Always Search for Ways to Make Your Money Go Further by Getting More Value from Each Dollar You Spend

So, the basic principles of successful financial management are clear-cut: On the one hand, taking on debt that cannot be paid off results in financial ruin; on the other hand, saving money and taking on debt wisely results in financial success. Fortunate people who have made successful educational and career choices enjoy an improving financial situation over time that allows them to use their higher incomes to simultaneously pay off their student and other loans, start a savings plan, begin the process of home ownership, and make other kinds of wealth-building investments.

The dividing line between financial success and failure is often fragile, however. If the ordinary person is to succeed, it is usually necessary to deny oneself many of the short-term pleasures that result from spending one's available money and time now in enjoyable ways. The term *delayed gratification* is used to describe people who have the ability to look ahead and force themselves to forgo spending their time and money in ways that increase their short-term utility but do not maximize their future utility. Delayed gratification has been found to be associated with career and financial success.

Of course, being able to delay your gratification and save money is good. But being able use your money to earn more money is even better. Managing money is a skill that you can develop over time by devoting just a little bit of energy to the endeavor. Just reading the daily or Sunday business section of your newspaper can provide you with a great deal of financial knowledge, as can occasionally picking up a magazine like *Money* or *Kiplinger's*. Many Internet sites are also available to help explain the many issues that surround successful savings and investing. For example, Yahoo!, MSN, and The Motley Fool

offer a rich array of resources. Initially you might not understand all of the terms and information you read in these magazines or on these Web sites, but eventually you will. And because so many people pay scant attention to their finances, it's quite possible that over time you will become more financially savvy than anyone you know—and probably wealthier, too.

In the meantime, there are some basic ways you can stay out of debt and get more for your money so you can save for the future. As the adage goes, if a person "takes care of the pennies, the dollars will take care of themselves."

1. Develop an appreciation of the value of goods and services by comparing the quality of similar or competing products. Take advantage of publications like *Consumer Reports,* a nonprofit product evaluation magazine available in libraries that objectively rates competing products.

2. Always shop around for the best prices and use the Internet to compare the prices of different products. Always think carefully about why you are making a particular purchase and what utility you will gain from the purchase. Then evaluate this utility against the price. If the product costs, say, twice as much as a similar product, is it truly twice as good? Will it make you twice as happy or provide you twice the utility? If not, buy the cheaper product.

3. Avoid impulse purchases. Resist the urge to buy products at the checkout stand, and never go into just one store and buy the first item you see. Before finally purchasing a product, visit the store a second time to evaluate the product again to ensure it is a good value for your money.

4. Always try to buy products on sale, often at the end of the season even though you might not use the products until the following year. Also, compare a product's everyday price in different stores to be sure the sale being advertised is a "real one" and not just a gimmick to make the product seem lower priced.

5. Use eBay to buy a wide variety of merchandise including books, clothing, toiletries, electronics, and so forth. eBay is a huge market with thousands of sellers, so prices on eBay are likely to be the best available. To ensure sellers are honest, check their approval ratings. eBay sellers want to avoid negative feedback, so most buyers who use the site have few problems with their purchases.

6. Shop in thrift or charity stores to find interesting things that can be obtained inexpensively but provide great utility. Items such as interesting furniture, kitchen equipment, china, workout equipment, and clothes are often available at extremely low prices in thrift stores.

7. Never buy new cars, furniture or large ticket items unless you are in a secure financial position because once these products are purchased, their value plummets. For example, the value of a new car drops 10% as soon as it is driven off the lot; the value of new furniture drops 60% as soon as it is in your home; and the value of clothes drops 90% as soon as you cut the tags off. So, be very careful that you are buying things that you like and will get utility from over an extended period.

8. Only establish one checking and savings account at a financial institution. Search out the best deals such as free checking with no monthly fees. If you can, join a credit union. Credit union members often pay lower fees and earn higher interest rates on the money saved in their accounts. Never write a check with insufficient funds and avoid any temptation to do so. Use a debit card to make purchases whenever possible.

9. Do not obtain a credit card until you have built up sufficient savings to pay off the credit card balance you accumulate at the end of every month. Then use only one credit card—a card that has no yearly fees and offers a "cash back" bonus. For example, the Discover credit card currently has no fees and offers 1% back on each dollar charged on the card. Many credit unions and banks are also currently developing such cards. Always use a cash-back card versus one offering frequent flier miles or other company-specific benefits.

10. Try to save at least 10% of your monthly income whenever feasible given your changing financial situation.

11. Assuming you do have money to invest, only invest it in products that you are *knowledgeable* about. For example, never buy the stock of individual companies unless you know a lot about the company, have studied it for several years, understand its industry and its competitors, and can analyze its current financial situation. Similarly, do not buy individual bonds or invest in commodities like real estate, jewelry, coins, currency, metals, and so on unless you have expertise in these products.

12. If you have no specialized knowledge about potential investments, pick one or two large mutual fund companies to invest your money in. Choose funds that have low annual maintenance fees and funds that have received high performance ratings by publications such as *Morningstar* and *The Wall Street Journal*. Choose a selection of stock or bond funds according to your personal risk preferences, and then leave the money in the fund for a period of a few years, monitoring its performance every year or so. Avoid switching funds frequently because you may have to pay extra fees to do so and because the performance of any fund is unpredictable over a short time period.

13. Reinvest any dividends you receive from the mutual funds you own and add money to the funds regularly as you can afford it.

14. Consider using your savings to purchase a dwelling as soon as it becomes financially feasible, but be careful to look at hundreds of different properties to find one you recognize as being undervalued and a good deal.

15. Continually be aware of the need to build your human capital and seek higher degrees or qualifications whenever it is clear that your income will not increase significantly or that your skills are becoming outdated. Politely ask your mentors and peers who appear to be doing well if they would be willing to tell you what they earn and how they got their jobs. Many of them will, indeed, give you this information as well as offer you advice about how to succeed in their businesses or careers.

In conclusion, managing your money and personal finances is a complex and difficult activity, but it can be one of the most rewarding. Financial success ultimately results from hard work, becoming financially informed, some luck, and the ability to understand the future consequences of the spending and saving decisions you make today. Not so coincidentally, these are the same factors that result in success or failure in the great game of business.

Glossary

A

ACCOUNTING   The process of collecting financial data, organizing and analyzing it using agreed-upon accounting rules, and reporting the results in financial statements.

ACCOUNTING SYSTEM   The financial information system a company uses to measure, record, analyze, and report all the transactions involved in its value-creation process.

ACCRUAL BASIS OF ACCOUNTING The principle that a company's income statement should reflect the revenue received when the company makes a sale, not when payment is actually received.

ADVERTISING   The paid, nonpersonal promotion of a company's goods and services using mass media to influence consumers.

AGENCY PROBLEM   The problem that arises because of the separation of the ownership and control of a business. It occurs when the firm's owner delegates authority to managers.

AGENT   A person or intermediary acting on behalf of a final customer.

ANTITRUST LAWS   Laws passed to curb the power of big business and make it illegal for companies to conspire with one another to limit supply to keep prices high.

ARBITRATION   A conflict resolution method that involves the use of a neutral third party to negotiate and impose a binding agreement on labor and management.

ARISTOCRACY   People given the right by a ruler to control a country's resources, including its land and labor.

ARTIFICIAL INTELLIGENCE   An IT system that reasons and learns like a human being.

ASSET TURNOVER RATIO   A measure of how well a company's assets are turned over or being put to use to generate sales.

ASSETS   The productive resources a company owns as well as all of its financial investments.

ATTITUDINAL STRUCTURING   The attempt by negotiators on each side to influence each other's attitudes during the bargaining process.

AUDIT   The formal evaluation of the fairness and reliability of a company's financial statements.

B

B2B MARKETPLACE   An industry-specific trading platform set up to connect buyers and sellers using the Internet.

BALANCE SHEET   A summary of the financial condition of a business at the end of a day of a specific reporting period.

BANKERS   The people who estimate the risks associated with a new venture and determine the way profits from a venture should be shared.

BARTER   The exchange of one product for another product.

BENCHMARKING   The practice of comparing a business's strengths and weaknesses to those of its competitors.

BENEFITS   The monetary rewards, such as paid health care, life insurance, sick and vacation pay, and pensions, employees receive because they are a member of a company.

BEST PRACTICES   The set of skill-based competencies that allow a particular function to perform at its optimal level.

BEST-OF-BREED SOLUTION   The highest-performing IT hardware or software application currently available for managing a particular information processing or multimedia task.

BOARD OF DIRECTORS   Experienced business executives from inside and outside of a company who are elected by a company's shareholders to act as their representatives.

BONDS   Common types of debt securities issued by a company for a period of more than one year.

BONUS PAY   A one-time reward employees receive for accomplishing a specific goal.

BOOKKEEPING   The record-keeping activities needed to monitor and track all of the financial transactions related to making and selling goods and services.

BOTTOM-LINE PROFIT   The amount of net income, profit, or earnings a company reports on the bottom line of its income statement.

BRAND LOYALTY   The tendency of customers to consistently purchase a particular product over time because they believe it can best satisfy their needs.

BRAND MANAGER   A manager responsible for managing a brand-name product.

BRAND NAME   The specific name, sign, or symbol a company uses to distinguish and legally protect the identity of its products.

BREAKEVEN POINT   The sales level that just covers all of a project's costs but where no profit is earned.

BROADBAND TECHNOLOGY   A type of communications hardware that allows for the rapid transmission of vast amounts of information.

BUDGET   A set of financial constraints limiting how much money can be spent to meet a predetermined target, such as a profit goal.

BUSINESS   Goal-directed behavior aimed at getting and using productive resources to buy, make, trade, and sell goods and services that can be sold at a profit.

BUSINESS COMMERCE   The process by which people produce and exchange valuable goods and services that fulfill their wants and needs.

BUSINESS MODEL   A company's plan about the way it will use its resources to create a product giving it a competitive advantage.

BUSINESS OCCUPATION   The acquired set of specialized skills that enable a person to create valuable goods and services that can be traded at a profit.

BUSINESS ORGANIZATION   A tool that empowers people to shape and control the behavior of other people to produce goods and services.

BUSINESS SYSTEM   The combination of commerce, occupations, and organizations that result in the production and distribution of goods and services people value.

BUSINESS VISION (BUSINESS MISSION)   A brief statement of a company's business model that tells stakeholders *why* the firm is in business, *how* it intends to satisfy customer needs, and *why* it will satisfy their needs better than its competitors.

BUSINESS-TO-BUSINESS (B2B) NETWORKS   Electronic markets that link suppliers to companies that assemble or manufacture products.

BUSINESS-TO-CUSTOMER (B2C) NETWORKS   Electronic systems that connect companies that make finished products directly to the final customers who use them.

BUYER'S REMORSE   A phenomenon that occurs when a customer believes he or she made a poor purchasing choice.

C

CALL PROVISION   A company's legal right to buy its bonds back early from bondholders to avoid high interest-rate payments.

CAPITAL   The total monetary value of a company's financial assets such as its cash, property, land, stock, patents, and brand names.

CAPITAL BUDGET   A set of rules for allocating funds to the different functions of a firm to achieve a predetermined rate of return on its investment.

CAPITAL FINANCING   The development of a financial plan to allow a company to obtain the money it needs to fund its activities at the lowest possible cost.

CAPITAL INVESTMENT AND BUDGETING   The development of a financial plan and budget to manage and invest capital so that it leads to the highest return on invested capital that can be obtained.

CAPITAL STRUCTURE   The balance between the amount of capital a company raises through debt and the amount it raises through equity.

CAPITALISM   The economic or business system in which the private ownership of resources becomes the basis for the production and distribution of goods and services.

CAPITALISTS   People who personally own or control the physical capital of industrial production such as machinery, factories, distribution networks, raw materials, and technology.

CASH   The value of a company's assets that be converted into cash immediately.

CASH FLOW STATEMENT   A financial report showing how much cash a company generated during a specific time period, including where the cash came from and how it was used.

CERTIFIED PUBLIC ACCOUNTANTS   People who have taken 150 semester hours of accounting courses and have passed the CPA exam administered by the American Institute of Certified Public Accountants.

CHAPTER 11 BANKRUPTCY   The dissolution of a company whereby it is legally protected from its creditors and allowed to develop a viable new business model.

CHAPTER 7 BANKRUPTCY   The dissolution of a business whereby its assets are sold to repay its creditors and owners.

CHARISMATIC LEADER   An exceptionally effective leader whose referent and expert power results in followers perceiving them as someone who personifies a company and what it stands for.

CHIEF EXECUTIVE OFFICER   A company's top manager. The CEO is responsible for overseeing the operations of the company and ensuring its capital is used to create the most profit possible.

CHIEF INFORMATION OFFICER   The top manager of a company's IT function.

CLASS SYSTEM   A social ranking of people based upon the amount of their capital and wealth, and because of factors such as heredity, kinship, fame, and occupation.

COERCIVE POWER   A leader's ability to sanction or punish employees who fail to meet job and company requirements.

COLD CALL   The first contact a salesperson has with a customer, either by e-mail, phone, or in person.

COLLECTIVE BARGAINING   The process through which union representatives and managers negotiate a binding labor agreement over work-related issues, such as pay, benefits, and grievance procedures.

COMMAND ECONOMY   Economic system in which the quantity and price of goods and services that a country produces is planned by the government.

COMMERCIAL PAPER   Short-term, unsecured debts or notes issued at a certain rate of interest for up to nine months.

COMMISSION SYSTEMS   Pay plans that link the pay employees receive to the amount of revenue they earn by selling a company's products.

COMMUNICATION   The transmission and sharing of information between people or groups so that each party understands what the other is trying to achieve.

COMMUNISM   A one-party totalitarian system based on the dogma that all property should be owned by the state and that no individual should have the right to own private property.

COMMUNITY   The physical society in which a company is located.

COMPANY NORMS   Beliefs, attitudes, and behaviors that specify how a company's members should behave.

COMPANY VALUES   The shared standards a company's members use to evaluate whether or not they have helped the company achieve its goals.

COMPETITIVE ADVANTAGE   The ability of a company to offer customers a more highly valued product than their competitors can produce.

COMPLEX PRODUCTS   Products with qualities and characteristics that make them difficult for customers to evaluate.

COMPUTER VIRUS   Software code deliberately written to harm hardware and software and corrupt files and databases.

COMPUTER-AIDED MATERIALS MANAGEMENT   A technique that relies on computers to manage the flow of raw materials and component parts into and out of a company's operating system.

COMPUTER-INTEGRATED MANUFACTURING   A manufacturing technique that controls the changeover of machines from one operation to another via computer software.

CONNOISSEUR   A person with immense knowledge about a particular type of product and who can identify the qualities that make it valuable.

CONTINGENCY APPROACH TO ORGANIZATIONAL DESIGN A type of organizational design that depends on the changing forces in a firm's competitive environment.

CONTINGENCY THEORY OF LEADERSHIP The theory that effective leadership occurs when managers adopt a leadership approach that matches the characteristics of their employees and the work setting.

CONTROLLING The process of evaluating whether or not a company is achieving its goals and taking action if it is not.

COPYRIGHTS Legal documents that give their owners the right to own and profit from intellectual property such as written or visual media.

CRAFT GUILD A group of skilled artisans organized to control and govern different aspects of its trade.

CRAFTSPEOPLE Workers or artisans with the skills to produce higher-quality goods and services.

CREATIVE SELLING Selling that requires salespeople to combine their technical knowledge and personal selling experience to craft creative and unique ways to better meet the needs of their customers.

CROSS-FUNCTIONAL TEAM A group of people from the different functions who work together on a particular project.

CURRENT ASSETS The total value of a company's cash, accounts receivable, inventory, and prepaid expenses.

CURRENT LIABILITIES Debts that are payable within one year's time, including accounts payable and accrued expenses.

CURRENT YIELD A financial measure of a bond's current rate of return. It is obtained by dividing the bond's original interest rate by its current closing price.

CUSTOMER GROUPS Groups of people who have a similar need for a particular product because the product satisfies several different kinds of needs.

CUSTOMER NEEDS Consumer needs that can be satisfied by the qualities or features of a good or service.

CUSTOMER RELATIONSHIP MANAGEMENT The process of tracking the demand and satisfaction of customers in an effort to develop products they will want to buy on an ongoing basis.

CUSTOMER RELATIONSHIP MANAGEMENT SYSTEM An IT-based knowledge management system designed to track a company's customers–what they are buying, how satisfied they are, and how their demands are changing.

CUSTOMIZED PRODUCTS Products designed to match the needs of individual customers.

D

DEBT SECURITIES Investment documents that provide evidence of a company's legal obligation to repay within a certain period of time the money it borrows and make regular interest payments on that money in the meantime.

DELEGATE Giving up decision-making authority to other people.

DEMOGRAPHIC FORCES Changes in the characteristics of a country's population, such as its age, gender, ethnic origin, race, and sexual orientation.

DEPRECIATE The act of calculating the reduced value of the assets a company uses to make and sell its products.

DEVIL'S ADVOCATE Someone who tries to convince others that an idea or plan is flawed.

DIMINISHING MARGINAL UTILITY The principle that the value people receive from an additional unit of a product declines as they obtain more of the product.

DIRECT DISTRIBUTION Distribution channels used to deliver and sell products directly to the final customer.

DISTRIBUTION The selection of the distribution channels to reach and deliver products to customers most efficiently and effectively.

DISTRIBUTION CHANNEL The specific method a company uses to sell and deliver its products to customers.

DISTRIBUTION COSTS The cost of getting products to customers.

DISTRIBUTION MIX The combination of channels a company selects to place, promote, sell, and deliver its products to customers.

DISTRIBUTORS Firms that link the companies that make products with the customers who buy them.

DIVISIONAL STRUCTURE A structure that groups employees by function but allows them to focus their activities on a particular product line or type of customer.

DOUBLE ENTRY BOOKKEEPING A method of recording the dual effects of a business's financial transaction so that the company's assets, liabilities, and owners' equity are always in balance.

DOWNSTREAM VALUE CHAIN All of the activities related to managing a product from the time it is made to the time it is delivered and used by customers.

E

EARNINGS PER SHARE A measure of how much profit a company has earned for each share of its stock issued.

E-COMMERCE Trade that takes place between companies and individual customers via the Internet (or other IT systems).

EFFECTIVE LEADER A person who can persuade his or her subordinates to work hard and perform at high levels.

EFFECTIVENESS A revenue-focused measure of how competitive the firm's business model is.

EFFICIENCY A cost-focused measure of how productively a company's resources are being used to produce goods and services.

EMPLOYEE STOCK OWNERSHIP PLAN A plan that allows employees to buy a company's shares at below-market prices.

EMPOWERMENT Expanding employees' tasks and responsibilities to allow them more freedom and autonomy over the way work is performed.

ENTERPRISE RESOURCE PLANNING SYSTEMS Multimodule applications software packages that coordinate all of a company's functional activities.

ENTREPRENEUR A person ready to supply the enterprise–energy, boldness, courage, spirit, expertise–necessary to start and grow a business.

ENTREPRENEURSHIP The phenomenon that occurs when someone finds a new way to use or combine resources to make better goods and services.

EQUITY SECURITIES   The capital stock certificates a company issues giving shareholders the legal right to its assets and dividends from its profits.

EQUITY THEORY   A theory that argues that employees will be motivated to achieve a goal only if they believe they will be rewarded equitably relative to their co-workers.

ETHERNET   A local-area communication technology that transmits information between computers at speeds of between 10 and 100 million MBPs using coaxial or fiber optic cable.

ETHICAL DILEMMA   The quandary people experience when they must decide whether or not they should act in a way that benefits someone else even if it harms others and isn't in their own self-interest.

ETHICS   The inner-guiding moral principles and values people use to analyze a situation and decide what is "right."

EXCLUSIVE DEALERSHIPS   Distributors that are licensed to stock and sell only one brand of a product.

EXPATRIATE MANAGERS   Domestic managers who work for their companies abroad.

EXPECTANCY THEORY   A theory that argues that the motivation of employees depends upon whether or not they believe that performing at a high level will lead to the rewards they desire.

EXPERT POWER   A person's recognized expertise or superior skill in a particular functional area of business.

EXPERT SYSTEM   An advanced IT system that can reason through a company's information, diagnose problems, and suggest solutions.

EXPORTING   Selling domestically produced goods and services to customers in countries abroad.

EXTERNAL RECRUITMENT   A policy of filling advanced job positions with applicants from outside of a company.

F

FEUDALISM   The business or economic system in which one class of people, aristocrats, control the property rights to all valuable resources, including people.

FINAL CUSTOMER   The person who actually uses or consumes a product.

FINANCE   The set of activities people and companies engages in to decide how to invest their capital so that it generates more cash, profit, and wealth.

FINANCIAL ACCOUNTANTS   Accountants who specialize in preparing financial data, following GAAP rules, for use by outside stakeholders.

FINANCIAL RATIOS   Ratios that measure different aspects of a company's performance.

FIRST MOVER ADVANTAGE   The competitive advantage gained be being first to develop a new product or process.

FIRST-LINE MANAGERS   Employees at the base of the managerial hierarchy. They are often called *supervisors*.

FLEXIBLE PRODUCTION   An advanced operating system that combines the benefits of mass production with the benefits of small-batch production.

FLEXIBLE WORK TEAM   A team of self-managed employees who assume responsibility for performing the operating tasks necessary to make a part, or all, of a product.

FOCUS GROUP   A group of people brought together to share their thoughts and feelings about a particular product and why it may or may not meet their needs.

FORMAL APPRAISALS   Appraisals conducted on a regular basis to provide employees with ongoing performance feedback.

FRANCHISING   A business practice whereby investors are allowed to purchase the right to own and operate a business using a company's name and business model.

FREE-MARKET ECONOMY   Economic system in which the production of goods and services is left in the hands of private enterprise.

FREE-TRADE AGREEMENTS   Joint decisions by countries to reduce or eliminate trade barriers that impede the flow of products between nations.

FREE-TRADE AREA   A group of countries that agree to promote the free flow of goods and services between them.

FUNCTIONAL ACTIVITIES   The task-specific operations needed to convert resources into finished goods and services sold to customers.

FUNCTIONAL STRUCTURE   A structure that groups people together because by virtue of their expertise of the type of activity they do (typically into departments).

FUNCTIONAL TEAM   People grouped together by virtue of their expertise, typically, by departments.

G

GATT   An international treaty between nations following WWII, dramatically fueling free trade.

GENERALLY ACCEPTED ACCOUNTING PRINCIPLES   A set of accounting rules and procedures U.S. companies must follow to ensure their financial standing is being reported accurately and honestly.

GEOGRAPHIC STRUCTURE   A structure in which divisions are created to serve the needs of customers in a particular region, country, or world area.

GLOBAL ENVIRONMENT   The set of forces surrounding a company that determines its ability to obtain productive resources—land, labor, capital and enterprise.

GLOBAL NETWORK   A set of task and reporting relationships among managers, functions, and operating units around the world.

GLOBAL OUTSOURCING   The process of purchasing inputs from throughout the world to take advantage of differences in the cost and quality of resources.

GLOBAL SUPPLY CHAIN MANAGEMENT   The coordination of the flow of raw materials, semifinished goods, and finished products around the world.

GOAL-SETTING THEORY   A theory that suggests that if goals are to motivate employees, they should be specific, challenging, measurable, results oriented, and specify a timeframe for completion.

GOVERNMENT   The political system chosen to create and manage the set of laws, rules, and regulations that control the actions of people and companies that operate in a society.

GRIEVANCE PROCEDURES   Labor-contract rules used to resolve disputes between companies and their employees.

GROSS MARGIN   A measure of how much of each sales dollar is left over after a firm pays for the cost of goods sold.

GROSS PROFIT The amount of money left over after a firm deducts the cost of the goods it has sold from the revenues earned from them.

GROUP A collection of people who follow similar work rules and norms and work towards a common, specific, and measurable goal.

GROUP COHESIVENESS The attractiveness of a team to its members.

H

HACKERS People who seek to invade a company's databases and steal the information for malicious or illegal reasons.

HEDGE FUNDS Mutual funds that use highly leveraged investments to try to rapidly increase investors' capital returns.

HIERARCHY OF AUTHORITY The ranking of people according to their relative rights and responsibilities to control and utilize resources.

HOST-COUNTRY NATIONALS Natives of a foreign country hired to manage a multinational's divisions there.

HUMAN CAPITAL A person's stock of knowledge, skills, experience, judgment, personality, and abilities.

HUMAN RESOURCE MANAGEMENT The set of activities designed to recruit high-quality employees and then improve their skills and capabilities.

HUMAN RESOURCE PLANNING The process of forecasting the type and number of employees a company will require in the future to meet the objectives of its business model.

HUMAN RESOURCES The people a company employs, from its CEO and top managers, the middle managers throughout its functions, to its nonmanagerial employees.

I

INCENTIVE PAY The extra rewards employees receive when they achieve specific work goals.

INCENTIVE SYSTEM A system of rewards and sanctions that shapes, influences, and controls the way employees behave at work.

INCOME STATEMENT The financial report that summarizes the results of a company's profit-making activities in a specific time period.

INDIVIDUAL ETHICS A person's standards and values that determine how he or she should act in situations when his or her own self-interest is at stake.

INDUSTRIAL CONFLICT The clash that occurs when workers and unions attempt to obtain a greater share of a company's profits at the expense of other stakeholders.

INDUSTRIAL REVOLUTION An era in the eighteenth and nineteenth centuries that marked improved production and trade brought about by advances in technology.

INDUSTRY A group of companies that make similar products and compete for the same customers.

INDUSTRY STANDARD A predominant type of technology used in an industry. Other technologies must be compatible with the industry standard in order to be widely adopted.

INFORMAL APPRAISALS Appraisals that take place as managers and subordinates meet from time to time to discuss important work issues.

INFORMATION A set of data, facts, numbers, and words that has been organized in such a way that it provides its users with knowledge.

INFORMATION OVERLOAD A situation in which managers have to process so much information it actually reduces their understanding of a situation.

INFORMATION TECHNOLOGY The many different kinds of computer and communications hardware and software and the skills of their designers, programmers, managers, and technicians who create and manage it.

INITIAL PUBLIC OFFERING The first time the owners of a company's stock offer it for sale to the general public.

INNOVATION The development of new and improved products and new and improved methods to create them.

INTEGRATING MECHANISMS Organizing tools that managers use to increase communication and coordination among a company's functions and divisions.

INTEGRATIVE BARGAINING SOLUTION A "win-win" solution that allows both parties to benefit from the labor contract agreed upon.

INTERMEDIARY A company such as a merchant, broker, or wholesaler that buys the products of one company and sells them to other companies.

INTERNAL RECRUITMENT A policy of promoting employees who already work for a company.

INTRANET A company's internal system of computers and Web sites accessible only by its employees.

INTRAPRENEURSHIP Entrepreneurial activity that takes place inside of an established company.

INVENTORY The resources—materials, supplies, and goods—a company holds in stock.

INVENTORY TURNOVER RATIO A measure of how quickly a firm's inventory is being sold.

INVISIBLE HAND The principle that the pursuit of self-interest in the marketplace naturally leads to the improved well-being of society in general.

IT CONSULTANTS Expert employees who use their knowledge and learning to solve their customers' IT problems.

J

JOB ANALYSIS The process of obtaining detailed information about the tasks and responsibilities involved in each job in a company.

JOB DESCRIPTION A list of the specific tasks, duties, and responsibilities that make up a particular job.

JOB ENLARGEMENT Motivating employees by expanding the range of tasks they do.

JOB ENRICHMENT THEORY A theory that argues that employees will be more motivated if they have more control over the way they do their jobs.

JOB SPECIFICATIONS A written list of the required skills, abilities, and knowledge needed to do a particular job.

JOINT VENTURE An alliance in which companies from different countries agree to pool their skills and resources to make and distribute a product together.

JUSTICE RULE   A rule stating that an ethical decision is one that distributes benefit and harms among people in a fair or impartial way

JUST-IN-TIME INVENTORY SYSTEM   An inventory management system whereby inputs are delivered to the firm just when they are needed rather than being purchased and warehoused prior to their use.

K

KNOWLEDGE   What a person perceives, recognizes, identifies, or discovers from analyzing data and information.

KNOWLEDGE MANAGEMENT SYSTEM   An IT system that analyzes the information collected from the TP system but filters and analyzes it to make it more useful to managers.

L

LABOR RELATIONS   The process of working with employees, or the unions that represent them, to create work rules and a negotiation process to resolve disputes between them.

LAW OF DEMAND   The principle that states that as the price of a product rises, consumers will buy less of it, and that as the price of it falls, consumers will buy more of it.

LAW OF SUPPLY   The principle that states that as the price of a product rises, producers will supply more of it, and that as the price of it falls, producers will supply less of it.

LEADERSHIP   The use of one's personality, beliefs, values, social skills, knowledge, and power to influence other peoples' thoughts, feelings, and behavior.

LEADING   The ability to develop a plan and motivate others to pursue it.

LEADING CUSTOMERS   Companies that improvise their own solutions to business problems because no products currently exist that can do so.

LEADING PROVIDERS   People or companies that believe their new products will better satisfy customer needs even though they have no sure proof of this.

LEARNING   An increase in the store or stock of people's expertise or knowledge.

LEGACY SYSTEM   The hardware and software components of a company's IT system at any one point in time.

LEGAL FORCES   Changes in a country's laws and regulations that often occur because of changes in the political and ethical attitudes within a society.

LEGITIMATE POWER   The rightful authority to direct and control employees' activities.

LEVERAGE   The ability to use borrowed capital in ways that have the potential to lead to high rates of return.

LIABILITIES   The financial obligations a company incurs by borrowing money or buying productive resources on credit.

LICENSED DISTRIBUTORS OR DEALERS   Independent companies that buy the rights to distribute, sell, and service a company's products within a specific geographical area.

LICENSING   Contracting with companies in other countries in order to give them the right to use a company's brand name and business model.

LIMITED LIABILITY   A legal system that prevents creditors from seizing the personal wealth of a company's stockholders to pay a company's debts.

LINE OF CREDIT   A short-term, unsecured loan a company can draw against as its accounts payable become due.

LIQUIDITY   Assets listed in the firm's balance sheet in order of how fast they can be converted into cash.

LOCKOUT   When managers decide to shut down a company's operations until workers are willing to accept the employment conditions being offered to them.

LONG-TERM CAPITAL BUDGETING   The financial decisions involved when a company chooses how to invest capital for extended periods of time.

M

MANAGEMENT BY EXCEPTION   The use of rules and standard operating procedures to coordinate operations whereby managers only intervene to take corrective action.

MANAGEMENT BY OBJECTIVES   A work-performance review system that involves setting specific and challenging goals and then reviewing employees' progress towards achieving those goals.

MANAGERIAL ACCOUNTANTS   Accountants who specialize in preparing and analyzing the financial data used by managers.

MANAGERS   Employees to whom a company's owners delegate responsibility for using its resources to create profitable goods and services.

MAQUILADORAS   U.S. companies' manufacturing plants in cities along the Mexican border.

MARKET   Buyers and sellers for a particular product.

MARKET SEGMENT   A group of customers the firm targets based on their need for its products.

MARKET SHARE   The total percentage of a product a company sells in a particular market.

MARKET STRUCTURE   A structure that groups functions into divisions that serve different types of customers.

MARKETING   An organizational function and a set of processes for creating, communicating, and delivering value to customers and for managing customer relationships in ways that benefit the organization and its stakeholders.

MARKETING MESSAGE   A product-related message the firm's marketing department sends to customers about how and why a product will better satisfy their needs.

MARKETING MIX   The combination of a product's qualities and features, its price, the way it is promoted and sold, and the places at which it is sold.

MARKETING RESEARCH   The systematic search for information that uncovers met and unmet customer needs, the different needs of different customer groups, and whether or not a product's marketing mix appeals to customers.

MASLOW'S NEEDS HIERARCHY THEORY   A theory that specifies why and how people try to satisfy their needs through their behaviors at work.

MASS PRODUCTION   An operating system based on the use of automated machines and standard operating procedures to make work routine and create a large number of standardized products.

MATCHING PRINCIPLE   An accounting rule that requires that the expenses incurred to make and sell products be deducted from the revenues generated by their sale during the same accounting period.

MATERIALS MANAGEMENT   The set of activities that control the flow of resources into and out of a firm's operating system.

MATRIX STRUCTURE   A structure that groups people and resources in two ways simultaneously: by function and by product.

MEDIATION   A conflict resolution method that involves the use of a neutral third party, or mediator, to help labor and management resolve their differences and reach an agreement.

MENTOR   A person who provides advice, guidance, and technical knowledge to other people *(mentees)* in order to help them advance their careers.

MERCANTILISM   The business system in which a product's price differences are exploited by trading the product across markets and countries.

MERCHANT   A trader who uses the discrepancy between the value and price of a product in one market and another to trade goods for profit.

MERIT PAY   A pay system that links superior performance directly to higher permanent rewards, such as a certain percentage increase in salary.

MIDDLE MANAGERS   Employees in charge of a company's various functions and responsible for using the company's functional resources productively to increase its profitability.

MINIMUM CHAIN-OF-COMMAND PRINCIPLE   The principle that a company's structure should be designed with as few managerial levels as possible.

MISSIONARY SELLING   Selling that occurs when a salesperson educates customers, builds goodwill, and performs promotional activities to encourage them to purchase a product at a later date.

MIXED ECONOMY   Economic system in which certain goods and services are produced by private enterprise and others are provided via centralized government planning.

MONOPOLY   A situation in which one company controls the supply of a product and can charge an artificially high price for it.

MORAL RIGHTS RULE   A rule stating that an ethical decision is one that best maintains and protects the fundamental, inalienable rights and privileges of the people affected by it.

MULTINATIONAL COMPANIES   Companies that operate and trade in many different countries around the world.

N

NATIONAL CULTURE   The particular set of economic, political, and social values and norms that exist in a particular country.

NEGOTIATION AND BARGAINING   A technique managers use to increase the chances that conflicting parties will reach a compromise.

NET INCOME   A company's total profit after deducting the cost of the goods it has sold as well as all of its other expenses.

NET PRESENT VALUE ANALYSIS   The financial analysis needed to determine the true rate of return of a proposed capital investment. It tells managers how much a long-term project would earn in today's dollars if it were undertaken.

NETWORK STRUCTURE   A system of task and reporting relationships based on the use of electronic ties that links suppliers, manufactures, and distributors.

NONPROFIT ORGANIZATION   An organization that is not in business to make profit but to provide value to the people and groups it serves.

NORMS   Unwritten codes of conduct that prescribe how people in a particular culture should act in certain situations.

O

OCCUPATIONAL ETHICS   Standards that govern how members of a profession, trade, or craft, should conduct themselves when performing work-related activities.

ON-THE-JOB TRAINING   Training employees receive in the course of doing their jobs.

OPERATING COSTS   The costs of acquiring and using productive resources to make and sell goods and services.

OPERATIONS   A company's system of value-creation activities used to transform inputs into finished goods and services.

ORGANIZATION BONUS SYSTEMS   The one-time rewards employees receive if a company achieves cost savings, quality increases, and so on, in a specified time period.

ORGANIZATIONAL CONFLICT   The discord that ensues when stakeholders thwart each other's attempts to achieve their goals and objectives.

ORGANIZATIONAL CULTURE   The set of shared company values and norms that shape the way employees and groups interact with one another.

ORGANIZATIONAL DESIGN   The process of creating an organizational structure and culture so that a company can pursue its business model profitably.

ORGANIZATIONAL ETHICS   The practices and beliefs that guide an organization's behavior towards its stakeholders.

ORGANIZATIONAL LEARNING   Managing information and knowledge to achieve a better fit between a company's business model and the forces in its environment.

ORGANIZATIONAL POLITICS   The activities managers and employees engage in to increase their power and persuade others to achieve their personal goals and objectives.

ORGANIZATIONAL SOCIALIZATION   The process by which newcomers learn and absorb a company's values and norms and acquire the work behaviors and attitudes necessary to perform their jobs effectively.

ORGANIZATIONAL STRUCTURE   The framework of task-and-authority relationships in a company that coordinates and motivates employees to work together towards a common goal.

ORGANIZING   A process managers use to create a company's organizational structure.

P

PARTNERSHIP   Two or more skilled professionals who agree to pool their talents and capital to establish a company in which they are the stockholders and owners.

PATENTS   Legal documents that give their owners the right to use, control, license, and profit for a 20-year period from new products or processes they have created.

PAY   The monetary rewards, such as wages, bonuses, and salaries, associated with a particular job.

PAY LEVEL   The average salary a company chooses to pay its employees compared to other companies in its industry.

PAY STRUCTURE   The relative pay and benefits received by employees doing different types of jobs or jobs at different levels in a company's hierarchy.

PERFORMANCE APPRAISAL   The process of formally evaluating the contributions an employee has made toward a company's functional and corporate-wide goals.

PERFORMANCE FEEDBACK   The communication of performance appraisal information to employees to influence their future performance levels.

PERSONAL SELLING   Direct face-to-face communication by salespeople with existing and potential customers to promote a company's products.

PERSUASIVE COMMUNICATION   The attempt by a party to share information with another party in order to get them to understand their objectives and work toward them.

PIECEWORK PLANS   Pay plans that link the pay employees receive to the number of units of a product an employee makes.

PLACE   The distribution and sales channels used to get both a product and its marketing message to the customer.

PLANNING   A process that managers use to select the best business model and goals for their company.

POLITICAL TACTICS   The specific strategies managers and employees engage in to gain the support of an organization's members.

POLITICAL-ECONOMIC FORCES Changes that occur in the form of a country's social and political systems.

POSITION ANALYSIS QUESTIONNAIRE A written method of job analysis that asks jobholders and their managers to answer detailed questions about the skills and abilities employees need to do a particular job.

POWER   The ability of one person to make other people or groups do something that they would *not* have otherwise done.

PRACTICAL RULE   A rule stating that an ethical decision is one that a manager can communicate to society because the typical person would think it is acceptable.

PREMIUM PRICE   The higher price a seller is able to charge versus what its competitors can charge.

PRICE   A way to measure the value of a product to customers.

PRICE-TO-EARNING RATIO   A way of valuing a stock by dividing its closing price by its annual earnings per share.

PRIMARY FUNCTIONS   Functions directly responsible for utilizing scarce resources most efficiently and effectively to create goods and services.

PRINCIPAL   The amount of money originally borrowed.

PRODUCT   Any kind of good or service that people value and want to buy.

PRODUCT BRANDING   Using a unique name, design, symbol, or other element to differentiate a product from its competitors.

PRODUCT DEVELOPMENT   The set of technical, scientific, and engineering processes involved in creating new or improved products to better satisfy customer needs.

PRODUCT DIFFERENTIATION   The process of setting a product apart from its competitors by designing and marketing it to better satisfy customers' needs.

PRODUCT LIFE CYCLE   The typical sequence of changes in demand for a product that occur over time.

PRODUCT POSITIONING   The process of customizing or tailoring a product to a specific market segment.

PRODUCT STRUCTURE   A structure that groups functions into divisions that specialize in certain products.

PRODUCTION LAYOUT   The way teams of employees are physically grouped into work cells or pods to assemble a product.

PRODUCTIVE RESOURCES   The four crucial ingredients–land, labor, capital, and enterprise–needed to profit from business.

PROFIT   The total amount of money left over after operating costs have been deducted from a company's sales revenues.

PROFIT MARGIN   A measure of how much profit a company generates from its sales.

PROFIT SHARING PLANS   Pay plans that reward employees on the basis of the profit a company earns in a particular period, usually a year.

PROFITABILITY   A measurement of how well a company is making use of its resources relative to its competitors.

PROLETARIAT   The class of unskilled workers who have no capital and only possess the rights to sell their own labor.

PROMOTION   The way in which a company advertises, announces, publicizes, and pushes its products.

PROMOTIONAL MIX   The combination of advertising, sales promotions, public relations, and personal selling used to reach and persuade customers to buy a product.

PROPERTY RIGHTS   The right of people to own, use, or sell valuable resources.

PROSPECTS   Potential customers for the goods and services a salesperson is offering.

PUBLIC INTEREST   Country-specific standards used to evaluate how a proposed course of action affects the welfare of society.

PUBLIC RELATIONS   The practice of conveying messages to the public through the media to influence people's opinions about the company and its products.

Q

QUALITY CONTROL CIRCLES   Team meetings in which production employees discuss ways to improve operating quality and productivity

QUOTAS   Restrictions on the amount of a good or service that can be imported into a country.

R

REAL-TIME INFORMATION   Information that is constantly updated.

RECEIVER   The party that receives the information transmitted by a sender.

RECRUITMENT   The process of identifying and attracting a pool of qualified job applicants.

REFERENT POWER   A leader's ability to influence and persuade other people because of personal qualities that make them attractive to others and effective in social situations.

REPRESENTATIVE DEMOCRACY   A form of government in which citizens periodically elect individuals to represent their interests.

REPUTATION The trust, goodwill, and confidence others have in a company that leads them to want to do business with it.

RESPONSIVENESS TO CUSTOMERS A measure of a company's ability to anticipate changing customer needs, resolve problems customers have with a product, and provide fast after-sales service.

RETAIL SELLING Selling to the final customer–the person who buys a product for his or her own use.

RETAILERS Intermediaries who sell other companies' products to the final customer.

RETURN ON EQUITY A measure of how much profit a company has earned on each $100 of stockholders' equity invested in the business.

RETURN ON INVESTED CAPITAL A measure of how much profit a company generates for each dollar invested in its business.

REVERSE ENGINEERING The process of examining the products of one's competitors in depth in order to figure out what makes them successful.

REWARD POWER A leader's ability to recognize and acknowledge employees who perform their jobs in a way that meets or exceeds the requirements of their job and company.

RISK The possibility of incurring future financial losses because of one's investment decisions.

RISK PREMIUM The extra reward investors demand for bearing the additional risks associated with a speculative investment.

ROLE The set of tasks a person is expected to perform because of the position he or she holds in an organization.

ROUTER Hardware and software that electronically transfers data between networks to its intended destination, such as a specific Web page or computer.

S

SALES The development and use of techniques to inform customers about the value of a company's products in order to persuade them to buy them.

SALES PROMOTIONS Nonpersonal, persuasive efforts designed to boost a company's sales immediately.

SALES REVENUE Money or income generated from the sale of a product.

SECONDARY FUNCTIONS Functions not directly responsible for getting products to customers but whose activities contribute to the efficiency and effectiveness of other functions.

SECURED LOAN A loan backed by valuable fixed or current assets.

SELECTION Creating the set of job- and company-specific criteria that determine which job applicants are the best match for a particular job and company.

SELF-ACTUALIZATION The desire for personal self-fulfillment; that is, a person's desire to become the best he or she is capable of becoming.

SELF-EFFICACY The belief a person holds about his or her ability to succeed at a certain task or in a particular situation.

SELF-MANAGED TEAMS Groups of employees who are given the responsibility to supervise their own activities and to monitor the quality of the goods and services they provide.

SENDER The party that transmits a message or other information to a receiver.

SHORT-TERM CAPITAL MANAGEMENT The financial decisions involved when a company purchases resources to make products that will be sold within a one-year period.

SMALL-BATCH PRODUCTION An operating system designed to make one-of-a-kind or small quantities of customized products.

SOCIETAL ETHICS Standards that govern how members of a society should deal with one another in matters involving issues such as fairness, justice, poverty, and the rights of the individual.

SOCIOCULTURAL FORCES Changes in the social structure of a country and in its class structure, culture, customs, and beliefs.

SOLE PROPRIETORSHIP A non-incorporated business entirely owned by one person.

SPECIALIZATION The process by which people become more skilled and productive when they perform a narrowly defined range of tasks specific to an occupation or job.

SPECIFIC FORCES Forces in the global environment that directly increase or decrease a company's sales revenues or operating costs, and thus its profitability.

STAKEHOLDERS People or groups of people who supply a company with its productive resources and thereby have an interest in how the company behaves.

STANDARDIZED PRODUCTS Products that are identical.

STOCK OPTIONS The right to buy a stock at a certain price and to benefit from increases in the stock's value in the future by selling it.

STOCKHOLDERS' EQUITY The total capital invested in a company over time as well as the past profits it has retained in its business.

STRETCH GOALS Highly ambitious goals put in place to motivate employees to perform at higher levels.

STRIKE A situation that arises when workers refuse to do their jobs in an attempt to bring the work process to a halt.

SUPPLIERS The individuals and companies that provide a company with the resources that it needs to produce goods and services.

T

TARGET PRICE The price a typical customer will be willing to pay for a product with a particular set of qualities and features.

TARIFFS Taxes or duties on imported products that raise the price at which they must be sold in foreign markets.

TEAM A group of people who are jointly responsible for creating, managing, and changing work rules and norms to find better ways to achieve current and future goals.

TEAMWORK A phenomenon that occurs when people pool their skills to create more valuable products than they could create alone.

TECHNICAL SELLING Selling that requires a company's sales representatives to impart detailed technical information to their customers.

TELEMARKETING A sales method used to contact prospective customers exclusively by phone.

THIRD-COUNTRY NATIONALS Managers who are native neither to the country the multinational is headquartered in nor the foreign country in which it operates.

360-DEGREE PERFORMANCE APPRAISAL The process of using multiple sources of information to appraise an employee's performance.

TOP MANAGEMENT TEAM A group consisting of the top managers of a company's major functions or business units.

TOP MANAGERS Employees who are responsible for developing a company's business model and who, along with the CEO, are ultimately responsible for its success or failure.

TOTAL EQUITY The sum of the capital stock invested in a business in addition to its retained earnings.

TOTAL QUALITY MANAGEMENT An operations technique used to continuously improve the production process, increase the quality of products, and help companies lower their operating costs.

TOTALITARIAN GOVERNMENT A form of government in which a person or group of people attempt to exercises absolute control over all forms of business activity.

TRADE The exchange of products through the use of money.

TRADE SELLING Selling done through intermediaries, such as wholesalers and retailers, which manage the sale of a company's products to other companies.

TRADE UNIONS Organizations that represent the interests of employees who hold similar types of jobs in a particular industry.

TRADEMARKS Property rights to the name of a product or the company that produces it.

TRAINING AND DEVELOPMENT The process through which companies increase their employees' work skills and knowledge to improve their job performance.

TRAINING GAP A specific type training an employee needs to acquire.

TRAINING-NEEDS ANALYSIS A method of identifying the kinds of employee training that will result in the greatest performance gains.

TRANSACTION COSTS The costs of bargaining, negotiating, monitoring, and regulating exchanges between people in business.

TRANSACTION PROCESSING SYSTEM An IT system designed to collect, record, and manipulate the data related to a company's day-to-day business operations.

TREASURY STOCK Stock a company buys back from the public and becomes part of stockholders' equity on the firm's balance sheet.

TRUST A combination of companies linked by legal titles and property rights that allow them to function like one large company. *Also,* A person's confidence and faith in another person's goodwill.

U

UNLIMITED LIABILITY A legal system in which the personal capital and wealth of all of a company's stockholders can be seized to pay its debts.

UNSECURED LOAN A loan not backed by valuable assets pledged to guarantee the loan will be paid back

UTILITARIAN RULE A rule stating that an ethical decision is one that produces the greatest well-being for the greatest number of people.

V

VALUE How well a product satisfies customers' desires or needs.

VALUE CHAIN The coordinated series or sequence of functional activities necessary to transform resources into the products customers want to buy.

VALUES General standards and guiding principles that people in a society use to determine which kinds of behaviors are right or wrong.

VARIABLE COSTS Costs that are only incurred when the firm makes and sells products.

VIRTUAL TEAMS Teams whose members are connected by e-mail, the Internet, instant messaging, wireless laptops, and video teleconferencing.

W

WEALTH The sum total of the resources, assets, and material possessions owned by people and groups in society.

WHISTLEBLOWER A stakeholder who reveals an organization's misdeeds to the public.

WHOLESALER An intermediary or broker that buys products from manufacturers and then resells them to other companies, such as retailers, which in turn distribute them to the final customer.

WHOLLY OWNED SUBSIDIARIES Business units established in countries abroad to manufacture and distribute a multinational's products.

WI-FI A type of Ethernet technology that allows computer users to access the Internet wirelessly.

WORK GOAL Something specific an employee is trying to accomplish when doing a job.

WORK MOTIVATION The psychological force within people that arouses their interest, directs their attention, and causes them to persist to achieve their work goals.

WORKING CAPITAL The amount of cash left over after a company subtracts its current liabilities from its current assets.

WORKING-TO-RULE When workers perform their jobs exactly as specified in their employment contracts but do no more.

WORK-IN-PROCESS GOODS The semifinished goods and services that move through a company's production process.

Notes

Chapter 1

1. "Kroger Profit Rises, Calif. Stores Rebound," *Yahoo News*, September 13, 2005, http://news.yahoo.com; Tracy Mullin, "Reinventing Supermarkets: The Nation's Grocery Chains Are Turning the Tables on the Competition," *Chain Store Age*, July 2005, downloaded from Infotrac at http://web5.infotrac.galegroup.com; Jon Springer, "Kroger Reaps Benefits of Aggressive Pricing Strategy," *Supermarket News*, June 27, 2005, http://web5.infotrac.galegroup.com; Elliot Zwiebach, "Kroger Seeks Sales Growth without Margin Sacrifice," *Supermarket News*, March 14, 2005, http://web5.infotrac.galegroup.com; and Christopher Steiner, "Fighting the Borg," *Forbes*, December 27, 2004, http://web5.infotrac.galegroup.com.

2. Blockbuster Inc., "About Blockbuster: Company Profile," "About Blockbuster: Company History," and financial statements, Blockbuster Web site, www.blockbuster.com, accessed September 20, 2005; Daniel McGinn, "Rewinding a Video Giant," *Newsweek*, June 27, 2005, downloaded from Infotrac at http://web5.infotrac.galegroup.com; and Subrata N. Chakravarty, "Give 'Em Variety," *Forbes*, May 2, 1988, http://web5.infotrac.galegroup.com.

3. Paul Matus (1999). "American Ground Transport-GM and the Streetcar." The Third Rail online. http://www.thethirdrail.net/9905/agt1.htm (accessed July 12, 2005)

4. The World Factbook 2005, US Central Intelligence Agency. http://www.cia.gov/cia/publications/factbook/index.html (accessed July 12, 2005)

5. Brian Grow, "Thinking Outside the Big Box," *Business Week*, October 25, 2004, downloaded from Infotrac at http://web5.infotrac.galegroup.com; Bob Nardelli, Patricia Sellers, and Julie Schlosser, "It's His Home Depot Now," *Fortune*, September 20, 2004, http://web5.infotrac.galegroup.com; and Chana R. Schoenberger, "House Call," *Forbes*, September 6, 2004, http://web5.infotrac.galegroup.com.

6. "Economies Grow in All States in 2004," U.S. Bureau of Economic Analysis. http://www.bea.doc.gov/bea/newsrel/GSPNewsRelease.htm (accessed July 12, 2005)

7. *1998 Human Development Report*. New York: Oxford University Press for the United Nations Development Programme.

8. http://www.census.gov/epcd/www/naics.html

Chapter 2

1. Kenneth Warren, "Carnegie," *Business History Review* 78(3) (Autumn 2004), downloaded at http://firstsearch.oclc.org; "Carnegie, Andrew," Biography.com database, www.biography.com, accessed September 23, 2005; "Meet Andrew Carnegie," *The American Experience*, PBS, www.pbs.org, 1999 (accessed September 23, 2005); and Ron Chernow, "Blessed Barons," *Time*, December 7, 1998, http://firstsearch.oclc.org.

2. James Watson, Stanley Tambiah, and William Fisher, "Gifting and Feasting in the Northwest Coast Potlatch," Peabody Museum, www.peabody.harvard.edu, 1999 (accessed September 26, 2005); Dorothee Schreiber, "Our Wealth Sits on the Table," *American Indian Quarterly* (Summer 2002), downloaded from Infotrac at http://web6.infotrac.galegroup.com; and Joyce Gregory Wyels, "Sharing the Box of Treasures," *Americas* (English ed.) 56 (January–February 2004), http://web6.infotrac.galegroup.com.

3. William T. O'Hara and Peter Mandel, "The World's Oldest Family Companies," *Family Business*. http://www.familybusinessmagazine.com/oldworld.html (accessed July 13, 2005)

4. Allen Brooke, "The White Queen?" *New Criterion* (February 2005), review of *Catherine de Medici: Renaissance Queen of France*, by Leonie Frieda, downloaded from Infotrac at http://web7.infotrac.galegroup.com; Paul Halsall, "The Massacre of St. Bartholomew's Day, August 24, 1572," *Modern History Sourcebook*, April 1998, www.fordham.edu/halsall/mod/1572stbarts.html; Niccolò Capponi, "*Le Palle di Marte*: Military Strategy and Diplomacy in the Grand Duchy of Tuscany under Ferdinand II de' Medici (1621–1670)," *Journal of Military History* 68(4) (October 2004), http://firstsearch.oclc.org; and Robert Knecht, "Chateaux of Ill Fortune," *History Today* (June 2004), http://web7.infotrac.galegroup.com.

5. *Standard Oil Co. of New Jersey v. United States*, 221 U.S. 1 (1911), www.oyez.org (accessed September 26, 2005); Steve Schifferes, "Trustbusters: A History Lesson," BBC News Online, February 15, 2000, http://news.bbc.co.uk; "The Rockefellers," *The American Experience*, PBS, www.pbs.org, 1999–2000 (accessed September 23, 2005); and Ida M. Tarbell, *The History of the Standard Oil Company* (1904), converted to electronic format by Nalinda Sapukotana, June 26, 1996, www.history.rochester.edu/fuels/tarbell/.

6. Anthony Sampson (1995). *Company Man: The Rise and Fall of Corporate Life*. New York: Times Business/Random House, page 19.

Chapter 3

1. Yahoo! Inc., "Company Overview: The Company" and "The History of Yahoo! How It All Started," Media Relations page of Yahoo! Web site, http://docs.yahoo.com, accessed September 21, 2005; "Historical Prices for Yahoo! Inc. (YHOO)," Yahoo! Finance, http://finance.yahoo.com, accessed September 21, 2005; Fred Vogelstein and Kate Bonamici, "Yahoo's Brilliant Solution," *Fortune*, August 8, 2005, downloaded from Infotrac at http://web3.infotrac.galegroup.com; and Don Valentine, "Don Valentine, Sequoia Capital," in *Done Deals: Venture Capitalists Tell Their Stories*, edited by Udayan Gupta (Harvard Business School Press, 2000), accessed at Sequoia Capital Web site, www.sequoiacap.com//perspective/articles/valentine.html.

2. Stephen Evans, "Rolled Gold for Stones Inc.," BBC News, May 17, 2005, http://newsvote.bbc.co.uk; Michael Endelman, "Making Bank . . . on Beer Koozies, T-Shirts, and Trucker Hats," *Entertainment Weekly*, December 17, 2004, downloaded from Infotrac at http://web4.infotrac.galegroup.com; and Andy Serwer, "Inside the Rolling Stones Inc.," *Fortune*, September 30, 2002, http://web4.infotrac.galegroup.com.

3. Anthony Sampson (1995). *Company Man: The Rise and Fall of Corporate Life*. New York: Times Business/Random House, page 22.

4. Gem Consortium; http://www.gemconsortium.org/document.asp?id=389 (accessed June 10, 2005)

5. Ford Motor Company, "Ford Marks 100 Years of Advancing Diversity at African American Business Conference," news release, June 19, 2003, http://media.ford.com; Marjorie Sorge, "Time to Take the Lead: WAW, McCall's Honor Top Women Automakers," *Ward's Auto World*, May 1995, pp. 65–66; and Cynthia Hanson, "No More Junkers for Debra Kent: She's on the Fast Track at Ford," *Chicago Tribune*, March 19, 1995.

9. Michael Kammen (ed.) (1973). *"What is the good of history?"* Selected letters of Carl L. Becker, 1900–1945. Ithaca, NY: Cornell University Press.

6. Louise Lee, "Too Many Surveys, Too Little Passion?" *Business Week*, August 1, 2005, downloaded from Infotrac at http://web5.infotrac.galegroup.com; "Historical Prices for Gap Inc. (GPS)" and "Income Statement for Gap Inc. (GPS)," Yahoo! Finance, http://finance.yahoo.com, accessed September 22, 2005; and Louise Lee, "The Gap Has Reason to Dance Again," *Business Week*, April 19, 2004, http://web5.infotrac.galegroup.com.

7. Donna Fenn (1999). "Grand Plans: How to Start a Company for $1,000 or Less," Inc. 21(11), August, pp. 43-46.

8. www.francise.org.

9. "SBA Small Business Frequently Asked Questions;" http://www.sba.gov/advo/research (accessed June 11, 2005)

Chapter 4

1. Nestlé S.A., "All about Nestlé," Nestlé Web site, www.nestle.com, accessed September 30, 2005; Graeme Evans, "No Break in Profit for Nestle," *Birmingham Post*, August 18, 2005, downloaded from the Business & Company Resource Center, http://galenet.galegroup.com; Carol Matlack, "Nestlé Is Starting to Slim Down at Last," *Business Week* (October 27, 2003), downloaded from Infotrac at http://web5.infotrac.galegroup.com; and Ben Worthen, "Nestlé's ERP Odyssey," *CIO* (May 15, 2002), www.cio.com.

2. The World Factbook 2005, US Central Intelligence Agency. http://www.cia.gov/cia/publications/factbook/index.html (accessed July 8, 2005)

3. Peter Lewis, "A Perpetual Crisis Machine," *Fortune* (September 19, 2005), downloaded from Infotrac at http://web3.infotrac.com; David Rocks and Moon Ihlwan, "Samsung Design," *Business Week* (December 6, 2004), http://web3.infotrac.galegroup.com; and Samsung Group, "Annual Financial Summary," and 2004 Annual Report, Samsung Web site, www.samsung.com, accessed September 30, 2005.

4. United Nations Population Fund, *State of the World Population 2004,* New York: UNFPA; http://www.unfpa.org/swp/swpmain.htm (accessed July 8, 2005)

5. Ryanair, "About Us," Ryanair Web site, www.ryanair.com, accessed September 30, 2005; Carol Matlack, "Fare Wars: A Great Time to Be a Tourist," *Business Week* (February 16, 2004), downloaded from Infotrac at http://web3.infotrac.galegroup.com; and Kerry Capell, "Ryanair Rising," *Business Week* (June 2, 2003), http://web3.infotrac.galegroup.com.

6. Erick Schonfeld, "The World According to eBay," *Business 2.0* (January–February 2005), downloaded from Infotrac at http://web2.infotrac.galegroup.com;

Timothy J. Mullaney and Robert D. Hof, "E-tailing Finally Hits Its Stride," *Business Week* (December 20, 2004), http://web2.infotrac.galegroup.com; Ian Rowley and Hiroko Tashiro, "Logging On to Online," *Business Week* (September 6, 2004), http://web2.infotrac.galegroup.com; and Robert D. Hof, "Reprogramming Amazon," *Business Week* (December 22, 2003), http://web2.infotrac.com.

7. Caitlin Kiernan, "No longer 'Made in America': Patriotic Shoppers Have Little Choice," *Times Herald-Record*, June 21, 2005; http://www.recordonline.com/archive/2005/06/21/america1.htm (accessed July 13, 2005)

8. http://www.ykk.com/english/index.html (accessed July 8, 2005)

Chapter 5

1. Jim Collins, "The 10 Greatest CEOs of All Time," *Fortune* (July 21, 2003), downloaded from Infotrac at http://web6.infotrac.galegroup.com; Joseph Weber, "How Andersen Turned to the Dark Side," *Business Week* (March 17, 2003), review of *Final Accounting*, by Barbara Ley Toffler, http://web6.infotrac.galegroup.com; and Joseph Nocera, "Dow Corning Succumbs," *Fortune* (October 30, 1995), http://web6.infotrac.galegroup.com.

2. "Hanging the Pirates," *Forbes* (January 31, 2005), downloaded from Infotrac at http://web6.infotrac.galegroup.com; Heather Green and Lorraine Woellert, "Coming to Grips with Grokster," *Business Week* (July 11, 2005), http://web6.infotrac.galegroup.com; IFPI, "Music Pirate Sales Hit Record 1.1 Billion Discs but Spread of Fake CD Trade Slows," news release, July 22, 2004, www.ifpi.org; and Jack Ewing and Tom Lowry, "It Seemed Like a Good Idea," *Business Week* (August 9, 2004), http://web6.infotrac.galegroup.com.

3. Ronald Grover, "Calming the Crowd after Eisner's Thrill Ride," *Business Week* (October 3, 2005), downloaded from Infotrac at http://web6.infotrac.galegroup.com; Charles Fishman, "For Disney, the Story Not Told," *Fast Company* (May 2004), http://web6.infotrac.galegroup.com; Ronald Grover and Tom Lowry, "Now It's Time to Say Goodbye," *Business Week* (March 15, 2004), http://web6.infotrac.galegroup.com; and Marc Gunther, "Eisner's Last Act," *Fortune* (March 8, 2004), http://web6.infotrac.galegroup.com.

4. Marc Gunther, "Cops of the Global Village," *Fortune* (June 27, 2005), downloaded from Infotrac at http://web6.infotrac.galegroup.com; David Drickhamer, "Under Fire," *Industry Week* (June 2002), http://web6.infotrac.galegroup.com; "Economics Focus: Sickness or Symptom?" *The Economist* (February 7,

2004), p. 73; and Robert B. Reich, "Trade: A Third Way," *The American Prospect Online* (May 22, 2000), www.prospect.org.

5. World Bank and Forbes Magazine; http://www.worldbank.org/data/quickreference/quickref.html (accessed July 13, 2005); http://www.forbes.com/lists/2003/02/26/billionaireland.html (accessed July 13, 2005)

6. Eric Schlosser (2002). *Fast Food Nation: The Dark Side of the All-American Meal,* New York: Perennial, p. 54.

7. Mike Allen, "Bidders Begin Assessing the Value of Metabolife," *San Diego Business Journal* (July 25, 2005), downloaded from Business & Company Resource Center, http://galenet.galegroup.com; John Carey, "Ephedra: One Down, More to Go," *Business Week* (January 19, 2004), downloaded from Infotrac at http://web2.infotrac.galegroup.com; and Arlene Weintraub and John Carey, "Diet Pills and Pols: A Dangerous Mix," *Business Week* (September 2, 2002), http://web2.infotrac.galegroup.com.

8. Bart A. Lazar, "Descriptive Marks allow Competitive Use," *Marketing News,* January 15, 2005, p. 6.

Chapter 6

1. Microsoft, threedegrees Web site, 2004, archived at http://web.archive.org/web/20040103063458/http://threedegrees.com/; Kim Peterson, "Microsoft Messaging System Is Geared to Youth," *Knight Ridder/Tribune Business News*, February 19, 2003, downloaded at Business & Company Resource Center, http://galenet.galegroup.com; and Christine Y. Chen, "Chasing the Net Generation," *Fortune* (September 4, 2000), http://galenet.galegroup.com.

2. "Executive Survey: 'Compassion' is Important for Future Business Leaders." *The Cornell Chronicle,* October 24, 1996. http://www.news.cornell.edu/Chronicle/96/10.24.96/executive_survey.html (accessed July 13, 2005).

3. Janice Jorgensen (ed.) (1974). *Encyclopedia of Consumer Brands*. Detroit: St. James Press, p. 513.

4. Marcia Dunn, "Remaking NASA One Step at a Time," MSNBC, October 12, 2003, www.msnbc.msn.com; James Glanz and John Schwartz, "Dogged Engineer's Effort to Assess Shuttle Damage," *New York Times*, September 26, 2003, downloaded from Factiva at http://integrate.factiva.com; and Matthew L. Wald with John Schwartz, "NASA Chief Promises Shift in Attitude," *New York Times*, August 28, 2003, http://integrate.factiva.com.

5. William C. Symonds and Peter Burrows, "A Digital Warrior for Kodak," *Business Week* (May 23, 2005), downloaded from Infotrac at http://web2.infotrac.galegroup.com; William Symonds and Faith Arner, "Not Exactly a Kodak Moment," *Business*

Week (November 24, 2003), http://web2. infotrac.galegroup.com; Subrata N. Chakravarty and Joanne Gordon, "Vindication," *Forbes* (September 7, 1998), http://web2.infotrac.galegroup.com; and Subrata N. Chakravarty and Amy Feldman, "The Road Not Taken," *Forbes* (August 30, 1993), http://web2.infotrac.galegroup.com.

Chapter 7

1. Dick's Drive-In Restaurants, Inc., Home page and "Working for Dick's," www.ddir.com, accessed October 4, 2005; Lynda V. Mapes, "Good Business," *Seattle Times,* January 31, 2005, downloaded from Infotrac at http://web2.infotrac. galegroup.com; and Sheryll Poe, "Seattle Restaurant Attracts Employees with Job Perks, Benefits," *Seattle Times,* August 4, 2001, http://web2.infotrac.galegroup.com.

2. Abraham H. Maslow (1954/1970). *Motivation and Personality* (2nd ed.). New York: Harper & Row, pp 48-51.

3. Deere and Company, "Our Past Leaders: Hans Becherer, Chairman and CEO, 1990–2000," Deere Web site, www.deere. com, accessed October 5, 2005; Bruce Upbin, "Bucking the Downtrend," *Forbes* (November 2, 1998), downloaded from Infotrac at http://web2.infotrac.galegroup. com; and Kevin Kelly, "The New Soul of John Deere," *Business Week* (January 31, 1994), www.businessweek.com.

4. Sharyn Bernard, "Rubbermaid Fine-Tunes Home Products Growth Plan," *HFN*, May 5, 2003, downloaded from Business & Company Resource Center, http://galenet.galegroup.com; Jean-Philippe Deschamps and P. Ranganath Nayak, "Fomenting a Customer Obsession," *National Productivity Review* (Autumn 1995), http://galenet.galegroup. com; and Marshall Loeb, "How to Grow a New Product Every Day," *Fortune* (November 14, 1994), http://galenet.galegroup.com.

5. Michelle Celarier, "Fixer-Upper: John Mack Faces the Challenge of His Life at CSFB," *Investment Dealers' Digest* (March 24, 2003), downloaded from FirstSearch at http://firstsearch.oclc.org; Anita Raghavan, "Credit Suisse Unit to Delay Telling Its Staff of Bonuses," *The Wall Street Journal,* December 21, 1998, http://online.wsj.com; and "Troubles at Credit Suisse First Boston," *The Economist* (April 10, 1993), downloaded from Factiva at http://integrate.factiva.com.

Chapter 8

1. Sony Corporation, "Sony Corporate Information: Organization Data," and "Sony History," Sony corporate Web site, www.sony.net, accessed October 6, 2005; Brent Schlender, "Inside the Shakeup at Sony," *Fortune* (April 4, 2005), downloaded from Infotrac at http://web4.infotrac. galegroup.com; and Brent Schlender, "Sony Plays to Win," *Fortune* (May 1, 2000), http://web4.infotrac.galegroup.com.

2. Michael Dell, *Direct from Dell: Strategies That Revolutionized an Industry* (New York: HarperBusiness, 1999), chap. 5–6; Daniel Lyons, "Make the Little Guys Feel Big," *Forbes* (April 17, 2000), downloaded from Infotrac at http://web4.infotrac.galegroup. com; Dell Computer Corporation, Annual Report 1999, downloaded from Dell corporate Web site, www1.us.dell.com.

3. Anthony Sampson (1995). *Company Man: The Rise and Fall of Corporate Life.* New York: Times Business/Random House, page 71.

4. "Running the Tightest Ships on the Net," *Business Week* (January 29, 2001), downloaded from Infotrac at http://web4.infotrac.galegroup.com; Steve Antonoff, "Management at Your Service," *Internet Week* (July 9, 2001), www.internetweek.com; and Larry Greenemeier, "Companies Want Management Metrics They Can Tally," *Information Week* (August 7, 2000), http://informationweek.com.

5. Andrew Park, "What You Don't Know about Dell," *Business Week* (November 3, 2003), downloaded from Infotrac at http://web4.infotrac.galegroup.com; Richard Craver, "Dell Computer Assemblers Receive Extensive, Sustained Training," *Winston-Salem Journal,* December 8, 2004, downloaded from Business & Company Resource Center, http://galenet. galegroup.com; and Carla Joinson, "Moving at the Speed of Dell," *HRMagazine* (April 1999), http://galenet.galegroup.com.

6. Thomas D. Seeley (1995). *The Wisdom of the Hive: The Social Physiology of Honey Bee Colonies,* Cambridge, MA: Harvard University Press, p. 246.

Chapter 9

1. IBM, "The Who, What, When, Where, Why and How of Becoming an On Demand Business," brochure downloaded from IBM Web site, www.ibm.com, October 11, 2005; Brian Thomas Eck and Murray Mitchell, "Transformation," *Supply Chain Management Review* (November–December 2003), downloaded from Infotrac at http://web1. infotrac.galegroup.com; and Spencer E. Ante, "Computing Power Sold Like Electricity," *Business Week* (November 11, 2002), http://web1.infotrac.galegroup.com.

2. http://www.gs1us.org/upc_background. html (accessed July 12, 2005)

3. G. R. Jones "SAP and the Enterprise Resource Planning Industry," in *Strategic Management: An Integrated Approach,* 6th ed., edited by C. W. L. Hill and G. R. Jones (Boston: Houghton Mifflin, 2003); SAP, "mySAP ERP" (2005), brochure downloaded from "mySAP ERP: Brochures and White Papers" page of SAP Web site, www.sap.com, October 11, 2005; and "SAP Rolls Out Next Generation of ERP to Customers," *Wireless News* (March 13, 2005), downloaded from Business & Company Resource Center, http://galenet. galegroup.com.

4. Andy Reinhardt, "A New Wireless Order," *Business Week* (October 3, 2005), downloaded from Infotrac at http://web4. infotrac.galegroup.com; Andy Reinhardt, "The Next Big Thing for Wireless?" *Business Week* (January 19, 2004), http://web4. infotrac.galegroup.com; and Aaron Ricadela and Paul Travis, "One on One with Paul Otellini," *Information Week* (March 21, 2003), http://web4.infotrac.galegroup.com.

5. "Enterprise Server OS Market Shares," ZDNet Research, August 17, 2005, http:// blogs.zdnet.com; Steve Hamm, "Linux Inc.," *Business Week* (January 31, 2005), downloaded from Infotrac at http://web4. infotrac.galegroup.com; Michael Maiello and Susan Kitchens, "Kill Bill," *Forbes* (June 7, 2004), http://web4.infotrac.galegroup. com; and Fred Vogelstein, "Bringing Linux to the Masses," *Fortune* (February 3, 2003), http://web4.infotrac.galegroup.com.

6. Phrase coined by Intel; examples from: http://pcbunn.cacr.caltech.edu/presentatio ns/giod_status_sep97/sld013.htm (accessed June 3, 2005); http://www.wisegeek.com/ how-much-text-is-in-a-kilobyte-or-megabyte.htm (accessed July 13, 2005)

Chapter 10

1. David Welch, "Running Out of Gas," *Business Week* (March 28, 2005), downloaded from Infotrac at http://web6.infotrac. galegroup.com; Alex Taylor III, "GM's Saturn Problem," *Fortune* (December 13, 2004), http://web6.infotrac.galegroup.com; and Alex Taylor III, "GM Gets Its Act Together," *Fortune* (April 5, 2004), http:// web6.infotrac.galegroup.com.

2. Michael Arndt, "3M's Rising Star," *Business Week* (April 12, 2004), downloaded from Infotrac at http://web6.infotrac. galegroup.com; 3M Company, *A Century of Innovation: The 3M Story* (St. Paul, Minn.: 3M, 2002), downloaded at http://solutions. 3m.com; and Jerry Useem, "[3M] + [General Electric] = ?," *Fortune* (August 12, 2002), http://web6.infotrac.galegroup.com.

3. Joël Glenn Brenner (1999), *The Emperors of Chocolate: Inside the Secret World of Hershey and Mars.* New York: Random House, page 46.

4. Connie Mabin, "Cardmakers Find Groups Pay More for Niche Greeting Cards," *Marketing News,* March 15, 2005, p. 15.

5. Matthew Boyle, "Digital Deals Pit Xerox against Kodak," *Fortune* (November 29, 2004), downloaded from Infotrac at http://web6.infotrac.galegroup.com; Alex Taylor III, "Kodak Scrambles to Refocus,"

Fortune (March 3, 1986), http://web6.infotrac.galegroup.com; and Subrata N. Chakravarty and Ruth Simon, "Has the World Passed Kodak By?" *Forbes* (November 5, 1984), http://web6.infotrac.galegroup.com.

6. Eric Schlosser (2002). *Fast Food Nation: The Dark Side of the All-American Meal,* New York: Perennial, p. 3.

7. Booz-Allen and Hamilton (1982). *New Product Management of the 1980s.* New York: Booz-Allen and Hamilton. Quoted in Robert G. Cooper (2001). *Winning at New Products: Accelerating the Process from Idea to Launch.* New York: Basic Books, p. 11.

8. www.gatorade.com (accessed July 13, 2005)

9. Thomas Edison. From unknown work, but widely quoted.

10. Polo Ralph Lauren Corporation, "Corporate Overview," investor relations pages of Polo Ralph Lauren Web site, http://investor.polo.com/, accessed October 12, 2005; Phyllis Berman, "The Wall Street Fashion Game," *Forbes* (March 4, 2002), downloaded from Infotrac at http://web6.infotrac.galegroup.com; and Susan Caminiti, "Ralph Lauren: The Emperor Has Clothes," *Fortune* (November 11, 1996), http://web6.infotrac.galegroup.com.

Chapter 11

1. Avon Products, 2004 Annual Report, www.avoncompany.com, accessed October 13, 2005; Kate Bonamici, "Not Just Cosmetic Changes," *Fortune* (August 23, 2004), downloaded from Infotrac at http://web3.infotrac.galegroup.com; Katrina Brooker, "It Took a Lady to Save Avon," *Fortune* (October 15, 2001), http://web3.infotrac.galegroup.com; and "Avon: The New Calling," *Business Week* (September 18, 2000), http://web3.infotrac.galegroup.com.

2. James P. Womack and Daniel T. Jones (2003). *Lean Thinking: Banish Waste and Create Wealth in Your Corporation* (rev. ed.). New York: Free Press, p. 43.

3. Kelly Devine Thomas, "Christie's and Sotheby's: On the Champagne Trail," *ARTnews Online* (September 2005), www.artnewsonline.com; Meredith Kahn, "Masterpiece Theater," *W* (June 2004), downloaded from Infotrac at http://web3.infotrac.galegroup.com; Christopher Mason, "That Cool, That Suit: Sotheby's 007," *New York Times* (May 20, 2001), downloaded from Business & Company Resource Center, http://galenet.galegroup.com; and Walter Robinson, "$17-Million Marilyn," *Artnet* (May 15, 1998), www.artnet.com.

4. Federal Trade Commission, "National Do Not Call Registry Celebrates One-Year Anniversary," news release, June 24, 2004, www.ftc.gov; Scott Reeves, "Door-to-Door Sales Make Comeback," *Oakland Tribune,*

November 11, 2003, downloaded from LookSmart FindArticles, www.findarticles.com; and "TeleZapper Disconnects Telemarketers," CNN, August 26, 2002, http://archives.cnn.com.

5. Siegried Giedion (1948). *Mechanization Takes Command: A Contribution to Anonymous History.* New York: Norton, pp. 77-96.

6. Carrier Corp.; http://www.global.carrier.com/ (accessed July 13, 2005)

7. Empire HealthChoice Assurance, "Selling Empire" and "Broker Online Services" at Brokers pages, Empire Web site, www.empireblue.com, accessed October 13, 2005; Empire HealthChoice Assurance, "Empire Broker Online Services Adds Group Renewals and Multi-Region Quotes," news release, November 23, 2004, www.empireblue.com; and Gary Baldwin, "Cutting through the Maze," *Internet Health Care* (March 2001), downloaded from Business & Company Resource Center, http://galenet.galegroup.com.

Chapter 12

1. Diane Brady, "The Unsung CEO," *Business Week* (November 1, 2004), downloaded from Infotrac at http://web3.infotrac.galegroup.com; Brett Nelson, "The Thinker," *Forbes* (March 3, 2003), http://web3.infotrac.galegroup.com; and John S. McClenahen, "UTC's Master of Principle," *Industry Week* (January 2003), http://web3.infotrac.galegroup.com.

2. "The Skinny on Packaging Size Preferences," In: Fact, Synovate Ltd., May 2004. http://www.synovate.com/en/publications/infact/may2004/ (accessed July 8, 2005)

3. Krispy Kreme Doughnuts, press kit (June 2004), downloaded from Krispy Kreme Web site, www.krispykreme.com; Monica Gagnier, "Krispy Gets Kremed," *Business Week* (December 6, 2004), downloaded from Infotrac at http://web3.infotrac.galegroup.com; Christina Dyrness, "Krispy Kreme Adds New Technologies to Its Arsenal," *Knight Ridder/Tribune Business News,* April 23, 2003, downloaded from Business & Company Resource Center, http://galenet.galegroup.com; and Catharine Skipp, "Hot Bytes, by the Dozen," *Newsweek* (April 19, 2003), downloaded from MSNBC.com at http://msnbc.msn.com.

4. Direct Marketing Association (2004). *Statistical Fact Book.* New York: Direct Marketing Association.

5. Stephen Pounds, "Motorola Closes Last Boynton Beach, Florida, Building," *Knight Ridder/Tribune Business News,* December 17, 2004, downloaded from Business & Company Resource Center, http://galenet.galegroup.com; Mohsen Attaran, "CIM: Getting Set for Implementation," *Industrial*

Management & Data Systems (January 1997), http://galenet.galegroup.com; and Gene Bylinsky, "The Digital Factory," *Fortune* (November 14, 1994), http://galenet.galegroup.com.

6. *Progressive Grocer,* 72nd Annual Report of the Grocery Industry, April 2005, p. 54.

7. William Atkinson, "Does JIT II Still Work in the Internet Age?" *Purchasing* (September 6, 2001), www.purchasing.com; Fred Hewitt, "After Supply Chains, Think Demand Pipelines," *Supply Chain Management Review* (May 2001), downloaded from Business & Company Resource Center, http://galenet.galegroup.com; Tim Minahan, "The Supply Chain as Inventory," *Purchasing* (October 17, 1996), http://galenet.galegroup.com; and Sherwin Greenblatt, "Continuous Improvement in Supply Chain Management," *Chief Executive* (June 1993), downloaded from LookSmart FindArticles at www.findarticles.com.

8. Chester Dawson, "Blazing the Toyota Way," *Business Week* (May 24, 2004), downloaded from Business & Company Resource Center, http://galenet.galegroup.com; Lindsay Chappell, "Toyota's Triumph," *Automotive News* (August 5, 2002), http://galenet.galegroup.com; and Peter Strozniak, "Toyota Alters Face of Production," *Industry Week* (August 13, 2001), http://galenet.galegroup.com.

Chapter 13

1. General Electric Company, "Careers at GE," www.gecareers.com, and "Business Directory," www.ge.com, accessed October 18, 2005; Edward E. Lawler III, *Treat People Right!* (San Francisco: Jossey-Bass, 2003); Matthew Boyle, "Performance Reviews: Perilous Curves Ahead," *Fortune* (May 28, 2001), downloaded from Infotrac at http://web5.infotrac.galegroup.com; and Glenn Rifkin, "Leadership: Can It Be Learned?" *Forbes* (April 8, 1996), http://web5.infotrac.galegroup.com.

2. David Kirkpatrick, "IBM Shares Its Secrets," *Fortune* (September 5, 2005), downloaded from Infotrac at http://web5.infotrac.galegroup.com; Elizabeth Corcoran, "Unoutsourcing," *Forbes* (May 10, 2004), http://web5.infotrac.galegroup.com; and Justin Fox, "Where Your Job Is Going," *Fortune* (November 24, 2003), http://web5.infotrac.galegroup.com.

3. Les Krantz (2002), *Jobs Rated Almanac: The Best and Worst Jobs - 250 in All - Ranked by More Than a Dozen Vital Factors Including Salary, Stress, Benefits, and More* (6th ed.), New York: Barricade Books.

4. Jim McTague, "Presumed Guilty?" *Barron's,* March 22, 2004, http://online.barrons.com; Jon Chesto, "Wall Street Brokerages to Pay $1.4B Settlement," *Boston Herald,* December 21, 2002, downloaded

from Business & Company Resource Center, http://galenet.galegroup.com; Securities and Exchange Commission, "Ten of Nation's Top Investment Firms Settle Enforcement Actions Involving Conflicts of Interest between Research and Investment Banking," news release, April 28, 2003, www.sec.gov; and Nicholas Varchaver and Katherine Bonamici, "The Perils of E-mail," *Fortune* (February 17, 2003), downloaded from Infotrac at http://web5.infotrac.galegroup.com.

5. Japan Institute for Labour Policy and Training, "New Moves in Performance-Based Compensation," *Japan Labor Flash*, March 15, 2005, www.jil.go.jp; Michael Kanellos, "Keiretsu Dynasties Give Way," *CNET News.com*, December 7, 2004, http://news.com.com; and Neil Weinberg, "Cracks in the Iron Rice Bowl," *Forbes* (November 2, 1998), downloaded from Infotrac at http://web4.infotrac.galegroup.com.

Chapter 14

1. Matthew Maier, "How to Beat Wal-Mart," *Business 2.0* (May 2005), downloaded from Infotrac at http://web7.infotrac.galegroup.com; "For Every Sporting-Goods Season: Turn, Turn, Turn," *Chain Store Age* (March 2004), downloaded from Business & Company Resource Center at http://galenet.galegroup.com; and Dick's Sporting Goods, Annual Report, 2003, accessed at Investor Relations pages of company Web site, www.dickssportinggoods.com.

2. http://www.manhattanda.org/office_overview/index.html (accessed July 8, 2005)

3. http://www.sec.gov/

4. Monica Roman, "Freddie's Frenetic Year," *Business Week* (July 12, 2004), downloaded from Infotrac at http://web7.infotrac.galegroup.com; Monica Roman, "Freddie Gets Fingered," *Business Week* (December 22, 2003), http://web7.infotrac.galegroup.com; Carol J. Loomis, "Freddie Finally Gets Fingered," *Fortune* (December 22, 2003), http://web7.infotrac.galegroup.com; and David Henry and Laura Cohn, "Why Freddie's Mess Matters," *Business Week* (June 23, 2003), http://web7.infotrac.galegroup.com.

5. Andrew Park, "Thomas Ryan: The Death Business Becomes Him," *Business Week* (July 18, 2005), downloaded from Infotrac at http://web7.infotrac.galegroup.com; Brian Grow, "What's Killing the Undertakers," *Business Week* (March 24, 2003), http://web7.infotrac.galegroup.com; and David Whitford, "Funeral Roll-Ups Face a Slow, Painful Death," *Fortune* (February 5, 2001), downloaded from Business & Company Resource Center at http://galenet.galegroup.com.

Chapter 15

1. Brett Pulley, "Last Days of the Lion King," *Forbes* (October 17, 2005), downloaded from Infotrac at http://web7.infotrac.galegroup.com; "Michael Eisner; Walt Disney," *Business Week* (January 10, 2005), http://web7.infotrac.galegroup.com; Marc Gunther, "Eisner's Last Act," *Fortune* (March 8, 2004), http://web7.infotrac.galegroup.com; and Marc Gunther, "For Roy Disney, the Company Founded by His Uncle Walt Is Much More than a Business," *Fortune* (January 12, 2004), http://web7.infotrac.galegroup.com.

2. http://www.moneyfactory.com/document.cfm/18/106 (accessed July 8, 2005).

3. California Public Employees' Retirement System, "Facts at a Glance," www.calpers.ca.gov, accessed October 20, 2005; Steven Brull, "A Truly Civil Servant," *Institutional Investor* (June 2005), downloaded from Infotrac at http://web2.infotrac.galegroup.com; and Marc Gunther, "Calpers Rides Again," *Fortune* (December 8, 2003), http://web2.infotrac.galegroup.com.

4. http://www.moneyfactory.com/document.cfm/18/106 (accessed July 8, 2005).

5. Carol J. Loomis, "How the HP Board KO'd Carly," *Fortune* (March 7, 2005), downloaded from Infotrac at http://web2.infotrac.galegroup.com; Carol J. Loomis, "Why Carly's Big Bet Is Failing," *Fortune* (February 7, 2005), http://web2.infotrac.galegroup.com; and Quentin Hardy, "We Did It," *Forbes* (August 11, 2003), http://web2.infotrac.galegroup.com.

6. Neil Weinberg, "Healing Thyself," *Forbes* (March 17, 2003), downloaded from Infotrac at http://web2.infotrac.galegroup.com; Susan J. Stabile, "Health Care Plan Litigation," *Employee Rights Quarterly* (Winter 2003), downloaded from Business & Company Resource Center at http://galenet.galegroup.com; and Phyllis Berman and Bernard Condon, "Columbia Health Care versus Managed Care," *Forbes* (June 3, 1996), http://web2.infotrac.galegroup.com.

Photo Credits

Chapter 1

page **5**: © Pam Francis//Time Life Pictures/ Getty Images; page **7**: © Dennis Blachut/ CORBIS ; page **9**: © Craig Mitchelldyer/ Getty Images; page **16**: © William Thomas Cain/Getty Images; page **19**: © Tom Stewart/CORBIS; page **24**: © L. Nelson/ Stock Photos/Corbis

Chapter 2

page **35**: © Topham/The Image Works; page **42**: © Christie's Images/CORBIS; page **44**: © Don Farrall/Getty Images; page **45**: © Bettmann/CORBIS; page **47**: © Arte & Immagini srl/CORBIS ; page **49**: © James Shaffer/PhotoEdit; page **51**: © Bettmann/CORBIS; page **52**: © Bettmann/CORBIS; page **56**: © Bryan F. Peterson/CORBIS

Chapter 3

page **65**: © Spencer Platt/Getty Images; page **69**: © Scott Gries/Getty Images; page **70**: © Kevin Fleming/CORBIS; page **72**: © Najlah Feanny/Corbis ; page **82**: © JEFF HAYNES/AFP/Getty Images; page **83**: © Will & Deni McIntyre / Photo Researchers, Inc.; page **86**: © Getty Images; page **88**: © Stuart Pearce/AGE Fotostock

Chapter 4

page **103**: © AP Photo/Keystone/Fabrice Coffrini; page **105**: © DIBYANGSHU SARKAR/AFP/Getty Images; page **108**: © Tim Boyle/Getty Images; page **111**: © Norbert von der Groeben/The Image Works; page **114**: © AP Photo/Song Kyeong Seok, Pool; page **117**: © Peter Blakely/CORBIS SABA ; page **119**: © DE MALGLAIVE ETIENNE/GAMMA; page **124**: © MARTIN OESER/AFP/Getty Images; page **125**: © Lee Stone/The Image Works; page **127**: © SEBASTIAN D'SOUZA/AFP/Getty Images

Chapter 5

page **139**: © Osterreicher, M./ Stockphoto.com; page **141**: © Bill Fritsch/AGE Fotostock; page **142**: © AP Photo/Damian Dovarganes; page **143**: © McGraw-Hill; page **147**: © AP Photo/ Ric Francis; page **151**: © Erik S. Lesser/ Liaison/Getty Images; page **155**: © AVENTURIER PATRICK/GAMMA; page **160**: © AP Photo/Matthew Cavanaugh; page **161**: of Hasbro/Getty Images; page **162**: © Russel Gordon; page **164**: © NEEMA FREDERIC /GAMMA

Chapter 6

page **175**: © McGraw-Hill; page **176**: © Reuters/CORBIS; page **178**: © 8383/ GAMMA; page **181**: © Jeffrey Greenberg / Photo Researchers, Inc.; page **184**: © Mark Garfinkel/ The Boston Herald; page **185**: © Royalty-Free/Corbis; page **187**: © John Henley/CORBIS; page **190**: © Rob Crandall/The Image Works; page **193**: © Folio/Omni-Photo; page **195**: © 8383/ GAMMA; page **198**: © TOSHIFUMI KITAMURA/AFP/Getty Images

Chapter 7

page **209**: © John Carver; page **213**: © Proles Productions/AGE Fotostock; page **214**: © Marc Romanelli/Getty Images; page **219**: © ROUNTREE ADAM/ GAMMA; page **222**: © JOERG BOETHLING/Peter Arnold, Inc.; page **225**: © Business Wire/Getty Images; page **226**: © Royalty Free/Masterfile; page **229**: © Richard Levine

Chapter 8

page **239**: © Stephen Shugerman/Getty Images; **page 245**: © AP Photo/Eric Risberg; page **245**: © Jeff Greenberg/ PhotoEdit; page **247**: © Scott Olson; page **253**: © Eiji Miyazawa/Black Star; page **255**: © AP Photo/Tim Sharp; page **256**: © Royalty Free/Masterfile; page **261**: © Ed Kashi/CORBIS; page **261**: © Frank Herholdt/Stone/Getty

Chapter 9

page **273**: © David Young-Wolff/PhotoEdit; page **280**: © Bob Pardue; page **282**: © Ralph Orlowski/Getty Images; page **283**: © Ryan McVay/Getty Images; page **286**: © SSPL/The Image Works; page **287**: © James L. Fly/Unicorn Stock Photos; page **290**: © Justin Sullivan/Getty Images; page **291**: © Science Museum/SSPL/The Image Works

Chapter 10

page **305**: © SuperStock/AGE Photo; page **305**: © Jim West/The Image Works; page **307**: © Roy Ooms/Masterfile; page **310**: © AP Photo/Jim Mone; page **315**: © Richard Levine; page **317**: © Peter Kramer/Getty Images; page **319**: © Norm Reid; page **326**: © AP Photo/Kathy Willens; page **327**: © Peter Frischmuth/ Peter Arnold, Inc.; page **330**: © AP Photo/ Julie Jacobson

Chapter 11

page **341**: © Mario Tama/Getty Images; page **346**: © Michael Newman/PhotoEdit; **349**: © Mario Ruiz//Time Life Pictures/ Getty Images; page **352**: © Shannon Stapleton/REUTERS/Corbis ; page **354**: © Matthew Borkoski/Index Stock; page **356**: © STAPLETON SHANNON/ GAMMA; page **358**: © Bob Daemmrich/ PhotoEdit; page **361**: © Stockbyte/Getty; page **362**: © Digital Vision/Age Fotostock

Chapter 12

page **371**: © Najlah Feanny/Corbis; page **373**: © Superstock/AGE Fotostock; page **377**: © Reed Saxon/AP Photo; page **379**: © ROBYN BECK/AFP/Getty Images; page **381**: © Les Stone / The Image Works; page **383**: © Jeff Greenberg/AGE Fotostock; page **384**: © Marc Asnin/ CORBIS SABA; page **388**: © John A. Rizzo/AGE Fotostock; page **390**: © PhotoLink/Getty Images

Chapter 13

page **399**: © Brownie Harris/CORBIS; page **403**: © Bill Varie/CORBIS; page **405**: Courtesy of Korn/Ferry International; page **408**: © ROUSSEL MARC/Gamma; page **417**: © G. Baden/zefa/Corbis; page **419**: © James Leynse/CORBIS; page **421**: © Junji Kurokawa/AP Photo; page **422**: © John Bazemore/ AP Photo; page **425**: © Helen King/CORBIS

Chapter 14

page **435**: © Susan Van Etten/PhotoEdit; page **438**: © Keith Dannemiller/CORBIS; page **439**: Copyright ©2005 by the American Institute of Certified Public Accountants, Inc. Reprinted with permission; page **442**: © Erik S. Lesser/Getty Images; page **443**: © Paul Sakuma/AP Photo; page **448**: Courtesy of General Mills; page **453**: © Digital Vision/Age Fotostock; page **458**: © Service Corporation International

Chapter 15

page **471**: © Stephen Chernin/Getty Images; page **473**: © Dennis MacDonald/ PhotoEdit; page **475**: © Tim Boyle/Getty Images; page **476**: Courtesy of CalPERS; page **483**: © Robin Weiner/Wirepix/The Image Works; page **485**: © Eric Risberg/ AP Photo; page **488**: Courtesy of International Business Machines Corporation; page **491**: © Andrew Holbrooke/Corbis; page **493**: © Ryan McVay/Getty Images

Index

Names

Subjects

Companies